SCOTLAND AT
150

A CENTURY AND A HALF
OF INTERNATIONAL FOOTBALL

SCOTLAND AT

A CENTURY AND A HALF OF INTERNATIONAL FOOTBALL

First published in 2023
by Jicks Publishing,
4 Hayfield Lane, Lerwick, Shetland, ZE1 0QD.

Copyright © Jim Tait, 2023

All rights reserved. No part of this publication may be reproduced, stored in a retrieval system, or transmitted in any form, or by any means, electronic, mechanical, photocopying, recording or otherwise, without permission in writing from the publisher.

ISBN 978-1-3999-4506-6

Printed by The Shetland Times Ltd, Lerwick, Shetland

CONTENTS

Foreword vii

Introduction... ix

List of featured matches x

Chapter One: 1873-1914 1

Chapter Two: 1920-1939 21

Chapter Three: 1946-1959 35

Chapter Four: 1960-1969 53

Chapter Five: 1970-1979 69

Chapter Six: 1980-1989 89

Chapter Seven: 1990-1999 109

Chapter Eight: 2000-2009 131

Chapter Nine: 2010-2019 151

Chapter Ten: 2020-2023 171

List of players 185

Most appearances 194

Top scorers 195

Head to head against opposition 196

The managers 202

Scottish League XI action 204

Women's internationals 205

Teams of the decades 207

Greatest side of my lifetime 211

Thanks and acknowledgments 213

PLAYERS FEATURED ON FRONT COVER

Alan Morton	1920-1932
Hughie Gallacher	1924-1935
Billy Liddell	1946-1955
Gordon Smith	1946-1957
George Young	1946-1957
Billy Steel	1947-1953
Lawrie Reilly	1948-1958
Denis Law	1958-1974
John White	1959-1964
Jim Baxter	1960-1967
Billy McNeill	1961-1972
Alan Gilzean	1963-1971
John Greig	1964-1975
Jimmy Johnstone	1964-1974
Billy Bremner	1965-1975
Tommy Gemmell	1966-1971
Eddie Gray	1969-1977
Martin Buchan	1971-1978
Kenny Dalglish	1971-1986
Joe Jordan	1973-1982
Danny McGrain	1973-1982
Graeme Souness	1974-1986
Willie Miller	1975-1989
Alan Hansen	1979-1987
Alex McLeish	1980-1994
Gordon Strachan	1980-1992
Andy Goram	1985-1998
Gary McAllister	1990-1999
Craig Gordon	2004-2022
Andrew Robertson	2014-2023
John McGinn	2016-2023

FOREWORD

The researching, and subsequent writing, of this superb publication was undoubtedly a labour of love for author Jim Tait. Without devotion to the national team and genuine interest I doubt if anyone could possibly have produced such accurate, inspirational and captivating material.

As someone who was privileged to be in charge of the national team on a record number of occasions and who, before that, was honoured to join Sir Alex Ferguson and Andy Roxburgh in the technical area, I had a ring-side view of around 138 of the matches so accurately recorded in chapters six, seven and eight. This enabled me to underpin the aspiration of respective managers, myself included, and groups of selected players.

Needless to say, I am in full agreement with everything which has been written and I know my friend, Sir Alex, would support Jim when he identified Denis Law as Scotland's best ever player. My assertion is that Sir Alex has been the best manager on the planet, so when I had to say a few words at the Aberdeen Town House event when Denis was being inducted as a Freeman of the city, I called Manchester United to seek information about Denis from the "great man" himself.

Sir Alex endorsed the excellent credentials of Denis by telling me that in conversation with the world's best ever player, the late Pele told him that the only British, not just Scottish, but British player who could have played for Brazil was Denis Law. Significantly, author Jim is in total agreement with the world's outstanding manager and the recently deceased player.

If ever reinforcement of Jim's opinion required credibility, surely agreement of such luminaries is evidence aplenty. It would be asinine to dispute the opinion of the world's two greatest football men. The fact that there is unanimity on this potentially contentious issue surely confirms that no other claim by the writer should be contested.

Jim has done his bit as a fan for the past 50 years. Now he has done his bit as a writer. We have, in this production, a Scottish football book which is without equal and to be thoroughly enjoyed.

Craig Brown CBE
Former Scotland manager
(1940 - 2023)

NOTES ON STYLE

- In the scoreline the home team is named first, and at major tournaments Scotland is always listed as the away side.
- A semi-colon is used to separate the different lines of team formation.
- In the "scorers" line the team which opens the scoring is listed first.
- In earlier matches where the time of the goal is unknown the symbol # is used.
- In featured matches the number preceding the player's name denotes the appearance.
- For reasons of simplicity no foreign letters, glyphs or diacritics are used.
- Full names of clubs are used except in certain cases, e.g. Celtic, Hearts or Rangers.
- Players are usually given the Christian name they are known by, although that may not be the case with older eras.
- The more technically correct "Netherlands" is used, rather than the equally common "Holland".
- "Soviet Union" is favoured over the alternative and often used "USSR" (Union of Soviet Socialist Republics).
- In some matches, particularly from earlier periods, the captain of the away team is unknown.

INTRODUCTION

It has been an ambition for many years to write a book charting the history of the Scottish international men's football team, with relevant information from each match played.

It all began in 1872 with the first game against England. That took place at the Kennington Oval in London, now of course one of the great cricket venues in the country. Friendly matches with the "auld enemy" were staged annually until in 1884 the Home Championship was formed, with Wales, England and Scotland playing each other. The following year Ireland joined the competition, which was to run for 100 years before it was abandoned.

Games continued up to 1914 when the First World War brought a halt to the action, and resumed again in 1920. The first matches against opposition other than the home countries were in 1929, when Scotland went on a European tour and played Norway, Germany and the Netherlands.

International football was again stopped for six years during the Second War, but began again in 1946 and has continued ever since.

My own interest began as a boy in the mid-1960s when I started to listen to matches on the radio. In 1967 I became completely hooked. At club level that year Glasgow Celtic were the first British team to lift the European Cup and Glasgow Rangers reached the final of the European Cup Winners Cup, while Scotland inflicted a famous 3-2 defeat on world champions England at Wembley.

My favourite player was Denis Law, and I would scour the back pages of my aunt and uncle's *Press & Journal* for match reports. In those days a goal scorer's name was printed in capital letters and inevitably my hero would be featured.

In 1968 Manchester United followed Celtic to become European club champions, although for me the victory in the final over Benfica was dampened somewhat due to the fact that Law was missing because of injury.

Scotland games were what really mattered though, and I began to keep a record of results, team line-ups and goal scorers. That diary is long lost, but I guess that distant memories of it prompted me to think of compiling this book.

The first international I attended was in November 1972 where thankfully there was a happy outcome, a 2-0 win over Denmark at Hampden Park. That followed a victory in the reverse fixture in Copenhagen the previous month and set the Scots up for what would ultimately be qualification for the 1974 World Cup.

That tournament in Germany was undoubtedly a high point, albeit that the Scots failed to get beyond the group stages. Failure to put more goals past Zaire was their undoing, as the players came home early but were the only unbeaten side in the whole competition.

World Cup qualification was almost a given in the following years, as Scotland headed to Argentina in 1978, Spain in 1982, Mexico in 1986 and Italy in 1990. Not making it to the USA in 1994 was but a minor setback, as that was sandwiched between successive European Championships at Sweden in 1992 and England in 1996, and the Scots were back in France for the 1998 World Cup.

The following two decades were to bear little fruit, with 10 more qualification failures and the one highlight being making the 2020 European Championship.

This book is made up of several different sections. Chapters 1-10 have details of every game played, including the competition, venue, attendance, team lines and scorers. To coincide with the 150th anniversary, short match reports from 150 of the most vital and memorable fixtures are also included.

The various sources from which I have gained information are listed in the acknowledgments, but for details on matches I generally used the archives of *The Scotsman*, courtesy of the National Library in Edinburgh. Over the years that newspaper had some excellent chief football reporters, including Hugh McIlvanney, John Rafferty and my own particular favourite Glenn Gibbons.

Subsequent chapters cover a list of all the players who have represented the country, some details of Scottish League internationals, and a list of managers who have been in charge. I have also taken the liberty of selecting my own "teams of the decades" and "greatest team of my lifetime". You may or may not agree with my choices but they might provoke some discussion.

I still firmly believe that Law was the greatest player ever to wear a Scottish shirt. For me he had everything – speed, skill, unbelievable sharpness and amazing bravery. He is also apparently one of the nicest men you could come across, but sadly I have never had the opportunity to find out for myself.

Many managers have taken on the task of bringing out the best from Scottish players over the years, starting with Andy Beattie in the 1950s, and they have had varying degrees of success.

The longest serving, and one of the best, was Craig Brown. He was in charge for 70 matches, from 1993 to 2001, and I am greatly indebted to him for writing a foreword for this book. Very sadly he passed away just a few weeks before publication, but I am sure he would have agreed that the current manager, Steve Clarke, and his team have provided a new sense of optimism. We wish them every success for the future, and here's to the next 150 years.

Jim Tait

LIST OF FEATURED MATCHES

1872	SCOTLAND 0, England 0	1
1876	SCOTLAND 4, Wales 0	2
1881	England 1, SCOTLAND 6	3
1884	Ireland 0, SCOTLAND 5	5
1901	SCOTLAND 11, Ireland 0	13
1902	England 2, SCOTLAND 2	14
1914	SCOTLAND 3, England 1	20
1920	Wales 1, SCOTLAND 1	21
1928	England 1, SCOTLAND 5	25
1929	Norway 3, SCOTLAND 7	26
1932	France 1, SCOTLAND 3	28
1933	SCOTLAND 2, England 1	29
1936	SCOTLAND 2, Germany 0	31
1937	SCOTLAND 3, England 1	32
1938	England 0, SCOTLAND 1	33
1939	SCOTLAND 1, England 2	34
1946	SCOTLAND 2, Belgium 2	35
1946	SCOTLAND 3, Switzerland 1	35
1949	England 1, SCOTLAND 3	37
1949	Ireland 2, SCOTLAND 8	38
1950	SCOTLAND 6, Northern Ireland 1	39
1951	England 2, SCOTLAND 3	40
1951	Belgium 0, SCOTLAND 5	40
1952	SCOTLAND 6, USA 0	41
1953	England 2, SCOTLAND 2	42
1954	SCOTLAND 2, England 4	43
1954	Austria 1, SCOTLAND 0	44
1954	Uruguay 7, SCOTLAND 0	44
1955	Austria 1, SCOTLAND 4	45
1956	SCOTLAND 1, England 1	46
1957	SCOTLAND 4, Spain 2	47
1957	SCOTLAND 3, Switzerland 2	48
1958	Yugoslavia 1, SCOTLAND 1	49
1958	SCOTLAND 2, Paraguay 3	50
1958	France 2, SCOTLAND 1	50
1958	Wales 0, SCOTLAND 3	51
1959	SCOTLAND 3, West Germany 2	51
1959	Northern Ireland 0, SCOTLAND 4	52
1961	England 9, SCOTLAND 3	54
1961	Republic of Ireland 0, SCOTLAND 3	55
1961	SCOTLAND 3, Czechoslovakia 2	55
1961	Czechoslovakia 4, SCOTLAND 2	56
1962	SCOTLAND 2, England 0	56
1962	SCOTLAND 5, Northern Ireland 1	57
1963	England 1, SCOTLAND 2	57
1963	Spain 2, SCOTLAND 6	58
1963	SCOTLAND 6, Norway 1	59
1964	SCOTLAND 1, England 0	59
1964	West Germany 2, SCOTLAND 2	60
1965	England 2, SCOTLAND 2	61
1965	SCOTLAND 1, Italy 0	62
1966	SCOTLAND 1, Brazil 1	63
1967	England 2, SCOTLAND 3	64
1967	Israel 1, SCOTLAND 2	65
1968	SCOTLAND 1, England 1	66
1969	SCOTLAND 8, Cyprus 0	68
1969	West Germany 3, SCOTLAND 2	68
1971	SCOTLAND 2, Portugal 1	71
1971	SCOTLAND 1, Belgium 0	71
1972	Yugoslavia 2, SCOTLAND 2	72
1972	SCOTLAND 2, Denmark 0	73
1973	SCOTLAND 0, England 5	74
1973	SCOTLAND 2, Czechoslovakia 1	75
1974	SCOTLAND 2, England 0	76
1974	Zaire 0, SCOTLAND 2	77
1974	Brazil 0, SCOTLAND 0	78
1974	Yugoslavia 1, SCOTLAND 1	78
1975	SCOTLAND 1, Romania 1	80
1976	SCOTLAND 2, England 1	81
1976	SCOTLAND 6, Finland 0	81
1977	England 1, SCOTLAND 2	83
1977	Argentina 1, SCOTLAND 1	83
1977	Wales 0, SCOTLAND 2	84
1978	Peru 3, SCOTLAND 1	85
1978	Iran 1, SCOTLAND 1	86
1978	Netherlands 2, SCOTLAND 3	86
1978	SCOTLAND 3, Norway 2	87
1980	SCOTLAND 4, Portugal 1	89
1981	England 0, SCOTLAND 1	91
1981	SCOTLAND 2, Sweden 0	91
1982	New Zealand 2, SCOTLAND 5	93
1982	Brazil 4, SCOTLAND 1	94
1982	Soviet Union 2, SCOTLAND 2	94
1984	SCOTLAND 1, England 1	97
1984	SCOTLAND 6, Yugoslavia 1	98
1984	SCOTLAND 3, Spain 1	98
1985	SCOTLAND 1, England 0	99
1985	Wales 1, SCOTLAND 1	100
1985	SCOTLAND 2, Australia 0	100
1986	SCOTLAND 3, Romania 0	101
1986	Denmark 1, SCOTLAND 0	102
1986	West Germany 2, SCOTLAND 1	102
1986	Uruguay 0, SCOTLAND 0	103
1986	SCOTLAND 3, Luxembourg 0	103
1987	SCOTLAND 2, Belgium 0	105
1989	SCOTLAND 2, France 0	107
1989	SCOTLAND 1, Norway 1	108
1990	Costa Rica 1, SCOTLAND 0	110
1990	Sweden 1, SCOTLAND 2	110
1990	Brazil 1, SCOTLAND 0	111

LIST OF FEATURED MATCHES

1991	SCOTLAND 4, San Marino 0	113
1992	Netherlands 1, SCOTLAND 0	114
1992	Germany 2, SCOTLAND 0	114
1992	CIS 0, SCOTLAND 3	115
1993	Malta 0, SCOTLAND 2	117
1995	SCOTLAND 5, San Marino 0	120
1996	Netherlands 0, SCOTLAND 0	121
1996	England 2, SCOTLAND 0	122
1996	Switzerland 0, SCOTLAND 1	122
1997	SCOTLAND 2, Austria 0	123
1997	SCOTLAND 2, Latvia 0	125
1998	Brazil 2, SCOTLAND 1	126
1998	Norway 1, SCOTLAND 1	127
1998	Morocco 3, SCOTLAND 0	127
1999	Germany 0, SCOTLAND 1	128
1999	SCOTLAND 3, Lithuania 0	130
1999	England 0, SCOTLAND 1	130
2001	SCOTLAND 2, Latvia 1	133
2001	France 5, SCOTLAND 0	133
2003	SCOTLAND 1, Lithuania 0	137
2003	SCOTLAND 1, Netherlands 0	138
2005	Slovenia 0, SCOTLAND 3	142
2006	Bulgaria 1, SCOTLAND 5	143
2006	SCOTLAND 6, Faroe Islands 0	144
2006	SCOTLAND 1, France 0	144
2007	France 0, SCOTLAND 1	146
2007	SCOTLAND 1, Italy 2	147
2009	SCOTLAND 0, Netherlands 1	150
2010	SCOTLAND 2, Spain 3	152
2011	Wales 1, SCOTLAND 3	153
2011	Spain 3, SCOTLAND 1	154
2013	England 3, SCOTLAND 2	157
2013	SCOTLAND 2, Croatia 0	158
2015	Gibraltar 0, SCOTLAND 6	162
2017	SCOTLAND 2, England 2	165
2017	Slovenia 2, SCOTLAND 2	166
2018	Albania 0, SCOTLAND 4	168
2019	SCOTLAND 6, San Marino 0	170
2019	SCOTLAND 3, Kazakhstan 1	170
2020	SCOTLAND 0, Israel 0	171
2020	Serbia 1, SCOTLAND 1	172
2020	Israel 1, SCOTLAND 0	173
2021	SCOTLAND 0, Czech Republic 2	175
2021	England 0, SCOTLAND 0	175
2021	SCOTLAND 1, Croatia 3	176
2021	SCOTLAND 2, Denmark 0	177
2022	SCOTLAND 1, Ukraine 3	178
2022	SCOTLAND 3, Ukraine 0	179
2022	Ukraine 0, SCOTLAND 0	180
2023	SCOTLAND 2, Spain 0	181

Denis Law, in the author's opinion Scotland's best ever player, opens the scoring in the memorable 3-2 victory over world champions England in 1967.

Drawings of the first match in 1872. *Courtesy of Scottish Football Museum*

CHAPTER ONE
1873-1914

30 November 1872   Friendly   Hamilton Crescent   Attendance 4,000

1   **SCOTLAND 0, England 0**
Referee: William Keay (Scotland)

Scotland (2-3-5):
1 Robert Gardner (Queen's Park, captain);
1 William Ker (Queen's Park)
1 Robert Leckie (Queen's Park);
1 William MacKinnon (Queen's Park)
1 Alexander Rhind (Queen's Park)
1 Robert Smith (Queen's Park);
1 James Smith (Queen's Park)
1 Joseph Taylor (Queen's Park)
1 James Thomson (Queen's Park)
1 James Weir (Queen's Park)
1 David Wotherspoon (Queen's Park)

The first official Scotland international match was, as were the following four, against the "Auld Enemy" at the West of Scotland Cricket Ground, Hamilton Crescent, Glasgow. According to the scarce reports available, it was a fairly dull affair. The English side was drawn from "nine of the crack clubs" of the country whereas the Scottish 11, although not comprising "so many brilliant players" and all from Queen's Park, worked well together from first to last. The home side was judged to have the best of the first half while the visitors, helped by some "pretty dribbling" from the captain Ottaway, came more into it after the break. Weir, Leckie, Rhind and Wotherspoon were said to have stood out for Scotland, but no goals were to be scored by either side.

England: Robert Barker; John Maynard, Frederick Chappell; Ernest Greenhalgh, John Brockbank, Charles Cheney; John Clegg, Charles Morice, Cuthbert Ottaway (captain), Arnold Smith, Reginald De Courtenay Welch.

---

8 March 1873   Friendly   Kennington Oval, London   Attendance 3,000

2   **England 4, SCOTLAND 2**
Referee: Theodore Lloyd

Scotland: Robert Gardner (Queen's Park, captain); William Ker (Queen's Park), John Blackburn (Royal Engineers); William Gibb (Clydesdale), Arthur Kinnaird (The Wanderers), William MacKinnon (Queen's Park); Henry Renny-Tailyour (Royal Engineers), Robert Smith (Queen's Park), Joseph Taylor (Queen's Park), James Thomson (Queen's Park), David Wotherspoon (Queen's Park).

England: Alec Morten (captain); Alfred Goodwin, Leonard Howell; William Clegg, Ernest Greenhalgh, Alexander Bonsor; Charles Chenery, George "Hubert" Heron, William Kenton-Slaney, Walpole Vidal, Pelham George von Donop.

Scorers: England: Kenyon-Slaney 1, 75; Bonsor 10; Chenery 85   Scotland: Renny-Tailyour 25; Gibb 70

---

7 March 1874   Friendly   Hamilton Crescent, Glasgow   Attendance: 7,000

3   **SCOTLAND 2, ENGLAND 1**
Referee: Archibald Rae (Scotland)

Scotland: Robert Gardner (Clydesdale); John Hunter (Third Lanark), Joseph Taylor (Queen's Park); Charles Campbell (Queen's Park), James Thomson (Queen's Park, captain), James Weir (Queen's Park); John Ferguson (Vale of Leven), Henry McNeil (Queen's Park), William MacKinnon (Queen's Park), Angus MacKinnon (Queen's Park), Frederick Anderson (Clydesdale).

England: Reginald Welch; Robert Ogilvie, Alfred Stratford; Cuthbert Ottaway (captain), Francis Birley, Charles Wollaston; Robert Kingsford, John Edwards, Charles Chenery, George Heron, John Owen.

Scorers: England: Kingsford 28   Scotland: Anderson 42; Angus MacKinnon 47

The Scottish team which lost 4-2 to England in 1873. Back (from left): William Gibb, Robert Smith, Henry Renny-Tailyour, James Thomson, William Ker, William MacKinnon. Front: David Wotherspoon, John Blackburn, Robert Gardner, Arthur Kinnaird, Joseph Taylor. Renny-Tailyour is wearing a different top – the rugby shirt he wore when representing Scotland against England the previous year.
Photo courtesy of Scottish Football Museum

| 6 March 1875 | Friendly | Kennington Oval | Attendance: 2,000 |

4 **England 2, SCOTLAND 2** *Referee: Francis Marindin (England)*

Scotland: Robert Gardner (Clydesdale); John Hunter (Eastern), Joseph Taylor (Queen's Park, captain); Alexander Kennedy (Eastern), Alexander McLintock (Vale of Leven), James Weir (Queen's Park); William MacKinnon (Queen's Park), Henry McNeil (Queen's Park), Thomas Highet (Queen's Park), Peter Andrews (Eastern), John McPherson (Clydesdale).

England: William Carr; Edward Haygarth, William Rawson; Francis Birley, Pelham Von Donop, Charles Wollaston; Charles Alcock (captain), Herbert Rawson, Alexander Bonsor, George Heron, Richard Geaves.

Scorers: England: Wollaston 5; Alcock 70   Scotland: McNeil 30; Andrews 75

| 4 March 1876 | Friendly | Hamilton Crescent, Glasgow | Attendance: 15,000 |

5 **SCOTLAND 3, England 0** *Referee: William Mitchell (Scotland)*

Scotland: Alexander McGeoch (Dumbreck); Joseph Taylor (Queen's Park, captain), John Hunter (Third Lanark); Alexander McLintock (Vale of Leven), Alexander Kennedy (Eastern), Henry McNeil (Queen's Park); William MacKinnon (Queen's Park), Thomas Highet (Queen's Park), William Miller (Third Lanark), John Ferguson (Vale of Leven), John Baird (Vale of Leven).

England: Arthur Savage; Edgar Field, Frederick Green; Beaumont Jarrett, Ernest Bambridge, Walter Buchanan; George Heron, Charles Smith, William Maynard, Charles Heron (captain), Arthur Cursham.

Scorers: Scotland: MacKinnon 8; McNeil 12; Highet 16

| 25 March 1876 | Friendly | Hamilton Crescent, Glasgow | Attendance: 17,000 |

6 **SCOTLAND 4, Wales 0** *Referee: Robert Gardner (Scotland)*

Scotland (2-3-5):
2 Alexander McGeoch (Dumbreck);
6 Joseph Taylor (Queen's Park);
1 Robert Neill (Queen's Park);
3 Alexander Kennedy (Eastern)
2 Charles Campbell (Queen's Park, captain)
3 Thomas Highet (Queen's Park);
3 John Ferguson (Vale of Leven)
1 James Lang (Clydesdale)
6 William MacKinnon (Queen's Park)
1 Moses McNeil (Rangers)
4 Henry McNeil (Queen's Park)

The first game against opposition other than England was again played at Hamilton Crescent, home of the West of Scotland cricket team. A very good crowd turned out to witness a fairly one-sided match, with the Scots running out winners by four goals to nil. The report in *The Scotsman* described the home team's passing and dribbling ability as being a key to victory, particularly evident in players such as the Queen's Park trio of Thomas Highet, William MacKinnon and Henry McNeil. It was John Ferguson of Vale of Leven who opened the scoring near the end of the first half, and James Lang of Clydesdale added another before both MacKinnon and McNeil got in on the act. The Welsh fought hard but were just no match for the home side.

Wales: David Thomson; William Evans, Samuel Kenrick; Edwin Cross, William Williams, Daniel Grey; William Davies, George Thomson, John Edwards, John Jones, Alfred Davies.

Scorers: Scotland: Ferguson 40; Lang 48; MacKinnon 53; Henry McNeil 70

| 3 March 1877 | Friendly | Kennington Oval, London | Attendance: 2,000 |

7 **England 1, SCOTLAND 3** *Referee: Robert Ogilvie (England)*

Scotland: Alexander McGeoch (Dumbreck); Robert Neill (Queen's Park), Thomas Vallance (Rangers); Charles Campbell (Queen's Park, captain), James Phillips (Queen's Park), James Richmond (Clydesdale); William MacKinnon (Queen's Park), John McGregor (Vale of Leven), John McDougall (Vale of Leven), John Smith (Mauchline), John Ferguson (Vale of Leven).

England: Morton Betts; William Lindsay, Lindsay Bury; Beaumont Jarrett, William Rawson, Charles Wollaston; Alfred Lyttleton, William Mosforth, Arthur Cursham, John Bain, Cecil Wingfield-Stratford.

Scorers: Scotland: Richmond 48; Ferguson #, 86   England: Lyttleton 55

| 5 March 1877 | Friendly | The Racecourse, Wrexham | Attendance: 4,000 |

8 **Wales 0, SCOTLAND 2** *Referee: William Dick (Scotland)*

Scotland: Alexander McGeoch (Dumbreck); Robert Neill (Queen's Park), Thomas Vallance (Rangers); James Phillips (Queen's Park), Charles Campbell (Queen's Park, captain), John Smith (Mauchline); John McGregor (Vale of Leven), John Ferguson (Vale of Leven), John McDougall (Vale of Leven), Henry McNeil (Queen's Park), John Hunter (Third Lanark).

Wales: Thomas Burnett; William Evans, Samuel Kenrick; John Morgan, Edwin Cross, William Davies; Alfred Davies, John Price, Alexander Jones, John Hughes, George Thomson.

Scorers: Scotland: Campbell 55; Evans 75 (own goal)

| 2 March 1878 | Friendly | First Hampden Park, Glasgow | Attendance: 10,000 |

9 **SCOTLAND 7, England 2** *Referee: William Dick (Scotland)*

Scotland: Robert Gardner (Clydesdale); Andrew McIntyre (Vale of Leven), Thomas Vallance (Rangers); Charles Campbell (Queen's Park, captain), Alexander Kennedy (Queen's Park), James Richmond (Queen's Park); John McGregor (Vale of Leven), John McDougall (Vale of Leven), Thomas Highet (Queen's Park), William MacKinnon (Queen's Park), Henry McNeil (Queen's Park).

England: Conrad Warner; John Hunter, Edward Lyttleton; Beaumont Jarrett, Norman Bailey, Arthur Cursham (captain); Percy Fairclough, John Wylie, Henry Wace, George Heron, William Mosforth.

Scorers: Scotland: McDougall 7, 41, 46; McGregor 32; McNeil 39, 70; MacKinnon 62   England: Wylie 65; Cursham 75

Chapter one: 1873-1914

23 March 1878	Friendly	First Hampden Park, Glasgow	Attendance: 6,000

10 SCOTLAND 9, Wales 0   *Referee: Robert Gardner (Scotland)*

Scotland: Robert Parlane (Vale of Leven); James Duncan (Alexandra Athletic), Robert Neill (Queen's Park, captain); James Phillips (Queen's Park), David Davidson (Queen's Park), John Ferguson (Vale of Leven); John Baird (Vale of Leven), James Lang (Third Lanark), James Weir (Queen's Park), James Watson (Rangers), Peter Campbell (Rangers).

Wales: Edward Phennah; George Higham, John Powell; Henry Edwards, William Williams, George Savin; James Davies, Daniel Grey, Thomas Britten, John Price, Charles Edwards.

Scorers: Scotland: Campbell 4, 18; Weir 15, 42; Baird 37; Ferguson 38, 50; Watson #; Lang #

5 April 1879	Friendly	Kennington Oval, London	Attendance: 4,500

11 England 5, SCOTLAND 4   *Referee: Charles Wollaston (England)*

Scotland: Robert Parlane (Vale of Leven); William Somers (Third Lanark), Henry McNeil (Queen's Park); Thomas Vallance (Rangers), Charles Campbell (Queen's Park, captain), John McPherson (Vale of Leven); William Beveridge (Ayr Academy), John Smith (Mauchline), John McDougall (Vale of Leven), Robert Paton (Vale of Leven), William MacKinnon (Queen's Park).

England: Reginald Birkett; Edward Christian, Harold Morse; James Prinsep, Norman Bailey, Arnold Hills; Arthur Goodyer, Henry Wace, Francis Sparks, William Mosforth, Edward Bambridge.

Scorers: England: Mosforth 5; Bambridge 48, 83; Goodyer 60, Bailey 75   Scotland: MacKinnon 15, 41; McDougall 23; Smith 26

7 April 1879	Friendly	The Racecourse, Wrexham	Attendance: 2,000

12 Wales 0, SCOTLAND 3   *Referee: John Cooper (Wales)*

Scotland: Robert Parlane (Vale of Leven); Thomas Vallance (Rangers), William Somers (Third Lanark); John McPherson (Vale of Leven), David Davidson (Queen's Park), Henry McNeil (Queen's Park); John McDougall (Vale of Leven, captain), Peter Campbell (Rangers), Robert Paton (Vale of Leven), William Beveridge (Ayr Academy), John Smith (Mauchline).

Wales: John Davies; Samuel Kenrick, John Morgan; Knyvett Crosse, William Williams, James Lloyd; George Woosnam, John Hughes, John Roberts, William Roberts, John Vaughan.

Scorers: Scotland: Campbell 34; Smith #, #

13 March 1880	Friendly	First Hampden Park	Attendance: 12,000

13 SCOTLAND 5, England 4   *Referee: Donald Hamilton (Scotland)*

Scotland: Archibald Rowan (Caledonian); Alexander McLintock (Vale of Leven), Robert Neill (Queen's Park, captain); Charles Campbell (Queen's Park), John McPherson (Vale of Leven), John Smith (Edinburgh University); Moses McNeil (Rangers), George Ker (Queen's Park), John McGregor (Vale of Leven), John Baird (Vale of Leven), John Kay (Queen's Park).

England: Harold Swepstone; Edwin Huntley, Thomas Brindle; Norman Bailey, John Hunter, Segar Bastard; Charles Wollaston, Samuel Widdowson, Francis Sparks, William Mosforth, Edward Bambridge.

Scorers: Scotland: Ker 4, 44, 48, 67; Baird 39   England: Mosforth 8; Bambridge 12, 87; Sparks 89

27 March 1880	Friendly	First Hampden Park	Attendance: 2,000

14 SCOTLAND 5, Wales 1   *Referee: Alexander Stuart (Scotland)*

Scotland: George Gillespie (Rangers); William Somers (Queen's Park), Archibald Lang (Dumbarton); David Davidson (Queen's Park, captain), Hugh McIntyre (Rangers), James Douglas (Renfrew); J. McAdam (Third Lanark), Malcolm Fraser (Queen's Park), Joseph Lindsay (Dumbarton), John Campbell (South Western), William Beveridge (Edinburgh University).

Wales: Harold Hibbott; John Morgan, John Powell; Edward Bowen, Henry Edwards, William Owen; William Roberts, John Roberts, John Price, Thomas Britten, John Vaughan.

Scorers: Scotland: Davidson 38; Beveridge 40; Lindsay #; McAdam #; Campbell #   Wales: William Roberts #

12 March 1881	Friendly	Kennington Oval, London	Attendance: 8,500

15 England 1, SCOTLAND 6   *Referee: Francis Marindin (England)*

Scotland (2-3-5):

2 George Gillespie (Rangers);
1 Andrew Watson (Queen's Park)
6 Thomas Vallance (Rangers);
8 Charles Campbell (Queen's Park, captain)
4 David Davidson (Queen's Park)
1 David Hill (Rangers);
1 William McGuire (Beith)
2 George Ker (Queen's Park)
2 Joseph Lindsay (Dumbarton)
9 Henry McNeil (Queen's Park)
6 John Smith (Edinburgh University)

Wearing rose and primrose shirts, the Scots were heartily applauded as they took to the field at the Surrey County Cricket Ground. They had most of the play in the first half but only scored once, John Smith finishing off a William McGuire cross. The game saw the debut of the first black international player, Scottish full back Andrew Watson, and he was involved in a move before David Hill made it 2-0 just after the break. The goals flowed after that with George Ker getting a third, Edward Bambridge pulling one back for England and Smith restoring the three-goal advantage. Smith completed his hat trick following a goalmouth "scrimmage" and Ker added his own second in the final minute. After the match the Scots were entertained by the Football Association at the Freemasons' Tavern, and left the next day for Wrexham where they would take on Wales.

England: John Hawtrey; Edgar Field, Claude Wilson; Norman Bailey, John Hunter, George Holden; Thurston Rostron, Reginald MacAulay, Clement Mitchell, John Hargreaves, Edward Bambridge.

Scorers: Scotland: Smith 10, 69, 79; Hill 53; Ker 74, 89   England: Bambridge 64

The 1882 team resplendent in their primrose and pink shirts (the racing colours of SFA honorary president Lord Rosebery) and wearing caps for the first time before beating England 5-1 at the first Hampden Park in Glasgow. Andrew Watson, the first black international footballer, is third from left in the back row. Other players (positions unknown) are George Gillespie, Thomas Vallance, Charles Campbell, David Davidson, David Hill, William McGuire, George Ker, Joseph Lindsay, Henry McNeil and John Smith. The team had won 6-1 against England at the Kennington Oval in London the previous year. *Photo courtesy of Scottish Football Museum*

14 March 1881   Friendly   The Racecourse, Wrexham   Attendance: 1,500

16 Wales 1, SCOTLAND 5
Referee: Samuel Kenrick (Wales)

Scotland: George Gillespie (Rangers); Andrew Watson (Queen's Park), Thomas Vallance (Rangers); John McPherson (Vale of Leven), David Davidson (Queen's Park, captain), William McGuire (Beith); David Hill (Rangers), George Ker (Queen's Park), Joseph Lindsay (Dumbarton), Henry McNeil (Queen's Park), John Smith (Edinburgh University).

Wales: Robert McMillan; John Morgan, John Roberts; William Williams, William Bell, William Owen; Thomas Lewis, John Price, Knyvett Crosse, William Roberts, John Vaughan.

Scorers: Wales: Crosse 5   Scotland: Ker 7, 44; McNeil 9; Bell 10 (own goal); Morgan 52 (own goal)

11 March 1882   Friendly   First Hampden Park   Attendance: 10,000

17 SCOTLAND 5, England 1
Referee: John Wallace (Scotland)

Scotland: George Gillespie (Rangers); Andrew Watson (Queen's Park), Andrew McIntyre (Vale of Leven); Charles Campbell (Queen's Park, captain), Peter Miller (Dumbarton), Malcolm Fraser (Queen's Park); William Anderson (Queen's Park), George Ker (Queen's Park), William Harrower (Queen's Park), John Kay (Queen's Park), Robert McPherson (Arthurlie).

England: Harold Swepstone; Haydock Greenwood, Alfred Jones; Norman Bailey, John Hunter, Henry Cursham; Edward Parry, Oliver Vaughton, Arthur Brown, William Mosforth, Edward Bambridge.

Scorers: Scotland: Harrower 15; Ker 43, 70, 85; McPherson 46   England: Vaughton 35

25 March 1882   Friendly   First Hampden Park   Attendance: 5,000

18 SCOTLAND 5, Wales 0
Referee: Donald Hamilton (Scotland)

Scotland: Archibald Rowan (Queen's Park, captain); Andrew Holm (Queen's Park), James Duncan (Alexandra Athletic); Charles Campbell (Queen's Park), Alexander Kennedy (Third Lanark), Malcolm Fraser (Queen's Park); David Hill (Rangers), George Ker (Queen's Park), James McAulay (Dumbarton), John Kay (Queen's Park), James Richmond (Queen's Park).

Wales: Henry Phoenix; John Morgan, John Powell; Henry Edwards, William Williams, John Roberts; William Owen, Walter Roberts, John Price, John Roberts, John Vaughan.

Scorers: Scotland: Kay 25; Ker #; Fraser #, #; McAulay 88

Chapter one: 1873-1914

| 10 March 1883 | Friendly | Bramall Lane, Sheffield | Attendance: 7,000 |

19 England 2, SCOTLAND 3 *Referee: John Sinclair (Ireland)*

Scotland: James McAulay (Dumbarton); Andrew Holm (Queen's Park, captain), Michael Paton (Dumbarton); Peter Miller (Dumbarton), John McPherson (Vale of Leven), Malcolm Fraser (Queen's Park); William Anderson (Queen's Park), John Smith (Queen's Park), John Inglis (Rangers), John Kay (Queen's Park), William McKinnon (Dumbarton).
England: Harold Swepstone; Percy De Paravincini, Alfred Jones; Norman Bailey, Stuart Macrae, Oliver Whately; Arthur Cursham, Harold Goodhart, Clement Mitchell, Henry Cursham, William Cobbold.
Scorers: Scotland: Smith 22, 39; Fraser 86   England: Mitchell 24; Cobbold 43

| 12 March 1883 | Friendly | The Racecourse, Wrexham | Attendance: 2,000 |

20 Wales 0, SCOTLAND 3 *Referee: Robert Lythgoe (England)*

Scotland: James McAulay (Dumbarton); Andrew Holm (Queen's Park, captain), Walter Arnott (Queen's Park); Peter Miller (Dumbarton), John McPherson (Vale of Leven), Malcolm Fraser (Queen's Park); William Anderson (Queen's Park), John Smith (Queen's Park), John Inglis (Rangers), John Kay (Queen's Park), William McKinnon (Dumbarton).
Wales: Richard Gough; Frederick Hughes, John Powell; Edward Bowen, Henry Edwards, John Jones; William Owen, Walter Roberts, John Price, William Roberts, John Vaughan.
Scorers: Scotland: Smith 35; Fraser 38; Anderson #

| 26 January 1884 | Home Championship | Ballynafeigh Park, Belfast | Attendance: 2,000 |

21 Ireland 0, SCOTLAND 5 *Referee: Thomas Hindle (England)*

Scotland (2-3-5):
1 John Inglis (Kilmarnock Athletic);
1 John Forbes (Vale of Leven)
2 Walter Arnott (Queen's Park, captain);
1 John Graham (Annbank)
1 William Fulton (Abercorn)
1 Robert Brown (Dumbarton);
1 Samuel Thomson (Boswell)
1 James Gossland (Rangers)
1 John Goudie (Abercorn)
2 William Harrower (Queen's Park)
1 John McAulay (Arthurlie)

Scotland's first ever game against Ireland was also the inaugural match in the British Home Championship, which was to run until a century later. The Scots were the first winners and along with England dominated the competition for the rest of the 19th century. Although Ireland was partitioned in 1921 and Northern Ireland and the Irish Republic were created, the team stuck to the original name until finally becoming Northern Ireland in 1954. Apart from periods during the First and Second World Wars the competition ran until 1984, with Northern Ireland being the final winners. In that first match 100 years earlier, the Scots enjoyed a 5-0 victory in Belfast, with goals coming from William Harrower (2), James Gossland (2) and John Goudie.

Ireland: Robert Hunter; Robert Wilson, William Crone; John Hastings, Thomas Molyneux, Alexander Dill; Arthur Spiller, John Gibb, William Morrow, John Davison, Arthur Gaussen.
Scorers: Scotland: Harrower 12, 86; Gossland 33, 72; Goudie 60

| 15 March 1884 | Home Championship | Cathkin Park, Glasgow | Attendance: 10,000 |

22 SCOTLAND 1, England 0 *Referee: John Sinclair (Ireland)*

Scotland: James McAulay (Dumbarton); Walter Arnott (Queen's Park), John Forbes (Vale of Leven); Charles Campbell (Queen's Park, captain), John McPherson (Vale of Leven), William Anderson (Queen's Park); Francis Shaw (Pollockshields Athletic), John Smith (Queen's Park), Joseph Lindsay (Dumbarton), Robert Christie (Queen's Park), William McKinnon (Dumbarton).
England: William Rose; Joseph Beverley, Alfred Dobson; Stuart Macrae, Norman Bailey, Charles Wilson; George Holden, Oliver Vaughton, William Bromley-Davenport, Edward Bambridge, William Gunn.
Scorer: Scotland: Smith 7

| 29 March 1884 | Home Championship | Cathkin Park, Glasgow | Attendance: 5,000 |

23 SCOTLAND 4, Wales 1 *Referee: Robert Sloane (England)*

Scotland: Thomas Turner (Arthurlie); Michael Paton (Dumbarton, captain), John Forbes (Vale of Leven); Alexander Kennedy (Third Lanark), James McIntyre (Rangers), Robert Brown (Dumbarton); Francis Shaw (Pollockshields Athletic), Samuel Thomson (Boswell), Joseph Lindsay (Dumbarton), John Kay (Queen's Park), William McKinnon (Dumbarton).
Wales: Elias Owen; Robert Roberts, Charles Conde; Frederick Hughes, Thomas Burke, John Jones; William Owen, Walter Roberts, Edward Shaw, John Eyton-Jones, Robert Jones.
Scorers: Scotland: Lindsay 22; Shaw 49; Kay 65, 87   Wales: Robert Roberts 7

| 14 March 1885 | Home Championship | First Hampden Park | Attendance: 6,000 |

24 SCOTLAND 8, Ireland 2 *Referee: William Dix (England)*

Scotland: William Chalmers (Rangers); Hugh McHardy (Rangers), James Niven (Moffat); Robert Kelso (Renton), John McPherson (Vale of Leven, captain), Alexander Barbour (Renton); John Marshall (Third Lanark), William Turner (Pollockshields Athletic), Alexander Higgins (Kilmarnock), Robert Calderwood (Cartvale), Walter Lamont (Pilgrims).
Ireland: Anthony Henderson; George Hewison, Samuel Johnston; Robert Muir, William Houston, William Eames; Thomas McLean, Joseph Sherrard, John Gibb, George McGee, Alexander Dill.
Scorers: Scotland: Lamont 10; Turner 12; Calderwood 15; Marshall 35; Higgins 51, #, #; Barbour 53   Ireland: Gibb 81, 89

| 21 March 1885 | Home Championship | Kennington Oval, London | Attendance: 8,000 |

25 England 1, SCOTLAND 1
Referee: John Sinclair (Ireland)

Scotland: James McAulay (Dumbarton); Walter Arnott (Queen's Park), Michael Paton (Dumbarton); Charles Campbell (Queen's Park, captain), John Gow (Queen's Park), William Anderson (Queen's Park); Alexander Hamilton (Queen's Park), William Sellar (Battlefield), Joseph Lindsay (Dumbarton), David Allan (Queen's Park), Robert Calderwood (Cartvale).

England: William Arthur; Arthur Walters, Percy Walters; Andrew Amos, Norman Bailey, James Forrest; Joseph Lofthouse, Thomas Danks, James Brown, William Cobbold, Edward Bambridge.

Scorers: Scotland: Lindsay 20   England: Bambridge 57

| 23 March 1885 | Home Championship | The Racecourse, Wrexham | Attendance: 2,000 |

26 Wales 1, SCOTLAND 8
Referee: Robert Sloane (England)

Scotland: James McAulay (Dumbarton); Walter Arnott (Queen's Park), Michael Paton (Dumbarton, captain); Robert Kelso (Renton), Leitch Keir (Renton), Alexander Hamilton (Queen's Park); William Anderson (Queen's Park), Joseph Lindsay (Dumbarton), Robert Calderwood (Cartvale), Robert Brown (Dumbarton), David Allan (Queen's Park).

Wales: Robert Mills-Roberts; George Thomas, Seth Powell; Thomas Burke, William Foulkes, Humphrey Jones; James Lloyd, Job Wilding, Harold Hibbott, George Farmer, Robert Jones.

Scorers: Scotland: Calderwood 8, #; Anderson #, #; Allan #; Lindsay 56, #, #   Wales: Robert Jones 54

| 20 March 1886 | Home Championship | Ballynafeigh Park, Belfast | Attendance: 3,000 |

27 Ireland 2, SCOTLAND 7
Referee: Jack Wolstenholme (Ireland)

Scotland: James Connor (Airdrie); Andrew Thomson (Arthurlie), William McLeod (Queen's Park); John Cameron (Rangers), Leitch Keir (Dumbarton), Robert Fleming (Morton); John Lambie (Queen's Park, captain), Charles Heggie (Rangers), William Turner (Pollockshields Athletic), James Gourlay (Cambuslang), Michael Dunbar (Cartvale).

Ireland: Shaw Gillespie; James Watson, William Crone; Thomas Molyneux, Oliver Devine, John Hastings; John McClatchey, Samuel Johnston, John Gibb, John Condy, William Turner.

Scorers: Scotland: Heggie 15, 18, #, #; Lambie #; Dunbar #; Gourlay #   Ireland: Condy #; Johnston 44

| 27 March 1886 | Home Championship | First Hampden Park | Attendance: 11,000 |

28 SCOTLAND 1, England 1
Referee: Alexander Hunter (Wales)

Scotland: James McAulay (Dumbarton); Walter Arnott (Queen's Park, captain), Michael Paton (Dumbarton); Charles Campbell (Queen's Park), John MacDonald (Edinburgh University), Alexander Hamilton (Queen's Park); William Sellar (Battlefield), George Somerville (Queen's Park), Joseph Lindsay (Dumbarton), Woodville Gray (Pollockshields Athletic), Ralph Aitken (Dumbarton).

England: William Arthur; Arthur Walters, Percy Walters; Norman Bailey (captain), Ralph Squire, James Forrest; Benjamin Spilsbury, George Brann, Tinsley Lindley, William Cobbold, Edward Bambridge.

Scorers: England: Lindley 35   Scotland: Somerville 80

| 10 April 1886 | Home Championship | First Hampden Park | Attendance: 5,500 |

29 SCOTLAND 4, Wales 1
Referee: John Sinclair (Ireland)

Scotland: George Gillespie (Queen's Park); James Lundie (Hibernian), William Semple (Cambuslang, captain); Robert Kelso (Renton), Andrew Jackson (Cambuslang), John Marshall (Third Lanark); Robert McCormick (Abercorn), James McGhee (Hibernian), William Harrower (Queen's Park), David Allan (Queen's Park), James McCall (Renton).

Wales: Albert Hersee; Alfred Davies, Frederick Jones; John Vaughan, William Bell, Humphrey Jones; Richard Williams, William Roberts, John Doughty, Herbert Sisson, William Lewis.

Scorers: Scotland: McCormick 30; McCall 47; Allan 53; Harrower 56   Wales: Vaughan 88

| 19 February 1887 | Home Championship | First Hampden Park | Attendance: 1,000 |

30 SCOTLAND 4, Ireland 1
Referee: Alexander Hunter (Wales)

Scotland: John Doig (Arbroath); Andrew Whitelaw (Vale of Leven), Robert Smellie (Queen's Park); John Weir (Third Lanark), Thomas McMillan (Dumbarton), James Hutton (St Bernard's); Thomas Jenkinson (Hearts), John Lambie (Queen's Park, captain), William Watt (Queen's Park), James Lowe (St Bernard's), William Johnstone (Third Lanark).

Ireland: Shaw Gillespie; William Fox, John Watson; Robert Moore, Archibald Rosbotham, Robert Baxter; John Reid, Olphert Stanfield, Frederick Browne, John Peden, John Gibb (captain).

Scorers: Scotland: Watt 5; Jenkinson 43; Johnstone 55; Lowe 75   Ireland: Browne 41

| 19 March 1887 | Home Championship | Leamington Road, Blackburn | Attendance: 12,000 |

31 England 2, SCOTLAND 3
Referee: John Sinclair (Ireland)

Scotland: James McAulay (Dumbarton, captain); Walter Arnott (Queen's Park), John Forbes (Vale of Leven); Robert Kelso (Renton), John Auld (Third Lanark), Leitch Keir (Dumbarton); John Marshall (Third Lanark), William Robertson (Dumbarton), William Sellar (Battlefield), James McCall (Renton), James Allan (Queen's Park).

England: Robert Roberts; Percy Walters, Arthur Walters; Norman Bailey, George Haworth, James Forrest; Edward Bambridge, William Cobbold, Joseph Lofthouse, Frederick Dewhurst, Tinsley Lindley.

Scorers: Scotland: McCall 30; Keir 68; Allan 70   England: Lindley 32; Dewhurst 69

Chapter one: 1873-1914

| 21 March 1887 | Home Championship | The Racecourse, Wrexham | Attendance: 2,000 |

32 **Wales 0, SCOTLAND 2** *Referee: Alfred Hull (England)*

Scotland: James McAulay (Dumbarton, captain); Walter Arnott (Queen's Park), John Forbes (Vale of Leven); Robert Kelso (Renton), John Auld (Third Lanark), Leitch Keir (Dumbarton); John Marshall (Third Lanark), William Robertson (Dumbarton), William Sellar (Battlefield), James McCall (Renton), James Allan (Queen's Park).

Wales: James Trainer; Alfred Davies, John Powell; Robert Roberts, James Morris, Thomas Burke; John Challen, Richard Jones, William Pryce-Jones, William Lewis, John Doughty.

Scorers: Scotland: Robertson 40; Allan 80

| 10 March 1888 | Home Championship | Easter Road, Edinburgh | Attendance: 8,000 |

33 **SCOTLAND 5, Wales 1** *Referee: John Clegg (England)*

Scotland: James Wilson (Vale of Leven); Andrew Hannah (Renton), Robert Smellie (Queen's Park, captain); James Johnstone (Abercorn), James Gourlay (Cambuslang), James McLaren (Hibernian); Alexander Latta (Dumbarton Athletic), William Groves (Hibernian), William Paul (Partick Thistle), John McPherson (Kilmarnock), Neil Munro (Abercorn).

Wales: James Trainer; David Jones, John Powell; Thomas Burke, Joseph Davies, Robert Roberts; William Pryce-Jones, Job Wilding, John Doughty, George Owen, Roger Doughty.

Scorers: Scotland: Paul 6; Munro 30; Latta 33, 75; Groves 65   Wales: John Doughty 41

| 17 March 1888 | Home Championship | First Hampden Park | Attendance: 10,000 |

34 **SCOTLAND 0, England 5** *Referee: John Sinclair (Ireland)*

Scotland: John Lindsay (Renton); Walter Arnott (Queen's Park), Donald Gow (Rangers, captain); James Kelly (Renton), Leitch Keir (Dumbarton), Robert Kelso (Renton); Alexander Hamilton (Queen's Park), William Berry (Queen's Park), William Sellar (Battlefield), James McCall (Renton), John Lambie (Queen's Park).

England: William Moon; Robert Howarth, Percy Walters; Henry Allen, George Haworth, Cecil Holden-White; George Woodhall, John Goodall, Tinsley Lindley, Dennis Hodgetts, Frederick Dewhurst.

Scorers: England: Lindley 32; Hodgetts 34; Dewhurst 40, 49; Goodall 43

| 24 March 1888 | Home Championship | Solitude, Belfast | Attendance: 5,000 |

35 **Ireland 2, SCOTLAND 10** *Referee: Robert Parlane (Scotland)*

Scotland: John McLeod (Dumbarton); Duncan Stewart (Dumbarton, captain), Archibald McCall (Renton); Allan Stewart (Queen's Park), George Dewar (Dumbarton), Andrew Jackson (Cambuslang); Neil McCallum (Renton), John Gow (Rangers), William Dickson (Strathmore), Thomas Breckenridge (Hearts), Ralph Aitken (Dumbarton).

Ireland: Ralph Lawther; Robert Wilson, Frederick Browne; James Forsythe, Archibald Rosbotham, Thomas Molyneux; William Dalton, Olphert Stanfield, John Barry, John Lemon, William Turner.

Scorers: Scotland: Dewar 5; Dickson 8, 33, 40, 45; Breckenridge 15; Aitken #; McCallum 53; Wilson 77 (own goal); Allan Stewart 83
Ireland: Dalton #, #

| 9 March 1889 | Home Championship | Ibrox Park, Glasgow | Attendance: 6,000 |

36 **SCOTLAND 7, Ireland 0** *Referee: William Stacey (England)*

Scotland: John Doig (Arbroath); James Adams (Hearts), Thomas McKeown (Celtic); Thomas Robertson (Queen's Park, captain), David Calderhead (Queen of the South Wanderers), John Buchanan (Cambuslang); Francis Watt (Kilbirnie), Thomas McInnes (Cowlairs), William Groves (Celtic), Robert Boyd (Mossend Swifts), David Black (Hurlford).

Ireland: John Clugston; John McVicker, Robert Crone; John Thompson, James Christian, William Crone; Samuel Torrans, Olphert Stanfield, John Gibb, James Wilton, John Peden.

Scorers: Scotland: Watt 7, 10; Black 25; Groves 32, 50, 71; McInnes 88

| 13 April 1889 | Home Championship | Kennington Oval, London | Attendance: 10,000 |

37 **England 2, SCOTLAND 3** *Referee: John Sinclair (Ireland)*

Scotland: James Wilson (Vale of Leven); Robert Smellie (Queen's Park, captain), Walter Arnott (Queen's Park); James Kelly (Celtic), George Dewar (Dumbarton), James McLaren (Celtic); James Oswald (Third Lanark), William Berry (Queen's Park), Alexander Latta (Dumbarton Athletic), John McPherson (Cowlairs), Neil Munro (Abercorn).

England: William Moon; Arthur Walters, Percy Walters; Henry Hammond, Henry Allen, James Forrest; William Bassett, John Goodall, John Brodie, David Weir, Tinsley Lindley.

Scorers: England: Bassett 15; Weir 17   Scotland: Munro 55; Oswald 82; McPherson 90

| 15 April 1889 | Home Championship | The Racecourse, Wrexham | Attendance: 6,000 |

38 **Wales 0, SCOTLAND 0** *Referee: John Sinclair (Ireland)*

Scotland: John McLeod (Dumbarton); Andrew Thomson (Third Lanark, captain), James Rae (Third Lanark); Allan Stewart (Queen's Park), Alexander Lochhead (Third Lanark), John Auld (Third Lanark); Francis Watt (Kilbirnie), Henry Campbell (Renton), William Paul (Partick Thistle), William Johnstone (Third Lanark), James Hannah (Third Lanark).

Wales: Allen Pugh; Alfred Davies, David Jones; Robert Roberts, Joseph Davies, Humphrey Jones; Joseph Davies, William Owen, John Doughty, George Owen, William Lewis. Substitute: Samuel Gillam (for Pugh 30).

| 22 March 1890 | Home Championship | Underwood Park, Paisley | Attendance: 7,500 |

39 SCOTLAND 5, Wales 0

Referee: William Findlay (Ireland)

Scotland: George Gillespie (Rangers, captain); Andrew Whitelaw (Vale of Leven), John Murray (Vale of Leven); Matthew McQueen (Leith Athletic), Andrew Brown (St Mirren), Hugh Wilson (Newmilns); J. Brown (Cambuslang), Francis Watt (Kilbirnie), William Paul (Partick Thistle), James Dunlop (St Mirren), Daniel Bruce (Vale of Leven).

Wales: James Trainer; William Jones, Samuel Jones; Peter Griffiths, Humphrey Jones, Robert Roberts; David Lewis, Oswald Davies, William Owen, Richard Jarrett, William Turner.

Scorers: Scotland: Wilson #; Paul 36, 43, #, 70

| 29 March 1890 | Home Championship | Ballynafeigh Park, Belfast | Attendance: 5,000 |

40 Ireland 1, SCOTLAND 4

Referee: William Stacey (England)

Scotland: John McLeod (Dumbarton, captain); Richard Hunter (St Mirren), James Rae (Third Lanark); John Russell (Cambuslang), Isaac Begbie (Hearts), David Mitchell (Rangers); Thomas Wylie (Rangers), Gilbert Rankin (Vale of Leven), John McPherson (Cowlairs), John Bell (Dumbarton), David Baird (Hearts).

Ireland: John Clugston; Robert Stewart, Robert Crone; John Reid, Samuel Spencer, Samuel Cooke; William Dalton, George Gaffikin, Olphert Stanfield, Samuel Torrans, John Peden.

Scorers: Scotland: Rankin 10, #; Wylie 50; McPherson #   Ireland: Peden #

| 5 April 1890 | Home Championship | Second Hampden Park | Attendance: 26,379 |

41 SCOTLAND 1, England 1

Referee: John Reid (Ireland)

Scotland: James Wilson (Vale of Leven); Walter Arnott (Queen's Park), Thomas McKeown (Celtic); Thomas Robertson (Queen's Park), James Kelly (Celtic), James McLaren (Celtic, captain); William Groves (Celtic), William Berry (Queen's Park), William Johnstone (Third Lanark), John McPherson (Cowlairs), James McCall (Renton).

England: William Moon; Arthur Walters, Percy Walters; George Haworth, Henry Allen, Alfred Shelton; William Bassett, Edward Currey, Tinsley Lindley, Harold Wood, Harold Daft.

Scorers: England: Wood 17   Scotland: McPherson 37

| 21 March 1891 | Home Championship | The Racecourse, Wrexham | Attendance: 4,000 |

42 Wales 3, SCOTLAND 4

Referee: Charles Crump (England)

Scotland: John McCorkindale (Partick Thistle); Archibald Ritchie (East Stirlingshire), James Hepburn (Alloa Athletic); Matthew McQueen (Leith Athletic), Andrew Brown (St Mirren), Thomas Robertson (Queen's Park, captain); William Gulliland (Queen's Park), Robert Buchanan (Abercorn), James Logan (Ayr United), Robert Boyd (Mossend Swifts), Alexander Keillor (Montrose).

Wales: James Trainer; Seth Powell, David Jones; Arthur Lea, Humphrey Jones, Charles Parry; Joseph Davies, William Owen, William Turner, John Bowdler, William Lewis.

Scorers: Scotland: Logan #; Buchanan #; Boyd #, #   Wales: Bowdler #, #; Owen #

The smart-looking team of 1891. The positions of the players in the photograph are unknown.

Photo courtesy of Scottish Football Museum

Chapter one: 1873-1914

| 28 March 1891 | Home Championship | Celtic Park, Glasgow | Attendance: 8,000 |

43 SCOTLAND 2, Ireland 1 *Referee: William Stacey (England)*

Scotland: George Gillespie (Queen's Park, captain); Donald Sillars (Queen's Park), William Paul (Dykebar); Thomas Hamilton (Hurlford), James Cleland (Royal Albert), James Campbell (Kilmarnock); James Low (Cambuslang), Robert Clements (Leith Athletic), William Bowie (Linthouse), Thomas Waddell (Queen's Park), James Fraser (Moffat).
Ireland: Joseph Loyal; William Gordon, George Forbes; Alexander Crawford, John Reynolds, Richard Moore; William Dalton, George Gaffikin, Olphert Stanfield, David Brisby, Samuel Torrans.
Scorers: Scotland: Low 6; Waddell 60   Ireland: Stanfield 85

| 4 April 1891 | Home Championship | Ewood Park, Blackburn | Attendance: 31,000 |

44 England 2, SCOTLAND 1 *Referee: William Morrow (Ireland)*

Scotland: James Wilson (Vale of Leven); Walter Arnott (Queen's Park, captain), Robert Smellie (Queen's Park); Isaac Begbie (Hearts), John McPherson (Hearts), John Hill (Hearts); Gilbert Rankin (Vale of Leven), Francis Watt (Kilbirnie), William Sellar (Queen's Park), William Berry (Queen's Park), David Baird (Hearts).
England: William Moon; Robert Howarth, Robert Holmes; Albert Smith, John Holt, Alfred Shelton; William Bassett, John Goodall, Frederick Geary, Edgar Chadwick, Alfred Milward.
Scorers: England: Goodall 20; Chadwick 30   Scotland: Watt 85

| 19 March 1892 | Home Championship | Solitude, Belfast | Attendance: 10,500 |

45 Ireland 2, SCOTLAND 3 *Referee: John Taylor (Wales)*

Scotland: Andrew Baird (Queen's Park); George Bowman (Montrose), John Drummond (Falkirk); Robert Marshall (Rangers), Thomas Robertson (Queen's Park, captain), Peter Dowds (Celtic); William Gulliland (Queen's Park), David McPherson (Kilmarnock), James Ellis (Mossend Swifts), William Lambie (Queen's Park), Alexander Keillor (Montrose).
Ireland: John Clugston; William Gordon, Robert Stewart; Nathaniel McKeown, Samuel Spencer, William Cunningham; William Dalton, George Gaffikin, James Williamson, Olphert Stanfield, Samuel Torrans.
Scorers: Scotland: Keillor 17; Lambie 28; Ellis #   Ireland: Williamson 42; Gaffikin 86

| 26 March 1892 | Home Championship | Tynecastle Park, Edinburgh | Attendance: 600 |

46 SCOTLAND 6, Wales 1 *Referee: John Reid (Ireland)*

Scotland: Robert Downie (Third Lanark); James Adams (Hearts), James Orr (Kilmarnock); Isaac Begbie (Hearts), James Campbell (Kilmarnock), John Hill (Hearts, captain); John Taylor (Dumbarton), William Thomson (Dumbarton), James Hamilton (Queen's Park), John McPherson (Rangers), David Baird (Hearts).
Wales: James Trainer; Smart Arridge, Seth Powell; William Hughes, Caesar Jenkins, Robert Roberts; Job Wilding, William Owen, William Lewis, Thomas Egan, Benjamin Lewis.
Scorers: Scotland: Thomson 1; Hamilton #, #; McPherson 15, 44; Baird #   Wales: Benjamin Lewis 87

| 2 April 1892 | Home Championship | Ibrox Park, Glasgow | Attendance: 20,000 |

47 SCOTLAND 1, England 4 *Referee: John Smith (Scotland)*

Scotland: John McLeod (Dumbarton); Daniel Doyle (Celtic), Walter Arnott (Queen's Park); James Kelly (Celtic), William Sellar (Queen's Park, captain), David Mitchell (Rangers); Donald Sillars (Queen's Park), William Taylor (Hearts), Thomas Waddell (Queen's Park), Alexander McMahon (Celtic), John Bell (Dumbarton).
England: George Toone; Arthur Dunn (captain), Robert Holmes; John Reynolds, John Holt, Alfred Shelton; William Bassett, John Goodall, John Southworth, Edgar Chadwick, Dennis Hodgetts.
Scorers: England: Chadwick 1; Goodall 20, 26; Southworth 25   Scotland: Bell 80

| 18 March 1893 | Home Championship | The Racecourse, Wrexham | Attendance: 4,500 |

48 Wales 0, SCOTLAND 8 *Referee: William Stacey (England)*

Scotland: John McLeod (Dumbarton); Daniel Doyle (Celtic), Robert Foyers (St Bernard's); Donald Sillars (Queen's Park, captain), Andrew McCreadie (Rangers), David Stewart (Queen's Park); John Taylor (Dumbarton), William Thomson (Dumbarton), John Madden (Celtic), John Barker (Rangers), William Lambie (Queen's Park).
Wales: Samuel Jones; Oliver Taylor, Frederick Jones; George Williams, Edwin Williams, Edward Morris; William Owen, James Vaughan, John Butler, Benjamin Lewis, Harold Bowdler.
Scorers: Scotland: Madden 4, 20, 47, 89; Barker #, #, #; Lambie #

| 25 March 1893 | Home Championship | Celtic Park, Glasgow | Attendance: 12,000 |

49 SCOTLAND 6, Ireland 1 *Referee: John Taylor (Wales)*

Scotland: John Lindsay (Renton); James Adams (Hearts), Robert Smellie (Queen's Park); William Maley (Celtic), James Kelly (Celtic, captain), David Mitchell (Rangers); William Sellar (Queen's Park), Thomas Waddell (Queen's Park), James Hamilton (Queen's Park), Alexander McMahon (Celtic), John Campbell (Celtic).
Ireland: John Clugston; William Gordon, Robert Torrans; Nathaniel McKeown, Samuel Johnston, Samuel Torrans; James Small, George Gaffikin, James Williamson, James Wilton, John Peden.
Scorers: Scotland: Sellar 10, 27; Samuel Torrans 20 (own goal); McMahon 28; Kelly #; Hamilton #   Ireland: Gaffikin 44

1 April 1893 Home Championship Richmond Athletic Ground, London Attendance: 16,000

50 England 5, SCOTLAND 2
Referee: John Clegg (England)

Scotland: John Lindsay (Renton); Walter Arnott (Queen's Park), Robert Smellie (Queen's Park); William Maley (Celtic), James Kelly (Celtic, captain), David Mitchell (Rangers); William Sellar (Queen's Park), Thomas Waddell (Queen's Park), James Hamilton (Queen's Park), Alexander McMahon (Celtic), John Campbell (Celtic).

England: Leslie Gay; Alban Harrison, Robert Holmes; John Reynolds, John Holt, George Kinsey; William Bassett, Robert Gosling, George Cotterill (captain), Edgar Chadwick, Frederick Spiksley,

Scorers: England: Gosling 15; Cotterill 65; Spiksley 75, 80; Reynolds 86   Scotland: Sellar 20, 47

24 March 1894 Home Championship Rugby Park, Kilmarnock Attendance: 10,000

51 SCOTLAND 5, Wales 2
Referee: Joseph McBride (Ireland)

Scotland: Andrew Baird (Queen's Park); David Crawford (St Mirren), Robert Foyers (St Bernard's); Edward McBain (St Mirren), James Kelly (Celtic, captain), John Johnstone (Kilmarnock); Andrew Stewart (Third Lanark), Thomas Chambers (Hearts), David Alexander (East Stirlingshire), Davidson Berry (Queen's Park), John Barker (Rangers).

Wales: Samuel Gillam; Oliver Taylor, Abel Hughes; George Williams, Thomas Chapman, Thomas Worthington; Hugh Morris, Benjamin Lewis, William Lewis, John Rea, Edwin James.

Scorers: Scotland: Berry 42; Barker 44; Chambers 70; Alexander #; Johnstone #   Wales: Morris #, #

31 March 1894 Home Championship Solitude, Belfast Attendance: 6,000

52 Ireland 1, SCOTLAND 2
Referee: Edward Phennah (Wales)

Scotland: Francis Barrett (Dundee); David Crawford (St Mirren), John Drummond (Rangers), Robert Marshall (Rangers, captain), William Longair (Dundee), David Stewart (Queen's Park); John Taylor (Dumbarton), James Blessington (Celtic), David Alexander (East Stirlingshire), Robert Scott (Airdrie), Alexander Keillor (Dundee).

Ireland: Thomas Scott; Robert Stewart, Samuel Torrans; Nathaniel McKeown, John Burnett, Robert Milne; William Dalton, George Gaffikin, Olphert Stanfield, William Gibson, James Barron.

Scorers: Scotland: Torrans 25 (own goal); Taylor 28   Ireland: Stanfield #

7 April 1894 Home Championship Celtic Park, Glasgow Attendance: 45,107

53 SCOTLAND 2, England 2
Referee: John Reid (Ireland)

Scotland: David Haddow (Rangers); Donald Sillars (Queen's Park), Daniel Doyle (Celtic, captain); Isaac Begbie (Hearts), Andrew McCreadie (Rangers), David Mitchell (Rangers); William Gulliland (Queen's Park), James Blessington (Celtic), Alexander McMahon (Celtic), John McPherson (Rangers), William Lambie (Queen's Park).

England: Leslie Gay; Thomas Clare, Frederick Pelly; John Reynolds, John Holt, Ernest Needham; William Bassett, John Goodall (captain), Gilbert Smith, Edgar Chadwick, Frederick Spiksley.

Scorers: Scotland: Lambie 7; McMahon 75   England: Goodall 35; Reynolds 85

23 March 1895 Home Championship The Racecourse, Wrexham Attendance 4,000

54 Wales 2, SCOTLAND 2
Referee: William Jope (England)

Scotland: Francis Barrett (Dundee); Donald Sillars (Queen's Park, captain), Robert Glen (Renton); James Simpson (Third Lanark), William McColl (Renton), Alexander Keillor (Dundee); John Fife (Third Lanark), John Murray (Renton), John Madden (Celtic), William Sawers (Dundee), John Divers (Celtic).

Wales: Samuel Jones; Robert Lloyd, Charles Parry; George Williams, Thomas Chapman, John Jones; Joseph Davies, Benjamin Lewis, Harold Trainer, William Lewis, John Rea.

Scorers: Wales: William Lewis #; Chapman #   Scotland: Madden #; Divers 39

30 March 1895 Home Championship Celtic Park, Glasgow Attendance: 15,000

55 SCOTLAND 3, Ireland 1
Referee: Thomas Mitchell (England)

Scotland: Daniel McArthur (Celtic); John Drummond (Rangers, captain), Daniel Doyle (Celtic); James Simpson (Third Lanark), David Russell (Hearts), Neil Gibson (Rangers); John Taylor (St Mirren), Thomas Waddell (Queen's Park), John McPherson (Rangers), John Walker (Hearts), William Lambie (Queen's Park).

Ireland: Thomas Scott; John Ponsonby, Lewis Scott; Hymie McKee, Thomas Alexander, Thomas McClatchey; Thomas Morrison, William Sherrard, Olphert Stanfield, William Gibson, James Barron.

Scorers: Scotland: Lambie 1; Walker #, #   Ireland: Sherrard #

6 April 1895 Home Championship Goodison Park, Liverpool Attendance: 42,500

56 England 3, SCOTLAND 0
Referee: John Reid (Ireland)

Scotland: Daniel McArthur (Celtic); John Drummond (Rangers), Daniel Doyle (Celtic); David Russell (Hearts), James Simpson (Third Lanark), Neil Gibson (Rangers); William Lambie (Queen's Park), John McPherson (Rangers), James Oswald (St Bernard's, captain), Thomas Waddell (Queen's Park), William Gulliland (Queen's Park).

England: John Sutcliffe; Lewis Lodge, James Crabtree; John Reynolds, John Holt, Ernest Needham; William Bassett, Stephen Bloomer, John Goodall (captain), Robert Gosling, Stephen Smith.

Scorers: England: Bloomer 30; Gibson 35 (own goal); Smith 44

Chapter one: 1873-1914

The team which played England in 1895. Back (from left): R. F. Harrison (SFA vice-president), John Drummond, William Lambie, Archibald Sliman (SFA president), David Russell, Neil Gibson, R. Dixon (SFA treasurer). Middle: William Gulliland, James Simpson, Thomas Waddell, James Oswald, John McPherson, Daniel Doyle, Daniel McArthur. Front: Robert Foyers, John McDowall (SFA secretary), J. Taylor (trainer).

| 21 March 1896 | Home Championship | Carolina Port, Dundee | Attendance: 11,700 |

57 SCOTLAND 4, Wales 0
Referee: Joseph McBride (Ireland)

Scotland: Robert MacFarlane (Morton); Duncan McLean (St Bernard's), Robert Glen (Renton); John Gillespie (Queen's Park, captain), Robert Neil (Hibernian), William Blair (Third Lanark); William Thomson (Dundee), Daniel Paton (St Bernard's), Robert McColl (Queen's Park), Alexander King (Hearts), Alexander Keillor (Dundee).

Wales: James Trainer; Charles Parry, John Matthias; Joseph Rogers, Caesar Jenkyns, John Jones; David Pugh, John Garner, Arthur Morris, John Rea, William Lewis.

Scorers: Scotland: Neil #, #; Keillor #; Paton #

| 28 March 1896 | Home Championship | Solitude, Belfast | Attendance: 8,000 |

58 Ireland 3, SCOTLAND 3
Referee: James Cooper (England)

Scotland: Kenneth Anderson (Queen's Park); Peter Meechan (Celtic), John Drummond (Rangers); Neil Gibson (Rangers), James Kelly (Celtic, captain), George Hogg (Hearts); Patrick Murray (Hibernian), James Blessington (Celtic), Robert McColl (Queen's Park), John Cameron (Queen's Park), William Lambie (Queen's Park).

Ireland: Thomas Scott; John Ponsonby, Samuel Torrans; Hugh Gordon, Robert Milne, James Fitzpatrick; Giddy Baird, Donald Morrogh, Olphert Stanfield, James Barron, John Peden.

Scorers: Scotland: McColl 7, #; Murray 78   Ireland: Barron #, #; Milne #

| 4 April 1896 | Home Championship | Celtic Park, Glasgow | Attendance: 56,500 |

59 SCOTLAND 2, England 1
Referee: Humphrey Jones (Wales)

Scotland: John Doig (Sunderland); John Drummond (Rangers, captain), Thomas Brandon (Blackburn Rovers); George Hogg (Hearts), James Cowan (Aston Villa), Neil Gibson (Rangers); Alexander King (Hearts), William Lambie (Queen's Park), Thomas Hyslop (Stoke City), James Blessington (Celtic), John Bell (Everton).

England: George Raikes; Lewis Lodge, William Oakley; Arthur Henfrey, Thomas Crawshaw, James Crabtree; William Bassett, John Goodall, Gilbert Smith (captain), Harold Wood, Cuthbert Burnup.

Scorers: Scotland: Lambie 22; Bell 33   England: Bassett 80

| 20 March 1897 | Home Championship | The Racecourse, Wrexham | Attendance: 5,000 |

60 Wales 2, SCOTLAND 2
Referee: Thomas Armitt (England)

Scotland: John Patrick (St Mirren); John Ritchie (Queen's Park, captain), David Gardner (Third Lanark); Bernard Breslin (Hibernian), David Russell (Celtic), Alexander Keillor (Dundee); John Kennedy (Hibernian), Patrick Murray (Hibernian), James Oswald (Rangers), James McMillan (St Bernard's), John Walker (Hearts).

Wales: James Trainer; William Jones, John Matthias; Sydney Darvell, John Mates, John Jones; William Meredith, David Pugh, Morgan Morgan-Owen; John Rea, William Lewis.

Scorers: Scotland: Ritchie 11 (pen); Walker #   Wales: Morgan-Owen 40; Pugh #

27 March 1897 Home Championship Ibrox Park, Glasgow Attendance: 15,000

61 SCOTLAND 5, Ireland 1 *Referee: James Cooper (England)*

Scotland: Matthew Dickie (Rangers); Duncan McLean (St Bernard's), John Drummond (Rangers, captain); Neil Gibson (Rangers), William Baird (St Bernard's), David Stewart (Queen's Park); Thomas Low (Rangers), John McPherson (Rangers), Robert McColl (Queen's Park), Alexander King (Celtic), William Lambie (Queen's Park).

Ireland: James Thompson; John Ponsonby, Samuel Torrans; John Pyper, Robert Milne, George McMaster; James Campbell, Olphert Stanfield, James Pyper, John Darling, John Peden.

Scorers: Scotland: McPherson #, #; Gibson #; McColl #; King #   Ireland: James Pyper #

3 April 1897 Home Championship Crystal Palace, London Attendance: 35,000

62 England 1, SCOTLAND 2 *Referee: Richard Gough (Wales)*

Scotland: John Patrick (St Mirren); Nicol Smith (Rangers), Daniel Doyle (Celtic); Neil Gibson (Rangers), James Cowan (Aston Villa), Hugh Wilson (Sunderland); John Bell (Everton), James Millar (Rangers), George Allan (Liverpool), Thomas Hyslop (Rangers), William Lambie (Queen's Park, captain).

England: John Robinson; Howard Spencer, William Oakley; John Reynolds, Thomas Crawshaw, Ernest Needham; William Athersmith, Stephen Bloomer, Gilbert Smith (captain), Edgar Chadwick, Alfred Milward.

Scorers: England: Bloomer 19   Scotland: Hyslop 27; Millar 83

19 March 1898 Home Championship Fir Park, Motherwell Attendance: 3,500

63 SCOTLAND 5, Wales 2 *Referee: William Stacey (England)*

Scotland: William Watson (Falkirk); Nicol Smith (Rangers), Matthew Scott (Airdrie, captain); William Thomson (Dumbarton), Alexander Christie (Queen's Park), Peter Campbell (Morton); James Gillespie (Third Lanark), James Millar (Rangers), James McKie (East Stirlingshire), Hugh Morgan (St Mirren), Robert Findlay (Kilmarnock).

Wales: James Trainer; Charles Parry, David Jones; Richard Jones, Caesar Jenkyns, John Jones; Edwin James, Thomas Thomas, Morgan Morgan-Owen, Arthur Morris, Alfred Watkins.

Scorers: Scotland: Gillespie 12, #, #; McKie #, 40   Wales: Thomas 44; Morgan-Owen #

26 March 1898 Home Championship Solitude, Belfast Attendance: 5,000

64 Ireland 0, SCOTLAND 3 *Referee: John Lewis (England)*

Scotland: Kenneth Anderson (Queen's Park); Robert Kelso (Dundee, captain), Daniel Doyle (Celtic); William Thomson (Dumbarton), David Russell (Celtic), Alexander King (Celtic); William Stewart (Queen's Park), John Campbell (Celtic), Robert McColl (Queen's Park), John Walker (Hearts), Thomas Robertson (Hearts).

Ireland: Thomas Scott; William Gibson, Samuel Torrans; William Anderson, Robert Milne, Michael Cochrane; James Campbell, John Mercer, James Pyper, James McCashin, John Peden.

Scorers: Scotland: Robertson 30; McColl 42; Stewart 70

2 April 1898 Home Championship Celtic Park, Glasgow Attendance: 40,000

65 SCOTLAND 1, England 3 *Referee: Thomas Robertson (Scotland)*

Scotland: Kenneth Anderson (Queen's Park); John Drummond (Rangers), Daniel Doyle (Celtic); Neil Gibson (Rangers), James Cowan (Aston Villa, captain), John Robertson (Everton); John Bell (Everton), John Campbell (Celtic), William Maxwell (Stoke City), James Millar (Rangers), Alexander Smith (Rangers).

England: John Robinson; William Oakley, William Williams; Frank Forman, Charles Wreford-Brown, Ernest Needham; William Athersmith, Stephen Bloomer, Gilbert Smith (captain), George Wheldon, Frederick Spiksley.

Scorers: England: Wheldon 3; Bloomer 23, 72   Scotland: Millar 48

18 March 1899 Home Championship The Racecourse, Wrexham Attendance: 12,000

66 Wales 0, SCOTLAND 6 *Referee: Charles Sutcliffe (England)*

Scotland: Daniel McArthur (Celtic); Nicol Smith (Rangers, captain), David Storrier (Celtic); Neil Gibson (Rangers), Harold Marshall (Celtic), Alexander King (Celtic); John Campbell (Rangers), Robert Hamilton (Rangers), Robert McColl (Queen's Park), John Bell (Celtic), Davidson Berry (Queen's Park).

Wales: James Trainer; John Matthias, Horace Blew; George Richards, John Jones, Edward Hughes; Frederick Kelly, Trevor Owen, Morgan Morgan-Owen, Ralph Jones, Arthur Morris.

Scorers: Scotland: Campbell 22, #; McColl 50, #, #; Marshall #

25 March 1899 Home Championship Celtic Park, Glasgow Attendance: 12,000

67 SCOTLAND 9, Ireland 1 *Referee: Charles Sutcliffe (England)*

Scotland: Matthew Dickie (Rangers); Nicol Smith (Rangers), David Storrier (Celtic, captain); Neil Gibson (Rangers), Alexander Christie (Queen's Park), Alexander King (Celtic); John Campbell (Rangers), Robert Hamilton (Rangers), Robert McColl (Queen's Park), Davidson Berry (Queen's Park), John Bell (Celtic).

Ireland: James Lewis; Samuel Swan, Thomas Foreman; William Anderson, Archibald Goodall, John McShane; George Sheehan, James Mellon, James Pyper, James McCashin, Joseph McAllen.

Scorers: Scotland: McColl, 5, 22, 47; Christie 6; Hamilton 33, 60; Bell 41; Berry 74; Campbell 82   Ireland: Goodall 58

Chapter one: 1873-1914

| 8 April 1899 | Home Championship | Villa Park, Birmingham | Attendance: 25,590 |

68 England 2, SCOTLAND 1 *Referee: James Torrans (Ireland)*

Scotland: John Doig (Sunderland); Nicol Smith (Rangers, captain), David Storrier (Celtic); Neil Gibson (Rangers), Alexander Christie (Queen's Park), John Robertson (Southampton); John Campbell (Rangers), Robert Hamilton (Rangers), Robert McColl (Queen's Park), Hugh Morgan (Liverpool), John Bell (Celtic).
England: John Robinson; Henry Thickett, James Crabtree; Raby Howell, Frank Forman, Ernest Needham; William Athersmith, Stephen Bloomer, Gilbert Smith (captain), James Settle, Frederick Forman.
Scorers: England: Smith 25, 40   Scotland: Hamilton 52

| 3 February 1900 | Home Championship | Pittodrie, Aberdeen | Attendance: 12,500 |

69 SCOTLAND 5, Wales 2 *Referee: Charles Sutcliffe (England)*

Scotland: Matthew Dickie (Rangers); Nicol Smith (Rangers), David Crawford (Rangers); James Irons (Queen's Park), Robert Neil (Rangers), John Robertson (Rangers); John Bell (Celtic), David Wilson (Queen's Park), Robert McColl (Queen's Park), Robert Hamilton (Rangers, captain), Alexander Smith (Rangers).
Wales: Frederick Griffiths; Charles Thomas, Charles Morris; Samuel Meredith, John Jones, William Harrison; David Pugh, William Butler, Richard Jones, Thomas Parry, Alfred Watkins.
Scorers: Scotland: Bell 2; Wilson 7, 35; Hamilton 37; Alexander Smith 60   Wales: Parry 44; Butler 52

| 3 March 1900 | Home Championship | Solitude, Belfast | Attendance: 6,000 |

70 Ireland 0, SCOTLAND 3 *Referee: Charles Sutcliffe (England)*

Scotland: Henry Rennie (Hearts); Nicol Smith (Rangers), Robert Glen (Hibernian); Neil Gibson (Rangers), Harold Marshall (Celtic, captain), William Orr (Celtic); William Stewart (Queen's Park), Robert Walker (Hearts), John Campbell (Celtic), Patrick Callaghan (Dunfermline), Alexander Smith (Rangers).
Ireland: James Lewis; John Pyper, Michael Cochrane; John McShane, John Barry, Hugh Maginnis; James Campbell, John Darling, Patrick McAuley, Alfred Kearns, Joseph McAllan.
Scorers: Scotland: Campbell 8, 83; Alexander Smith 23

| 7 April 1900 | Home Championship | Celtic Park, Glasgow | Attendance: 63,000 |

71 SCOTLAND 4, England 1 *Referee: James Torrans (Ireland)*

Scotland: Henry Rennie (Hearts); Nicol Smith (Rangers), John Drummond (Rangers); Neil Gibson (Rangers), Alexander Raisbeck (Liverpool), John Robertson (Rangers, captain); John Bell (Celtic), Robert Walker (Hearts), Robert McColl (Queen's Park), John Campbell (Celtic), Alexander Smith (Rangers).
England: John Robinson; William Oakley, James Crabtree; William Johnson, Arthur Chadwick, Ernest Needham; William Athersmith, Stephen Bloomer, Gilbert Smith (captain), George Wilson, John Plant.
Scorers: Scotland: McColl 1, 25, 44; Bell 6   England: Bloomer 35

| 23 February 1901 | Home Championship | Celtic Park, Glasgow | Attendance: 15,000 |

72 SCOTLAND 11, Ireland 0 *Referee: Richard Gough (Wales)*

Scotland (2-3-5):
1 George McWattie (Queen's Park);
9 Nicol Smith (Rangers)
1 Bernard Battles (Celtic);
5 David Russell (Celtic)
1 George Anderson (Kilmarnock)
5 John Robertson (Rangers);
7 John Campbell (Celtic)
4 John Campbell (Rangers)
5 Robert Hamilton (Rangers, captain)
5 Alexander McMahon (Celtic)
5 Alexander Smith (Rangers)

Of the 16 previous matches between the sides, Scotland had won 15 with one draw, so the visitors were always going to be up against it. The Scots ran away handsome winners in front of a crowd at Celtic Park in Glasgow estimated at 15,000. Rangers centre forward Robert Hamilton, who had scored twice in the 9-1 victory of 1899, this time bagged a personal tally of four, while Celtic inside left Alexander McMahon did likewise. There were two John Campbells in the side, the Celtic player on the right wing and his Rangers namesake at inside right, and it was the former who also found the net twice. The final goal was delivered by right half David Russell, another playing on his home ground. The final score of 11-0 remains Scotland's biggest ever victory.

Ireland: Samuel McAlpine; William Gibson, Samuel Torrans; Patrick Farrell, James Connor, Michael Cochrane; James Scott, James Smith, James Campbell, Harold O'Reilly, Robert Clarke.
Scorers: Scotland: McMahon 6, #, #, #; Russell #; Campbell (Celtic) 30, #; Hamilton #, #, #, #

| 2 March 1901 | Home Championship | The Racecourse, Wrexham | Attendance: 5,000 |

73 Wales 1, SCOTLAND 1 *Referee: Charles Sutcliffe (England)*

Scotland: George McWattie (Queen's Park); Nicol Smith (Rangers), Bernard Battles (Celtic); Neil Gibson (Rangers), David Russell (Celtic), John Robertson (Rangers, captain); Mark Bell (Hearts), Robert Walker (Hearts), Robert McColl (Queen's Park), John Campbell (Celtic), Alexander Smith (Rangers).
Wales: Leigh Roose; Samuel Meredith, Charles Morris; Maurice Parry, William Jones, Edward Hughes; David Pugh, John Jones, Morgan Morgan-Jones, Thomas Parry, Ephraim Williams.
Scorers: Scotland: Robertson 74   Wales: Thomas Parry 78

| 30 March 1901 | Home Championship | Crystal Palace, London | Attendance: 18,520 |

74 England 2, SCOTLAND 2 *Referee: James Torrans (Ireland)*

Scotland: Henry Rennie (Hibernian); Bernard Battles (Celtic), John Drummond (Rangers); Andrew Aitken (Newcastle United), Alexander Raisbeck (Liverpool), John Robertson (Rangers, captain); Robert Walker (Hearts), John Campbell (Celtic), Robert McColl (Queen's Park), Robert Hamilton (Rangers), Alexander Smith (Rangers).

England: John Sutcliffe; James Iremonger, William Oakley; Albert Wilkes, Frank Forman, Ernest Needham; Walter Bennett, Stephen Bloomer, Gilbert Smith (captain), Reginald Foster, Frederick Blackburn.

Scorers: England: Blackburn 36; Bloomer 80   Scotland: Campbell 48; Hamilton 75

| 1 March 1902 | Home Championship | Grosvenor Park, Belfast | Attendance: 15,000 |

75 Ireland 1, SCOTLAND 5 *Referee: Frederick Bye (England)*

Scotland: Henry Rennie (Hibernian); Nicol Smith (Rangers), John Drummond (Rangers); George Key (Hearts), Albert Buick (Hearts, captain), John Robertson (Rangers); William McCartney (Hibernian), Robert Walker (Hearts), Robert Hamilton (Rangers), John Campbell (Celtic), Alexander Smith (Rangers).

Ireland: James Nolan-Whelan; William Gibson, John Pyper; John Darling, Archibald Goodall, Robert Milne; James Campbell, Thomas Morrison, Andrew Gara, Alfred Kearns, Joseph McAllen.

Scorers: Scotland: Hamilton 43, 70 74; Walker 49; Buick 76   Ireland: Milne 89

| 15 March 1902 | Home Championship | Cappielow, Greenock | Attendance: 5,284 |

76 SCOTLAND 5, Wales 1 *Referee: Joseph McBride (Ireland)*

Scotland: Henry Rennie (Hibernian); Henry Allan (Hearts), John Drummond (Rangers); Hugh Wilson (Third Lanark), Albert Buick (Hearts), John Robertson (Rangers); John Campbell (Celtic, captain), Robert Walker (Hearts), Robert Hamilton (Rangers), Alexander McMahon (Celtic), Alexander Smith (Rangers).

Wales: Leigh Roose; Horace Blew, Robert Morris; Maurice Parry, John Jones, William Jones; William Meredith, Llewelyn Griffiths, Hugh Morgan-Owen, Richard Morris, Joseph Owens.

Scorers: Scotland: Smith #, #, 88; Buick #; Drummond #   Wales: Morgan-Owen #

| 3 May 1902 | Home Championship | Villa Park, Birmingham | Attendance: 15,000 |

77 England 2, SCOTLAND 2 *Referee: James Torrans (Ireland)*

Scotland (2-3-5):

6	Henry Rennie (Hibernian);
12	Nicol Smith (Rangers)
13	John Drummond (Rangers);
2	Andrew Aitken (Newcastle United, captain)
3	Alexander Raisbeck (Liverpool)
10	John Robertson (Rangers);
1	Robert Templeton (Aston Villa)
7	Robert Walker (Hearts)
7	Robert McColl (Newcastle United)
1	Ronald Orr (Newcastle United)
10	Alexander Smith (Rangers).

The 1902 game against England was replayed at Villa Park in Birmingham. It followed the disaster at Ibrox Park in Glasgow the previous month when a collapsed stand claimed the lives of 25 supporters and injured over 500 more. It was agreed by both the Scottish and English associations that that game would be null and void. Scotland got the best possible start when in the third minute Robert Templeton of Aston Villa beat the English keeper with a deceptive shot from long range. Ronald Orr of Newcastle made it 2-0 in the 28th minute, catching the ball on the drop following a corner and finding the net. The home side's play improved immeasurably after half-time and two goals in quick succession midway through the half by Settle and Wilkes meant a share of the points.

England: William George; Robert Crompton, George Molyneux; Albert Wilkes, Frank Forman, Albert Houlker; William Hogg, Stephen Bloomer (captain), William Beats, James Settle, John Cox.

Scorers: Scotland: Templeton 3; Orr 28   England: Settle 65; Wilkes 67

| 9 March 1903 | Home Championship | Cardiff Arms Park | Attendance: 11,000 |

78 Wales 0, SCOTLAND 1 *Referee: Frederick Kirkham (England)*

Scotland: Henry Rennie (Hibernian); Andrew McCombie (Sunderland), James Watson (Sunderland); Andrew Aitken (Newcastle United), Alexander Raisbeck (Liverpool, captain), John Robertson (Rangers); Robert Templeton (Newcastle United), Robert Walker (Hearts), John Campbell (Celtic), Finlay Speedie (Rangers), Alexander Smith (Rangers).

Wales: Robert Evans; Horace Blew, Charles Morris; Maurice Parry, Morgan Morgan-Owen, Thomas Davies; William Meredith, Walter Watkins, Arthur Morris, Richard Morris, Robert Atherton.

Scorer: Scotland: Speedie 25

| 21 March 1903 | Home Championship | Celtic Park, Glasgow | Attendance: 17,000 |

79 SCOTLAND 0, Ireland 2 *Referee: Frederick Kirkham (England)*

Scotland: Henry Rennie (Hibernian); Archibald Gray (Hibernian), John Drummond (Rangers, captain); John Cross (Third Lanark), Peter Robertson (Dundee), William Orr (Celtic); David Lindsay (St Mirren), Robert Walker (Hearts), William Porteous (Hearts), Finlay Speedie (Rangers), Alexander Smith (Rangers).

Ireland: William Scott; Alexander McCartney, Peter Boyle; John Darling, Robert Milne, Hugh Maginnis; John Mercer, James Sheridan, Maurice Connor, Thomas Shanks, John Kirwan.

Scorers: Ireland: Connor 9; Kirwan 83

Chapter one: 1873-1914

| 4 April 1903 | Home Championship | Bramall Lane, Sheffield | Attendance: 32,000 |

80 **England 1, SCOTLAND 2** *Referee: William Nunnerley (Wales)*

Scotland: John Doig (Sunderland); Andrew McCombie (Sunderland), James Watson (Sunderland); Andrew Aitken (Newcastle United), Alexander Raisbeck (Liverpool, captain), John Robertson (Rangers); Robert Templeton (Newcastle United), Robert Walker (Hearts), Robert Hamilton (Rangers), Finlay Speedie (Rangers), Alexander Smith (Rangers).

England: Thomas Baddeley; Robert Crompton (captain), George Molyneux; William Johnson, Thomas Booth, Albert Houlker; Henry Davis, Percival Humphreys, Vivian Woodward, Arthur Capes, John Cox.

Scorers: England: Woodward 10   Scotland: Speedie 57; Walker 59

| 12 March 1904 | Home Championship | Dens Park, Dundee | Attendance: 12,000 |

81 **SCOTLAND 1, Wales 1** *Referee: Frederick Kirkham (England)*

Scotland: Leslie Skene (Queen's Park); Thomas Jackson (St Mirren), James Sharp (Dundee, captain); William Orr (Celtic), Thomas Sloan (Third Lanark), John Robertson (Rangers); John Walker (Rangers), Robert Walker (Hearts), Alexander Bennett (Celtic), Alexander MacFarlane (Dundee), George Wilson (Hearts).

Wales: David Davies; Horace Blew, Thomas Davies; George Richards, Edward Hughes, John Jones; Arthur Davies, Walter Watkins, Arthur Green, Richard Morris, Robert Atherton.

Scorers: Scotland: Robert Walker 5   Wales: Atherton 65

| 26 March 1904 | Home Championship | Dalymount Park, Dublin | Attendance: 1,000 |

82 **Ireland 1, SCOTLAND 1** *Referee: Frederick Kirkham (England)*

Scotland: Henry Rennie (Hibernian); Thomas Jackson (St Mirren), John Cameron (St Mirren); George Henderson (Rangers), Charles Thomson (Rangers), John Robertson (Rangers, captain); John Walker (Rangers), Robert Walker (Hearts), Robert Hamilton (Rangers), Hugh Wilson (Third Lanark), Alexander Smith (Rangers).

Ireland: William Scott; William McCracken, Alexander McCartney; English McConnell, Robert Milne, Hugh Maginnis; James Campbell, James Sheridan, Harry O'Reilly, Harold Sloan, John Kirwan.

Scorers: Scotland: Hamilton 22   Ireland: Sheridan 74

| 9 April 1904 | Home Championship | Celtic Park, Glasgow | Attendance: 45,000 |

83 **SCOTLAND 0, England 1** *Referee: William Nunnerley (Wales)*

Scotland: Peter McBride (Preston North End); Thomas Jackson (St Mirren), James Watson (Sunderland); Andrew Aitken (Newcastle United), Alexander Raisbeck (Liverpool), John Robertson (Rangers, captain); Thomas Niblo (Aston Villa), Robert Walker (Hearts), Alexander Brown (Middlesbrough), Ronald Orr (Newcastle United), Robert Templeton (Newcastle United).

England: Thomas Baddeley; Robert Crompton (captain), Herbert Burgess; Samuel Wolstenholme, Bernard Wilkinson, Alexander Leake; John Rutherford, Stephen Bloomer, Vivian Woodward, Stanley Harris, Frederick Blackburn.

Scorer: England: Bloomer 64

| 6 March 1905 | Home Championship | The Racecourse, Wrexham | Attendance: 6,000 |

84 **Wales 3, SCOTLAND 1** *Referee: Frederick Kirkham (England)*

Scotland: Henry Rennie (Hibernian); Andrew McCombie (Newcastle United), Thomas Jackson (St Mirren, captain); Andrew Aitken (Newcastle United), Charles Thomson (Hearts), John Robertson (Rangers); Robert Templeton (Arsenal), Robert Walker (Hearts), Samuel Kennedy (Partick Thistle), Thomas Fitchie (Arsenal), Alexander Smith (Rangers).

Wales: Leigh Roose; Horace Blew, Charles Morris; George Latham, Edward Hughes, John Hughes; William Meredith, Arthur Davies, Walter Watkins, Arthur Morris, Alfred Oliver.

Scorers: Wales: Watkins 30; Arthur Morris 47; Meredith 76   Scotland: Robertson 86

| 18 March 1905 | Home Championship | Celtic Park, Glasgow | Attendance: 35,000 |

85 **SCOTLAND 4, Ireland 0** *Referee: Frederick Kirkham (England)*

Scotland: William Howden (Partick Thistle); Donald McLeod (Celtic), William McIntosh (Third Lanark); Neil Gibson (Partick Thistle, captain), Charles Thomson (Hearts), James Hay (Celtic); James "Napoleon" McMenemy (Celtic), Robert Walker (Hearts), James Quinn (Celtic), Peter Somers (Celtic), George Wilson (Hearts).

Ireland: William Scott; William McCracken, Alexander McCartney; John Darling, James Connor, English McConnell; John Mercer, James Maxwell, Neill Murphy, Charles O'Hagan, John Kirwan.

Scorers: Scotland: Thomson 14 (pen), 61 (pen); Walker 35; Quinn 50

| 1 April 1905 | Home Championship | Crystal Palace, London | Attendance: 32,000 |

86 **England 1, SCOTLAND 0** *Referee: William Nunnerley (Wales)*

Scotland: John Lyall (Sheffield Wednesday); Andrew McCombie (Newcastle United), James Watson (Sunderland); Andrew Aitken (Newcastle United), Charles Thomson (Hearts, captain), Peter McWilliam (Newcastle United); Robert Walker (Hearts), James Howie (Newcastle United), Alexander Young (Everton), Peter Somers (Celtic), George Wilson (Hearts).

England: James Linacre; Howard Spencer (captain), Herbert Smith; Herod Ruddlesdin, Charles Roberts, Alexander Leake; John Sharp, Stephen Bloomer, Vivian Woodward, Joseph Bache, George Bridgett.

Scorer: England: Bache 80

3 March 1906   Home Championship   Tynecastle, Edinburgh   Attendance: 25,000

87 SCOTLAND 0, Wales 2   *Referee: John Lewis (England)*

Scotland: James Raeside (Third Lanark); Donald McLeod (Celtic), Andrew Richmond (Queen's Park); Alexander McNair (Celtic), Charles Thomson (Hearts, captain), John May (Rangers); George Stewart (Hibernian), Alexander McFarlane (Dundee), James Quinn (Celtic), Thomas Fitchie (Arsenal), George Wilson (Hearts).

Wales: Leigh Roose; Horace Blew, Charles Morris; Edwin Hughes, Morgan Morgan-Owen, George Latham; William Jones, Richard Morris, John Jones, Richard Jones, Robert Evans.

Scorers: Wales: William Jones 50; John Jones 65

17 March 1906   Home Championship   Dalymount Park, Dublin   Attendance: 8,000

88 Ireland 0, SCOTLAND 1   *Referee: Frederick Bye (England)*

Scotland: Henry Rennie (Hibernian); Donald McLeod (Celtic), David Hill (Third Lanark); James Young (Celtic), Charles Thomson (Hearts, captain), John May (Rangers); Gladstone Hamilton (Port Glasgow Athletic), Robert Walker (Hearts), James Quinn (Celtic), Thomas Fitchie (Arsenal), Alexander Smith (Rangers).

Ireland: Frederick McKee; George Willis, John Darling; John Wright, Robert Milne, Joseph Ledwidge; Andrew Hunter, Thomas Mulholland, Thomas Waddell, Charles O'Hagan, John Kirwan.

Scorer: Scotland: Fitchie 52

7 April 1906   Home Championship   Hampden Park   Attendance: 102,741

89 SCOTLAND 2, England 1   *Referee: William Nunnerley (Wales)*

Scotland: Peter McBride (Preston North End); Donald McLeod (Celtic), William Dunlop (Liverpool); Andrew Aitken (Newcastle United), Alexander Raisbeck (Liverpool, captain), Peter McWilliam (Newcastle United); George Stewart (Hibernian), James Howie (Newcastle United), Alexander Menzies (Hearts), George Livingston (Manchester City), Alexander Smith (Rangers).

England: James Ashcroft; Robert Crompton, Herbert Burgess; Benjamin Warren, Colin Veitch, Joseph Makepeace; Richard Bond, Samuel Day, Albert Shepherd, Stanley Harris, James Conlin.

Scorers: Scotland: Howie 44, 55   England: Shepherd 81

4 March 1907   Home Championship   The Racecourse, Wrexham   Attendance: 7,715

90 Wales 1, SCOTLAND 0   *Referee: James Mason (England)*

Scotland: Peter McBride (Preston North End); Thomas Jackson (St Mirren), James Sharp (Arsenal); Andrew Aitken (Middlesbrough), Charles Thomson (Hearts, captain), Peter McWilliam (Newcastle United); George Stewart (Manchester City), George Livingston (Rangers), Alexander Young (Everton), Thomas Fitchie (Queen's Park), Alexander Smith (Rangers).

Wales: Leigh Roose; Horace Blew, Charles Morris; George Latham, Lloyd Davies, Ioan Price; William Meredith, William Jones, Hugh Morgan-Owen, Arthur Morris, Gordon Jones.

Scorer: Wales: Arthur Morris 50

Before the 3-0 home win over Ireland at Celtic Park in 1907. Back from left: T. Watson (linesman), Robert Walker, J. Wilson (linesman), William Muir, W. T. McCulloch (official), Willam Agnew, J. Liddell (official), Alexander McNair, Frank O'Rourke, John Lewis (referee). Front: William Key, Thomas Jackson, Charles Thomson, Peter Somers, Alexander Bennett, John Fraser, J. K. McDowall (official).

Photo courtesy of Scottish Football Museum

Chapter one: 1873-1914

| 16 March 1907 | Home Championship | Celtic Park, Glasgow | Attendance: 26,000 |

91 SCOTLAND 3, Ireland 0   *Referee: John Lewis (England)*

Scotland: William Muir (Dundee); Thomas Jackson (St Mirren), William Agnew (Kilmarnock); William Key (Queen's Park), Charles Thomson (Hearts, captain), Alexander McNair (Celtic); Alexander Bennett (Celtic), Robert Walker (Hearts), Frank O'Rourke (Airdrie), Peter Somers (Celtic), John Fraser (Dundee).
Ireland: William Scott; George Willis, Alexander McCartney; John Wright, James Connor, George McClure; John Blair, James Maxwell, Edward McGuire, Charles O'Hagan, Samuel Young.
Scorers: Scotland: O'Rourke 40; Walker 48; Thomson 82 (pen)

| 6 April 1907 | Home Championship | St James' Park, Newcastle | Attendance: 35,829 |

92 England 1, SCOTLAND 1   *Referee: Thomas Robertson (Scotland)*

Scotland: Peter McBride (Preston North End); Charles Thomson (Hearts, captain), James Sharp (Arsenal); Andrew Aitken (Middlesbrough), Alexander Raisbeck (Liverpool), Peter McWilliam (Newcastle United); George Stewart (Manchester City), Robert Walker (Hearts), Andrew Wilson (Sheffield Wednesday), Walter White (Bolton Wanderers), George Wilson (Everton).
England: Sam Hardy; Robert Crompton (captain), Jesse Pennington; Benjamin Warren, William Wedlock, Colin Veitch; John Rutherford, Stephen Bloomer, Vivian Woodward, James Stewart, Harold Hardman.
Scorers: Scotland: Crompton 2 (own goal)   England: Bloomer 42

| 7 March 1908 | Home Championship | Dens Park, Dundee | Attendance: 18,000 |

93 SCOTLAND 2, Wales 1   *Referee: James Mason (England)*

Scotland: Henry Rennie (Hibernian); William Agnew (Kilmarnock), George Chaplin (Dundee); Alexander McNair (Celtic), Charles Thomson (Hearts, captain), James Galt (Rangers); Alexander Bennett (Celtic), Robert Walker (Hearts), James Speirs (Rangers), Alexander MacFarlane (Dundee), William Lennie (Aberdeen).
Wales: Leigh Roose; Horace Blew, Charles Morris; Maurice Parry, Edwin Hughes, Lloyd Davies; William C. Davies, William Jones, William Davies, Arthur Green, Robert Evans.
Scorers: Wales: Jones 30   Scotland: Bennett 60; Lennie 87

| 14 March 1908 | Home Championship | Dalymount Park, Dublin | Attendance: 9,000 |

94 Ireland 0, SCOTLAND 5   *Referee: James Ibbotson (England)*

Scotland: Henry Rennie (Hibernian); James Mitchell (Kilmarnock), William Agnew (Kilmarnock); John May (Rangers), Charles Thomson (Hearts, captain), James Galt (Rangers); Robert Templeton (Kilmarnock), Robert Walker (Hearts), James Quinn (Celtic), Robert McColl (Queen's Park), William Lennie (Aberdeen).
Ireland: William Scott (captain); Alexander Craig, Alexander McCartney; Valentine Harris, James Connor, English McConnell; John Blair, Dennis Hannon, William Andrews, Charles O'Hagan, Samuel Young.
Scorers: Scotland: Quinn 3, #, 70, 75; Galt 23

| 4 April 1908 | Home Championship | Hampden Park | Attendance: 121,452 |

95 SCOTLAND 1, England 1   *Referee: James Mason (England)*

Scotland: Peter McBride (Preston North End); Alexander McNair (Celtic), James Sharp (Arsenal); Andrew Aitken (Middlesbrough), Charles Thomson (Hearts, captain), John May (Rangers); James Howie (Newcastle United), Robert Walker (Hearts), Andrew Wilson (Sheffield Wednesday), Walter White (Bolton Wanderers), James Quinn (Celtic).
England: Sam Hardy; Robert Crompton, Jesse Pennington; Benjamin Warren, William Wedlock, Evelyn Lintott; John Rutherford, Vivian Woodward (captain), George Hilsdon, James Windridge, George Bridgett.
Scorers: Scotland: Wilson 27   England: Windridge 75

| 1 March 1909 | Home Championship | The Racecourse, Wrexham | Attendance: 6,000 |

96 Wales 3, SCOTLAND 2   *Referee: Thomas Campbell (England)*

Scotland: Peter McBride (Preston North End); Thomas Collins (Hearts), James Sharp (Fulham); John May (Rangers), Charles Thomson (Sunderland, captain), Peter McWilliam (Newcastle United); Alexander Bennett (Rangers), John Hunter (Dundee), Robert Walker (Hearts), Peter Somers (Celtic), Harold Paul (Queen's Park).
Wales: Leigh Roose; Horace Blew, Charles Morris; Maurice Parry, Ernest Peake, Ioan Price; William Meredith (captain), George Wynn, William Davies, William Jones, Robert Evans.
Scorers: Wales: Davies 25, 39; Jones 29   Scotland: Walker 70; Paul 73

| 15 March 1909 | Home Championship | Ibrox Park, Glasgow | Attendance: 24,000 |

97 SCOTLAND 5, Ireland 0   *Referee: James Mason (England)*

Scotland: James Brownlie (Third Lanark); James Main (Hibernian), James Watson (Middlesbrough); William Walker (Clyde), James Stark (Rangers, captain); Alexander Bennett (Rangers), James Hay (Celtic); James "Napoleon" McMenemy (Celtic), Alexander Thomson (Airdrie), Alexander MacFarlane (Dundee), Harold Paul (Queen's Park).
Ireland: William Scott; Alexander Craig, Alexander McCartney; Valentine Harris (captain), English McConnell, Harold Sloan; Andrew Hunter, William Lacey, William Greer, Charles Webb, John Kirwan.
Scorers: Scotland: McMenemy 15, 77; MacFarlane 20; Thomson 48; Paul 84

3 April 1909   Home Championship   Crystal Palace, London   Attendance: 27,000

98 England 2, SCOTLAND 0
Referee: James Stark (Scotland)

Scotland: James Brownlie (Third Lanark); John Cameron (Chelsea), James Watson (Middlesbrough); Alexander McNair (Celtic), James Stark (Rangers, captain), Peter McWilliam (Newcastle United); Alexander Bennett (Rangers), Robert Walker (Hearts), James Quinn (Celtic), George Wilson (Newcastle United), Harold Paul (Queen's Park).

England: Samuel Hardy; Robert Crompton (captain), Jesse Pennington; Benjamin Warren, William Wedlock, Evelyn Lintott; Frederick Pentland, Harold Fleming, Bertram Freeman, George Holley, George Wall.

Scorer: England: Wall 3, 10

5 March 1910   Home Championship   Rugby Park, Kilmarnock   Attendance: 22,000

99 SCOTLAND 1, Wales 0
Referee: Herbert Bamlett (England)

Scotland: James Brownlie (Third Lanark); George Law (Rangers), James Mitchell (Kilmarnock); Alexander McNair (Celtic), William Loney (Celtic), James Hay (Celtic, captain); Alexander Bennett (Rangers), James "Napoleon" McMenemy (Celtic), James Quinn (Celtic), Archibald Devine (Falkirk), George Robertson (Motherwell).

Wales: Leigh Roose; Jeffrey Jones, Charles Morris (captain); Edwin Hughes, Ernest Peake, Llewelyn Davies; William Meredith, William Davies, Evan Jones, Arthur Morris, Robert Evans.

Scorer: Scotland: Devine 86

19 March 1910   Home Championship   Windsor Park, Belfast   Attendance: 17,000

100 Ireland 1, SCOTLAND 0
Referee: John Howcroft (England)

Scotland: James Brownlie (Third Lanark); George Law (Rangers), James Mitchell (Kilmarnock); William Walker (Clyde), William Loney (Celtic), James Hay (Celtic, captain); George Sinclair (Hearts), John McTavish (Falkirk), James Quinn (Celtic), Alexander Higgins (Newcastle United), Robert Templeton (Kilmarnock).

Ireland: William Scott (captain); Samuel Burniston, Patrick McCann; Valentine Harris, English McConnell, John Darling; William Renneville, William Lacey, John Murray, John Murphy, Francis Thompson.

Scorer: Ireland: Thompson 54

2 April 1910   Home Championship   Hampden Park   Attendance: 106,205

101 SCOTLAND 2, England 0
Referee: James Mason (England)

Scotland: James Brownlie (Third Lanark); George Law (Rangers), James Hay (Celtic); Andrew Aitken (Leicester Fosse), Charles Thomson (Sunderland, captain), Peter McWilliam (Newcastle United); Alexander Bennett (Rangers), James "Napoleon" McMenemy (Celtic), James Quinn (Celtic), Alexander Higgins (Newcastle United), Robert Templeton (Kilmarnock).

England: Samuel Hardy; Robert Crompton (captain), Jesse Pennington; Andrew Ducat, William Wedlock, Joseph "Henry" Makepeace; Richard Bond, William Hibbert, John Parkinson, Harold Hardinge, George Wall.

Scorers: Scotland: McMenemy 20; Quinn 32

Prior to an excellent 2-0 home win over England at Hampden. Back (from left): H. S. McLachlan (SFA), W. Lorimer (SFA president), A. M. Robertson (SFA). Middle: J. K. McDowall (SFA secretary), J. Nutt (trainer), George Law, James Hay, James Brownlie, James "Napoleon" McMenemy, Robert Templeton, Peter McWilliam, T. Steen (SFA treasurer), James Mason (referee). Front: Alexander Bennett, James Quinn, Charles Thomson, Alexander Higgins, Andrew Aitken.   *Photo courtesy of Scottish Football Museum*

Chapter one: 1873-1914

| 6 March 1911 | Home Championship | Ninian Park, Cardiff | Attendance: 14,000 |

102 Wales 2, SCOTLAND 2   *Referee: James Mason (England)*

Scotland: James Brownlie (Third Lanark); Donald Colman (Aberdeen), John Walker (Swindon Town); Thomas Tait (Sunderland), Wilfred Low (Newcastle United), Peter McWilliam (Newcastle United, captain); Alexander Bennett (Rangers), James "Napoleon" McMenemy (Celtic), William Reid (Rangers), Alexander MacFarlane (Dundee), Robert Hamilton (Dundee).

Wales: Leigh Roose; Charles Morris (captain), Thomas Hewitt; Edwin Hughes, Lloyd Davies, Llewelyn Davies; William Meredith, Evan Jones, William Davies, Arthur Morris, Edward Vizard.

Scorers: Wales: Arthur Morris 20, 67   Scotland: Hamilton 35, 89

| 18 March 1911 | Home Championship | Celtic Park, Glasgow | Attendance: 32,000 |

103 SCOTLAND 2, Ireland 0   *Referee: Herbert Bamlett (England)*

Scotland: James Brownlie (Third Lanark); Donald Colman (Aberdeen), John Walker (Swindon Town); Andrew Aitken (Leicester Fosse, captain), Charles Thomson (Sunderland), James Hay (Celtic); Angus Douglas (Chelsea), James "Napoleon" McMenemy (Celtic), William Reid (Rangers), Alexander Higgins (Newcastle United), Alexander Smith (Rangers).

Ireland: William Scott (captain); Samuel Burnison, Patrick McCann; Valentine Harris, James Connor, Harold Hampton; William Lacey, Denis Hannon, John McDonnell, Charles Webb, Thomas Walker.

Scorers: Scotland: Reid 23; McMenemy 53

| 1 April 1911 | Home Championship | Goodison Park, Liverpool | Attendance: 38,000 |

104 England 1, SCOTLAND 1   *Referee: William Nunnerley (Wales)*

Scotland: James Lawrence (Newcastle United); Donald Colman (Aberdeen), John Walker (Swindon Town); Andrew Aitken (Leicester Fosse), Wilfred Low (Newcastle United), James Hay (Celtic, captain); Alexander Bennett (Rangers), James "Napoleon" McMenemy (Celtic), William Reid (Rangers), Alexander Higgins (Newcastle United), Alexander Smith (Rangers).

England: Reginald Williamson; Robert Crompton (captain), Jesse Pennington; Benjamin Warren, William Wedlock, Kenneth Hunt; John Simpson, James Stewart, George Webb, Joseph Bache, Robert Evans.

Scorers: England: Stewart 20   Scotland: Higgins 88

| 2 March 1912 | Home Championship | Tynecastle, Edinburgh | Attendance: 32,000 |

105 SCOTLAND 1, Wales 0   *Referee: James Mason (England)*

Scotland: James Brownlie (Third Lanark); Alexander McNair (Celtic), John Walker (Swindon Town); Robert Mercer (Hearts), Charles Thomson (Sunderland, captain), James Hay (Celtic); George Sinclair (Hearts), James "Napoleon" McMenemy (Celtic), James Quinn (Celtic), Robert Walker (Hearts), George Robertson (Sheffield Wednesday).

Wales: Robert Evans; Llewelyn Davies (captain), Lloyd Davies; Joseph Jones, Edwin Hughes, Moses Russell; William Meredith, George Wynn, Evan Jones, John Williams, Edward Vizard.

Scorer: Scotland: Quinn 87

| 16 March 1912 | Home Championship | Windsor Park, Belfast | Attendance: 12,000 |

106 Ireland 1, SCOTLAND 4   *Referee: Herbert Bamlett (England)*

Scotland: James Brownlie (Third Lanark); Alexander McNair (Celtic, captain), John Walker (Swindon Town); James Gordon (Rangers), Wilfred Low (Newcastle United), Alexander Bell (Manchester United); George Sinclair (Hearts), Robert Walker (Hearts), William Reid (Rangers), Walter Aitkenhead (Blackburn Rovers), Robert Templeton (Kilmarnock).

Ireland: James Hanna; George Willis, Alexander Craig; John Darling, Patrick O'Connell, Joseph Moran; John Houston, James McKnight, James McAulay, Joseph Enright, Samuel Young.

Scorers: Scotland: Aitkenhead 8, 23; Reid 60; Robert Walker 70   Ireland: McKnight 42 (pen)

| 23 March 1912 | Home Championship | Hampden Park | Attendance: 127,307 |

107 SCOTLAND 1, England 1   *Referee: James Mason (England)*

Scotland: James Brownlie (Third Lanark); Alexander McNair (Celtic, captain), John Walker (Swindon Town); James Gordon (Rangers), Charles Thomson (Sunderland), James Hay (Newcastle United); Robert Templeton (Kilmarnock), Robert Walker (Hearts), David McLean (Sheffield Wednesday), Andrew Wilson (Sheffield Wednesday), James Quinn (Celtic).

England: Reginald Williamson; Robert Crompton (captain), Jesse Pennington; John Brittleton, William Wedlock, Joseph Makepeace; John Simpson, Frank Jefferis, Bertram Freeman, George Holley, George Wall.

Scorers: Scotland: Wilson 7   England: Holley 13

| 3 March 1913 | Home Championship | The Racecourse, Wrexham | Attendance: 8,000 |

108 Wales 0, SCOTLAND 0   *Referee: Isaac Baker (England)*

Scotland: James Brownlie (Third Lanark); Robert Orrock (Falkirk), John Walker (Swindon Town); James Gordon (Rangers), Charles Thomson (Sunderland, captain), James Campbell (Sheffield Wednesday); Andrew McAtee (Celtic), Robert Walker (Hearts), William Reid (Rangers), Andrew Wilson (Sheffield Wednesday), Robert Templeton (Kilmarnock).

Wales: William Bailiff; Thomas Hewitt, Llewelyn Davies (captain); Edwin Hughes, Lloyd Davies, William Jones; William Meredith, George Wynn, Walter Davies, James Roberts, Edward Vizard.

15 March 1913 Home Championship Dalymount Park, Dublin Attendance: 12,000

109 Ireland 1, SCOTLAND 2 *Referee: Arthur Adams (England)*

Scotland: James Brownlie (Third Lanark); Donald Colman (Aberdeen, captain), John Walker (Swindon Town); Robert Mercer (Hearts), Thomas Logan (Falkirk), Peter Nellies (Hearts); Alexander Bennett (Rangers), James Gordon (Rangers), William Reid (Rangers), James Croal (Falkirk), George Robertson (Sheffield Wednesday).

Ireland: William Scott; William McConnell, Peter Warren; William Andrews, Valentine Harris (captain), Henry Hampton; John Houston, James McKnight, William Gillespie, James McAuley, Francis Thompson.

Scorers: Scotland: Reid 16; Bennett 32   Ireland: McKnight 42

5 April 1913 Home Championship Stamford Bridge, London Attendance: 52,500

110 England 1, SCOTLAND 0 *Referee: Alexander Jackson (Scotland)*

Scotland: James Brownlie (Third Lanark); Alexander McNair (Celtic), John Walker (Swindon Town); James Gordon (Rangers), Charles Thomson (Sunderland, captain), David Wilson (Oldham Athletic); Joseph Donnachie (Oldham Athletic), Robert Walker (Hearts), William Reid (Rangers), Andrew Wilson (Sheffield Wednesday), George Robertson (Sheffield Wednesday).

England: Sam Hardy; Robert Crompton (captain), Jesse Pennington; John Brittleton, Joseph McCall, William Watson; John Simpson, Harold Fleming, Joseph Hampton, George Holley, Joseph Hodkinson.

Scorer: England: Hampton 37

28 February 1914 Home Championship Celtic Park, Glasgow Attendance: 10,000

111 SCOTLAND 0, Wales 0 *Referee: Harold Taylor (England)*

Scotland: James Brownlie (Third Lanark); Thomas Kelso (Dundee), Joseph Dodds (Celtic); Peter Nellies (Hearts, captain), Peter Pursell (Queen's Park), Henry Anderson (Raith Rovers); Alexander Donaldson (Bolton Wanderers), James "Napoleon" McMenemy (Celtic), James Reid (Airdrie), James Croal (Falkirk), John Browning (Celtic).

Wales: Edward Peers; Thomas Hewitt, William Jennings; Thomas Matthias, Lloyd Davies (captain), Joseph Jones; William Meredith, George Wynn, Walter Davies, William Jones, John Evans.

14 March 1914 Home Championship Windsor Park, Belfast Attendance: 31,000

112 Ireland 1, SCOTLAND 1 *Referee: Herbert Bamlett (England)*

Scotland: James Brownlie (Third Lanark); Joseph Dodds (Celtic), Alexander McNair (Celtic, captain); James Gordon (Rangers), Charles Thomson (Sunderland), James Hay (Newcastle United); Alexander Donaldson (Bolton Wanderers), James "Napoleon" McMenemy (Celtic), William Reid (Rangers), Andrew Wilson (Sheffield Wednesday), Joseph Donnachie (Oldham Athletic).

Ireland: Frederick McKee; William McConnell, Alexander Craig; Valentine Harris, Patrick O'Connell (captain), Michael Hamill; John Houston, Robert Nixon, Samuel Young, William Lacey, Francis Thompson.

Scorers: Scotland: Donnachie 70   Ireland: Young 89

4 April 1914 Home Championship Hampden Park Attendance: 105,000

113 SCOTLAND 3, England 1 *Referee: Herbert Bamlett (England)*

Scotland (2-3-5):

16 James Brownlie (Third Lanark);
12 Alexander McNair (Celtic)
3 Joseph Dodds (Celtic);
7 James Gordon (Rangers, captain)
21 Charles Thomson (Sunderland)
11 John Hay (Newcastle United);
3 Alexander Donaldson (Bolton Wanderers)
11 James "Napoleon" McMenemy (Celtic)
9 William Reid (Rangers)
3 James Croal (Falkirk)
3 Joseph Donnachie (Oldham Athletic)

The final match before the First World War saw Scotland record one of the most convincing victories over England for some considerable time, being more dominant than the 3-1 score suggests. A superb goal from Sunderland's Charles Thomson opened the scoring in the second minute, when following a corner the ball broke to him and the centre half thundered it home from 20 yards. England equalised through Fleming in the 15th minute, taking advantage of slackness in the Scottish defence. In the second half the home side took over and put on a superb display. Inside right James "Napoleon" McMenemy of Celtic and Rangers centre forward William Reid both scored but England were by all accounts lucky not to concede more. Inside left James Croal of Falkirk also had a fine match with his dynamism standing out.

England: Samuel Hardy; Robert Crompton, Jesse Pennington; Albert Sturgess, Joseph McCall, Robert McNeal; Frederick Walden, Harold Fleming, Joseph Hampton, Joseph Smith, Edwin Mosscrop.

Scorers: Scotland: Thomson 2; McMenemy 50; Reid 67   England: Fleming 15

CHAPTER TWO
1920-1939

---

26 February 1920   Home Championship   Ninian Park, Cardiff   Attendance: 16,000

114   Wales 1, SCOTLAND 1

Referee: James Mason (England)

Scotland (2-3-5):
1   Kenneth Campbell (Liverpool);
13   Alexander McNair (Celtic)
1   David Thomson (Dundee);
8   James Gordon (Rangers)
1   William Cringan (Celtic, captain)
1   James McMullan (Partick Thistle);
2   James Reid (Airdrie)
1   John Crosbie (Ayr United)
1   Andrew Wilson (Dunfermline Athletic)
1   Thomas Cairns (Rangers)
1   Alan Morton (Queen's Park)

After the six-year break due to the First World War, the Home Championship action resumed in the spring of 1920 with a match at Ninian Park against Wales. Just three of the team who played in the last match in 1914 remained – experienced Celtic full back Alexander McNair who won his 13th cap, Rangers right half James Gordon who made his eighth appearance, and James Reid of Airdrie who turned out for the second time. Wales had more survivors from pre-war, including captain Billy Meredith who was making his 50th appearance, for which he received a special presentation, and claimed a deserved home draw. The hosts made the perfect start when left winger John Evans gave them the lead in the fifth minute, and it took until the 78th before the Scots replied through Rangers inside left Thomas Cairns. One of the Scottish debutants was left winger Alan Morton of Queen's Park, who was to go on to a memorable international career. Another new boy, Andrew Wilson of Dunfermline, went on to score an amazing 13 goals in the next 11 games.

Wales: Edward Peers; Harold Millership, Moses Russell; Thomas Matthias, Joseph Jones, William Jennings; William Meredith (captain), Ivor Jones, Stanley Davies, Richard Richards, John Evans.

Scorers: Wales: Evans 5   Scotland: Cairns 78

---

13 March 1920   Home Championship   Celtic Park, Glasgow   Attendance: 39,757

115   SCOTLAND 3, Ireland 0

Referee: James Mason (England)

Scotland: Kenneth Campbell (Liverpool); Alexander McNair (Celtic), James Blair (Sheffield Wednesday); James Bowie (Rangers), Wilfred Low (Newcastle United), James Gordon (Rangers); Alexander Donaldson (Bolton Wanderers), James "Napoleon" McMenemy (Celtic), Andrew Wilson (Dunfermline Athletic), Andrew Cunningham (Rangers), Alan Morton (Queen's Park).

Ireland: Elisha Scott; Robert Manderson, David Rollo; Michael Hamill, William Lacey, William Emerson (captain); Patrick Robinson, Patrick "Patsy" Gallacher, Edward Brooks, William Gillespie, James McCandless.

Scorers: Scotland: Wilson 8; Morton 42; Cunningham 55

---

10 April 1920   Home Championship   Hillsborough, Sheffield   Attendance: 35,000

116   England 5, SCOTLAND 4

Referee: Thomas Dougray (Scotland)

Scotland: Kenneth Campbell (Partick Thistle); Alexander McNair (Celtic, captain), James Blair (Sheffield Wednesday); James Bowie (Rangers), Wilfred Low (Newcastle United), James Gordon (Rangers); Alexander Donaldson (Bolton Wanderers), Thomas Miller (Liverpool), Andrew Wilson (Dunfermline Athletic), John Paterson (Leicester City), Alexander Troup (Dundee).

England: Sam Hardy; Ephraim Longworth, Jesse Pennington (captain); Andrew Ducat, Joseph McCall, Arthur Grimsdell; Charles Wallace, Robert Kelly, John Cock, Frederick Morris, Alfred Quantrill.

Scorers: England: Cock 9; Quantrill 15; Kelly 57, 73; Morris 67   Scotland: Miller 13, 40; Wilson 21; Donaldson 31

---

12 February 1921   Home Championship   Pittodrie, Aberdeen   Attendance: 20,824

117   SCOTLAND 2, Wales 1

Referee: James Mason (England)

Scotland: Kenneth Campbell (Partick Thistle, captain); John Marshall (Middlesbrough), William McStay (Celtic); Joseph Morris (Partick Thistle), Charles Pringle (St Mirren), James McMullan (Partick Thistle); Alexander Archibald (Rangers), Andrew Cunningham (Rangers), Andrew Wilson (Dunfermline Athletic), Joseph Cassidy (Celtic), Alexander Troup (Dundee).

Wales: Edward Peers; Harry Millership, Moses Russell; Frederick Keenor, Joseph Jones, Thomas Matthias; David Williams, David Collier, Francis Hoddinott, Stanley Davies, Edward Vizard.

Scorers: Scotland: Wilson 11, 46   Wales: Collier 30

---

26 February 1921   Home Championship   Windsor Park, Belfast   Attendance: 30,000

118   Ireland 0, SCOTLAND 2

Referee: Arthur Ward (England)

Scotland: Kenneth Campbell (Partick Thistle); John Marshall (Middlesbrough), William McStay (Celtic); Joseph Harris (Partick Thistle), John Graham (Arsenal), James McMullan (Partick Thistle); Alexander McNab (Morton), Thomas Miller (Manchester United), Andrew Wilson (Dunfermline Athletic, captain), Joseph Cassidy (Celtic), Alexander Troup (Dundee).

Ireland: Elisha Scott; James Mulligan, David Rollo; William Lacey (captain), Ernest Smith, Michael O'Brien; Samuel McGregor, James Ferris, Daniel McKinney, Michael Hamill, Louis "Bookman" Buckhalter.

Scorers: Scotland: Wilson 10; Cassidy 89

| 9 April 1921 | Home Championship | Hampden Park | Attendance: 85,000 |

119 SCOTLAND 3, England 0 *Referee: Arthur Ward (England)*

Scotland: John Ewart (Bradford City); John Marshall (Middlesbrough, captain), James Blair (Cardiff City); Stewart Davidson (Middlesbrough), George Brewster (Everton), James McMullan (Partick Thistle); Alexander McNab (Morton), Thomas Miller (Manchester United), Andrew Wilson (Dunfermline Athletic), Andrew Cunningham (Rangers), Alan Morton (Rangers).

England: Harold Gough; Thomas Smart, John Silcock; Bertram Smith, George Wilson, Arthur Grimsdell (captain); Samuel Chedgzoy, Robert Kelly, Henry Chambers, Herbert Bliss, James Dimmock.

Scorers: Scotland: Wilson 20; Morton 43; Cunningham 57

| 4 February 1922 | Home Championship | The Racecourse, Wrexham | Attendance: 8,000 |

120 Wales 2, SCOTLAND 1 *Referee: Arthur Ward (England)*

Scotland: Kenneth Campbell (Partick Thistle); John Marshall (Middlesbrough, captain), Donald McKinlay (Liverpool); David Meiklejohn (Rangers), Michael Gilhooley (Hull City), William Collier (Raith Rovers); Alexander Archibald (Rangers), John White (Albion Rovers), Andrew Wilson (Middlesbrough), Francis Walker (Third Lanark), Alan Morton (Rangers).

Wales: Edward Peers; Edward Parry, James Evans; Herbert Evans, Joseph Jones, Thomas Matthias; Stanley Davies, Ivor Jones, Leonard Davies, Richard Richards, Edward Vizard.

Scorers: Wales: Leonard Davies 7; Stanley Davies 25   Scotland: Archibald 65

| 4 March 1922 | Home Championship | Celtic Park, Glasgow | Attendance: 36,000 |

121 SCOTLAND 2, Ireland 1 *Referee: Arthur Ward (England)*

Scotland: Kenneth Campbell (Partick Thistle); John Marshall (Middlesbrough), Donald McKinlay (Liverpool); James Hogg (Ayr United), William Cringan (Celtic), Thomas Muirhead (Rangers); Alexander Donaldson (Bolton Wanderers), James Kinloch (Partick Thistle), Andrew Wilson (Middlesbrough), Andrew Cunningham (Rangers, captain), Alexander Troup (Dundee).

Ireland: Francis Collins; William McCracken (captain), William McCandless; Robert McCracken, Michael O'Brien, William Emerson; William Lacey, Patrick "Patsy" Gallacher, Robert Irvine, William Gillespie, David Lyner.

Scorers: Ireland: Gillespie 42   Scotland: Wilson 60, 83

| 8 April 1922 | Home Championship | Villa Park, Birmingham | Attendance: 33,646 |

122 England 0, SCOTLAND 1 *Referee: Thomas Dougray (Scotland)*

Scotland: Kenneth Campbell (Partick Thistle); John Marshall (Middlesbrough), James Blair (Cardiff City, captain); John Gilchrist (Celtic), William Cringan (Celtic), Neil McBain (Manchester United); Alexander Archibald (Rangers), John Crosbie (Birmingham), Andrew Wilson (Middlesbrough), Thomas Cairns (Rangers), Alan Morton (Rangers).

England: Jeremiah Dawson; Thomas Clay, Samuel Wadsworth; Frank Moss, George Wilson (captain), Thomas Bromilow; Richard York, Robert Kelly, William Rawlings, William Walker, William Smith.

Scorer: Scotland: Wilson 63

| 3 March 1923 | Home Championship | Windsor Park, Belfast | Attendance: 31,000 |

123 Ireland 0, SCOTLAND 1 *Referee: Arthur Ward (England)*

Scotland: William Harper (Hibernian); John Hutton (Aberdeen), James Blair (Cardiff City, captain); David Steele (Huddersfield Town), David Morris (Raith Rovers), Neil McBain (Everton); Alexander Archibald (Rangers), John White (Hearts), Andrew Wilson (Middlesbrough), Joseph Cassidy (Celtic), Alan Morton (Rangers).

Ireland: Thomas Farquharson; William McCracken, John Curran; Samuel Irving, George Moorhead, William Emerson; Hamilton McKenzie, Patrick "Patsy" Gallacher, George Reid, William Gillespie, William Moore.

Scorer: Scotland: Wilson 69

| 17 March 1923 | Home Championship | Love Street, Paisley | Attendance: 25,000 |

124 SCOTLAND 2, Wales 0 *Referee: Isaac Baker (England)*

Scotland: William Harper (Hibernian); John Hutton (Aberdeen), James Blair (Cardiff City); John McNab (Liverpool), William Cringan (Celtic, captain), David Steel (Huddersfield Town); Henry Ritchie (Hibernian), Andrew Cunningham (Rangers), Andrew Wilson (Middlesbrough), Thomas Cairns (Rangers), Alan Morton (Rangers).

Wales: George Godding; Moses Russell, James Evans; Thomas Matthias, Frederick Keenor, Robert John; David Williams, Robert Davies, Stanley Davies, Leonard Davies, David Nicholas.

Scorer: Scotland: Wilson 7, 55

| 14 April 1923 | Home Championship | Hampden Park | Attendance: 71,000 |

125 SCOTLAND 2, England 2 *Referee: Arthur Ward (England)*

Scotland: William Harper (Hibernian); John Hutton (Aberdeen), James Blair (Cardiff City); David Steele (Huddersfield Town), William Cringan (Celtic, captain), Thomas Muirhead (Rangers); Denis Lawson (St Mirren), Andrew Cunningham (Rangers), Andrew Wilson (Middlesbrough), Thomas Cairns (Rangers), Alan Morton (Rangers).

England: Edward Taylor; Ephraim Longworth, Samuel Wadsworth; Frederick Kean, George Wilson (captain), John Tresadern; Samuel Chedgzoy, Robert Kelly, Victor Watson, Henry Chambers, Frederick Tunstall.

Scorers: Scotland: Cunningham 28; Wilson 55   England: Kelly 31; Watson 42

Chapter two: 1920-1939

| 16 February 1924 | Home Championship | Ninian Park, Cardiff | Attendance: 26,000 |

126 Wales 2, SCOTLAND 0 *Referee: Herbert Andrews (England)*

Scotland: William Harper (Hibernian); John Marshall (Llanelli), James Blair (Cardiff City, captain); David Meiklejohn (Rangers), Neil McBain (Everton), Thomas Muirhead (Rangers); Alexander Archibald (Rangers), William Russell (Airdrie), Joseph Cassidy (Celtic), John McKay (Blackburn Rovers), Alan Morton (Rangers).

Wales: Albert Gray; Moses Russell, John Jenkins; Herbert Evans, Frederick Keenor, William Jennings; William Davies, Ivor Jones, Leonard Davies, Richard Richards, Edward Vizard.

Scorers: Wales: William Davies 61; Leonard Davies 72

| 1 March 1924 | Home Championship | Celtic Park, Glasgow | Attendance: 30,000 |

127 SCOTLAND 2, Ireland 0 *Referee: George Watson (England)*

Scotland: William Harper (Hibernian); John Hutton (Aberdeen, captain), James Hamilton (St Mirren); Peter Kerr (Hibernian), David Morris (Raith Rovers), James McMullan (Partick Thistle); James Reid (Airdrie), Andrew Cunningham (Rangers), Hughie Gallacher (Airdrie), Thomas Cairns (Rangers), Alan Morton (Rangers).

Ireland: Thomas Farquharson; David Rollo, William McCandless; Samuel Irving, Michael O'Brien, Gerald Morgan; Daniel McKinney, Patrick "Patsy" Gallacher, Robert Irvine, William Gillespie, John McGrillen.

Scorers: Scotland: Cunningham 86; Morris 88

| 12 April 1924 | Home Championship | Wembley, London | Attendance: 37,250 |

128 England 1, SCOTLAND 1 *Referee: Thomas Dougray (Scotland)*

Scotland: William Harper (Hibernian); John Smith (Ayr United), Philip McCloy (Ayr United); William Clunas (Sunderland), David Morris (Raith Rovers), James McMullan (Partick Thistle, captain); Alexander Archibald (Rangers), William Cowan (Newcastle United), Neil Harris (Newcastle United), Andrew Cunningham (Rangers), Alan Morton (Rangers).

England: Edward Taylor; Thomas Smart, Samuel Wadsworth; Frank Moss (captain), Charles Spencer, Percival Barton; William Butler, David Jack, Charles Buchan, William Walker, Frederick Tunstall.

Scorers: Scotland: Cowan 40   England: Walker 60

| 14 February 1925 | Home Championship | Tynecastle, Edinburgh | Attendance: 25,000 |

129 SCOTLAND 3, Wales 1 *Referee: Arthur Ward (England)*

Scotland: William Harper (Hibernian); James Nelson (Cardiff City), William McStay (Celtic); David Meiklejohn (Rangers), David Morris (Raith Rovers, captain), Robert Bennie (Airdrie); Alex Jackson (Aberdeen), James Dunn (Hibernian), Hughie Gallacher (Airdrie), Thomas Cairns (Rangers), Alan Morton (Rangers).

Wales: Albert Gray; John Jenkins, Moses Russell; Stanley Davies, Frederick Keenor, William Williams; William Davies, John Nicholls, Leonard Davies, George Beadles, Frederick Cook.

Scorers: Scotland: Meiklejohn 9; Gallacher 20, 61   Wales: Williams 43

| 28 February 1925 | Home Championship | Windsor Park, Belfast | Attendance: 41,000 |

130 Ireland 0, SCOTLAND 3 *Referee: George Watson (England)*

Scotland: William Harper (Hibernian); James Nelson (Cardiff City), William McStay (Celtic); David Meiklejohn (Rangers), David Morris (Raith Rovers, captain), Robert Bennie (Airdrie); Alex Jackson (Aberdeen), James Dunn (Hibernian), Hughie Gallacher (Airdrie), Thomas Cairns (Rangers), Alan Morton (Rangers).

Ireland: Thomas Farquharson; Robert Manderson, William McCandless; James Chatton, Michael O'Brien, Samuel Irving; David Martin, Patrick "Patsy" Gallacher, Edward Carroll, William Gillespie, Joseph Toner.

Scorers: Scotland: Meiklejohn 4; Gallacher 25; Dunn 35

| 4 April 1925 | Home Championship | Hampden Park | Attendance: 92,000 |

131 SCOTLAND 2, England 0 *Referee: Arthur Ward (England)*

Scotland: William Harper (Hibernian); William McStay (Celtic), Philip McCloy (Ayr United); David Meiklejohn (Rangers), David Morris (Raith Rovers, captain), James McMullan (Partick Thistle); Alex Jackson (Aberdeen), William Russell (Airdrie), Hughie Gallacher (Airdrie), Thomas Cairns (Rangers), Alan Morton (Rangers).

England: Richard Pym; William Ashurst, Samuel Wadsworth (captain); Thomas Magee, John Townrow, Leonard Graham; Robert Kelly, James Seed, Frank Roberts, William Walker, Frederick Tunstall.

Scorer: Scotland: Gallacher 36, 86

| 31 October 1925 | Home Championship | Ninian Park, Cardiff | Attendance: 18,000 |

132 Wales 0, SCOTLAND 3 *Referee: Ernest Pinkstone (England)*

Scotland: William Robb (Rangers); John Hutton (Aberdeen), William McStay (Celtic); William Clunas (Sunderland), William Townsley (Falkirk, captain), James McMullan (Partick Thistle); Alex Jackson (Huddersfield Town), John Duncan (Leicester City), Hughie Gallacher (Airdrie), Alex James (Preston North End), Adam McLean (Celtic).

Wales: Albert Gray; Moses Russell, John Jenkins; Samuel Bennion, Frederick Keenor, James Lewis; David Williams, William Davies, Stanley Davies, Richard Richards, Edward Vizard.

Scorers: Scotland: Duncan 70; McLean 80; Clunas 82

The team which defeated Wales 3-0 in 1926. Back (from left): J. Fleming (linesman), John Forshaw (referee), Thomas McInally, James Gibson, William Wiseman, Alan McClory, Andrew Cunningham, Robert Gillespie, G. Livingston (trainer). Front: Alex Jackson, James McMullan, William McStay, Adam McLean, Hughie Gallacher. *Photo courtesy of Scottish Football Museum*

27 February 1926   Home Championship   Ibrox Park, Glasgow   Attendance: 30,000
133 SCOTLAND 4, Ireland 0   *Referee: George Watson (England)*

Scotland: William Harper (Arsenal); John Hutton (Aberdeen), William McStay (Celtic, captain); Peter Wilson (Celtic), John McDougall (Airdrie), Robert Bennie (Airdrie); Alex Jackson (Huddersfield Town), Andrew Cunningham (Rangers), Hughie Gallacher (Newcastle United), Thomas McInally (Celtic), Adam McLean (Celtic).

Ireland: Elisha Scott; Robert Manderson, Thomas Watson; Samuel Irving, Joseph Gowdy, Thomas Sloan; Andrew Bothwell, Alexander Steele, Samuel Curran, William Gillespie, John Mahood.

Scorers: Scotland: Gallacher 13, 60, 66; Cunningham 40

17 April 1926   Home Championship   Old Trafford, Manchester   Attendance: 49,000
134 England 0, SCOTLAND 1   *Referee: Thomas Dougray (Scotland)*

Scotland: William Harper (Arsenal); John Hutton (Aberdeen), William McStay (Celtic, captain); James Gibson (Partick Thistle), William Summers (St Mirren), James McMullan (Manchester City); Alex Jackson (Huddersfield Town), Alex Thomson (Celtic), Hughie Gallacher (Newcastle United), Andrew Cunningham (Rangers), Alexander Troup (Everton).

England: Edward Taylor; Frederick Goodall, Thomas Mort; Willis Edwards, John Hill, George Green; Richard York, Sydney Puddefoot, Edward Harper (captain), William Walker, James Ruffell.

Scorer: Scotland: Jackson 37

30 October 1926   Home Championship   Ibrox Park, Glasgow   Attendance: 41,000
135 SCOTLAND 3, Wales 0   *Referee: John Forshaw (England)*

Scotland: Alan McClory (Motherwell); William McStay (Celtic, captain), William Wiseman (Queen's Park); James Gibson (Partick Thistle), Robert Gillespie (Queen's Park), James McMullan (Manchester City); Alex Jackson (Huddersfield Town), Andrew Cunningham (Rangers), Hughie Gallacher (Newcastle United), Thomas McInally (Celtic), Adam McLean (Celtic).

Wales: Albert Gray; Thomas Evans, John Jenkins; Samuel Bennion, Frederick Keenor, William Jennings; William Davies, Stanley Davies, John Fowler, Charles Jones, Edward Vizard.

Scorers: Scotland: Gallacher 20; Jackson 33, 73

26 February 1927   Home Championship   Windsor Park, Belfast   Attendance: 40,000
136 Ireland 0, SCOTLAND 2   *Referee: George Watson (England)*

Scotland: John Harkness (Queen's Park); John Hutton (Blackburn Rovers), William McStay (Celtic, captain); Thomas Muirhead (Rangers), James Gibson (Partick Thistle), Thomas "Tully" Craig (Rangers); Alex Jackson (Huddersfield Town), James Dunn (Hibernian), Hughie Gallacher (Newcastle United), James Howieson (St Mirren), Alan Morton (Rangers).

Ireland: Elisha Scott; Andrew McCluggage, William McConnell; Joseph Gowdy, Thomas Sloan, David McMullan; John McGrillen, Patrick "Patsy" Gallacher, Hugh Davey, Samuel Irving, Joseph Toner.

Scorer: Scotland: Morton 44, 88

Chapter two: 1920-1939

2 April 1927 Home Championship Hampden Park Attendance: 111,214

137 SCOTLAND 1, England 2 *Referee: Arthur Ward (England)*

Scotland: John Harkness (Queen's Park); William McStay (Celtic, captain), Robert Thomson (Falkirk); Thomas Morrison (St Mirren), James Gibson (Partick Thistle), James McMullan (Manchester City); Adam McLean (Celtic), Andrew Cunningham (Rangers), Hughie Gallacher (Newcastle United), Bobby McPhail (Airdrie), Alan Morton (Rangers).

England: John Brown; Frederick Goodall, Herbert Jones; Willis Edwards, John Hill (captain), Sidney Bishop; Joseph Hulme, William "Dixie" Dean, Arthur Rigby, George Brown, Louis Page.

Scorers: Scotland: Morton 53 England: Dean 69, 88

29 October 1927 Home Championship The Racecourse, Wrexham Attendance: 16,000

138 Wales 2, SCOTLAND 2 *Referee: Arthur Kingscott (England)*

Scotland: William Robb (Hibernian); John Hutton (Blackburn Rovers), William McStay (Celtic); David Meiklejohn (Rangers), James Gibson (Aston Villa), James McMullan (Manchester City, captain); Alex Jackson (Huddersfield Town), Robert McKay (Newcastle United), Hughie Gallacher (Newcastle United), George Stevenson (Motherwell), Alan Morton (Rangers).

Wales: Albert Gray; Moses Russell, Thomas Evans; Samuel Bennion, Frederick Keenor, Stanley Davies; William Hole, Leonard Davies, John Fowler, Ernest Curtis, Frederick Cook.

Scorers: Scotland: Gallacher 14; Hutton 16 (pen) Wales: Curtis 44; Gibson 76 (own goal)

25 February 1928 Home Championship Firhill Park, Glasgow Attendance: 55,000

139 SCOTLAND 0, Ireland 1 *Referee: Arthur Ward (England)*

Scotland: Allan McClory (Motherwell); John Hutton (Blackburn Rovers), William McStay (Celtic); Thomas Muirhead (Rangers, captain), David Meiklejohn (Rangers), Thomas "Tully" Craig (Rangers); Henry Ritchie (Hibernian), James Dunn (Hibernian), Jimmy McGrory (Celtic), George Stevenson (Motherwell), Alan Morton (Rangers).

Ireland: Elisha Scott; Andrew McCluggage, Robert Hamilton; Samuel Irving, George Moorhead, Gerald Morgan; James Chambers, Robert Irvine, Samuel Curran, James Ferris, John Mahood.

Scorer: Ireland: Chambers 10

31 March 1928 Home Championship Wembley, London Attendance 80,868

140 England 1, SCOTLAND 5 *Referee: William Bell (Scotland)*

Scotland (2-3-5):
3 John Harkness (Queen's Park);
3 James Nelson (Cardiff City)
1 Thomas Law (Chelsea);
6 James Gibson (Aston Villa)
1 Thomas Bradshaw (Bury)
13 James McMullan (Manchester City, captain);
10 Alex Jackson (Huddersfield Town)
5 James Dunn (Hibernian)
12 Hughie Gallacher (Newcastle United)
2 Alex James (Preston North End)
19 Alan Morton (Rangers)

Scotland's greatest ever victory over England saw the victorious side dubbed the "Wembley Wizards", and by all accounts the scoreline did not flatter the visitors. Huddersfield Town winger Alex Jackson gave the Scots the lead in the fourth minute, heading in an Alan Morton cross, and inside left Alex James made it two just before half-time after a clever turn and shot. Midway through the second half Jackson headed home another Morton cross and James added his own second a few minutes later. Five minutes before the end Jackson got his hat trick, with a terrific first-time shot following yet another Morton assist. In the final minute Robert Kelly reduced the leeway for England from a free kick, the last goal of a remarkable game. A big surprise was that the great Hughie Gallacher, usually such a prolific marksman, was not among the scorers.

England: Arthur Hufton; Frederick Goodall (captain), Herbert Jones; Willis Edwards, Thomas Wilson, Henry Healless; Joseph Hulme, Robert Kelly, William "Dixie" Dean, Joseph Bradford, William Smith.

Scorers: Scotland: Jackson 4, 65, 85; James 44, 66 England: Kelly 89

27 October 1928 Home Championship Ibrox Park, Glasgow Attendance: 55,000

141 SCOTLAND 4, Wales 2 *Referee: Arthur Kingscott (England)*

Scotland: John Harkness (Hearts); Douglas Gray (Rangers), Daniel Blair (Clyde); Thomas Muirhead (Rangers), William King (Queen's Park), James McMullan (Manchester City, captain); Alex Jackson (Huddersfield Town), James Dunn (Everton), Hughie Gallacher (Newcastle United), Bobby McPhail (Rangers), Alan Morton (Rangers).

Wales: Albert Gray; Ernest Morley, William Jennings; Samuel Bennion, Frederick Keenor, David Evans; William Hole, William Davies, Wilfred Lewis, Leonard Davies, David Williams.

Scorers: Wales: William Davies 12, 75 Scotland: Gallacher 25, 42, 49; Dunn 56

23 February 1929 Home Championship Windsor Park, Belfast Attendance 35,000

142 Ireland 3, SCOTLAND 7 *Referee: Albert Fogg (England)*

Scotland: John Harkness (Hearts); Douglas Gray (Rangers), Daniel Blair (Clyde); Thomas Muirhead (Rangers), David Meiklejohn (Rangers), James McMullan (Manchester City, captain); Alex Jackson (Huddersfield Town), William Chalmers (Queen's Park), Hughie Gallacher (Newcastle United), Alex James (Preston North End), Alan Morton (Rangers).

Ireland: Elisha Scott; Andrew McCluggage, Hugh Flack; Joseph Miller, George Moorhead, Alexander Steele; James Chambers, Richard Rowley, Joseph Bambrick, Lawrence Cumming, John Mahood.

Scorers: Scotland: Gallacher 3, 9, 14, 51, 76; Jackson 36, 82 Ireland: Rowley 16, 42; Bambrick 58

| 13 April 1929 | Home Championship | Hampden Park | Attendance: 110,512 |

143 SCOTLAND 1, England 0
Referee: Arthur Joseph (England)

Scotland: John Harkness (Hearts); James Crapnell (Airdrie), Joseph Nibloe (Kilmarnock); John Buchanan (Rangers), David Meiklejohn (Rangers), James McMullan (Manchester City, captain); Alex Jackson (Huddersfield Town), Alexander Cheyne (Aberdeen), Hughie Gallacher (Newcastle United), Alex James (Preston North End), Alan Morton (Rangers).

England: John Hacking; Thomas Cooper, Ernest Blenkinsop; Willis Edwards, James Seddon, Henry Nuttall; John Bruton, George Brown, William "Dixie" Dean, William Wainscoat, James Ruffell.

Scorer: Scotland: Cheyne 90

| 26 May 1929 | Friendly | Brann, Bergen | Attendance: 4,000 |

144 Norway 3, SCOTLAND 7
Referee: Fredrik Schielderop (Norway)

Scotland (2-3-5):
1 Alexander McLaren (St Johnstone);
2 James Crapnell (Airdrie)
2 Joseph Nibloe (Kilmarnock);
1 William Imrie (St Johnstone)
1 Allan Craig (Motherwell)
3 Thomas "Tully" Craig (Rangers, captain);
1 James Nisbet (Ayr United)
2 Alexander Cheyne (Aberdeen)
1 David McCrae (St Mirren)
1 Robert Rankin (St Mirren)
1 Robert Howe (Hamilton Academical)

A Scottish team played four matches during a European tour. Two were against Norway and one each against the Netherlands and Germany, but only the second encounter with the Norwegians was registered as a full international. It was the first official game against opposition other than England, Wales or Ireland. The first game against Norway finished 4-0 to the Scots and although their opponents did better in the second the visitors were still victorious by a four-goal margin. Alex Cheyne of Aberdeen netted a hat trick, James Nisbet got two and Robert Rankin and captain Thomas Craig one apiece. Cheyne has been credited in some quarters for starting the famous "Hampden Roar" in the previous match with his late winner against England.

Norway: Hugo Hoftstad; Haakon Walde, Egil Lund; Ravn Tollefsen, Alexander Olsen, Kjeld Kjos; Kaare Kongsvik, Oscar Thortensen, Rolf Brodahl, Kaare Lie, Sverre Berg-Johannesen.

Scorers: Norway: Kongsvik 4, 76; Berg-Johannesen 37   Scotland: Rankin 6; Craig 27; Cheyne 30, 64, 68; Nisbet 47, 52

| 1 June 1929 | Friendly | Deutsches Stadion, Berlin | Attendance: 40,000 |

145 Germany 1, SCOTLAND 1
Referee: Otto Ohlsson (Sweden)

Scotland: Alexander McLaren (St Johnstone); Douglas Gray (Rangers), James Crapnell (Airdrie); Hugh Morton (Kilmarnock), William Imrie (St Johnstone), Thomas "Tully" Craig (Rangers, captain); James Nisbet (Ayr United), Alexander Cheyne (Aberdeen), David McCrae (St Mirren), Robert Rankin (St Mirren), James Fleming (Rangers).

Germany: Heinrich Stuhlfauth; Franz Schutz, Hans Brunke; Hans Geiger, Hans Gruber, Conrad Heidkamp; Hans Ruch, Johannes Sobeck, Josef Pottinger, Richard Hofmann, Ludwig Hoffman.

Scorers: Germany: Ruch 49   Scotland: Imrie 87

| 4 June 1929 | Friendly | Olympic Stadion, Amsterdam | Attendance: 24,000 |

146 Netherlands 0, SCOTLAND 2
Referee: John Langenus (Belgium)

Scotland: Alexander McLaren (St Johnstone); Douglas Gray (Rangers), Joseph Nibloe (Kilmarnock); Hugh Morton (Kilmarnock), Allan Craig (Motherwell), Thomas "Tully" Craig (Rangers, captain); James Nisbet (Ayr United), Alexander Cheyne (Aberdeen), James Fleming (Rangers), Robert Rankin (St Mirren), Robert Howe (Hamilton Academical).

Netherlands: Gejus van der Meulen; Sjaak de Bruijn, Dolf van Kol; Hueb de Leeuw, Maarten Grobbe, Koos van der Wildt; Gep Landaal, Felix Smeets, Wim Tap, Cor Kools, Frans Homborg.

Scorers: Scotland: Fleming 31; Rankin 44 (pen)

| 26 October 1929 | Home Championship | Ninian Park, Cardiff | Attendance: 25,000 |

147 Wales 2, SCOTLAND 4
Referee: William McLean (Northern Ireland)

Scotland: John Harkness (Hearts); Douglas Gray (Rangers), Joseph Nibloe (Kilmarnock); James Gibson (Aston Villa), John Johnstone (Hearts), Thomas "Tully" Craig (Rangers); Alex Jackson (Huddersfield Town), Thomas Muirhead (Rangers, captain), Hughie Gallacher (Newcastle United), Alex James (Arsenal), Alan Morton (Rangers).

Wales: Albert Gray; Benjamin Williams, Arthur Lumberg; Samuel Bennion, Frederick Keenor, Robert John; William Davies, Eugene O'Callaghan, Leonard Davies, Charles Jones, Frederick Cook.

Scorers: Scotland: Gallacher 7, 20; James 74; Gibson 77   Wales: O'Callaghan 55; Leonard Davies 63

| 22 February 1930 | Home Championship | Celtic Park, Glasgow | Attendance: 30,000 |

148 SCOTLAND 3, Ireland 1
Referee: Arthur Joseph (England)

Scotland: Robert Middleton (Cowdenbeath); Douglas Gray (Rangers), William Wiseman (Queen's Park); James Gibson (Aston Villa), David Meiklejohn (Rangers, captain), Thomas "Tully" Craig (Rangers); Alex Jackson (Huddersfield Town), George Stevenson (Motherwell), Hughie Gallacher (Newcastle United), Alex James (Arsenal), Alan Morton (Rangers).

Ireland: Alfred Gardiner; Samuel Russell, Robert Hamilton; Robert McDonald, John Jones, Thomas Sloan; James Chambers, Robert Irvine, Joseph Bambrick, James McCambridge, Harold McCaw.

Scorers: Scotland: Gallacher 32, 61; Stevenson 70   Ireland: McCaw 40

Chapter two: 1920-1939

5 April 1930　　　　Home Championship　　　　Wembley, London　　　　Attendance: 87,375

149　England 5, SCOTLAND 2　　　　*Referee: William McLean (Northern Ireland)*

Scotland: John Harkness (Hearts); Douglas Gray (Rangers), Thomas Law (Chelsea); John Buchanan (Rangers), David Meiklejohn (Rangers, captain), Thomas "Tully" Craig (Rangers); Alex Jackson (Huddersfield Town), Alex James (Arsenal), James Fleming (Rangers), George Stevenson (Motherwell), Alan Morton (Rangers).

England: Henry Hibbs; Frederick Goodall, Ernest Blenkinsop; Alfred Strange, Maurice Webster, William Marsden; Samuel Crooks, David Jack, Victor Watson, Joseph Bradford, Ellis Rimmer.

Scorers: England: Watson 12, 28; Rimmer 30, 54; Jack 33　　Scotland: Fleming 48, 62

18 May 1930　　　　Friendly　　　　Yves du Manoir, Colombes, Paris　　　　Attendance: 25,000

150　France 0, SCOTLAND 2　　　　*Referee: Raphael Van Praag (Belgium)*

Scotland: John Thomson (Celtic); James Nelson (Cardiff City), James Crapnell (Airdrie, captain); Peter Wilson (Celtic), George Walker (St Mirren), Frank Hill (Aberdeen); Alex Jackson (Huddersfield Town), Alexander Cheyne (Aberdeen), Hughie Gallacher (Newcastle United), George Stevenson (Motherwell), James Connor (Sunderland).

France: Alexis Thepot; Manuel Anatol, Marcel Capelle; Jean Laurent, Maurice Banide, Augustin Chantrel; Marcel Kauffman, Henri Pavillard, Marcel Pinel, Edmond Delfour, Pierre Korb.

Scorer: Scotland: Gallacher 42, 85

25 October 1930　　　　Home Championship　　　　Ibrox Park, Glasgow　　　　Attendance 23,106

151　SCOTLAND 1, Wales 1　　　　*Referee: Charles Lines (England)*

Scotland: John Thomson (Celtic); Douglas Gray (Rangers), John Gilmour (Dundee); Colin McNab (Dundee), Robert Gillespie (Queen's Park, captain), Frank Hill (Aberdeen); Daniel McRorie (Morton), George Brown (Rangers), Bernard Battles (Hearts), George Stevenson (Motherwell), Alan Morton (Rangers).

Wales: Leonard Evans; Frederick Dewey, Wynne Crompton; William Rogers, Frederick Keenor, Emrys Ellis; William Collins, John Neal, Thomas Bamford, Walter Robbins, William Thomas.

Scorers: Wales: Bamford 6　　Scotland: Battles 37

21 February 1931　　　　Home Championship　　　　Windsor Park, Belfast　　　　Attendance: 20,000

152　Ireland 0, SCOTLAND 0　　　　*Referee: Herbert Hull (England)*

Scotland: John Thomson (Celtic); James Crapnell (Airdrie), Joseph Nibloe (Kilmarnock); Peter Wilson (Celtic), George Walker (St Mirren), Frank Hill (Aberdeen); John Murdoch (Motherwell), Peter Scarff (Celtic), Benny Yorston (Aberdeen), Bobby McPhail (Rangers), Alan Morton (Rangers, captain).

Ireland: Alfred Gardiner; John McNinch, Robert Fulton; William McCleery, John Jones, Thomas Sloan; Hugh Blair, Edward Falloon, Frederick Roberts, John Geary, Harold McCaw.

28 March 1931　　　　Home Championship　　　　Hampden Park　　　　Attendance: 129,810

153　SCOTLAND 2, England 0　　　　*Referee: Alfred Atwood (Wales)*

Scotland: John Thomson (Celtic); Daniel Blair (Clyde), Joseph Nibloe (Kilmarnock); Colin McNab (Dundee), David Meiklejohn (Rangers, captain), John Miller (St Mirren); Alexander Archibald (Rangers), George Stevenson (Motherwell), Jimmy McGrory (Celtic), Bobby McPhail (Rangers), Alan Morton (Rangers).

England: Henry Hibbs; Frederick Goodall (captain), Ernest Blenkinsop; Alfred Strange, Herbert Roberts, Austin Campbell; Samuel Crooks, Gordon Hodgson, William "Dixie" Dean, Harold Burgess, John Crawford.

Scorers: Scotland: Stevenson 60; McGrory 62

16 May 1931　　　　Friendly　　　　Hohe Warte Stadion, Vienna　　　　Attendance: 45,000

154　Austria 5, SCOTLAND 0　　　　*Referee: Paul Ruoff (Switzerland)*

Scotland: John Jackson (Partick Thistle); Daniel Blair (Clyde, captain), Joseph Nibloe (Kilmarnock); Colin McNab (Dundee), James McDougall (Liverpool), George Walker (St Mirren); Andrew Love (Aberdeen), James Paterson (Cowdenbeath), James Easson (Portsmouth), James Robertson (Dundee), Daniel Liddle (East Fife).

Austria: Rudolf Hiden; Roman Schramseis, Josef Blum; Georg Braun, Josef Smistik, Karl Gall; Karl Zischek, Friedrich Gschweidl, Matthias Sindelar, Anton Schall, Adolf Vogel.

Scorers: Austria: Schall 8; Zischek 13, 69; Vogel 49; Sindelar 77

20 May 1931　　　　Friendly　　　　Stadio Nazionale, Rome　　　　Attendance: 25,000

155　Italy 3, SCOTLAND 0　　　　*Referee: Peco Bauwens (Germany)*

Scotland: John Jackson (Partick Thistle); Daniel Blair (Clyde), Joseph Nibloe (Kilmarnock); Colin McNab (Dundee), James McDougall (Liverpool, captain), John Miller (St Mirren); Andrew Love (Aberdeen), James Paterson (Cowdenbeath), William Boyd (Clyde), James Robertson (Dundee), Daniel Liddle (East Fife).

Italy: Giampiero Combi; Eraldo Monzeglio, Umberto Caligaris; Attilio Ferraris, Fulvio Bernardini, Luigi Bertolini; Raffaele Costantino, Renato Cesarini, Giuseppe Meazza, Giovanni Ferrari, Raimondo Orsi.

Scorers: Italy: Costantino 6; Meazza 42; Orsi 87

| 24 May 1931 | Friendly | Parc des Charmilles, Geneva | Attendance: 10,000 |

156 Switzerland 2, SCOTLAND 3   *Referee: Albino Carraro (Italy)*

Scotland: John Jackson (Partick Thistle); James Crapnell (Airdrie, captain), Joseph Nibloe (Kilmarnock); Colin McNab (Dundee), George Walker (St Mirren), John Miller (St Mirren); Andrew Love (Aberdeen), James Paterson (Cowdenbeath), William Boyd (Clyde), James Easson (Portsmouth), Daniel Liddle (East Fife).

Switzerland: Charles Pasche; Severino Minelli, Rudolf Ramseyer; Edmond Loichot, Otto Imhof, Gabriele Gilardoni; Edmond Kramer, Andre Syrvet, Albert Buche, Andre Abegglen, Max Fauguel.

Scorers: Scotland: Easson 22; Boyd 24; Love 89   Switzerland: Buche 31; Fauguel 66

| 19 September 1931 | Home Championship | Ibrox Park, Glasgow | Attendance: 40,000 |

157 SCOTLAND 3, Ireland 1   *Referee: Isaac Caswell (England)*

Scotland: Robert Hepburn (Ayr United); Daniel Blair (Clyde), Robert McAulay (Rangers); Alexander Massie (Hearts), David Meiklejohn (Rangers), George Brown (Rangers); James Crawford (Queen's Park), George Stevenson (Motherwell), Jimmy McGrory (Celtic), Bobby McPhail (Rangers), James Connor (Sunderland).

Ireland: Alfred Gardiner; John McNinch, Robert Hamilton; William McCreery, John Jones, William Gowdy; Hugh Blair, Richard Rowley, James Dunne, John Geary, James Chambers.

Scorers: Scotland: Stevenson 5; McGrory 34; McPhail 72   Ireland: Dunne 20

| 31 October 1931 | Home Championship | The Racecourse, Wrexham | Attendance: 10,860 |

158 Wales 2, SCOTLAND 3   *Referee: Isaac Caswell (England)*

Scotland: John Harkness (Hearts); Daniel Blair (Clyde), Robert McAulay (Rangers); Alexander Massie (Hearts), David Meiklejohn (Rangers, captain), George Brown (Rangers); Robert Thomson (Celtic), George Stevenson (Motherwell), Jimmy McGrory (Celtic), Bobby McPhail (Rangers), Alan Morton (Rangers).

Wales: Albert Gray; Aneurin Richards, Arthur Lumberg; Thomas Edwards, Thomas Griffiths, Edward Lawrence; Philip Griffiths, Eugene O'Callaghan, Ernest Glover, Walter Robbins, Ernest Curtis.

Scorers: Wales: Curtis 15 (pen); O'Callaghan 78   Scotland: Stevenson 25; Thomson 31; McGrory 55

| 9 April 1932 | Home Championship | Wembley, London | Attendance: 92,180 |

159 England 3, SCOTLAND 0   *Referee: Samuel Thompson (Northern Ireland)*

Scotland: Thomas Hamilton (Rangers); James Crapnell (Airdrie, captain), Joseph Nibloe (Kilmarnock); Colin McNab (Dundee), Allan Craig (Motherwell), George Brown (Rangers); Alexander Archibald (Rangers), James Marshall (Rangers), Neil Dewar (Third Lanark), Charles Napier (Celtic), Alan Morton (Rangers).

England: Harold Pearson; George Shaw, Ernest Blenkinsop (captain); Alfred Strange, James O'Dowd, Samuel Weaver; Samuel Crooks, Robert Barclay, Thomas Waring, Thomas Johnson, William Houghton.

Scorers: England: Waring 36; Barclay 79; Crooks 88

| 8 May 1932 | Friendly | Stade Olympique, Paris | Attendance: 20,000 |

160 France 1, SCOTLAND 3   *Referee: Albino Carraro (Italy)*

Scotland (2-3-5):

10 John Harkness (Hearts);
8 James Crapnell (Airdrie)
11 Joseph Nibloe (Kilmarnock);
3 Alexander Massie (Hearts)
3 Robert Gillespie (Queen's Park, captain)
4 John Miller (St Mirren);
2 James Crawford (Queen's Park)
2 Alexander Thomson (Celtic)
2 Neil Dewar (Third Lanark)
7 Bobby McPhail (Rangers)
31 Alan Morton (Rangers)

For this friendly match the players on both sides wore black armbands in honour of French President Paul Doumer, who had been assassinated the previous day. Although a much more sombre occasion than expected, the Scots rose to the task in fine style and registered an impressive victory. It was a personal triumph for Third Lanark centre forward Neil Dewar who scored all three goals. The Rangers left-sided pairing of Bobby McPhail and Alan Morton also had fine games, exchanging clever passing and providing the assists for all of Dewar's strikes. Marcel Langiller pulled one back from the penalty spot just before half-time and that proved the end of the scoring, with the second half more of a dull affair.

France: Alexis Thepot; Manuel Anatol, Andre Chardar; Emile Scharwath, Joseph Kaucsar, Jean Laurent; Ernest Liberati, Joseph Alcazar, Robert Mercier, Rene Gerard, Marcel Langiller.

Scorers: Scotland: Dewar 14, 27, 40   France: Langiller 43 (pen)

| 17 September 1932 | Home Championship | Windsor Park, Belfast | Attendance: 40,000 |

161 Ireland 0, SCOTLAND 4   *Referee: William Harper (England)*

Scotland: Alexander McLaren (St Johnstone); Douglas Gray (Rangers), James Crapnell (Airdrie, captain); Alexander Massie (Hearts), John Johnstone (Hearts), William Telfer (Motherwell); James Crawford (Queen's Park), George Stevenson (Motherwell), Jimmy McGrory (Celtic), Bobby McPhail (Rangers), James King (Hamilton Academical).

Ireland: Elisha Scott; William Cook, Robert Fulton; Edward Falloon, John Jones, William Gowdy; Edward Mitchell, Thomas Priestley, William Millar, Samuel English, James Kelly.

Scorers: Scotland: King 3; McPhail 35, 67; McGrory 75

Chapter two: 1920-1939

26 October 1932   Home Championship   Tynecastle, Edinburgh   Attendance: 31,000

162 SCOTLAND 2, Wales 5
Referee: William Harper (England)

Scotland: Alexander McLaren (St Johnstone); Douglas Gray (Rangers), Daniel Blair (Aston Villa); Hugh Wales (Motherwell), John Johnstone (Hearts, captain), John Thomson (Everton); James Crawford (Queen's Park), Alexander Thomson (Celtic), Neil Dewar (Third Lanark), Alex James (Arsenal), Douglas Duncan (Derby County).

Wales: William John; Benjamin Williams, Benjamin Ellis; Frederick Keenor, Thomas Griffiths, David Richards; Cuthbert Phillips, Eugene O'Callaghan, David Astley, Walter Robbins, David Lewis.

Scorers: Wales: John Thomson 9 (own goal); Griffiths 20; O'Callaghan 25, 46; Astley 43   Scotland: Dewar 63; Duncan 70

---

1 April 1933   Home Championship   Hampden Park   Attendance: 134,170

163 SCOTLAND 2, England 1
Referee: Samuel Thompson (Northern Ireland)

Scotland (2-3-5):
4 John Jackson (Partick Thistle);
1 Andrew Anderson (Hearts),
1 Peter McGonagle (Celtic);
4 Peter Wilson (Celtic),
4 Robert Gillespie (Queen's Park, captain),
5 George Brown (Rangers);
5 James Crawford (Queen's Park),
2 James Marshall (Rangers),
6 Jimmy McGrory (Celtic),
9 Bobby McPhail (Rangers),
2 Douglas Duncan (Derby County)

Celtic centre forward Jimmy McGrory gave Scotland the lead in only the fourth minute, breaking free from a ruck of defenders to sweep the ball home at the far post. England were more than a match for the home side in the first half and deservedly equalised on the half-hour mark when George Hunt scored with a fine left-foot drive. After half-time the Scottish side began to take control, and were unlucky not to find the net before McGrory finally made it 2-1 with just under 10 minutes left. Bobby McPhail, who also had a fine game, gave him a perfect pass and McGrory gave the English keeper no chance with what proved to be the winner. Others who impressed were Hearts right back Andrew Anderson, on his debut, and left winger Douglas "Dally" Duncan from Derby County. While Alex Cheyne had been credited in some quarters for starting the famous "Hampden Roar" with his late winner against England in 1929, others say it was inspired by McGrory's efforts in this match.

England: Henry Hibbs; Thomas Cooper, Ernest Blenkinsop (captain); Alfred Strange, Ernest Hart, Samuel Weaver; Joseph Hulme, Ronald Starling, George Hunt, John Pickering, John Arnold.

Scorers: Scotland: McGrory 4, 81   England: Hunt 30

The team which defeated England in 1933. Back (players only, from left); Peter Wilson, Robert Gillespie, George Brown, John Jackson, Andrew Anderson, Peter McGonagle. Front: James Crawford, James Marshall, Jimmy McGrory, Bobby McPhail, Douglas Duncan.

---

16 September 1933   Home Championship   Celtic Park, Glasgow   Attendance: 27,131

164 SCOTLAND 1, Ireland 2
Referee: Edward Wood (England)

Scotland: John Harkness (Hearts); Andrew Anderson (Hearts), Peter McGonagle (Celtic, captain); Alexander Massie (Hearts), Alexander Low (Falkirk), William Telfer (Motherwell); James Boyd (Newcastle United), Alexander Venters (Cowdenbeath), Jimmy McGrory (Celtic), Bobby McPhail (Rangers), James King (Hamilton Academical).

Ireland: Elisha Scott (captain); Thomas Willighan, Robert Fulton; John McMahon, John Jones, William Mitchell; Hugh Blair, Alexander Stevenson, David Martin, John Coulter, John Mahood.

Scorers: Ireland: Martin 8, 13   Scotland: McPhail 60

4 October 1933   Home Championship   Ninian Park, Cardiff   Attendance: 40,000

165 Wales 3, SCOTLAND 2   *Referee: Edward Wood (England)*

Scotland: John Harkness (Hearts); Andrew Anderson (Hearts, captain), Duncan Urquhart (Hibernian); Matt Busby (Manchester City), John Blair (Motherwell), Jimmy McLuckie (Manchester City); Francis McGurk (Birmingham City), John McMenemy (Motherwell), William McFadyen (Motherwell), James Easson (Portsmouth), Douglas Duncan (Derby County).

Wales: William John; Sidney Lawrence, Benjamin Ellis; James Murphy, Thomas Griffiths (captain), David Richards; Cuthbert Phillips, Eugene O'Callaghan, David Astley, Walter Robbins, William Evans.

Scorers: Wales: Evans 25; Robbins 35; Astley 56   Scotland: McFadyen 76; Duncan 81

29 November 1933   Friendly   Hampden Park   Attendance: 62,000

166 SCOTLAND 2, Austria 2   *Referee: John Langenus (Belgium)*

Scotland: James Kennaway (Celtic); Andrew Anderson (Hearts), Peter McGonagle (Celtic); David Meiklejohn (Rangers, captain), Philip Watson (Blackpool), George Brown (Rangers); Duncan Ogilvie (Motherwell), Robert Bruce (Middlesbrough), William McFadyen (Motherwell), Bobby McPhail (Rangers), Douglas Duncan (Derby County).

Austria: Peter Platzer; Anton Janda, Karl Sesta; Franz Wagner, Josef Smistik, Walter Nausch (captain); Karl Zischek, Josef Bican, Matthias Sindelar, Anton Schall, Ralf Viertel.

Scorers: Scotland: Meiklejohn 7; McFadyen 49   Austria: Zischek 41; Schall 53

14 April 1934   Home Championship   Wembley, London   Attendance: 92,363

167 England 3, SCOTLAND 0   *Referee: Samuel Thompson (Northern Ireland)*

Scotland: John Jackson (Chelsea); Andrew Anderson (Hearts), Peter McGonagle (Celtic); Alexander Massie (Hearts, captain), Thomas Smith (Kilmarnock), John Miller (St Mirren); William Cook (Bolton Wanderers), James Marshall (Rangers), Hughie Gallacher (Chelsea), George Stevenson (Motherwell), James Connor (Sunderland).

England: Frank Moss; Thomas Cooper (captain), Eddie Hapgood; Lewis Stoker, Ernest Hart, Wilfred Copping; Samuel Crooks, Horatio "Raich" Carter, John Bowers, Cliff Bastin, Eric Brook.

Scorers: England: Bastin 43; Brook 80; Bowers 88

20 October 1934   Home Championship   Windsor Park, Belfast   Attendance: 39,752

168 Ireland 2, SCOTLAND 1   *Referee: Henry Mee (England)*

Scotland: James Dawson (Rangers); Andrew Anderson (Hearts), Peter McGonagle (Celtic); Alexander Massie (Hearts, captain), James Simpson (Rangers), Andrew Herd (Hearts); William Cook (Bolton Wanderers), George Stevenson (Motherwell), James Smith (Rangers), Patrick Gallacher (Sunderland), James Connor (Sunderland).

Ireland: Elisha Scott; James Mackie, Robert Fulton; Walter McMillen, John Jones (captain), William Mitchell; Harold Duggan, William Gowdy, David Martin, Alexander Stevenson, John Coulter.

Scorers: Scotland: Gallacher 43   Ireland: Martin 76; Coulter 89

21 November 1934   Home Championship   Pittodrie, Aberdeen   Attendance: 26,334

169 SCOTLAND 3, Wales 2   *Referee: Samuel Thompson (Northern Ireland)*

Scotland: Allan McGrory (Motherwell); Andrew Anderson (Hearts), Peter McGonagle (Celtic); Alexander Massie (Hearts), James Simpson (Rangers, captain), George Brown (Rangers); William Cook (Bolton Wanderers), Tommy Walker (Hearts), David McCulloch (Hearts), Charles Napier (Celtic), Douglas Duncan (Derby County).

Wales: William John; Sidney Lawrence, David Jones; James Murphy, Harold Hanford, David Richards; Idris Hopkins, Ronald Williams, David Astley (captain), Thomas Mills, Cuthbert Phillips.

Scorers: Scotland: Duncan 23; Napier 46, 85   Wales: Phillips 73; Astley 88

6 April 1935   Home Championship   Hampden Park   Attendance: 129,693

170 SCOTLAND 2, England 0   *Referee: Samuel Thompson (Northern Ireland)*

Scotland: John Jackson (Chelsea); Andrew Anderson (Hearts), George Cummings (Partick Thistle); Alexander Massie (Hearts), James Simpson (Rangers, captain), George Brown (Rangers); Charles Napier (Celtic), Tommy Walker (Hearts), Hughie Gallacher (Derby County), Bobby McPhail (Rangers), Douglas Duncan (Derby County).

England: Henry Hibbs; Charles Male, Eddie Hapgood (captain); Clifford Britton, John Barker, Walter Alsford; Albert Geldard, Cliff Bastin, Robert Gurney, Raymond Westwood, Eric Brook.

Scorer: Scotland: Duncan 43, 50

5 October 1935   Home Championship   Ninian Park, Cardiff   Attendance: 35,004

171 Wales 1, SCOTLAND 1   *Referee: Albert Caseley (England)*

Scotland: John Jackson (Chelsea); Andrew Anderson (Hearts), George Cummings (Partick Thistle); Alexander Massie (Hearts), James Simpson (Rangers, captain), George Brown (Rangers); James Delaney (Celtic), Tommy Walker (Hearts), Matthew Armstrong (Aberdeen), William Mills (Aberdeen), Douglas Duncan (Derby County).

Wales: William John; Sidney Lawrence, Robert John; James Murphy, Thomas Griffiths (captain), David Richards; Cuthbert Phillips, Brynmor Jones, Ernest Glover, Leslie Jones, Walter Robbins.

Scorers: Scotland: Duncan 35   Wales: Phillips 42

The Scottish players are introduced to the Prince of Wales (later to become King George VI) before the 1935 game against England.

13 November 1935   Home Championship   Tynecastle, Edinburgh   Attendance: 30,000

172 SCOTLAND 2, Ireland 1   *Referee: Harry Nattrass (England)*

Scotland: John Jackson (Chelsea); Andrew Anderson (Hearts), George Cummings (Partick Thistle); Alexander Massie (Hearts), James Simpson (Rangers, captain), Alexander Hastings (Sunderland); James Delaney (Celtic), Tommy Walker (Hearts), Matthew Armstrong (Aberdeen), William Mills (Aberdeen), Douglas Duncan (Derby County).

Ireland: Elisha Scott; William Cook, Robert Fulton; Keiller McCullough, John Jones, William Mitchell; Harold Duggan, Alexander Stevenson, Joseph Bambrick, Peter Doherty, James Kelly.

Scorers: Ireland: Kelly 49   Scotland: Walker 58; Duncan 89

4 April 1936   Home Championship   Wembley, London   Attendance: 93,267

173 England 1, SCOTLAND 1   *Referee: William Hamilton (Northern Ireland)*

Scotland: James Dawson (Rangers); Andrew Anderson (Hearts), George Cummings (Aston Villa); Alexander Massie (Aston Villa), James Simpson (Rangers, captain), George Brown (Rangers); John Crum (Celtic), Tommy Walker (Hearts), David McCulloch (Brentford), Alexander Venters (Rangers), Douglas Duncan (Derby County).

England: Edward Sagar; Charles Male, Eddie Hapgood (captain); William Crayston, John Barker, John Bray; Samuel Crooks, Robert Barclay, George Camsell, Cliff Bastin, Eric Brook.

Scorers: England: Camsell 30   Scotland: Walker 77 (pen)

14 October 1936   Friendly   Ibrox Park, Glasgow   Attendance: 50,000

174 SCOTLAND 2, Germany 0   *Referee: Harry Nattrass (England)*

Scotland (2-3-5):
3 James Dawson (Rangers);
12 Andrew Anderson (Hearts)
5 George Cummings (Aston Villa);
13 Alexander Massie (Aston Villa)
7 James Simpson (Rangers, captain)
11 George Brown (Rangers);
3 James Delaney (Celtic)
6 Tommy Walker (Hearts)
3 Matthew Armstrong (Aberdeen)
13 Bobby McPhail (Rangers)
10 Douglas Duncan (Derby County)

Strangely most of the plaudits were given to the German players, who gave the Nazi salute both before and after the game, and chancellor Adolf Hitler was praised for his efforts to foster relations between the two countries. *The Scotsman* reported that the Scottish team was seldom dangerous as an attacking force, and deserved the win principally on account of territorial advantage. Jimmy Delaney of Celtic proved the man for the occasion with both goals, pouncing for his first in the 67th minute after German goalkeeper Hans Jakob had fumbled the ball, and then angling home a shot with seven minutes left after Tommy Walker had provided the opening with a lob. Walker was the pick of the home side, according to the newspaper, with keeper Jimmy Dawson, full back Andrew Anderson and wing half George Brown the only others to escape criticism.

Germany: Hans Jakob; Reinhold Munzenberg, Andreas Munkert; Paul Janes, Ludwig Goldbrunner, Albin Kitzinger; Franz Elbern, Rudolf Gellesch, Otto Siffling, Fritz Szepan (captain), Adolf Urban.

Scorer: Scotland: Delaney 67, 83

| 31 October 1936 | Home Championship | Windsor Park, Belfast | Attendance: 45,000 |

175 Ireland 1, SCOTLAND 3
Referee: Thomas Thompson (England)

Scotland: James Dawson (Rangers); Andrew Anderson (Hearts), Bobby Ancell (Newcastle United); Alexander Massie (Aston Villa), James Simpson (Rangers, captain), George Brown (Rangers); Alexander Munro (Hearts), Tommy Walker (Hearts), David McCulloch (Brentford), Charles Napier (Derby County), Douglas Duncan (Derby County).

Ireland: Thomas Breen; William Cook (captain), Robert Fulton; Walter McMillen, John Jones, William Mitchell; Noel Kernaghan, Keiller McCullough, David Martin, John Coulter, James Kelly.

Scorers: Ireland: Kernaghan 25   Scotland: Napier 27; Munro 47; McCulloch 63

| 2 December 1936 | Home Championship | Dens Park, Dundee | Attendance: 23,858 |

176 SCOTLAND 1, Wales 2
Referee: Arthur Barton (England)

Scotland: James Dawson (Rangers); Andrew Anderson (Hearts), Bobby Ancell (Newcastle United); Alexander Massie (Aston Villa), James Simpson (Rangers, captain), George Brown (Rangers); Alexander Munro (Hearts), Tommy Walker (Hearts), David McCulloch (Brentford), William Mills (Aberdeen), Douglas Duncan (Derby County).

Wales: Albert Gray; Herbert Turner, Benjamin Ellis; James Murphy, Thomas Griffiths (captain), David Richards; Idris Hopkins, Brynmor Jones, Ernest Glover, Leslie Jones, Seymour Morris.

Scorers: Wales: Glover 22, 77   Scotland: Walker 59

| 17 April 1937 | Home Championship | Hampden Park | Attendance: 149,547 |

177 SCOTLAND 3, England 1
Referee: William McLean (Northern Ireland)

Scotland (2-3-5):
6 James Dawson (Rangers);
15 Andrew Anderson (Hearts)
1 Andrew Beattie (Preston North End);
16 Alexander Massie (Aston Villa)
10 James Simpson (Rangers, captain)
14 George Brown (Rangers);
4 James Delaney (Celtic)
9 Tommy Walker (Hearts)
1 Francis O'Donnell (Preston North End)
14 Bobby McPhail (Rangers)
13 Douglas Duncan (Derby County)

The record crowd for a football match in Great Britain was listed at just under 150,000, but was thought to exceed that figure. They witnessed a thrilling game in which Scotland fought back from a goal behind at half-time and won with two late efforts by Rangers inside left Bobby McPhail. Frederick Steele gave England the lead as the match approached half-time but an excellently worked goal finished by Preston's Francis O'Donnell squared things just after the interval. Scotland were superior from then on but missed many chances and could have been made to pay when England created two of their own. However, keeper James Dawson saved well on both occasions and it was McPhail who put the Scots ahead from a narrow angle with 10 minutes left. The Rangers player made the game safe with a fine header not long afterwards.

England: Victor Woodley; Charles Male (captain), Samuel Barkas; Clifford Britton, Alfred Young, John Bray; Stanley Matthews, Horatio "Raich" Carter, Frederick Steele, Ronald Starling, Joseph Johnson.

Scorers: England: Steele 40   Scotland: O'Donnell 47; McPhail 80, 88

Huge crowds, well in excess of 100,000, were commonplace at Hampden Park in the 1930s and 1940s. This was the scene in 1935.
Photo courtesy of Scottish Football Museum

Chapter two: 1920-1939

| 9 May 1937 | Friendly | Prater Stadion, Vienna | Attendance: 63,000 |

178 Austria 1, SCOTLAND 1 *Referee: John Langenus (Belgium)*

Scotland: James Dawson (Rangers); Andrew Anderson (Hearts), Andrew Beattie (Preston North End); Alexander Massie (Aston Villa), James Simpson (Rangers, captain), Alexander McNab (Sunderland); James Delaney (Celtic), Tommy Walker (Hearts), Francis O'Donnell (Preston North End), Charles Napier (Derby County), Torrance "Torry" Gillick (Everton).

Austria: Peter Platzer; Karl Sesta, Willibald Schmaus; Karl Adamec, Josef Pekarek, Walter Nausch; Rudolf Geiter, Josef Stroh, Matthias Sindelar, Camillo Jerusalem, Johann Pesser.

Scorers: Austria: Jerusalem 78   Scotland: O'Donnell 80

| 15 May 1937 | Friendly | Sparta Stadion, Prague | Attendance: 35,000 |

179 Czechoslovakia 1, SCOTLAND 3 *Referee: Peco Bauwens (Germany)*

Scotland: James Dawson (Rangers); Bobby Hogg (Celtic), Andrew Beattie (Preston North End); Charles Thomson (Sunderland), James Simpson (Rangers, captain), George Brown (Rangers); James Delaney (Celtic), Tommy Walker (Hearts), Francis O'Donnell (Preston North End), Bobby McPhail (Rangers), Torrance "Torry" Gillick (Everton).

Czechoslovakia: Frantisek Planicka; Jaroslav Burgr, Josef Cytroky; Josef Kostalek, Jaroslav Boucek, Karel Kolsky; Vilem Zlatnik, Frantisek Svoboda, Jiri Sobotka, Vlastimil Kopecky, Antonin Puc.

Scorers: Scotland: Simpson 14; McPhail 32; Gillick 69   Czechoslovakia: Puc 31

| 30 October 1937 | Home Championship | Ninian Park, Cardiff | Attendance: 41,800 |

180 Wales 2, SCOTLAND 1 *Referee: Charles Argent (England)*

Scotland: James Dawson (Rangers); Andrew Anderson (Hearts), George Cummings (Aston Villa); Alexander Massie (Aston Villa), James Simpson (Rangers, captain), George Brown (Rangers); Robert Main (Rangers), Tommy Walker (Hearts), Francis O'Donnell (Preston North End), Bobby McPhail (Rangers), Douglas Duncan (Derby County).

Wales: Albert Gray; Herbert Turner, William Hughes; James Murphy, Harold Hanford, David Richards; Cuthbert Phillips, Leslie Jones, Edwin Perry, Brynmor Jones, Seymour Morris.

Scorers: Wales: Brynmor Jones 26; Morris 51   Scotland: Massie 72

| 10 November 1937 | Home Championship | Pittodrie, Aberdeen | Attendance: 21,878 |

181 SCOTLAND 1, Ireland 1 *Referee: Arthur Jewell (England)*

Scotland: James Dawson (Rangers); Andrew Anderson (Hearts), George Cummings (Aston Villa); Duncan McKenzie (Brentford), James Simpson (Rangers, captain), Alexander Hastings (Sunderland); James Delaney (Celtic), Tommy Walker (Hearts), James Smith (Rangers), Bobby McPhail (Rangers), Robert Reid (Brentford).

Ireland: Thomas Breen; William Hayes, William Cook; Matthew Doherty, Walter McMillen, William Mitchell; John Brown, James McAlinden, David Martin, Peter Doherty, John Coulter.

Scorers: Ireland: Peter Doherty 14   Scotland: Smith 49

| 8 December 1937 | Friendly | Hampden Park | Attendance: 41,000 |

182 SCOTLAND 5, Czechoslovakia 0 *Referee: Thomas Thompson (England)*

Scotland: William Waugh (Hearts); Andrew Anderson (Hearts, captain), George Cummings (Aston Villa); George Robertson (Kilmarnock), Robert Johnston (Sunderland), George Brown (Rangers); Peter Buchanan (Chelsea), Tommy Walker (Hearts), David McCulloch (Brentford), Andrew Black (Hearts), David Kinnear (Rangers).

Czechoslovakia: Frantisek Planicka; Josef Kostalek, Ferdinand Daucik; Antonin Vodicka, Jaroslav Boucek, Karel Kolsky; Jan Riha, Jiri Sobotka, Josef Zeman, Oldrich Nejedly, Antonin Puc.

Scorers: Scotland: Black 1; McCulloch 30, 62; Buchanan 38; Kinnear 70

| 9 April 1938 | Home Championship | Wembley, London | Attendance: 93,267 |

183 England 0, SCOTLAND 1 *Referee: William Hamilton (Northern Ireland)*

Scotland (2-3-5):
1 David Cumming (Middlesbrough);
20 Andrew Anderson (Hearts)
4 Andrew Beattie (Preston North End);
1 Bill Shankly (Preston North End)
2 Thomas Smith (Preston North End)
18 George Brown (Rangers, captain);
1 John Milne (Middlesbrough)
15 Tommy Walker (Hearts)
5 Francis O'Donnell (Blackpool)
1 George Mutch (Preston North End)
2 Robert Reid (Brentford)

A glorious goal by inside right Tommy Walker of Hearts, just six minutes into the game, gave Scotland a first victory at Wembley in 10 years. The selectors' choice of eight "Anglo Scots" was said to be justified, although the three home-based players were judged the backbone of the side. George Brown played a captain's game, Walker got his "picture goal" and Andrew Anderson managed to subdue the dangerous Cliff Bastin on the English left wing. One of those making their debut was Bill Shankly of Preston North End, who went on to become the legendary manager of Liverpool. Walker's goal saw him tear through the middle, superbly control a bouncing pass from Francis O'Donnell and fire the ball past keeper Victor Woodley from 15 yards.

England: Victor Woodley; Bert Sproston, Eddie Hapgood (captain), Charles Willingham, Stan Cullis, Wilfred Copping; Stanley Matthews, George Hall, Michael Fenton, Joseph Stephenson, Cliff Bastin.

Scorer: Scotland: Walker 6

| 21 May 1938 | Friendly | Olympisch Stadion, Amsterdam | Attendance: 50,000 |

184 Netherlands 1, SCOTLAND 3
Referee: Charles Argent (England)

Scotland: James Dawson (Rangers); Andrew Anderson (Hearts), James Carabine (Third Lanark); Thomas McKillop (Rangers), James Dykes (Hearts), George Brown (Rangers, captain); Alexander Munro (Blackpool), Tommy Walker (Hearts), Francis O'Donnell (Blackpool), Andrew Black (Hearts), Francis Murphy (Celtic).

Netherlands: Adrianus van Male; Bartholomeus Weber, Hubertus Caldenhove; Jacob Paauwe, Willem Anderiesen, Gerardus van Heel; Frank Wels, Hendrik van Spaandonck, Leendert Vente, Frederick van der Veen, Hubertus de Harder.

Scorers: Scotland: Black 52; Murphy 56; Walker 70   Netherlands: Vente 85

| 8 October 1938 | Home Championship | Windsor Park, Belfast | Attendance: 40,000 |

185 Ireland 0, SCOTLAND 2
Referee: Herbert Mortimer (England)

Scotland: James Dawson (Rangers); James Carabine (Third Lanark, captain), Andrew Beattie (Preston North End); Bill Shankly (Preston North End), James Dykes (Hearts), George Paterson (Celtic); James Delaney (Celtic), Tommy Walker (Hearts), John Crum (Celtic), John Divers (Celtic), Torrance "Torry" Gillick (Everton).

Ireland: Thomas Breen; William Hayes, William Cook; Walter McMillen, Matthew O'Mahoney, Robert Browne; John Brown, James McAlinden, David Martin, Alexander Stevenson, John Coulter.

Scorers: Scotland: Delaney 33; Walker 48

| 9 November 1938 | Home Championship | Tynecastle, Edinburgh | Attendance: 34,810 |

186 SCOTLAND 3, Wales 2
Referee: Thomas Thompson (England)

Scotland: John Brown (Clyde); Andrew Anderson (Hearts, captain), Andrew Beattie (Preston North End); Bill Shankly (Preston North End), Robert Baxter (Middlesbrough), Archibald Miller (Hearts); James Delaney (Celtic), Tommy Walker (Hearts), David McCulloch (Derby County), Robert Beattie (Preston North End), Torrance "Torry" Gillick (Everton).

Wales: William John; William Whatley, William Hughes; Donald Dearson, Thomas Jones, David Richards; Idris Hopkins, Leslie Jones, David Astley, Brynmor Jones, Reginald Cumner.

Scorers: Wales: Astley 20; Leslie Jones 86   Scotland: Gillick 38; Walker 83, 84

| 7 December 1938 | Friendly | Ibrox Park, Glasgow | Attendance: 23,000 |

187 SCOTLAND 3, Hungary 1
Referee: Charles Nattrass (England)

Scotland: James Dawson (Rangers); Andrew Anderson (Hearts, captain), Andrew Beattie (Preston North End); Bill Shankly (Preston North End), Robert Baxter (Middlesbrough), James "Scot" Symon (Rangers); Alex McSpadyen (Partick Thistle), Tommy Walker (Hearts), David McCulloch (Derby County), Andrew Black (Hearts), Torrance "Torry" Gillick (Everton).

Hungary: Antal Szabo; Lagos Koranyi, Sandro Biro; Gyula Polgar, Jozsef Turay, Gyula Dudas; Pal Titkos, Laszlo Cseh, Gyorgy Sarosi, Geza Toldi, Laszlo Gyetvai.

Scorers: Scotland: Walker 19 (pen); Black 27; Gillick 28   Hungary: Sarosi 72 (pen)

| 15 April 1939 | Home Championship | Hampden Park | Attendance: 149,269 |

188 SCOTLAND 1, England 2
Referee: William Hamilton (Northern Ireland)

Scotland (2-3-5):
- 14 James Dawson (Rangers);
- 3 James Carabine (Third Lanark)
- 9 George Cummings (Aston Villa);
- 5 Bill Shankly (Preston North End)
- 3 Bob Baxter (Middlesbrough)
- 2 Alex McNab (West Bromwich Albion);
- 2 Alex McSpadyen (Partick Thistle)
- 20 Tommy Walker (Hearts)
- 1 James Dougall (Preston North End, captain)
- 3 Alexander Venters (Rangers)
- 2 John Milne (Middlesbrough)

In the final international match before the Second World War, England gained a fighting victory, their first in the Home Championship over the Scots for five years and their first north of the border for 12 years. A crowd officially listed at 149,269 crammed into Hampden Park for the game, and they were delighted when James Dougall gave Scotland the lead in the 21st minute, lobbing the ball into an empty net after good work by Tommy Walker and Alex Venters. England struck back after half-time, with Albert Beasley volleying the ball into the roof of the net after taking a pass from Tommy Lawton. It was Lawton, the most feared centre forward in England at the time, who got the winner. Stanley Matthews, who had a fine game on the right wing and had previously created chances which weren't taken, laid on the goal.

England: Victor Woodley; William Morris, Eddie Hapgood (captain); Charles Willingham, Stan Cullis, Joe Mercer; Stanley Matthews, George Hall, Tommy Lawton, Leonard Goulden, Albert Beasley.

Scorers: Scotland: Dougall 21   England: Beasley 66; Lawton 88

CHAPTER THREE
1946-1959

---

23 January 1946   Friendly (victory international)   Hampden Park   Attendance: 46,000

189 SCOTLAND 2, Belgium 2
Referee: Joseph Jackson (Scotland)

Scotland (2-3-5):
- 1 Bobby Brown (Rangers);
- 1 James McGowan (Partick Thistle)
- 1 John Shaw (Rangers, captain);
- 1 James Campbell (Morton)
- 1 Andrew Paton (Motherwell)
- 2 George Paterson (Celtic);
- 1 Gordon Smith (Hibernian)
- 1 Archie Baird (Aberdeen)
- 10 James Delaney (Manchester United)
- 1 John Deakin (St Mirren)
- 1 James Walker (Hearts)

The first match following a six-year break due to the Second World War saw Scotland record a fairly unconvincing home draw with Belgium. This game, and the following against Switzerland, were not originally recognised as full internationals but that was later rectified. There were first caps for nine of the players with only the experienced Jimmy Delaney of Manchester United, making his 10th appearance, and his former Celtic team mate George Paterson surviving from pre-war. It took a last-minute penalty by Delaney to level things up. He had given the Scots the lead early in the second half but the Belgians pulled ahead through Lemberechts and D'Aguilar. A thick fog had descended on Hampden during the game and many of the spectators were unable to see what was happening across the field. A number of the players were discarded after just one cap and many changes made for the next game.

Belgium: Francois Daenen; Robert Paverick (captain), Joseph Pannaye; Antoine Puttaert, Marcel Vercammen, Rene Devos; Victor Lemberechts, Henri Coppens, Albert De Cleyn, Frederic D'Aguilar, Francois Sermon. *Coach:* Francois Demol.

Scorers: Scotland: Delaney 50, 90 (pen)   Belgium: Lemberechts 60; D'Aguilar 73

---

15 May 1946   Friendly (victory international)   Hampden Park   Attendance: 113,000

190 SCOTLAND 3, Switzerland 1
Referee: Percy Stevens (England)

Scotland (2-3-5):
- 2 Bobby Brown (Rangers);
- 1 David Shaw (Hibernian)
- 2 John Shaw (Rangers, captain);
- 1 Willie Campbell (Morton)
- 1 Frank Brennan (Newcastle United)
- 1 Jackie Husband (Partick Thistle);
- 1 Willie Waddell (Rangers)
- 1 Willie Thornton (Rangers)
- 11 James Delaney (Manchester United)
- 21 Tommy Walker (Hearts)
- 1 Billy Liddell (Liverpool)

Substitute:
- 1 George Young (Rangers, for Campbell 42)

Scotland played well enough to see off Switzerland at home, but according to reports the match was lacking in artistry and the over 100,000 fans had little to cheer about. A little known fact was that George Young of Rangers was the first ever substitute in an international for Scotland, replacing the injured Willie Campbell, but did not initially receive a cap for his trouble. Switzerland scored in the first minute through Aeby but by half-time the Scots were two in front. Left winger Billy Liddell got the equaliser and three minutes later made it 2-1 with the goal of the match when he ran through and lobbed the advancing keeper. Jimmy Delaney got the third when he finished off a Liddell cross. The play deteriorated in the second half, although right back David Shaw twice had solo runs and shots which brought good saves out of Ballabio.

Switzerland: Erwin Ballabio; Rudolf Gyger, Willy Steffen; Franz Rickenbach, Franco Andreoli, Roger Bocquet; Lauro Amado (captain), Walter Fink, Hans-Peter Friedlander, Rene Maillard, Georges Aeby. *Trainer:* Karl Rappan.

Scorers: Switzerland: Aeby 1   Scotland: Liddell 25, 28; Delaney 35

---

19 October 1946   Home Championship   The Racecourse, Wrexham   Attendance: 29,568

191 Wales 3, SCOTLAND 1
Referee: William Evans (England)

Scotland: William Miller (Celtic); James Stephen (Bradford City, captain), David Shaw (Hibernian); Hugh Brown (Partick Thistle), Frank Brennan (Newcastle United), Jackie Husband (Partick Thistle); Willie Waddell (Rangers), Cornelius "Neil" Dougall (Birmingham City), Willie Thornton (Rangers), James Blair (Blackpool), Billy Liddell (Liverpool).

Wales: Cyril Sidlow; Raymond Lambert, William Hughes (captain); Douglas Witcomb, Thomas Jones, Ronald Burgess; William Jones, Aubrey Powell, Trevor Ford, Brynmor Jones, George Edwards.

Scorers: Scotland: Waddell 49 (pen)   Wales: Brynmor Jones 52; Ford 78; Stephen 87 (own goal)

---

27 November 1946   Home Championship   Hampden Park   Attendance: 98,776

192 SCOTLAND 0, Ireland 0
Referee: George Reader (England)

Scotland: Bobby Brown (Rangers); George Young (Rangers), David Shaw (Hibernian, captain); William Campbell (Morton), Frank Brennan (Newcastle United), Hugh Long (Clyde); Gordon Smith (Hibernian), George Hamilton (Aberdeen), Willie Thornton (Rangers), James Duncanson (Rangers), Billy Liddell (Liverpool).

Ireland: Edward Hinton; William Gorman, James Feeney; Cornelius Martin, John Vernon, Peter Farrell; David Cochrane, John Carey, David Walsh, Alexander Stevenson (captain), Thomas Eglington.

| 12 April 1947 | Home Championship | Wembley, London | Attendance: 98,200 |

193 England 1, SCOTLAND 1 *Referee: Charles Dalasaille (France)*

Scotland: William Miller (Celtic); George Young (Rangers), John Shaw (Rangers, captain); Archibald MacAuley (Brentford), Willie Woodburn (Rangers), Alex Forbes (Sheffield United); Gordon Smith (Hibernian), Andrew McLaren (Preston North End), James Delaney (Manchester United), Billy Steel (Morton), Thomas Pearson (Newcastle United).

England: Frank Swift; Lawrence Scott, George Hardwick (captain); Billy Wright, Neil Franklin, Harold Johnston; Stanley Matthews, Horatio "Raich" Carter, Tommy Lawton, Wilf Mannion, James Mullen. *Manager:* Walter Winterbottom.

Scorers: Scotland: McLaren 16   England: Carter 56

| 18 May 1947 | Friendly | Heysel Stadion, Brussels | Attendance: 51,161 |

194 Belgium 2, SCOTLAND 1 *Referee: Valdemar Laursen (Denmark)*

Scotland: William Miller (Celtic); George Young (Rangers), John Shaw (Rangers, captain); Hugh Brown (Partick Thistle), Willie Woodburn (Rangers), Alex Forbes (Sheffield United); Robert Campbell (Falkirk), Andrew McLaren (Preston North End), Bobby Flavell (Airdrie), Billy Steel (Morton), Thomas Pearson (Newcastle United).

Belgium: Francois Daenen; Leon Aernaudts, Joseph Pannaye; Alfons de Buck, Jules Henriet, Fernand Massay; Victor Lemberechts, Henri Coppens, Albert de Cleyn (captain), Leopold Anoul, Rene Thirifays. *Coach:* William Gormlie.

Scorers: Belgium: Anoul 28, 77   Scotland: Steel 64

| 24 May 1947 | Friendly | Stade Municipal, Luxembourg-Ville | Attendance: 4,000 |

195 Luxembourg 0, SCOTLAND 6 *Referee: Jean Wouters (Belgium)*

Scotland: William Miller (Celtic); George Young (Rangers), John Shaw (Rangers, captain); Hugh Brown (Partick Thistle), Willie Woodburn (Rangers), Alex Forbes (Sheffield United); William MacFarlane (Hearts), Andrew MacLaren (Preston North End), Bobby Flavell (Airdrie), Billy Steel (Morton), Robert Campbell (Falkirk).

Luxembourg: Bernard Michaux; Rene Marchetti, Francois Dumont; Alphonse Feyder, Arnold Kieffer, Remy Wagner; Paul Feller, Camille Libar (captain), Nicolas Kettel, Marcel Rewenig, Leon Letsch. *Substitute:* Fernand Guth (for Letsch 82).

Scorers: Scotland: Flavell 6, 69; Steel 13, 48; McLaren 60; Forbes 86

| 4 October 1947 | Home Championship | Windsor Park, Belfast | Attendance: 52,000 |

196 Ireland 2, SCOTLAND 0 *Referee: Thomas Smith (England)*

Scotland: William Miller (Celtic); George Young (Rangers), John Shaw (Rangers, captain); Archibald MacAuley (Arsenal), Willie Woodburn (Rangers), Alex Forbes (Sheffield United); James Delaney (Manchester United), James Watson (Motherwell), Willie Thornton (Rangers), Billy Steel (Derby County), Billy Liddell (Liverpool).

Ireland: Edward Hinton; Cornelius Martin, Thomas Aherne; William Walsh, John Vernon (captain), Peter Farrell; David Cochrane, Samuel Smyth, David Walsh, Alexander Stevenson, Thomas Eglington.

Scorer: Ireland: Smyth 35, 54

| 12 November 1947 | Home Championship | Hampden Park | Attendance: 88,000 |

197 SCOTLAND 1, Wales 2 *Referee: Arthur Ellis (England)*

Scotland: William Miller (Celtic); Jock Govan (Hibernian), James Stephen (Bradford City); Archibald MacAuley (Arsenal), Willie Woodburn (Rangers), Alex Forbes (Sheffield United); Gordon Smith (Hibernian), Andrew McLaren (Preston North End), James Delaney (Manchester United), Billy Steel (Derby County), Billy Liddell (Liverpool).

Wales: Cyril Sidlow; Alfred Sherwood, Walley Barnes; Ivor Powell, Thomas Jones, Ronald Burgess (captain); Sidney Thomas, Aubrey Powell, Trevor Ford, George Lowrie, George Edwards.

Scorers: Scotland: McLaren 10   Wales: Ford 35; Lowrie 42

| 10 April 1948 | Home Championship | Hampden Park | Attendance: 135,376 |

198 SCOTLAND 0, England 2 *Referee: David Maxwell (Northern Ireland)*

Scotland: Ian Black (Southampton); Jock Govan (Hibernian), David Shaw (Hibernian); William Campbell (Morton), George Young (Rangers, captain), Archibald MacAuley (Arsenal); James Delaney (Manchester United), Bobby Combe (Hibernian), Willie Thornton (Rangers), Billy Steel (Derby County), Billy Liddell (Liverpool).

England: Frank Swift; Lawrence Scott, George Hardwick (captain); Billy Wright, Neil Franklin, Henry Cockburn; Stanley Matthews, Stan Mortensen, Tommy Lawton, Stanley Pearson, Tom Finney. *Manager:* Walter Winterbottom.

Scorers: England: Finney 44; Mortensen 62

| 28 April 1948 | Friendly | Hampden Park | Attendance: 70,000 |

199 SCOTLAND 2, Belgium 0 *Referee: William Ling (England)*

Scotland: Jimmy Cowan (Morton); Jock Govan (Hibernian), David Shaw (Hibernian); William Campbell (Morton), George Young (Rangers, captain), Archibald MacAuley (Arsenal); Gordon Smith (Hibernian), Bobby Combe (Hibernian), Leslie Johnston (Clyde), Eddie Turnbull (Hibernian), David Duncan (East Fife).

Belgium: Francois Daenen; Leon Aernaudts, Leopold Anoul; Alfons de Buck, Victor Erroelen, Jules Henriet (captain); Victor Lemberechts, Henri Govard, Jozef Mermans, August van Steenlant, Albert de Cleyn.

Scorers: Scotland: Combe 25; Duncan 59

Chapter three: 1946-1959

| 17 May 1948 | Friendly | Wankdorf Stadion, Berne | Attendance: 30,000 |

200 Switzerland 2, SCOTLAND 1 *Referee: Alois Beranech (Austria)*

Scotland: Jimmy Cowan (Morton); Jock Govan (Hibernian), David Shaw (Hibernian); William Campbell (Morton), George Young (Rangers, captain), Archibald MacAuley (Arsenal); Gordon Smith (Hibernian), Bobby Combe (Hibernian), Leslie Johnston (Clyde), Eddie Turnbull (Hibernian), David Duncan (East Fife).

Switzerland: Eugenio Corrodi; Andre Belli, Willy Steffen; Gerhard Lusenti, Olivier Eggimann, Roger Bocquet; Alfred Bickel, Hans-Peter Friedlander, Lauro Amado (captain), Rene Maillard, Jacques Fatton. Substitute: Jean Tamini (for Bickel 46). *Coach:* Karl Rappan.

Scorers: Scotland: Johnston 19   Switzerland: Maillard 45; Fatton 78

| 23 May 1948 | Friendly | Stade Olympique, Paris | Attendance: 46,032 |

201 France 3, SCOTLAND 0 *Referee: Karel van der Meer (Netherlands)*

Scotland: Jimmy Cowan (Morton); Jock Govan (Hibernian), David Shaw (Hibernian); William Campbell (Morton), George Young (Rangers, captain), Archibald MacAuley (Arsenal); Edward Rutherford (Rangers), Billy Steel (Derby County), Gordon Smith (Hibernian), Sammy Cox (Rangers), David Duncan (East Fife).

France: Julien Darui (captain); Guy Huguet, Roger Marche; Antoine Cuissard, Jean Gregoire, Jean Prouff; Georges Sesia, Jean Baratte, Emile Bongiorni, Larbi Ben Barek, Pierre Flamion.

Scorers: France: Bongiorni 55; Flamion 60; Baratte 79

| 23 October 1948 | Home Championship | Ninian Park, Cardiff | Attendance: 59,911 |

202 Wales 1, SCOTLAND 3 *Referee: David Maxwell (Northern Ireland)*

Scotland: Jimmy Cowan (Morton); Hugh Howie (Hibernian), David Shaw (Hibernian); Bobby Evans (Celtic), George Young (Rangers, captain), Willie Redpath (Motherwell); Willie Waddell (Rangers), Jimmy Mason (Third Lanark), Lawrie Reilly (Hibernian), Billy Steel (Derby County), John Kelly (Barnsley).

Wales: Cyril Sidlow; Alfred Sherwood, Walley Barnes; Roy Paul, Frederick Stansfield, Ronald Burgess (captain); Sidney Thomas, William Lucas, Trevor Ford, Brynmor Jones, William Jones.

Scorers: Scotland: Howie 15; Waddell 20, 30   Wales: Brynmor Jones 22

| 17 November 1948 | Home Championship | Hampden Park | Attendance: 93,182 |

203 SCOTLAND 3, Ireland 2 *Referee: William Evans (England)*

Scotland: Bobby Brown (Rangers); Jock Govan (Hibernian), David Shaw (Hibernian); Bobby Evans (Celtic), George Young (Rangers, captain), Willie Redpath (Motherwell); Willie Waddell (Rangers), Jimmy Mason (Third Lanark), Willie Houliston (Queen of the South), Billy Steel (Derby County), John Kelly (Barnsley).

Ireland: William Smyth; John Carey (captain), Rory Keane; James McCabe, John Vernon, William Walsh; David Cochrane, Samuel Smyth, David Walsh, Peter Doherty, John O'Driscoll.

Scorers: Scotland: Houliston 27, 89; Mason 72

| 9 April 1949 | Home Championship | Wembley, London | Attendance: 98,188 |

204 England 1, SCOTLAND 3 *Referee: Mervyn Griffiths (Wales)*

Scotland (2-3-5):
- 5 Jimmy Cowan (Morton);
- 13 George Young (Rangers, captain)
- 2 Sammy Cox (Rangers);
- 3 Bobby Evans (Celtic)
- 6 Willie Woodburn (Rangers)
- 1 George Aitken (East Fife);
- 5 Willie Waddell (Rangers)
- 3 Jimmy Mason (Third Lanark)
- 2 Willie Houliston (Queen of the South)
- 10 Billy Steel (Derby County)
- 2 Lawrie Reilly (Hibernian)

A memorable win over England at Wembley secured the Home Championship for the first time since 1936. It was the first time for 20 years that all three teams had been beaten, following 3-1 and 3-2 wins over Wales and Ireland. For half an hour the English dominated, but the Scots weathered the storm and scored in the 28th minute through Jimmy Mason. Jimmy Cowan made several fine saves to deny an equaliser and after half-time the game swung in Scotland's favour. With full backs George Young and Sammy Cox coping well with Tom Finney and Stanley Matthews, they got the upper hand and it was no surprise when Billy Steel made it 2-0. A brilliant run ended in him playing a one-two with Willie Houliston before rifling the ball home. Lawrie Reilly got a third, heading home a Willie Waddell cross, before England's consolation by Jackie Milburn.

England: Frank Swift; John Aston, John Howe; Billy Wright (captain), Neil Franklin, Henry Cockburn; Stanley Matthews, Stan Mortensen, Jackie Milburn, Stan Pearson, Tom Finney. *Manager:* Walter Winterbottom.

Scorers: Scotland: Mason 28; Steel 52; Reilly 61   England: Milburn 75

| 27 April 1949 | Friendly | Hampden Park | Attendance: 125,683 |

205 SCOTLAND 2, France 0 *Referee: William Ling (England)*

Scotland: Jimmy Cowan (Morton); George Young (Rangers, captain), Sammy Cox (Rangers); Bobby Evans (Celtic), Willie Woodburn (Rangers), George Aitken (East Fife); Willie Waddell (Rangers), Willie Thornton (Rangers), Willie Houliston (Queen of the South), Billy Steel (Derby County), Lawrie Reilly (Hibernian).

France: Rene Vignal; Marcel Salva, Roger Marche; Robert Jonquet, Roger Mindonnet, Louis Hon; Roger Gabet, Antoine Cuissard, Jean Baratte, Albert Batteux, Pierre Flamion.

Scorer: Scotland: Steel 37, 80

1 October 1949 Home Championship/World Cup qualifying Windsor Park, Belfast Attendance: 55,000

206 Ireland 2, SCOTLAND 8
Referee: Reginald Mortimer (England)

Scotland (2-3-5):

- 7 Jimmy Cowan (Morton);
- 15 George Young (Rangers, captain)
- 4 Sammy Cox (Rangers);
- 5 Bobby Evans (Celtic)
- 8 Willie Woodburn (Rangers)
- 3 George Aitken (East Fife);
- 7 Willie Waddell (Rangers)
- 4 Jimmy Mason (Third Lanark)
- 1 Henry Morris (East Fife)
- 12 Billy Steel (Derby County)
- 4 Lawrie Reilly (Hibernian)

One of Scotland's best away wins over Ireland was a personal triumph for centre forward Henry Morris of East Fife, who netted a hat trick in his only appearance for the national team. He opened the scoring in the second minute and Willie Waddell quickly made it 2-0. Then goals from Billy Steel, Lawrie Reilly and a Waddell penalty put the Scots out of sight at half-time. The Irish staged a mini-fightback after the break with a double from Samuel Smyth but the visitors regained their superiority with Morris and Jimmy Mason finding the net before Morris completed his treble. Scotland finished second behind England in the Home Championship table which should have meant qualification for the 1950 World Cup. However, the Scottish Football Association had ruled that it would only accept the invitation if the team finished top. Scottish captain George Young, supported by his English counterpart Billy Wright, pleaded with the SFA to change its mind but the authority was not for budging.

Ireland: Patrick Kelly; Gerard Bowler, Alfred McMichael; Danny Blanchflower, John Vernon, Roy Ferris; David Cochrane, Samuel Smyth, Robert Brennan, Edward Crossan, John McKenna.

Scorers: Scotland: Morris 2, 70, 89; Waddell 5, 42 (pen); Steel 25; Reilly 26; Mason 80

Ireland: Smyth 50, 59

HOME CHAMPIONSHIP/FIFA WORLD CUP QUALIFYING – GROUP ONE

	P	W	D	L	F	A	Pts
England	3	3	0	0	14	3	6
Scotland	3	2	0	1	10	3	4
Wales	3	0	1	2	1	6	1
Ireland	3	0	1	2	4	17	1

---

9 November 1949 Home Championship/World Cup qualifying Hampden Park Attendance: 73,781

207 SCOTLAND 2, Wales 0
Referee: Samuel Law (England)

Scotland: Jimmy Cowan (Morton); George Young (Rangers, captain), Sammy Cox (Rangers); Bobby Evans (Celtic), Willie Woodburn (Rangers), George Aitken (East Fife); Billy Liddell (Liverpool), John McPhail (Celtic), Alexander Linwood (Clyde), Billy Steel (Derby County), Lawrie Reilly (Hibernian).

Wales: Keith Jones; Walley Barnes, Alfred Sherwood; Ivor Powell, Thomas Jones, Ronald Burgess (captain); Maldwyn Griffiths, Roy Paul, Trevor Ford, Royston Clarke, George Edwards.

Scorers: Scotland: McPhail 25; Linwood 78

---

15 April 1950 Home Championship/World Cup qualifying Hampden Park Attendance: 133,300

208 SCOTLAND 0, England 1
Referee: Reginald Leafe (England)

Scotland: Jimmy Cowan (Morton); George Young (Rangers, captain), Sammy Cox (Rangers); Ian McColl (Rangers), Willie Woodburn (Rangers), Alex Forbes (Arsenal); Willie Waddell (Rangers), William Moir (Bolton Wanderers), Willie Bauld (Hearts), Billy Steel (Derby County), Billy Liddell (Liverpool).

England: Fred Williams; Alf Ramsey, John Aston; Billy Wright (captain), Neil Franklin, Jimmy Dickinson; Tom Finney, Wilf Mannion, Stan Mortensen, Roy Bentley, Robert Langton. *Manager:* Walter Winterbottom.

Scorer: England: Bentley 64

---

26 April 1950 Friendly Hampden Park Attendance: 123,751

209 SCOTLAND 3, Switzerland 1
Referee: George Reader (England)

Scotland: Jimmy Cowan (Morton); George Young (Rangers, captain), Sammy Cox (Rangers); Bobby Evans (Celtic), Robert Dougan (Hearts), George Aitken (East Fife); Robert Campbell (Chelsea), Allan Brown (East Fife), Willie Bauld (Hearts), Billy Steel (Derby County), Lawrie Reilly (Hibernian).

Switzerland: Georges Stuber; Rudolf Gyger, Willy Steffen; Andre Neury, Olivier Eggimann, Roger Bocquet; Alfred Bickel (captain), Charles Antenen, Jean Tamini, Rene Bader, Jacques Fatton.

Scorers: Scotland: Bauld 9; Campbell 38; Brown 44   Switzerland: Antenen 20

---

21 May 1950 Friendly Estadio Nacional, Lisbon Attendance: 68,000

210 Portugal 2, SCOTLAND 2
Referee: Ramon Azon (Spain)

Scotland: Jimmy Cowan (Morton); George Young (Rangers, captain), Sammy Cox (Rangers); Bobby Evans (Celtic), Willie Woodburn (Rangers), Alex Forbes (Arsenal); Robert Campbell (Chelsea), Allan Brown (East Fife), Willie Bauld (Hearts), Billy Steel (Derby County), Billy Liddell (Liverpool).

Portugal: Ernesto Oliveira; Octavio Barrosa (captain), Angelo Carvalho; Carlos Canario, Felix Antunes, Serafim Batista; Mario Nobre, Manuel Vasques, Henrique Ben David, Jose Travacos, Albano Pereira. *Coach:* Salvador do Carmo.

Scorers: Portugal: Travacos 9; Albano 29   Scotland: Bauld 20; Brown 23

Chapter three: 1946-1959

| 27 May 1950 | Friendly | Stade Olympique, Paris | Attendance: 35,568 |

211 France 0, SCOTLAND 1
Referee: Julian Arque Martin (Spain)

Scotland: Jimmy Cowan (Morton); George Young (Rangers, captain), Sammy Cox (Rangers); Ian McColl (Rangers), Willie Woodburn (Rangers), Alex Forbes (Arsenal); Robert Campbell (Chelsea), Allan Brown (East Fife), Lawrie Reilly (Hibernian), Billy Steel (Derby County), Billy Liddell (Liverpool).

France: Abderrahman Ibrir; Guy Huguet, Roger Marche; Jean Gregoire, Roger Lamy, Antoine Cuissard; Henri Baillot, Andre Strappe, Jean Baratte (captain), Jean Grumellon, Georges Dard.

Scorer: Scotland: Brown 69

| 21 October 1950 | Home Championship | Ninian Park, Cardiff | Attendance: 50,000 |

212 Wales 1, SCOTLAND 3
Referee: Arthur Ellis (England)

Scotland: Jimmy Cowan (Morton); George Young (Rangers, captain), Willie McNaught (Raith Rovers); Ian McColl (Rangers), Willie Woodburn (Rangers), Alex Forbes (Arsenal); Bobby Collins (Celtic), John McPhail (Celtic), Lawrie Reilly (Hibernian), Billy Steel (Dundee), Billy Liddell (Liverpool).

Wales: Brynley Parry; Walley Barnes, Alfred Sherwood; Ivor Powell, Roy Paul, Ronald Burgess (captain); Harold Williams, Brynley Allen, Trevor Ford, Aubrey Powell, Royston Clarke.

Scorers: Scotland: Reilly 23, 65; Liddell 72   Wales: Aubrey Powell 68

The team which beat Wales 3-1 at Cardiff in 1950. Back (from left): Willie Woodburn, Ian McColl, Jimmy Cowan, John McPhail, Alex Forbes, Willie McNaught. Front: Bobby Collins, Lawrie Reilly, George Young, Billy Steel, Billy Liddell.

| 1 November 1950 | Home Championship | Hampden Park | Attendance: 83,142 |

213 SCOTLAND 6, Ireland 1
Referee: Benjamin Griffiths (Wales)

Scotland (2-3-5):
14 Jimmy Cowan (Morton);
22 George Young (Rangers, captain)
2   Willie McNaught (Raith Rovers);
4   Ian McColl (Rangers)
14 Willie Woodburn (Rangers)
10 Alex Forbes (Arsenal);
2   Bobby Collins (Celtic)
5   Jimmy Mason (Third Lanark)
3   John McPhail (Celtic)
19 Billy Steel (Dundee)
12 Billy Liddell (Liverpool)

Scotland overwhelmed Northern Ireland with a scintillating display at Hampden, with Billy Steel of Dundee the obvious man of the match with his dazzling play and four goals. Celtic centre forward John McPhail, in for the injured Lawrie Reilly, grabbed the other two. Other standouts were Ian McColl at right half, inside right Jimmy Mason and left winger Billy Liddell, who set up four of the goals. Scotland were two up after 13 minutes, both from McPhail, but Northern Ireland fought back and scored through McGarry just before half-time. Steel was irrepressible after the interval, netting four times, while Liddell supplied the crosses for three of his finishes.

Northern Ireland: Hugh Kelly; Charles Gallogly, Alfred McMichael; Danny Blanchflower, John Vernon (captain), Wilbur Cush; John Campbell, Kevin McGarry, Eddie McMorran, Peter Doherty, John McKenna.

Scorers: Scotland: McPhail 8, 13; Steel 53, 57, 66, 79   Northern Ireland: McGarry 43

| 13 December 1950 | Friendly | Hampden Park | Attendance: 68,000 |

214 SCOTLAND 0, Austria 1

Referee: William Ling (England)

Scotland: Jimmy Cowan (Morton); George Young (Rangers, captain), Willie McNaught (Raith Rovers); Bobby Evans (Celtic), Willie Woodburn (Rangers), Alex Forbes (Arsenal); Bobby Collins (Celtic), Eddie Turnbull (Hibernian), John McPhail (Celtic), Billy Steel (Dundee), Billy Liddell (Liverpool).

Austria: Walter Zeman; Rudolf Rockl, Ernst Happel; Gerhard Hanappi, Ernst Ocwirk, Leopold Gernhardt; Ernst Melchior, Karl Decker (captain), Theodor Wagner, Ernst Stojaspal, Lukas Aurednik. *Coach:* Walter Nausch.

Scorer: Austria: Melchior 26

| 14 April 1951 | Home Championship | Wembley, London | Attendance: 98,000 |

215 England 2, SCOTLAND 3

Referee: George Mitchell (Scotland)

Scotland (2-3-5):

16 Jimmy Cowan (Morton);
24 George Young (Rangers, captain)
10 Sammy Cox (Rangers);
10 Bobby Evans (Celtic)
16 Willie Woodburn (Rangers)
3 Willie Redpath (Motherwell);
9 Willie Waddell (Rangers)
1 Bobby Johnstone (Hibernian)
9 Lawrie Reilly (Hearts)
21 Billy Steel (Dundee)
14 Billy Liddell (Liverpool)

The Wembley victory was easier than the score suggests, as England lost inside forward Wilf Mannion in the 12th minute. A clash of heads with Billy Liddell resulted in Mannion being knocked out and later found to have suffered a fractured cheekbone. The 10 English players strove manfully against the odds after that. Lawrie Reilly, in his second game against England, was the Scots' best player and again on the scoresheet. Billy Liddell and Billy Steel also had fine matches. Harold Hassall gave England the lead with a powerful drive from 25 yards, but Scotland soon equalised when Bobby Johnstone finished off a Reilly pass. The turning point came just after the interval, Reilly returning the compliment from a Johnstone pass and Liddell making it 3-1. A terrific individual goal by Tom Finney reduced the deficit again to one goal 10 minutes later.

England: Bert Williams; Alf Ramsey, William Eckersley; Henry Johnston, John Froggatt, Billy Wright (captain); Stanley Matthews, Wilf Mannion, Stan Mortenson, Harold Hassall, Tom Finney. *Manager:* Walter Winterbottom.

Scorers: England: Hassall 26; Finney 63   Scotland: Johnstone 33; Reilly 47; Liddell 53

| 12 May 1951 | Friendly | Hampden Park | Attendance: 75,000 |

216 SCOTLAND 3, Denmark 1

Referee: William Evans (England)

Scotland: Jimmy Cowan (Morton); George Young (Rangers, captain), Sammy Cox (Rangers); Jimmy Scoular (Portsmouth), Willie Woodburn (Rangers), Willie Redpath (Motherwell); Willie Waddell (Rangers), Bobby Johnstone (Hibernian), Lawrie Reilly (Hibernian), Billy Steel (Dundee), Bobby Mitchell (Newcastle United).

Denmark: Eigil Nielsen; Dan Ohland-Andersen, Poul Petersen; Erik Hansen, Edvin Hansen, Steen Blicher; James Ronvang, Jorgen Wagner Hansen, Jens Torstensen, Knud Lundberg (captain), Jens Peder Hansen.

Scorers: Denmark: Jorgen Wagner Hansen 6   Scotland: Steel 33; Reilly 59; Mitchell 86

| 16 May 1951 | Friendly | Hampden Park | Attendance: 75,394 |

217 SCOTLAND 1, France 0

Referee: Reginald Mortimer (England)

Scotland: Jimmy Cowan (Morton); George Young (Rangers, captain), Sammy Cox (Rangers); Jimmy Scoular (Portsmouth), Willie Woodburn (Rangers), Willie Redpath (Motherwell); Willie Waddell (Rangers), Bobby Johnstone (Hibernian), Lawrie Reilly (Hibernian), Billy Steel (Dundee), Bobby Mitchell (Newcastle United).

France: Stephane Dawoski; Guy Huguet, Roger Marche (captain); Antoine Bonifaci, Robert Jonquet, Antoine Cuissard; Rene Alpsteg, Andre Strappe, Jean Baratte, Edouard Kargu, Edmond Haan.

Scorer: Scotland: Reilly 78

| 20 May 1951 | Friendly | Heysel, Brussels | Attendance: 55,135 |

218 Belgium 0, SCOTLAND 5

Referee: Louis Fauquemberghe (France)

Scotland (2-3-5):

19 Jimmy Cowan (Morton);
27 George Young (Rangers, captain)
13 Sammy Cox (Rangers);
5 Ian McColl (Rangers)
19 Willie Woodburn (Rangers)
6 Willie Redpath (Motherwell);
12 Willie Waddell (Rangers)
6 Jimmy Mason (Third Lanark)
2 George Hamilton (Aberdeen)
24 Billy Steel (Dundee)
12 Lawrie Reilly (Hibernian)

The third of a four-match European tour, in which the Scots defeated Denmark, France and Belgium but then lost heavily to Austria, was a personal triumph for George Hamilton. The veteran Aberdeen centre forward netted three of the five goals, heading in the opener in the eighth minute after a cross from Willie Waddell. Jimmy Mason added a second nine minutes later and Hamilton got his second after half-time with a great shot following a George Young clearance out of defence. He completed his hat trick soon after, following up after the keeper had saved a Billy Steel effort. Waddell got the fifth towards the end after Steel, Hamilton and Mason had scattered the defence with a lovely passing movement.

Belgium: Henri Meert; Arsene Vaillant, Leopold Anoul; Jan van der Auwera, Louis Carre, Victor Mees; Victor Lemberechts, Frederic D'Aguilar, Rik Coppens, Josef Mermans, Francois Sermon. *Trainer:* William Gormlie (England).

Scorers: Scotland: Hamilton 8, 58, 65; Mason 17; Waddell 81

Chapter three: 1946-1959

| 27 May 1951 | Friendly | Praterstadion, Vienna | Attendance: 65,000 |

219 Austria 4, SCOTLAND 0 *Referee: Jean Lutz (Switzerland)*

Scotland: Jimmy Cowan (Morton); George Young (Rangers, captain), Sammy Cox (Rangers); Jimmy Scoular (Portsmouth), Willie Woodburn (Rangers), Willie Redpath (Motherwell); Willie Waddell (Rangers), Jimmy Mason (Third Lanark), George Hamilton (Aberdeen), Billy Steel (Dundee), Lawrie Reilly (Hibernian).

Austria: Walter Zeman; Rudolf Rockl, Ernst Happel; Gerhard Hanappi, Ernst Ocwirk, Leopold Gernhardt (captain); Ernst Melchior, Hans Riegler, Theodor Wagner, Erich Probst, Alfred Korner. *Coach:* Walter Nausch.

Scorers: Austria: Hanappi 42, 56; Wagner 69 (pen), 88

| 6 October 1951 | Home Championship | Windsor Park, Belfast | Attendance: 56,946 |

220 Ireland 0, SCOTLAND 3 *Referee: William Evans (England)*

Scotland: Jimmy Cowan (Morton); George Young (Rangers, captain), Sammy Cox (Rangers); Bobby Evans (Celtic), Willie Woodburn (Rangers), Willie Redpath (Motherwell); Willie Waddell (Rangers), Bobby Johnstone (Hibernian), Lawrie Reilly (Hibernian), Tommy Orr (Morton), Billy Liddell (Liverpool).

Ireland: Norman Uprichard; Leonard Graham, Alfred McMichael; William Dickson, John Vernon, Roy Ferris; Billy Bingham, Jimmy McIlroy, Edward McMorran, Bertie Peacock, Charlie Tully. *Manager:* Peter Doherty.

Scorers: Scotland: Orr 32; Johnstone 44, 62

| 14 November 1951 | Home Championship | Hampden Park | Attendance: 71,272 |

221 SCOTLAND 0, Wales 1 *Referee: Patrick Morris (Ireland)*

Scotland: Jimmy Cowan (Morton); George Young (Rangers, captain), Sammy Cox (Rangers); Tommy Docherty (Preston North End), Willie Woodburn (Rangers), Alex Forbes (Arsenal); Willie Waddell (Rangers), Tommy Orr (Morton), Lawrie Reilly (Hibernian), Billy Steel (Dundee), Billy Liddell (Liverpool).

Wales: William Shortt; Walley Barnes, Alfred Sherwood; Roy Paul, Raymond Daniel, Ronald Burgess (captain); William Foulkes, William Morris, Trevor Ford, Ivor Allchurch, Royston Clarke.

Scorer: Wales: Allchurch 89

| 5 April 1952 | Home Championship | Hampden Park | Attendance: 133,991 |

222 SCOTLAND 1, England 2 *Referee: Patrick Morris (Ireland)*

Scotland: Bobby Brown (Rangers); George Young (Rangers, captain), Willie McNaught (Raith Rovers); Jimmy Scoular (Portsmouth), Willie Woodburn (Rangers), Willie Redpath (Motherwell); Gordon Smith (Hibernian), Bobby Johnstone (Hibernian), Lawrie Reilly (Hibernian), Ian McMillan (Airdrie), Billy Liddell (Liverpool).

England: Gilbert Merrick; Alf Ramsey, Thomas Garrett; Billy Wright (captain), John Froggatt, Jimmy Dickinson; Tom Finney, Ivan Broadis, Nat Lofthouse, Stan Pearson, John Rowley. *Manager:* Walter Winterbottom.

Scorers: England: Pearson 9, 44   Scotland: Reilly 77

| 30 April 1952 | Friendly | Hampden Park | Attendance: 107,765 |

223 SCOTLAND 6, USA 0 *Referee: Douglas Gerrard (Scotland)*

Scotland (2-3-5):
- 23 Jimmy Cowan (Morton);
- 32 George Young (Rangers, captain),
- 17 Sammy Cox (Rangers);
- 5 Jimmy Scoular (Portsmouth),
- 24 Willie Woodburn (Rangers),
- 1 Hugh Kelly (Blackpool);
- 9 Gordon Smith (Hibernian),
- 2 Ian McMillan (Airdrie),
- 17 Lawrie Reilly (Hibernian),
- 4 Allan Brown (Blackpool),
- 18 Billy Liddell (Liverpool).

The USA, although containing over half of the side which defeated England 1-0 at the 1950 World Cup, were soundly beaten in the first ever meeting between the teams. Hibernian centre forward Lawrie Reilly was the star of the show with a masterful hat trick, while 20-year-old Ian McMillan of Airdrie scored twice on his second appearance. The Americans were praised for their effort and sportsmanship, with tricky forward John Souza and goalkeeper Frank Borghi getting special mentions, but in truth they were no match for the Scots. Jimmy Cowan in goal was rarely troubled and in defence the Rangers trio of George Young, Willie Woodburn and Sammy Cox were commanding, but overall there were no weak links.

USA: Frank Borghi; John O'Connell, Harold Keough; William Shepell, Charles Colombo, Walter Bahr; Lloyd Monsen, Ed Souza, Richard Roberts, John Souza, Ben McLaughlin.

Scorers: Scotland: Reilly 9, 10, 34; McMillan 29, 89; O'Connell 60 (own goal)

| 25 May 1952 | Friendly | Idraetsparken, Copenhagen | Attendance: 39,000 |

224 Denmark 1, SCOTLAND 2 *Referee: Sten Ahlner (Sweden)*

Scotland: Jimmy Cowan (Morton); George Young (Rangers, captain), Sammy Cox (Rangers); Jimmy Scoular (Portsmouth), Andrew Paton (Motherwell), Alex Forbes (Arsenal); Lawrie Reilly (Hibernian), Ian McMillan (Airdrie), Willie Thornton (Rangers), Allan Brown (Blackpool), Billy Liddell (Liverpool).

Denmark: Kaj Jorgensen; Poul Petersen, Svend Nielsen; Erik Terkelsen, Christen Brogger, Steen Blicher; Carl Holm, Poul Rasmussen, Jens Torstensen, Knud Lundberg, Holger Seebach.

Scorers: Scotland: Thornton 49; Reilly 71   Denmark: Rasmussen 63

| 30 May 1952 | Friendly | Rasunda Stadion, Stockholm | Attendance: 32,122 |

225 Sweden 3, SCOTLAND 1
Referee: Karel van der Meer (Netherlands)

Scotland: Jimmy Cowan (Morton); George Young (Rangers, captain), Sammy Cox (Rangers); Jimmy Scoular (Portsmouth), Andrew Paton (Motherwell), Alex Forbes (Arsenal); Lawrie Reilly (Hibernian), Wilson Humphries (Motherwell), Willie Thornton (Rangers), Allan Brown (Blackpool), Billy Liddell (Liverpool).

Sweden: Karl Svensson; Lennart Samuelsson, Erik Nilsson; Holger Hansson, Bengt Gustavsson, Gosta Lindh; Sylve Bengtsson, Gosta Lofgren, Lars Eriksson, Yngve Brodd, Gosta Sandberg.

Scorers: Sweden: Sandberg 2; Lofgren 3; Bengtsson 68 Scotland: Liddell 6

| 18 October 1952 | Home Championship | Ninian Park, Cardiff | Attendance 60,261 |

226 Wales 1, SCOTLAND 2
Referee: Alfred Bond (England)

Scotland: George Farm (Blackpool); George Young (Rangers, captain), Sammy Cox (Rangers); Jimmy Scoular (Portsmouth), Frank Brennan (Newcastle United), George Aitken (Sunderland); Tommy Wright (Sunderland), Allan Brown (Blackpool), Lawrie Reilly (Hibernian), Billy Steel (Dundee), Billy Liddell (Liverpool).

Wales: William Shortt; Arthur Lever, Alfred Sherwood; Roy Paul, Raymond Daniel, Ronald Burgess (captain); William Foulkes, Ellis Davies, Trevor Ford, Ivor Allchurch, Royston Clarke.

Scorers: Wales: Ford 23 Scotland: Brown 32; Liddell 69

| 5 November 1952 | Home Championship | Hampden Park | Attendance: 65,057 |

227 SCOTLAND 1, Ireland 1
Referee: Robert Smith (Wales)

Scotland: George Farm (Blackpool); George Young (Rangers, captain), Sammy Cox (Rangers); Jimmy Scoular (Portsmouth), Frank Brennan (Newcastle United), George Aitken (Sunderland); Tommy Wright (Sunderland), James Logie (Arsenal), Lawrie Reilly (Hibernian), Billy Steel (Dundee), Billy Liddell (Liverpool).

Ireland: Norman Uprichard; Leonard Graham, Alfred McMichael; Danny Blanchflower, William Dickson, Frank McCourt; Billy Bingham, Seamus D'Arcy, Edward McMorran, Jimmy McIlroy, Charlie Tully.

Scorers: Ireland: D'Arcy 80 Scotland: Reilly 90

| 18 April 1953 | Home Championship | Wembley, London | Attendance: 97,000 |

228 England 2, SCOTLAND 2
Referee: Thomas Mitchell (Northern Ireland)

Scotland (2-3-5):
- 3 George Farm (Blackpool);
- 37 George Young (Rangers, captain)
- 22 Sammy Cox (Rangers);
- 2 Tommy Docherty (Preston North End)
- 6 Frank Brennan (Newcastle United)
- 1 Doug Cowie (Dundee);
- 3 Tommy Wright (Sunderland)
- 6 Bobby Johnstone (Hibernian)
- 22 Lawrie Reilly (Hibernian)
- 29 Billy Steel (Dundee)
- 23 BIlly Liddell (Liverpool)

A battling display, with captain George Young setting the example, saw the Scots twice fight back after going a goal behind to take a deserved draw back from London. When Sammy Cox was carried off injured with 20 minutes remaining, and England 2-1 ahead, things looked bleak. But the Scottish players rolled up their sleeves like never before and Lawrie Reilly played a one-two with his Hibs team mate Bobby Johnstone before lobbing keeper Merrick to make it 2-2. Ivan Broadis had twice given England the lead with fine goals and it was Reilly who also notched the first equaliser. He showed great awareness to find the net in a crowded penalty area after Billy Steel had set up Johnstone whose shot had rebounded off the bar. Reilly played seven times against England in the 1950s, scoring six goals, a record to be proud of indeed.

England: Gilbert Merrick; Alf Ramsey, Lionel Smith; Billy Wright (captain), Malcolm Barrass, Jimmy Dickinson; Tom Finney, Ivan Broadis, Nat Lofthouse, Redfern Froggatt, John Froggatt. *Manager:* Walter Winterbottom.

Scorers: England: Broadis 18, 70 Scotland: Reilly 54, 89

| 6 May 1953 | Friendly | Hampden Park | Attendance: 83,800 |

229 SCOTLAND 1, Sweden 2
Referee: William Ling (England)

Scotland: George Farm (Blackpool); George Young (Rangers, captain), John Little (Rangers); Bobby Evans (Celtic), Doug Cowie (Dundee), Tommy Docherty (Preston North End); John Henderson (Portsmouth), Bobby Johnstone (Hibernian), Lawrie Reilly (Hibernian), Billy Steel (Dundee), Tommy Ring (Clyde).

Sweden: Karl Svensson; Lennart Samuelsson, Orvar Bergmark; Sven-Ove Svensson, Bengt Gustavsson, Gosta Lindh; Sylve Bengtsson, Gosta Lofgren, Lars Eriksson, Hans Andersson-Tvilling, Gosta Sandberg.

Scorers: Sweden: Lofgren 33; Eriksson 55 Scotland: Johnstone 41

| 3 October 1953 | Home Championship/World Cup qualifying | Windsor Park, Belfast | Attendance: 58,248 |

230 Ireland 1, SCOTLAND 3
Referee: Arthur Ellis (England)

Scotland: George Farm (Blackpool); George Young (Rangers, captain), Sammy Cox (Rangers); Bobby Evans (Celtic), Frank Brennan (Newcastle United), Doug Cowie (Dundee); Willie Waddell (Rangers), Charles Fleming (East Fife), John McPhail (Celtic), James Watson (Huddersfield Town), John Henderson (Portsmouth).

Ireland: William Smyth; William Cunningham, Alfred McMichael; Danny Blanchflower, James McCabe, Wilbur Cush; Billy Bingham, Jimmy McIlroy, William Simpson, Charlie Tully, Norman Lockhart. *Manager:* Peter Doherty.

Scorers: Scotland: Fleming 47, 69; Henderson 89 Ireland: Lockhart 72 (pen)

4 November 1953　　　Home Championship/World Cup qualifying　　　Hampden Park　　　Attendance: 71,387

231　SCOTLAND 3, Wales 3
Referee: Thomas Mitchell (Northern Ireland)

Scotland: George Farm (Blackpool); George Young (Rangers, captain), Sammy Cox (Rangers); Bobby Evans (Celtic), Willie Telfer (St Mirren), Doug Cowie (Dundee); John MacKenzie (Partick Thistle), Bobby Johnstone (Hibernian), Lawrie Reilly (Hibernian), Allan Brown (Blackpool), Billy Liddell (Liverpool).

Wales: Ron Howells; Walley Barnes (captain), Alfred Sherwood; Roy Paul, Raymond Daniel, Ronald Burgess; William Foulkes, Ellis Davies, John Charles, Ivor Allchurch, Royston Clarke.

Scorers: Scotland: Brown 19; Johnstone 42; Reilly 58　　　Wales: Charles 49, 88; Allchurch 73

---

3 April 1954　　　Home Championship/World Cup qualifying　　　Hampden Park　　　Attendance: 134,544

232　SCOTLAND 2, England 4
Referee: Thomas Mitchell (Northern Ireland)

Scotland (2-3-5):

7　George Farm (Blackpool);
1　Michael Haughney (Celtic)
25　Sammy Cox (Rangers, captain);
15　Bobby Evans (Celtic)
8　Frank Brennan (Newcastle United)
8　George Aitken (Sunderland);
2　John MacKenzie (Partick Thistle)
9　Bobby Johnstone (Hibernian)
3　John Henderson (Portsmouth)
9　Allan Brown (Blackpool)
1　Willie Ormond (Hibernian)

Manager: Andy Beattie

England went away from Glasgow with a hard-fought 4-2 win but neither side was said to have enhanced their prospects for the forthcoming World Cup in Switzerland. Scotland, who were missing the likes of George Young, Willie Woodburn and Lawrie Reilly, started well enough and took the lead early on when Allan Brown headed in a corner by John MacKenzie. However, England quickly equalised when Ivan Broadis put away a well-taken goal. After half-time the visitors went ahead quickly through John Nicholls and further emphasised their superiority with goals by Ronald Allen and James Mullen. Scotland got one back near the finish when left winger Willie Ormond found the net. Next up before the World Cup were two friendlies against Norway and one with Finland.

England: Gilbert Merrick; Ron Staniforth, Roger Byrne; Billy Wright (captain), Henry Clarke, Jimmy Dickinson; Tom Finney, Ivan Broadis, Ronald Allen, John Nicholls, James Mullen. *Manager:* Walter Winterbottom.

Scorers: Scotland: Brown 7, Ormond 89

England: Broadis 14; Nicholls 51; Allen 68; Mullen 83

HOME CHAMPIONSHIP/FIFA WORLD CUP QUALIFYING – GROUP THREE

	P	W	D	L	F	A	Pts
England	3	3	0	0	11	4	6
Scotland	3	1	1	1	8	8	3
N. Ireland	3	1	0	2	4	7	2
Wales	3	0	1	2	5	9	1

---

5 May 1954　　　Friendly　　　Hampden Park　　　Attendance: 25,897

233　SCOTLAND 1, Norway 0
Referee: John Clough (England)

Scotland: Fred Martin (Aberdeen); Willie Cunningham (Preston North End), Jock Aird (Burnley); Tommy Docherty (Preston North End, captain), James Davidson (Partick Thistle), Bobby Evans (Celtic); Bobby Johnstone (Hibernian), George Hamilton (Aberdeen), Patrick Buckley (Aberdeen), Allan Brown (Blackpool), Willie Ormond (Hibernian). *Manager:* Andy Beattie.

Norway: Asbjorn Hansen; Oddvar Hansen, Harry Karlsen (captain); Thorleif Olsen, Tor Hernes, Arne Natland; Willy Fossli, Gunnar Thoresen, Arne Kotte, Hans Nordahl, Gunnar Dybwad. *Coach:* Willibald Hahn.

Scorer: Scotland: Hamilton 34

---

19 May 1954　　　Friendly　　　Ullevaal Stadion, Oslo　　　Attendance: 25,000

234　Norway 1, SCOTLAND 1
Referee: John Erik Andersson (Sweden)

Scotland: Fred Martin (Aberdeen); Willie Cunningham (Preston North End), Jock Aird (Burnley); Tommy Docherty (Preston North End, captain), James Davidson (Partick Thistle), Doug Cowie (Dundee); John MacKenzie (Partick Thistle), George Hamilton (Aberdeen), John Henderson (Portsmouth), Allan Brown (Blackpool), Neil Mochan (Celtic). *Manager:* Andy Beattie.

Norway: Asbjorn Hansen; Oddvar Hansen, Harry Karlsen; Thorleif Olsen, Thorbjorn Svenssen (captain), Tor Hernes; Ragnar Hvidsten, Gunnar Thoresen, Arne Kotte, Gunnar Arnesen, Harry Kure. *Substitute:* Arne Natland (for Hernes 58). *Coach:* Willibald Hahn.

Scorers: Scotland: MacKenzie 56　　　Norway: Kure 88

---

25 May 1954　　　Friendly　　　Olympia Stadion, Helsinki　　　Attendance: 21,675

235　Finland 1, SCOTLAND 2
Referee: Sten Ahlner (Sweden)

Scotland: John Anderson (Leicester City); Alexander Wilson (Portsmouth), Willie Cunningham (Preston North End, captain); Bobby Evans (Celtic), Doug Cowie (Dundee), David Mathers (Partick Thistle); John MacKenzie (Partick Thistle), Bobby Johnstone (Hibernian), Allan Brown (Blackpool), Willie Fernie (Celtic), Willie Ormond (Hibernian). *Manager:* Andy Beattie.

Finland: Mauro Rintanen (captain); Ake Lindman, Lauri Lehtinen; Ibert Henriksson, Turkka Sundback, Aimo Sommarberg; Pertti Vanhanen, Matti Hiltunen, Rainer Forss, Olavi Lahtinen, Borje Nygard. *Substitute:* Aarre Klinga (for Rintanen 48).

Scorers: Scotland: Ormond 10; Johnstone 47　　　Finland: Lahtinen 86

| 16 June 1954 | FIFA World Cup (group stages) | Sportsplatz Hardturm, Zurich | Attendance: 25,000 |

236 Austria 1, SCOTLAND 0

Referee: Laurent Franken (Belgium)

Scotland (2-3-5):

- 3 Fred Martin (Aberdeen);
- 4 Willie Cunningham (Preston North End, captain)
- 3 Jock Aird (Burnley);
- 6 Tommy Docherty (Preston North End)
- 3 James Davidson (Partick Thistle)
- 7 Doug Cowie (Dundee);
- 5 John MacKenzie (Partick Thistle)
- 2 Willie Fernie (Celtic)
- 2 Neil Mochan (Celtic)
- 13 Allan Brown (Blackpool)
- 4 Willie Ormond (Hibernian)

Manager: Andy Beattie

"Scotland unlucky in World Cup" ran the headline in *The Scotsman*, which in all honesty could have been used for most of the subsequent campaigns. The first foray into the competition in Switzerland in 1954, with a largely experimental and inexperienced line-up, was said to have been a victim of unfair tactics and bad refereeing. Neil Mochan was particularly unlucky when he was right through and saw his shot just clear the bar, then a couple of minutes later he was fouled in the box and the referee gave an indirect free kick. To compound the Scots' misery Austria took the lead shortly after when Probst scored. Scotland came within inches of equalising when Willie Ormond's header went just over, but it was not to be and a stiff test lay in wait against world champions Uruguay in the second match.

Austria: Kurt Schmied; Gerhard Harappa, Leopold Barschandt; Ernst Ocwirk, Ernst Happel, Karl Koller; Robert Korner, Walter Schleger, Robert Dienst, Erich Probst, Alfred Korner. *Trainer:* Walter Nausch.

Scorer: Austria: Probst 32

| 19 June 1954 | FIFA World Cup (group stages) | St Jakob Stadion, Basle | Attendance 34,000 |

237 Uruguay 7, SCOTLAND 0

Referee: Vincenzo Orlandini (Italy)

Scotland (2-3-5):

- 4 Fred Martin (Aberdeen);
- 5 Willie Cunningham (Preston North End, captain)
- 4 Jock Aird (Burnley);
- 7 Tommy Docherty (Preston North End)
- 4 James Davidson (Partick Thistle)
- 8 Doug Cowie (Dundee);
- 6 John MacKenzie (Partick Thistle)
- 3 Willie Fernie (Celtic)
- 3 Neil Mochan (Celtic)
- 14 Allan Brown (Blackpool)
- 5 Willie Ormond (Hibernian)

Manager: Andy Beattie

Following the narrow 1-0 defeat against Austria in the first of Scotland's two matches the team was completely outplayed by the highly fancied Uruguayans in the second game. Playing with heavy cotton shirts in scorching heat did not help. Wingers Carlos Borge and Julio Abbadie were chiefly responsible for inflicting most of the damage, with Borges claiming a hat trick and his colleague scoring twice. Centre forward Omar Miguez also weighed in with two goals, while Scottish full backs Willie Cunningham and John Aird were heavily criticised in the media. Manager Andy Beattie resigned on the day of the match although the Scots badly missed the injured Lawrie Reilly of Hibs and Rangers stalwart George Young.

Uruguay: Roque Maspoli; Jose Santamaria, William Martinez; Victor Andrade, Obdulio Varela (captain), Luis Cruz, Julio Abbadie; Javier Ambrois, Omar Miguez, Juan Schiaffino, Carlos Borges. *Trainer:* Juan Lopez.

Scorers: Uruguay: Borges 17, 48, 58; Miguez 31, 82; Abbadie 55, 87

*With Uruguay and Austria having qualified and Scotland out of the running, the remaining two matches were not played.

1954 FIFA WORLD CUP GROUP THREE*

	P	W	D	L	F	A	Pts
Uruguay	2	2	0	0	9	0	4
Austria	2	2	0	0	6	0	4
Czechoslovakia	2	0	1	2	0	7	0
Scotland	2	0	0	2	0	8	0

| 16 October 1954 | Home Championship | Ninian Park, Cardiff | Attendance: 53,000 |

238 Wales 0, SCOTLAND 1

Referee: William Ling (England)

Scotland: William Fraser (Sunderland); George Young (Rangers, captain), Willie Cunningham (Preston North End); Tommy Docherty (Preston North End), James Davidson (Partick Thistle), Doug Cowie (Dundee); Willie Waddell (Rangers), Harry Yorston (Aberdeen), Patrick Buckley (Aberdeen), Willie Fernie (Celtic), Tommy Ring (Clyde).

Wales: John Kelsey; Walley Barnes (captain), Alfred Sherwood; Roy Paul, John Charles, David Bowen; William Reed, Derek Tapscott, Trevor Ford, Ivor Allchurch, Royston Clarke.

Scorer: Scotland: Buckley 70

| 3 November 1954 | Home Championship | Hampden Park | Attendance: 46,200 |

239 SCOTLAND 2, Northern Ireland 2

Referee: Alfred Bond (England)

Scotland: William Fraser (Sunderland); George Young (Rangers, captain), Willie McNaught (Raith Rovers); Bobby Evans (Celtic), James Davidson (Partick Thistle), Doug Cowie (Dundee); Willie Waddell (Rangers), Bobby Johnstone (Hibernian), Patrick Buckley (Aberdeen), Willie Fernie (Celtic), Tommy Ring (Clyde).

Northern Ireland: Norman Uprichard; Leonard Graham, William Cunningham; Danny Blanchflower, Terry McCavana, Bertie Peacock; Billy Bingham, Jackie Blanchflower, William McAdams, Jimmy McIlroy, Peter McParland. *Manager:* Peter Doherty.

Scorers: Scotland: Davidson 22; Johnstone 74   Northern Ireland: Bingham 24; McAdams 44

Chapter three: 1946-1959

| 8 December 1954 | Friendly | Hampden Park | Attendance: 113,146 |

240 SCOTLAND 2, Hungary 4   *Referee: Leopold Horn (Netherlands)*

Scotland: Fred Martin (Aberdeen); Willie Cunningham (Preston North End, captain), Harry Haddock (Clyde); Tommy Docherty (Preston North End), James Davidson (Partick Thistle), John Cumming (Hearts); John MacKenzie (Partick Thistle), Bobby Johnstone (Hibernian), Lawrie Reilly (Hibernian), Jimmy Wardhaugh (Hearts), Tommy Ring (Clyde).

Hungary: Lajos Farago; Jeno Buzanszky, Guyula Lorant; Mihaly Lantos, Jozsef Bozsik, Ferenc Szojka; Karoly Sandor, Sandor Kocsis, Nandor Hidegkuti, Ferenc Puskas (captain), Mate Fenyvesi. *Coach:* Gusztav Sebes.

Scorers: Hungary: Bozsik 20; Hidegkuti 26; Sandor 44; Kocsis 90   Scotland: Ring 36; Johnstone 46

| 2 April 1955 | Home Championship | Wembley, London | Attendance: 96,847 |

241 England 7, SCOTLAND 2   *Referee: Benjamin Griffiths (Wales)*

Scotland: Fred Martin (Aberdeen); Willie Cunningham (Preston North End, captain), Harry Haddock (Clyde); Tommy Docherty (Preston North End), James Davidson (Partick Thistle), John Cumming (Hearts); John MacKenzie (Partick Thistle), Bobby Johnstone (Manchester City), Lawrie Reilly (Hibernian), Ian McMillan (Airdrie), Tommy Ring (Clyde).

England: Fred Williams; James Meadows, Roger Byrne; Kenneth Armstrong, Billy Wright (captain), Duncan Edwards; Stanley Matthews, Don Revie, Nat Lofthouse, Dennis Wilshaw, Frank Blunstone. *Manager:* Walter Winterbottom.

Scorers: England: Wilshaw 1, 70, 73, 80; Lofthouse 7, 27; Revie 25   Scotland: Reilly 15; Docherty 85

| 4 May 1955 | Friendly | Hampden Park | Attendance: 20,858 |

242 SCOTLAND 3, Portugal 0   *Referee: Juan Gardeazabal (Spain)*

Scotland: Tommy Younger (Hibernian); Alex Parker (Falkirk), Harry Haddock (Clyde); Bobby Evans (Celtic), George Young (Rangers, captain), John Cumming (Hearts); Gordon Smith (Hibernian), Archie Robertson (Clyde), Lawrie Reilly (Hibernian), Thomas Gemmell (St Mirren), Billy Liddell (Liverpool).

Portugal: Carlos Gomes; Manuel Caldeira, Angelo Carvalho; Fernando Caiado, Manuel Passos (captain), Emilio Graca; Jose Aguas, Lucas Matateu, Mario Coluna, Jose Trevacos, Joao Martins. *Coach:* Joao da Silva.

Scorers: Scotland: Gemmell 7; Liddell 36; Reilly 86

| 15 May 1955 | Friendly | JNA Stadium, Belgrade | Attendance: 20,000 |

243 Yugoslavia 2, SCOTLAND 2   *Referee: Vincenzo Orlandini (Italy)*

Scotland: Tommy Younger (Hibernian); Alex Parker (Falkirk), Harry Haddock (Clyde); Bobby Evans (Celtic), George Young (Rangers, captain), John Cumming (Hearts); Gordon Smith (Hibernian), Bobby Collins (Celtic), Lawrie Reilly (Hibernian), Thomas Gemmell (St Mirren), Billy Liddell (Liverpool).

Yugoslavia: Vladimir Beara; Bruno Belin, Milan Zekovic; Zlatko Cajkovski, Suad Svraka, Vujadin Boskov; Todor Veselinovic, Milos Milutinovic, Bernard Vukas, Stjepan Bobek (captain), Branko Zebec. *Substitute:* Branko Kralj (for Beara 68). *Trainer:* Aleksandar Tirnanic.

Scorers: Yugoslavia: Veselinovic 13; Vukas 38   Scotland: Reilly 30; Smith 40

| 19 May 1955 | Friendly | Prater Stadion, Vienna | Attendance: 65,000 |

244 Austria 1, SCOTLAND 4   *Referee: Giorgio Bernardi (Italy)*

Scotland (2-3-5):
- 3 Tommy Younger (Hibernian);
- 3 Alex Parker (Falkirk);
- 1 Andrew Kerr (Partick Thistle);
- 11 Tommy Docherty (Preston North End)
- 21 Bobby Evans (Celtic)
- 11 Doug Cowie (Dundee);
- 12 Gordon Smith (Hibernian, captain)
- 5 Bobby Collins (Celtic)
- 29 Lawrie Reilly (Hibernian)
- 2 Archie Robertson (Clyde)
- 27 Billy Liddell (Liverpool)

The first ever win over Austria came in the second match of the continental tour of 1955, after a tough encounter in which the referee at times struggled to keep control. Archie Robertson opened the scoring with only seconds gone, flicking the ball home after a dazzling move, and Gordon Smith volleyed home in the final minute of the first half. It was an excellent display and the only surprise was that the lead was not greater. As the Austrians failed to make any headway their play became more and more rough, but the Scots kept their cool and Billy Liddell's unstoppable drive made it 3-0. Austria pulled one back through Ernst Ocwirk with just two minutes remaining but Lawrie Reilly restored the three-goal advantage almost straight away.

Austria: Kurt Schmied; Paul Halla, Leopold Barschandt; Gerhard Hanappi, Rudolf Rockl, Ernst Ocwirk; Ernst Hofbauer, Theodor Wagner, Richard Brousek, Erich Probst, Walter Schleger. *Substitute:* Robert Dienst (for Brousek 42). *Trainer:* Karl Geyer.

Scorers: Scotland: Robertson 1; Smith 44; Liddell 70; Reilly 89   Austria: Ocwirk 88

| 29 May 1955 | Friendly | Nep Stadion Budapest | Attendance: 102,000 |

245 Hungary 3, SCOTLAND 1   *Referee: Friedrich Seipelt (Austria)*

Scotland: Tommy Younger (Hibernian); Andrew Kerr (Partick Thistle), Harry Haddock (Clyde); Tommy Docherty (Preston North End), Bobby Evans (Celtic), Doug Cowie (Dundee); Gordon Smith (Hibernian, captain), Bobby Collins (Celtic), Lawrie Reilly (Hibernian), Archie Robertson (Clyde), Billy Liddell (Liverpool).

Hungary: Imre Danka; Jeno Buzanszky, Pal Varhidi; Mihaly Lantos, Jozsef Bozsik, Ferenc Szojka; Karoly Sandor, Nandor Hidegkuti, Sandor Kocsis, Ferenc Puskas (captain), Mate Fenyvesi. *Substitutes:* Peter Palotas (for Sandor 44); Lajos Farago (for Danka 46). *Trainer:* Gusztav Sebes.

Scorers: Scotland: Smith 42   Hungary: Hidegkuti 51; Kocsis 59; Fenyvesi 68

| 8 October 1955 | Home Championship | Windsor Park, Belfast | Attendance: 48,000 |

246 Northern Ireland 2, SCOTLAND 1 *Referee: John Kelly (England)*

Scotland: Tommy Younger (Hibernian); Alex Parker (Falkirk), Joseph McDonald (Sunderland); Bobby Evans (Celtic), George Young (Rangers, captain), Archie Glen (Aberdeen); Gordon Smith (Hibernian), Bobby Collins (Celtic), Lawrie Reilly (Hibernian), Bobby Johnstone (Manchester City), Billy Liddell (Liverpool).

Northern Ireland: Norman Uprichard; Leonard Graham, Willie Cunningham; Danny Blanchflower (captain), Terry McCavana, Bertie Peacock; Billy Bingham, Jackie Blanchflower, Francis Coyle, Jimmy McIlroy, Peter McParland. *Manager:* Peter Doherty.

Scorers: Northern Ireland: Jackie Blanchflower 7; Bingham 16 Scotland: Reilly 62

| 9 November 1955 | Home Championship | Hampden Park | Attendance: 53,887 |

247 SCOTLAND 2, Wales 0 *Referee: Reginald Leafe (England)*

Scotland: Tommy Younger (Hibernian); Alex Parker (Falkirk), Joseph McDonald (Sunderland); Bobby Evans (Celtic), George Young (Rangers, captain), Doug Cowie (Dundee); Gordon Smith (Hibernian), Bobby Johnstone (Manchester City), Lawrie Reilly (Hibernian), Bobby Collins (Celtic), John Henderson (Portsmouth).

Wales: John Kelsey; Stuart Williams, Alfred Sherwood (captain); Mel Charles, John Charles, Roy Paul; Derek Tapscott, Noel Kinsey, Trevor Ford, Ivor Allchurch, Cliff Jones. *Manager:* Walley Barnes.

Scorer: Scotland: Johnstone 14, 25

| 14 April 1956 | Home Championship | Hampden Park | Attendance: 132,817 |

248 SCOTLAND 1, England 1 *Referee: Leo Callaghan (Wales)*

Scotland (2-3-5):
7 Tommy Younger (Hibernian);
6 Alex Parker (Falkirk)
1 John Hewie (Charlton Athletic);
25 Bobby Evans (Celtic)
47 George Young (Rangers, captain)
2 Archie Glen (Aberdeen);
1 Graham Leggat (Aberdeen)
17 Bobby Johnstone (Manchester City)
33 Lawrie Reilly (Hibernian)
5 Ian McMillan (Airdrie)
16 Gordon Smith (Hibernian)

A last-minute effort by Johnny Haynes deprived Scotland of another home win over England, but in all honesty the visitors were worthy of the draw. The supporters obviously did not think so, however, and there was stunned silence when the final whistle blew. The Scots had taken the lead on the hour mark, when Aberdeen winger Graham Leggat grabbed a memorable goal. Drifting infield, he brought the ball down with one foot and lobbed goalkeeper Reg Matthews with the other. The pass was provided by South African-born left back John Hewie, who was a stand-out for his side. Others to impress were centre half George Young, who handled his English opponent Nat Lofthouse well, and wing halves Bobby Evans and Archie Glen.

England: Reg Matthews; Jeffrey Hall, Roger Byrne; Jimmy Dickinson, Billy Wright (captain), Duncan Edwards; Tom Finney, Tommy Taylor, Nat Lofthouse, Johnny Haynes, William Perry. *Manager:* Walter Winterbottom.

Scorers: Scotland: Leggat 60 England: Haynes 89

| 2 May 1956 | Friendly | Hampden Park | Attendance: 80,509 |

249 SCOTLAND 1, Austria 1 *Referee: Johannes Bronkhorst (Netherlands)*

Scotland: Tommy Younger (Hibernian); Alex Parker (Falkirk), John Hewie (Charlton Athletic); Bobby Evans (Celtic), George Young (Rangers, captain), Doug Cowie (Dundee); John MacKenzie (Partick Thistle), Alfie Conn (Hearts), Lawrie Reilly (Hibernian), Hugh Baird (Airdrie), Michael Cullen (Luton Town).

Austria: Bruno Engelmeier; Paul Halla, Leopold Barschandt; Ernst Ocwirk (captain), Walter Kollmann, Karl Koller; Herbert Grohs, Theodor Wagner, Gerhard Hanappi, Alfred Korner, Walter Haummer. *Coach:* Josef Argauer.

Scorers: Scotland: Conn 12 Austria: Wagner 14

| 20 October 1956 | Home Championship | Ninian Park, Cardiff | Attendance: 60,000 |

250 Wales 2, SCOTLAND 2 *Referee: Robert Mann (England)*

Scotland: Tommy Younger (Liverpool); Alex Parker (Falkirk), John Hewie (Charlton Athletic); Ian McColl (Rangers), George Young (Rangers, captain), Doug Cowie (Dundee); Graham Leggat (Aberdeen), Jackie Mudie (Blackpool), Lawrie Reilly (Hibernian), Bobby Collins (Celtic), Willie Fernie (Celtic).

Wales: John Kelsey; Alfred Sherwood, Mel Hopkins; Alan Harrington, Raymond Daniel, Derrick Sullivan; Terry Medwin, John Charles, Trevor Ford, Ivor Allchurch, Cliff Jones. *Manager:* Jimmy Murphy.

Scorers: Wales: Ford 7; Medwin 32 Scotland: Fernie 22; Reilly 36

| 7 November 1956 | Home Championship | Hampden Park | Attendance: 62,035 |

251 SCOTLAND 1, Northern Ireland 0 *Referee: Reginald Leafe (England)*

Scotland: Tommy Younger (Liverpool); Alex Parker (Falkirk), John Hewie (Charlton Athletic); Ian McColl (Rangers), George Young (Rangers, captain), Doug Cowie (Dundee); Alex Scott (Rangers), Jackie Mudie (Blackpool), Lawrie Reilly (Hibernian), Jimmy Wardhaugh (Hearts), Willie Fernie (Celtic).

Northern Ireland: Harry Gregg; Willie Cunningham, Alfred McMichael; Danny Blanchflower (captain), Jackie Blanchflower, Thomas Casey; Billy Bingham, Jimmy McIlroy, Bruce Shields, Thomas Dickson, Peter McParland. *Manager:* Peter Doherty.

Scorer: Scotland: Scott 25

Chapter three: 1946-1959

The team before the draw with Wales in 1956. Back (from left): Alex Parker, Ian McColl, Tommy Younger, John Hewie, Doug Cowie. Front: Graham Leggat, Jackie Mudie, Lawrie Reilly, George Young, Bobby Collins, Willie Fernie.

| 21 November 1956 | Friendly | Hampden Park | Attendance: 55,521 |

252 SCOTLAND 2, Yugoslavia 0

Referee: Pieter Roomer (Netherlands)

Scotland: Tommy Younger (Liverpool); Alex Parker (Falkirk), John Hewie (Charlton Athletic); Ian McColl (Rangers), George Young (Rangers, captain), Tommy Docherty (Preston North End); Alex Scott (Rangers), Jackie Mudie (Blackpool), Lawrie Reilly (Hibernian), Sammy Baird (Rangers), Willie Fernie (Celtic).

Yugoslavia: Vladimir Beara; Bruno Belin, Branko Stankovic, Lazar Tasic, Ivan Horvat, Vujadin Boskov; Aleksandar Petakovic, Milos Milutinovic, Tihomir Ognjanovic, Bernard Vukas, Branko Zebec. *Coach:* Aleksandar Tirnanic.

Scorers: Scotland: Mudie 36; Baird 55

| 6 April 1957 | Home Championship | Wembley, London | Attendance: 97,520 |

253 England 2, SCOTLAND 1

Referee: Pieter Roomer (Netherlands)

Scotland: Tommy Younger (Liverpool); Eric Caldow (Rangers), John Hewie (Charlton Athletic); Ian McColl (Rangers), George Young (Rangers, captain), Tommy Docherty (Preston North End); Bobby Collins (Celtic), Willie Fernie (Celtic), Lawrie Reilly (Hibernian), Jackie Mudie (Blackpool), Tommy Ring (Clyde).

England: Alan Hodgkinson; Jeffrey Hall, Roger Byrne; Ron Clayton, Billy Wright (captain), Duncan Edwards; Stanley Matthews, Thomas Thompson, Tom Finney, Derek Kevan, Colin Grainger. *Manager:* Walter Winterbottom.

Scorers: Scotland: Ring 1   England: Kevan 63; Edwards 80

| 8 May 1957 | FIFA World Cup qualifying | Hampden Park | Attendance: 88,890 |

254 SCOTLAND 4, Spain 2

Referee: Albert Dusch (West Germany)

Scotland (2-3-5):

13 Tommy Younger (Liverpool);
2   Eric Caldow (Rangers)
7   John Hewie (Charlton Athletic);
10 Ian McColl (Rangers)
53 George Young (Rangers, captain)
15 Tommy Docherty (Preston North End);
17 Gordon Smith (Hibernian)
11 Bobby Collins (Celtic)
5   Jackie Mudie (Blackpool)
2   Sammy Baird (Rangers)
7   Tommy Ring (Clyde)

Scotland boosted their chances of qualifying for the 1958 World Cup in Sweden with a fine home win over a Spanish side whose tactics, according to the press, were more suited to the bull ring than a football pitch. The star of the show was Blackpool centre forward Jackie Mudie, who grabbed a fine hat trick. Full back John Hewie completed the scoring from the penalty spot. A special mention was made of captain George Young, who was making his final home appearance for the national side. Young had celebrated winning his 50th cap the previous November against Northern Ireland. His Rangers team mate Eric Caldow at right back had a fine game against the Spanish maestro Gento.

Spain: Antonio Ramallets; Fernando Olivella, Marcelino Campanal; Jesus Garay (captain), Martin Verges, Jose Zarraga; Miguel Gonzalez, Ladislao Kubala, Alfredo di Stefano, Luis Suarez, Francisco Gento. *Trainer:* Manuel Vallina.

Scorers: Scotland: Mudie 22, 70, 79; Hewie 41 (pen)   Spain: Kubala 30; Suarez 50

| 19 May 1957 | World Cup qualifying | Sankt Jakob Stadion, Basle | Attendance: 48,000 |

255 Switzerland 1, SCOTLAND 2
Referee: Friedrich Seipelt (Austria)

Scotland: Tommy Younger (Liverpool); Eric Caldow (Rangers), John Hewie (Charlton Athletic); Ian McColl (Rangers), George Young (Rangers, captain), Tommy Docherty (Preston North End); Gordon Smith (Hibernian), Bobby Collins (Celtic), Jackie Mudie (Blackpool), Sammy Baird (Rangers), Tommy Ring (Clyde).

Switzerland: Eugene Parlier; Willy Kernen, Harry Koch; Andre Grobety, Ivo Frosio, Heinz Schneiter; Charles Antenen, Eugen Meier, Roger Vonlanthen, Robert Ballaman (captain), Fernando Riva. *Coach:* Jacques Spagnoli.

Scorers: Switzerland: Vonlanthen 12   Scotland: Mudie 33; Collins 71

| 22 May 1957 | Friendly | Neckar Stadion, Stuttgart | Attendance: 80,000 |

256 West Germany 1, SCOTLAND 3
Referee: Gottfried Dienst (Switzerland)

Scotland: Tommy Younger (Liverpool); Eric Caldow (Rangers), John Hewie (Charlton Athletic); Ian McColl (Rangers), Bobby Evans (Celtic), Tommy Docherty (Preston North End, captain); Alex Scott (Rangers), Bobby Collins (Celtic), Jackie Mudie (Blackpool), Sammy Baird (Rangers), Tommy Ring (Clyde).

West Germany: Hans Tilkowski; Willi Gerdau, Erich Juskowiak; Georg Stollenwerk, Heinz Wewers, Horst Szymaniak; Helmut Rahn (captain), Willi Schroder, Alfred Kelbassa, Alfred Schmidt, Gerhard Siedl. *Coach:* Josef Herberger.

Scorers: Scotland: Collins 20, 54; Mudie 33   West Germany: Siedl 70

| 26 May 1957 | World Cup qualifying | Estadio Bernabeu, Madrid | Attendance: 90,000 |

257 Spain 4, SCOTLAND 1
Referee: Reginald Leafe (England)

Scotland: Tommy Younger (Liverpool); Eric Caldow (Rangers), John Hewie (Charlton Athletic); Dave Mackay (Hearts), Bobby Evans (Celtic), Tommy Docherty (Preston North End, captain); Gordon Smith (Hibernian), Bobby Collins (Celtic), Jackie Mudie (Blackpool), Sammy Baird (Rangers), Tommy Ring (Clyde).

Spain: Antonio Ramallets; Juan Quincoces, Jesus Garay; Juan Segarra, Martin Verges, Enrique Gensana; Estanislao Basora, Ladislao Kubala, Alfredo di Stefano, Enrique Mateos, Francisco Gento. *Coach:* Meana Vallina.

Scorers: Spain: Mateos 13; Kubala 20; Basora 57, 85   Scotland: Smith 79

| 5 October 1957 | Home Championship | Windsor Park, Belfast | Attendance: 50,000 |

258 Northern Ireland 1, SCOTLAND 1
Referee: Leo Callaghan (Wales)

Scotland: Tommy Younger (Liverpool); Alex Parker (Falkirk), Eric Caldow (Rangers); Ian McColl (Rangers), Bobby Evans (Celtic), Tommy Docherty (Preston North End, captain); Graham Leggat (Aberdeen), Bobby Collins (Celtic), Jackie Mudie (Blackpool), Sammy Baird (Rangers), Tommy Ring (Clyde).

Northern Ireland: Norman Uprichard; Willie Cunningham, Alfred McMichael; Danny Blanchflower (captain), Jackie Blanchflower, Bertie Peacock; Billy Bingham, William Simpson, William McAdams, Jimmy McIlroy, Peter McParland. *Manager:* Peter Doherty.

Scorers: Northern Ireland: Simpson 47   Scotland: Leggat 58

| 6 November 1957 | World Cup qualifying | Hampden Park | Attendance: 58,811 |

259 SCOTLAND 3, Switzerland 2
Referee: Reginald Leafe (England)

Scotland (2-3-5):

- 18 Tommy Younger (Liverpool);
- 12 Alex Parker (Falkirk);
- 7   Eric Caldow (Rangers);
- 10 Willie Fernie (Celtic)
- 30 Bobby Evans (Celtic)
- 20 Tommy Docherty (Preston North End, captain);
- 4   Alex Scott (Rangers)
- 16 Bobby Collins (Celtic)
- 10 Jackie Mudie (Blackpool)
- 4   Archie Robertson (Clyde)
- 12 Tommy Ring (Clyde)

Scotland duly qualified for the World Cup finals in Sweden, but it was apparently a somewhat fortunate victory with the Swiss more difficult to overcome as "one of their own Alpine peaks". The home side took the lead in the 29th minute when Archie Robertson scored following a Tommy Docherty through ball. The Scottish captain was at fault for the equaliser, however, with his misplaced pass going to Riva who lobbed Tommy Younger to find the net. After the break Willie Fernie set up Jackie Mudie for the goal of the match, his cross turned smartly in by the Blackpool man. The Scots looked easy qualifiers when Alex Scott made it 3-1 after 70 minutes, but Vonlanden pulling another back made it a difficult but successful end to the game.

Switzerland: Eugene Parlier; Willy Kernen, Fritz Morf; Andre Grobety, Harry Koch, Heinz Schneiter; Francesco Chiesa, Robert Ballaman, Eugen Meier, Marcel Vonlanden, Fernando Riva. *Trainer:* Jaques Spagnoli.

Scorers: Scotland: Robertson 29; Mudie 52, Scott 70

Switzerland: Riva 35, Vonlanden 80

FIFA WORLD CUP QUALIFYING GROUP ONE

	P	W	D	L	F	A	Pts
Scotland	4	3	0	1	10	9	6
Spain	4	2	1	1	12	8	5
Switzerland	4	0	1	3	6	11	1

Chapter three: 1946-1959

13 November 1957   Home Championship   Hampden Park   Attendance: 42,918

260 SCOTLAND 1, Wales 1   *Referee: John Clough (England)*

Scotland: Tommy Younger (Liverpool); Alex Parker (Falkirk), Eric Caldow (Rangers); Tommy Docherty (Preston North End, captain), Bobby Evans (Celtic), Willie Fernie (Celtic); Alex Scott (Rangers), Bobby Collins (Celtic), James Gardiner (Motherwell), Jackie Mudie (Blackpool), Tommy Ewing (Partick Thistle).

Wales: John Kelsey; Stuart Williams, Mel Hopkins; Alan Harrington, Mel Charles, David Bowen; Len Allchurch, William Harris, Terry Medwin, Roy Vernon, Cliff Jones. *Manager:* Jimmy Murphy.

Scorers: Scotland: Collins 14   Wales: Medwin 76

19 April 1958   Home Championship   Hampden Park   Attendance: 127,874

261 *SCOTLAND 0, England 4   *Referee: Albert Dusch (West Germany)*

Scotland: Tommy Younger (Liverpool); Alex Parker (Falkirk), Harry Haddock (Clyde); Ian McColl (Rangers), Bobby Evans (Celtic), Tommy Docherty (Preston North End, captain); George Herd (Clyde), Jimmy Murray (Hearts), Jackie Mudie (Blackpool), James Forrest (Motherwell), Tommy Ewing (Partick Thistle). *Manager:* Dawson Walker.

England: Eddie Hopkinson; Don Howe, Ernest Langley; Ron Clayton, Billy Wright (captain), Bill Slater; Bryan Douglas, Bobby Charlton, Derek Kevan, Johnny Haynes, Tom Finney. *Manager:* Walter Winterbottom.

Scorers: England: Douglas 20; Kevan 33, 75; Charlton 67

*Manchester United manager Matt Busby had agreed to take on the role of team manager on a part-time basis. However, he was seriously injured in the Munich air disaster and trainer Dawson Walker was left in charge of the players.

7 May 1958   Friendly   Hampden Park   Attendance: 54,900

262 SCOTLAND 1, Hungary 1   *Referee: John Clough (England)*

Scotland: Tommy Younger (Liverpool, captain); Eric Caldow (Rangers), John Hewie (Charlton Athletic); Eddie Turnbull (Hibernian), Bobby Evans (Celtic), Doug Cowie (Dundee); Graham Leggat (Aberdeen), Jimmy Murray (Hearts), Jackie Mudie (Blackpool), Bobby Collins (Celtic), Stewart Imlach (Nottingham Forest). *Manager:* Dawson Walker.

Hungary: Gyula Grosics; Sandor Matrai, Ferenc Sipos; Laszlo Sarosi, Jozsef Bozsik (captain), Pal Berendi; Laszlo Budai, Ferenc Machos, Lajos Tichy, Deszo Bundzsak, Mate Fenyvesi. *Coach:* Lajos Baroti.

Scorers: Scotland: Mudie 14   Hungary: Fenyvesi 52

1 June 1958   Friendly   Dziesiciolecia Stadion, Warsaw   Attendance: 70,000

263 Poland 1, SCOTLAND 2   *Referee: Jeno Szranko (Hungary)*

Scotland: Tommy Younger (Liverpool, captain); Eric Caldow (Rangers), John Hewie (Charlton Athletic); Eddie Turnbull (Hibernian), Bobby Evans (Celtic), Doug Cowie (Dundee); Graham Leggat (Aberdeen), Jimmy Murray (Hearts), Jackie Mudie (Blackpool), Bobby Collins (Celtic), Stewart Imlach (Nottingham Forest). *Manager:* Dawson Walker.

Poland: Edward Szymkowiak; Henryk Szcepanski, Roman Korynt; Jerry Wozniak, Witold Majewski, Edmund Zientara; Marian Nowara, Marian Norkowski, Henryk Kempny, Gerard Cieslik (captain), Roman Lentner. *Trainers:* Henryk Reyman, Feliks Dyrda and Stanislaw Szymaniak.

Scorers: Scotland: Collins 21, 53   Poland: Cieslik 84

8 June 1958   FIFA World Cup (group stages)   Arosvallen, Vasteras   Attendance: 9,591

264 Yugoslavia 1, SCOTLAND 1   *Referee: Paul Wyssling (Switzerland)*

Scotland (2-3-5):
- 23 Tommy Younger (Liverpool, captain);
- 11 Eric Caldow (Rangers)
- 13 John Hewie (Charlton Athletic);
- 7 Eddie Turnbull (Hibernian)
- 35 Bobby Evans (Celtic)
- 19 Doug Cowie (Dundee);
- 6 Graham Leggat (Aberdeen)
- 4 Jimmy Murray (Hearts)
- 15 Jackie Mudie (Blackpool)
- 20 Bobby Collins (Celtic)
- 3 Stewart Imlach (Nottingham Forest)

Manager: Dawson Walker

Scotland began the 1958 World Cup finals in Sweden with a fighting display to take a point against Yugoslavia. Although they were outplayed in the first half against a side rated number two in the world, the Scots roared back after the break, playing some brilliant football, and were unlucky not to take full points. There was a double blow in the early stages when Stewart Imlach was injured and then Petakovic opened the scoring with a rasping low drive. The Yugoslavians could have gone further ahead but the Scots defended well, and then equalised a few minutes into the second half. It was a goal made in Edinburgh with Eddie Turnbull of Hibernian sending in a perfect free kick and Hearts inside forward Jimmy Murray heading home. Graham Leggat could have won it with 10 minutes remaining, but for a brilliant save by keeper Beara.

Yugoslavia: Vladimir Beara; Tomislav Crnkovic, Vasilije Sijakovic; Dobrosav Krstic, Branko Zebec (captain), Vujadin Boskov; Aleksandar Petakovic, Todor Veselinovic, Milos Milutinovic, Dragoslav Sekularac, Zdravko Rajkov. *Trainer:* Aleksandar Tirnanic.

Scorers: Yugoslavia: Petakovic 6   Scotland: Murray 51

| 11 June 1958 | FIFA World Cup (group stages) | Idrottsparken, Norrkoping | Attendance: 11,665 |

265 Paraguay 3, SCOTLAND 2

Referee: Vincenzo Orlandini (Italy)

Scotland (2-3-5):

- 24 Tommy Younger (Liverpool, captain);
- 15 Alex Parker (Everton)
- 12 Eric Caldow (Rangers);
- 8 Eddie Turnbull (Hibernian)
- 36 Bobby Evans (Celtic)
- 20 Doug Cowie (Dundee);
- 7 Graham Leggat (Aberdeen)
- 21 Bobby Collins (Celtic)
- 16 Jackie Mudie (Blackpool)
- 5 Archie Robertson (Clyde)
- 12 Willie Fernie (Celtic)

Manager: Dawson Walker

Several injury-enforced changes appeared to upset the balance for the second match, and the Scots were a shadow of the team which held Yugoslavia in the opening tie. Again they found themselves a goal down early on, when Aguero put Paraguay ahead with only three minutes on the clock. However, Jackie Mudie equalised halfway through the half after a great passing move. Ramirez restored Paraguay's lead with a minute remaining until the break and from then on the South American side began to dominate. Parodi got a third in the 74th minute and although Bobby Collins pulled one back it was never to be. They now needed to beat France in the third match to retain any hopes of making the quarter-finals.

Paraguay: Samuel Aguilar; Edelmiro Arevalo, Juan Vicente Lezcano; Eligio Echague, Salvador Villalba, Ignacio Achucarro; Juan Bautista Aguero (captain), Jose del Rosario Parodi, Jorgelino Romero, Cayetano Re Ramirez, Florencio Amarilla. *Trainer:* Aurelio Gonzalez.

Scorers: Scotland: Mudie 23; Collins 76   Paraguay: Aguero 3; Ramirez 44; Parodi 75

| 15 June 1958 | FIFA World Cup (group stages) | Eyravallen, Orebro | Attendance: 13,554 |

266 France 2, SCOTLAND 1

Referee: Juan Brozzi (Argentina)

Scotland (2-3-5):

- 1 Bill Brown (Dundee);
- 13 Eric Caldow (Rangers)
- 14 John Hewie (Charlton Athletic);
- 9 Eddie Turnbull (Hibernian)
- 37 Bobby Evans (Celtic, captain)
- 2 Dave Mackay (Hearts);
- 22 Bobby Collins (Celtic)
- 5 Jimmy Murray (Hearts)
- 17 Jackie Mudie (Blackpool)
- 7 Sammy Baird (Rangers)
- 4 Stewart Imlach (Nottingham Forest)

Manager: Dawson Walker

For the first time at a World Cup tournament, it was a case of "what could have been" for the Scots. Despite conceding an early goal to French centre forward Raymond Kopa, they rallied in fine style and were unlucky in the 29th minute when John Hewie hit the post from the penalty spot. Just Fontaine, who ended up as top scorer in the competition with an amazing 13 goals in six matches, made it 2-0 with seconds remaining of the first half. Scotland eventually got a deserved goal when Sammy Baird raced through on to a Jimmy Murray pass and scored in the 66th minute, but despite tremendous late pressure the French held on for the win. Goalkeeper Bill Brown, who gained his first cap, Dave MacKay, Bobby Collins and Eddie Turnbull all had fine games.

France: Claude Abbes; Raymond Kaelbel, Robert Jonquet (captain); Andre Lerond, Armand Penverne, Jean-Jaques Marcel; Maryan Wisnieski, Just Fontaine, Raymond Kopa, Roger Piantoni, Jean Vincent. *Trainer:* Albert Batteux.

Scorers: France: Kopa 22; Fontaine 45   Scotland: Baird 66

1958 FIFA WORLD CUP GROUP TWO

	P	W	D	L	F	A	Pts
France	3	2	0	1	11	7	4
Yugoslavia	3	1	2	0	7	6	4
Paraguay	3	1	1	1	9	12	3
Scotland	3	0	1	2	4	6	1

Some of the 1958 World Cup squad pose for a photo during a break from training. From left: Bobby Collins, Eric Caldow, John Hewie, Tommy Younger, Jackie Mudie, Alex Parker, Alex Scott, Ian Gardiner, Tommy Ewing, Tommy Docherty, Willie Fernie, Bobby Evans, Dawson Walker (manager).

18 October 1958 Home Championship   Ninian Park, Cardiff   Attendance: 59,162

267 Wales 0, SCOTLAND 3   *Referee: Reginald Leafe (England)*

Scotland (2-3-5):
2   Bill Brown (Dundee);
1   John Grant (Hibernian)
14 Eric Caldow (Rangers);
3   Dave Mackay (Hearts, captain)
1   Willie Toner (Kilmarnock)
23 Tommy Docherty (Arsenal);
8   Graham Leggat (Fulham)
23 Bobby Collins (Everton)
1   David Herd (Arsenal)
1   Denis Law (Huddersfield Town)
6   John Henderson (Arsenal)
Manager: Matt Busby

A tough match was expected in Cardiff after the respective fortunes of the two sides at the 1958 World Cup. While the Scots finished bottom of their group and failed to progress to the knockout stages, their opponents reached the quarter-finals where they lost by a single goal to eventual winners Brazil. The doubters needn't have worried, however, as a tremendous performance resulted in a 3-0 win. Eighteen-year-old Denis Law marked his debut with a goal while Graham Leggat and Bobby Collins were also on target. It was said that Law, more than anyone else, symbolised the new hope for Scottish football. His subtlety, agility, stamina and surprising strength made him the standout player of the game. Dave Mackay, who missed a penalty in the first minute, was also impressive, along with his fellow wing half Tommy Docherty, keeper Bill Brown and full back Eric Caldow.

Wales: John Kelsey; Stuart Williams, Mel Hopkins; Derrick Sullivan, Mel Charles, David Bowen; Len Allchurch, Roy Vernon, Terry Medwin, Ivor Allchurch, Phil Woosnam. *Manager:* Jimmy Murphy.

Scorers: Scotland: Leggat 30; Law 70; Collins 82

5 November 1958 Home Championship   Hampden Park   Attendance: 72,732

268 SCOTLAND 2, Northern Ireland 2   *Referee: John Clough (England)*

Scotland: Bill Brown (Dundee); John Grant (Hibernian), Eric Caldow (Rangers); Dave Mackay (Hearts, captain), Willie Toner (Kilmarnock), Tommy Docherty (Arsenal); Graham Leggat (Fulham), Bobby Collins (Everton), David Herd (Arsenal), Denis Law (Huddersfield Town), John Henderson (Arsenal). *Manager:* Matt Busby.

Northern Ireland: Norman Uprichard; Richard Keith, Alfred McMichael; Danny Blanchflower (captain), Willie Cunningham, Bertie Peacock; Billy Bingham, Wilbur Cush, William Simpson, Jimmy McIlroy, Peter McParland. *Manager:* Peter Doherty.

Scorers: Scotland: Herd 51; Collins 54   Northern Ireland: Caldow 72 (own goal); McIlroy 76

11 April 1959 Home Championship   Wembley, London   Attendance: 98,329

269 England 1, SCOTLAND 0   *Referee: Joaquim Campos (Portugal)*

Scotland: Bill Brown (Dundee); Duncan MacKay (Celtic), Eric Caldow (Rangers); Tommy Docherty (Arsenal), Bobby Evans (Celtic, captain), Dave Mackay (Tottenham Hotspur); Graham Leggat (Fulham), Bobby Collins (Everton), David Herd (Arsenal), John Dick (West Ham), Willie Ormond (Hibernian). *Manager:* Andy Beattie.

England: Eddie Hopkinson; Don Howe, Graham Shaw; Ron Clayton, Billy Wright (captain), Ron Flowers; Bryan Douglas, Peter Broadbent, Bobby Charlton, Johnny Haynes, Doug Holden. *Manager:* Walter Winterbottom.

Scorer: England: Charlton 59

6 May 1959 Friendly   Hampden Park   Attendance: 103,415

270 SCOTLAND 3, West Germany 2   *Referee: Arthur Ellis (England)*

Scotland (2-3-5):
8   George Farm (Blackpool);
2   Duncan Mackay (Celtic)
17 Eric Caldow (Rangers);
6   Dave MacKay (Tottenham Hotspur)
39 Bobby Evans (Celtic, captain)
1   Bert McCann (Motherwell);
11 Graham Leggat (Fulham)
1   John White (Falkirk)
1   Ian St John (Motherwell)
26 Bobby Collins (Everton)
1   Andy Weir (Motherwell)
Manager: Andy Beattie

A youthful Scottish side recorded one of the best victories for several years over a strong West German eleven, with all the goals coming in the first half. John White gave the Scots the lead in the opening minute, with a low shot after a head flick from Ian St John. Just five minutes later it was two, with Andy Weir stabbing the ball home after the keeper had palmed away a cross from Graham Leggat. The Germans were stunned but Seeler gave them hope when he glided through the middle to place a shot past the advancing Farm. In the 23rd minute the two-goal advantage was restored when Leggat scored with a fine header from a Weir corner. Nine minutes from the break the visitors hit back again when Eric Caldow handled in the box and Juskowiak scored from the spot. West Germany pressed hard in the second half but to no avail. White was judged man of the match.

West Germany: Gunter Sawitzki; Erich Juskowiak, Karl-Heinz Schnellinger; Helmut Benthaus, Herbert Erhardt, Horst Szymaniak; Helmut Rahn (captain), Rolf Geiger, Uwe Seeler, Alfred Schmidt, Hans Schafer. *Trainer:* Josef Herberger.

Scorers: Scotland: White 1; Weir 6; Leggat 23   West Germany: Seeler 14; Juskowiak 36 (pen)

| 27 May 1959 | Friendly | Olympisch, Amsterdam | Attendance: 55,000 |

271 Netherlands 1, SCOTLAND 2
Referee: Joaquim Campos (Portugal)

Scotland: George Farm (Blackpool); Duncan Mackay (Celtic), Eric Caldow (Rangers); Eric Smith (Celtic), Bobby Evans (Celtic, captain), John Hewie (Charlton Athletic); Graham Leggat (Fulham), Bobby Collins (Everton), John White (Falkirk), Denis Law (Huddersfield Town), Bertie Auld (Celtic). *Manager:* Andy Beattie.

Netherlands: Franz de Munck; Roelof Wiersma, Johannes Kraay; Jan Notermans, Cornelius van der Hart (captain), Jean Klassens; Pieter van der Kuil, Cornelis Rijvers, Leopold Canjels, Cornelis van der Gijp, Coenraad Moulijn. *Trainer:* Elek Schwartz.

Scorers: Netherlands: van der Gijp 18   Scotland: Collins 61; Leggat 65

| 3 June 1959 | Friendly | Estadio Jose Alvalade, Lisbon | Attendance: 30,000 |

272 Portugal 1, SCOTLAND 0
Referee: Daniel Zariquilgui (Spain)

Scotland: George Farm (Blackpool); Duncan MacKay (Celtic), Eric Caldow (Rangers); Eric Smith (Celtic), Bobby Evans (Celtic, captain), John Hewie (Charlton Athletic); Alex Scott (Rangers), Bobby Collins (Everton), John White (Falkirk), Denis Law (Huddersfield Town), Bertie Auld (Celtic). *Manager:* Andy Beattie.

Portugal: Acurcio Carrelo; Virgilio Mendes, Angelo Martins; Fernando Mendes, Raul Figueiredo, Vicente Lucas; Carlos Duarte, Mario Coluna, Lucas Matateu, Augusto Rocha, Hernani Da Silva. *Trainer:* Jose Maria Antunes.

Scorer: Portugal: Matateu 25

| 3 October 1959 | Home Championship | Windsor Park, Belfast | Attendance: 59,000 |

273 Northern Ireland 0, SCOTLAND 4
Referee: Reginald Leafe (England)

Scotland (2-3-5):

- 5 Bill Brown (Tottenham Hotspur);
- 20 Eric Caldow (Rangers)
- 17 John Hewie (Charlton Athletic);
- 7 Dave Mackay (Tottenham Hotspur)
- 42 Bobby Evans (Celtic, captain)
- 2 Bert McCann (Motherwell);
- 13 Graham Leggat (Fulham)
- 4 John White (Falkirk)
- 2 Ian St John (Motherwell)
- 5 Denis Law (Huddersfield Town)
- 1 George Mulhall (Aberdeen)

Manager: Andy Beattie

Scotland's biggest win for seven years came at Windsor Park, Belfast, over an Irish side that contained more than a few players at the veteran stage. Graham Leggat, now of Fulham, got the opener halfway through the first half, after a fine move involving centre forward Ian St John and left back John Hewie. Nine minutes later Hewie converted a penalty after Leggat had been taken down and young John White showed great agility to make it three with the half coming to an end. The Irish were rarely in it after the break but the Scots were only able to add one more to the tally, left winger George Mulhall shooting home in the 54th minute. Keeper Bill Brown had a fine game, as did Denis Law who was unlucky not to get his name on the score sheet.

Northern Ireland: Harry Gregg; Richard Keith, Alfred McMichael; Danny Blanchflower (captain), Willie Cunningham, Bertie Peacock; Billy Bingham, Wilbur Cush, Derek Dougan, Jimmy McIlroy, Peter McParland. *Manager:* Peter Doherty.

Scorers: Scotland: Leggat 25; Hewie 34 (pen); White 41; Mulhall 54

| 4 November 1959 | Home Championship | Hampden Park | Attendance: 55,813 |

274 SCOTLAND 1, Wales 1
Referee: Kevin Howley (England)

Scotland: Bill Brown (Tottenham Hotspur); Eric Caldow (Rangers), John Hewie (Charlton Athletic); Dave Mackay (Tottenham Hotspur), Bobby Evans (Celtic, captain), Bert McCann (Motherwell); Graham Leggat (Fulham), John White (Tottenham Hotspur), Ian St John (Motherwell), Denis Law (Huddersfield Town), Bertie Auld (Celtic). *Manager:* Andy Beattie.

Wales: John Kelsey; Stuart Williams (captain), Mel Hopkins; Derrick Sullivan, John Charles, Colin Baker; Terry Medwin, Phil Woosnam, Graham Moore, Ivor Allchurch, Cliff Jones. *Manager:* Jimmy Murphy.

Scorers: Wales: Charles 8   Scotland: Leggat 46

Denis Law about to cross the ball during the 1960 match against England, with Ronnie Clayton bearing down on him and Bill Slater on the right.

CHAPTER FOUR
1960-1969

9 April 1960   Home Championship   Hampden Park   Attendance: 129,783

275 SCOTLAND 1, England 1
Referee: Jeno Szranko (Hungary)

Scotland: Frank Haffey (Celtic); Duncan MacKay (Celtic), Eric Caldow (Rangers); John Cumming (Hearts), Bobby Evans (Celtic, captain), Bert McCann (Motherwell); Graham Leggat (Fulham), Alex Young (Hearts), Ian St John (Motherwell), Denis Law (Manchester City), Andy Weir (Motherwell). *Manager:* Andy Beattie.

England: Ron Springett; Jimmy Armfield, Ray Wilson; Ronnie Clayton (captain), Bill Slater, Ron Flowers; John Connelly, Peter Broadbent, Joe Baker, Ray Parry, Bobby Charlton. *Manager:* Walter Winterbottom.

Scorers: Scotland: Leggat 16   England: Charlton 50 (pen)

4 May 1960   Friendly   Hampden Park   Attendance: 26,643

276 SCOTLAND 2, Poland 3
Referee: Arthur Holland (England)

Scotland: Bill Brown (Tottenham Hotspur); Duncan MacKay (Celtic), John Hewie (Charlton Athletic); Dave Mackay (Tottenham Hotspur), Bobby Evans (Celtic, captain), John Cumming (Hearts); Graham Leggat (Fulham), John White (Tottenham Hotspur), Ian St John (Motherwell), Denis Law (Manchester City), Andy Weir (Motherwell). *Manager:* Andy Beattie.

Poland: Tomasz Stefaniszyn; Henryk Szczepanski, Henryk Grzybowski; Fryderyk Monica, Adam Michel, Edmund Zientara (captain); Jan Kowalski, Luzjan Brychczy, Stanislaw Hachorek, Ernest Pol, Krzysztof Baszkiewicz. *Substitute:* Edward Szymkowiak (for Stefaniszyn 77). *Trainer:* Czeslaw Krug.

Scorers: Poland: Baszkiewicz 11; Brychczy 29; Pol 60   Scotland: Law 23; St John 46

29 May 1960   Friendly   Prater Stadion, Vienna   Attendance: 60,000

277 Austria 4, SCOTLAND 1
Referee: Albert Dusch (West Germany)

Scotland: Bill Brown (Tottenham Hotspur); Duncan MacKay (Celtic), Eric Caldow (Rangers); Dave Mackay (Tottenham Hotspur), Bobby Evans (Chelsea, captain), John Cumming (Hearts); Graham Leggat (Fulham), John White (Tottenham Hotspur), Ian St John (Motherwell), Denis Law (Manchester City), Andy Weir (Motherwell). *Substitute:* Alex Young (Hearts, for Law 12). *Manager:* Andy Beattie.

Austria: Walter Zeman; Erich Hasenkopf, Franz Swoboda; Walter Skocik, Walter Glechner, Karl Koller; Rudolf Flogel, Gerhard Hanappi, Erich Hof, Josef Hamerl, Karl Skerlan. *Trainer:* Karl Decker.

Scorers: Austria: Hanappi 26, 31; Hof 44, 63   Scotland: Dave Mackay 76

5 June 1960   Friendly   Nep Stadion, Budapest   Attendance: 90,000

278 Hungary 3, SCOTLAND 3
Referee: Arthur Ellis (England)

Scotland: Bill Brown (Tottenham Hotspur); Duncan MacKay (Celtic), Eric Caldow (Rangers); John Cumming (Hearts), Bobby Evans (Chelsea, captain), Dave Mackay (Tottenham Hotspur); Graham Leggat (Fulham), George Herd (Clyde), Alex Young (Hearts), Willie Hunter (Motherwell), Andy Weir (Motherwell). *Manager:* Andy Beattie.

Hungary: Gyula Grosics (captain); Sandor Matrai, Ferenc Sipos; Jeno Dalnoki, Deszo Bundzsak, Antal Kotasz; Karoly Sandor, Janos Gorocs, Florian Albert, Lajos Tichy, Mate Fenyvesi. *Trainer:* Lajos Baroti.

Scorers: Hungary: Sandor 19; Gorocs 77; Tichy 90   Scotland: Hunter 34; Herd 62; Young 66

8 June 1960   Friendly   Mayis Stadyum, Ankara   Attendance: 22,500

279 Turkey 4, SCOTLAND 2
Referee: Erich Steiner (Austria)

Scotland: Bill Brown (Tottenham Hotspur); Duncan MacKay (Celtic), Eric Caldow (Rangers); Dave Mackay (Tottenham Hotspur), Bobby Evans (Chelsea, captain), John Cumming (Hearts); John White (Tottenham Hotspur), George Herd (Clyde), Alex Young (Hearts), Willie Hunter (Motherwell), Andy Weir (Motherwell). *Manager:* Andy Beattie.

Turkey: Turgay Seren (captain); Naci Erdem, Basri Dirimlili; Suat Mamat, Ergun Ercina, Kaya Kostepen; Lefter Kucukandonyadis, Can Bartu, Metin Oktay, Birol Pekel, Senol Birol. *Trainer:* Ignac Molnar (Hungary).

Scorers: Turkey: Metin 8; Lefter 32, 35; Senol 62   Scotland: Caldow 12 (pen); Young 72

22 October 1960   Home Championship   Ninian Park, Cardiff   Attendance: 55,000

280 Wales 2, SCOTLAND 0
Referee: Arthur Holland (England)

Scotland: Lawrie Leslie (Airdrie); Duncan MacKay (Celtic), Eric Caldow (Rangers, captain); Jimmy Gabriel (Everton), John Martis (Motherwell), Dave Mackay (Tottenham Hotspur); George Herd (Clyde), John White (Tottenham Hotspur), Alex Young (Hearts), Willie Hunter (Motherwell), Davie Wilson (Rangers). *Manager:* Dawson Walker.

Wales: John Kelsey; Alan Harrington, Graham Williams; Victor Crowe (captain), Mel Nurse, Colin Baker; Terry Medwin, Phil Woosnam, Kenneth Leek, Roy Vernon, Cliff Jones. *Manager:* Jimmy Murphy.

Scorers: Wales: Jones 43; Vernon 72

9 November 1960   Home Championship   Hampden Park   Attendance: 34,564

281 SCOTLAND 5, Northern Ireland 2   *Referee: Kevin Howley (England)*

Scotland: Lawrie Leslie (Airdrie); Duncan MacKay (Celtic), Eric Caldow (Rangers, captain); Dave Mackay (Tottenham Hotspur), Jackie Plenderleith (Manchester City), Jim Baxter (Rangers); George Herd (Clyde), Denis Law (Manchester City), Alex Young (Hearts), Ralph Brand (Rangers), Davie Wilson (Rangers). *Manager:* Ian McColl.

Northern Ireland: Harry Gregg; Richard Keith, Alex Elder; Danny Blanchflower (captain), Thomas Forde, Bertie Peacock; Billy Bingham, Walter Bruce, William McAdams, Jimmy Nicholson, Peter McParland. *Manager:* Peter Doherty.

Scorers: Scotland: Law 8; Caldow 43 (pen); Young 78; Brand 81, 90   Northern Ireland: Blanchflower 48 (pen); McParland 84

---

15 April 1961   Home Championship   Wembley, London   Attendance: 97,350

282 England 9, SCOTLAND 3   *Referee: Marcel Lequesne (France)*

Scotland (2-3-5):

2 Frank Haffey (Celtic);
1 Bobby Shearer (Rangers)
28 Eric Caldow (Rangers, captain);
15 Dave Mackay (Hearts)
1 Billy McNeill (Celtic)
5 Bert McCann (Motherwell);
1 John MacLeod (Hibernian)
11 Denis Law (Manchester City)
7 Ian St John (Motherwell)
1 Pat Quinn (Motherwell)
3 Davie Wilson (Rangers)

Manager: Ian McColl

The "greatest humiliation in the 90 years of international football", wrote Hugh McIlvanney in *The Scotsman*, and indeed it was a low point in the country's fortunes. However, it should not be forgotten that the score was only 5-3 to England with 15 minutes remaining, and only a late collapse led to the record books being troubled. The reporter praised the destructive qualities of Jimmy Greaves, who netted a hat trick, and Johnny Haynes, and fairly laid into the weaknesses of the likes of Dave MacKay, Bert McCann and Frank Haffey. The Celtic keeper, who had played well the previous year in a 1-1 draw with England, was never to represent his country again. Denis Law was also criticised for indiscipline, with only Celtic centre half Billy McNeill getting pass marks for his display.

England: Ron Springett; Jimmy Armfield, Mick McNeil; Bobby Robson, Peter Swan, Ron Flowers; Bryan Douglas, Jimmy Greaves, Bobby Smith, Johnny Haynes (captain), Bobby Charlton. *Manager:* Walter Winterbottom.

Scorers: England: Robson 8; Greaves 20, 29, 83; Douglas 55; Smith 74, 85; Haynes 80, 82

Scotland: Mackay 49; Wilson 53; Quinn 75

---

3 May 1961   World Cup qualifying   Hampden Park   Attendance: 46,696

283 SCOTLAND 4, Republic of Ireland 1   *Referee: Maurice Guigue (France)*

Scotland: Lawrie Leslie (Airdrie); Bobby Shearer (Rangers), Eric Caldow (Rangers, captain); Pat Crerand (Celtic), Billy McNeill (Celtic), Jim Baxter (Rangers); John MacLeod (Hibernian), Pat Quinn (Motherwell), David Herd (Arsenal), Ralph Brand (Rangers), Davie Wilson (Rangers). *Manager:* Ian McColl.

Republic of Ireland: Noel Dwyer; John McNally, Noel Cantwell (captain); Matthew McEvoy, Charlie Hurley, Patrick Saward; Johnny Giles, Ambrose Fogarty, Dermot Curtis, George Cummins, Joseph Haverty.

Scorers: Scotland: Brand 14, 40; Herd 59, 85   Republic of Ireland: Haverty 52

Jim Baxter (left) and Denis Law practice before an international match against Northern Ireland in the early 1960s.

Chapter four: 1960-1969

7 May 1961	World Cup qualifying	Dalymount Park, Dublin	Attendance: 45,000

284 Republic of Ireland 0, SCOTLAND 3   *Referee: Gaston Grandain (Belgium)*

Scotland (2-3-5):

4   Lawrie Leslie (Airdrie);
3   Bobby Shearer (Rangers)
30   Eric Caldow (Rangers, captain);
2   Pat Crerand (Celtic)
3   Billy McNeill (Celtic)
3   Jim Baxter (Rangers);
3   John Macleod (Hibernian)
3   Pat Quinn (Motherwell)
7   Alex Young (Everton)
3   Ralph Brand (Rangers)
5   Davie Wilson (Rangers)

Manager: Ian McColl

Scotland completed the double over the Republic of Ireland, following the 4-1 home win four days earlier. Against what was described as a mediocre Irish outfit, they were 2-0 ahead after 16 minutes. Both goals came from Alex Young of Everton, brought in as a late replacement after David Herd of Arsenal was taken ill. Ralph Brand of Rangers added a late third to make the score fairly comfortable and Celtic right half Pat Crerand got the plaudits as the standout player on the field. The result set the Scots up nicely with two games to come against the strong Czechoslovakian side.

Republic of Ireland: Noel Dwyer; James Kelly, Noel Cantwell (captain); Matthew McEvoy, Charlie Hurley, Michael Meagan; Fionan Fagan, Johnny Giles, Peter Fitzgerald, George Cummins, Joe Haverty.

Scorers: Scotland: Young 4, 16; Brand 86

---

14 May 1961	World Cup qualifying	Tehelne Pole, Bratislava	Attendance: 50,000

285 Czechoslovakia 4, SCOTLAND 0   *Referee: Erich Steiner (Austria)*

Scotland: Lawrie Leslie (Airdrie); Bobby Shearer (Rangers), Eric Caldow (Rangers, captain); Pat Crerand (Celtic), Billy McNeill (Celtic), Jim Baxter (Rangers); John MacLeod (Hibernian), Ian McMillan (Rangers), David Herd (Arsenal), Ralph Brand (Rangers), Davie Wilson (Rangers). *Manager:* Ian McColl.

Czechoslovakia: Viliam Schrojf; Frantisek Safranek, Jan Popluhar; Jiri Tichy, Svatopluk Pluskal, Josef Masopust (captain); Tomas Pospichal, Adolf Scherer, Josef Kadrada, Andrej Kvasnak, Vaclav Masek. *Trainer:* Rudolf Vytlacil.

Scorers: Czechoslovakia: Pospichal 7, 85; Kvasnak 12 (pen); Kadrada 44

---

29 September 1961	World Cup qualifying	Hampden Park	Attendance: 51,590

286 SCOTLAND 3, Czechoslovakia 2   *Referee: Leif Gulliksen (Norway)*

Scotland (2-3-5):

11   Bill Brown (Tottenham Hotspur);
12   Duncan MacKay (Celtic)
32   Eric Caldow (Rangers, captain);
4   Pat Crerand (Celtic)
5   Billy McNeill (Celtic)
5   Jim Baxter (Rangers);
7   Alex Scott (Rangers)
10   John White (Tottenham Hotspur)
8   Ian St John (Liverpool)
12   Denis Law (Torino)
7   Davie Wilson (Rangers)

Manager: Ian McColl

The Scots gained revenge for a 4-0 mauling in Bratislava four months earlier and Denis Law, restored to the side and now with Italian side Torino, was described as putting on a "world-class display". The visitors were ahead twice, first to an early strike by Andrej Kvasnak and again just after the break when Adolf Scherer found the net. But goals by Ian St John and a first for Law had got Scotland deservedly back on equal terms. Law's decisive winner put the teams level at the top of the table on six points apiece, and although the Czechs had a superior goal difference a play-off was necessary.

Czechoslovakia: Viliam Schrojf; Jozef Bamba, Jan Popluhar; Ladislav Novak (captain), Titus Bubernik, Josef Masopust; Tomas Pospichal, Adolf Scherer, Josef Kadrada, Andrej Kvasnak, Vaclav Masek. *Trainer:* Rudolf Vytlacil.

Scorers: Czechoslovakia: Kvasnak 6, Scherer 51

Scotland: St John 21; Law 62, 83

FIFA WORLD CUP QUALIFYING GROUP EIGHT

	P	W	D	L	F	A	Pts
Czechoslovakia	4	3	0	1	16	5	6
Scotland	4	3	0	1	10	7	6
Rep of Ireland	4	0	0	4	3	17	0

---

7 October 1961	Home Championship	Windsor Park, Belfast	Attendance: 41,000

287 Northern Ireland 1, SCOTLAND 6   *Referee: James Finney (England)*

Scotland: Bill Brown (Tottenham Hotspur); Duncan MacKay (Celtic), Eric Caldow (Rangers, captain); Pat Crerand (Celtic), Billy McNeill (Celtic), Jim Baxter (Rangers); Alex Scott (Rangers), John White (Tottenham Hotspur), Ian St John (Liverpool), Ralph Brand (Rangers), Davie Wilson (Rangers). *Manager:* Ian McColl.

Northern Ireland: Harry Gregg; Eddie Magill, Alex Elder; Danny Blanchflower, Terry Neill, Bertie Peacock; Sammy Wilson, Jimmy McIlroy, William Lawther, Matthew Hill, James McLaughlin.

Scorers: Scotland: Wilson 14; Scott 34, 53, 79; Brand 38, 69   Northern Ireland: McLaughlin 17

| 8 November 1961 | Home Championship | Hampden Park | Attendance: 74,329 |

288 SCOTLAND 2, Wales 0
Referee: Arthur Holland (England)

Scotland: Bill Brown (Tottenham Hotspur); Alex Hamilton (Dundee), Eric Caldow (Rangers, captain); Pat Crerand (Celtic), Ian Ure (Dundee), Jim Baxter (Rangers); Alex Scott (Rangers), John White (Tottenham Hotspur), Ian St John (Liverpool), Ralph Brand (Rangers), Davie Wilson (Rangers). *Manager:* Ian McColl.

Wales: John Kelsey; Alan Harrington, Stuart Williams; Victor Crowe, Mel Charles, Colin Baker; Len Allchurch, Phil Woosnam, Kenneth Leek, Ivor Allchurch, Cliff Jones. *Manager:* Jimmy Murphy.

Scorer: Scotland: St John 22, 50

| 29 November 1961 | World Cup qualifying (play-off) | Heysel, Brussels, Belgium | Attendance: 7,000 |

289 Czechoslovakia 4, SCOTLAND 2
(after extra time, 2-2 at full time)
Referee: Gerard Versyp (Belgium)

Scotland (2-3-5):
- 1 Eddie Connachan (Dunfermline);
- 2 Alex Hamilton (Dundee)
- 35 Eric Caldow (Rangers, captain);
- 7 Pat Crerand (Celtic)
- 2 Ian Ure (Dundee)
- 8 Jim Baxter (Rangers);
- 7 Ralph Brand (Rangers)
- 13 John White (Tottenham Hotspur)
- 11 Ian St John (Liverpool)
- 13 Denis Law (Torino)
- 1 Hugh Robertson (Dundee)

Manager: Ian McColl

Extra-time against the Czechs proved a step too far for Scotland, having taken the lead twice only to see it wiped out on both occasions. Ian St John of Liverpool, who got both goals, was widely acclaimed as man of the match. His first came in the 35th minute, heading in an expertly curled free kick by Jim Baxter. It took until the 70th minute for the Czechs to find an equaliser through Hledik, but the game had barely restarted when St John got his second following a Ralph Brand free kick. With just under 10 minutes remaining the Czechs got the second equaliser through Scherer after a bout of pressure. The Scots faded in extra time, allowing Pospichal and Kvasnak to put their side out of sight and through to the World Cup finals in Chile. According to media reports several of the Scottish players, notably Denis Law and Jim Baxter, were below par, and the Czechs deployed rough-house tactics which were not punished by the referee.

Czechoslovakia: Viliam Schrojf; Jiri Hledik, Jan Popluhar; Jiri Tichy (captain), Svatopluk Pluskal, Josef Masopust; Tomas Pospichal, Adolf Scherer, Andrej Kvasnak, Rudolf Kucera, Josef Jelinek II. *Trainer:* Rudolf Vytlacil.

Scorers: Scotland: St John 35, 71   Czechoslovakia: Hledik 70, Scherer 82, Pospichal 95, Kvasnak 105

| 14 April 1962 | Home Championship | Hampden Park | Attendance: 132,431 |

290 SCOTLAND 2, England 0
Referee: Leopold Horn (Netherlands)

Scotland (2-3-5):
- 14 Bill Brown (Tottenham Hotspur);
- 3 Alex Hamilton (Dundee)
- 36 Eric Caldow (Rangers, captain);
- 8 Pat Crerand (Celtic)
- 7 Billy McNeill (Celtic)
- 9 Jim Baxter (Rangers);
- 10 Alex Scott (Rangers)
- 14 John White (Tottenham Hotspur)
- 12 Ian St John (Liverpool)
- 14 Denis Law (Torino)
- 10 Davie Wilson (Rangers)

Manager: Ian McColl

Scotland defeated England for the first time on home soil since 1937 with a performance to savour. Misfortune had prevented Ian McColl's side from heading to the forthcoming World Cup in Chile, but it was obvious that the Scots were superior to those who English manager Walter Winterbottom would be taking to the finals. Denis Law and Jim Baxter were simply brilliant, putting on displays which no-one in the opposing team could match, while others who excelled were Pat Crerand, Billy McNeill and Ian St John. It was left winger Davie Wilson who opened the scoring in the 13th minute, firing a deflected shot past the keeper, and from there on the Scots never looked back. In truth, everyone in the side did their bit, and the only surprise was that it took until the final two minutes before the score was doubled. Eric Caldow did the honours from the penalty spot, following a handball after yet another spell of fierce Scottish pressure.

England: Ron Springett; Jimmy Armfield, Ray Wilson; Stan Anderson, Peter Swan, Ron Flowers; Bryan Douglas, Jimmy Greaves, Bobby Smith, Johnny Haynes (captain), Bobby Charlton. *Manager:* Walter Winterbottom.

Scorers: Scotland: Wilson 13; Caldow 88 (pen)

| 2 May 1962 | Friendly | Hampden Park | Attendance: 67,181 |

291 SCOTLAND 2, Uruguay 3
Referee: Arthur Holland (England)

Scotland: Eddie Connachan (Dunfermline Athletic); Alex Hamilton (Dundee), Eric Caldow (Rangers, captain); Pat Crerand (Celtic), Billy McNeill (Celtic), Jim Baxter (Rangers); Alex Scott (Rangers), Pat Quinn (Motherwell), Ian St John (Liverpool), Ralph Brand (Rangers), Davie Wilson (Rangers). *Manager:* Ian McColl.

Uruguay: Roberto Sosa; Horacio Troche, Ruben Soria; Edgardo Gonzalez, Nestor Goncalvez, Pedro Cubilla; Ronald Langon, Julio Cortes, Vladas Douksas, Jose Sacia, Luis Cubilla. *Coach:* Juan Carlos Corazzo.

Scorers: Uruguay: Sacia 37; Luis Cubilla 45, 47   Scotland: Baxter 81; Brand 88

Chapter four: 1960-1969

20 October 1962   Home Championship   Ninian Park, Cardiff   Attendance: 58,000

292 Wales 2, SCOTLAND 3   *Referee: Kenneth Dagnall (England)*

Scotland: Bill Brown (Tottenham Hotspur); Alex Hamilton (Dundee), Eric Caldow (Rangers, captain); Pat Crerand (Celtic), Ian Ure (Dundee), Jim Baxter (Rangers); Willie Henderson (Rangers), John White (Tottenham Hotspur), Ian St John (Liverpool), Denis Law (Manchester United), Davie Wilson (Rangers). *Manager:* Ian McColl.

Wales: Tony Millington; Stuart Williams, Mel Hopkins; Terry Hennessey, John Charles (captain), Malcolm Lucas; Barrie Jones, Ivor Allchurch, Mel Charles, Roy Vernon, Cliff Jones. *Manager:* Jimmy Murphy.

Scorers: Scotland: Caldow 19 (pen); Law 63; Henderson 79   Wales: Allchurch 40; John Charles 88

7 November 1962   Home Championship   Hampden Park   Attendance 58,734

293 SCOTLAND 5, Northern Ireland 1   *Referee: James Finney (England)*

Scotland (2-3-5):

16 Bill Brown (Tottenham Hotspur);
6   Alex Hamilton (Dundee)
39 Eric Caldow (Rangers, captain);
11 Pat Crerand (Celtic)
4   Ian Ure (Dundee)
12 Jim Baxter (Rangers);
2   Willie Henderson (Rangers)
16 John White (Tottenham Hotspur)
15 Ian St John (Liverpool)
16 Denis Law (Manchester United)
2   George Mulhall (Sunderland)

Manager: Ian McColl

This was Denis Law's game, as his skill and speed dazzled the crowd and completely overwhelmed the opposition. The Irish had started in good fashion, with Billy Bingham scoring in the eighth minute – when Scottish keeper Bill Brown fished the ball out of the net it was the first time he had touched it. Law got a memorable equaliser with five minutes of the first half left, hooking the ball over his shoulder after a fine Willie Henderson cross. Law got his second in the 64th minute, again following a Henderson cross, and claimed his hat trick not long after, this time George Mulhall providing the assist. Henderson got the goal his play deserved with just over 10 minutes remaining, and Law (who else?) hooked the ball home near the end for number five.

Northern Ireland: Bobby Irvine; Eddie Magill, Alex Elder, Danny Blanchflower, Samuel Hatton, Jimmy Nicolson; Billy Humphries, Sammy McMillan, Derek Dougan, Jimmy McIlroy, Billy Bingham. *Manager:* Bertie Peacock.

Scorers: Northern Ireland: Bingham 8   Scotland: Law 40, 64, 77, 87; Henderson 79

6 April 1963   Home Championship   Wembley, London   Attendance: 98,606

294 England 1, SCOTLAND 2   *Referee: Leopold Horn (Netherlands)*

Scotland (2-3-5):

17 Bill Brown (Tottenham Hotspur);
7   Alex Hamilton (Dundee)
40 Eric Caldow (Rangers, captain);
17 Dave MacKay (Tottenham Hotspur)
5   Ian Ure (Dundee)
13 Jim Baxter (Rangers);
3   Willie Henderson (Rangers)
17 John White (Tottenham Hotspur)
16 Ian St John (Liverpool)
17 Denis Law (Manchester United)
13 Davie Wilson (Rangers)

Manager: Ian McColl

Such was the apparent standard of the Scottish international side in 1963 that a 2-1 win at Wembley was considered a below-par performance, while the game was overshadowed by the broken leg sustained by captain Eric Caldow in the fifth minute. He was injured in a tackle by English centre forward Bobby Smith, which ended his international career on 40 caps, but Caldow assured his opponent later that it was "an accident, pure and simple". The Scots played the rest of the game with 10 players, but Smith was also hurt and only able to hobble on the wing for the duration. Jim Baxter was the standout player, scoring both goals and turning in an excellent performance, while a late goal by England's Bryan Douglas was probably no more than his side deserved.

England: Gordon Banks; Jimmy Armfield (captain), Gerry Byrne; Bobby Moore, Maurice Norman, Ron Flowers; Bryan Douglas, Jimmy Greaves, Bobby Smith, Jimmy Melia, Bobby Charlton. *Manager:* Alf Ramsey.

Scorers: Scotland: Baxter 29, 31 (pen)   England: Douglas 79

8 May 1963   Friendly   Hampden Park   Attendance: 94,596

295 SCOTLAND 4, Austria 1*   *Referee: James Finney (England)*

Scotland: Bill Brown (Tottenham Hotspur); Alex Hamilton (Dundee), Davie Holt (Hearts); Dave Mackay (Tottenham Hotspur, captain), Ian Ure (Dundee), Jim Baxter (Rangers); Willie Henderson (Rangers), Davie Gibson (Leicester City), Jimmy Millar (Rangers), Denis Law (Manchester United), Davie Wilson (Rangers). *Manager:* Ian McColl.

Austria: Gernot Fraydl; Ferdinand Kolarik, Erich Hasenkopf; Alfred Gager, Walter Glechner, Karl Koller; Anton Linhart, Erich Hof, Horst Nemec, Ernst Fiala, Friedrich Rafreider. *Trainer:* Karl Decker.

Scorers: Scotland: Wilson 16, 26; Law 33, 71   Austria: Linhart 72

*The match was abandoned after 79 minutes. Two Austrian players had been sent off, Horst Nemec for spitting and Erich Hof for a dangerous tackle, and referee James Finney decided to end the contest in the interests of safety. The result stood as an official international.

Jim Baxter scores the second of his two goals, with a penalty, in the 2-1 victory over England at Wembley in 1963.

| 4 June 1963 | Friendly | Brann Stadion, Bergen | Attendance: 23,000 |

296 Norway 4, SCOTLAND 3 Referee: Haukur Oskarsson (Iceland)

Scotland: Adam Blacklaw (Burnley); Alex Hamilton (Dundee), Davie Holt (Hearts); Dave Mackay (Tottenham Hotspur, captain), Ian Ure (Dundee), Jim Baxter (Rangers); Willie Henderson (Rangers), Davie Gibson (Leicester City), Ian St John (Liverpool), Denis Law (Manchester United), Davie Wilson (Rangers). *Substitute:* Frank McLintock (Leicester City, for Mackay 78). *Manager:* Ian McColl.

Norway: Sverre Andersen; Erik Hagen, Edgar Stakseth, Roar Johansen, Finn Thorsen, Arild Gulden; Roald Jensen, Arne Pedersen, John Krogh, Olav Nilsen, Erik Johansen. *Trainer:* Ragnar Larsen.

Scorers: Norway: Nilsen 5; Erik Johansen 60; Pedersen 81; Krogh 83   Scotland: Law 14, 22, 76

| 9 June 1963 | Friendly | Dalymount Park, Dublin | Attendance: 30,000 |

297 Republic of Ireland 1, SCOTLAND 0 Referee: Kevin Howley (England)

Scotland: Tommy Lawrence (Liverpool); Alex Hamilton (Dundee), Davie Holt (Hearts); Frank McLintock (Leicester City), Billy McNeill (Celtic), Jim Baxter (Rangers); Willie Henderson (Rangers), Davie Gibson (Leicester City), Jimmy Millar (Rangers), Denis Law (Manchester United, captain), Davie Wilson (Rangers). *Substitute:* Ian St John (Liverpool, for Miller 44). *Manager:* Ian McColl.

Republic of Ireland: Alan Kelly; Tony Dunne, Tommy Traynor; Andy McEvoy, Charlie Hurley, Mick McGrath; Johnny Giles, Patrick Turner, Noel Cantwell (captain), Noel Peyton, Joe Haverty. *Substitute:* Ambrose Fogarty (for Peyton 44).

Scorer: Republic of Ireland: Cantwell 6

| 13 June 1963 | Friendly | Bernabeu, Madrid | Attendance: 40,000 |

298 Spain 2, SCOTLAND 6 Referee: Guilio Campanati (Italy)

Scotland (2-3-5):

- 2 Adam Blacklaw (Burnley);
- 10 Billy McNeill (Celtic)
- 4 Davie Holt (Hearts);
- 3 Frank McLintock (Leicester City)
- 8 Ian Ure (Dundee)
- 17 Jim Baxter (Rangers);
- 7 Willie Henderson (Rangers)
- 4 Davie Gibson (Leicester City)
- 19 Ian St John (Liverpool)
- 21 Denis Law (Manchester United)
- 17 Davie Wilson (Rangers)

Manager: Ian McColl

After two shock defeats to Norway and the Republic of Ireland on their "European tour", Scotland produced a memorable performance in Madrid to roundly dispose of the home side. The goals were shared round with all five of the forwards on target. The Scots had a nervous start and Adelardo Rodriguez scored an early goal. However, Denis Law equalised in the 16th minute, Leicester City pair Frank McLintock and Davie Gibson both found the net and Davie Wilson made it 4-1. Spain pulled another back just before the break through Jose Veloso but Scottish superiority in the second half led to further goals by Willie Henderson and Ian St John. The three tour matches were notable for allowing the novelty of substitutes, although Scotland only took advantage in the first two games.

Spain: Jose Train; Feliciano Rivilla (captain), Jose Mignorance; Severina Reija, Luis Koldo Aguirre, Jesus Glaria; Amancio Amara, Adelardo Rodriguez, Jose Veloso, Vicente Guillot, Carlos Lapetra. Substitutes: Carmelo Cedrun (for Train 46), Ignacio Zoco (for Mignorance 32). *Trainer:* Jose Villalonga.

Scorers: Spain: Adelardo 8; Veloso 43   Scotland: Law 16; Gibson 17; McLintock 20; Wilson 33; Henderson 51; St John 83

Chapter four: 1960-1969

12 October 1963   Home Championship   Windsor Park, Belfast   Attendance: 39,000

299 Northern Ireland 2, SCOTLAND 1
Referee: Jack Taylor (England)

Scotland: Bill Brown (Tottenham Hotspur); Alex Hamilton (Dundee), Davie Provan (Rangers); Pat Crerand (Manchester United), Ian Ure (Arsenal), Dave Mackay (Tottenham Hotspur, captain); Willie Henderson (Rangers), John White (Tottenham Hotspur), Ian St John (Liverpool), Davie Gibson (Leicester City), George Mulhall (Sunderland). *Manager:* Ian McColl.

Northern Ireland: Harry Gregg; Eddie Magill, John Parke; Martin Harvey, Terry Neill, Willie McCullough; Billy Bingham (captain), Billy Humphries, Sammy Wilson, Johnny Crossan, Jimmy Hill. *Manager:* Bertie Peacock.

Scorers: Northern Ireland: Bingham 25; Wilson 63   Scotland: St John 49

---

7 November 1963   Friendly   Hampden Park   Attendance: 35,416

300 SCOTLAND 6, Norway 1
Referee: Kevin Howley (England)

Scotland (2-3-5):
- 20 Bill Brown (Tottenham Hotspur);
- 12 Alex Hamilton (Dundee)
- 2 Davie Provan (Rangers);
- 20 Dave MacKay (Tottenham Hotspur, captain)
- 10 Ian Ure (Arsenal)
- 12 Jim Baxter (Rangers);
- 18 Alex Scott (Everton)
- 19 John White (Tottenham Hotspur)
- 1 Alan Gilzean (Dundee)
- 22 Denis Law (Manchester United)
- 9 Willie Henderson (Rangers)

Substitute: 1 Jimmy Gabriel (Everton, for Baxter 46)

Manager: Ian McColl

Denis Law, who had scored a hat trick against Norway in Bergen five months earlier but ended up on the losing side, stamped his mark all over the return match and went one better with four goals. The Norwegians actually took the lead when Kristoffersen scored in the eighth minute, but from there on it was a superb display. Alan Gilzean, playing at centre forward, had a hand in several of the goals, starting with the equaliser in the 19th minute when he nodded on for Law to score. The same pair were involved just before half-time when the Scots deservedly took the lead, and Law got his hat trick following a corner kick 15 minutes after the break. Dave MacKay then hit home two long-range shots before Law completed the scoring. Along with Law and Gilzean there was a great performance by inside right John White, whose passing was a sight to behold.

Norway: Sverre Andersen; Erik Hagen, Edgar Stakseth; Roar Johansen, Finn Thorsen, Arild Gulden; Roald Jensen, Arne Pedersen, Per Kristoffersen, Olaf Nielsen, Erik Johansen. *Substitute:* Kjell Kaspersen (for Andersen 78). *Trainer:* Ragnar Larssen,

Scorers: Norway: Kristoffersen 8   Scotland: Law 19, 44, 59, 82; MacKay 74, 76

---

20 November 1963   Home Championship   Hampden Park   Attendance: 56,167

301 SCOTLAND 2, Wales 1
Referee: William Clements (England)

Scotland: Bill Brown (Tottenham Hotspur); Alex Hamilton (Dundee), Jim Kennedy (Celtic); Dave Mackay (Tottenham Hotspur, captain), Billy McNeill (Celtic), Jim Baxter (Rangers); Willie Henderson (Rangers), John White (Tottenham Hotspur), Alan Gilzean (Dundee), Denis Law (Manchester United), Alex Scott (Everton). *Manager:* Ian McColl.

Wales: Gary Sprake; Stuart Williams (captain), Graham Williams; Terry Hennessey, Mike England, Mel Nurse; Barrie Jones, Graham Moore, John Charles, Roy Vernon, Cliff Jones. *Manager:* Jimmy Murphy.

Scorers: Scotland: White 44; Law 47   Wales: Barrie Jones 57

---

11 April 1964   Home Championship   Hampden Park   Attendance: 133,245

302 SCOTLAND 1, England 0
Referee: Leopold Sylvain Horn (Netherlands)

Scotland (2-3-5):
- 1 Campbell Forsyth (Kilmarnock);
- 14 Alex Hamilton (Dundee)
- 2 Jim Kennedy (Celtic);
- 1 John Greig (Rangers)
- 12 Billy McNeill (Celtic, captain)
- 20 Jim Baxter (Rangers);
- 11 Willie Henderson (Rangers)
- 21 John White (Tottenham Hotspur)
- 3 Alan Gilzean (Dundee)
- 24 Denis Law (Manchester United)
- 18 Davie Wilson (Rangers)

Manager: Ian McColl

The victory was only by one goal but it was the most convincing of the three in a row since that terrible match of 1961. Many of the Scottish players had superb games, from John Greig, making his debut, and Billy McNeill in defence, to the underrated John White in the middle of the park and Alan Gilzean and Willie Henderson up front. The heading ability of Gilzean, who proved the perfect foil for Denis Law, was a real asset and it was fitting that the man from Coupar Angus got the only goal of the game in the 72nd minute. Challenged by the English keeper Gordon Banks and centre Maurice Norman, he beat them both in the air before heading home.

England: Gordon Banks; Jimmy Armfield (captain), Ray Wilson; Gordon Milne, Maurice Norman, Bobby Moore; Terry Paine, Roger Hunt, Johnny Byrne, George Eastham, Bobby Charlton. *Manager:* Alf Ramsey.

Scorer: Scotland: Gilzean 72

12 May 1964　　Friendly　　Niedersachsen Stadion, Hanover　　Attendance: 75,000
303 West Germany 2, SCOTLAND 2
Referee: Tonny Poulsen (Denmark)

Scotland (2-3-5):

1　Jim Cruickshank (Hearts);
15　Alex Hamilton (Dundee)
3　Jim Kennedy (Celtic);
2　John Greig (Rangers)
13　Billy McNeill (Celtic, captain)
21　Jim Baxter (Rangers);
12　Willie Henderson (Rangers)
22　John White (Tottenham Hotspur)
4　Alan Gilzean (Dundee)
25　Denis Law (Manchester United)
19　Davie Wilson (Rangers)

Substitute: 1 Davie Holt (Hearts, for Hamilton 40)

Manager: Ian McColl

Scotland preserved the impressive record of never having lost a match in Germany – but only just. It took two late goals by Alan Gilzean to level the score, in a match that was played in near tropical heat at Hanover. Captain Uwe Seeler had given his side the lead, with two thunderous shots in as many minutes, and that remained the score at half-time. The Scots were a bit unlucky to be two down and in the 70th minute Gilzean headed home a smart goal. Davie Wilson had the ball in the net just afterwards but was ruled offside, as an equaliser was sought. With just six minutes left it duly arrived. Willie Henderson crossed from the right, Denis Law hit the post and Gilzean charged in on the rebound. Manager Ian McColl conceded that although it was a good result his team had played badly, although very impressive were keeper Jim Cruickshank, John Greig and Billy McNeill in defence and substitute Davie Holt, who replaced the injured Alex Hamilton. It was the final appearance for John White, who was tragically killed by lightning in July 1964. He was sheltering under a tree at a golf course in Enfield, London.

West Germany: Hans Tilkowski; Hans Nowak, Rudolf Steiner; Horst Szymaniak, Willi Giesemann, Wolfgang Weber; Reinhard Libuda, Alfred Schmidt, Uwe Seeler, Rolf Geiger, Gerhard Dorfel. *Substitute:* Stefan Reisch (for Schmidt 25). *Trainer:* Josef Herberger.

Scorers: West Germany: Seeler 32, 33　　Scotland: Gilzean 70, 84

3 October 1964　　Home Championship　　Ninian Park, Cardiff　　Attendance: 37,093
304 Wales 3, SCOTLAND 2
Referee: Kevin Howley (England)

Scotland: Campbell Forsyth (Kilmarnock); Alex Hamilton (Dundee), Jim Kennedy (Celtic); John Greig (Rangers), Ron Yeats (Liverpool), Jim Baxter (Rangers); Jimmy Johnstone (Celtic), Davie Gibson (Leicester City), Steve Chalmers (Celtic), Denis Law (Manchester United, captain), Jimmy Robertson (Tottenham Hotspur). *Manager:* Ian McColl.

Wales: Gary Sprake; Stuart Williams (captain), Graham Williams; Barry Hole, John Charles, Terry Hennessey; Cliff Jones, Kenneth Leek, Wyn Davies, Ivor Allchurch, Ron Rees. *Manager:* Dave Bowen.

Scorers: Wales: Davies 6; Leek 87, 89　　Scotland: Chalmers 28; Gibson 29

21 October 1964　　World Cup qualifying　　Hampden Park　　Attendance: 54,332
305 SCOTLAND 3, Finland 1
Referee: Joseph Hannet (Belgium)

Scotland: Campbell Forsyth (Kilmarnock); Alex Hamilton (Dundee), Jim Kennedy (Celtic); John Greig (Rangers), Jackie McGrory (Kilmarnock), Jim Baxter (Rangers); Jimmy Johnstone (Celtic), Davie Gibson (Leicester City), Steve Chalmers (Celtic), Denis Law (Manchester United, captain), Alex Scott (Everton). *Manager:* Ian McColl.

Finland: Martti Halme; Pertti Makipaa, Tirno Kautonen; Stig Holmqvist (captain), Aarno Rinne, Veijo Valtonen; Harri Jarvi, Juhani Peltonen, Arto Tolsa, Simo Syrjavaara, Martti Hyvarinen. *Trainer:* Kaarlo Laaksonen.

Scorers: Scotland: Law 2; Chalmers 38; Gibson 42　　Finland: Peltonen 70

The team which drew 2-2 with England at Wembley in 1965. Back (from left): Ian McColl (manager), Alex Hamilton, Bill Brown, Pat Crerand, Billy McNeill, John Greig, Eddie McCreadie. Front: Ian St John, Willie Henderson, Bobby Collins, Billy Bremner (unused), Denis Law, Davie Wilson.

Chapter four: 1960-1969

25 November 1964	Home Championship	Hampden Park	Attendance: 48,752

306 SCOTLAND 3, Northern Ireland 2 *Referee: Geoffrey Powell (Wales)*

Scotland: Campbell Forsyth (Kilmarnock); Alex Hamilton (Dundee), Jim Kennedy (Celtic); John Greig (Rangers), Jackie McGrory (Kilmarnock), Frank McLintock (Arsenal); Willie Wallace (Hearts), Denis Law (Manchester United), Alan Gilzean (Dundee), Jim Baxter (Rangers, captain), Davie Wilson (Rangers). *Manager:* Ian McColl.

Northern Ireland: Pat Jennings; Eddie Magill, Alex Elder; Martin Harvey, Terry Neill (captain), John Parke; George Best, Billy Humphries, Willie Irvine, Johnny Crossan, Bobby Braithewaite. *Manager:* Bertie Peacock.

Scorers: Northern Ireland: Best 9; Irvine 19   Scotland: Wilson 10, 31; Gilzean 17

10 April 1965	Home Championship	Wembley, London	Attendance: 98,199

307 England 2, SCOTLAND 2 *Referee: Istvan Zsolt (Hungary)*

Scotland (2-3-5):
22 Bill Brown (Tottenham Hotspur);
19 Alex Hamilton (Dundee)
1   Eddie McCreadie (Chelsea);
13 Pat Crerand (Manchester United)
14 Billy McNeill (Celtic, captain)
6   John Greig (Rangers);
13 Willie Henderson (Rangers)
29 Bobby Collins (Leeds United)
21 Ian St John (Liverpool)
29 Denis Law (Manchester United)
21 Davie Wilson (Rangers)
Manager: Ian McColl

In most circumstances coming away from Wembley with a draw would be considered an achievement, but the press really laid into Scotland for not defeating a team which lost two players to injury. England got a lucky break in the 25th minute when Bobby Charlton's shot deflected off Alex Hamilton and deceived keeper Bill Brown, and when Jimmy Greaves made it two things looked bleak. But Denis Law's goal just before the break, which made him Scotland's top scorer, gave hope for the second period. Ian St John equalised from close range on the hour mark but by then England had lost Ray Wilson and Gerry Byrne to injury. The latter eventually came back on but was only able to limp around. John Greig was the only Scottish player to play with distinction and Law was not his usual energetic self.

England: Gordon Banks; George Cohen, Ray Wilson; Nobby Stiles, Jack Charlton, Bobby Moore (captain); Peter Thompson, Jimmy Greaves, Barry Bridges, Johnny Byrne, Bobby Charlton. *Manager:* Alf Ramsey.

Scorers: England: Bobby Charlton 25; Greaves 35   Scotland: Law 41; St John 59

8 May 1965	Friendly	Hampden Park	Attendance: 60,146

308 SCOTLAND 0, Spain 0 *Referee: Kevin Howley (England)*

Scotland: Bill Brown (Tottenham Hotspur); Alex Hamilton (Dundee), Eddie McCreadie (Chelsea); Billy Bremner (Leeds United), Billy McNeill (Celtic, captain), John Greig (Rangers); Willie Henderson (Rangers), Bobby Collins (Leeds United), Denis Law (Manchester United), Alan Gilzean (Tottenham Hotspur), John Hughes (Celtic). *Manager:* Ian McColl.

Spain: Jose Iribar; Feliciano Rivilla, Fernando Olivella (captain); Severino Reija, Ignacio Zoco, Jesus Glaria; Jose Ufarte, Luis Aragones, Marcelino Martinez, Koldo Aguirre, Carlos Lapetra. *Trainer:* Jose Luis Villalonga.

23 May 1965	World Cup qualifying	Slaski Stadion, Chorzow	Attendance: 67,462

309 Poland 1, SCOTLAND 1 *Referee: Sergey Alimov (Soviet Union)*

Scotland: Bill Brown (Tottenham Hotspur); Alex Hamilton (Dundee), Eddie McCreadie (Chelsea); John Greig (Rangers), Billy McNeill (Celtic, captain), Pat Crerand (Manchester United); Willie Henderson (Rangers), Bobby Collins (Leeds United), Neil Martin (Hibernian), Denis Law (Manchester United), John Hughes (Celtic). *Manager:* Jock Stein.

Poland: Edward Szymkowiak; Henryk Szczepanski (captain), Jacek Gmoch; Stanislaw Oslizlo, Roman Bazan, Ryszard Grzegorczyk; Antoni Nieroba, Jan Banas, Jan Liberda, Ernest Pol, Roman Lenther. *Trainers:* Wieslaw Motoczynski, Ryszard Koncewicz and Karol Krawczyk.

Scorers: Poland: Lenther 52   Scotland: Law 76

27 May 1965	World Cup qualifying	Olympiastadion, Helsinki	Attendance: 20,162

310 Finland 1, SCOTLAND 2 *Referee: Erwin Vetter (East Germany)*

Scotland: Bill Brown (Tottenham Hotspur); Alex Hamilton (Dundee), Eddie McCreadie (Chelsea); Pat Crerand (Manchester United), Billy McNeill (Celtic, captain), John Greig (Rangers); Willie Henderson (Rangers), Denis Law (Manchester United, Neil Martin (Hibernian), Willie Hamilton (Hibernian), Davie Wilson (Rangers). *Manager:* Jock Stein.

Finland: Lars Nasman; Pertti Makipaa, Timo Kautonen; Stig Holmqvist, Aarno Rinne, Ollie Heinonen (captain); Markku Kumpulampi, Juhani Peltonen, Martti Hyvarinen, Rauno Ruotsalainen, Semi Nuoranen. *Trainer:* Kaarlo Laaksonen.

Scorers: Finland: Hyvarinen 5   Scotland: Wilson 37; Greig 50

2 October 1965	Home Championship	Windsor Park, Belfast	Attendance: 53,000

311 Northern Ireland 3, SCOTLAND 2 *Referee: Jack Taylor (England)*

Scotland: Bill Brown (Tottenham Hotspur); Alex Hamilton (Dundee), Eddie McCreadie (Chelsea); Dave Mackay (Tottenham Hotspur), Billy McNeill (Celtic, captain), John Greig (Rangers); Willie Henderson (Rangers), Denis Law (Manchester United), Alan Gilzean (Tottenham Hotspur), Jim Baxter (Sunderland), John Hughes (Celtic). *Manager:* Jock Stein.

Northern Ireland: Pat Jennings; Eddie Magill, Alex Elder; Martin Harvey, Terry Neill (captain), Jimmy Nicholson; Jimmy McIlroy, Johnny Crossan, Willie Irvine, Derek Dougan, George Best. *Manager:* Bertie Peacock.

Scorers: Scotland: Gilzean 17, 81   Northern Ireland: Dougan 42; Crossan 59; Irvine 89

| 13 October 1965 | World Cup qualifying | Hampden Park | Attendance: 107,508 |

312 SCOTLAND 1, Poland 2
Referee: Hans Carlsson (Sweden)

Scotland: Bill Brown (Tottenham Hotspur); Alex Hamilton (Dundee), Eddie McCreadie (Chelsea); Pat Crerand (Manchester United), Billy McNeill (Celtic, captain), John Greig (Rangers); Willie Henderson (Rangers), Billy Bremner (Leeds United), Alan Gilzean (Tottenham Hotspur), Denis Law (Manchester United), Willie Johnston (Rangers). *Manager:* Jock Stein.

Poland: Konrad Kornek; Henryk Szczepanski (captain), Jacek Gmoch; Stanislaw Oslizlo, Zygmunt Anczok, Antoni Nieroba; Zygfryd Szoltysik, Jerzy Sadek, Ernest Pol, Jan Liberda, Eugeniusz Faber. *Trainers:* Wieslaw Motoczynski, Ryszard Koncewicz and Karol Krawczyk.

Scorers: Scotland: McNeill 14   Poland: Pol 84; Sadek 86

| 9 November 1965 | World Cup qualifying | Hampden Park | Attendance: 100,393 |

313 SCOTLAND 1, Italy 0
Referee: Rudolf Kreitlein (West Germany)

Scotland (2-3-5):

- 28 Bill Brown (Tottenham Hotspur);
- 12 John Greig (Rangers)
- 3 Davie Provan (Rangers);
- 1 Bobby Murdoch (Celtic)
- 1 Ron McKinnon (Rangers)
- 26 Jim Baxter (Sunderland, captain);
- 19 Willie Henderson (Rangers)
- 3 Billy Bremner (Leeds United)
- 9 Alan Gilzean (Tottenham Hotspur)
- 3 Neil Martin (Sunderland)
- 4 John Hughes (Celtic)

Manager: Jock Stein

Having started the eighth World Cup qualifying campaign in indifferent fashion, beating Finland home and away but drawing and losing to Poland, a win for the Scots was a must if they were to retain hopes of making it across the border for the finals in England. And a win was what they got, courtesy of a John Greig goal with just two minutes remaining. It was manager Jock Stein's fifth game since replacing Ian McColl, and the huge crowd went into raptures when Greig's thundering shot hit the net. Jim Baxter, again in fine form, had floated through the middle, swerved past the Italian centre half, and then laid the ball off to his former Rangers team mate. Scotland also had earlier chances through Neil Martin and Alan Gilzean, while Billy Bremner had a fine game marking Italian maestro Gianni Rivera. Unfortunately Scotland could not complete the job in Napoli the following month, however, and narrowly missed out on qualification again.

Italy: William Negri; Tarcisio Burgnich, Giacinto Facchetti; Aristide Guarneri, Sandro Salvadore (captain), Roberto Rosato; Giovanni Lodetti, Giacomo Burgarelli, Sandro Mazzola, Gianni Rivera, Paolo Barison. *Trainer:* Edmondo Fabbri.

Scorer: Scotland: Greig 88

FIFA WORLD CUP QUALIFYING GROUP EIGHT

	P	W	D	L	F	A	Pts
Italy	6	4	1	1	17	3	9
Scotland	6	3	1	2	8	8	7
Poland	6	2	2	2	11	10	6
Finland	6	1	0	5	5	20	2

| 24 November 1965 | Home Championship | Hampden Park | Attendance: 49,888 |

314 SCOTLAND 4, Wales 1
Referee: James Finney (England)

Scotland: Bobby Ferguson (Kilmarnock); John Greig (Rangers), Eddie McCreadie (Chelsea); Bobby Murdoch (Celtic), Ron McKinnon (Rangers), Jim Baxter (Sunderland, captain); Willie Henderson (Rangers), Charlie Cooke (Dundee), Jim Forrest (Rangers), Alan Gilzean (Tottenham Hotspur), Willie Johnston (Rangers). *Manager:* Jock Stein.

Wales: David Hollins; Peter Rodrigues, Colin Green; Terry Hennessy, Mike England (captain), Barrie Hole; Ronnie Rees, Tom Vernon, Wyn Davies, Ivor Allchurch, Gil Reece. *Manager:* Dave Bowen.

Scorers: Scotland: Murdoch 10, 29; Henderson 13; Greig 86   Wales: Allchurch 12

| 7 December 1965 | World Cup qualifying | San Paulo, Napoli | Attendance: 68,873 |

315 Italy 3, SCOTLAND 0
Referee: Istvan Zsolt (Hungary)

Scotland: Adam Blacklaw (Burnley); Davie Provan (Rangers), Eddie McCreadie (Rangers); Bobby Murdoch (Celtic), Ron McKinnon (Rangers), John Greig (Rangers, captain); Jim Forrest (Rangers), Billy Bremner (Leeds United), Ron Yeats (Liverpool), Charlie Cooke (Dundee), John Hughes (Celtic). *Manager:* Jock Stein.

Italy: Enrico Albertosi; Tarcisio Burgnich, Giacinto Facchetti; Roberto Rosato, Sandro Salvadore, Giovanni Lodetti; Bruno Mora, Giacomo Bulgarelli, Sandro Mazzola, Gianni Rivera, Ezio Pascutti. *Trainer:* Edmondo Fabbri.

Scorers: Italy: Pascutti 38; Facchetti 74; Mora 85

| 2 April 1966 | Home Championship | Hampden Park | Attendance: 123,052 |

316 SCOTLAND 3, England 4
Referee: Henri Faucheux (France)

Scotland: Bobby Ferguson (Kilmarnock); John Greig (Rangers, captain), Tommy Gemmell (Celtic); Bobby Murdoch (Celtic), Ron McKinnon (Rangers), Jim Baxter (Sunderland); Jimmy Johnstone (Celtic), Denis Law (Manchester United), Willie Wallace (Hearts), Billy Bremner (Leeds United), Willie Johnston (Rangers). *Manager:* John Prentice.

England: Gordon Banks; George Cohen, Keith Newton; Nobby Stiles, Jack Charlton, Bobby Moore (captain); Alan Ball, Roger Hunt, Bobby Charlton, Geoff Hurst, John Connelly. *Manager:* Alf Ramsey.

Scorers: England: Hurst 18; Hunt 34, 47; Bobby Charlton 73   Scotland: Law 42; Jimmy Johnstone 57, 82

Chapter four: 1960-1969

| 11 May 1966 | Friendly | Hampden Park | Attendance: 16,513 |

317 SCOTLAND 0, Netherlands 3
Referee: Kevin Howley (England)

Scotland: Bobby Ferguson (Kilmarnock); John Greig (Rangers, captain), Davie Provan (Rangers); Pat Stanton (Hibernian), Ron McKinnon (Rangers), Dave Smith (Aberdeen); Willie Henderson (Rangers), Andy Penman (Dundee), Jim Scott (Hibernian), Willie Wallace (Hearts), Willie Johnston (Rangers). *Manager:* John Prentice.

Netherlands: Eduard Graafland; Frederik Flinkevleugel, Emil Pijs; Daniel Schrijvers (captain), Cornelis Veldhoen, Wilhelmus Dullens; Benardus Muller, Jesaia Swart, Wilhelmus Van der Kuijlen, Klaas Nuninga, Pieter Keizer. *Trainer:* Georg Kessler.

Scorers: Netherlands: Nuninga 15; Van der Kuijlen 53, 84

| 18 June 1966 | Friendly | Hampden Park | Attendance: 23,321 |

318 SCOTLAND 0, Portugal 1
Referee: George McCabe (England)

Scotland: Bobby Ferguson (Kilmarnock); Willie Bell (Leeds United), Eddie McCreadie (Chelsea); John Greig (Rangers, captain), Jackie McGrory (Kilmarnock), Billy Bremner (Leeds United); Alex Scott (Everton), Charlie Cooke (Chelsea), Alex Young (Everton), Jim Baxter (Sunderland), Jackie Sinclair (Leicester City). *Substitute:* Steve Chalmers (Celtic, for Young 46). *Manager:* John Prentice.

Portugal: Jose Pereira; Joao Morais, Alexandre Baptista; Vicente Lucas, Hilario Da Conceicao, Jaime Graca; Mario Coluna (captain), Jose Augusto, Eusebio Ferreira, Jose Torres, Antonio Simoes. *Substitute:* Fernando Peres (for Augusto 80). *Trainer:* Otto Martins Gloria (Brazil).

Scorer: Portugal: Torres 72

| 25 June 1966 | Friendly | Hampden Park | Attendance: 74,933 |

319 SCOTLAND 1, Brazil 1
Referee: James Finney (England)

Scotland (2-3-5):

5	Bobby Ferguson (Kilmarnock);
18	John Greig (Rangers, captain)
2	Willie Bell (Leeds United);
7	Billy Bremner (Leeds United)
6	Ron McKinnon (Rangers)
1	John Clark (Celtic);
16	Alex Scott (Everton)
4	Charlie Cooke (Chelsea)
4	Steve Chalmers (Celtic)
30	Jim Baxter (Sunderland)
1	Peter Cormack (Hibernian)

Manager: John Prentice

A somewhat depleted team gave world champions Brazil a game to remember and with a bit more luck could have claimed a memorable victory. Scotland got the perfect start in the opening minute when a great bit of play between Jim Baxter and Steve Chalmers ended in the latter shooting home. Baxter was on fine form, easily matching the Brazilians with his range of passing, while the great Pele was basically marked out of the game by Billy Bremner. Young Peter Cormack of Hibernian was another to impress, running himself into the ground, while Celtic's John Clark defended stoutly all game. Brazil equalised through Servilio but had few more chances, and the Scots could have won it had Gilmar not saved superbly from Chalmers.

Brazil: Gilmar; Fidelis, Paulo Henrique; Orlando, Bellini (captain), Zito; Jairzinho, Gerson, Servilio, Pele, Amarildo. *Substitute:* Valter Machado (for Servilio 46). *Trainer:* Vicente Feola.

Scorers: Scotland: Chalmers 1   Brazil: Servilio 16

The great Brazilian, Pele, makes a point to Scotland's John Clark during the 1-1 draw of 1966. Also pictured are (from left) John Greig, Servilio, Charlie Cooke and Ron McKinnon.

| 22 October 1966 | Home Championship/European qualifying | Ninian Park, Cardiff | Attendance: 33,269 |

320 Wales 1, SCOTLAND 1
Referee: Kenneth Dagnall (England)

Scotland: Bobby Ferguson (Kilmarnock); John Greig (Rangers, captain), Tommy Gemmell (Celtic); Billy Bremner (Leeds United), Ron McKinnon (Rangers), John Clark (Celtic); Jimmy Johnstone (Celtic), Denis Law (Manchester United), Joe McBride (Celtic), Jim Baxter (Sunderland), Willie Henderson (Rangers). *Manager:* Malcolm MacDonald.

Wales: Gary Sprake; Peter Rodrigues, Graham Williams; Terry Hennessey, Mike England (captain), Barry Hole; Gil Reece, Wyn Davies, Ron Davies, Cliff Jones, Alan Jarvis. *Manager:* Dave Bowen.

Scorers: Wales: Ron Davies 76   Scotland: Law 86

| 16 November 1966 | Home Championship/European qualifying | Hampden Park | Attendance: 45,281 |

321 SCOTLAND 2, Northern Ireland 1
Referee: Jack Taylor (England)

Scotland: Bobby Ferguson (Kilmarnock); John Greig (Rangers, captain), Tommy Gemmell (Celtic); Billy Bremner (Leeds United), Ron McKinnon (Rangers), John Clark (Celtic); Willie Henderson (Rangers), Bobby Murdoch (Celtic), Joe McBride (Celtic), Steve Chalmers (Celtic), Bobby Lennox (Celtic). *Manager:* Malcolm MacDonald.

Northern Ireland: Pat Jennings; John Parke, Alex Elder (captain); Martin Harvey, Terry Neill, Jimmy Nicholson; Sammy Wilson, Johnny Crossan, Willie Irvine, Derek Dougan, Dave Clements. *Manager:* Bertie Peacock.

Scorers: Northern Ireland: Nicholson 9   Scotland: Murdoch 14; Lennox 35

| 15 April 1967 | Home Championship/European qualifying | Wembley, London | Attendance: 99,063 |

322 England 2, SCOTLAND 3
Referee: Gerhard Schulenburg (West Germany)

Scotland (2-3-5):
1 Ronnie Simpson (Celtic);
4 Tommy Gemmell (Celtic)
10 Eddie McCreadie (Chelsea);
21 John Greig (Rangers, captain)
9 Ron McKinnon (Rangers)
32 Jim Baxter (Sunderland);
4 Willie Wallace (Celtic)
10 Billy Bremner (Leeds United)
1 Jim McCalliog (Sheffield Wednesday)
37 Denis Law (Manchester United)
2 Bobby Lennox (Celtic)
Manager: Bobby Brown

A remarkable day at Wembley saw the world champions subdued, tormented and outclassed, as Scotland recorded one of the most memorable victories ever. Arguably it was an even better England side than that which won the World Cup the previous year, as Jimmy Greaves was restored to the side. Remarkably four of the five goals came in the last 12 minutes, after Denis Law had given the Scots the lead in the 27th minute, finishing in rapier style after a series of attacks. The home side's cause was not helped by an injury to centre half Jack Charlton, who spent the remainder of the match on the wing, but in truth the victory was much deserved. Jim Baxter was again in sparkling form, actually playing "keepie-uppie" at one stage in the second half as he teased the English. Law was said to be unhappy at what he termed a casual approach, as he fancied Scotland could have recorded a much more convincing score had they been more ruthless. Bobby Lennox made it 2-0 in the 78th minute before Jack Charlton pulled one back, but debutant Jim McCalliog quickly restored the two-goal advantage. A Geoff Hurst effort made it 3-2 but the English had been reduced to mediocrity.

England: Gordon Banks; George Cohen, Ray Wilson; Nobby Stiles, Jack Charlton, Bobby Moore; Alan Ball, Jimmy Greaves, Bobby Charlton, Geoff Hurst, Martin Peters. *Manager:* Alf Ramsey.

Scorers: Scotland: Law 27; Lennox 78; McCalliog 87   England: Jack Charlton 84; Hurst 88

Captains John Greig and Bobby Moore lead the teams out at Wembley in 1967.

Chapter four: 1960-1969

| 10 May 1967 | Friendly | Hampden Park | Attendance: 53,497 |

323 SCOTLAND 0, Soviet Union 2   *Referee: Laurens van Ravens (Netherlands)*

Scotland: Ronnie Simpson (Celtic); Tommy Gemmell (Celtic), Eddie McCreadie (Chelsea); John Clark (Celtic), Billy McNeill (Celtic), Jim Baxter (Sunderland, captain); Jimmy Johnstone (Celtic), Frank McLintock (Arsenal), Jim McCalliog (Sheffield Wednesday), Denis Law (Manchester United), Bobby Lennox (Celtic). *Substitute:* Willie Wallace (Celtic, for Law 46). *Manager:* Bobby Brown.

Soviet Union: Lev Yashin; Valentin Afonin, Albert Shesternev (captain); Murtaz Khurtzilava, Vasiliy Danilov, Valeriy Voronin; Igor Chislenko, Jozsef Sabo, Fedor Medvid, Eduard Streltsov, Eduard Malofeev. *Trainer:* Mikhael Yakushin.

Scorers: Soviet Union: Gemmell 17 (own goal); Medvid 41

| 16 May 1967 | Friendly | Ramat-Gan, Tel Aviv | Attendance: 27,000 |

324 Israel 1, SCOTLAND 2   *Referee: Moshe Mizrahi (Israel)*

Scotland (2-3-5):
1 Harry Thomson (Burnley);
1 Willie Callaghan (Dunfermline)
1 Eddie Colquhoun (Sheffield United);
1 Alan Anderson (Hearts)
11 Ian Ure (Arsenal, captain)
1 Doug Fraser (West Bromwich Albion);
1 Andy Penman (Rangers)
1 Bobby Hope (West Bromwich Albion)
3 Jim McCalliog (Sheffield Wednesday)
1 Alex Ferguson (Dunfermline)
1 Willie Morgan (Burnley)

Substitute: 1 Harry Hood (Clyde, for Penman)
Manager: Bobby Brown

A Scottish squad embarked on a tour of Asia, Oceana and North America in May of 1967 and included a young and largely inexperienced group of players. Five of the games, against Israel, Australia (three) and Canada were eventually upgraded to full internationals by the Scottish Football Association in 2021. The other matches were against Hong Kong, a New Zealand under-23 side, an Auckland XI and a Vancouver XI. Several of the players, who had never been classified as internationals before, were finally awarded caps 44 years later. They were Alan Anderson, Alex Ferguson, Harry Hood, Jim Townsend, Harry Thomson and Hugh Tinney. The only player on the tour who did not play in one of the official internationals was John Woodward of York City. Joe Harper netted five times in the 7-2 win over Canada while Ferguson got three in the matches against Australia. Unfortunately the squad captain, Ian Ure, suffered a broken jaw in the first match and was forced to return home early.

Israel: Itzik Visoker; Yehoshua Feigenbaum, Itzhak Droker; Menahem Bello, Moshe Litzinski, Mordechai Piker; Rahamim Talbi, Giovanni Spiegeleisen, Yehezkel Hazoun, Moshe Assis, Reuven Young. *Substitute:* George Borba (for Assis). *Trainer:* Milovan Ciric.

Scorers: Scotland: Morgan 21; Colquhoun 83   Israel: Spiegel 40

| 28 May 1967 | Friendly | Sydney Showground | Attendance: 34,792 |

325 Australia 0, SCOTLAND 1   *Referee: Bill Hosie (South Australia)*

Scotland: Harry Thomson (Burnley); Willie Callaghan (Dunfermline), Eddie Colquhoun (Sheffield United); Jim Townsend (Hearts), Alan Anderson (Hearts), Doug Fraser (West Bromwich Albion); Willie Morgan (Burnley), Bobby Hope (West Bromwich Albion), Jim McCalliog (Sheffield Wednesday), Alex Ferguson (Dunfermline), Harry Hood (Clyde). *Manager:* Bobby Brown.

Australia: Peter Fuzes; George Nuttall, Alan Marnoch; John Watkiss, Billy Cook, Pat Hughes; Alan Westwater, Ron Giles, John Warren, Ray Baartz, Archie Blue. *Substitute:* John Giacometti (for Giles). *Coach:* Joe Venglos.

Scorer: Scotland: Ferguson 31

| 31 May 1967 | Friendly | Norwood Oval, Adelaide | Attendance: 20,000 |

326 Australia 1, SCOTLAND 2   *Referee: Des Maitland (Victoria)*

Scotland: Jim Cruickshank (Hearts); Willie Callaghan (Dunfermline), Jim Townsend (Hearts); Alan Anderson (Hearts), Jackie McGrory (Kilmarnock), Doug Fraser (West Bromwich Albion); Tommy McLean (Kilmarnock), Bobby Hope (West Bromwich Albion), Jim McCalliog (Sheffield Wednesday), Alex Ferguson (Dunfermline), Willie Morgan (Burnley). *Manager:* Bobby Brown.

Australia: Bill Rorke; Cliff van Blerk, Alan Marnoch; Billy Cook, Nigel Shepherd, Pat Hughes; Alan Westwater, Hammy McMeechan, John Watkiss, Ray Baartz, John Giacometti. *Substitute:* Archie Blue (for McMeechan). *Coach:* Joe Venglos.

Scorers: Scotland: Townsend 25; Morgan 68   Australia: Baartz 34

| 3 June 1967 | Friendly | Olympic Park, Melbourne | Attendance: 22,138 |

327 Australia 0, SCOTLAND 2   *Referee: Tony Boskovic (New South Wales)*

Scotland: Jim Cruickshank (Hearts); Willie Callaghan (Dunfermline), Jim Townsend (Hearts); Alan Anderson (Hearts), Jackie McGrory (Kilmarnock), Doug Fraser (West Bromwich Albion); Tommy McLean (Kilmarnock), Bobby Hope (West Bromwich Albion), Jim McCalliog (Sheffield Wednesday), Alex Ferguson (Dunfermline), Willie Morgan (Burnley). *Substitutes:* Hugh Tinney (Bury, for Fraser); Andy Penman (Rangers, for McLean). *Manager:* Bobby Brown.

Australia: Peter Fuzes; Cliff van Blerk, Alan Marnoch; Billy Rice, Nigel Shepherd, Pat Hughes (captain); John Warren, John Watkiss, Atti Abonyi, Alan Westwater, Bruce Morrow. *Substitute:* Bill Rorke (for Fuzes 65). *Coach:* Joe Venglos.

Scorers: Scotland: Ferguson 61, 80

13 June 1967　　　　　Friendly　　　　　　　　　　Alexander Park, Winnipeg　　　　　Attendance: 3,000

328　Canada 2, SCOTLAND 7
Referee: Danny McClure

Scotland: Jim Cruickshank (Hearts); Jim Townsend (Hearts), Hugh Tinney (Bury); Alan Anderson (Hearts), Jackie McGrory (Kilmarnock), Doug Fraser (West Bromwich Albion); Willie Morgan (Burnley), Bobby Hope (West Bromwich Albion), Joe Harper (Morton), Harry Hood (Clyde), Tommy McLean (Kilmarnock). *Substitutes:* Andy Penman (Rangers, for Fraser); Jim McCalliog (Sheffield Wednesday, for Hood). *Manager:* Bobby Brown.

Canada: Art Kussner; Jim Berry, Bob DiLuca; Jim Baird (captain), Karl Kauck, Russ Hillman; Harold Hansen, Robbie Goodheart, Ike MacKay, Ralph McPate, Sergio Zanatta. *Substitutes:* Norman Patterson, Tony Adams.

Scorers: Scotland: Harper 20, 22, #, #, #; Hope 46; Morgan 90　　　Canada: Adams #, MacKay #

The timing of the Canadian substitutions, the Canadian goals and three of Joe Harper's efforts remains unclarified.

21 October 1967　　　Home Championship/European qualifying　　　Windsor Park, Belfast　　Attendance: 55,000

329　Northern Ireland 1, SCOTLAND 0
Referee: James Finney (England)

Scotland: Ronnie Simpson (Celtic); Tommy Gemmell (Celtic), Eddie McCreadie (Chelsea); John Greig (Rangers, captain), Ron McKinnon (Rangers), Ian Ure (Arsenal); Willie Wallace (Celtic), Bobby Murdoch (Celtic), Jim McCalliog (Sheffield Wednesday), Denis Law (Manchester United), Willie Morgan (Burnley). *Manager:* Bobby Brown.

Northern Ireland: Pat Jennings; Billy McKeag, John Parke; Arthur Stewart, Terry Neill (captain), Dave Clements; Billy Campbell, Johnny Crossan, Derek Dougan, Jimmy Nicholson, George Best. *Manager:* Billy Bingham.

Scorer: Northern Ireland: Clements 68

22 November 1967　　Home Championship/European qualifying　　　Hampden Park　　　Attendance: 57,472

330　SCOTLAND 3, Wales 2
Referee: James Finney (England)

Scotland: Bobby Clark (Aberdeen); Jim Craig (Celtic), Eddie McCreadie (Chelsea); John Greig (Rangers, captain), Ron McKinnon (Rangers), Jim Baxter (Sunderland); Jimmy Johnstone (Celtic), Billy Bremner (Leeds United), Alan Gilzean (Tottenham Hotspur), Willie Johnston (Rangers), Bobby Lennox (Celtic). *Manager:* Bobby Brown.

Wales: Gary Sprake; Peter Rodrigues, Colin Green; Terry Hennessey, Eddie James, Barry Hole; Ronnie Rees, Wyn Davies, Ron Davies, Alan Durban, Cliff Jones. *Manager:* Dave Bowen.

Scorers: Scotland: Gilzean 15, 65; McKinnon 78　　　Wales: Ron Davies 18; Durban 49

24 February 1968　　Home Championship/European qualifying　　　Hampden Park　　　Attendance: 134,000

331　SCOTLAND 1, England 1
Referee: Laurens van Ravens (Netherlands)

Scotland (2-3-5):
- 4　Ronnie Simpson (Celtic);
- 7　Tommy Gemmell (Celtic)
- 14　Eddie McCreadie (Chelsea);
- 21　Billy McNeill (Celtic),
- 12　Ron McKinnon (Rangers)
- 24　John Greig (Rangers, captain);
- 5　Charlie Cooke (Chelsea)
- 12　Billy Bremner (Leeds United)
- 6　John Hughes (Celtic)
- 6　Willie Johnston (Rangers)
- 5　Bobby Lennox (Celtic)

Manager: Bobby Brown

A home draw was unfortunately not enough for the Scots to qualify for the forthcoming European Championships. Having beaten England at Wembley the previous year, a bad defeat to Northern Ireland in Belfast likely put paid to the chances. It was also an understrength team which took to the field, minus several injured players and the suspended Jimmy Johnstone. England manager Alf Ramsey proclaimed afterwards that his side had "outclassed" their opponents, and had been unlucky not to score more goals. However, the Scots also had chances to win it, with Chelsea winger Charlie Cooke outstanding, and the only English player who really stood out was Bobby Charlton. Martin Peters gave the visitors the lead with an angled shot in the 20th minute, while a rare John Hughes headed goal levelled things up as half-time approached.

England: Gordon Banks; Keith Newton, Ray Wilson; Alan Mullery, Brian Labone, Bobby Moore (captain); Alan Ball, Geoff Hurst, Mike Summerbee, Bobby Charlton, Martin Peters. *Manager:* Alf Ramsey.

Scorers: England: Peters 20　　Scotland: Hughes 39

30 May 1968　　　　　Friendly　　　　　　　　　Olympisch Stadion, Amsterdam　　　Attendance: 19,000

332　Netherlands 0, SCOTLAND 0
Referee: Karl Riegg (West Germany)

Scotland: Bobby Clark (Aberdeen); Doug Fraser (West Bromwich Albion), Eddie McCreadie (Chelsea); Bobby Moncur (Newcastle United), Ron McKinnon (Rangers), Dave Smith (Rangers); Willie Henderson (Rangers), Bobby Hope (West Bromwich Albion), George McLean (Dundee), John Greig (Rangers, captain), Charlie Cooke (Chelsea). *Substitute:* Jimmy Smith (Aberdeen, for Hope 12). *Manager:* Bobby Brown.

Netherlands: Jan Van Beveren; Pieter Romeun, Rinus Israel; Johan Eijkenbroek (captain), Hendrik Warnas, Wim Jansen; Hendrik Gloot, Jan Klijnjan, Wilhelmus van der Kuijlen, Wim van Hanegem, Rob Rensenbrink. *Trainer:* Georg Kessler.

Chapter four: 1960-1969

| 16 October 1968 | Friendly | Idraetsparken, Copenhagen | Attendance: 11,900 |

333 Denmark 0, SCOTLAND 1
Referee: Hans Carlsson (Sweden)

Scotland: Jim Herriot (Birmingham City); Tommy Gemmell (Celtic), Eddie McCreadie (Chelsea); Billy Bremner (Leeds United, captain), Ron McKinnon (Rangers), John Greig (Rangers); Tommy McLean (Kilmarnock), Jim McCalliog (Sheffield Wednesday), Colin Stein (Rangers), Bobby Hope (West Bromwich Albion), Bobby Lennox (Celtic). S*ubstitute:* Peter Cormack (Hibernian, for McCalliog 87). *Manager:* Bobby Brown.

Denmark: Knud Engedahl; Jan Larsen, Niels Yde; Leif Sorensen, Henning Munk-Jensen, Borge Enemark (captain); Flemming Mortensen, Finn Wiberg, Bent Jensen, Ole Steffensen, Ulrik le Fevre.

Scorer: Scotland: Lennox 70

| 6 November 1968 | World Cup qualifying | Hampden Park | Attendance: 80,856 |

334 SCOTLAND 2, Austria 1
Referee: Curt Liedberg (Sweden)

Scotland: Ronnie Simpson (Celtic); Tommy Gemmell (Celtic), Eddie McCreadie (Chelsea); Billy Bremner (Leeds United), Ron McKinnon (Rangers), John Greig (Rangers, captain); Jimmy Johnstone (Celtic), Charlie Cooke (Chelsea), John Hughes (Celtic), Denis Law (Manchester United), Bobby Lennox (Celtic). *Substitute:* Alan Gilzean (Tottenham Hotspur, for Law 75). *Manager:* Bobby Brown.

Austria: Gerald Fuchsbichler; Walter Gebhardt, Gerhard Sturmberger (captain); Johann Eigenstiller, Peter Pumm, Franz Hasil; August Starek, Johann Ettmayer, Helmut Matzler, Helmut Siber, Helmut Redl. *Substitute:* Helmut Koglberger (for Redl 46). *Trainer:* Leopold Stastny.

Scorers: Austria: Starek 2   Scotland: Law 7; Bremner 75

| 11 December 1968 | World Cup qualifying | GSP Stadhion, Nicosia | Attendance: 5,895 |

335 Cyprus 0, SCOTLAND 5
Referee: Paul Bonnet (Malta)

Scotland: Jim Herriot (Birmingham City); Doug Fraser (West Bromwich Albion), Eddie McCreadie (Chelsea); Billy Bremner (Leeds United, captain), Ron McKinnon (Rangers), John Greig (Rangers); Tommy McLean (Kilmarnock), Bobby Murdoch (Celtic), Colin Stein (Rangers), Alan Gilzean (Tottenham Hotspur), Charlie Cooke (Chelsea). *Substitutes:* Billy McNeill (Celtic, for McKinnon 46); Bobby Lennox (Celtic, for Cooke 80). *Manager:* Bobby Brown.

Cyprus: Michalakis Alkiviadis; Panikos Iakovou, Lakis Theodorou; Michael Stefanos, Kyriakos Koureas, Kostas Panayiotou; Panikos Efthymiadis, Panikos Krystallis, Melis Asprou, Andreas Pakkos, Andreas Stylianou. *Substitutes:* Marcos Markou (for Pakkos 6); Yiannis Xypolitas (for Krystallis 46). *Trainer:* Pambos Avraamides.

Scorers: Scotland: Gilzean 3, 30; Murdoch 23; Stein 40, 43

| 19 April 1969 | World Cup qualifying | Hampden Park | Attendance: 95,951 |

336 SCOTLAND 1, West Germany 1
Referee: Juan Gardeazabal (Spain)

Scotland: Tommy Lawrence (Liverpool); Tommy Gemmell (Celtic), Eddie McCreadie (Chelsea); Bobby Murdoch (Celtic), Ron McKinnon (Rangers), John Greig (Rangers); Jimmy Johnstone (Celtic), Billy Bremner (Leeds United, captain), Denis Law (Manchester United), Alan Gilzean (Tottenham Hotspur), Bobby Lennox (Celtic). *Substitute:* Charlie Cooke (Chelsea, for Lennox 63). *Manager:* Bobby Brown.

West Germany: Horst Wolter; Berti Vogts, Karl-Heinz Schnellinger; Franz Beckenbauer, Willie Schultz (captain), Bernhardn Patzke; Bernhard Dorfel, Helmut Haller, Gerd Muller, Wolfgang Overath, Siegfried Held. *Substitutes:* Sep Maier (for Wolter 46); Max Lorenz (for Overath 79). *Trainer:* Helmut Schon.

Scorers: West Germany: Muller 39   Scotland: Murdoch 88

| 3 May 1969 | Home Championship | The Racecourse, Wrexham | Attendance: 18,765 |

337 Wales 3, SCOTLAND 5
Referee: James Finney (England)

Scotland: Tommy Lawrence (Liverpool); Tommy Gemmell (Celtic), Eddie McCreadie (Chelsea); Billy Bremner (Leeds United, captain), Billy McNeill (Celtic), John Greig (Rangers); Tommy McLean (Kilmarnock), Bobby Murdoch (Celtic), Colin Stein (Rangers), Alan Gilzean (Tottenham Hotspur), Charlie Cooke (Chelsea). *Substitute:* Jim Herriot (Birmingham City, for Lawrence 46). *Manager:* Bobby Brown.

Wales: Gary Sprake; Stephen Derrett, Colin Green; Alan Durban (captain), Alwyn Burton, Dave Powell; Graham Moore, John Toshack, Ron Davies, Wyn Davies, Barrie Jones. *Substitute:* Ronnie Rees (for Derrett 78). *Manager:* Dave Bowen.

Scorers: Scotland: McNeill 12; Stein 16; Gilzean 55; Bremner 72; McLean 87   Wales: Ron Davies 29, 57; Toshack 44

| 6 May 1969 | Home Championship | Hampden Park | Attendance: 7,483 |

338 SCOTLAND 1, Northern Ireland 1
Referee: David Smith (England)

Scotland: Jim Herriot (Birmingham City); Tommy Gemmell (Celtic), Eddie McCreadie (Chelsea); Billy Bremner (Leeds United, captain), John Greig (Rangers), Pat Stanton (Hibernian); Willie Henderson (Rangers), Bobby Murdoch (Celtic), Colin Stein (Rangers), Denis Law (Manchester United), Charlie Cooke (Chelsea). *Substitute:* Willie Johnston (Rangers, for Cooke 75). *Manager:* Bobby Brown.

Northern Ireland: Pat Jennings; David Craig, Alex Elder; Sammy Todd, Terry Neill (captain), Jimmy Nicholson; George Best, Eric McMordie, Derek Dougan, Tommy Jackson, Dave Clements. *Manager:* Billy Bingham.

Scorers: Northern Ireland: McMordie 11   Scotland: Stein 53

| 10 May 1969 | Home Championship | Wembley, London | Attendance: 89,902 |

339 England 4, SCOTLAND 1
Referee: Robert Helies (France)

Scotland: Jim Herriot (Birmingham City); Tommy Gemmell (Celtic), Eddie McCreadie (Chelsea); Bobby Murdoch (Celtic), Billy McNeill (Celtic), John Greig (Rangers); Willie Henderson (Rangers), Billy Bremner (Leeds United, captain), Colin Stein (Rangers), Alan Gilzean (Tottenham Hotspur), Eddie Gray (Leeds United). *Substitute:* Willie Wallace (Celtic, for Gilzean 57). *Manager:* Bobby Brown.

England: Gordon Banks; Keith Newton, Terry Cooper; Alan Mullery, Brian Labone, Bobby Moore (captain); Francis Lee, Alan Ball, Bobby Charlton, Geoff Hurst, Martin Peters. *Manager:* Alf Ramsey.

Scorers: England: Peters 16, 64; Hurst 20, 60 (pen)   Scotland: Stein 43

| 17 May 1969 | World Cup qualifying | Hampden Park | Attendance: 39,095 |

340 SCOTLAND 8, Cyprus 0   *Referee: Peter Coates (Republic of Ireland)*

Scotland (2-3-5):
6   Jim Herriot (Birmingham City);
14 Tommy Gemmell (Celtic)
23 Eddie McCreadie (Chelsea);
20 Billy Bremner (Leeds United, captain)
25 Billy McNeill (Celtic)
33 John Greig (Rangers);
27 Willie Henderson (Rangers)
12 Charlie Cooke (Chelsea)
6   Colin Stein (Rangers)
17 Alan Gilzean (Tottenham Hotspur)
2   Eddie Gray (Leeds United)

Manager: Bobby Brown

Scotland made hay against a poor Cypriot team as they warmed up for the vital away tie in Germany five months later. They racked up eight goals, the most for decades, and the only question among a crowd approaching 40,000 was whether it would end in double figures. Eddie Gray of Leeds United opened the scoring in the 15th minute and from then on the score increased regularly. Billy McNeill made it two before Rangers striker Colin Stein took over, finding the net four times. Willie Henderson got the seventh and when a penalty was awarded the talk was whether Stein could equal Hughie Gallacher's record of five goals in a match. Professionalism prevailed, however. Regular penalty-taker Tommy Gemmell was handed the ball and he made no mistake.

Cyprus: Michalakis Alkiviadis; Ioannis Andreou, Andreas Konstantinou; Georgiou Sotirakis, Kyriakos Koureas, Michael Stefanos; Marcos Markou, Panikos Efthymiadis, Panikos Krystallis (captain), Melis Asprou, Andreas Stylianou. *Substitutes:* Demos Kavazis (for Konstantinou 46); Paschalis Fokis (for Sotirakis 46). *Trainer:* Pambos Avraamides.

Scorers: Scotland: Gray 15; McNeill 20; Stein 28, 49, 59, 67; Henderson 70; Gemmell 76 (pen)

| 21 September 1969 | Friendly | Dalymount Park, Dublin | Attendance: 27,000 |

341 Republic of Ireland 1, SCOTLAND 1   *Referee: Norman Burtenshaw (England)*

Scotland: Ernie McGarr (Aberdeen); John Greig (Rangers), Tommy Gemmell (Celtic); Pat Stanton (Hibernian), Ron McKinnon (Rangers), Bobby Moncur (Newcastle United); Willie Henderson (Rangers), Billy Bremner (Leeds United, captain), Colin Stein (Rangers), Peter Cormack (Hibernian), John Hughes (Celtic). *Substitutes:* Jim Herriot (Birmingham City, for McGarr 24); Willie Callaghan (Dunfermline, for Gemmell 46). *Manager:* Bobby Brown.

Republic of Ireland: Alan Kelly; Shay Brennan, Mick Meagan; Al Finucane, Paddy Mulligan, John Conway; Eamon Rogers, Johnny Giles, Don Givens, Alfie Hale, Ray Treacy. *Manager:* Mick Meagan.

Scorers: Scotland: Stein 8   Republic of Ireland: Givens 27

| 22 October 1969 | World Cup qualifying | Volkspark, Hamburg | Attendance: 72,000 |

342 West Germany 3, SCOTLAND 2   *Referee: Gilbert Droz (Switzerland)*

Scotland (4-2-4):
8   Jim Herriot (Birmingham City);
35 John Greig (Rangers)
19 Ron McKinnon (Rangers)
26 Billy McNeill (Celtic)
16 Tommy Gemmell (Celtic);
22 Billy Bremner (Leeds United, captain)
4   Peter Cormack (Hibernian);
9   Jimmy Johnstone (Celtic)
18 Alan Gilzean (Tottenham Hotspur)
8   Colin Stein (Rangers)
3   Eddie Gray (Leeds United)

Manager: Bobby Brown

Bobby Brown's injury-hit side, needing a win to stay on course for qualification, put on a thrilling performance before being edged out. Hibernian midfielder Peter Cormack, one of those brought in at the last minute, was a standout, racing and harrying in midfield, while Eddie Gray and Alan Gilzean were also on fine form. In the third minute Jimmy Johnstone made it 1-0 after keeper Maier was unable to hold a fierce drive from Gray, but the Germans equalised near the end of the half through Fichtel. When ace marksman Gerd Muller put the home side ahead in the 58th minute after a flick-on from fellow striker Uwe Seeler all hopes looked lost, but a masterly header by Gilzean six minutes later restored parity. A draw looked likely before Libuda got a fine goal with 10 minutes left. Two minutes later Tommy Gemmell was badly fouled as he raced in on goal. He got up, delivered a perfectly placed kick to the perpetrator's backside, and was inevitably ordered off.

West Germany: Sepp Maier; Horst-Dieter Hottges, Franz Beckenbauer, Willi Schulz, Berti Vogts; Klaus Fichte, Wolfgang Overath, Helmut Haller; Reinhard Libuda, Uwe Seeler (captain), Gerd Muller. *Trainer:* Helmut Schon.

Scorers: Scotland: Johnstone 3; Gilzean 64

West Germany: Fichtel 37; Muller 58; Libuda 80

FIFA WORLD CUP QUALIFYING GROUP SEVEN

	P	W	D	L	F	A	Pts
West Germany	6	5	1	0	20	3	11
Scotland	6	3	1	2	18	7	7
Austria	6	3	0	3	12	7	6
Cyprus	6	0	0	6	2	35	0

| 5 November 1969 | World Cup qualifying | Prater, Vienna | Attendance: 10,091 |

343 Austria 2, SCOTLAND 0   *Referee: Karlo Kruashvili (Soviet Union)*

Scotland: Ernie McGarr (Aberdeen); John Greig (Rangers), Ron McKinnon (Rangers), Pat Stanton (Hibernian), Francis Burns (Manchester United); Bobby Murdoch (Celtic), Billy Bremner (Leeds United, captain); Charlie Cooke (Chelsea), Alan Gilzean (Tottenham Hotspur), Hugh Curran (Wolverhampton Wanderers), Eddie Gray (Leeds United). *Substitutes:* Peter Lorimer (Leeds United, for Curran 54); Colin Stein (Rangers, for Cooke 72). *Manager:* Bobby Brown.

Austria: Wilhelm Harreither; Helmut Wallner, Gerhard Sturmberger (captain); Johann Schmidradner, Erich Fak, Johann Geyer; Norbert Hof, Johann Ettmayer, Thomas Parits, Robert Kaiser, Helmut Redl. *Substitute:* Josef Hickersberger (for Kaiser 60). *Trainer:* Leopold Stastny.

Scorers: Austria: Redl 15, 52

CHAPTER FIVE
1970-1979

18 April 1970   Home Championship   Windsor Park, Belfast   Attendance: 31,000

344 Northern Ireland 0, SCOTLAND 1
Referee: Eric Jennings (England)

Scotland: Bobby Clark (Aberdeen); David Hay (Celtic), Billy Dickson (Kilmarnock); Frank McLintock (Arsenal, captain), Ron McKinnon (Rangers), Bobby Moncur (Newcastle United); Tommy McLean (Kilmarnock), Willie Carr (Coventry City), John O'Hare (Derby County), Alan Gilzean (Tottenham Hotspur), Willie Johnston (Rangers). *Substitute:* Colin Stein (Rangers, for Gilzean 70). *Manager:* Bobby Brown.

Northern Ireland: Pat Jennings; David Craig, Dave Clements; Sammy Todd, Terry Neill (captain), Jimmy Nicholson; Billy Campbell, Bertie Lutton, Derek Dougan, Eric McMordie, George Best. *Substitutes:* Liam O'Kane (for Todd 46); Desmond Dickson (for Campbell 75). *Manager:* Billy Bingham.

Scorer: Scotland: O'Hare 58

22 April 1970   Home Championship   Hampden Park   Attendance: 30,434

345 SCOTLAND 0, Wales 0
Referee: David Smith (England)

Scotland: Jim Cruickshank (Hearts); Willie Callaghan (Dunfermline Athletic), Billy Dickson (Kilmarnock); John Greig (Rangers, captain), Ron McKinnon (Rangers), Bobby Moncur (Newcastle United); Tommy McLean (Kilmarnock), David Hay (Celtic), John O'Hare (Derby County), Colin Stein (Rangers), Willie Carr (Coventry City). *Substitute:* Bobby Lennox (Celtic, for McLean 70). *Manager:* Bobby Brown.

Wales: Tony Millington; Peter Rodrigues, Rod Thomas; Terry Hennessey (captain), Mike England, Dave Powell; Dick Krzywicki, Alan Durban, Ron Davies, Graham Moore, Ron Rees. *Manager:* Dave Bowen.

25 April 1970   Home Championship   Hampden Park   Attendance: 137,438

346 SCOTLAND 0, England 0
Referee: Gerhard Schulenburg (West Germany)

Scotland: Jim Cruickshank (Hearts); Tommy Gemmell (Celtic), Billy Dickson (Kilmarnock); John Greig (Rangers, captain), Ron McKinnon (Rangers), Bobby Moncur (Newcastle United); Jimmy Johnstone (Celtic), David Hay (Celtic), Colin Stein (Rangers), John O'Hare (Derby County), Willie Carr (Coventry City). *Substitute:* Alan Gilzean (Tottenham Hotspur, for Moncur 82). *Manager:* Bobby Brown.

England: Gordon Banks; Keith Newton, Emlyn Hughes; Nobby Stiles, Brian Labone, Bobby Moore (captain); Peter Thompson, Alan Ball, Jeff Astle, Geoff Hurst, Martin Peters. *Substitute:* Alan Mullery (for Thompson 58). *Manager:* Alf Ramsey.

11 November 1970   European Championship qualifying   Hampden Park   Attendance: 24,618

347 SCOTLAND 1, Denmark 0
Referee: Erich Linemayr (Austria)

Scotland: Jim Cruickshank (Hearts); David Hay (Celtic), John Greig (Rangers); Pat Stanton (Hibernian), Ron McKinnon (Rangers), Bobby Moncur (Newcastle United, captain); Jimmy Johnstone (Celtic), Willie Carr (Coventry City), Colin Stein (Rangers), John O'Hare (Derby County), Willie Johnston (Rangers). *Substitutes:* Peter Cormack (Nottingham Forest, for O'Hare 75); Sandy Jardine (Rangers, for Hay 77). *Manager:* Bobby Brown.

Denmark: Kaj Poulsen; Torben Nielsen, Poul-Henning Frederiksen; Erik Sandvad, Flemming Pedersen, Jens-Jorgen Hansen; Bent Outzen, Kristen Nygaard, Morten Olsen, Keld Pedersen, Benny Nielsen. *Substitute:* Poul-Erik Thygesen (for Olsen 46). *Trainer:* Rudolf Strittich (Austria).

Scorer: Scotland: O'Hare 14

3 February 1971   European Championship qualifying   Stade Sclessin, Liege   Attendance: 13,931

348 Belgium 3, SCOTLAND 0
Referee: Antonio Sbardella (Italy)

Scotland: Jim Cruickshank (Hearts); David Hay (Celtic), John Greig (Rangers), Ron McKinnon (Rangers), Tommy Gemmell (Celtic); Pat Stanton (Hibernian), Bobby Moncur (Newcastle United, captain), Archie Gemmill (Derby County); Charlie Cooke (Chelsea), Colin Stein (Rangers), John O'Hare (Derby County). *Substitutes:* Tony Green (Blackpool, for Stanton 46); Jim Forrest (Aberdeen, for Stein 46). *Manager:* Bobby Brown.

Belgium: Christian Piot; Georges Heylens, Nicolas Dewalque, Jean Plaskie, Jean Thissen; Wilfried Van Moer, Erwin Vandendaele, Leon Semmeling; Henri Depireux, Andre Denul, Paul Van Himst. *Trainer:* Raymond Goethals.

Scorers: Belgium: McKinnon 36 (own goal); Van Himst 55, 83 (pen)

21 April 1971   European Championship qualifying   Estadio de Luz, Lisbon   Attendance: 35,463

349 Portugal 2, SCOTLAND 0
Referee: Michel Kitabjian (France)

Scotland: Bobby Clark (Aberdeen); David Hay (Celtic), Ron McKinnon (Rangers), Bobby Moncur (Newcastle United, captain), Jim Brogan (Celtic); Pat Stanton (Hibernian), Davie Robb (Aberdeen), Peter Cormack (Nottingham Forest); Willie Henderson (Rangers), Jim McCalliog (Wolverhampton Wanderers), Alan Gilzean (Tottenham Hotspur). *Substitutes:* Drew Jarvie (Airdrie, for McCalliog 63); Tony Green (Blackpool, for Stanton 75). *Manager:* Bobby Brown.

Portugal: Vitor Damas; Malta Da Silva, Humberto Coelho; Jose Carlos, Adolfo Calisto, Rui Rodrigues; Fernando Peres, Antonio Simoes, Tamagnini Nene, Vitor Baptista, Eusebio. *Substitutes:* Artur Jorge (for Baptista 76); Fernando Neves (for Nene 86). *Trainer:* Jose Gomes da Silva.

Scorers: Portugal: Stanton 22 (own goal); Eusebio 82

— 69 —

15 May 1971   Home Championship   Ninian Park, Cardiff   Attendance: 19,068

350   Wales 0, SCOTLAND 0
Referee: Jack Taylor (England)

Scotland: Bobby Clark (Aberdeen); David Hay (Celtic), Frank McLintock (Arsenal), Bobby Moncur (Newcastle United, captain), Jim Brogan (Celtic); Billy Bremner (Leeds United), Peter Cormack (Nottingham Forest), Davie Robb (Aberdeen); Peter Lorimer (Leeds United), John O'Hare (Derby County), Eddie Gray (Leeds United). *Substitute:* John Greig (Rangers, for Bremner 72). *Manager:* Bobby Brown.

Wales: Gary Sprake; Peter Rodrigues, Glyn James, John Roberts, Rod Thomas; Terry Yorath, Alan Durban, Leighton Phillips; Gil Reece, John Toshack, Ron Davies. *Manager:* Dave Bowen.

18 May 1971   Home Championship   Hampden Park   Attendance: 31,643

351   SCOTLAND 0, Northern Ireland 1
Referee: Clive Thomas (Wales)

Scotland: Bobby Clark (Aberdeen); David Hay (Celtic), Frank McLintock (Arsenal), Bobby Moncur (Newcastle United, captain), Jim Brogan (Celtic); John Greig (Rangers), Tony Green (Blackpool), Eddie Gray (Leeds United); Peter Lorimer (Leeds United), Hugh Curran (Wolverhampton Wanderers), John O'Hare (Derby County). *Substitutes:* Drew Jarvie (Airdrie, for O'Hare 46); Frank Munro (Wolverhampton Wanderers, for McLintock 71). *Manager:* Bobby Brown.

Northern Ireland: Pat Jennings; Pat Rice, Liam O'Kane, Allan Hunter, Sammy Nelson; Jimmy Nicholson, Bryan Hamilton, Eric McMordie; Dave Clements, Derek Dougan, George Best. *Substitute:* David Craig (for McMordie 67). *Manager:* Billy Bingham.

Scorer: Northern Ireland: Greig 14 (own goal)

22 May 1971   Home Championship   Wembley, London   Attendance: 91,469

352   England 3, SCOTLAND 1
Referee: Jef Dorpmans (Netherlands)

Scotland: Bobby Clark (Aberdeen); John Greig (Rangers), Frank McLintock (Arsenal), Bobby Moncur (Newcastle United, captain), Jim Brogan (Celtic); Billy Bremner (Leeds United), Tony Green (Blackpool), Peter Cormack (Nottingham Forest); Jimmy Johnstone (Celtic), Davie Robb (Aberdeen), Hugh Curran (Wolverhampton Wanderers). *Substitutes:* Frank Munro (Wolverhampton Wanderers, for Curran 46); Drew Jarvie (Airdrie, for Green 82). *Manager:* Bobby Brown.

England: Gordon Banks; Chris Lawler, Roy McFarland, Bobby Moore (captain), Terry Cooper; Alan Ball, Peter Storey, Martin Peters; Francis Lee, Geoff Hurst, Martin Chivers. *Substitute:* Allan Clarke (for Lee 73). *Manager:* Alf Ramsey.

Scorers: England: Peters 9; Chivers 30, 40   Scotland: Curran 11

9 June 1971   European Championship qualifying   Idraetsparken, Copenhagen   Attendance: 37,682

353   Denmark 1, SCOTLAND 0
Referee: Wolfgang Riedel (East Germany)

Scotland: Bobby Clark (Aberdeen); Frank Munro (Wolverhampton Wanderers), Ron McKinnon (Rangers), Bobby Moncur (Newcastle United, captain), Billy Dickson (Kilmarnock); Pat Stanton (Hibernian), Tom Forsyth (Motherwell); Tommy McLean (Kilmarnock), Jim Forrest (Aberdeen), Colin Stein (Rangers), Hugh Curran (Wolverhampton Wanderers). *Substitutes:* Davie Robb (Aberdeen, for Forsyth 46); Jocky Scott (Dundee, for Forrest 70). *Manager:* Bobby Brown.

Denmark: Erik Sorensen; Torben Nielsen, Mogens Berg; Preben Arentoft, Jorgen Rasmussen, Kersten Bjerre; Finn Laudrup, Ole Bjornmose, Ulrik Le Fevre, Benny Nielsen, Jorgen Kristensen. *Substitutes:* Keld Pedersen (for Benny Nielsen 46); Bent Outzen (for Laudrup 75). *Trainer:* Rudolf Strittich (Austria).

Scorer: Denmark: Laudrup 44

Manager Tommy Docherty with the two goalkeepers in his squad, Bobby Clark (left) and Bob Wilson.

Chapter five: 1970-1979

| 14 June 1971 | Friendly | Lenin Stadion, Moscow | Attendance: 20,000 |

354 Soviet Union 1, SCOTLAND 0

Referee: Ferdinand Marschall (Austria)

Scotland: Bobby Clark (Aberdeen); John Brownlie (Hibernian), Frank Munro (Wolverhampton Wanderers), Ron McKinnon (Rangers), Billy Dickson (Kilmarnock); Pat Stanton (Hibernian), Bobby Watson (Motherwell), Davie Robb (Aberdeen); Jim Forrest (Aberdeen), Colin Stein (Rangers), Jocky Scott (Dundee). *Substitute:* Hugh Curran (Wolverhampton Wanderers, for Stein 71). *Manager:* Bobby Brown.

Soviet Union: Yevgeni Rudakov; Iurij Istomin, Albert Shesternev (captain), Viktor Matvienko, Vladimir Kaplichni; Victor Kolotov, Anatolij Konkov, Givi Nodija; Vladimir Fedotov, Vitalij Shevchenko, Gennadij Yevryuzhikhin. *Substitutes:* Vitalij Khmelnitski (for Yevryuzhikhin 46); Nikolai Dolgov (for Nodija 70). *Trainer:* Vladimir Nikolaev.

Scorer: Soviet Union: Yevryuzhikhin 24

| 13 October 1971 | European Championship qualifying | Hampden Park | Attendance: 58,612 |

355 SCOTLAND 2, Portugal 1

Referee: Bruno Piotrowicz (Poland)

Scotland (4-4-2):

1 Bob Wilson (Arsenal);
2 Sandy Jardine (Rangers)
10 Pat Stanton (Hibernian);
3 Eddie Colquhoun (Sheffield United)
9 David Hay (Celtic);
26 Billy Bremner (Leeds United, captain)
2 Archie Gemmill (Derby County)
1 George Graham (Arsenal)
1 Alex Cropley (Hibernian);
13 Jimmy Johnstone (Celtic)
8 John O'Hare (Derby County)

Substitute: 1 Martin Buchan (Aberdeen, for Colquhoun 60)

Manager: Tommy Docherty

Having already lost to Denmark and Portugal in the qualifying tournament, interim manager Tommy Docherty's task was to get the team playing to their potential. That was the case in his first match as the Hampden roar returned with an excellent win over the Portuguese, who again included the legendary Eusebio in their line-up. It was the Derby County pair John O'Hare and Archie Gemmill who were on the score sheet, the former netting a header halfway through the opening half. Rodrigues equalised for Portugal in the 57th minute but the game had hardly restarted when Gemmill restored the lead, winning a header in the box as he reached the ball just before the advancing keeper. There were several other fine performances for Docherty's first game in charge, including new keeper Bob Wilson, centre back Pat Stanton and his Hibs team mate Alex Cropley.

Portugal: Vitor Damas; Malta da Silva, Francisco Calo; Rui Rodrigues, Adolfo Calisto, Jaime Graca; Rolando Goncalves, Antonio Simoes, Tamagnini Nene, Vitor Baptista, Eusebio. *Substitutes:* Artur Jorge (for Eusebio 46); Fernando Perez (for Calo 66). *Trainer:* Jose da Silva.

Scorers: Scotland: O'Hare 23; Gemmill 58   Portugal: Rodrigues 57

| 10 November 1971 | European Championship qualifying | Pittodrie, Aberdeen | Attendance: 36,500 |

356 SCOTLAND 1, Belgium 0

Referee: Einar Bostrom (Sweden)

Scotland (4-3-3):

10 Bobby Clark (Aberdeen);
3 Sandy Jardine (Rangers)
11 Pat Stanton (Hibernian);
2 Martin Buchan (Aberdeen)
10 David Hay (Celtic);
27 Billy Bremner (Leeds United, captain)
1 Steve Murray (Aberdeen)
2 Alex Cropley (Hibernian);
14 Jimmy Johnstone (Celtic)
9 John O'Hare (Derby County)
7 Eddie Gray (Leeds United)

Substitutes: 1 Kenny Dalglish (Celtic, for Cropley 48);
1 John Hansen (Partick Thistle, for Johnstone 79)

Manager: Tommy Docherty

The Scots recorded their second consecutive win under Tommy Docherty, who was officially confirmed as manager a few days later, with a very competent display against group winners Belgium. The match saw the debut of Kenny Dalglish of Celtic, who was to go on and gain a record number of caps, as he replaced Alex Cropley off the bench in the second half. John O'Hare got the only goal in the sixth minute, flicking home a cross after magical wing play from Jimmy Johnstone. There were several other fine performances including full back Sandy Jardine, who marked the dangerous Paul Van Himst out of the game, Pat Stanton and Martin Buchan in central defence, midfielders Billy Bremner and Steve Murray and Eddie Gray on the left flank.

Belgium: Christian Piot; Georges Heylens, Nicolas Dewalque, Andre Stassart, Leon Dolmans; Wilfried Van Moer, Erwin Vandensaele, Wilfried Puis; Leon Semmeling, Johan Devrindt, Paul Van Himst. *Substitutes:* Maurice Martens (for Van Moer 57); Raoul Lambert (for Puis 69). *Trainer:* Raymond Goethals.

Scorer: Scotland: O'Hare 6

EUROPEAN CHAMPIONSHIP QUALIFYING
GROUP FIVE

	P	W	D	L	F	A	Pts
Belgium	6	4	1	1	11	3	9
Portugal	6	3	1	2	10	6	7
Scotland	6	3	0	4	4	7	6
Denmark	6	1	0	5	2	11	2

| 1 December 1971 | Friendly | Olympisch Stadion, Amsterdam | Attendance: 18,000 |

357 Netherlands 2, SCOTLAND 1

Referee: Ferdinand Biwersi (West Germany)

Scotland: Bob Wilson (Arsenal); Sandy Jardine (Rangers), Pat Stanton (Hibernian), Eddie Colquhoun (Sheffield United), David Hay (Celtic); Billy Bremner (Leeds United, captain), Archie Gemmill (Derby County), George Graham (Arsenal); Jimmy Johnstone (Celtic), Kenny Dalglish (Celtic), Eddie Gray (Leeds United). *Substitutes:* John O'Hare (Derby County, for Johnstone 56); Peter Cormack (Nottingham Forest, for Gray 84). *Manager:* Tommy Docherty.

Netherlands: Piet Schrijvers; Hans Venneker, Barry Hulshoff, Rinus Israel, Ruud Krol; Johan Neeskens, Wim van Hanegem, Henk Wery; Theo Pahlplatz, Johan Cruyff (captain), Piet Keizer. *Substitutes:* Wim Jansen (for Wery 46); Gerri Muhren (for Keizer 46). *Trainer:* Frantisek Fadrhonc (Czechoslovakia).

Scorers: Netherlands: Cruyff 5; Hulshoff 87   Scotland: Graham 58

| 26 April 1972 | Friendly | Hampden Park | Attendance: 21,001 |

358 SCOTLAND 2, Peru 0
Referee: Pat Partridge (England)

Scotland: Ally Hunter (Kilmarnock); John Brownlie (Hibernian), Billy McNeill (Celtic), Bobby Moncur (Newcastle United), Willie Donachie (Manchester City); Willie Carr (Coventry City), Asa Hartford (West Bromwich Albion), Archie Gemmill (Derby County); Willie Morgan (Manchester United), John O'Hare (Derby County), Denis Law (Manchester United, captain). *Manager:* Tommy Docherty.

Peru: Manuel Uribe; Rodolfo Manzo, Jose Velasquez, Hector Chumpitaz, Antonio Trigueros; Ramon Mifflin, Alfredo Quesada, Juan Munante; Teofilo Cubillas, Percy Rojas, Juan Orbegozo. *Substitute:* Hugo Sotil (for Rojas 46). *Trainer:* Lajos Baroti (Hungary).

Scorers: Scotland: O'Hare 47; Law 65

| 20 May 1972 | Home Championship | Hampden Park* | Attendance: 39,710 |

359 SCOTLAND 2, Northern Ireland 0
Referee: Clive Thomas (Wales)

Scotland: Bobby Clark (Aberdeen); John Brownlie (Hibernian), Billy McNeill (Celtic), Bobby Moncur (Newcastle United), Willie Donachie (Manchester City); Billy Bremner (Leeds United, captain), Archie Gemmill (Derby County), George Graham (Arsenal); Jimmy Johnstone (Celtic), John O'Hare (Derby County), Denis Law (Manchester United). *Substitute:* Peter Lorimer (Leeds United, for Johnstone 61). *Manager:* Tommy Docherty.

Northern Ireland: Pat Jennings; Pat Rice, Terry Neill (captain), Allan Hunter, Sammy Nelson; Dave Clements, Danny Hegan, Eric McMordie; Tommy Jackson, Willie Irvine, Derek Dougan. *Substitutes:* Sammy McIlroy (for McMordie 68); David Craig (for Clements 83). *Manager:* Terry Neill.

Scorers: Scotland: Law 86; Lorimer 89

*The tie should have been played in Belfast but was switched to Glasgow because of the troubles in Northern Ireland. That remained the case until 1980 when the match returned to Windsor Park.

| 25 May 1972 | Home Championship | Hampden Park | Attendance: 21,332 |

360 SCOTLAND 1, Wales 0
Referee: James Lawther (Northern Ireland)

Scotland: Bobby Clark (Aberdeen); Pat Stanton (Hibernian), Billy McNeill (Celtic), Bobby Moncur (Newcastle United), Martin Buchan (Manchester United); Billy Bremner (Leeds United, captain), Archie Gemmill (Derby County), Tony Green (Newcastle United); Peter Lorimer (Leeds United), John O'Hare (Derby County), Denis Law (Manchester United). *Substitutes:* Asa Hartford (West Bromwich Albion, for Gemmill 35); Lou Macari (Celtic, for O'Hare 56). *Manager:* Tommy Docherty.

Wales: Gary Sprake; Malcolm Page, Terry Hennessey (captain), Mike England, Rod Thomas; Terry Yorath, Alan Durban, Leighton Phillips; Gil Reece, Wyn Davies, Ron Davies. *Substitute:* Leighton James (for Hennessey 74). *Manager:* Dave Bowen.

Scorer: Scotland: Lorimer 72

| 27 May 1972 | Home Championship | Hampden Park | Attendance: 119,325 |

361 SCOTLAND 0, England 1
Referee: Sergio Gonella (Italy)

Scotland: Bobby Clark (Aberdeen); John Brownlie (Hibernian), Billy McNeill (Celtic), Bobby Moncur (Newcastle United), Willie Donachie (Manchester City); Billy Bremner (Leeds United, captain), Archie Gemmill (Derby County), Asa Hartford (West Bromwich Albion); Peter Lorimer (Leeds United), Denis Law (Manchester United), Lou Macari (Celtic). *Substitutes:* Jimmy Johnstone (Celtic, for Gemmill 49); Tony Green (Newcastle United, for Donachie 74). *Manager:* Tommy Docherty.

England: Gordon Banks; Paul Madeley, Roy McFarland, Bobby Moore (captain), Emlyn Hughes; Alan Ball, Colin Bell, Norman Hunter, Peter Storey; Rodney Marsh, Martin Chivers. *Substitute:* Malcolm MacDonald (for Marsh 84). *Manager:* Alf Ramsey.

Scorer: England: Ball 28

| 29 June 1972 | Brazilian Independence Cup (final group stage) | Belo Horizonte | Attendance: 4,000 |

362 Yugoslavia 2, SCOTLAND 2
Referee: Angel Coerezza (Argentina)

Scotland (4-3-3):
- 2 Ally Hunter (Kilmarnock);
- 1 Alex Forsyth (Partick Thistle)
- 5 Eddie Colquhoun (Sheffield United)
- 4 Martin Buchan (Manchester United)
- 4 Willie Donachie (Manchester City);
- 32 Billy Bremner (Leeds United, captain)
- 4 Asa Hartford (West Bromwich Albion)
- 4 George Graham (Arsenal);
- 8 Willie Morgan (Manchester United)
- 47 Denis Law (Manchester United)
- 3 Lou Macari (Celtic)

Substitutes: 2 John Hansen (Partick Thistle, for Forsyth 46); 1 Jimmy Bone (Norwich City, for Law 76)

Manager: Tommy Docherty

Yugoslavia: Rizah Meskovic; Petar Krivokuca, Miroslav Boskovic, Miroslav Pavlovic, Blagoje Paunovic; Josip Katalinski, Danilo Popivoda, Branko Oblak; Jovan Acimovic, Dusan Bajevic, Dragan Dzajic. *Substitutes:* Slobodan Santrac (for Boskovic 38); Jure Jerkovic (for Paunovic 46). *Trainer:* Vujadin Boskov.

Scorers: Scotland: Macari 40, 64   Yugoslavia: Bajevic 61; Jerkovic 86

A late goal by Yugoslavia denied Scotland a win in their opening match of the Brazilian Independence Cup. As one of the European entrants the Scots were automatically in the final group stage where the other members were Czechoslovakia and the host country. Lou Macari, playing up front with Denis Law, opened the scoring in the 40th minute but the Yugoslavs equalised through the dangerous Dusan Bajevic after the break. Within three minutes Macari restored the lead and with Scotland appearing well in command they gained a penalty when substitute Jimmy Bone was fouled. Unfortunately Willie Morgan, who had set up both Macari's goals, saw his shot saved. Then with just four minutes left substitute Jure Jerkovic struck to salvage a point for his side. The second match against the Czechs ended goal-less and in the final deciding game Jairzinho's goal put Brazil through as group winners and consigned Scotland to third place.

BRAZILIAN INDEPENDENCE CUP FINAL STAGES – GROUP A

	P	W	D	L	F	A	Pts
Brazil	3	2	1	0	4	0	5
Yugoslavia	3	1	1	1	4	6	3
Scotland	3	0	2	1	2	3	2
Czechoslovakia	3	0	2	1	1	2	2

Chapter five: 1970-1979

2 July 1972　　Brazilian Independence Cup (final group stage)　　Porto Alegre　　Attendance: 15,000

363　Czechoslovakia 0, SCOTLAND 0
Referee: Armando Marquez (Brazil)

Scotland: Bobby Clark (Aberdeen); Alex Forsyth (Partick Thistle), Eddie Colquhoun (Sheffield United), Martin Buchan (Manchester United), Willie Donachie (Manchester City); Billy Bremner (Leeds United, captain), Asa Hartford (West Bromwich Albion), George Graham (Arsenal); Willie Morgan (Manchester United), Denis Law (Manchester United), Lou Macari (Celtic). *Substitute:* Colin Stein (Rangers, for Law 78). *Manager:* Tommy Docherty.

Czechoslovakia: Ivo Viktor; Karol Dobias, Ludevit Zlocha, Vladimir Hagara, Jan Pivarnik; Jan Medvid, Ladislav Kuna, Jaroslav Pollak; Vladimir Terneny, Jozef Adamec, Dusan Kabat. *Substitutes:* Jan Capkovic (for Kabat 60); Anton Hrusecky (for Terneny 70). *Trainers:* Ladislav Novak and Ladislav Kacani.

5 July 1972　　Brazilian Independence Cup (final group stage)　　Maracana, Rio de Janeiro　　Attendance: 130,000

364　Brazil 1, SCOTLAND 0
Referee: Abraham Klein (Israel)

Scotland: Bobby Clark (Aberdeen); Alex Forsyth (Partick Thistle), Eddie Colquhoun (Sheffield United), Martin Buchan (Manchester United), Willie Donachie (Manchester City); Billy Bremner (Leeds United, captain), Asa Hartford (West Bromwich Albion), George Graham (Arsenal); Willie Morgan (Manchester United), Denis Law (Manchester United), Lou Macari (Celtic). *Manager:* Tommy Docherty.

Brazil: Emerson Leao; Ze Maria, Brito, Vantuir, Marco Antonio; Clodoaldo, Gerson, Rivelino; Tostao, Leivinha, Jairzinho. *Substitute:* Dario (for Leivinha 63). *Coach:* Mario Zagallo.

Scorer: Jairzinho 80

18 October 1972　　World Cup qualifying　　Idraetsparken, Copenhagen　　Attendance: 31,200

365　Denmark 1, SCOTLAND 4
Referee: Tofik Bakhramov (Soviet Union)

Scotland: Bobby Clark (Aberdeen); John Brownlie (Hibernian), Eddie Colquhoun (Sheffield United), Martin Buchan (Manchester United), Alex Forsyth (Partick Thistle); Billy Bremner (Leeds United, captain), George Graham (Arsenal), Lou Macari (Celtic); Peter Lorimer (Leeds United), Jimmy Bone (Norwich City), Willie Morgan (Manchester United). *Substitutes:* Joe Harper (Aberdeen, for Bone 65); Kenny Dalglish (Celtic, for Macari 88). *Manager:* Tommy Docherty.

Denmark: Mogens Therkildsen; Torben Nielsen, Henning Munk-Jensen, Per Rontved (captain), Flemming Ahlberg; John Steen Olsen, Jack Hansen, Ole Bjornmose; Finn Laudrup, Eigil Nielsen, Henning Jensen. *Substitute:* Bent Jensen (for Hansen 58). *Coach:* Rudolf Strittich (Austria).

Scorers:　Scotland: Macari 17; Bone 19; Harper 80; Morgan 83　　Denmark: Laudrup 28

15 November 1972　　World Cup qualifying　　Hampden Park　　Attendance: 47,109

366　SCOTLAND 2, Denmark 0
Referee: Charles Corver (Netherlands)

Scotland (4-2-4):

1　David Harvey (Leeds United);
6　John Brownlie (Hibernian)
8　Martin Buchan (Manchester United)
10　Eddie Colquhoun (Sheffield United)
7　Willie Donachie (Manchester City);
36　Billy Bremner (Leeds United, captain)
8　George Graham (Arsenal);
8　Peter Lorimer (Leeds United)
4　Kenny Dalglish (Celtic)
3　Joe Harper (Aberdeen)
12　Willie Morgan (Manchester United)

Substitute: 6　Willie Carr (Coventry, for Dalglish 75)

Manager: Tommy Docherty

Having opened up the 10th World Cup qualifying campaign with an excellent 4-1 win in Denmark, the Scots completed the double with a fairly routine two-goal victory. An early goal by Kenny Dalglish set the tone, following a corner kick with Eddie Colquhoun and George Graham both involved. Scotland had to wait until the 48th minute to make the game safe, Peter Lorimer finishing off a pass from Dalglish, but rarely in the match was keeper David Harvey troubled. A bit of late drama saw Lorimer sent off for retaliating after a hacking tackle by Per Rontved. The Dane also received his marching orders. The victory set up Scotland nicely for the home and away matches with Czechoslovakia which would ultimately decide the group winners.

Denmark: Mogens Therkildsen; Flemming Ahlberg, Henning Munk-Jensen, Per Rontved, Johnny Hansen; Allan Michaelsen, John Olsen; Kersten Bjerre (captain), Jorgen Kristensen, Bent Jensen, Ulrik Le Fevre. *Substitutes:* Heinz Hildebrandt (for Thekildsen 46); Finn Laudrup (for Kristensen 73). *Trainer:* Rudolf Strittich (Austria).

Scorers:　Scotland: Dalglish 2; Lorimer 48

Action from the Brazilian Independence Cup match against the home side. From left: Tostao (Brazil), George Graham, Leivinha (Brazil), Martin Buchan and referee Abraham Klein.

| 14 February 1973 | Friendly (100th centenary) | Hampden Park | Attendance: 48,470 |

367 SCOTLAND 0, England 5   *Referee: Robert Wurstz (France)*

Scotland (4-2-4):
- 17 Bobby Clark (Aberdeen);
- 5   Alex Forsyth (Manchester United)
- 11 Eddie Colquhoun (Sheffield United)
- 9   Martin Buchan (Manchester United)
- 8   Willie Donachie (Manchester City);
- 37 Billy Bremner (Leeds United, captain)
- 9   George Graham (Manchester United);
- 9   Peter Lorimer (Leeds United)
- 5   Kenny Dalglish (Celtic)
- 7   Lou Macari (Manchester United)
- 13 Willie Morgan (Manchester United)

Substitute: 18 Colin Stein (Rangers, for Morgan 19)
Manager: Willie Ormond

The special match to celebrate the international centenary was one to forget on an icy Hampden surface. It was the worst possible start when Peter Lorimer deflected a harmless looking shot into his own net in the sixth minute, and from there on England simply adapted to the conditions better. Their three-pronged attack of Mick Channon, Alan Clarke and Martin Chivers took full advantage of hesitant defending and found the net four times between them. The Scots did play well at times and could have scored two or three times themselves had it not been for either bad luck or brilliant goalkeeping from Peter Shilton.

England: Peter Shilton; Paul Madeley, Peter Storey, Bobby Moore (captain), Emlyn Hughes; Alan Ball, Colin Bell, Martin Peters; Mick Channon, Martin Chivers, Allan Clarke. *Manager:* Alf Ramsey.

Scorers: England: Lorimer 6 (own goal); Clarke 12, 85; Channon 15; Chivers 76

| 12 May 1973 | Home Championship | The Racecourse, Wrexham | Attendance: 18,682 |

368 Wales 0, SCOTLAND 2   *Referee: James Lawther (Northern Ireland)*

Scotland: Peter McCloy (Rangers); Danny McGrain (Celtic), Jim Holton (Manchester United), Derek Johnstone (Rangers), Willie Donachie (Manchester City); Pat Stanton (Hibernian, captain), George Graham (Manchester United), David Hay (Celtic); Willie Morgan (Manchester United), Kenny Dalglish (Celtic), Derek Parlane (Rangers). *Substitutes:* Colin Stein (Coventry City, for Parlane 80); Lou Macari (Manchester United, for Dalglish 84). *Manager:* Willie Ormond.

Wales: Gary Sprake; Peter Rodrigues, Mike England (captain), John Roberts, Rod Thomas; Trevor Hockey, Terry Yorath, Brian Evans; John Mahoney, John Toshack, Leighton James. *Substitutes:* Wyn Davies (for Yorath 69); Peter O'Sullivan (for Evans 78). *Manager:* Dave Bowen.

Scorer: Scotland: Graham 18, 80

| 16 May 1973 | Home Championship | Hampden Park | Attendance: 39,018 |

369 SCOTLAND 1, Northern Ireland 2   *Referee: Kenneth Burns (England)*

Scotland: Peter McCloy (Rangers); Danny McGrain (Celtic), Jim Holton (Manchester United), Derek Johnstone (Rangers), Willie Donachie (Manchester City); Pat Stanton (Hibernian, captain), George Graham (Manchester United), David Hay (Celtic); Willie Morgan (Manchester United), Colin Stein (Coventry City), Kenny Dalglish (Celtic). *Substitutes:* Billy Bremner (Leeds United, for Stanton 50); Lou Macari (Manchester United, for Graham 77). *Manager:* Willie Ormond.

Northern Ireland: Pat Jennings; Pat Rice, Terry Neill (captain), Allan Hunter, David Craig; Dave Clements, Martin O'Neill, Bryan Hamilton; Tommy Jackson, Sammy Morgan, Trevor Anderson. *Substitute:* Bertie Lutton (for Anderson 65). *Manager:* Terry Neill.

Scorers: Northern Ireland: O'Neill 3; Anderson 17   Scotland: Dalglish 89

| 19 May 1973 | Home Championship | Wembley, London | Attendance: 95,950 |

370 England 1, SCOTLAND 0   *Referee: Kurt Tschenscher (West Germany)*

Scotland: Ally Hunter (Celtic); Sandy Jardine (Rangers), Jim Holton (Manchester United), Derek Johnstone (Rangers), Danny McGrain (Celtic); Billy Bremner (Leeds United, captain), Lou Macari (Manchester United), David Hay (Celtic); Peter Lorimer (Leeds United), Kenny Dalglish (Celtic), Willie Morgan (Manchester United). *Substitutes:* Joe Jordan (Leeds United, for Macari 74); Colin Stein (Coventry City, for Lorimer 80). *Manager:* Willie Ormond.

England: Peter Shilton; Peter Storey, Roy McFarland, Bobby Moore (captain), Emlyn Hughes; Alan Ball, Colin Bell, Martin Peters; Mick Channon, Martin Chivers, Allan Clarke. *Manager:* Alf Ramsey.

Scorer: England: Peters 55

| 22 June 1973 | Friendly | Wankdorf Stadion, Berne | Attendance: 10,000 |

371 Switzerland 1, SCOTLAND 0   *Referee: Achille Verbeke (France)*

Scotland: Peter McCloy (Rangers); Sandy Jardine (Rangers), Jim Holton (Manchester United), Derek Johnstone (Rangers), Danny McGrain (Celtic); Billy Bremner (Leeds United, captain), David Hay (Celtic), Kenny Dalglish (Celtic), Willie Morgan (Manchester United), Derek Parlane (Rangers), John Connolly (Everton). *Substitute:* Joe Jordan (Leeds United, for Connolly 46). *Manager:* Willie Ormond.

Switzerland: Erich Burgener; Walter Mundschin, Jean-Yves Valentini, Peter Ramseier, Rene Hasler; Karl Odermatt (captain), Jakob Kuhn, Rolf Blattler; Walter Balmer, Fernand Luisier, Otto Demarmels. *Substitutes:* Rene-Pierre Quentin (for Blattler 25); Uli Wegmann (for Ramseier 46). *Trainer:* Rene Hussy.

Scorer: Switzerland: Mundschin 62

30 June 1973 Friendly Hampden Park Attendance: 78,181

372 SCOTLAND 0, Brazil 1
Referee: Kenneth Burns (England)

Scotland: Peter McCloy (Rangers); Sandy Jardine (Rangers), Jim Holton (Manchester United), Derek Johnstone (Rangers), Danny McGrain (Celtic); Billy Bremner (Leeds United, captain), David Hay (Celtic), Kenny Dalglish (Celtic); Willie Morgan (Manchester United), Joe Jordan (Leeds United), Derek Parlane (Rangers). *Substitute:* George Graham (Manchester United, for Dalglish 70). *Manager:* Willie Ormond.

Brazil: Emerson Leao; Luis Pereira, Wilson Piazza (captain), Ze Maria, Marco Antonio; Clodoaldo, Paolo Cesar Lima, Rivelino; Valdomiro, Jairzinho, Dirceu. *Trainer:* Mario Zagallo.

Scorer: Brazil: Johnstone 33 (own goal)

---

26 September 1973 World Cup qualifying Hampden Park Attendance: 95,786

373 SCOTLAND 2, Czechoslovakia 1
Referee: Henry Oberg (Norway)

Scotland (4-3-3):

4 Ally Hunter (Celtic);
8 Sandy Jardine (Rangers),
6 Jim Holton (Manchester United),
1 George Connelly (Celtic),
6 Danny McGrain (Celtic);
42 Billy Bremner (Leeds United, captain),
17 David Hay (Celtic),
1 Tommy Hutchison (Coventry City);
19 Willie Morgan (Manchester United),
11 Kenny Dalglish (Celtic),
50 Denis Law (Manchester City)

Substitute: 4 Joe Jordan (Leeds United, for Dalglish 63)

Manager: Willie Ormond

A night to cap all nights at the old stadium saw Scotland qualify for the World Cup finals in Germany, reaching the tournament for the first time since 1958. Having gone a goal behind in the 33rd minute, the Scots replied quickly with a Jim Holton header from a corner kick. The corner had been won by Denis Law, who had been brought back into the side for his 50th appearance and displayed an all-action performance. In the second half Scotland piled on the pressure, but it took until the 75th minute before the magical moment arrived. A free kick ended with Billy Bremner hitting the post and the ball rolling across the line and apparently to safety, but Willie Morgan turned it back across goal and substitute Joe Jordan headed home. Great scenes after the match saw Bremner raised aloft by his team mates, with a German adventure beckoning the following year.

Czechoslovakia: Ivo Viktor; Jan Pivarnik, Vaclav Samek, Ludovit Zlocha, Jaroslav Bendl; Premysl Bicovsky, Antonin Panenka, Ladislav Kuna (captain); Jozef Adamec, Zdenek Nehoda, Pavel Stratil. *Substitutes:* Karel Dobias (for Kuna 21); Jan Capkovic (for Panenka 78). *Trainer:* Vaclav Jezek.

Scorers: Czechoslovakia: Nehoda 33 Scotland: Holton 40; Jordan 75

FIFA WORLD CUP QUALIFYING FINAL STAGES – GROUP A

	P	W	D	L	F	A	Pts
Scotland	4	3	0	1	8	3	6
Czechoslovakia	4	2	1	1	9	3	5
Denmark	4	0	1	3	2	13	1

Captain Billy Bremner is held aloft by his team mates after the win over Czechoslovakia which made sure of qualification for the 1974 World Cup. From left: Willie Morgan, Joe Jordan, Danny McGrain, Tommy Hutchison, Denis Law, Sandy Jardine, Jim Holton, Ally Hunter and Kenny Dalglish.

---

17 October 1973 World Cup qualifying Tehelne Pole Stadion, Bratislava Attendance: 15,000

374 Czechoslovakia 1, SCOTLAND 0
Referee: Ferdinand Biwerski (West Germany)

Scotland: David Harvey (Leeds United); Sandy Jardine (Rangers), Tom Forsyth (Rangers), John Blackley (Hibernian), Danny McGrain (Celtic); Kenny Dalglish (Celtic), David Hay (Celtic), Tommy Hutchison (Coventry City); Willie Morgan (Manchester United), Joe Jordan (Leeds United), Denis Law (Manchester City). *Substitute:* Donald Ford (Hearts, for Law 58). *Manager:* Willie Ormond.

Czechoslovakia: Ivo Viktor (captain); Jan Pivarnik, Vaclav Samek, Karel Dvorak, Vladimir Hagara; Premysl Bicovski, Jaroslav Pollak, Miroslav Gajdusek; Frantisek Vesely, Zdenek Nehoda, Jan Capkovic. *Substitutes:* Jiri Klement (for Vesely 61); Antonin Panenka (for Capkovic 78). *Trainer:* Vaclav Jezek.

Scorer: Czechoslovakia: Nehoda 17 (pen)

| 14 November 1973 | Friendly | Hampden Park | Attendance: 58,235 |

375 SCOTLAND 1, West Germany 1
Referee: Jack Taylor (England)

Scotland: David Harvey (Leeds United); Sandy Jardine (Rangers), Jim Holton (Manchester United), George Connelly (Celtic), Danny McGrain (Celtic); Billy Bremner (Leeds United, captain), Kenny Dalglish (Celtic), Jimmy Smith (Newcastle United); Willie Morgan (Manchester United), Denis Law (Manchester City), Tommy Hutchison (Coventry City). *Substitutes:* Peter Lorimer (Leeds United, for Smith 81); Joe Jordan (Leeds United, for Law 87). *Manager:* Willie Ormond.

West Germany: Wolfgang Kleff; Berti Vogts, Horst-Dieter Hottges, Franz Beckenbauer (captain), Wolfgang Weber; Uli Hoeness, Gunter Netzer, Herbert Wimmer; Jurgen Grabowski, Sigi Held, Erwin Kremers. *Substitutes:* Sepp Maier (for Kleff 46); Josef Heynckes (for Kremers 46); Bernhard Cullmann (for Wimmer 75); Heinz Flohe (for Held 75). *Trainer:* Helmut Schon.

Scorers: Scotland: Holton 7   West Germany: Hoeness 80

| 27 March 1974 | Friendly | Wald Stadion, Frankfurt | Attendance: 62,000 |

376 West Germany 2, SCOTLAND 1
Referee: Paul Schiller (Austria)

Scotland: Thomson Allan (Dundee); Sandy Jardine (Rangers), Kenny Burns (Birmingham City), Martin Buchan (Manchester United), Erich Schaedler (Hibernian); Pat Stanton (Hibernian), David Hay (Celtic, captain), Tommy Hutchison (Coventry City); Willie Morgan (Manchester United), Kenny Dalglish (Celtic), Denis Law (Manchester City). *Substitutes:* Donald Ford (Hearts, for Law 59); Bobby Robinson (Dundee, for Burns 59). *Manager:* Willie Ormond.

West Germany: Sepp Maier; Berti Vogts, Georg Schwartzenbeck, Franz Beckenbauer (captain), Paul Breitner; Bernhard Cullmann, Uli Hoeness, Herbert Wimmer; Jurgen Grabowski, Gerd Muller, Dieter Hertzog. *Trainer:* Helmut Schon.

Scorers: West Germany: Breitner 33 (pen); Grabowski 35   Scotland: Dalglish 77

| 11 May 1974 | Home Championship | Hampden Park | Attendance: 53,775 |

377 SCOTLAND 0, Northern Ireland 1
Referee: Iorwerth Price-Jones (Wales)

Scotland: David Harvey (Leeds United); Sandy Jardine (Rangers), Jim Holton (Manchester United), Martin Buchan (Manchester United), Willie Donachie (Manchester City); Billy Bremner (Leeds United, captain), David Hay (Celtic), Tommy Hutchison (Coventry City); Willie Morgan (Manchester United), Kenny Dalglish (Celtic), Denis Law (Manchester City). *Substitutes:* Jimmy Smith (Newcastle United, for Donachie 46); Joe Jordan (Leeds United, for Law 65). *Manager:* Willie Ormond.

Northern Ireland: Pat Jennings; Pat Rice, Liam O'Kane, Allan Hunter, Sammy Nelson; Bryan Hamilton, Dave Clements (captain), Sammy Morgan; Sammy McIlroy, Tommy Cassidy, Chris McGrath. *Substitute:* Tommy Jackson (for Hamilton 48). *Manager:* Terry Neill.

Scorer: Northern Ireland: Cassidy 40

| 14 May 1974 | Home Championship | Hampden Park | Attendance: 41,969 |

378 SCOTLAND 2, Wales 0
Referee: Malcolm Wright (Northern Ireland)

Scotland: David Harvey (Leeds United); Sandy Jardine (Rangers), Jim Holton (Manchester United), Martin Buchan (Manchester United), David Hay (Celtic); Billy Bremner (Leeds United, captain), Kenny Dalglish (Celtic), Tommy Hutchison (Coventry City); Jimmy Johnstone (Celtic), Joe Jordan (Leeds United), Donald Ford (Hearts). *Substitutes:* Jimmy Smith (Newcastle United, for Hutchison 6); Danny McGrain (Celtic, for Buchan 76). *Manager:* Willie Ormond.

Wales: Gary Sprake; Rod Thomas, John Roberts, Dave Roberts, Malcolm Page; John Mahoney, Terry Yorath, Tony Villars; Gil Reece, Les Cartwright, Leighton James. *Substitute:* David Smallman (for Reece 46). *Manager:* Dave Bowen.

Scorers: Scotland: Dalglish 24; Jardine 44 (pen)

| 18 May 1974 | Home Championship | Hampden Park | Attendance: 94,487 |

379 SCOTLAND 2, England 0
Referee: Leonardus van der Kroft (Netherlands)

Scotland (4-3-3):

6   David Harvey (Leeds United);
14 Sandy Jardine (Rangers)
10 Jim Holton (Manchester United)
2   John Blackley (Hibernian)
10 Danny McGrain (Celtic);
46 Billy Bremner (Leeds United, captain)
22 David Hay (Celtic)
17 Kenny Dalglish (Celtic);
19 Jimmy Johnstone (Celtic)
9   Joe Jordan (Leeds United)
12 Peter Lorimer (Leeds United)

Manager: Willie Ormond

A victory over the "auld enemy" was just what the doctor ordered, with the World Cup in Germany only a month away. Joe Jordan got the opening goal in the fifth minute and Scotland were never seriously in trouble after that. When Colin Todd put through his own goal just after half an hour the result was pretty much secure. Sweeper John Blackley, stepping in to replace the injured Martin Buchan, took to the role with aplomb, David Hay was an inspiration in midfield, as was captain Billy Bremner, full backs Sandy Jardine and Danny McGrain excelled and Jimmy Johnstone was at his exciting best on the wing. With just two more friendly matches to come against Belgium and Norway, the sights began to turn to the big stuff in June.

England: Peter Shilton; David Nish, Norman Hunter, Colin Todd, Mike Pejic; Emlyn Hughes (captain), Colin Bell, Martin Peters; Mick Channon, Frank Worthington, Keith Weller. *Substitutes:* Dave Watson (for Hunter 46); Malcolm MacDonald (for Worthington 70). *Manager:* Joe Mercer.

Scorers: Scotland: Jordan 5; Todd (own goal) 31

Chapter five: 1970-1979

| 1 June 1974 | Friendly | Klokke Stadion, Bruges | Attendance: 7,769 |

380 Belgium 2, SCOTLAND 1
Referee: Klaus Ohmsen (West Germany)

Scotland: David Harvey (Leeds United); Sandy Jardine (Rangers), Gordon McQueen (Leeds United), John Blackley (Hibernian), Danny McGrain (Celtic); Billy Bremner (Leeds United, captain), David Hay (Celtic), Kenny Dalglish (Celtic); Jimmy Johnstone (Celtic), Joe Jordan (Leeds United), Peter Lorimer (Leeds United). *Substitutes:* Willie Morgan (Manchester United, for Johnstone 69); Tommy Hutchison (Coventry City, for Dalglish 80). *Manager:* Willie Ormond.

Belgium: Christian Piot; Gilbert Van Binst, Nicolas Dewalque, Erwin Vandendaele, Maurice Martens; Wilfried Van Moer, Jan Verheyen, Ivo Van Herp; Roger Henrotay, Paul Van Himst (captain), Raoul Lambert. *Substitutes:* Jean Thissen (for Dewalque 40); Julien Cools (for Henrotay 68). *Trainer:* Raymond Goethals.

Scorers: Belgium: Henrotay 23; Lambert 83 (pen)   Scotland: Johnstone 41

| 6 June 1974 | Friendly | Ullevaal Stadion, Oslo | Attendance: 18,432 |

381 Norway 1, SCOTLAND 2
Referee: Arne Axelsson (Sweden)

Scotland: Thomson Allan (Dundee); Sandy Jardine (Rangers), Jim Holton (Manchester United), Martin Buchan (Manchester United), Danny McGrain (Celtic); Billy Bremner (Leeds United, captain), David Hay (Celtic), Tommy Hutchison (Coventry City); Jimmy Johnstone (Celtic), Joe Jordan (Leeds United), Peter Lorimer (Leeds United). *Substitute:* Kenny Dalglish (Celtic, for Johnstone 70). *Manager:* Willie Ormond.

Norway: Gier Karlsen; Oystein Wormdahl, Jan Birkelund, Tore Kordahl, Svein Grondalen; Harald Berg, Tor-Egil Johansen, Svein Kvia (captain); Helge Skuseth, Tom Lund, Harry Hestad. *Substitute:* Stein Thunberg (for Berg 70). *Trainer:* George Curtis (England).

Scorers: Norway: Lund 19   Scotland: Jordan 74; Dalglish 86

| 14 June 1974 | FIFA World Cup (group stages) | Westfalen, Dortmund | Attendance: 25,800 |

382 Zaire 0, SCOTLAND 2
Referee: Gerhard Schulenburg (West Germany)

Scotland (4-3-3):
8   David Harvey (Leeds United);
17 Sandy Jardine (Rangers)
12 Jim Holton (Manchester United)
4   John Blackley (Hibernian)
13 Danny McGrain (Celtic);
49 Billy Bremner (Leeds United, captain)
25 David Hay (Celtic)
20 Kenny Dalglish (Celtic);
15 Peter Lorimer (Leeds United)
12 Joe Jordan (Leeds United)
55 Denis Law (Manchester City)

Substitute: 9 Tommy Hutchison (Coventry City, for Dalglish 75)

Manager: Willie Ormond

A "win but no wild celebrations" ran the newspaper headline, and it was indeed a disappointing start to the tournament. The African champions' all-round ability was much better than expected, while the Scottish players appeared to take their collective foot off the gas after the victory was in the bag. The first goal was a routine one – Danny McGrain's cross was flicked on by Joe Jordan and Peter Lorimer volleyed the ball home – and seven minutes later it was two. This time captain Billy Bremner clipped in a free kick and with the Zaire players crowding round the dangerous Jim Holton, Jordan found himself in a clear position to head home. There were several chances in the second half to increase the lead further but competent defending and some excellent saves by keeper Kazadi kept the score at 2-0. Would goal difference come back to haunt the Scots? Denis Law, on his final appearance, moved ahead of George Young's previous record of 54 caps.

Zaire: Mwamba Kazadi; Ilungu Mwepu, Mwanza Mukombo, Tshimen Buhanga, Boba Lobilo; Massamba Kilasu, Mulamba N'Daye, Mantantu Kidumu (captain); Mabwene Mana, Maku Mayanga, Etepe Kalolo. *Substitutes:* Uba Kembo (for Mayanga 64); Mafu Kibonge (for Kidumu 75). *Trainer:* Blagoje Vidinic (Yugoslavia).

Scorers: Scotland: Lorimer 26, Jordan 33

The team before the opening 1974 World Cup game against Zaire. Back (from left): David Harvey, Jim Holton, Joe Jordan, Danny McGrain, John Blackley. Front: Kenny Dalglish, Sandy Jardine, Peter Lorimer, Billy Bremner, David Hay, Denis Law.

| 18 June 1974 | FIFA World Cup (group stages) | Waldstadion, Frankfurt | Attendance: 62,000 |

383 Brazil 0, SCOTLAND 0

Referee: Arie van Gemert (Netherlands)

Scotland (4-3-3):
9 David Harvey (Leeds United);
18 Sandy Jardine (Rangers)
13 Jim Holton (Manchester United)
14 Martin Buchan (Manchester United)
14 Danny McGrain (Celtic);
50 Billy Bremner (Leeds United, captain)
26 David Hay (Celtic)
21 Kenny Dalglish (Celtic);
25 Willie Morgan (Manchester United)
13 Joe Jordan (Leeds United)
16 Peter Lorimer (Leeds United)
Manager: Willie Ormond

It was a travesty that the Scots did not get more than a point against the reigning world champions, as Brazil appeared a shadow of the thrilling 1970 side. Poor refereeing by the Dutch official was said to be a factor, allowing the Brazilians to get away with blatant fouling, but missed chances – Billy Bremner incredibly from about six inches – were really the downfall. No-one in the Scottish side looked out of place at this level, from goalkeeper David Harvey and the stylish Martin Buchan, to David Hay and the magnificent Bremner in midfield, winning his 50th cap, who held their own in a fierce area of the ground. Manager Willie Ormond praised his players, suggesting that Rivelino should have been ordered off when he fouled three Scots after being booked, while the Brazilian great Pele, watching from the stands, criticised his countrymen for not being able to keep their cool. With goal difference now looking to play a part, only a victory against Yugoslavia in the final group two match would likely suffice.

Brazil: Emerson Leao; Nelinho, Luis Pereira, Mario Perez, Francisco Marinho; Wilson Piazza (captain), Roberto Rivelino; Jairzinho, Leivinha, Mirandinha, Paolo Cesar Lima. *Substitutes:* Paulo Cesar Carpegiani (for Leivinha 66). *Trainer:* Mario Zagallo.

| 22 June 1974 | FIFA World Cup (group stages) | Waldstadion, Frankfurt | Attendance: 54,000 |

384 Yugoslavia 1, SCOTLAND 1

Referee: Alfonso Gonzalez (Mexico)

Scotland (4-3-3):
10 David Harvey (Leeds United);
19 Sandy Jardine (Rangers)
14 Jim Holton (Manchester United)
15 Martin Buchan (Manchester United)
15 Danny McGrain (Celtic);
51 Billy Bremner (Leeds United, captain)
27 David Hay (Celtic)
22 Kenny Dalglish (Celtic);
26 Willie Morgan (Manchester United)
14 Joe Jordan (Leeds United)
17 Peter Lorimer (Leeds United)
Substitute: 10 Tommy Hutchison (Coventry City, for Dalglish 65)
Manager: Willie Ormond

Of all the glorious failures over the years the events in West Germany in 1974 must be at the top. Scotland missed making the knockout stages on goal difference, ended up the only unbeaten side in the entire competition, and conceded just one goal in three matches. Try as they may they could not overcome the Yugoslavs, and when Karasi scored against the run of play in the 83rd minute it was all but over. Joe Jordan's late equaliser gave a glimmer of hope but it was only that – and the players headed home with their heads high. Many of them received lavish praise including keeper David Harvey, full backs Sandy Jardine and Danny McGrain, Jim Holton and Martin Buchan in central defence, and captain Billy Bremner and David Hay in midfield. There is no doubt it was a great experience for players and supporters alike, but sadly a case of "what may have been".

Yugoslavia: Enver Maric; Ivan Buljan, Enver Hadziabdic, Brando Oblak, Josip Katalinski; Vladislav Bogicevic, Ilija Petkovic, Jovan Acimovic; Dusan Bajevic, Ivan Surjak, Dragan Dzajic (captain). *Substitute:* Stanislav Karasi (for Bajevic 72). *Selection committee:* Milan Miljanic, Milan Ribar, Sulejman Rebac, Tomislav Ivic and Milovan Ciric.

Scorers: Yugoslovia: Karasi 83   Scotland: Jordan 89

1974 FIFA WORLD CUP GROUP TWO

	P	W	D	L	F	A	Pts
Yugoslavia	3	1	2	0	10	1	4
Brazil	3	1	2	0	3	0	4
Scotland	3	1	2	0	3	1	4
Zaire	3	0	0	3	0	14	0

| 30 October 1974 | Friendly | Hampden Park | Attendance: 39,445 |

385 SCOTLAND 3, East Germany 0

Referee: Jack Taylor (England)

Scotland: David Harvey (Leeds United); Sandy Jardine (Rangers, captain), Jim Holton (Manchester United), Martin Buchan (Manchester United), Alex Forsyth (Manchester United); Kenny Dalglish (Celtic), Graeme Souness (Middlesbrough), Tommy Hutchison (Coventry City); Jimmy Johnstone (Celtic), Joe Jordan (Leeds United), John "Dixie" Deans (Celtic). *Substitutes:* Kenny Burns (Birmingham City, for Holton 12); Derek Johnstone (Rangers, for Dalglish 86). *Manager:* Willie Ormond.

East Germany: Jurgen Croy; Bernhard Bransch (captain), Gerhard Kische, Konrad Weise, Siegmar Watzlich; Lothar Kurbjuweit, Reinhard Hafner, Reinhard Lauck; Hans-Jurgen Kreische, Jurgen Sparwasser, Martin Hoffmann. *Substitutes:* Manfred Zapf (for Bransch 38); Harald Irmscher (for Kurbjuweit 56); Joachim Streich (for Lauck 73). *Trainer:* Georg Buschner.

Scorers: Scotland: Hutchison 34 (pen); Burns 36; Dalglish 75

| 20 November 1974 | European Championship qualifying | Hampden Park | Attendance: 94,331 |

386 SCOTLAND 1, Spain 2

Referee: Erich Linemayr (Austria)

Scotland: David Harvey (Leeds United); Sandy Jardine (Rangers), Gordon McQueen (Leeds United), Kenny Burns (Birmingham City), Alex Forsyth (Manchester United); Billy Bremner (Leeds United, captain), Graeme Souness (Middlesbrough), Tommy Hutchison (Coventry City); Jimmy Johnstone (Celtic), Joe Jordan (Leeds United), John "Dixie" Deans (Celtic). *Substitutes:* Kenny Dalglish (Celtic, for Hutchison 65); Peter Lorimer (Leeds United, for Deans 65). *Manager:* Willie Ormond.

Spain: Jose Iribar; Angel Castellanos, Gregorio Benito, Jose Capon, Miguel Bianqueti; Enrique Costas, Roberto Martinez, Angel Villar, Carlos Rexach (captain), Javier Planas, Enrique Castro. *Substitute:* Juan Sol (for Bianqueti 75). *Trainer:* Ladislao Kubala.

Scorers: Scotland: Bremner 11   Spain: Castro 36, 61

Chapter five: 1970-1979

5 February 1975 European Championship qualifying Estadio Luis Casanova, Valencia Attendance: 40,952

387 Spain 1, SCOTLAND 1
Referee: Alfred Delcourt (Belgium)

Scotland: David Harvey (Leeds United); Sandy Jardine (Rangers), Gordon McQueen (Leeds United), Martin Buchan (Manchester United), Danny McGrain (Celtic); Charlie Cooke (Chelsea), Billy Bremner (Leeds United, captain), Kenny Burns (Birmingham City), Tommy Hutchison (Coventry City); Kenny Dalglish (Celtic), Joe Jordan (Leeds United). *Substitutes:* Derek Parlane (Rangers, for Jordan 66); Paul Wilson (Celtic, for Burns 79). *Manager:* Willie Ormond.

Spain: Jose Iribar; Gregorio Benito, Jose Camacho, Juan Sol, Enrique Costas; Jose Claramunt (captain), Angel Villar, Juan Asensi; Carlos Rexach, Jose Garate, Enrique Castro. *Substitutes:* Alfredo Mejido (for Garate 66); Miguel Bianqueti (for Costas 70). *Trainer:* Ladislao Kubala.

Scorers: Scotland: Jordan 2 Spain: Mejido 67

16 April 1975 Friendly Ullevi Stadion, Gothenburg Attendance: 15,574

388 Sweden 1, SCOTLAND 1
Referee: Svein Thima (Norway)

Scotland: Stewart Kennedy (Rangers); Sandy Jardine (Rangers, captain), Frank Munro (Wolverhampton Wanderers), Colin Jackson (Rangers), Danny McGrain (Celtic); Bobby Robinson (Dundee), Graeme Souness (Middlesbrough), Kenny Dalglish (Celtic); Lou Macari (Manchester United), Derek Parlane (Rangers), Ted MacDougall (Norwich City). *Substitutes:* Derek Johnstone (Rangers, for Macari 54); Billy Hughes (Sunderland, for Souness 54). *Manager:* Willie Ormond.

Sweden: Goran Hagberg; Bjorn Andersson, Kent Karlsson, Bjorn Nordqvist (captain), Jorgen Augustsson; Eine Fredriksson, Conny Torstensson; Ralf Edstrom, Thomas Ahlstrom, Jan Matsson, Thomas Sjoberg. *Substitutes:* Roy Andersson (for Nordqvist 46); Anders Linderoth (for Edstrom 46); Thomas Nordahl (for Ahlstrom 65). *Trainer:* Georg Eriksson.

Scorers: Sweden: Sjoberg 44 Scotland: MacDougall 86

13 May 1975 Friendly Hampden Park Attendance: 34,307

389 SCOTLAND 1, Portugal 0
Referee: Robert Mathewson (England)

Scotland: Stewart Kennedy (Rangers); Sandy Jardine (Rangers, captain); Gordon McQueen (Leeds United), Martin Buchan (Manchester United), Danny McGrain (Celtic); Charlie Cooke (Chelsea), Bruce Rioch (Derby County), Kenny Dalglish (Celtic), Tommy Hutchison (Coventry City); Derek Parlane (Rangers), Ted MacDougall (Norwich City). *Substitutes:* Colin Jackson (Rangers, for Buchan 27); Lou Macari (Manchester United, for Cooke 77); Arthur Duncan (Hibernian, for Rioch 77). *Manager:* Willie Ormond.

Portugal: Vitor Damas; Artur Correia, Humberto Coelho (captain), Carlos Alhinho, Antonio Barras; Octavio Machado, Samuel Fraguito, Antonio Oliveira; Mario Moinhos, Joao Alves, Tamagnini Nene. *Substitutes:* Vitor Pereira (for Alves 66); Fernando Gomes (for Nene 66); Romeu da Silva (for Moinhos 66). *Trainer:* Jose Maria Pedroto.

Scorer: Scotland: Artur 43 (own goal)

17 May 1975 Home Championship Ninian Park, Cardiff Attendance: 23,509

390 Wales 2, SCOTLAND 2
Referee: Malcolm Wright (Northern Ireland)

Scotland: Stewart Kennedy (Rangers); Sandy Jardine (Rangers, captain), Gordon McQueen (Leeds United), Colin Jackson (Rangers), Danny McGrain (Celtic); Bruce Rioch (Derby County), Lou Macari (Manchester United), Kenny Dalglish (Celtic); Derek Parlane (Rangers), Ted MacDougall (Norwich City), Arthur Duncan (Hibernian). *Substitute:* Frank Munro (Wolverhampton Wanderers, for Jackson 77). *Manager:* Willie Ormond.

Wales: Dai Davies; Rod Thomas, Terry Yorath (captain), John Roberts, Malcolm Page; Gil Reece, John Mahoney, Brian Flynn, Leighton Phillips; John Toshack, Leighton James. *Manager:* Mike Smith.

Scorers: Wales: Toshack 28; Flynn 35 Scotland: Jackson 54; Rioch 62

20 May 1975 Home Championship Hampden Park Attendance: 64,696

391 SCOTLAND 3, Northern Ireland 0
Referee: Pat Partridge (England)

Scotland: Stewart Kennedy (Rangers); Sandy Jardine (Rangers, captain), Frank Munro (Wolverhampton Wanderers), Gordon McQueen (Leeds United), Danny McGrain (Celtic); Bobby Robinson (Dundee), Bruce Rioch (Derby County), Kenny Dalglish (Celtic); Derek Parlane (Rangers), Ted MacDougall (Norwich City), Arthur Duncan (Hibernian). *Substitutes:* Alfie Conn (Tottenham Hotspur, for Robinson 76); Alex Forsyth (Manchester United, for Jardine 89). *Manager:* Willie Ormond.

Northern Ireland: Pat Jennings; Pat Rice, Chris Nicholl, Allan Hunter, Liam O'Kane; Dave Clements (captain), Martin O'Neill, Tommy Finney; Tommy Jackson, Derek Spence, Sammy McIlroy. *Substitutes:* Ronnie Blair (for Hunter 83); Trevor Anderson (for O'Neill 87). *Manager:* Dave Clements.

Scorers: Scotland: MacDougall 15; Dalglish 21; Parlane 80

24 May 1975 Home Championship Wembley, London Attendance: 98,241

392 England 5, SCOTLAND 1
Referee: Rudolf Glockner (East Germany)

Scotland: Stewart Kennedy (Rangers); Sandy Jardine (Rangers, captain), Frank Munro (Wolverhampton Wanderers), Gordon McQueen (Leeds United), Danny McGrain (Celtic); Alfie Conn (Tottenham Hotspur), Bruce Rioch (Derby County), Kenny Dalglish (Celtic); Derek Parlane (Rangers), Ted MacDougall (Norwich City), Arthur Duncan (Hibernian). *Substitutes:* Tommy Hutchison (Coventry City, for Duncan 61); Lou Macari (Manchester United, for MacDougall 71). *Manager:* Willie Ormond.

England: Ray Clemence; Steve Whitworth, Colin Todd, Dave Watson, Kevin Beattie; Alan Ball (captain), Colin Bell, Gerry Francis; Mick Channon, Kevin Keegan, David Johnson. *Substitute:* Dave Thomas (for Keegan 85). *Manager:* Don Revie.

Scorers: England: Francis 6, 65; Beattie 8; Bell 40; Johnson 75 Scotland: Rioch 41 (pen)

1 June 1975   European Championship qualifying   23 August Stadionul, Bucharest   Attendance: 52,203

393 Romania 1, SCOTLAND 1
Referee: Ertugrul Gilek (Turkey)

Scotland: Jim Brown (Sheffield United); Danny McGrain (Celtic), Frank Munro (Wolverhampton Wanderers), Gordon McQueen (Leeds United, captain), Alex Forsyth (Manchester United); Bruce Rioch (Derby County), Willie Miller (Aberdeen), Kenny Dalglish (Celtic); Lou Macari (Manchester United), Derek Parlane (Rangers), Arthur Duncan (Hibernian). *Substitutes:* Tommy Hutchison (Coventry City, for Rioch 67); Bobby Robinson (Dundee, for Macari 67). *Manager:* Willie Ormond.

Romania: Necula Raducanu; Florin Cheran, Gabriel Sandu, Alexandru Satmareanu, Teodor Anghelini; Ioan Dumitru, Cornel Dinu (captain), Nicolae Dobrin; Zoltan Crisan, Dudu Georgescu, Mircea Lucescu. *Substitutes:* Ilie Balaci (for Georgescu 37); Attila Kun (for Dobrin 82). *Trainer:* Valentin Stanescu.

Scorers: Romania: Georgescu 22   Scotland: McQueen 89

3 September 1975   European Championship qualifying   Idraetsparken, Copenhagen   Attendance: 40,300

394 Denmark 0, SCOTLAND 1
Referee: Robert Schaut (Belgium)

Scotland: David Harvey (Leeds United); Danny McGrain (Celtic), Gordon McQueen (Leeds United), Martin Buchan (Manchester United), Alex Forsyth (Manchester United); Billy Bremner (Leeds United, captain), Bruce Rioch (Derby County), Tommy Hutchison (Coventry City); Peter Lorimer (Leeds United), Joe Harper (Hibernian), Kenny Dalglish (Celtic). *Substitute:* Arthur Duncan (Hibernian, for Hutchison 71). *Manager:* Willie Ormond.

Denmark: Birger Jensen; Flemming Mortensen, Henning Munk-Jensen, Lars Larsen, Niels Hansen; Ove Bjerg, Ole Bjornmose, Benny Nielsen; Allan Simonsen, Henning Jensen, Ulrik Le Fevre (captain). *Trainer:* Rudolf Strittich (Austria).

Scorer: Scotland: Harper 51

29 October 1975   European Championship qualifying   Hampden Park   Attendance: 48,021

395 SCOTLAND 3, Denmark 1
Referee: Rolf Nyhus (Norway)

Scotland: David Harvey (Leeds United); Danny McGrain (Celtic), John Greig (Rangers, captain), Colin Jackson (Rangers), Stewart Houston (Manchester United); Asa Hartford (Manchester City), Bruce Rioch (Derby County), Archie Gemmill (Derby County); Peter Lorimer (Leeds United), Ted MacDougall (Norwich City), Kenny Dalglish (Celtic). *Substitute:* Derek Parlane (Rangers, for MacDougall 85). *Manager:* Willie Ormond.

Denmark: Benno Larsen; John Andersen, Henning Munk-Jensen (captain), Lars Larsen, Niels Hansen; Johnny Hansen, Heino Hansen, Kristen Nygaard; Niels Sorensen, Lars Barstrup, Jens Kolding. *Substitute:* Frank Nielsen (for Niels Hansen 68). *Trainer:* Rudolf Strittich (Austria).

Scorers: Denmark: Bastrup 21   Scotland: Dalglish 48; Rioch 54; MacDougall 61

17 December 1975   European Championship qualifying   Hampden Park   Attendance: 11,375

396 SCOTLAND 1, Romania 1
Referee: Adolf Prokop (East Germany)

Scotland (4-3-3):
- 9 Jim Cruickshank (Hearts);
- 7 John Brownlie (Hibernian)
- 5 Colin Jackson (Rangers)
- 20 Martin Buchan (Manchester United, captain)
- 12 Willie Donachie (Manchester City);
- 8 Bruce Rioch (Derby County)
- 8 Asa Hartford (Manchester City)
- 9 Archie Gemmill (Derby County);
- 1 John Doyle (Ayr United)
- 1 Andy Gray (Aston Villa)
- 34 Kenny Dalglish (Celtic)

Scotland dominated but were unable to press home their advantage and the result was the same 1-1 draw as in the reverse fixture in Bucharest six months earlier. Having beaten Denmark home and away, it was the defeat at Hampden against Spain which ultimately deprived the Scots of qualification for the final stages. Romania used destructive tactics and John Doyle and Asa Hartford were both under considerable attack. Young Andy Gray up front found little support and Kenny Dalglish was often outmuscled. Bruce Rioch, who scored the opening goal from a free kick in the 39th minute, and Archie Gemmill both battled hard in the middle of the park. In the 73rd minute, however, a rare attack found the Scots short at the back and substitute Crisan stroked the ball home.

Substitutes: 21 Peter Lorimer (Leeds United, for Doyle 73); 7 Ted MacDougall (Norwich City, for Dalglish 73)
Manager: Willie Ormond

Romania: Necula Raducanu; Florin Cheran, Gabriel Sandu, Alexandru Satmareanu, Teodor Anghelini; Mihai Romila, Cornel Dinu (captain), Ladislau Boloni; Mircea Lucescu, Dudu Georgescu, Anghel Iordanescu. *Substitutes:* Iuliu Hajnal (for Romila 58); Zoltan Crisan (for Lucescu 60). *Trainer:* Cornel Dragusin.

Scorers: Scotland: Rioch 39   Romania: Crisan 73

EUROPEAN CHAMPIONSHIP QUALIFYING GROUP FOUR

	P	W	D	L	F	A	Pts
Spain	6	3	3	0	10	6	9
Romania	6	1	5	0	11	6	7
Scotland	6	2	3	1	8	6	7
Denmark	6	0	1	5	3	14	1

7 April 1976   Friendly   Hampden Park   Attendance: 15,531

397 SCOTLAND 1, Switzerland 0
Referee: Pat Partridge (England)

Scotland: Alan Rough (Partick Thistle); Danny McGrain (Celtic), Tom Forsyth (Rangers, captain), John Blackley (Hibernian), Frank Gray (Leeds United); Tommy Craig (Newcastle United), Alex MacDonald (Rangers), Kenny Dalglish (Celtic); Willie Pettigrew (Motherwell), Andy Gray (Aston Villa), Derek Johnstone (Rangers). *Substitutes:* Bobby McKean (Rangers, for Pettigrew 46); Des Bremner (Hibernian, for Dalglish 46). *Manager:* Willie Ormond.

Switzerland: Erich Burgener; Gilbert Guyot, Jorg Stohler, Lucio Bizzini (captain), Pius Fischbach; Rene Hasler, Rene Botteron, Rudolf Elsener; Kurt Muller, Peter Risi, Daniel Jeandupeux. *Substitutes:* Claude Andrey (for Hasler 53); Marc Schnyder (for Elsener 64). *Trainer:* Rene Hussy.

Scorer: Scotland: Pettigrew 2

Chapter five: 1970-1979

6 May 1976   Home Championship   Hampden Park   Attendance: 35,000

398 SCOTLAND 3, Wales 1   *Referee: Malcolm Wright (Northern Ireland)*

Scotland: Alan Rough (Partick Thistle); Danny McGrain (Celtic), Tom Forsyth (Rangers), Colin Jackson (Rangers), Willie Donachie (Manchester City); Archie Gemmill (Derby County, captain), Don Masson (Queens Park Rangers), Bruce Rioch (Derby County); Willie Pettigrew (Motherwell), Joe Jordan (Leeds United), Eddie Gray (Leeds United). *Manager:* Willie Ormond.
Wales: Brian Lloyd; Dave Jones, Dave Roberts, John Roberts, Joey Jones; Carl Harris, Terry Yorath (captain), Arfon Griffiths; Alan Curtis, Peter O'Sullivan, Leighton James. *Substitute:* Les Cartwright (for Harris 46). *Manager:* Mike Smith.
Scorers: Scotland: Pettigrew 38; Rioch 44; Gray 69   Wales: Griffiths 61 (pen)

8 May 1976   Home Championship   Hampden Park   Attendance: 49,897

399 SCOTLAND 3, Northern Ireland 0   *Referee: Thomas Reynolds (Wales)*

Scotland: Alan Rough (Partick Thistle); Danny McGrain (Celtic), Tom Forsyth (Rangers), Colin Jackson (Rangers), Willie Donachie (Manchester City); Archie Gemmill (Derby County, captain), Don Masson (Queen's Park Rangers), Bruce Rioch (Derby County); Kenny Dalglish (Celtic), Joe Jordan (Leeds United), Willie Pettigrew (Motherwell). *Substitutes:* Asa Hartford (Manchester City, for Rioch 56); Derek Johnstone (Rangers, for Pettigrew 66). *Manager:* Willie Ormond.
Northern Ireland: Pat Jennings; Pat Rice, Chris Nicholl, Allan Hunter (captain), Peter Scott; Tommy Finney, Bryan Hamilton, Pat Sharkey; Tommy Cassidy, Sammy McIlroy, Sammy Morgan. *Substitutes:* David McCreery (for Sharkey 61); Derek Spence (for Morgan 85). *Manager:* Dave Clements.
Scorers: Scotland: Gemmill 23; Masson 47; Dalglish 52

15 May 1976   Home Championship   Hampden Park   Attendance: 85,165

400 SCOTLAND 2, England 1   *Referee: Karoly Palotai (Hungary)*

Scotland (4-3-3):
4   Alan Rough (Partick Thistle);
28 Danny McGrain (Celtic)
6   Tom Forsyth (Rangers)
8   Colin Jackson (Rangers)
15 Willie Donachie (Manchester City);
12 Archie Gemmill (Derby County, captain)
3   Don Masson (Queens Park Rangers)
11 Bruce Rioch (Derby County);
37 Kenny Dalglish (Celtic)
20 Joe Jordan (Leeds United)
10 Eddie Gray (Leeds United)

Substitute: 10 Derek Johnstone (Rangers, for Gray 79)

Manager: Willie Ormond

The men in dark blue came from behind to record a deserved victory over England and clinch the Home Championship trophy once more. Mick Channon opened the scoring early on with a fine header but to their credit the Scots did not let their heads go down and the classy Don Masson equalised just seven minutes later. Kenny Dalglish, who had one of his best games for his country, got the winner just after the break when the ball went through the legs of keeper Ray Clemence. Other than those two there were several other excellent displays including full backs Danny McGrain and Willie Donachie, Tom Forsyth in central defence, captain Archie Gemmill and Joe Jordan up front.

England: Ray Clemence; Colin Todd, Phil Thompson, Roy McFarland, Mick Mills; Ray Kennedy, Gerry Francis (captain), Peter Taylor; Kevin Keegan, Mick Channon, Stuart Pearson. *Substitutes:* Trevor Cherry (for Pearson 46); Mike Doyle (for McFarland 70). *Manager:* Don Revie.
Scorers: England: Channon 11   Scotland: Masson 18; Dalglish 49

8 September 1976   Friendly   Hampden Park   Attendance: 16,338

401 SCOTLAND 6, Finland 0   *Referee: Gordon Kew (England)*

Scotland (4-3-3):
5   Alan Rough (Partick Thistle);
29 Danny McGrain (Celtic)
6   Tom Forsyth (Rangers)
21 Martin Buchan (Manchester United)
16 Willie Donachie (Manchester City);
13 Archie Gemmill (Derby County, captain)
4   Don Masson (Queens Park Rangers)
12 Bruce Rioch (Derby County);
38 Kenny Dalglish (Celtic)
3   Andy Gray (Aston Villa)
11 Eddie Gray (Leeds United)

Substitute: 16 David Harvey (Leeds United, for Rough 46)

Manager: Willie Ormond

An eight-match unbeaten run since the 5-1 hammering by England at Wembley was extended to nine with a masterful display against Finland at Hampden Park. Although the visitors were a fairly weak side, it was still a confidence-boosting win before Willie Ormond's men faced a difficult away World Cup qualifier in Czechoslovakia. Bruce Rioch was man of the match with a great performance in midfield, and it was he who opened the scoring in the seventh minute with a spectacular drive. Don Masson made it two with a penalty before Kenny Dalglish and Andy Gray put the Scots out of sight before half-time. Eddie Gray, another who starred, got the goal he deserved in the 68th minute before his namesake Andy finished things off by chesting down and volleying home a Dalglish cross. The only poor aspect of the evening was the disappointing crowd of just over 16,000.

Finland: Pertti Alaja; Teppo Heikkinen, Erkki Vihtila; Ari Makynen, Esko Ranta, Pertti Jantunen; Jouko Suomalainen, Mikka Toivola, Olavi Rissanen, Juha Dahllund, Matti Paatelainen (captain). *Substitutes:* Jyrki Nieminen (for Paatellainen 39); Goram Enckelman (for Alaja 46); Matti Ahonen (for Heikkinen 75). *Trainer:* Aulis Rytkonen.
Scorers: Scotland: Rioch 7; Masson 16 (pen); Dalglish 23; Andy Gray 44, 80; Eddie Gray 68

13 October 1976   World Cup qualifying   Sparta Stadion, Prague   Attendance: 38,000

402 Czechoslovakia 2, SCOTLAND 0
Referee: Alberto Michelotti (Italy)

Scotland: Alan Rough (Partick Thistle); Danny McGrain (Celtic), Martin Buchan (Manchester United), Gordon McQueen (Leeds United), Willie Donachie (Manchester City); Archie Gemmill (Derby County, captain), Don Masson (Queens Park Rangers), Bruce Rioch (Derby County); Kenny Dalglish (Celtic), Andy Gray (Aston Villa), Joe Jordan (Leeds United). *Substitutes:* Kenny Burns (Birmingham City, for Dalglish 56); Asa Hartford (Manchester City, for Masson 68). *Manager:* Willie Ormond.

Czechoslovakia: Alexander Vencel; Patel Biros, Jozef Capkovic, Anton Ondrus (captain), Koloman Gogh; Jaroslav Pollak, Karol Dobias, Antonin Panenka; Marian Masny, Zdenek Nehoda, Ladislav Petras. *Substitutes:* Jan Kozak (for Gogh 13); Ladislav Jurkemik (for Capkovic 68). *Trainer:* Vaclav Jesek.

Scorers: Czechoslovakia: Panenka 46; Petras 48

17 November 1976   World Cup qualifying   Hampden Park   Attendance: 63,233

403 SCOTLAND 1, Wales 0
Referee: Ferdinand Biwerski (West Germany)

Scotland: Alan Rough (Partick Thistle); Danny McGrain (Celtic), John Blackley (Hibernian), Gordon McQueen (Leeds United), Willie Donachie (Manchester City); Archie Gemmill (Derby County, captain), Kenny Burns (Birmingham City), Bruce Rioch (Derby County); Kenny Dalglish (Celtic), Joe Jordan (Leeds United), Eddie Gray (Leeds United). *Substitutes:* Asa Hartford (Manchester City, for Rioch 67); Willie Pettigrew (Motherwell, for Gray 84). *Manager:* Willie Ormond.

Wales: Dai Davies; Malcolm Page, Leighton Phillips, Ian Evans, Joey Jones; Arfon Griffiths, Terry Yorath (captain), Brian Flynn; Mickey Thomas, John Toshack, Leighton James. *Substitute:* Alan Curtis (for James 74). *Manager:* Mike Smith.

Scorer: Scotland: Evans 15 (own goal)

27 April 1977   Friendly   Hampden Park   Attendance: 22,659

404 SCOTLAND 3, Sweden 1
Referee: Jack Taylor (England)

Scotland: Alan Rough (Partick Thistle); Danny McGrain (Celtic), Tom Forsyth (Rangers), John Blackley (Hibernian), Willie Donachie (Manchester City); Ronnie Glavin (Celtic), Kenny Burns (Birmingham City), Asa Hartford (Manchester City); Kenny Dalglish (Celtic, captain), Willie Pettigrew (Motherwell), Willie Johnston (West Bromwich Albion). *Substitutes:* Sandy Jardine (Rangers, for Glavin 58); David Narey (Dundee United, for Blackley 76); Joe Craig (Celtic, for Burns 76). *Manager:* Willie Ormond.

Sweden: Ronnie Hellstrom; Magnus Andersson, Bjorn Andersson, Bjorn Nordqvist (captain), Roy Andersson; Lennart Larsson, Conny Torstensson, Bo Borjesson; Sigvard Johansson, Benny Wendt, Thomas Sjoberg. *Substitutes:* Hasse Borg (for Torstensson 55); Anders Ljungberg (for Borjesson 65); Olle Nordin (for Johansson 71). *Trainer:* Georg Eriksson.

Scorers: Scotland: Hellstrom 30 (own goal); Dalglish 56; Craig 79   Sweden: Wendt 51

28 May 1977   Home Championship   The Racecourse, Wrexham   Attendance: 14,469

405 Wales 0, SCOTLAND 0
Referee: Malcolm Moffat (Northern Ireland)

Scotland: Alan Rough (Partick Thistle); Danny McGrain (Celtic), Tom Forsyth (Rangers), Gordon McQueen (Leeds United), Willie Donachie (Manchester City); Archie Gemmill (Derby County), Don Masson (Queens Park Rangers), Bruce Rioch (Everton, captain), Asa Hartford (Manchester City); Kenny Dalglish (Celtic), Derek Parlane (Rangers). *Substitutes:* Willie Johnston (West Bromwich Albion, for Rioch 65); Kenny Burns (Birmingham City, for Parlane 74). *Manager:* Ally MacLeod.

Wales: Dai Davies; Rod Thomas, Leighton Phillips, Ian Evans, Joey Jones; Peter Sayer, John Mahoney, Terry Yorath (captain), Brian Flynn; Nick Deacy, Leighton James. *Substitute:* Mickey Thomas (for James 67). *Manager:* Mike Smith.

Fans invade the pitch at Wembley after the 2-1 win of 1977. Many souvenirs, either a piece of turf or net, were taken back to Scotland.

| 1 June 1977 | Home Championship | Hampden Park | Attendance: 44,699 |

406 SCOTLAND 3, Northern Ireland 0
Referee: William Gow (Wales)

Scotland: Alan Rough (Partick Thistle); Danny McGrain (Celtic), Tom Forsyth (Rangers), Gordon McQueen (Leeds United), Willie Donachie (Manchester City); Don Masson (Queens Park Rangers), Bruce Rioch (Everton, captain), Asa Hartford (Manchester City); Kenny Dalglish (Celtic), Joe Jordan (Leeds United), Willie Johnston (West Bromwich Albion). *Substitutes:* Lou Macari (Manchester United, for Jordan 69); Archie Gemmill (Derby County, for Johnston 86). *Manager:* Ally MacLeod.

Northern Ireland: Pat Jennings; Jimmy Nicholl, Tommy Jackson, Allan Hunter (captain), Pat Rice; Bryan Hamilton, Martin O'Neill, David McCreery; Sammy McIlroy, Chris McGrath, Trevor Anderson. *Substitute:* Derek Spence (for Anderson 56). *Manager:* Danny Blanchflower.

Scorers: Scotland: Dalglish 37, 79; McQueen 61

| 4 June 1977 | Home Championship | Wembley, London | Attendance: 98,103 |

407 England 1, SCOTLAND 2
Referee: Karoly Palotai (Hungary)

Scotland (4-3-3):

11 Alan Rough (Partick Thistle);
35 Danny McGrain (Celtic)
11 Tom Forsyth (Rangers)
14 Gordon McQueen (Leeds United)
22 Willie Donachie (Manchester City);
8 Don Masson (Queens Park Rangers)
17 Bruce Rioch (Derby County, captain)
15 Asa Hartford (Manchester City);
44 Kenny Dalglish (Celtic)
24 Joe Jordan (Leeds United)
13 Willie Johnston (West Bromwich Albion)

Substitutes: 17 Lou Macari (Manchester United, for Jordan 43);
18 Archie Gemmill (Derby County, for Masson 83)

Manager: Ally MacLeod

Three matches into the managerial reign of Ally MacLeod and a thrilling victory at Wembley clinched the Home Championship for a second successive year. Don Masson of Queen's Park Rangers, a late arrival to the squad, was man of the match as he controlled the spread of play for over an hour. As half-time approached and the Scots well on top, centre back Gordon McQueen headed home Asa Hartford's free kick for a worthy opener. The Scottish fans were in dreamland when, in the 61st minute, Kenny Dalglish got the second. As it turned out, it was Dalglish's second winning goal against the English in succession. A late penalty by Mick Channon took some of the gloss off the victory but it was definitely still one to savour. Spectators thronged on to the pitch at full time, many taking home a souvenir piece of turf or a bit of the net. The spectacle would have been disappointing to the organisers, but it was not unexpected.

England: Ray Clemence; Phil Neal, Emlyn Hughes (captain), Dave Watson, Mick Mills; Brian Greenhoff, Ray Kennedy, Brian Talbot; Mick Channon, Trevor Francis, Stuart Pearson. *Substitutes:* Trevor Cherry (for Greenhoff 57); Dennis Tueart (for Kennedy 67). *Manager:* Don Revie.

Scorers: Scotland: McQueen 43; Dalglish 61   England: Channon 87 (pen)

| 15 June 1977 | Friendly | Estadio Nacional, Santiago | Attendance: 60,000 |

408 Chile 2, SCOTLAND 4
Referee: Juan Silvagno (Chile)

Scotland: Alan Rough (Partick Thistle); Danny McGrain (Celtic), Tom Forsyth (Rangers), Martin Buchan (Manchester United), Willie Donachie (Manchester City); Don Masson (Queens Park Rangers), Bruce Rioch (Everton, captain), Asa Hartford (Manchester City); Lou Macari (Manchester United), Kenny Dalglish (Celtic), Willie Johnston (West Bromwich Albion). *Substitutes:* Jim Stewart (Kilmarnock, for Rough 46); Archie Gemmill (Derby County, for Rioch 46); Sandy Jardine (Rangers, for Hartford 80). *Manager:* Ally MacLeod.

Chile: Adolfo Nef; Juan Machuca, Enzo Escobar, Elias Figueroa, Alberto Quintana; Waldo Quiroz, Eddio Inostroza, Juan Soto; Leonardo Veliz, Rogelio Farias, Hector Pinto. *Substitutes:* Julio Crisosto (for Soto 37); Gustavo Moscoso (for Veliz 79). *Trainer:* Luis Santibanez.

Scorers: Scotland: Dalglish 19; Macari 30, 57; Hartford 37   Chile: Crisosto 49, 72

| 18 June 1977 | Friendly | Estadio Boca Juniors, Buenos Aires | Attendance: 57,000 |

409 Argentina 1, SCOTLAND 1
Referee: Romualdo Filho (Brazil)

Scotland (4-3-3):

13 Alan Rough (Partick Thistle);
37 Danny McGrain (Celtic)
13 Tom Forsyth (Rangers)
24 Martin Buchan (Manchester United, captain)
24 Willie Donachie (Manchester City);
10 Don Masson (Queens Park Rangers)
20 Archie Gemmill (Derby County)
17 Asa Hartford (Manchester City);
19 Lou Macari (Manchester United)
46 Kenny Dalglish (Celtic)
15 Willie Johnston (West Bromwich Albion)

Manager: Ally MacLeod

The second match of the South American tour was marred by an unacceptable display of brutality by a team who would go on to win the World Cup the following year. President of the Argentinian Football Association, Dr Alfredo Cantilo, apologised afterwards, saying he was ashamed by the conduct of some of his country's players. Vicente Pernia, who had fouled Willie Johnston on numerous occasions and spat in his face, elbowed him in the kidneys in the 56th minute and finally received his marching orders. Incredibly, the Brazilian referee also saw fit to dismiss Johnston, which saw the winger leave the field in tears. The goals were both penalties, Don Masson for Scotland in the 77th minute and Daniel Passarella for the hosts four minutes later. The best Scottish performers were Archie Gemmill and Asa Hartford in midfield.

Argentina: Hector Baley; Vicente Pernia, Daniel Killer, Daniel Passarella, Jorge Carrascosa (captain); Osvaldo Ardiles, Americo Gallego, Omar Larrosa; Pedro Gonzalez, Leopoldo Luque, Rene Houseman. *Substitutes:* Alberto Tarantini (for Gonzalez 59); Victor Trossero (for Larrosa 70). *Coach:* Cesar Luis Menotti.

Scorers: Scotland: Masson 77 (pen)   Argentina: Passarella 81 (pen)

| 23 June 1977 | Friendly | Estadio Maracana, Rio de Janeiro | Attendance: 60,763 |

410 Brazil 2, SCOTLAND 0
Referee: Oscar Scolfaro (Brazil)

Scotland: Alan Rough (Partick Thistle); Danny McGrain (Celtic), Tom Forsyth (Rangers), Martin Buchan (Manchester United), Willie Donachie (Manchester City); Don Masson (Queens Park Rangers), Bruce Rioch (Everton, captain), Archie Gemmill (Derby County), Asa Hartford (Manchester City); Kenny Dalglish (Celtic), Willie Johnston (West Bromwich Albion). *Substitute:* Sandy Jardine (Rangers, for Johnston 61). *Manager:* Ally MacLeod.

Brazil: Emerson Leao; Ze Maria, Luis Pereira, Edinho, Francisco Marinho; Paulo Isidoro, Toninho Cerezo, Rivelino (captain); Paulo Cesar Lima, Gil, Reinaldo. *Substitute:* Zico (for Gil 46). *Trainer:* Claudio Coutinho.

Scorers: Brazil: Zico 70; Cerezo 75

| 7 September 1977 | Friendly | Weltjugend Stadion, East Berlin | Attendance: 50,000 |

411 East Germany 1, SCOTLAND 0
Referee: Martin Horbas (Czechoslovakia)

Scotland: David Stewart (Leeds United); Danny McGrain (Celtic), Gordon McQueen (Leeds United), Martin Buchan (Manchester United), Willie Donachie (Manchester City); Don Masson (Queens Park Rangers, captain), Asa Hartford (Manchester City), Lou Macari (Manchester United); Kenny Dalglish (Liverpool), Joe Jordan (Leeds United), Willie Johnston (West Bromwich Albion). *Substitutes:* Arthur Graham (Leeds United, for Johnston 59); Archie Gemmill (Derby County, for Hartford 65). *Manager:* Ally MacLeod.

East Germany: Jurgen Croy; Hans-Jurgen Dorner (captain), Gerhard Kische, Konrad Weise, Gerhard Weber; Reinhard Hafner, Hartmut Schade, Lutz Lindemann, Gerhard Heidler, Jurgen Sparwasser, Joachim Streich. *Substitutes:* Peter Kotte (for Sparwasser 46); Martin Hoffmann (for Streich 46). *Trainer:* Georg Buschner.

Scorer: East Germany: Schade 59

| 21 September 1977 | World Cup qualifying | Hampden Park | Attendance: 85,000 |

412 SCOTLAND 3, Czechoslovakia 1
Referee: Francis Rion (Belgium)

Scotland: Alan Rough (Partick Thistle); Sandy Jardine (Rangers), Tom Forsyth (Rangers), Gordon McQueen (Leeds United), Danny McGrain (Celtic); Don Masson (Queens Park Rangers), Bruce Rioch (Everton, captain), Asa Hartford (Manchester City); Kenny Dalglish (Liverpool), Joe Jordan (Leeds United), Willie Johnston (West Bromwich Albion). *Manager:* Ally MacLeod.

Czechoslovakia: Pavol Michalik; Miroslav Paurik, Jozef Capkovic, Karel Dvorak, Koloman Gogh; Karol Dobias, Jaroslav Pollak (captain), Jozef Moder; Miroslav Gajdusek, Marian Masny, Zdenek Nehoda. *Substitutes:* Lubomir Knapp (for Moder 46); Peter Gallis (for Dobias 69). *Trainer:* Vaclav Jesek.

Scorers: Scotland: Jordan 19; Hartford 35; Dalglish 54   Czechoslovakia: Gajdusek 80

| 12 October 1977 | World Cup qualifying | Anfield, Liverpool | Attendance: 50,850 |

413 Wales 0, SCOTLAND 2
Referee: Robert Wurtz (France)

Scotland (4-3-3):
16 Alan Rough (Partick Thistle);
32 Sandy Jardine (Rangers)
17 Gordon McQueen (Leeds United)
16 Tom Forsyth (Rangers)
27 Willie Donachie (Manchester City);
14 Don Masson (Queens Park Rangers, captain)
21 Asa Hartford (Manchester City)
21 Lou Macari (Manchester United);
50 Kenny Dalglish (Liverpool)
27 Joe Jordan (Leeds United)
19 Willie Johnston (West Bromwich Albion).

Substitute: 27 Martin Buchan (Manchester United, for Jardine 57)

Manager: Ally MacLeod

Wales: Dai Davies; Rod Thomas, Dave Jones, Leighton Phillips, Joey Jones; John Mahoney, Terry Yorath (captain), Brian Flynn; Peter Sayer, John Toshack, Mickey Thomas. *Substitute:* Nick Deacy (for Sayer 75). *Manager:* Mike Smith.

Scorers: Scotland: Masson 79 (pen); Dalglish 87

"Que, sera, sera, we're going to Argentine" sang the tartan hordes as Scotland saw off Wales in Liverpool to reach the second World Cup finals in a row. The result was in doubt, however, until 12 minutes from the end when Wales conceded an unfortunate penalty. Dave Jones was judged to have handled in the box under pressure from Joe Jordan, and although there was a degree of doubt over whose hand had actually touched the ball, Don Masson made an excellent job of converting the spot kick. With time running out the Scots made sure of the result. Substitute Martin Buchan, in unfamiliar territory at right back, provided a cross and Kenny Dalglish scored a flying header at his own club ground to clinch a memorable victory.

FIFA WORLD CUP QUALIFYING GROUP SEVEN

	P	W	D	L	F	A	Pts
Scotland	4	3	0	1	6	3	6
Czechoslovakia	4	2	0	2	4	6	4
Wales	4	1	0	3	3	4	2

| 22 February 1978 | Friendly | Hampden Park | Attendance: 59,524 |

414 SCOTLAND 2, Bulgaria 1
Referee: Pat Partridge (England)

Scotland: Jim Blyth (Coventry City); Stuart Kennedy (Aberdeen), Gordon McQueen (Manchester United), Willie Miller (Aberdeen), Willie Donachie (Manchester City); Archie Gemmill (Nottingham Forest, captain), Graeme Souness (Liverpool), Asa Hartford (Manchester City); Kenny Dalglish (Liverpool), Joe Jordan (Manchester United), Lou Macari (Manchester United). *Substitutes:* Ian Wallace (Coventry City, for Dalglish 65); Derek Johnstone (Rangers, for Jordan 65). *Manager:* Ally MacLeod.

Bulgaria: Stefan Staikov; Plamen Nikolev, Dimitar Enchev, Georgi Bonev, Ivan Iliev; Kantcho Kasherov, Aleksander Ivanov, Georgi Slavkov; Radoslav Zdravkov, Andrei Jeliazkov (captain), Stoicho Mladenov. *Substitute:* Ivan Tishanski (for Slavkov 68). *Trainer:* Tsvetan Ilchev.

Scorers: Bulgaria: Mladenov 8   Scotland: Gemmill 41 (pen); Wallace 85

Chapter five: 1970-1979

| 13 May 1978 | Home Championship | Hampden Park | Attendance: 64,433 |

415 SCOTLAND 1, Northern Ireland 1
Referee: William Gow (Wales)

Scotland: Alan Rough (Partick Thistle); Sandy Jardine (Rangers), Tom Forsyth (Rangers), Gordon McQueen (Manchester United), Martin Buchan (Manchester United); Don Masson (Derby County), Bruce Rioch (Derby County, captain), Archie Gemmill (Nottingham Forest); Derek Johnstone (Rangers), Joe Jordan (Manchester United), John Robertson (Nottingham Forest). *Substitutes:* Kenny Burns (Nottingham Forest, for Buchan 37); Kenny Dalglish (Liverpool, for Jordan 46). *Manager:* Ally MacLeod.

Northern Ireland: Jim Platt; Jimmy Nicholl, Peter Scott, Allan Hunter, David McCreery; Sammy McIlroy, Martin O'Neill, Bryan Hamilton (captain); Chris McGrath, Gerry Armstrong, Trevor Anderson. *Substitutes:* Billy Hamilton (for McGrath 63); Terry Cochrane (for Anderson 77). *Manager:* Danny Blanchflower.

Scorers: Northern Ireland: O'Neill 26 Scotland: Johnstone 36

| 17 May 1978 | Home Championship | Hampden Park | Attendance: 70,241 |

416 SCOTLAND 1, Wales 1
Referee: Malcolm Wright (Northern Ireland)

Scotland: Jim Blyth; Stuart Kennedy (Aberdeen), Kenny Burns (Nottingham Forest), Gordon McQueen (Manchester United), Willie Donachie (Manchester City); Archie Gemmill (Nottingham Forest, captain), Graeme Souness (Liverpool), Asa Hartford (Manchester City); Kenny Dalglish (Liverpool), Derek Johnstone (Rangers), Willie Johnston (West Bromwich Albion). *Substitutes:* Tom Forsyth (Rangers, for McQueen 32); John Robertson (Nottingham Forest, for Johnston 85). *Manager:* Ally MacLeod.

Wales: Dai Davies; Malcolm Page, Leighton Phillips, Dave Roberts, Joey Jones; Carl Harris, John Mahoney, Terry Yorath (captain), Brian Flynn; Phil Dwyer, Alan Curtis. *Substitute:* Nick Deacy (for Page 76). *Manager:* Mike Smith.

Scorers: Scotland: Johnstone 12 Wales: Donachie 89 (own goal)

| 20 May 1978 | Home Championship | Hampden Park | Attendance: 88,319 |

417 SCOTLAND 0, England 1
Referee: Georges Konrath (France)

Scotland: Alan Rough (Partick Thistle); Stuart Kennedy (Aberdeen), Tom Forsyth (Rangers), Kenny Burns (Nottingham Forest), Willie Donachie (Manchester City); Don Masson (Derby County), Bruce Rioch (Derby County, captain), Asa Hartford (Manchester City); Kenny Dalglish (Liverpool), Joe Jordan (Manchester United), Willie Johnston (West Bromwich Albion). *Substitutes:* Graeme Souness (Liverpool, for Rioch 74); Archie Gemmill (Nottingham Forest, for Masson 74). *Manager:* Ally MacLeod.

England: Ray Clemence; Phil Neal, Emlyn Hughes (captain), Dave Watson, Mick Mills; Steve Coppell, Tony Currie, Ray Wilkins, Peter Barnes; Paul Mariner, Trevor Francis. *Substitutes:* Brian Greenhoff (for Hughes 73); Trevor Brooking (for Mariner 76). *Manager:* Ron Greenwood.

Scorer: England: Coppell 83

| 3 June 1978 | FIFA World Cup (group stages) | Chateu Carreras, Cordoba | Attendance: 37,792 |

418 Peru 3, SCOTLAND 1
Referee: Ulf Eriksson (Sweden)

Scotland (4-3-3):
19 Alan Rough (Partick Thistle);
4 Stuart Kennedy (Aberdeen)
20 Tom Forsyth (Rangers)
12 Kenny Burns (Nottingham Forest)
29 Martin Buchan (Manchester United);
17 Don Masson (Queens Park Rangers)
25 Asa Hartford (Manchester City)
23 Bruce Rioch (Derby County, captain);
55 Kenny Dalglish (Liverpool)
31 Joe Jordan (Manchester United)
22 Willie Johnston (West Brom)

Substitutes: 27 Archie Gemmill (Nottingham Forest, for Masson 70); 23 Lou Macari (Manchester United, for Rioch 70)

Manager: Ally MacLeod

Manager Ally MacLeod famously said prior to the tournament: "We might not win the World Cup, but we'll get a medal." His prediction came under considerable pressure after an appalling start by what was a fairly unprepared side. The skill of Munante and in particular Oblitas was simply too much for the inexperienced Stuart Kennedy and the out-of-position Martin Buchan at full backs. It started brightly enough when Joe Jordan scored in the 15th minute, but when the out-of-form Don Masson missed a penalty the writing was on the wall. Just before half-time Cueto got a deserved equaliser and two fabulous strikes from Cubillas in the second half consigned the sorry Scots to defeat. Most of the problems stemmed from midfield where Masson and Bruce Rioch, so impressive during the qualifying campaign, were fairly ineffective.

Peru: Ramon Quiroga; Jaime Huerta, Hector Chumpitaz (captain), Rodolfo Manzo, Ruben Diaz; Jose Velasquez, Cesar Cueto, Teofilio Cubillas; Juan Munante, Guillermo La Rosa, Juan Oblitas. *Substitutes:* Hugo Sotil (for Laguna 62); Percy Rojas (for Cueto 82). *Trainer:* Marcos Calderon.

Scorers: Scotland: Jordan 15 Peru: Cueto 42; Cubillas 71, 77

Keeper Alan Rough blocks a shot against Peru. He was unable to do anything against two superb strikes from Teofilio Cubillas, however, which put the game out of Scotland's reach.

7 June 1978   FIFA World Cup (group stages)   Chateu Carreras, Cordoba   Attendance: 7,938

419 Iran 1, SCOTLAND 1

Referee: Youssouf N'Diaye (Senegal)

Scotland (4-3-3):

20 Alan Rough (Partick Thistle);
34 Sandy Jardine (Rangers)
30 Martin Buchan (Manchester United)
13 Kenny Burns (Nottingham Forest)
31 Willie Donachie (Manchester City);
28 Archie Gemmill (Nottingham Forest, captain)
24 Lou Macari (Manchester United)
26 Asa Hartford (Manchester City);
56 Kenny Dalglish (Liverpool)
32 Joe Jordan (Manchester United)
3   John Robertson (Nottingham Forest)

Substitutes: 21 Tom Forsyth (Rangers, for Buchan 57);
5 Joe Harper (Aberdeen, for Dalglish 73)

Manager: Ally MacLeod

If the defeat by Peru was bad, the shame continued with a hapless display against a team described as the "nobodies of world football". A draw, courtesy of an Iranian own goal, was almost more than the Scots deserved and another early exit from the competition looked almost certain. Manager Ally MacLeod made several changes, one of which was enforced after winger Willie Johnston failed a drugs test and was immediately flown home. Archie Gemmill and Lou Macari started in midfield and both full backs were replaced with Martin Buchan moving to his more familiar central defensive role. The media, meanwhile, asked the question on most supporters' minds: Where was Graham Souness?

Iran: Nasser Hejazi; Hassan Nazari, Nasrollah Abdollahi, Hossein Kazerani, Andranik Eskandarian; Mohammed Sadeghi, Ali Parvin (captain), Ebrahim Ghassempour; Iraj Danaifar, Ghafoor D'jahani, Hossein Faraki. *Substitutes:* Hassan Nayeb-Agha (for Danaifar 80); Hassan Rowshan (for Faraki 83). *Manager:* Heshmat Mohajerani.

Scorers: Scotland: Eskandarian 43 (own goal)   Iran: Danaifar 60

---

11 June 1978   FIFA World Cup (group stages)   San Martin, Mendoza   Attendance: 35,130

420 Netherlands 2, SCOTLAND 3

Referee: Erich Linemayr (Austria)

Scotland (4-4-2):

21 Alan Rough (Partick Thistle);
5   Stuart Kennedy (Aberdeen)
31 Martin Buchan (Manchester United)
22 Tom Forsyth (Rangers)
32 Willie Donachie (Manchester City);
29 Archie Gemmill (Nottingham Forest)
24 Bruce Rioch (Derby County, captain)
7   Graeme Souness (Liverpool)
27 Asa Hartford (Manchester City);
57 Kenny Dalglish (Liverpool)
33 Joe Jordan (Manchester United)

Manager: Ally MacLeod

It was still mathematically possible for Scotland to qualify for the knockout stages, but to do so they would have to beat Netherlands by three clear goals. When Rob Rensenbrink converted a 34th minute penalty the task was made all the more impossible. But what happened after that was sensational, and would live long in the memories of those who witnessed it. With the Scots taking the game to their opponents, Kenny Dalglish grabbed a deserved goal just before the break after Joe Jordan had headed the ball on. Just after the interval the Dutch themselves conceded a penalty and when Archie Gemmill scored a glimmer of hope appeared. Then about halfway through the half came one of the greatest ever World Cup goals. Gemmill received the ball on the right wing, cut inside, dribbled past three players and lifted it past keeper Jongbloed. One more goal would do it. But reality returned and Rep's fantastic long-range effort in the 71st minute flew past Alan Rough and into the net for 3-2. For the second tournament in a row goal difference meant the Scots were out.

Netherlands: Jan Jongbloed; Wim Suurbier, Ruud Krol (captain), Wim Rijsbergen, Jan Poortvliet; Willy van de Kerkhof, Johan Neeskens, Wim Jansen, Rene van de Kerkhof; Johnny Rep, Rob Rensenbrink. *Substitutes:* Johannes Boskamp (for Neeskens 10); Piet Wildschut (for Rijsbergen, 46). *Trainer:* Ernst Happel (Austria).

Scorers: Netherlands: Rensenbrink 34 (pen); Rep 71
Scotland: Dalglish 44; Gemmill 46 (pen), 68

1978 FIFA WORLD CUP GROUP FOUR

	P	W	D	L	F	A	Pts
Peru	3	2	1	0	7	2	5
Netherlands	3	1	1	1	5	3	3
Scotland	3	1	1	1	5	6	3
Iran	3	0	1	2	2	8	1

Archie Gemmill celebrates after his great individual goal against the Netherlands.

---

20 September 1978   European Championship qualifying   Prater Stadion, Vienna   Attendance: 62,281

421 Austria 3, SCOTLAND 2

Referee: Alberto Michelotti (Italy)

Scotland: Alan Rough (Partick Thistle); Stuart Kennedy (Aberdeen), Gordon McQueen (Manchester United), Martin Buchan (Manchester United), Willie Donachie (Manchester City); Archie Gemmill (Nottingham Forest, captain), Graeme Souness (Liverpool), Asa Hartford (Manchester City); Kenny Dalglish (Liverpool), Joe Jordan (Manchester United), Andy Gray (Aston Villa). *Substitute:* Arthur Graham (Leeds United, for Jordan 61). *Manager:* Ally MacLeod.

Austria: Erwin Fuchsbichler; Robert Sara, Erich Obermayer, Heinrich Strasser, Bruno Pezzey; Heribert Weber, Kurt Jara, Herbert Prohaska; Walter Schachner, Wilhelm Kreuz, Hans Krankl. *Substitute:* Franz Oberacher (for Prohaska 87). *Trainer:* Karl Stotz.

Scorers: Austria: Pezzey 27; Schachner 48; Kreuz 64   Scotland: McQueen 65; Gray 77

Chapter five: 1970-1979

25 October 1978   European Championship qualifying   Hampden Park   Attendance: 65,372

422 SCOTLAND 3, Norway 2   *Referee: Vojtech Christov (Czechoslovakia)*

Scotland (4-3-3):
2   Jim Stewart (Middlesbrough);
34 Willie Donachie (Manchester City)
22 Gordon McQueen (Manchester United)
33 Martin Buchan (Manchester United)
2   Frank Gray (Leeds United);
31 Archie Gemmill (Nottingham Forest, captain)
9   Graeme Souness (Liverpool)
29 Asa Hartford (Manchester City);
59 Kenny Dalglish (Liverpool)
6   Andy Gray (Aston Villa)
3   Arthur Graham (Leeds United)
Manager: Jock Stein

Jock Stein, who had replaced Ally MacLeod as manager, was a relieved man after a late penalty by captain Archie Gemmill gave his side full points. Scotland got off to a poor start when defensive frailty led to Einar Aas scoring in only the third minute, but Kenny Dalglish headed home an equaliser on the half-hour mark. Several chances came and went either side of half-time before Arne Larsen-Okland put the visitors ahead again in the 64th minute. However, Dalglish fired home his second following a cute head-flick from Andy Gray and then Gemmill did the business from the spot after Arthur Graham was fouled in the box. Dalglish was the standout Scottish player, not just for his two goals but his all-round excellent display.

Norway: Tom-Rusz Jacobsen; Trond Pedersen, Jan Birkelund, Svein Grondalen, Einar Aas; Tore Kordahl, Tor-Egil Johansen (captain), Svein Mathisen; Tom Jacobsen, Arne Larsen-Okland, Hallvar Thoresen. *Substitutes:* Jan Hansen (for Tom Jacobsen 37); Helge Karlsen (for Pedersen 86). *Trainer:* Tor Roste Fossen.

Scorers: Norway: Aas 3; Larsen-Okland 64   Scotland: Dalglish 30, 82; Gemmill 87 (pen)

29 November 1978   European Championship qualifying   Estadio da Luz, Lisbon   Attendance: 70,000

423 Portugal 1, SCOTLAND 0   *Referee: Ernst Dolflinger (Switzerland)*

Scotland: Alan Rough (Partick Thistle); Stuart Kennedy (Aberdeen), Martin Buchan (Manchester United), Gordon McQueen (Manchester United), Frank Gray (Leeds United); David Narey (Dundee United), Archie Gemmill (Nottingham Forest, captain), Asa Hartford (Manchester City); Kenny Dalglish (Liverpool), Joe Jordan (Manchester United), John Robertson (Nottingham Forest). *Substitutes:* Willie Donachie (Manchester City, for Gray 65); Ian Wallace (Coventry City, for Jordan 78). *Manager:* Jock Stein.

Portugal: Manuel Bento; Artur Correia, Humberto Coelho (captain), Carlos Alhinho, Alberto Fonseca; Minervino Pietra, Antonio Oliveira, Joao Alves; Jose Costa, Tamagnini Nene, Fernando Gomes. *Substitutes:* Sheu Han (for Costa 46); Eurico Gomes (for Oliveira 82). *Trainer:* Mario Wilson.

Scorer: Portugal: Alberto 29

19 May 1979   Home Championship   Ninian Park, Cardiff   Attendance: 20,371

424 Wales 3, SCOTLAND 0   *Referee: Pat Partridge (England)*

Scotland: Alan Rough (Partick Thistle); George Burley (Ipswich Town), Alan Hansen (Liverpool), Paul Hegarty (Dundee United), Frank Gray (Leeds United); John Wark (Ipswich Town), Graeme Souness (Liverpool), Asa Hartford (Manchester City); Kenny Dalglish (Liverpool, captain), Ian Wallace (Coventry City), Arthur Graham (Leeds United). *Substitute:* Joe Jordan (Manchester United, for Wallace 55). *Manager:* Jock Stein.

Wales: Dai Davies; Byron Stevenson, Leighton Phillips, Phil Dwyer, Joey Jones; Robbie James, John Mahoney, Terry Yorath (captain), Brian Flynn; Alan Curtis, John Toshack. *Substitute:* Peter Nicholas (for Yorath 89). *Manager:* Mike Smith.

Scorer: Wales: Toshack 28, 35, 75

22 May 1979   Home Championship   Hampden Park   Attendance: 28,524

425 SCOTLAND 1, Northern Ireland 0   *Referee: Clive Thomas (Wales)*

Scotland: George Wood (Everton); George Burley (Ipswich Town), Gordon McQueen (Manchester United), Paul Hegarty (Dundee United), Frank Gray (Leeds United); John Wark (Ipswich Town), Graeme Souness (Liverpool), Asa Hartford (Manchester City); Kenny Dalglish (Liverpool, captain), Joe Jordan (Manchester United), Arthur Graham (Leeds United). *Substitutes:* David Narey (Dundee United, for Wark 46); Frank McGarvey (Liverpool, for Graham 89). *Manager:* Jock Stein.

Northern Ireland: Pat Jennings; Pat Rice, Jimmy Nicholl, Allan Hunter, Sammy Nelson; Victor Moreland, Bryan Hamilton (captain), Sammy McIlroy; Tommy Sloan, Derek Spence, Gerry Armstrong. *Substitutes:* Peter Scott (for Moreland 62); Billy Caskey (for Spence 77). *Manager:* Danny Blanchflower.

Scorer: Scotland: Graham 76

26 May 1979   Home Championship   Wembley, London   Attendance: 100,000

426 England 3, SCOTLAND 1   *Referee: Antonio Garrido (Portugal)*

Scotland: George Wood (Everton); George Burley (Ipswich Town), Gordon McQueen (Manchester United), Paul Hegarty (Dundee United), Frank Gray (Leeds United); John Wark (Ipswich Town), Graeme Souness (Liverpool), Asa Hartford (Manchester City); Kenny Dalglish (Liverpool, captain), Joe Jordan (Manchester United), Arthur Graham (Leeds United). *Manager:* Jock Stein.

England: Ray Clemence; Phil Neal, Phil Thompson, Dave Watson, Mick Mills; Steve Coppell, Ray Wilkins, Trevor Brooking, Peter Barnes; Kevin Keegan (captain), Bob Latchford. *Manager:* Ron Greenwood.

Scorers: Scotland: Wark 20   England: Barnes 44; Coppell 64; Keegan 70

2 June 1979	Friendly	Hampden Park	Attendance: 61,918

427 SCOTLAND 1, Argentina 3	*Referee: Pat Partridge (England)*

Scotland: Alan Rough (Partick Thistle); George Burley (Ipswich Town), Alan Hansen (Liverpool), Paul Hegarty (Dundee United), Iain Munro (St Mirren); David Narey (Dundee United), John Wark (Ipswich Town), Asa Hartford (Manchester City); Kenny Dalglish (Liverpool, captain), Frank McGarvey (Liverpool), Arthur Graham (Leeds United). *Substitutes:* George Wood (Everton, for Rough 46); Frank Gray (Leeds United, for Hartford 70). *Manager:* Jock Stein.

Argentina: Ubaldo Fillol; Jorge Olguin, Daniel Passarella (captain), Hugo Villaverde, Alberto Tarantini; Juan Barbas, Americo Gallego, Diego Maradona, Jose Valencia; Rene Houseman, Leopoldo Luque. *Substitutes:* Victor Trossero (for Villaverde 21); Norberto Outes (for Houseman 56). *Trainer:* Cesar Luis Menotti.

Scorers: Argentina: Luque 33, 60; Maradona 70   Scotland: Graham 85

7 June 1979	European Championship qualifying	Ullevaal Stadion, Oslo	Attendance: 17,269

428 Norway 0, SCOTLAND 4	*Referee: Ib Nielsen (Denmark)*

Scotland: Alan Rough (Partick Thistle); George Burley (Ipswich Town), Gordon McQueen (Manchester United), Kenny Burns (Nottingham Forest), Iain Munro (St Mirren); Arthur Graham (Leeds United), Archie Gemmill (Nottingham Forest, captain), Asa Hartford (Manchester City), John Robertson (Nottingham Forest); Kenny Dalglish (Liverpool), Joe Jordan (Manchester United). *Substitutes:* Paul Hegarty (Dundee United, for Burley 46); John Wark (Ipswich Town, for Hegarty 70). *Manager:* Jock Stein.

Norway: Tom-Rusz Jacobsen; Trond Pedersen, Helge Karlsen, Svein Grondalen, Einar Aas; Tore Kordahl, Roger Albertsen, Stein Thunberg; Svein Mathisen, Arne Larsen-Okland, Hallvar Thoresen. *Substitutes:* Jan Hansen (for Pedersen 67); Torbjorn Svendsen (for Thunberg 75). *Trainer:* Roste Fossen.

Scorers: Scotland: Jordan 32; Dalglish 39; Robertson 43; McQueen 55

12 September 1979	Friendly	Hampden Park	Attendance: 41,035

429 SCOTLAND 1, Peru 1	*Referee: George Courtney (England)*

Scotland: Alan Rough (Partick Thistle); Sandy Jardine (Rangers, captain), Gordon McQueen (Manchester United), Kenny Burns (Nottingham Forest), Iain Munro (St Mirren); John Wark (Ipswich Town), Graeme Souness (Liverpool), Asa Hartford (Manchester City); Davie Cooper (Rangers), Kenny Dalglish (Liverpool), John Robertson (Nottingham Forest). *Substitutes:* Roy Aitken (Celtic, for Wark 71); Arthur Graham (Leeds United, for Cooper 71). *Manager:* Jock Stein.

Peru: Eusebio Acasuzo; Hugo Gastulo, Jorge Olaechea, Hector Chumpitaz (captain), Toribio Diaz; Robert Mosquera, Jose Velasquez, Cesar Cueto; German Leguia, Ernesto Labarthe, Guillermo La Rosa. *Substitute:* Fredy Ravello (for Labarthe 46). *Trainer:* Jose Chiarella.

Scorers: Scotland: Hartford 4   Peru: Leguia 85

17 October 1979	European Championship qualifying	Hampden Park	Attendance: 67,895

430 SCOTLAND 1, Austria 1	*Referee: Karoly Palotai (Hungary)*

Scotland: Alan Rough (Partick Thistle); Sandy Jardine (Rangers), Gordon McQueen (Manchester United), Kenny Burns (Nottingham Forest), Iain Munro (St Mirren); John Wark (Ipswich Town), Graeme Souness (Liverpool), Archie Gemmill (Birmingham City, captain); Arthur Graham (Leeds United), Kenny Dalglish (Liverpool), John Robertson (Nottingham Forest). *Substitute:* Davie Cooper (Rangers, for Graham 61). *Manager:* Jock Stein.

Austria: Friedrich Koncilia; Robert Sara (captain), Dietmar Mirnegg, Roland Hattenberger, Bruno Pezzey; Heribert Weber, Kurt Jara, Herbert Prohaska; Walter Schachner, Wilhelm Kreuz, Hans Krankl. *Substitutes:* Gerhard Steinkogler (for Schachner 80); Reinhold Hintermaier (for Krankl 89). *Trainer:* Karl Stotz.

Scorers: Austria: Krankl 40   Scotland: Gemmill 75

21 November 1979	European Championship qualifying	Heysel Stadion, Brussels	Attendance: 14,289

431 Belgium 2, SCOTLAND 0	*Referee: Elzar Zade (Soviet Union)*

Scotland: Alan Rough (Partick Thistle); Sandy Jardine (Rangers, captain), Alan Hansen (Liverpool), Willie Miller (Aberdeen), Iain Munro (St Mirren); John Wark (Ipswich Town), Graeme Souness (Liverpool), Asa Hartford (Everton); Kenny Dalglish (Liverpool), Joe Jordan (Manchester United), John Robertson (Nottingham Forest). *Substitutes:* Frank Gray (Nottingham Forest, for Munro 61); Davie Provan (Celtic, for Jordan 61). *Manager:* Jock Stein.

Belgium: Theo Custers; Eric Gerets, Luc Millecamps, Walter Meeuws, Michel Renquin; Julien Cools (captain), Wilfried Van Moer, Rene Vandereycken; Francois Van der Elst, Jan Ceulemans, Eduard Voordeckers. *Substitute:* Rene Verheyen (for Van Moer 66). *Trainer:* Guy Thys.

Scorers: Belgium: Van der Elst 7; Voordeckers 46

19 December 1979	European Championship qualifying	Hampden Park	Attendance: 25,389

432 SCOTLAND 1, Belgium 3	*Referee: Heinz Aldinger (West Germany)*

Scotland: Alan Rough (Partick Thistle); Sandy Jardine (Rangers, captain), Gordon McQueen (Manchester United), Kenny Burns (Nottingham Forest), Danny McGrain (Celtic); Eamonn Bannon (Dundee United), Roy Aitken (Celtic), John Wark (Ipswich Town); Kenny Dalglish (Liverpool), Derek Johnstone (Rangers), John Robertson (Nottingham Forest). *Substitute:* Davie Provan (Celtic, for Bannon 46). *Manager:* Jock Stein.

Belgium: Theo Custers; Eric Gerets, Luc Millecamps, Walter Meeuws, Maurice Martens; Julien Cools (captain), Wilfried Van Moer, Rene Vandereycken; Francois Van der Elst, Jan Ceulemans, Erwin Vandenbergh. *Substitutes:* Gerard Plessers (for Van Moer 49); Guy Dardenne (for Vandenbergh 73). *Trainer:* Guy Thys.

Scorers: Belgium: Vandenbergh 18; Van der Elst 23, 29   Scotland: Robertson 55

CHAPTER SIX
1980-1989

26 March 1980   European Championship qualifying   Hampden Park   Attendance: 20,233

433 SCOTLAND 4, Portugal 1
Referee: Robert Wurtz (France)

Scotland (4-3-3):
- 31 Alan Rough (Partick Thistle);
- 6 George Burley (Ipswich Town)
- 4 Alan Hansen (Liverpool)
- 5 Dave Narey (Dundee United)
- 42 Danny McGrain (Celtic);
- 16 Graeme Souness (Liverpool)
- 1 Alex McLeish (Aberdeen)
- 35 Archie Gemmill (Birmingham City);
- 70 Kenny Dalglish (Liverpool)
- 7 Andy Gray (Wolverhampton Wanderers)
- 10 John Robertson (Nottingham Forest)

Substitutes: 1 Steve Archibald (Aberdeen, for Dalglish 48); 3 Davie Provan (Celtic, for Robertson 75)
Manager: Jock Stein

A fine home win over Portugal completed the qualifying group for the 1980 European Championships in Italy. In a strong group the Scots finished fourth behind qualifiers Belgium, Austria and Portugal, with Norway in last place. The game marked the debut of Aberdeen centre half Alex McLeish, playing in a midfield role, who was to go on to an illustrious Scottish international career and would also become manager. Kenny Dalglish put the Scots ahead after a fine move involving John Robertson and Andy Gray, and Gray himself got the second 20 minutes later. Aberdeen striker Steve Archibald, also making his debut, made the game safe in the 68th minute. Although Portugal pulled one back through Fernando Gomes shortly after, an Archie Gemmill penalty with six minutes remaining cemented an impressive result.

Portugal: Manuel Bento; Adelinho Teixeira, Humberto Coelho (captain), Carlos Simoes, Alberto Fonseca Junior; Antonio Frasco Vieira, Eurico Gomes, Jose Alberto Costa; Tamangini Nene, Fernando Gomes, Rui Jordao. *Substitutes:* Sheu Han (for Eurico Gomes 35; Carlos Manuel dos Santos (for Frasco Vieira 77). *Trainer:* Mario Wilson.

Scorers: Scotland: Dalglish 6; Gray 26; Archibald 68; Gemmill 84 (pen)
Portugal: Fernando Gomes 74

EUROPEAN CHAMPIONSHIP QUALIFYING GROUP TWO

	P	W	D	L	F	A	Pts
Belgium	8	4	4	0	12	5	12
Austria	8	4	3	1	14	7	11
Portugal	8	4	1	3	10	11	9
Scotland	8	3	1	4	15	13	7
Norway	8	0	1	7	5	20	1

---

16 May 1980   Home Championship   Windsor Park, Belfast   Attendance: 18,000

434 Northern Ireland 1, SCOTLAND 0
Referee: Clive Thomas (Wales)

Scotland: Billy Thomson (St Mirren); George Burley (Ipswich Town), David Narey (Dundee United), Alex McLeish (Aberdeen), Danny McGrain (Celtic); Gordon Strachan (Aberdeen), Graeme Souness (Liverpool), Archie Gemmill (Birmingham City, captain), Peter Weir (St Mirren); Kenny Dalglish (Liverpool), Steve Archibald (Tottenham Hotspur). *Substitutes:* Davie Provan (Celtic, for Weir 59); Joe Jordan (Manchester United, for Souness 59). *Manager:* Jock Stein.

Northern Ireland: Jim Platt; Jimmy Nicholl, John O'Neill, Chris Nicholl, Mal Donaghy; Tommy Cassidy, Sammy McIlroy (captain), Noel Brotherston, Tommy Finney; Billy Hamilton, Gerry Armstrong. *Substitutes:* John McClelland (for Hamilton 52); David McCreery (for Cassidy 70). *Manager:* Billy Bingham.

Scorer: Northern Ireland: Hamilton 36

---

21 May 1980   Home Championship   Hampden Park   Attendance: 31,359

435 SCOTLAND 1, Wales 0
Referee: Hugh Wilson (Northern Ireland)

Scotland: Alan Rough (Partick Thistle); Danny McGrain (Celtic), Paul Hegarty (Dundee United), Alex McLeish (Aberdeen), Iain Munro (St Mirren); Gordon Strachan (Aberdeen), Willie Miller (Aberdeen), Archie Gemmill (Birmingham City, captain), Peter Weir (St Mirren); Kenny Dalglish (Liverpool), Joe Jordan (Manchester United). *Substitute:* Roy Aitken (Celtic, for Weir 84). *Manager:* Jock Stein.

Wales: Dai Davies; Paul Price, Terry Yorath (captain), Keith Pontin, Joey Jones; Peter Nicholas, David Giles, Brian Flynn; Mickey Thomas, Ian Walsh, Leighton James. *Substitutes:* Ian Rush (for Walsh 15); Leighton Phillips (for Pontin 46). *Manager:* Mike England.

Scorer: Scotland: Miller 26

---

24 May 1980   Home Championship   Hampden Park   Attendance: 85,000

436 SCOTLAND 0, England 2
Referee: Antonio Garrido (Portugal)

Scotland: Alan Rough (Partick Thistle); Danny McGrain (Celtic), Paul Hegarty (Dundee United), Alex McLeish (Aberdeen), Iain Munro (St Mirren); Gordon Strachan (Aberdeen), Willie Miller (Aberdeen), Roy Aitken (Celtic), Archie Gemmill (Birmingham City, captain); Kenny Dalglish (Liverpool), Joe Jordan (Manchester United). *Substitutes:* Andy Gray (Wolverhampton Wanderers, for Aitken 53); George Burley (Ipswich Town, for Munro 62). *Manager:* Jock Stein.

England: Ray Clemence; Trevor Cherry, Phil Thompson (captain), Dave Watson, Kenny Sansom; Ray Wilkins, Trevor Brooking, Terry McDermott; Steve Coppell, David Johnson, Paul Mariner. *Substitute:* Emlyn Hughes (for Mariner 71). *Manager:* Ron Greenwood.

Scorers: England: Brooking 8; Coppell 75

28 May 1980   Friendly   Warta Stadion, Poznan   Attendance: 20,000

437 Poland 1, SCOTLAND 0
Referee: Ivan Josifov (Bulgaria)

Scotland: Alan Rough (Partick Thistle); George Burley (Ipswich Town), Willie Miller (Aberdeen), Alex McLeish (Aberdeen), Danny McGrain (Celtic, captain); Gordon Strachan (Aberdeen), David Narey (Dundee United), Roy Aitken (Celtic), Kenny Dalglish (Liverpool); Steve Archibald (Tottenham Hotspur), Joe Jordan (Manchester United). *Substitutes:* Alan Brazil (Ipswich Town, for Jordan 46); Peter Weir (St Mirren, for Dalglish 56); Ally Dawson (Rangers, for Burley 80). *Manager:* Jock Stein.

Poland: Piotr Mowlik; Marek Dziuba, Hieronim Barczak, Wladyslaw Zmuda, Pawel Janas; Adam Nawalka, Andrzej Palasz, Kazimierz Kmiecik; Leszek Lipka, Grzegorz Lato (captain), Zbigniew Boniek. *Substitutes:* Stanislaw Terlecki (for Palasz 46); Wlodzimierz Ciolek (for Dziuba 69). *Trainer:* Ryszard Kulesza.

Scorer: Poland: Boniek 69

31 August 1980   Friendly   Nep Stadion, Budapest   Attendance: 10,000

438 Hungary 3, SCOTLAND 1
Referee: Jakob Baumann (Switzerland)

Scotland: Alan Rough (Partick Thistle); Danny McGrain (Celtic), Willie Miller (Aberdeen), Alex McLeish (Aberdeen), Ally Dawson (Rangers); David Narey (Dundee United), Archie Gemmill (Birmingham City, captain), Kenny Dalglish (Liverpool); Alan Brazil (Ipswich Town), Steve Archibald (Tottenham Hotspur), Peter Weir (St Mirren). *Substitute:* Gordon Strachan (Aberdeen, for Brazil 46). *Manager:* Jock Stein.

Hungary: Ferenc Meszaros; Sandor Paroczai, Laszlo Balint (captain), Imre Garaba, Jozsef Toth; Jozsef Pasztor, Zoltan Kereki, Tibor Nyilasi; Ferenc Csongradi, Laszlo Kiss, Andras Torocsik. *Substitutes:* Gabor Szanto (for Paroczai 63); Marton Esterhazy (for Kiss 68). *Trainer:* Kalman Meszoly.

Scorers: Hungary: Torocsik 4, 65; Kereki 69   Scotland: Archibald 67

10 September 1980   World Cup qualifying   Rasunda Stadion, Stockholm   Attendance: 39,831

439 Sweden 0, SCOTLAND 1
Referee: Franz Wohrer (Austria)

Scotland: Alan Rough (Partick Thistle); Danny McGrain (Celtic), Willie Miller (Aberdeen), Alex McLeish (Aberdeen), Frank Gray (Nottingham Forest); Gordon Strachan (Aberdeen), Alan Hansen (Liverpool), Archie Gemmill (Birmingham City, captain), John Robertson (Nottingham Forest); Kenny Dalglish (Liverpool), Andy Gray (Wolverhampton Wanderers). *Substitute:* Steve Archibald (Tottenham Hotspur, for Dalglish 80). *Manager:* Jock Stein.

Sweden: Ronnie Hellstrom; Johnny Gustavsson, Hans Borg (captain), Per-Olof Bild, Haakan Arvidsson; Sten-Ove Ramberg, Ingemar Erlandsson, Mats Nordgren; Billy Ohlsson, Thomas Nilsson, Thomas Sjoberg. *Substitute:* Peter Nilsson (for Erlandsson 80). *Trainer:* Lars Arnesson.

Scorer: Scotland: Strachan 72

15 October 1980   World Cup qualifying   Hampden Park   Attendance: 60,765

440 SCOTLAND 0, Portugal 0
Referee: Jan Redelfs (West Germany)

Scotland: Alan Rough (Partick Thistle); Danny McGrain (Celtic), Willie Miller (Aberdeen), Alan Hansen (Liverpool), Frank Gray (Nottingham Forest); Gordon Strachan (Aberdeen), Graeme Souness (Liverpool), Archie Gemmill (Birmingham City, captain); Kenny Dalglish (Liverpool), Andy Gray (Wolverhampton Wanderers), John Robertson (Nottingham Forest). *Manager:* Jock Stein.

Portugal: Manuel Bento (captain); Gabriel Mendes, Joao Laranjeira, Carlos Simoes, Minervino Pietra; Eurico Gomes, Carlos Manuel, Fernando Chalana; Jose Costa, Rui Jordao, Manuel Hernandes. *Substitutes:* Sheu Han (for Chalana 60); Tamagnini Nene (for Jordao 60). *Trainer:* Julio "Jura" Pereira.

25 February 1981   World Cup qualifying   Ramat Gan Stadium, Tel Aviv   Attendance: 35,000

441 Israel 0, SCOTLAND 1
Referee: Otto Andreco (Romania)

Scotland: Alan Rough (Partick Thistle); Danny McGrain (Celtic), Kenny Burns (Nottingham Forest), Alex McLeish (Aberdeen), Frank Gray (Nottingham Forest); John Wark (Ipswich Town), Graeme Souness (Liverpool), Archie Gemmill (Birmingham City, captain); Kenny Dalglish (Liverpool), Steve Archibald (Tottenham Hotspur), John Robertson (Nottingham Forest). *Substitutes:* Willie Miller (Aberdeen, for Wark 46); Andy Gray (Wolverhampton Wanderers, for Dalglish 69). *Manager:* Jock Stein.

Israel: Shlomo Mitzrahi; Gad Machnes, Avi Cohen, Yaacov Cohen, Haim Bar; Ytszak Shum, Yaacov Ekhoiz, Moshe Sinai; Nissim Cohen, Beni Tabak, Gideon Damti (captain). *Trainer:* Jack Mansell (England).

Scorer: Scotland: Dalglish 54

25 March 1981   World Cup qualifying   Hampden Park   Attendance: 78,444

442 SCOTLAND 1, Northern Ireland 1
Referee: Klaus Scheurell (West Germany)

Scotland: Alan Rough (Partick Thistle); Danny McGrain (Celtic), Willie Miller (Aberdeen), Alex McLeish (Aberdeen), Frank Gray (Nottingham Forest); John Wark (Ipswich Town), Kenny Burns (Nottingham Forest), Archie Gemmill (Birmingham City, captain); Steve Archibald (Tottenham Hotspur), Andy Gray (Wolverhampton Wanderers), John Robertson (Nottingham Forest). *Substitutes:* Asa Hartford (Everton, for Burns 77); Billy Thomson (St Mirren, for Rough 80). *Manager:* Jock Stein.

Northern Ireland: Pat Jennings; Jimmy Nicholl, John O'Neill, Chris Nicholl, Sammy Nelson (captain); Terry Cochrane, John McClelland, David McCreery; Sammy McIlroy, Billy Hamilton, Gerry Armstrong. *Substitute:* Derek Spence (for Hamilton 78). *Manager:* Billy Bingham.

Scorers: Northern Ireland: Hamilton 70   Scotland: Wark 75

28 April 1981   World Cup qualifying   Hampden Park   Attendance: 61,489

443 SCOTLAND 3, Israel 1
Referee: Gudmundur Haroldsson (Iceland)

Scotland: Alan Rough (Partick Thistle); Danny McGrain (Celtic), Alan Hansen (Liverpool), Alex McLeish (Aberdeen), Frank Gray (Nottingham Forest); Davie Provan (Celtic), Graeme Souness (Liverpool), Asa Hartford (Everton), John Robertson (Nottingham Forest); Steve Archibald (Tottenham Hotspur), Joe Jordan (Manchester United). *Manager:* Jock Stein.

Israel: Shlomo Mitzrahi; Gad Machnes, Avi Cohen, Yaacov Cohen, Haim Bar; Ytszak Shum, Yaacov Ekhoiz, Moshe Sinai; Yaacov Zeituni, Beni Tabak, Gideon Damti (captain). *Trainer:* Jack Mansell (England).

Scorers: Scotland: Robertson 21 (pen), 30 (pen); Provan 53   Israel: Sinai 58

| 16 May 1981 | Home Championship | Vetch Field, Swansea | Attendance: 18,985 |

444 Wales 2, SCOTLAND 0
Referee: Oliver Donnelly (Northern Ireland)

Scotland: Alan Rough (Partick Thistle); Ray Stewart (West Ham), David Narey (Dundee United), Gordon McQueen (Manchester United), Frank Gray (Nottingham Forest); Davie Provan (Celtic), Willie Miller (Aberdeen), Kenny Burns (Nottingham Forest), Asa Hartford (Everton, captain); Arthur Graham (Leeds United), Joe Jordan (Manchester United). *Substitutes:* Danny McGrain (Celtic, for Gray 46); Paul Sturrock (Dundee United, for Graham 85). *Manager:* Jock Stein.

Wales: Dai Davies (captain); Paul Price, Leighton Phillips, Kevin Ratcliffe, Joey Jones; Carl Harris, Peter Nicholas, Brian Flynn; Mickey Thomas, Ian Walsh, Leighton James. *Substitutes:* Terry Boyle (for Jones 71); Jeremy Charles (for Walsh 76). *Manager:* Mike England.

Scorer: Wales: Walsh 17, 20

| 19 May 1981 | Home Championship | Hampden Park | Attendance: 22,248 |

445 SCOTLAND 2, Northern Ireland 0
Referee: Pat Partridge (England)

Scotland: Billy Thomson (St Mirren); Danny McGrain (Celtic, captain), Willie Miller (Aberdeen), Alex McLeish (Aberdeen), Frank Gray (Leeds United); Ray Stewart (West Ham), Tommy Burns (Celtic), Asa Hartford (Everton), Paul Sturrock (Dundee United), Steve Archibald (Tottenham Hotspur), John Robertson (Nottingham Forest). *Manager:* Jock Stein.

Northern Ireland: Pat Jennings; Jimmy Nicholl, John O'Neill, Chris Nicholl, Sammy Nelson; Terry Cochrane, John McClelland, Martin O'Neill (captain); Sammy McIlroy, Billy Hamilton, Gerry Armstrong. *Substitute:* Mal Donaghy (for Nelson 70). *Manager:* Billy Bingham.

Scorers: Scotland: Stewart 5; Archibald 49

| 23 May 1981 | Home Championship | Wembley, London | Attendance: 90,000 |

446 England 0, SCOTLAND 1
Referee: Robert Wurtz (France)

Scotland (4-4-2):
- 42 Alan Rough (Partick Thistle);
- 55 Danny McGrain (Celtic, captain)
- 14 Willie Miller (Aberdeen)
- 12 Alex McLeish (Aberdeen)
- 16 Frank Gray (Leeds United);
- 7 Davie Provan (Celtic)
- 3 Ray Stewart (West Ham)
- 42 Asa Hartford (Everton)
- 17 John Robertson (Nottingham Forest);
- 10 Steve Archibald (Tottenham Hotspur)
- 47 Joe Jordan (Manchester United)

Substitutes: 10 David Narey (Dundee United, for Hartford 27); 3 Paul Sturrock (Dundee United, for Provan 80)

Manager: Jock Stein

Although the solitary goal came via John Robertson's second-half penalty, this was a game which Scotland bossed and deserved to win by two or three goals. Robertson had a fine match, giving his Nottingham Forest team mate Viv Anderson a torrid time. In defence captain Danny McGrain was his usual immaculate self and on the other flank Frank Gray was as steady as they come. In the middle Alex McLeish was imperious while his Aberdeen team mate Willie Miller put down a serious claim for starting in preference to Alan Hansen. The Scots lost Asa Hartford to injury early on but his replacement, David Narey, came on in midfield and never put a foot wrong. Manager Jock Stein was delighted with the show, stressing that his team was thankfully becoming difficult to beat.

England: Joe Corrigan; Viv Anderson, Ray Wilkins, Dave Watson (captain), Kenny Sansom; Steve Coppell, Bryan Robson, Glenn Hoddle, Graham Rix; Peter Withe, Tony Woodcock. *Substitutes:* Alvin Martin (for Watson 46); Trevor Francis (for Woodcock 46). *Manager:* Ron Greenwood.

Scorer: Scotland: Robertson 64 (pen)

| 9 September 1981 | World Cup qualifying | Hampden Park | Attendance: 81,511 |

447 SCOTLAND 2, Sweden 0
Referee: Andre Daina (Switzerland)

Scotland (4-2-4):
- 43 Alan Rough (Partick Thistle);
- 56 Danny McGrain (Celtic, captain)
- 8 Alan Hansen (Liverpool)
- 13 Alex McLeish (Aberdeen)
- 17 Frank Gray (Leeds United);
- 12 John Wark (Ipswich Town)
- 43 Asa Hartford (Everton);
- 8 Davie Provan (Celtic)
- 79 Kenny Dalglish (Liverpool)
- 48 Joe Jordan (AC Milan)
- 18 John Robertson (Nottingham Forest)

Substitute: 14 Andy Gray (Wolverhampton Wanderers, for Dalglish 70)

Manager: Jock Stein

Sweden: Thomas Ravelli; Stig Fredriksson, Glenn Hysen, Bo Borjesson, Andreas Ravelli; Ingemar Erlandsson (captain), Hans Borg, Karl-Gunnar Bjorklund; Thomas Larsson, Jan Svensson, Thomas Sjoberg. *Substitutes:* Greger Hallen (for Fredriksson, 46); Tommy Holmgren (for Svensson, 73). *Trainer:* Lara Arnesson.

Scorers: Scotland: Jordan 20; Robertson 83 (pen)

Joe Jordan, whose autumn goals helped send Scotland to the 1974 World Cup finals in West Germany and the 1978 tournament in Argentina, repeated the trick against Sweden. The victory left the Scots needing just a point from the remaining two games to make sure of heading to the 1982 competition in Spain. The Swedes, who had won four matches in a row going into the Hampden encounter, proved stuffy and difficult opponents to break down, but Jordan's first-half goal was added to by a penalty in the 83rd minute, converted by John Robertson, to make the result safe. Jordan, now with AC Milan, powered in a header in the 20th minute, and it was substitute Andy Gray, introduced late for Kenny Dalglish, who caused panic in the Swedish defence which led to the late spot kick.

FIFA WORLD CUP QUALIFYING GROUP SIX

	P	W	D	L	F	A	Pts
Scotland	8	4	3	1	9	4	11
Northern Ireland	8	3	3	2	6	3	9
Sweden	8	3	2	3	7	8	8
Portugal	8	3	1	4	8	11	7
Israel	8	1	3	4	6	10	5

| 14 October 1981 | World Cup qualifying | Windsor Park, Belfast | Attendance: 22,248 |

448 Northern Ireland 0, SCOTLAND 0
Referee: Valeriy Butenko (Soviet Union)

Scotland: Alan Rough (Partick Thistle); Ray Stewart (West Ham), Willie Miller (Aberdeen), Alan Hansen (Liverpool), Frank Gray (Leeds United); Gordon Strachan (Aberdeen), Graeme Souness (Liverpool), Asa Hartford (Everton, captain); Kenny Dalglish (Liverpool), Steve Archibald (Tottenham Hotspur), John Robertson (Nottingham Forest). *Substitute:* Andy Gray (Wolverhampton Wanderers, for Souness 76). *Manager:* Jock Stein.

Northern Ireland: Pat Jennings; Jimmy Nicholl, Chris Nicholl, John O'Neill, Mal Donaghy; Martin O'Neill, Sammy McIlroy, David McCreery; Gerry Armstrong, Willie Hamilton, Noel Brotherston. *Manager:* Billy Bingham.

| 18 November 1981 | World Cup qualifying | Estadio da Luz, Lisbon | Attendance: 25,000 |

449 Portugal 2, SCOTLAND 1
Referee: Charles Corver (Netherlands)

Scotland: Billy Thomson (St Mirren); Ray Stewart (West Ham), Willie Miller (Aberdeen), Alan Hansen (Liverpool), Frank Gray (Leeds United); Gordon Strachan (Aberdeen), Graeme Souness (Liverpool), Asa Hartford (Everton, captain); Davie Provan (Celtic), Steve Archibald (Tottenham Hotspur), Paul Sturrock (Dundee United). *Substitutes:* Stuart Kennedy (Aberdeen, for Gray 42); Kenny Dalglish (Liverpool, for Archibald 75). *Manager:* Jock Stein.

Portugal: Manuel Bento (captain); Carlos Simoes, Gregorio Freixo, Eurico Gomes, Adelino Texeira; Eduardo Mendes, Jaime Magalhaes, Romeu Fernandes da Silva; Antonio Oliveira, Manuel Fernandes, Jose Alberto Costa. *Substitutes:* Diamantino Miranda (for Magalhaes 46); Antonio Veloso (for Freixo 50). *Trainer:* Julio Pereira.

Scorers: Scotland: Sturrock 9   Portugal: Fernandes 33, 56

| 24 February 1982 | Friendly | Estadio Luis Casanova, Valencia | Attendance: 30,000 |

450 Spain 3, SCOTLAND 0
Referee: Albert "Bep" Thomas (Netherlands)

Scotland: Alan Rough (Partick Thistle); Danny McGrain (Celtic, captain), Alan Hansen (Liverpool), Alex McLeish (Aberdeen), Frank Gray (Leeds United); Gordon Strachan (Aberdeen), Graeme Souness (Liverpool), Asa Hartford (Everton), John Wark (Ipswich Town); Kenny Dalglish (Liverpool), Alan Brazil (Ipswich Town). *Substitute:* Steve Archibald (Tottenham Hotspur, for Strachan 54). *Manager:* Jock Stein.

Spain: Luis Arconada (captain); Jose Camacho, Rafael Gordillo, Jose Alesanco, Miguel Tendillo; Jose Sanchez, Miguel Alonso, Victor Munoz; Roberto Lopez, Enrique Saura, Jesus Satrustegui. *Substitutes:* Enrique Castro (for Satrustegui 46); Ricardo Gallego (for Munoz 54). *Trainer:* Jose Emilio Santamaria.

Scorers: Spain: Munoz 26; Castro 83 (pen); Gallego 86

Part of the squad for the 1982 World Cup. Back (from left): Graeme Souness, Alan Rough, Alex McLeish, Alan Hansen, Billy Thomson (not chosen), David Narey. Middle: John Wark, Frank Gray, Willie Miller, Jock Stein (manager), Alan Brazil, Steve Archibald, Roy Aitken (not chosen). Front: Paul Sturrock, Gordon Strachan, Danny McGrain, Asa Hartford, Kenny Dalglish. Others in the final squad were Jim Leighton, George Wood, Allan Evans, George Burley, John Robertson, Davie Provan and Joe Jordan.

| 23 March 1982 | Friendly | Hampden Park | Attendance: 71,848 |

451 SCOTLAND 2, Netherlands 1
Referee: George Courtney (England)

Scotland: Alan Rough (Partick Thistle); Danny McGrain (Celtic, captain), Allan Evans (Aston Villa), Willie Miller (Aberdeen), Frank Gray (Leeds United); David Narey (Dundee United), Jim Bett (Rangers), John Wark (Ipswich Town); Kenny Dalglish (Liverpool), Joe Jordan (AC Milan), Steve Archibald (Tottenham Hotspur). *Substitutes:* Alan Brazil (Ipswich Town, for Dalglish 46); Tommy Burns (Celtic, for Archibald 46); Gordon Strachan (Aberdeen, for Jordan 62). *Manager:* Jock Stein.

Netherlands: Johannes Van Breukelen; Michael Van De Korput, Ronald Spelbos, Jonny Metgod, Ruud Krol (captain); Hugo Hovenkamp, Johan Peters, Frank Rijkaard; Arnold Muhren, Simon Tahamata, Wim Kieft. *Trainer:* Kees Rijvers.

Scorers: Scotland: Gray 13 (pen); Dalglish 21   Netherlands: Kieft 30

| 28 April 1982 | Home Championship | Windsor Park, Belfast | Attendance: 20,000 |

452 Northern Ireland 1, SCOTLAND 1
Referee: John Hunting (England)

Scotland: George Wood (Arsenal); Danny McGrain (Celtic, captain), Allan Evans (Aston Villa), Alex McLeish (Aberdeen), Arthur Albiston (Manchester United); Davie Provan (Celtic), John Wark (Ipswich Town), Asa Hartford (Manchester City); Kenny Dalglish (Liverpool), Alan Brazil (Ipswich Town), John Robertson (Nottingham Forest). *Substitutes:* Alan Hansen (Liverpool, for McLeish 75); Paul Sturrock (Dundee United, for Robertson 80). *Manager:* Jock Stein.

Northern Ireland: Jim Platt; Mal Donaghy, John O'Neill, John McClelland, Sammy Nelson; James Cleary, Felix Healy, Martin O'Neill (captain); Sammy McIlroy, Bobby Campbell, Noel Brotherston. *Manager:* Billy Bingham.

Scorers: Scotland: Wark 32   Northern Ireland: McIlroy 55

| 24 May 1982 | Home Championship | Hampden Park | Attendance: 25,284 |

453 SCOTLAND 1, Wales 0
Referee: Fred McKnight (Northern Ireland)

Scotland: Alan Rough (Partick Thistle); Ray Stewart (West Ham), David Narey (Dundee United), Alan Hansen (Liverpool), Frank Gray (Leeds United); Tommy Burns (Celtic), Graeme Souness (Liverpool, captain), Asa Hartford (Manchester City); Kenny Dalglish (Liverpool), Joe Jordan (AC Milan), Alan Brazil (Ipswich Town). *Substitutes:* George Burley (Ipswich Town, for Stewart 72); Paul Sturrock (Dundee United, for Jordan 72). *Manager:* Jock Stein.

Wales: Dai Davies; Byron Stevenson, Chris Marustik, Nigel Stevenson, Joey Jones; Robbie James, Peter Nicholas, Brian Flynn (captain); Alan Curtis, Ian Rush, Leighton James. *Substitutes:* Ian Walsh (for Curtis 75); Mickey Thomas (for Flynn 75). *Manager:* Mike England.

Scorer: Scotland: Hartford 7

| 29 May 1982 | Home Championship | Hampden Park | Attendance: 80,529 |

454 SCOTLAND 0, England 1
Referee: Jan Redelfs (West Germany)

Scotland: Alan Rough (Partick Thistle); George Burley (Ipswich Town), Allan Evans (Aston Villa), Alan Hansen (Liverpool), Danny McGrain (Celtic, captain); David Narey (Dundee United), Graeme Souness (Liverpool), Asa Hartford (Manchester City); Kenny Dalglish (Liverpool), Joe Jordan (AC Milan), Alan Brazil (Ipswich Town). *Substitutes:* John Robertson (Nottingham Forest, for Hartford 46); Paul Sturrock (Dundee United, for Jordan 63). *Manager:* Jock Stein.

England: Peter Shilton; Mick Mills, Phil Thompson, Terry Butcher, Kenny Sansom; Steve Coppell, Ray Wilkins, Bryan Robson, Trevor Brooking; Kevin Keegan (captain), Paul Mariner. *Substitutes:* Trevor Francis (for Mariner 46); Terry McDermott (for Keegan 56). *Manager:* Ron Greenwood.

Scorer: England: Mariner 13

| 15 June 1982 | FIFA World Cup (group stages) | La Rosaleda, Malaga | Attendance: 20,000 |

455 New Zealand 2, SCOTLAND 5
Referee: David Socha (USA)

Scotland (4-3-3):
49 Alan Rough (Partick Thistle);
61 Danny McGrain (Celtic, captain)
4 Allan Evans (Aston Villa)
15 Alan Hansen (Liverpool)
23 Frank Gray (Leeds United);
12 Gordon Strachan (Aberdeen)
26 Graeme Souness (Liverpool)
16 John Wark (Ipswich Town);
87 Kenny Dalglish (Liverpool)
8 Alan Brazil (Ipswich Town)
22 John Robertson (Nottingham Forest)

Substitutes: 15 Steve Archibald (Tottenham Hotspur, for Brazil 53); 14 David Narey (Dundee United, for Strachan 83)

Manager: Jock Stein

The World Cup finals in Spain started with the expected victory against group six underdogs New Zealand, but lapses in defence were worrying and something which would likely prove far more costly in the matches to come against Brazil and the Soviet Union. The first half saw an inspired performance by Aberdeen's Gordon Strachan, laying on goals for Kenny Dalglish and a John Wark double. The first followed a 40-yard run, the second after some midfield skills and the third saw a superb cross from the right wing. Sumner pulled a goal back after the break following an uncharacteristic Danny McGrain error and when Wooddin scored another from a suspiciously offside position the result was suddenly in jeopardy. However, John Robertson flighted home a direct free kick in the 73rd minute and Strachan provided another cross for a Steve Archibald header not long after. Strachan was substituted with seven minutes left and manager Jock Stein came out of the dugout to lead the applause. The job was done and boy, how he had contributed.

New Zealand: Frank van Hattum; John Hill, Robert Almond, Adrian Elrick, Samuel Malcolmson, Keith McKay, Allan Boath, Kenneth Cresswell; Steve Sumner, Wynton Rufer, Steve Wooddin. *Substitutes:* Ricki Herbert (for Almond 65); Duncan Cole (for Malcolmson 77). *Trainer:* John Adshead (England).

Scorers: Scotland: Dalglish 18; Wark 29, 32; Robertson 73; Archibald 80   New Zealand: Sumner 54; Wooddin 65

| 18 June 1982 | FIFA World Cup (group stages) | Benito Villamarin, Sevilla | Attendance: 47,379 |

456 Brazil 4, SCOTLAND 1

Referee: Luis Calderon (Costa Riva)

Scotland (4-3-3):
- 50 Alan Rough (Partick Thistle);
- 15 David Narey (Dundee United)
- 18 Willie Miller (Aberdeen)
- 16 Alan Hansen (Liverpool)
- 24 Frank Gray (Leeds United);
- 17 John Wark (Ipswich Town)
- 27 Graeme Souness (Liverpool, captain)
- 50 Asa Hartford (Everton);
- 13 Gordon Strachan (Aberdeen)
- 16 Steve Archibald (Tottenham Hotspur)
- 23 John Robertson (Nottingham Forest)

Substitutes: 88 Kenny Dalglish (Liverpool, for Strachan 65);
16 Alex McLeish (Aberdeen, for Hartford 69)

Manager: Jock Stein

A breathtaking display by Brazil completely floored Scotland after David Narey had opened the scoring in the 18th minute. The Scots played their part in an entertaining game but the South American players were simply too good and the shooting power so evident for all to see. Narey's goal was far from the "toe poke" it became popularly known as, more a superb first-time strike following excellent work by Graeme Souness and John Wark. The Brazilians unfortunately took offence at the audacity, however, and made their opponents pay in no uncertain terms. Zico, rated along with Maradona as the best in the world, proved it when he rifled home a superb free kick in the 33rd minute. After the break the Scots settled down again, with Souness having a fine game in midfield, and Perez made a fine save from Steve Archibald. The Brazilian players quickly regained their composure, however, and Oscar Bernardi headed home a Junior corner kick. Eder then chipped Alan Rough for number three and Falcao added the icing on the cake with a brilliant drive with just three minutes remaining. Keeper Alan Rough and midfielder Asa Hartford both made their 50th appearances.

Brazil: Valdir Peres; Leandro, Oscar Bernardi, Luisinho, Junior; Roberto Falcao, Socrates (captain), Zico; Toninho Cerezo, Serginho, Eder. *Substitute:* Paulo Isidoro (for Serginho 82). *Trainer:* Tele Santana.

Scorers: Scotland: Narey 18 Brazil: Zico 33; Oscar 48; Eder 64; Falcao 87

| 22 June 1982 | FIFA World Cup (group stages) | La Rosaleda, Malaga | Attendance: 45,000 |

457 Soviet Union 2, SCOTLAND 2

Referee: Nicolae Rainea (Romania)

Scotland (4-3-3):
- 51 Alan Rough (Partick Thistle);
- 16 David Narey (Dundee United)
- 19 Willie Miller (Aberdeen)
- 17 Alan Hansen (Liverpool)
- 25 Frank Gray (Leeds United);
- 14 Gordon Strachan (Aberdeen)
- 28 Graeme Souness (Liverpool, captain)
- 18 John Wark (Ipswich Town);
- 17 Steve Archibald (Tottenham Hotspur)
- 52 Joe Jordan (AC Milan)
- 24 John Robertson (Nottingham Forest)

Substitutes: 62 Danny McGrain (Celtic, for Strachan 71);
9 Alan Brazil (Ipswich Town, for Jordan 71)

Manager: Jock Stein

For the third World Cup finals in a row, Scotland were knocked out of the competition on goal difference. Defensive lapses, in particular the tangle between Willie Miller and Alan Hansen which led to the second goal, were ultimately to prove costly. The Scots started brightly enough and when Joe Jordan scored in his third tournament in a row qualification looked on. With Graeme Souness again running the show in midfield, and Gordon Strachan and John Robertson providing width in attack, things were looking very positive. Soviet keeper Dasaev made a fine save from Strachan to prevent number two but it was obvious his side were coming more into it and they deservedly equalised through Chivadze after the interval. The Scots were beginning to run out of steam towards the end and when Miller and Hansen fell over each other near the touchline it left Shengelia to run in on goal and make it 2-1. The Scots were not finished though and Souness hit back with a superb individual goal with just two minutes left. It was not enough to make the knockout stages for the first time but it had certainly salvaged some pride.

Soviet Union: Rinat Dasaev; Tengiz Sulakvelidze, Sergei Baltacha, Aleksandr Chivadze (captain), Anatoliy Demianenko; Andrei Bal, Sergei Borovski, Vladimir Bessonov; Ramaz Shengelia, Yuri Gavrilov, Oleg Blokhin. *Substitute:* Sergei Andreev (for Shengelia 89). *Trainer:* Konstantin Beskov.

Scorers: Scotland: Jordan 15; Souness 88

Soviet Union: Chivadze 59; Shengelia 85

1982 FIFA WORLD CUP GROUP SIX

	P	W	D	L	F	A	Pts
Brazil	3	3	0	0	10	2	6
Soviet Union	3	1	1	1	6	4	3
Scotland	3	1	1	1	8	8	3
New Zealand	3	0	0	3	2	12	0

| 13 October 1982 | European Championship qualifying | Hampden Park | Attendance: 40,335 |

458 SCOTLAND 2, East Germany 0

Referee: Georges Konrath (France)

Scotland: Jim Leighton (Aberdeen); David Narey (Dundee United), Willie Miller (Aberdeen), Alan Hansen (Liverpool), Frank Gray (Leeds United); Gordon Strachan (Aberdeen), Graeme Souness (Liverpool, captain), John Wark (Ipswich Town), John Robertson (Nottingham Forest); Steve Archibald (Tottenham Hotspur), Alan Brazil (Ipswich Town). *Substitute:* Paul Sturrock (Dundee United, for Brazil 71). *Manager:* Jock Stein.

East Germany: Bodo Rudwaleit; Ronald Kreer, Dirk Stahmann, Norbert Trieloff, Rudiger Schnuphase (captain); Reinhard Hafner, Frank Baum, Hans-Jurgen Dorner; Hans-Uwe Pilz, Hans-Jurgen Riediger, Joachim Streich. *Substitutes:* Matthias Liebers (for Hafner 72); Jurgen Pommerenke (for Dorner 72). *Trainer:* Rudolf Krause.

Scorers: Scotland: Wark 53; Sturrock 75

Chapter six: 1980-1989

17 November 1982   European Championship qualifying   Wankdorf Stadion, Berne   Attendance: 26,000

459 Switzerland 2, SCOTLAND 0
Referee: Vojtech Christov (Czechoslovakia)

Scotland: Jim Leighton (Aberdeen); David Narey (Dundee United), Alan Hansen (Liverpool), Willie Miller (Aberdeen), Frank Gray (Leeds United); Gordon Strachan (Aberdeen), Graeme Souness (Liverpool, captain), John Wark (Ipswich Town), John Robertson (Nottingham Forest); Paul Sturrock (Dundee United), Alan Brazil (Ipswich Town). *Substitute:* Steve Archibald (Tottenham Hotspur, for Sturrock, 46). *Manager:* Jock Stein.

Switzerland: Erich Burgener (captain); Heinz Ludi, Roger Wehrli, Andre Egli, Alain Geiger; Lucien Favre, Michel Decastel, Heinz Hermann; Raimondo Ponte, Rudolf Elsener, Claudio Sulser. *Substitutes:* Umberto Barberis (for Decastel 61); Hanspeter Zwicker (for Elsener 85). *Trainer:* Paul Wolfisberg.

Scorers: Switzerland: Sulser 49; Egli 60

15 December 1982   European Championship qualifying   Heysel Stadion, Brussels   Attendance: 48,877

460 Belgium 3, SCOTLAND 2
Referee: Antonio Garrido (Portugal)

Scotland: Jim Leighton (Aberdeen); David Narey (Dundee United), Alan Hansen (Liverpool), Alex McLeish (Aberdeen), Frank Gray (Leeds United); Gordon Strachan (Aberdeen), Graeme Souness (Liverpool, captain), Roy Aitken (Celtic), Jim Bett (Rangers); Kenny Dalglish (Liverpool), Steve Archibald (Tottenham Hotspur). *Substitutes:* Tommy Burns (Celtic, for Strachan 77); Paul Sturrock (Dundee United, for Bett 77). *Manager:* Jock Stein.

Belgium: Jean-Marie Pfaff; Eric Gerets (captain), Jos Daerden, Walter Meeuws, Marc Baecke; Guy Vandersmissen, Ludo Coeck, Frank Vercauteren; Jan Ceulemans, Francois Van der Elst, Erwin Vandenbergh. *Substitutes:* Rene Verheyen (for Vercauteren 63); Maurice De Schryver (for Vandenbergh 87). *Trainer:* Guy Thys.

Scorers: Scotland: Dalglish 13, 36   Belgium: Vandenbergh 26; Van der Elst 39, 63

30 March 1983   European Championship qualifying   Hampden Park   Attendance: 36,923

461 SCOTLAND 2, Switzerland 2
Referee: Charles Corver (Netherlands)

Scotland: Jim Leighton (Aberdeen); Richard Gough (Dundee United), Willie Miller (Aberdeen), Alan Hansen (Liverpool), Frank Gray (Leeds United); Gordon Strachan (Aberdeen), Graeme Souness (Liverpool, captain), John Wark (Ipswich Town), Peter Weir (Aberdeen); Kenny Dalglish (Liverpool), Charlie Nicholas (Celtic). *Substitute:* Alex McLeish (Aberdeen, for Hansen 46). *Manager:* Jock Stein.

Switzerland: Erich Burgener (captain); Heinz Ludi, Roger Wehrli, Andre Egli, Alain Geiger; Lucien Favre, Michel Decastel, Heinz Hermann; Raimondo Ponte, Rudolf Elsener, Claudio Sulser. *Substitutes:* Hanspeter Zwicker (for Hermann 69); Charles In-Albon (for Sulser 84). *Trainer:* Paul Wolfisberg.

Scorers: Switzerland: Egli 15; Hermann 58   Scotland: Wark 70; Nicholas 76

24 May 1983   Home Championship   Hampden Park   Attendance: 16,238

462 SCOTLAND 0, Northern Ireland 0
Referee: Keith Hackett (England)

Scotland: Billy Thomson (St Mirren); Richard Gough (Dundee United), David Narey (Dundee United), Paul Hegarty (Dundee United, captain), Ally Dawson (Rangers); Tommy Burns (Celtic), Neil Simpson (Aberdeen), John Wark (Ipswich Town), Eamonn Bannon (Dundee United); Andy Gray (Wolverhampton Wanderers), Charlie Nicholas (Celtic). *Substitute:* Gordon Strachan (Aberdeen, for Simpson 65). *Manager:* Jock Stein

Northern Ireland: Pat Jennings; Jimmy Nicholl, John O'Neill, John McClelland, Mal Donaghy; Gerry Mullen, Martin O'Neill (captain), Sammy McIlroy; Ian Stewart, Billy Hamilton, Gerry Armstrong. *Substitutes:* Chris Nicholl (for John O'Neill 46); Noel Brotherston (for Hamilton 89). *Manager:* Billy Bingham.

28 May 1983   Home Championship   Ninian Park, Cardiff   Attendance: 14,100

463 Wales 0, SCOTLAND 2
Referee: Malcolm Moffat (Northern Ireland)

Scotland: Jim Leighton (Aberdeen); Richard Gough (Dundee United), David Narey (Dundee United), Alex McLeish (Aberdeen), Frank Gray (Leeds United); Gordon Strachan (Aberdeen), Willie Miller (Aberdeen), Graeme Souness (Liverpool, captain), Eamonn Bannon (Dundee United); Andy Gray (Wolverhampton Wanderers), Alan Brazil (Tottenham Hotspur). *Manager:* Jock Stein.

Wales: Neville Southall; Neil Slatter, Paul Price, Kevin Ratcliffe, Joey Jones; Kenny Jackett, Peter Nicholas (captain), Jeremy Charles, Brian Flynn; Mickey Thomas, Gordon Davies. *Substitute:* Steve Lowndes (for Flynn 57). *Manager:* Mike England.

Scorers: Scotland: Andy Gray 11; Brazil 67

1 June 1983   Home Championship   Wembley, London   Attendance: 84,000

464 England 2, SCOTLAND 0
Referee: Erik Fredriksson (Sweden)

Scotland: Jim Leighton (Aberdeen); Richard Gough (Dundee United), David Narey (Dundee United), Alex McLeish (Aberdeen), Frank Gray (Leeds United); Gordon Strachan (Aberdeen), Willie Miller (Aberdeen), Graeme Souness (Liverpool, captain), Eamonn Bannon (Dundee United); Andy Gray (Wolverhampton Wanderers), Charlie Nicholas (Celtic). *Substitutes:* Alan Brazil (Tottenham Hotspur, for Bannon 53); John Wark (Ipswich Town, for Nicholas 67). *Manager:* Jock Stein.

England: Peter Shilton; Phil Neal, Graham Roberts, Terry Butcher, Kenny Sansom; Sammy Lee, Bryan Robson, Glenn Hoddle, Gordon Cowans; Peter Withe, Trevor Francis. *Substitutes:* Gary Mabbutt (for Robson 25); Luther Blissett (for Withe 46). *Manager:* Bobby Robson.

Scorers: England: Robson 12; Cowans 52

12 June 1983   Friendly   Empire Stadium, Vancouver   Attendance: 14,942

465 Canada 0, SCOTLAND 2
Referee: Philip Clarke (Canada)

Scotland: Billy Thomson (St Mirren); Richard Gough (Dundee United), David Narey (Dundee United), Alex McLeish (Aberdeen), Ally Dawson (Rangers); Gordon Strachan (Aberdeen), Willie Miller (Aberdeen, captain), Tommy Burns (Celtic), Eamonn Bannon (Dundee United); Paul Sturrock (Dundee United), Charlie Nicholas (Celtic). *Substitutes:* Mark McGhee (Aberdeen, for Nicholas 37); Graeme Souness (Liverpool, for Strachan 70). *Manager:* Jock Stein

Canada: Tino Lettieri; Robert Lenarduzzi, Robert Iarusci, Bruce Wilson, Randy Ragan; Ian Bridge, Peter Roe, Gerry Sweeney; Eddie McNally, Gerry Gray, Dale Mitchell. *Substitutes:* John Connor (for Roe 46); Terry Felix (for McNally 46). *Coach:* Tony Waiters (England).

Scorers: Scotland: Strachan 36 (pen); McGhee 75

16 June 1983   Friendly   Commonwealth Stadium, Edmonton   Attendance: 12,258

466 Canada 0, SCOTLAND 3
Referee: Rolando Fusco (Canada)

Scotland: Jim Leighton (Aberdeen); Richard Gough (Dundee United), David Narey (Dundee United), Alex McLeish (Aberdeen), Frank Gray (Leeds United); Gordon Strachan (Aberdeen), Willie Miller (Aberdeen), Graeme Souness (Liverpool, captain); Paul Sturrock (Dundee United), Mark McGhee (Aberdeen), Charlie Nicholas (Celtic). *Substitutes:* Roy Aitken (Celtic, for Strachan 46); Andy Gray (Wolverhampton Wanderers, for McGhee 54). *Manager:* Jock Stein.

Canada: Tino Lettieri; Robert Lenarduzzi, Robert Iarusci, Bruce Wilson, Randy Ragan; Ian Bridge, Peter Roe, Gerry Sweeney; Eddie McNally, Gerry Gray, Dale Mitchell. *Substitute:* Terry Felix (for Gray 46). *Coach:* Tony Waiters (England).

Scorers: Scotland: Nicholas 20; Gough 50; Souness 89

19 June 1983   Friendly   Varsity Stadion, Toronto   Attendance: 15,500

467 Canada 0, SCOTLAND 2
Referee: Antonio Evangelista (Canada)

Scotland: Jim Leighton (Aberdeen); Richard Gough (Dundee United), David Narey (Dundee United), Alex McLeish (Aberdeen), Ally Dawson (Rangers); Willie Miller (Aberdeen), Graeme Souness (Liverpool, captain), Roy Aitken (Celtic); Paul Sturrock (Dundee United), Andy Gray (Wolverhampton Wanderers), Charlie Nicholas (Celtic). *Substitutes:* Gordon Strachan (Aberdeen, for Gray 46); Tommy Burns (Celtic, for Narey 65). *Manager:* Jock Stein.

Canada: Chris Turner; Terry Moore, Colin Miller, Bruce Wilson, Paul Lee; Ian Bridge, Peter Roe, John Connor; Terry Felix, Gerry Gray, Dale Mitchell. *Substitutes:* Craig Martin (for Lee 46); Edward McNally (for Bridge 46). *Coach:* Tony Waiters (England).

Scorer: Scotland: Gray 17, 32

21 September 1983   Friendly   Hampden Park   Attendance: 20,545

468 SCOTLAND 2, Uruguay 0
Referee: David Richardson (England)

Scotland: Jim Leighton (Aberdeen); Richard Gough (Dundee United), Willie Miller (Aberdeen), Alex McLeish (Aberdeen), Arthur Albiston (Manchester United); John Wark (Ipswich Town), Paul McStay (Celtic), Graeme Souness (Liverpool, captain), John Robertson (Derby County); Kenny Dalglish (Liverpool), Frank McGarvey (Celtic). *Substitutes:* Davie Dodds (Dundee United, for McGarvey 17); Neil Simpson (Aberdeen, for McStay 77). *Manager:* Jock Stein.

Uruguay: Rudolfo Rodriguez (captain); Nelson Gutierrez, Eduardo Acevedo, Victor Diogo, Nelson Agresta; Venancio Ramos, Washington Gonzalez, Jorge Barrios; Luis Acosta, Alberto Santelli, Mario Saralegui. *Substitutes:* Alfredo de Los Santos (for Acosta 46); Nestor Montelongo (for Ramos 70); Carlos Aguilera (for Santelli 70). *Trainer:* Omar Borras.

Scorers: Scotland: Robertson 24 (pen); Dodds 55

12 October 1983   European Championship qualifying   Hampden Park   Attendance: 23,475

469 SCOTLAND 1, Belgium 1
Referee: Enzo Barbaresco (Italy)

Scotland: Jim Leighton (Aberdeen); Richard Gough (Dundee United), Willie Miller (Aberdeen, captain), Alex McLeish (Aberdeen), Arthur Albiston (Manchester United); John Wark (Ipswich Town), Paul McStay (Celtic), Jim Bett (Lokeren), John Robertson (Derby County); Kenny Dalglish (Liverpool), Charlie Nicholas (Arsenal). *Substitutes:* Frank McGarvey (Celtic, for Nicholas 74); Roy Aitken (Celtic, for Wark 80). *Manager:* Jock Stein.

Belgium: Jean-Marie Pfaff; Eric Gerets (captain), Luc Millecamps, Walter Meeuws, Michel Wintacq; Ludo Coeck, Frank Vercauteren, Nico Claesen; Jan Ceulemans, Francois Van der Elst, Eduard Voordeckers. *Substitute:* Michel De Wolf (for Meeuws 76). *Trainer:* Guy Thys.

Scorers: Belgium: Vercauteren 30   Scotland: Nicholas 49

16 November 1983   European Championship qualifying   Kurt Wabbel Stadion, Halle   Attendance: 18,000

470 East Germany 2, SCOTLAND 1
Referee: Franz Wohrer (Austria)

Scotland: Billy Thomson (St Mirren); Richard Gough (Dundee United), Willie Miller (Aberdeen, captain), Alex McLeish (Aberdeen), Arthur Albiston (Manchester United); Gordon Strachan (Aberdeen), John Wark (Ipswich Town), Paul McStay (Celtic), Eamonn Bannon (Dundee United); Kenny Dalglish (Liverpool), Steve Archibald (Tottenham Hotspur). *Substitute:* Frank McGarvey (Celtic, for McStay 60). *Manager:* Jock Stein.

East Germany: Bodo Rudwaleit; Ronald Kreer, Dirk Stahmann, Rainer Troppa, Uwe Zotzsche; Christian Backs, Wolfgang Steinbach, Hans-Uwe Pilz; Hans Richter, Rainer Ernst, Joachim Streich (captain). *Substitute:* Jurgen Raab (for Ernst 87). *Trainer:* Bernd Stange.

Scorers: East Germany: Kreer 33; Streich 42   Scotland: Bannon 78

Chapter six: 1980-1989

| 13 December 1983 | Home Championship | Windsor Park, Belfast | Attendance: 12,000 |

471 Northern Ireland 2, SCOTLAND 0
Referee: Neil Midgley (England)

Scotland: Jim Leighton (Aberdeen); Richard Gough (Dundee United), Roy Aitken (Celtic), Alex McLeish (Aberdeen), Doug Rougvie (Aberdeen); Gordon Strachan (Aberdeen), Paul McStay (Celtic), Graeme Souness (Liverpool, captain), Peter Weir (Aberdeen); Davie Dodds (Dundee United), Frank McGarvey (Celtic). *Substitute:* Mark McGhee (Aberdeen, for McGarvey 60). *Manager:* Jock Stein.

Northern Ireland: Pat Jennings; Jimmy Nicholl, John McClelland, Gerry McElhinney, Mal Donaghy; Terry Cochrane, Paul Ramsey, Sammy McIlroy (captain); Ian Stewart, Norman Whiteside, Billy Hamilton. *Substitute:* John O'Neill (for Cochrane 86). *Manager:* Billy Bingham.

Scorers: Northern Ireland: Whiteside 17; McIlroy 56

| 28 February 1984 | Home Championship | Hampden Park | Attendance: 21,542 |

472 SCOTLAND 2, Wales 1
Referee: Jack Poucher (Northern Ireland)

Scotland: Jim Leighton (Aberdeen); Richard Gough (Dundee United), Willie Miller (Aberdeen), Alex McLeish (Aberdeen), Arthur Albiston (Manchester United); Paul McStay (Celtic), Graeme Souness (Liverpool, captain), Jim Bett (Lokeren); Paul Sturrock (Dundee United), Frank McGarvey (Celtic), Davie Cooper (Rangers). *Substitutes:* Maurice Johnston (Watford, for McGarvey 46); Roy Aitken (Celtic, for McStay 64). *Manager:* Jock Stein.

Wales: Neville Southall; Jeff Hopkins, Jeremy Charles, Kevin Ratcliffe (captain), Joey Jones; Robbie James, Kenny Jackett, Brian Flynn; Mickey Thomas, Alan Curtis, Ian Rush. *Substitutes:* Gordon Davies (for Rush 64); Paul Price (for Curtis 84). *Manager:* Mike England.

Scorers: Scotland: Cooper 37 (pen); Johnston 78   Wales: James 47

| 25 May 1984 | Home Championship | Hampden Park | Attendance: 73,064 |

473 SCOTLAND 1, England 1
Referee: Paolo Casarin (Italy)

Scotland (4-3-3):

13 Jim Leighton (Aberdeen);
13 Richard Gough (Dundee United)
32 Willie Miller (Aberdeen, captain)
29 Alex McLeish (Aberdeen)
6   Arthur Albiston (Manchester United);
27 Gordon Strachan (Aberdeen)
5   Jim Bett (Lokeren)
27 John Wark (Liverpool);
22 Steve Archibald (Tottenham Hotspur)
4   Mark McGhee (Aberdeen)
4   Davie Cooper (Rangers)

Substitutes: 6 Paul McStay (Celtic, for Strachan 62);
2 Maurice Johnston (Celtic, for McGhee 62)

Manager: Jock Stein

With the Scottish side having missed out on qualification for the 1984 European Championships, the match against England had a special significance as it was the last ever in the Home Championship. The historic competition was winding down after 100 years, with Wales, Scotland and Northern Ireland keen to continue but the English association deciding to withdraw because of apparent fixture congestion. The final tie was something of a lacklustre affair, with the Scots deprived of the Liverpool contingent with the European Cup final looming and England also understrength. Mark McGhee opened the scoring with a header in the 13th minute and Tony Woodcock equalised with nine minutes remaining of the first half. The Scots had chances to win after the break, with superb Davie Cooper wing play before a Jim Bett volley was cleared off the line, and Steve Archibald missing an opportunity. England's Mark Chamberlain also scorned a chance after great work by Ray Wilkins and Bryan Robson, so a draw was probably just about the right result.

England: Peter Shilton; Mike Duxbury, Graham Roberts, Terry Fenwick, Kenny Sanson; Ray Wilkins, Bryan Robson (captain); Mark Chamberlain, Tony Woodcock, Luther Blissett, John Barnes. *Substitutes:* Gary Lineker (for Woodcock 72); Steve Hunt (for Chamberlain 74). *Manager:* Bobby Robson.

Scorers: Scotland: McGhee 13   England: Woodcock 36

Before the superb 6-1 win over Yugoslavia in 1984. From left: Graeme Souness, Jim Leighton, Kenny Dalglish, Steve Nicol, Jim Bett, Arthur Albiston, John Wark, Davie Cooper, Maurice Johnston, Willie Miller, Alex McLeish.

1 June 1984 Friendly Stade Velodrome, Marseille Attendance: 24,641

474 France 2, SCOTLAND 0 Referee: Luigi Agnolin (Italy)

Scotland: Jim Leighton (Aberdeen); Richard Gough (Dundee United), Willie Miller (Aberdeen), Alex McLeish (Aberdeen), Maurice Malpas (Dundee United); Gordon Strachan (Aberdeen), Ray Stewart (West Ham), John Wark (Liverpool), Jim Bett (Lokeren); Steve Archibald (Tottenham Hotspur), Maurice Johnston (Watford). *Substitutes:* Neil Simpson (Aberdeen, for Strachan 46); Charlie Nicholas (Arsenal, for Gough 67). *Manager:* Jock Stein.

France: Joel Bats; Manuel Amoros, Maxime Bossis, Patrick Battiston, Yvon Le Roux; Luis Fernandez, Jean Tigana, Alain Giresse, Michel Platini (captain); Bruno Bellone, Bernard Lacombe. *Substitutes:* Daniel Bravo (for Lacombe 46); Bernard Genghini (for Fernandez 67); Didier Six (for Bellone 67). *Trainer:* Michel Hidalgo.

Scorers: France: Giresse 14; Lacombe 29

---

12 September 1984 Friendly Hampden Park Attendance: 18,512

475 SCOTLAND 6, Yugoslavia 1 Referee: Keith Hackett (England)

Scotland (4-3-3):

15 Jim Leighton (Aberdeen);
1   Steve Nicol (Liverpool)
34 Willie Miller (Aberdeen)
31 Alex McLeish (Aberdeen)
7   Arthur Albiston (Manchester United);
29 John Wark (Liverpool)
41 Graeme Souness (Sampdoria, captain)
7   Jim Bett (Lokeren);
94 Kenny Dalglish (Liverpool)
4   Maurice Johnston (Celtic)
5   Davie Cooper (Rangers)

Manager Jock Stein was rightly pleased after his side racked up the best win in eight years – against formidable opposition in Yugoslavia. Despite conceding the first goal, the Scots roared back and Davie Cooper equalised in the next minute. Graeme Souness, outstanding in midfield, then put them ahead after Cooper had demonstrated fine wing play. Kenny Dalglish got a third before the break, with Cooper again providing the pass, and from then on it was really one-way traffic. Stein rang the changes after half-time but it made no difference, with Maurice Johnston and substitutes Paul Sturrock and Charlie Nicholas all finding the net to make it a total of six.

Substitutes: 7 Paul McStay (Celtic, for Wark 46); 15 Paul Sturrock (Dundee United, for Dalglish 55); 9 Charlie Nicholas (Arsenal, for Cooper 60)

Manager: Jock Stein

Yugoslavia: Dragan Pantelic; Branko Miljus, Mirsad Baljic, Miodrag Jesic, Vladimir Matijevic; Ljubomir Radanovic (captain), Edin Bahtic, Blaz Sliskovic; Zoran Batrovic, Fadilj Vokri, Petar Georgijevski. *Substitutes:* Ranko Stojic (for Pantelic 46); Darko Pancev (for Vokri 46); Nenad Gracan (for Georgijevski 46); Davor Jozic, for Matijevic 65). *Trainer:* Milos Milutinovic.

Scorers: Yugoslavia: Vokri 10   Scotland: Cooper 11; Souness 18; Dalglish 31; Sturrock 64; Johnston 66; Nicholas 80

---

17 October 1984 World Cup qualifying Hampden Park Attendance: 52,829

476 SCOTLAND 3, Iceland 0 Referee: Egbert Mulder (Netherlands)

Scotland: Jim Leighton (Aberdeen); Steve Nicol (Liverpool), Willie Miller (Aberdeen), Alex McLeish (Aberdeen), Arthur Albiston (Manchester United); Paul McStay (Celtic), Graeme Souness (Sampdoria, captain), Jim Bett (Lokeren); Kenny Dalglish (Liverpool), Maurice Johnston (Celtic), Davie Cooper (Rangers). *Substitute:* Charlie Nicholas (Arsenal, for Dalglish 68). *Manager:* Jock Stein.

Iceland: Bjarni Sigurdsson; Thorgrimur Thrainsson, Arni Sveinsson, Magnus Bergs, Saevar Jonsson; Attli Edvaldsson, Janus Gudlaugsson, Ragnar Margeirsson; Arnor Gudjohnsen, Petur Petursson, Asgeir Sigurvinsson (captain). *Trainer:* Tony Knapp (England).

Scorers: Scotland: McStay 22, 40; Nicholas 70

---

14 November 1984 World Cup qualifying Hampden Park Attendance: 74,299

477 SCOTLAND 3, Spain 1 Referee: Adolf Prokop (East Germany)

Scotland (4-3-3):

16 Jim Leighton (Aberdeen);
2   Steve Nicol (Liverpool)
35 Willie Miller (Aberdeen)
32 Alex McLeish (Aberdeen)
8   Arthur Albiston (Manchester United);
8   Paul McStay (Celtic)
42 Graeme Souness (Sampdoria, captain)
8   Jim Bett (Lokeren);
96 Kenny Dalglish (Liverpool)
5   Maurice Johnston (Celtic)
6   Davie Cooper (Rangers)

Manager: Jock Stein.

With one of the best performances in several years, Scotland defeated the European Championship runners-up to take a firm hold on group seven qualification for the 1986 World Cup. The goals came from youth and experience, with Maurice Johnston's double added to in the second half by Kenny Dalglish who equalled Denis Law's Scottish record of 30 on his 96th appearance. Graeme Souness was again the most influential player on the field, well backed up by midfield colleagues Paul McStay and Jim Bett. Johnston's first goal came after Spanish keeper Arconada had brilliantly blocked a Bett volley, and the young Celtic striker headed home a second nine minutes later. Spain were more dangerous in the second half and Goikoetxea's header gave them hope in the 65th minute. However, after Souness saw a spectacular volley sail just over the bar, Dalglish cut inside and curled home a magnificent left-foot effort to make it 3-1.

Spain: Luis Arconada (captain); Santiago Urquiaga, Andoni Goikoetxea, Antonio Maceda, Jose Camacho; Juan Antiono Senor, Victor Munoz, Rafael Vasquez; Carlos Santillana, Ismael Urtubi, Hipolito Rincon. *Substitutes:* Emilio Butragueno (for Rincon 46); Jose Carrasco (for Urtubi 80). *Trainer:* Miguel Munoz.

Scorers: Scotland: Johnston 33, 42; Dalglish 75   Spain: Goikoetxea 65

Chapter six: 1980-1989

27 February 1985   World Cup qualifying   Estadio Sanchez Pizjuan, Seville   Attendance: 70,410

478 Spain 1, SCOTLAND 0
Referee: Michel Vautrot (France)

Scotland: Jim Leighton (Aberdeen); Richard Gough (Dundee United), Willie Miller (Aberdeen), Alex McLeish (Aberdeen), Arthur Albiston (Manchester United); Paul McStay (Celtic), Graeme Souness (Sampdoria, captain), Jim Bett (Lokeren); Steve Archibald (Barcelona), Maurice Johnston (Celtic), Davie Cooper (Rangers). *Substitutes:* Gordon Strachan (Manchester United, for McStay 76); Charlie Nicholas (Arsenal, for Archibald 84). *Manager:* Jock Stein.

Spain: Luis Arconada (captain); Gerardo Miranda, Jose Camacho, Antonio Maceda, Andoni Goikoetxea; Rafael Gordillo, Ricardo Gallega, Roberto Fernandez; Juan Senor, Fernando Clos, Emilio Butragueno. *Substitute:* Julio Alberto (for Gallega 80). *Trainer:* Miguel Munoz.

Scorer: Spain: Clos 48

27 March 1985   World Cup qualifying   Hampden Park   Attendance: 62,424

479 SCOTLAND 0, Wales 1
Referee: Alexis Ponnet (Belgium)

Scotland: Jim Leighton (Aberdeen); Steve Nicol (Liverpool), Willie Miller (Aberdeen), Alex McLeish (Aberdeen), Arthur Albiston (Manchester United); Paul McStay (Celtic), Graeme Souness (Sampdoria, captain), Jim Bett (Lokeren); Kenny Dalglish (Liverpool), Maurice Johnston (Celtic), Davie Cooper (Rangers). *Substitutes:* Alan Hansen (Liverpool, for Albiston 57); Charlie Nicholas (Arsenal, for McStay 75). *Manager:* Jock Stein.

Wales: Neville Southall; Neil Slatter, Dave Phillips, Kevin Ratcliffe (captain), Joey Jones; Robbie James, Kenny Jackett, Peter Nicholas; Mickey Thomas, Ian Rush, Mark Hughes. *Manager:* Mike England.

Scorer: Wales: Rush 37

25 May 1985   Stanley Rous Cup   Hampden Park   Attendance: 66,489

480 SCOTLAND 1, England 0
Referee: Michel Vautrot (France)

Scotland (4-4-2):
20 Jim Leighton (Aberdeen);
16 Richard Gough (Dundee United)
39 Willie Miller (Aberdeen)
36 Alex McLeish (Aberdeen)
2 Maurice Malpas (Dundee United);
30 Gordon Strachan (Manchester United)
12 Roy Aitken (Celtic)
46 Graeme Souness (Sampdoria, captain)
12 Jim Bett (Lokeren);
25 Steve Archibald (Barcelona)
1 David Speedie (Chelsea)

Substitute: 1 Murdo MacLeod (Celtic, for Strachan 71)

Manager: Jock Stein

Captain Graeme Souness, having been on the losing side four times against England, finally got the victory he craved. Now with Sampdoria in Italy, he was again a star performer as Scotland saw off very strong opposition at Hampden Park. The competition was the Stanley Rous Cup, played for against England in 1985 and 1986 and then for three years against England and an invited side from South America before being discontinued. The game was notable for the number of players on both sides playing for foreign clubs – fairly uncommon at that time – with Souness in Italy, Steve Archibald in Spain and Jim Bett in Belgium and England having Trevor Francis, Mark Hateley and Ray Wilkins all with Italian sides. Richard Gough got the only goal of the match, making a late run to float a header past Peter Shilton from a Bett cross in the 68th minute. With two important World Cup qualifying games against Iceland and Wales looming, the result was the perfect send-off.

England: Peter Shilton; Viv Anderson, Terry Fenwick, Terry Butcher, Kenny Sansom; Glen Hoddle, Bryan Robson (captain), Ray Wilkins; Trevor Francis, Mark Hateley, John Barnes. *Substitutes:* Chris Waddle (for Barnes 63); Gary Lineker (for Hoddle 80). *Manager:* Bobby Robson.

Scorer: Scotland: Gough 68

With the Stanley Rous Cup in 1985. Back (from left): Alan Rough, Richard Gough, Alex McLeish, Roy Aitken, Jim Leighton, Maurice Malpas, David Speedie, Steve Archibald, Willie Miller, Maurice Johnston. Front: Jim Bett, Graeme Souness, Murdo MacLeod, Gordon Strachan.

SCOTLAND AT 150: A CENTURY AND A HALF OF INTERNATIONAL FOOTBALL

28 May 1985   World Cup qualifying   Reykjavik   Attendance: 15,052

481 Iceland 0, SCOTLAND 1   *Referee: Anatoliy Milchenko (Soviet Union)*

Scotland: Jim Leighton (Aberdeen); Richard Gough (Dundee United), Willie Miller (Aberdeen), Alex McLeish (Aberdeen), Maurice Malpas (Dundee United); Gordon Strachan (Aberdeen), Graeme Souness (Sampdoria, captain), Roy Aitken (Celtic), Jim Bett (Lokeren); Andy Gray (Aston Villa), Graeme Sharp (Everton). *Substitute:* Steve Archibald (Barcelona, for Gray 73). *Manager:* Jock Stein.

Iceland: Eggert Gudmundsson; Thorgrimur Thrainsson, Arni Sveinsson, Magnus Bergs, Saevar Jonsson; Janus Gudlaugsson, Petur Petursson, Atli Edvaldsson; Teitur Thordarson (captain), Sidurdur Jonsson, Gudmundur Thorbjornsson. *Substitutes:* Omar Torfason (for Sigurdur Jonsson 25); Sigurdur Gretarsson (for Thordarson 57). *Trainer:* Tony Knapp (England).

Scorer: Scotland: Bett 86

---

10 September 1985   World Cup qualifying   Ninian Park, Cardiff   Attendance: 39,500

482 Wales 1, SCOTLAND 1   *Referee: Johannes Keizer (Netherlands)*

Scotland (4-4-2):
22 Jim Leighton (Aberdeen);
18 Richard Gough (Dundee United)
41 Willie Miller (Aberdeen, captain)
38 Alex McLeish (Aberdeen)
4 Maurice Malpas (Dundee United);
32 Gordon Strachan (Aberdeen)
5 Steve Nicol (Liverpool)
14 Roy Aitken (Celtic)
14 Jim Bett (Aberdeen);
2 Graeme Sharp (Everton)
2 David Speedie (Chelsea)

Substitutes: 52 Alan Rough (Hibernian, for Leighton 46);
10 Davie Cooper (Rangers, for Strachan 61)

Manager: Jock Stein

Wales: Neville Southall; Joey Jones, Kevin Ratcliffe, Dave Phillips, Pat Van Den Hauwe; Robbie James, Kenny Jackett, Peter Nicholas; Mickey Thomas, Mark Hughes, Ian Rush. *Substitutes:* Steve Lovell (for James 80); Clayton Blackmore (for Thomas 83). *Manager:* Mike England.

Scorers: Wales: Hughes 13   Scotland: Cooper 81 (pen)

The Scots gained the point needed for possible qualification, courtesy of a Davie Cooper penalty, but the victory was marred by the death of manager Jock Stein shortly after the game. He suffered a heart attack in the dugout and was pronounced dead on the way to hospital. When Mark Hughes gave Wales the lead early on it left Scotland with an uphill struggle. Missing captain Graeme Souness, the side seemed to lack composure, and could easily have conceded a second when Hughes headed just over. The game was drifting away until the 81st minute when Phillips was penalised for handball and Cooper made an expert job of the spot kick. It could even have been a victory, had David Speedie managed to finish with only the keeper to beat. The result meant Scotland briefly led the table, but with Spain still to play Iceland at home second place and a play-off against the Oceanic group winners was the likely outcome.

FIFA WORLD CUP QUALIFYING GROUP SEVEN

	P	W	D	L	F	A	Pts
Spain	6	4	0	2	9	8	8
Scotland	6	3	1	2	8	4	7
Wales	6	3	1	2	7	6	7
Iceland	6	1	0	5	4	10	2

---

16 October 1985   Friendly   Hampden Park   Attendance: 41,114

483 SCOTLAND 0, East Germany 0   *Referee: Joseph Worrall (England)*

Scotland: Jim Leighton (Aberdeen); Richard Gough (Dundee United), Willie Miller (Aberdeen), Alex McLeish (Aberdeen); Arthur Albiston (Manchester United); Steve Nicol (Liverpool), Graeme Souness (Sampdoria, captain), Roy Aitken (Celtic); Kenny Dalglish (Liverpool), Maurice Johnston (Celtic), Davie Cooper (Rangers). *Substitutes:* Andy Goram (Oldham Athletic, for Leighton 49); David Speedie (Chelsea, for Johnston 65); Paul McStay (Celtic, for Aitken 81). *Manager:* Alex Ferguson.

East Germany: Rene Muller (captain); Frank Rohde, Ronald Kreer, Carsten Sanger, Uwe Zotzsche; Hans-Uwe Pilz, Matthias Liebers, Jorg Stubner, Andreas Thom; Ulf Kirsten, Rainer Ernst. *Substitutes:* Jorg Weissflog (for Muller 46); Andreas Bielau (for Ernst 70). *Trainer:* Bernd Stange.

---

20 November 1985   World Cup qualifying (play-off)   Hampden Park   Attendance: 61,920

484 SCOTLAND 2, Australia 0   *Referee: Vojtech Christov (Czechoslovakia)*

Scotland (4-3-3):
24 Jim Leighton (Aberdeen);
7 Steve Nicol (Liverpool)
43 Willie Miller (Aberdeen)
40 Alex McLeish (Aberdeen)
5 Maurice Malpas (Dundee United);
33 Gordon Strachan (Manchester United)
49 Graeme Souness (Sampdoria, captain)
16 Roy Aitken (Celtic);
99 Kenny Dalglish (Liverpool)
1 Frank McAvennie (West Ham)
12 Davie Cooper (Rangers)

Substitutes: 3 Graeme Sharp (Everton, for Dalglish 72); 15 Jim Bett (Aberdeen, for Strachan 84)

Manager: Alex Ferguson

Manager Alex Ferguson had suggested that a two-goal lead from the first leg could be good enough to take his side to the finals in Mexico, and that proved to be correct with the Scots achieving a goalless draw in Australia a fortnight later. The Australians were physically impressive and capable of playing an effective containing game, but seemed to run out of ideas in the opposition half of the field. But although enjoying the bulk of possession in the first period, it took until the hour mark for Scotland to put the game to bed. Davie Cooper got the opener with a trademark free kick and two minutes later Kenny Dalglish set up Frank McAvennie to make it 2-0. Dalglish, on his 99th appearance, had the chance to set a new scoring record of 31 goals but his shot was blocked on the line.

Australia: Terry Greedy; Charlie Yankos, Alan Davidson, David Ratcliffe, Graham Jennings; Steve O'Connor, Joe Watson, Ken Murphy; Oscar Crino, David Mitchell, John Kosmina (captain). *Substitutes:* Jimmy Patikas (for Watson 65); Robbie Dunn (for O'Connor 82). *Trainer:* Frank Arok.

Scorers: Scotland: Cooper 58; McAvennie 60

Chapter six: 1980-1989

| 4 December 1985 | World Cup qualifying (play-off) | Olympic Park, Melbourne | Attendance: 32,000 |

485 Australia 0, SCOTLAND 0 *Referee: Jose Wright (Brazil)*

Scotland: Jim Leighton (Aberdeen); Richard Gough (Dundee United), Willie Miller (Aberdeen), Alex McLeish (Aberdeen), Maurice Malpas (Dundee United); Roy Aitken (Celtic), Graeme Souness (Sampdoria, captain), Paul McStay (Celtic); David Speedie (Chelsea), Frank McAvennie (West Ham), Davie Cooper (Rangers). *Substitute:* Graeme Sharp (Everton, for Speedie 76). *Manager:* Alex Ferguson.

Australia: Terry Greedy; Alan Davidson, Graham Jennings, Charlie Yankos, David Ratcliffe; Robert Dunn, James Patikas, Kenny Murphy; Oscar Crino, David Mitchell, John Kosmina (captain). *Substitutes:* Zarko Odzakov (for Crino 68); Frank Farina (for Dunn 75). *Trainer:* Frank Arok.

| 28 January 1986 | Friendly | Ramat Gan Stadion, Tel Aviv | Attendance: 7,000 |

486 Israel 0, SCOTLAND 1 *Referee: Albert Thomas (Netherlands)*

Scotland: Jim Leighton (Aberdeen); Richard Gough (Dundee United), David Narey (Dundee United), Willie Miller (Aberdeen, captain), Maurice Malpas (Dundee United); Roy Aitken (Celtic), Paul McStay (Celtic), Jim Bett (Aberdeen), Eamonn Bannon (Dundee United); Graeme Sharp (Everton), Charlie Nicholas (Arsenal). *Substitute:* Paul Sturrock (Dundee United, for Sharp 68). *Manager:* Alex Ferguson.

Israel: Avi Ran; Eitan Aharoni, Avi Cohen (captain), Menashe Shiminov, Zion Marili; Rifat Turk, Motti Iwanir, Efraeem Davidi; Uri Malmillian, Zahi Armeli, Eli Ohana. *Substitutes:* Eli Cohen (for Turk 46); Eyal Begleibter (for Iwanir 46); Rony Rosenthal (for Ohana 57). *Trainer:* Yosef Mirmovich.

Scorer: Scotland: McStay 57

| 26 March 1986 | Friendly | Hampden Park | Attendance: 53,589 |

487 SCOTLAND 3, Romania 0 *Referee: Volker Roth (West Germany)*

Scotland (4-4-2):

2 Andy Goram (Oldham Athletic);
22 Richard Gough (Dundee United)
27 David Narey (Dundee United)
46 Willie Miller (Aberdeen)
8 Maurice Malpas (Dundee United);
34 Gordon Strachan (Manchester United)
19 Roy Aitken (Celtic)
51 Graeme Souness (Sampdoria)
8 Eamonn Bannon (Dundee United);
100 Kenny Dalglish (Liverpool, captain)
6 Graeme Sharp (Everton)

Substitutes: 14 Charlie Nicholas (Arsenal, for Sharp 46);
23 Alan Hansen (Liverpool, for Miller 60);
1 Pat Nevin (Chelsea, for Strachan 72)

Manager: Alex Ferguson

On the eve of Kenny Dalglish's 100th cap, the only Scot to reach that target at the time of writing, manager Alex Ferguson described him as being "electric" in training. Asked about the compliment, Dalglish quipped: "What Fergie meant to say was that I was shocking." Joking aside, the game was a huge milestone and fittingly drew an excellent crowd of nearly 54,000, more than at many competitive matches in recent years. Dalglish himself was on fine form, with also excellent wing play from Gordon Strachan, Eamonn Bannon and substitute Pat Nevin. Strachan chipped in the opener in the 18th minute, noticing the keeper was off his line, and he also provided the pass from which Richard Gough got the second 10 minutes later. Scotland were well on top after the break and Roy Aitken deservedly got number three near the end with a powerful drive after a Bannon cross had been headed down by Gough. Dalglish was presented with his 100th cap before the match by West German legend Franz Beckenbauer.

Romania: Silviu Lung; Mircea Rednic, Nicolae Ungureanu, Ion Andone, Gino Iorgulescu (captain); Lica Movila, Michael Klein, Gheorghe Hagi; Marcel Coras, Dorin Mateut, Rodion Camataru. *Substitutes:* Alexandru Nicolae (for Iorgulescu 46); Romulus Gabor (for Coras 70); Nita Cireasa (for Andone 75). *Trainer:* Mircea Lucescu.

Scorers: Scotland: Strachan 18; Gough 27; Aitken 81

| 23 April 1986 | Stanley Rous Cup | Wembley, London | Attendance: 68,357 |

488 England 2, SCOTLAND 1 *Referee: Michel Vautrot (France)*

Scotland: Alan Rough (Hibernian); Richard Gough (Dundee United), Willie Miller (Aberdeen), Alex McLeish (Aberdeen), Maurice Malpas (Dundee United); Steve Nicol (Liverpool), Graeme Souness (Sampdoria, captain), Roy Aitken (Celtic), Eamonn Bannon (Dundee United); David Speedie (Chelsea), Charlie Nicholas (Arsenal). *Substitute:* Pat Nevin (Chelsea, for Nicholas 58). *Manager:* Alex Ferguson.

England: Peter Shilton; Gary M. Stevens, Terry Butcher, Dave Watson, Kenny Sansom; Steve Hodge, Ray Wilkins (captain), Glenn Hoddle; Chris Waddle, Trevor Francis, Mark Hateley. *Substitutes:* Peter Reid (for Wilkins 46); Gary A. Stevens (for Hodge 75). *Manager:* Bobby Robson.

Scorers: England: Butcher 27; Hoddle 39   Scotland: Souness 57 (pen)

| 29 April 1986 | Friendly | Philips Stadion, Eindhoven | Attendance: 14,500 |

489 Netherlands 0, SCOTLAND 0 *Referee: Helmut Kohl (Austria)*

Scotland: Andy Goram (Oldham Athletic); Maurice Malpas (Dundee United), David Narey (Dundee United), Alex McLeish (Aberdeen), Arthur Albiston (Manchester United); Willie Miller (Aberdeen, captain), Jim Bett (Aberdeen), Robert Connor (Dundee), Paul Sturrock (Dundee United), Ally McCoist (Rangers), Davie Cooper (Rangers). *Manager:* Alex Ferguson.

Netherlands: Johannes Van Breukelen (captain); Jan Silooy, Andrianus Van Tiggelen, Ronald Koeman, Danny Blind; Gerald Vanenburg, Jan Wouters, Michel Valke; Johannes Van't Schip, Robert De Wit, Johannes Bosman. *Substitute:* Wilbert Suvrun (for Valke 72). *Trainer:* Leo Beenhakker.

4 June 1986   FIFA World Cup (group stages)   Nezahualcoyotl   Attendance: 18,000

490 Denmark 1, SCOTLAND 0

Referee: Lagos Nemeth (Hungary)

Scotland (4-4-2):
27 Jim Leighton (Aberdeen);
24 Richard Gough (Dundee United)
49 Willie Miller (Aberdeen)
44 Alex McLeish (Aberdeen)
11 Maurice Malpas (Dundee United);
35 Gordon Strachan (Manchester United)
21 Roy Aitken (Celtic)
53 Graeme Souness (Rangers, captain)
9 Steve Nicol (Liverpool);
18 Paul Sturrock (Dundee United)
16 Charlie Nicholas (Arsenal)

Substitutes: 3 Frank McAvennie (West Ham, for Sturrock 61);
10 Eamonn Bannon (Dundee United, for Strachan 74)

Manager: Alex Ferguson

It was the worst possible start to the 1986 World Cup in Mexico as the Scots lost by a single goal to Denmark, courtesy of Preben Elkjaer in the second half. With Kenny Dalglish injured and a lack of real firepower up front, there seemed no-one with the ability to break through the Danish rearguard. Some of the Scottish play was good, however, with Maurice Malpas in particular standing out in the first half. Charlie Nicholas had a couple of chances but his first shot was blocked and the second went just wide. At the other end the dangerous Michael Laudrup fired a shot just over the bar. After the break the Danes looked more dangerous and it took a couple of superb tackles by Willie Miller on Laudrup and Elkjaer to stop the threat. A goal looked likely though and in the 57th minute Elkjaer drilled a left-foot shot past Jim Leighton. The closest the Scots came to an equaliser was when Aitken had the ball in the net but he was correctly ruled offside. Having used both permitted substitutes, Scotland were reduced to 10 men when Nicholas was carried from the field after a brutal tackle by Berggreen who was booked.

Denmark: Troels Rasmussen; Soren Busk, Morten Olsen (captain), Ivan Nielsen, Klaus Berggreen; Frank Arnesen, Jens-Jorn Bertelsen, Soren Lerby, Jesper Olsen; Michael Laudrup, Preben Elkjaer. *Substitutes:* John Sivebaek (for Arnesen 75); Jan Molby (for Jesper Olsen 83). *Trainer:* Josef Piontek (West Germany).

Scorer: Denmark: Elkjaer 57

---

8 June 1986   FIFA World Cup (group stages)   Estadio Corregidora, Queretaro   Attendance: 25,000

491 West Germany 2, SCOTLAND 1

Referee: Ioan Igna (Romania)

Scotland (4-4-2):
28 Jim Leighton (Aberdeen);
25 Richard Gough (Dundee United)
29 David Narey (Dundee United)
50 Willie Miller (Aberdeen)
12 Maurice Malpas (Dundee United);
36 Gordon Strachan (Manchester United)
22 Roy Aitken (Celtic)
54 Graeme Souness (Rangers, captain)
10 Steve Nicol (Liverpool);
11 Eamonn Bannon (Dundee United)
27 Steve Archibald (Barcelona)

Substitutes: 4 Frank McAvennie (West Ham, for Nicol 59);
15 Davie Cooper (Rangers, for Bannon 74)

Manager: Alex Ferguson

Scotland's hopes took a second hammer blow when, after taking the lead through Gordon Strachan, West Germany replied with goals by Rudi Voller and Klaus Allofs. The result left the Scots with zero points after the first two matches. Apart from his goal Strachan had a tremendous first half, after the Scots weathered a difficult opening 10 minutes to take control of the match. After half-chances for Dundee United pair Maurice Malpas and Eamonn Bannon, Strachan sent the supporters wild when his angled shot from a Roy Aitken pass beat Schumacher in the 18th minute. The lead was not to last long, however, as Voller equalised from point-blank range four minutes later. The influential Magath, who was Germany's best player, had a hand in the goal. An unfortunate mix-up in the Scottish defence five minutes after half-time gave Allofs a chance and he took advantage to put his side 2-1 ahead. There were a couple of nervous moments for West Germany, notably when Richard Gough headed inches over after a cross from substitute Davie Cooper, but they held on for victory.

West Germany: Harald Schumacher (captain); Thomas Berthold, Norbert Eder, Karl-Heinz Forster, Klaus Augenthaler; Hans-Peter Briegel, Felix Magath, Lothar Matthaus; Pierre Littbarski, Klaus Allofs, Rudi Voller. *Substitutes:* Ditmar Jakobs (for Briegel 63); Karl-Heinz Rummenigge (for Littbarski 76). *Trainer:* Franz Beckenbauer.

Scorers: Scotland: Strachan 18   West Germany: Voller 22; Allofs 50

Gordon Strachan fires the ball home to open the scoring against Germany at the 1986 World Cup.

13 June 1986 FIFA World Cup (group stages) Nezahualcouyotl Attendance: 20,000

492 Uruguay 0, SCOTLAND 0
Referee: Joel Quiniou (France)

Scotland (4-4-2):
- 29 Jim Leighton (Aberdeen);
- 26 Richard Gough (Dundee United)
- 30 David Narey (Dundee United)
- 51 Willie Miller (Aberdeen, captain)
- 14 Arthur Albiston (Manchester United);
- 37 Gordon Strachan (Manchester United)
- 23 Roy Aitken (Celtic)
- 15 Paul McStay (Celtic)
- 11 Steve Nicol (Liverpool);
- 19 Paul Sturrock (Dundee United)
- 7 Graeme Sharp (Everton)

Substitutes: 16 Davie Cooper (Rangers, for Nicol 70); 17 Charlie Nicholas (Arsenal, for Sturrock 70)

Manager: Alex Ferguson

After losing both their opening games in the most difficult World Cup group the Scots still had a chance of qualification for the next round as one of the best four third-placed sides. To do so they would need to beat Uruguay and they got off to what should have been the perfect start when the Uruguayans had a man sent off with only a minute gone. Jose Batista hacked down Gordon Strachan on the left wing and French referee Joel Quiniou, rated one of the top three officials in the world, produced the red card. It was a brave decision but certainly the correct one. What happened after that was disappointing, however, as a strange lack of inspiration, allied to missed chances and questionable tactics by the opposition, left the game goalless. Paul Sturrock did have the ball in the net but was clearly offside, while Steve Nicol fluffed a chance when it looked easier to score.

Uruguay: Fernando Alvez; Nelson Gutierrez, Eduardo Acevedo, Victor Diogo, Jose Batista; Venancio Ramos, Jorge Barrios (captain), Alfonso Pereira; Sergio Santin, Wilmar Cabrera, Enzo Francescoli. *Substitutes:* Mario Saralegiu (for Ramos 71); Antonio Alzamendi (for Francescoli 84). *Trainer:* Omar Borras.

1986 FIFA WORLD CUP GROUP E

	P	W	D	L	F	A	Pts
Denmark	3	3	0	0	9	1	6
West Germany	3	1	1	1	3	4	3
Uruguay	3	0	2	1	2	7	2
Scotland	3	0	1	2	1	3	1

---

10 September 1986 European Championship qualifying Hampden Park Attendance: 35,070

493 SCOTLAND 0, Bulgaria 0
Referee: Erik Fredriksson (Sweden)

Scotland: Jim Leighton (Aberdeen); Richard Gough (Dundee United), David Narey (Dundee United), Willie Miller (Aberdeen, captain), Maurice Malpas (Dundee United); Gordon Strachan (Manchester United), Roy Aitken (Celtic), Paul McStay (Celtic); Maurice Johnston (Celtic), Charlie Nicholas (Arsenal), Davie Cooper (Rangers). *Substitute:* Kenny Dalglish (Liverpool, for Nicholas 53). *Manager:* Andy Roxburgh.

Bulgaria: Borislav Mihailov; Plamen Nikolov, Petar Petrov, Georgi Dimitrov (captain), Nikolai Iliev; Hristo Kolev, Plamen Simeonov, Anyo Sadkov; Iliya Voinov, Nasko Sirakov, Petar Aleksandrov. *Substitutes:* Georgi Karushev (for Simeonov 78); Lachezar Tanev (for Aleksandrov 87). *Trainer:* Hristo Mladenov.

---

15 October 1986 European Championship qualifying Lansdowne Road, Dublin Attendance: 48,000

494 Republic of Ireland 0, SCOTLAND 0
Referee: Einar Halle (Norway)

Scotland: Jim Leighton (Aberdeen); Richard Gough (Tottenham Hotspur), David Narey (Dundee United), Alan Hansen (Liverpool), Ray Stewart (West Ham); Gordon Strachan (Manchester United), Roy Aitken (Celtic, captain), Paul McStay (Celtic), Murdo MacLeod (Celtic); Graeme Sharp (Everton), Maurice Johnston (Celtic). *Manager:* Andy Roxburgh.

Republic of Ireland: Pat Bonner; Dave Langan, Mick McCarthy, Kevin Moran, Jim Beglin; Liam Brady, Paul McGrath, Ray Houghton, Kevin Sheedy; Frank Stapleton (captain), John Aldridge. *Substitute:* Gerry Daly (for Moran 71). *Manager:* Jack Charlton (England).

---

12 November 1986 European Championship qualifying Hampden Park Attendance: 35,078

495 SCOTLAND 3, Luxembourg 0
Referee: Eysteinn Gudmundsson (Iceland)

Scotland (4-4-2):
- 32 Jim Leighton (Aberdeen);
- 9 Ray Stewart (West Ham)
- 25 Alan Hansen (Liverpool)
- 29 Richard Gough (Tottenham Hotspur)
- 3 Murdo MacLeod (Celtic);
- 3 Pat Nevin (Chelsea)
- 1 Brian McClair (Celtic)
- 26 Roy Aitken (Celtic, captain)
- 18 Davie Cooper (Rangers);
- 102 Kenny Dalglish (Liverpool)
- 12 Maurice Johnston (Celtic

Substitutes: 18 Paul McStay (Celtic, for Hansen 46); 2 Ally McCoist (Rangers, for MacLeod 64)

Manager: Andy Roxburgh

With 0-0 draws against Bulgaria and the Republic of Ireland in their first European Championships qualifiying matches, Scotland finally got a win in the third tie of the campaign. It was Kenny Dalglish's 102nd and final international appearance, and a very attacking line-up selected by Andy Roxburgh still struggled to find the net. Davie Cooper got two goals in the first half, the first from the penalty spot, and Maurice Johnston added another in the second period. However, for most of the match there appeared to be insufficient ammunition to supply the players in the firing line with scoring opportunities. The stand-out player was centre back Alan Hansen, who displayed fine passing out of defence and was surprisingly replaced in the second half.

Luxembourg: John van Rijswijck; Marcel Bossi, Gianni Di Pentima, Hubert Meunier (captain), Laurent Schonckert; Guy Hellers, Carlo Weis, Jean-Pierre Barboni; Theo Scholten, Theo Malget, Robert Langers. *Substitutes:* Gerard Jeitz (for Malget 79); Jeff Saibene (for Scholten 89). *Trainer:* Paul Philipp.

Scorers: Scotland: Cooper 24 (pen), 38; Johnston 70

18 February 1987   European Championship qualifying   Hampden Park   Attendance: 45,081

496 SCOTLAND 0, Republic of Ireland 1
Referee: Henrik van Ettekoven (Netherlands)

Scotland: Jim Leighton (Aberdeen); Ray Stewart (West Ham), Alan Hansen (Liverpool), Richard Gough (Tottenham Hotspur), Maurice Malpas (Dundee United); Pat Nevin (Chelsea), Gordon Strachan (Manchester United), Roy Aitken (Celtic, captain), Davie Cooper (Rangers); Brian McClair (Celtic), Maurice Johnston (Celtic). *Substitutes:* Paul McStay (Celtic, for Cooper 46); Ally McCoist (Rangers, for Malpas 67). *Manager:* Andy Roxburgh.

Republic of Ireland: Pat Bonner; Paul McGrath, Mick McCarthy, Kevin Moran, Ronnie Whelan; Liam Brady, Mark Lawrenson, Ray Houghton; Tony Galvin, Frank Stapleton (captain), John Aldridge. *Substitute:* John Byrne (for Brady 60). *Manager:* Jack Charlton (England).

Scorer: Republic of Ireland: Lawrenson 8

1 April 1987   European Championship qualifying   Van den Stock Stadion, Brussels   Attendance: 26,650

497 Belgium 4, SCOTLAND 1
Referee: Michel Vautrot (France)

Scotland: Jim Leighton (Aberdeen); Richard Gough (Tottenham Hotspur), David Narey (Dundee United), Alex McLeish (Aberdeen), Maurice Malpas (Dundee United); Jim McInally (Dundee United), Paul McStay (Celtic), Roy Aitken (Celtic, captain), Jim Bett (Aberdeen); Paul Sturrock (Dundee United), Ally McCoist (Rangers). *Substitute:* Pat Nevin (Chelsea, for Bett 80). *Manager:* Andy Roxburgh.

Belgium: Jean-Marie Pfaff (captain); Georges Grun, Patrick Vervoort, Leo Clijsters, Stephane Demol; Frank Van der Elst, Frank Vercauteren, Enzo Scifo, Philippe Desmet; Nico Claesen, Erwin Vandenbergh. *Substitutes:* Leo Van der Elst (for Scifo 73); Guy Vandersmissen (for Frank Van der Elst 89). *Trainer:* Guy Thys.

Scorers: Belgium: Claesen 9, 55, 86; Vercauteren 74   Scotland: McStay 14

23 May 1987   Stanley Rous Cup   Hampden Park   Attendance: 64,713

498 SCOTLAND 0, England 0
Referee: Dieter Pauly (West Germany)

Scotland: Jim Leighton (Aberdeen); Richard Gough (Dundee United), Willie Miller (Aberdeen), Alex McLeish (Aberdeen), Murdo MacLeod (Celtic); Paul McStay (Celtic), Neil Simpson (Aberdeen), Roy Aitken (Celtic, captain), Ian Wilson (Leicester City); Brian McClair (Celtic), Ally McCoist (Rangers). *Substitute:* Charlie Nicholas (Arsenal, for McClair 58). *Manager:* Andy Roxburgh.

England: Chris Woods; Gary Stevens, Terry Butcher, Mark Wright, Stuart Pearce; Steve Hodge, Bryan Robson (captain), Glenn Hoddle, Chris Waddle; Peter Beardsley, Mark Hateley. *Manager:* Bobby Robson.

26 May 1987   Stanley Rous Cup   Hampden Park   Attendance: 41,384

499 SCOTLAND 0, Brazil 2
Referee: Luigi Agnolin (Italy)

Scotland: Andy Goram (Oldham Athletic); Richard Gough (Tottenham Hotspur), Willie Miller (Aberdeen), Alex McLeish (Aberdeen), Murdo MacLeod (Celtic); Paul McStay (Celtic), Jim McInally (Dundee United), Roy Aitken (Celtic, captain), Ian Wilson (Leicester City); Davie Cooper (Rangers), Ally McCoist (Rangers). *Substitute:* Brian McClair (Celtic, for McInally 59). *Manager:* Andy Roxburgh.

Brazil: Carlos; Josimar, Douglas, Ricardo Rocha, Geraldao (captain); Muller, Nelsinho, Rai; Edu, Valdo, Mirandinha. *Trainer:* Carlos Alberto Silva.

Scorers: Brazil: Rai 51; Valdo 62

Before taking on Belgium in October 1987. From left: Roy Aitken, Jim Leighton (hidden), Maurice Johnston, Ian Wilson, Paul McStay, Maurice Malpas, Gary Gillespie, Steve Clarke, Ian Durrant, Ally McCoist, Alex McLeish.

Chapter six: 1980-1989

9 September 1987   Friendly   Hampden Park   Attendance: 21,128

500 SCOTLAND 2, Hungary 0   *Referee: Jan Keizer (Netherlands)*

Scotland: Jim Leighton (Aberdeen); Steve Clarke (Chelsea), Willie Miller (Aberdeen), Alex McLeish (Aberdeen), Steve Nicol (Liverpool); Gordon Strachan (Manchester United), Paul McStay (Celtic), Roy Aitken (Celtic, captain), Ian Durrant (Rangers); Ally McCoist (Rangers), Maurice Johnston (Nantes). *Substitutes:* Eric Black (Metz, for Johnston 71); Jim Bett (Aberdeen, for McStay 77). *Manager:* Andy Roxburgh.

Hungary: Peter Disztl; Sandor Sallai, Arpad Toma, Jozsef Csuhay, Imre Garaba (captain); Zoltan Peter, Gyorgy Bognar, Jozsef Keller; Ferenc Meszaros, Kalman Kovacs, Gyula Hajszan. *Substitute:* Ferenc Lovasz (for Kovacs 87). *Trainer:* Jozsef Garami.

Scorer: Scotland: McCoist 34, 62

---

14 October 1987   European Championship qualifying   Hampden Park   Attendance: 20,052

501 SCOTLAND 2, Belgium 0   *Referee: Paolo Casarin (Italy)*

Scotland (4-4-2):

37 Jim Leighton (Aberdeen);
2   Steve Clarke (Chelsea)
1   Gary Gillespie (Liverpool)
48 Alex McLeish (Aberdeen)
16 Maurice Malpas (Dundee United);
24 Paul McStay (Celtic)
32 Roy Aitken (Celtic, captain)
2   Ian Durrant (Rangers)
3   Ian Wilson (Everton);
8   Ally McCoist (Rangers)
15 Maurice Johnston (Nantes)

Substitutes: 1 Derek Whyte (Celtic, for Malpas 53);
9 Graeme Sharp (Everton, for Johnston 72)

Manager: Andy Roxburgh

Belgium: Michel Preud'homme; Eric Gerets, Patrick Vervoort, Leo Clijsters, Georges Grun; Frank Van der Elst, Luc Beyens, Frank Vercauteren; Jan Ceulemans (captain), Marc Degrijse, Nico Claesen. *Substitute:* Philippe Desmet (for Beyens 55). *Trainer:* Guy Thys.

Scorers: Scotland: McCoist 14; McStay 79

The Scots had started the campaign well enough, drawing the first two matches 0-0 and beating Luxembourg, but unfortunately then lost to the Republic of Ireland and Belgium which ultimately was to cost them qualification. They got back on track again after that with a home victory over Belgium. Ally McCoist, who had scored both goals in the previous 2-0 win over Hungary in a friendly, got the opener after a move involving Steve Clarke, Ian Wilson and Maurice Johnston. Paul McStay, the game's outstanding player, made it 2-0 with just over 10 minutes left. Gaining possession on the edge of the Belgian box, he eased past a defender before firing into the corner of the net from 18 yards. The next game saw a fine away win over Bulgaria, which denied the hosts top spot and let the Republic of Ireland through, before finishing with a disappointing goalless draw with Luxembourg.

EUROPEAN CHAMPIONSHIP QUALIFYING GROUP SEVEN

	P	W	D	L	F	A	Pts
Rep of Ireland	8	4	3	1	10	5	11
Bulgaria	8	4	2	2	12	6	10
Belgium	8	3	3	2	16	8	9
Scotland	8	3	3	2	7	5	9
Luxembourg	8	0	1	7	2	23	1

---

11 November 1987   European Championship qualifying   Vasil Levski Stadion, Sofia   Attendance: 49,976

502 Bulgaria 0, SCOTLAND 1   *Referee: Helmut Kohl (Austria)*

Scotland: Jim Leighton (Aberdeen); Steve Clarke (Chelsea), Gary Gillespie (Liverpool), Alex McLeish (Aberdeen), Maurice Malpas (Dundee United); Steve Nicol (Liverpool), Paul McStay (Celtic), Roy Aitken (Celtic, captain), Ian Wilson (Everton); Brian McClair (Manchester United), Graeme Sharp (Everton). *Substitutes:* Gary MacKay (Hearts, for McStay 57); Gordon Durie (Chelsea, for Sharp 71). *Manager:* Andy Roxburgh.

Bulgaria: Borislav Mihailov; Plamen Nikolov, Krasimir Bezinski, Petar Petrov, Nikolai Iliev; Plamen Simeonov, Anyo Sadkov, Hristo Stoichkov; Bozhidar Iskrenov, Nasko Sirakov (captain), Petar Aleksandrov. *Substitutes:* Iliya Voinov (for Aleksandrov 42); Lyuboslav Penev (for Simeonov 88). *Trainer:* Hristo Mladenov.

Scorer: Scotland: MacKay 87

---

2 December 1987   European Championship qualifying   Esch-sur-Alzette   Attendance: 1,999

503 Luxembourg 0, SCOTLAND 0   *Referee: Manfred Neuner (West Germany)*

Scotland: Jim Leighton (Aberdeen); Derek Whyte (Celtic), Willie Miller (Aberdeen), Alex McLeish (Aberdeen, captain), Maurice Malpas (Dundee United); Pat Nevin (Chelsea), Paul McStay (Celtic), Roy Aitken (Celtic), Ian Wilson (Everton); Graeme Sharp (Everton), Maurice Johnston (Nantes). *Substitutes:* Gary MacKay (Hearts, for Whyte 60); Eric Black (Metz, for Nevin 60). *Manager:* Andy Roxburgh.

Luxembourg: John Van Rijswick; Marcel Bossi, Carlo Weis, Hubert Meunier (captain), Pierre Petry; Jean-Paul Girres, Jean-Pierre Barboni, Theo Scholten; Jeannot Reiter, Robert Langers, Gerard Jeitz. *Substitutes:* Armin Krings (for Reiter 54); Jeff Saibene (for Girres 87). *Trainer:* Paul Philipp.

---

17 February 1988   Friendly   King Fahd Stadium, Riyadh   Attendance: 35,000

504 Saudi Arabia 2, SCOTLAND 2   *Referee: Abdullah Al Nasir (Saudi Arabia)*

Scotland: Jim Leighton (Aberdeen); Steve Clarke (Chelsea), Willie Miller (Aberdeen), Richard Gough (Rangers), Maurice Malpas (Dundee United); Steve Nicol (Liverpool), Paul McStay (Celtic), Roy Aitken (Celtic, captain), John Collins (Hibernian); Frank McAvennie (Celtic), Maurice Johnston (Nantes). *Substitutes:* Henry Smith (Hearts, for Leighton 46); Alex McLeish (Aberdeen, for Miller 46); John Colquhoun (Hearts, for Nicol 46); Gary MacKay (Hearts, for McStay 63); Robert Connor (Aberdeen, for McAvennie 81). *Manager:* Andy Roxburgh.

Saudi Arabia: Abdullah Al-Diayye; Bandar Serour, Salah Naima, Ahmed Jamil, Mohamed Abdeljaquad; Khaled Messad, Zaki Saleh, Baasam Aboudaoud; Saal Al-Doussari, Youssef Jazaa, Abdullah Majed. *Substitutes:* Saad Moubarak (for Al-Doussari 46); Fahd Hrifi (for Majed 84). *Trainer:* Carlos Alberto Parreira (Brazil).

Scorers: Saudi Arabia: Jazaa 15; Majed 71   Scotland: Johnston 47; Collins 49

22 March 1988 Friendly Ta'Qali Stadium, Valletta Attendance: 8,000

505 Malta 1, SCOTLAND 1
Referee: George Courtney (England)

Scotland: Jim Leighton (Aberdeen); Steve Clarke (Chelsea), Willie Miller (Aberdeen), Alex McLeish (Aberdeen), Maurice Malpas (Dundee United); Gary MacKay (Hearts), Derek Ferguson (Rangers), Roy Aitken (Celtic, captain), Ian Durrant (Rangers); Graeme Sharp (Everton), Ally McCoist (Rangers). *Substitutes:* Brian McClair (Manchester United, for McCoist 51); Jim McInally (Dundee United, for MacKay 55); John Colquhoun (Hearts, for Durrant 75). *Manager:* Andy Roxburgh.

Malta: David Cluett; John Buttigieg, Joseph Brincat, Alex Azzopardi, Edwin Camilleri; Martin Scicluna, Raymond Vella (captain), David Carabott; Charles Micallef, Michael Degiorgio, Carmel Bussutil. *Substitute:* Charles Scerri (for Micallef 10). *Trainer:* Horst Heese (West Germany).

Scorers: Scotland: Sharp 21   Malta: Bussutil 53

27 April 1988 Friendly Bernabeu, Madrid Attendance: 15,000

506 Spain 0, SCOTLAND 0
Referee: Carlos Da Silva (Portugal)

Scotland: Jim Leighton (Aberdeen); Richard Gough (Rangers), Willie Miller (Aberdeen), Alex McLeish (Aberdeen), Steve Nicol (Liverpool); Gary Gillespie (Liverpool), Paul McStay (Celtic), Roy Aitken (Celtic, captain), Ian Durrant (Rangers); Ally McCoist (Rangers), Maurice Johnston (Nantes). *Substitute:* Brian McClair (Manchester United, for McCoist 69). *Manager:* Andy Roxburgh.

Spain: Andoni Zubizarreta; Pedro Renones, Miguel Soler, Victor Munoz, Manuel Sanchis; Rafael Gordillo (captain), Ricardo Gallego, Miguel Gonzalez; Rafael Vasquez, Julio Salinas, Emilio Butragueno. *Substitutes:* Miguel Tendillo (for Gallego 46); Eloy Olaya (for Salinas 78). *Trainer:* Miguel Munoz Mozun.

17 May 1988 Stanley Rous Cup Hampden Park Attendance: 20,487

507 SCOTLAND 0, Columbia 0
Referee: Joao Correia (Portugal)

Scotland: Jim Leighton (Aberdeen); Richard Gough (Rangers), Willie Miller (Aberdeen), Alex McLeish (Aberdeen), Steve Nicol (Liverpool); Paul McStay (Celtic), Roy Aitken (Celtic, captain), Murdo MacLeod (Borussia Dortmund); Kevin Gallacher (Dundee United), Ally McCoist (Rangers), Maurice Johnston (Nantes). *Substitutes:* Derek Ferguson (Rangers, for McCoist 59); Andy Walker (Celtic, for Gallacher 67). *Manager:* Andy Roxburgh.

Columbia: Jose Higuita; Andres Escobar, Leonel Alvarez, Luis Herrera, Carlos Hoyas; Luis Perea, Alexis Garcia, Carlos Valderrama (captain); Bernardo Redin, Arnoldo Iguaran, John Trellez. *Substitute:* Jaime Arango (for Trellez 78). *Trainer:* Francisco Maturana.

21 May 1988 Stanley Rous Cup Wembley, London Attendance: 70,480

508 England 1, SCOTLAND 0
Referee: Joel Quiniou (France)

Scotland: Jim Leighton (Aberdeen); Richard Gough (Rangers), Willie Miller (Aberdeen), Alex McLeish (Aberdeen), Steve Nicol (Liverpool); Neil Simpson (Aberdeen), Paul McStay (Celtic), Roy Aitken (Celtic, captain), Murdo MacLeod (Borussia Dortmund); Ally McCoist (Rangers), Maurice Johnston (Nantes). *Substitutes:* Tommy Burns (Celtic, for Simpson 74); Kevin Gallacher (Dundee United, for McCoist 77). *Manager:* Andy Roxburgh.

England: Peter Shilton; Gary Stevens, Tony Adams, Dave Watson, Kenny Sansom; Trevor Steven, Neil Webb, Bryan Robson (captain), John Barnes; Peter Beardsley, Gary Lineker. *Substitute:* Chris Waddle (for Steven 72). *Manager:* Bobby Robson.

Scorer: England: Beardsley 11

14 September 1988 World Cup qualifying Ullevaal Stadion, Oslo Attendance: 22,769

509 Norway 1, SCOTLAND 2
Referee: Luigi Agnolin (Italy)

Scotland: Jim Leighton (Manchester United); Steve Nicol (Liverpool), Willie Miller (Aberdeen), Alex McLeish (Aberdeen), Maurice Malpas (Dundee United); Gary Gillespie (Liverpool), Paul McStay (Celtic), Roy Aitken (Celtic, captain); Kevin Gallacher (Dundee United), Brian McClair (Manchester United), Maurice Johnston (Nantes). *Substitute:* Ian Durrant (Rangers, for Aitken 55). *Manager:* Andy Roxburgh.

Norway: Erik Thorstvedt; Hans Henriksen, Rune Bratseth, Erland Johnsen, Anders Giske (captain); Kjetil Osvold, Tom Sundby, Sverre Brandhaug, Karl-Peter Loken; Goran Sorloth, Jan-Aage Fjortoft. *Substitutes:* Orjan Berg (for Sundby 2); Jan-Ivar Jakobsen (for Berg 84). *Trainer:* Ingvar Stadheim.

Scorers: Scotland: McStay 14; Johnston 63   Norway: Fjortoft 44

19 October 1988 World Cup qualifying Hampden Park Attendance: 42,771

510 SCOTLAND 1, Yugoslavia 1
Referee: Karl-Heinz Trischler (West Germany)

Scotland: Andy Goram (Hibernian); Richard Gough (Rangers), Willie Miller (Aberdeen, captain), Alex McLeish (Aberdeen), Maurice Malpas (Dundee United); Steve Nicol (Liverpool), Paul McStay (Celtic), Roy Aitken (Celtic), Jim Bett (Aberdeen); Brian McClair (Manchester United), Maurice Johnston (Nantes). *Substitutes:* Ally McCoist (Rangers, for Bett 55); David Speedie (Coventry City, for Aitken 70). *Manager:* Andy Roxburgh.

Yugoslavia: Tomislav Ivkovic; Vujadin Stanojkovic, Predrag Spasic, Srecko Katanec, Faruk Hadzibegic; Davor Jozic, Ljubomir Radanovic, Mehmed Bazdarevic; Borislav Cvetkovic, Dragan Stojkovic, Zlatko Vujovic (captain). *Substitutes:* Dragoljub Brnovic (for Spasic 83); Refik Sabanadzovic (for Cvetkovic 89). *Trainer:* Ivan Osim.

Scorers: Scotland: Johnston 19   Yugoslavia: Katanec 36

Chapter six: 1980-1989

22 December 1988   Friendly   Stadio Renato Curi, Perugia   Attendance: 25,600

511 Italy 2, SCOTLAND 0
Referee: Alain Delmer (France)

Scotland: Andy Goram (Hibernian); Richard Gough (Rangers), David Narey (Dundee United), Alex McLeish (Aberdeen), Maurice Malpas (Dundee United); Ian Ferguson (Rangers), Paul McStay (Celtic), Roy Aitken (Celtic, captain), Murdo MacLeod (Borussia Dortmund); Kevin Gallacher (Dundee United), Maurice Johnston (Nantes). *Substitutes:* Brian McClair (Manchester United, for McStay 56); Gordon Durie (Chelsea, for Ferguson 71); David Speedie (Coventry City, for Gough 87). *Manager:* Andy Roxburgh.

Italy: Walter Zenga; Guiseppe Bergomi (captain), Franco Baresi, Riccardo Ferri, Paolo Maldini; Massimo Crippa, Nicola Berti, Guiseppe Giannini; Giancarlo Marocchi, Aldo Serena, Gianluca Vialli. *Substitutes:* Stefano Tacconi (for Zenga 50); Ciro Ferrara (for Bergomi 50). *Trainer:* Azeglio Vicini.

Scorers: Italy: Giannini 47 (pen); Berti 70

8 February 1989   World Cup qualifying   Tsirion Stadhion, Limassol   Attendance: 25,000

512 Cyprus 2, SCOTLAND 3
Referee: Siegfried Kirschen (East Germany)

Scotland: Jim Leighton (Manchester United); Richard Gough (Rangers), David Narey (Dundee United), Alex McLeish (Aberdeen), Maurice Malpas (Dundee United); Steve Nicol (Liverpool), Paul McStay (Celtic), Roy Aitken (Celtic, captain), David Speedie (Coventry City), Brian McClair (Manchester United), Maurice Johnston (Nantes). *Substitutes:* Ian Ferguson (Rangers, for Nicol 10); Alan McInally (Aston Villa, for Speedie 78). *Manager:* Andy Roxburgh.

Cyprus: Georgios Pantziaras; Charalambous Pittas, Kostas Miamiliotis, Georgios Christodoulou, Avraam Socratous; Yiannakis Yiangoudakis (captain), Christos Koliandris, Pavlos Savva; Floros Nicolaou, Georgios Savvides, Yiannos Ioannou. *Substitutes:* Kostas Petsas (for Savva 39); Antonis Andrellis (for Miamiliotis 77). *Trainer:* Panikos Iacovou.

Scorers: Scotland: Johnston 9; Gough 54, 90+6   Cyprus: Koliandris 14; Ioannou 47

8 March 1989   World Cup qualifying   Hampden Park   Attendance: 65,204

513 SCOTLAND 2, France 0
Referee: Jiri Stiegler (Czechoslovakia)

Scotland (4-4-2):
47 Jim Leighton (Manchester United);
42 Richard Gough (Rangers)
5   Gary Gillespie (Liverpool)
60 Alex McLeish (Aberdeen, captain)
25 Maurice Malpas (Dundee United);
3   Ian Ferguson (Rangers)
35 Paul McStay (Celtic)
44 Roy Aitken (Celtic)
21 Steve Nicol (Liverpool);
14 Ally McCoist (Rangers)
25 Maurice Johnston (Nantes).

Substitutes: 42 Gordon Strachan (Manchester United, for Ferguson 56); 12 Brian McClair (Manchester United, for McCoist 69)

Manager: Andy Roxburgh.

A great display at home saw off France to set up qualification for the 1990 World Cup in Italy and all but end the visitors' hopes of making it to the finals. Maurice Johnston, now playing in France himself at Nantes, got a goal in each half in a well-deserved victory while Liverpool centre back Gary Gillespie, in just his fifth appearance, right back Richard Gough and Paul McStay in midfield also stood out. It was from Gillespie's cross that the first goal came, Gough heading the ball down and Johnston finding the net after Ally McCoist's initial shot was blocked. Keeper Jim Leighton made a couple of timely saves to keep the French out before Johnston got his second just after half-time. Gough began the move and Steve Nicol's cross found Johnston whose header squirmed out of French goalkeeper Bats' hands and over the line.

France: Joel Bats; Manuel Amoros (captain), Frank Silvestre, Luc Sonor, Laurent Blanc, Patrick Battiston; Frank Sauzee, Jean-Philippe Durand, Thierry Laurey; Jean-Pierre Papin, Daniel Xuereb. *Substitutes:* Stephane Paille (for Durand 57); Christian Perez (for Xuereb 73). *Trainer:* Michel Platini.

Scorer: Scotland: Johnston 28, 52

26 April 1989   World Cup qualifying   Hampden Park   Attendance: 50,081

514 SCOTLAND 2, Cyprus 1
Referee: Gudmundur Haraldsson (Iceland)

Scotland: Jim Leighton (Manchester United); Richard Gough (Rangers), David McPherson (Hearts), Alex McLeish (Aberdeen), Maurice Malpas (Dundee United); Pat Nevin (Everton), Paul McStay (Celtic), Roy Aitken (Celtic, captain); Gordon Durie (Chelsea), Ally McCoist (Rangers), Maurice Johnston (Nantes). *Substitutes:* David Speedie (Coventry City, for Durie 59); Charlie Nicholas (Aberdeen, for Nevin 74). *Manager:* Andy Roxburgh.

Cyprus: Andreas Charitou; Charalambous Pittas, Spiros Kastanas, Georgios Christodoulou, Avraam Socratous; Yiannakis Yiangoudakis (captain), Christos Koliandris, Kostas Petsas; Floros Nicolaou, Georgios Savvides, Yiannos Ioannou. *Substitute:* Antonis Andrellis (for Pittas 64). *Trainer:* Panikos Iacovou.

Scorers: Scotland: Johnston 26; McCoist 63   Cyprus: Nicolaou 62

27 May 1989   Stanley Rous Cup   Hampden Park   Attendance: 63,282

515 SCOTLAND 0, England 2
Referee: Michel Vautrot (France)

Scotland: Jim Leighton (Manchester United); Stewart McKimmie (Aberdeen), David McPherson (Hearts), Alex McLeish (Aberdeen), Maurice Malpas (Dundee United); Pat Nevin (Everton), Paul McStay (Celtic), Roy Aitken (Celtic, captain), Robert Connor (Aberdeen); Ally McCoist (Rangers), Maurice Johnston (Nantes). *Substitute:* Peter Grant (Celtic, for Connor 57). *Manager:* Andy Roxburgh.

England: Peter Shilton; Gary Stevens, Terry Butcher, Des Walker, Stuart Pearce; Trevor Steven, Neil Webb, Bryan Robson (captain), Chris Waddle; John Fashanu, Tony Cottee. *Substitutes:* Steve Bull (for Fashanu 31); Paul Gascoigne (for Cottee 75). *Manager:* Bobby Robson.

Scorers: England: Waddle 20; Bull 80

30 May 1989   Stanley Rous Cup   Hampden Park   Attendance: 9,006

516 SCOTLAND 2, Chile 0

Referee: Alexis Ponnet (Belgium)

Scotland: Jim Leighton (Manchester United, captain); Stewart McKimmie (Aberdeen), Gary Gillespie (Liverpool), Alex McLeish (Aberdeen), Maurice Malpas (Dundee United); Peter Grant (Celtic), Paul McStay (Celtic), Roy Aitken (Celtic), Murdo MacLeod (Borussia Dortmund); David Speedie (Coventry City), Alan McInally (Aston Villa). *Substitutes:* Maurice Johnston (Nantes, for Speedie 46); Derek Whyte (Celtic, for Gillespie 70). *Manager:* Andy Roxburgh.

Chile: Roberto Rojas (captain); Oscar Reyes, Leonel Contreras, Hugo Gonzalez, Jaime Pizarro; Hugo Rubio, Jaime Vera, Juvenal Olmos; Alejandro Hisis, Juan Covarrubias, Hector Puebla. *Substitute:* Juan Letelier (for Covarrubias 46). *Trainer:* Orlando Aravena.

Scorers: Scotland: McInally 4; MacLeod 52

---

6 September 1989   World Cup qualifying   Maksimir Stadion, Zagreb   Attendance: 42,500

517 Yugoslavia 3, SCOTLAND 1

Referee: Marcel Van Langenhove (Belgium)

Scotland: Jim Leighton (Manchester United); Steve Nicol (Liverpool), Willie Miller (Aberdeen), Alex McLeish (Aberdeen), Maurice Malpas (Dundee United); Gary Gillespie (Liverpool), Paul McStay (Celtic), Roy Aitken (Celtic, captain), Murdo MacLeod (Borussia Dortmund); Gordon Durie (Chelsea), Ally McCoist (Rangers). *Substitute:* Alan McInally (Bayern Munich, for Durie 71). *Manager:* Andy Roxburgh.

Yugoslavia: Tomislav Ivkovic; Mirsad Baljic, Predrag Spasic, Srecko Katanec, Faruk Hadzibegic; Dragoljub Brnovic, Mehmed Bazdarevic, Dragan Stojkovic; Safet Susic, Dragan Jakovljevic, Zlatko Vujovic (captain). *Substitute:* Dejan Savicevic (for Jakovljevic 73). *Trainer:* Ivan Osim.

Scorers: Scotland: Durie 37   Yugoslavia: Katanec 52; Nicol 57 (own goal); Gillespie 59 (own goal)

---

11 October 1989   World Cup qualifying   Parc des Princes, Paris   Attendance: 25,000

518 France 3, SCOTLAND 0

Referee: Kurt Rothlisberger (Switzerland)

Scotland: Jim Leighton (Manchester United); Steve Nicol (Liverpool), Richard Gough (Rangers), Alex McLeish (Aberdeen), Maurice Malpas (Dundee United); Gordon Strachan (Manchester United), Paul McStay (Celtic), Roy Aitken (Celtic, captain), Murdo MacLeod (Borussia Dortmund); Ally McCoist (Rangers), Maurice Johnston (Rangers). *Substitutes:* Alan McInally (Bayern Munich, for Strachan 64); Jim Bett (Aberdeen, for MacLeod 75). *Manager:* Andy Roxburgh.

France: Joel Bats; Frank Silvestre, Eric Di Meco, Frank Sauzee, Yvon Le Roux; Jean-Philippe Durand, Bernard Pardo, Didier Deschamps; Christian Perez, Jean-Marc Ferreri, Eric Cantona. *Substitutes:* Bernard Casoni (for Le Roux 46); Daniel Bravo (for Perez 81). *Trainer:* Michel Platini.

Scorers: France: Deschamps 26; Cantona 63; Nicol 88 (own goal)

---

15 November 1989   World Cup qualifying   Hampden Park   Attendance: 63,987

519 SCOTLAND 1, Norway 1

Referee: Michal Listkiewicz (Poland)

Scotland (4-3-3):

53 Jim Leighton (Manchester United);
3 Dave McPherson (Hearts)
65 Willie Miller (Aberdeen)
66 Alex McLeish (Aberdeen)
31 Maurice Malpas (Dundee United);
41 Paul McStay (Celtic)
50 Roy Aitken (Celtic, captain)
22 Jim Bett (Aberdeen);
30 Maurice Johnston (Rangers)
19 Ally McCoist (Rangers)
21 Davie Cooper (Rangers)

Substitutes: 12 Murdo MacLeod (Borussia Dortmund, for Miller 67);
13 Brian McClair (Manchester United, for Cooper 74)

Manager: Andy Roxburgh

Norway: Erik Thorstvedt; Hugo Hansen, Rune Bratseth, Terje Kojedal, Erlend Johnsen; Stig Inge Bjornebye, Tom Gulbrandsen, Per Egil Ahlsen; Bent Skammelsrud, Goram Sorloth, Jan Age Fjortoft. *Substitutes:* Lars Bohinen, for Skammelsrud 58); Jan Halvorsen (for Kojedal 82). *Trainer:* Ingvar Stadheim.

Scorers: Scotland: McCoist 44   Norway: Johnsen 89

The late embarrassment of an unexpected equaliser by Norway took some of the gloss off the occasion as Scotland qualified for the World Cup finals for the fifth time in a row, finishing second in group five behind Yugoslavia. Although they would travel to Italy with few expectations, Andy Roxburgh's squad had a number of steady and experienced players who regularly gave their all. The opening goal came on the stroke of half-time, when ace predator Ally McCoist coolly lobbed the keeper after Maurice Malpas had headed the ball forward to him. Scotland lost Willie Miller midway through the second half and were forced to readjust, which may have stalled the momentum as they went for a second goal. Indeed it was Norway who got one back in the final minute when a speculative shot by Johnsen completely deceived Jim Leighton in goal. Captain Roy Aitken became the latest player to achieve 50 international caps.

FIFA WORLD CUP QUALIFYING GROUP FIVE

	P	W	D	L	F	A	Pts
Yugoslavia	8	6	2	0	16	6	14
Scotland	8	4	2	2	12	12	10
France	8	3	3	2	10	7	9
Norway	8	2	2	4	10	9	6
Cyprus	8	0	1	7	6	20	1

CHAPTER SEVEN
1990-1999

28 March 1990 Friendly Hampden Park Attendance: 51,537

520 SCOTLAND 1, Argentina 0
Referee: Frans Houben (Netherlands)

Scotland: Jim Leighton (Manchester United); Richard Gough (Rangers), Craig Levein (Hearts), Alex McLeish (Aberdeen, captain), Stewart McKimmie (Aberdeen); Jim Bett (Aberdeen), Stuart McCall (Everton), Paul McStay (Celtic), Murdo MacLeod (Borussia Dortmund); Robert Fleck (Norwich City), Alan McInally (Bayern Munich). *Substitutes:* Brian McClair (Manchester United, for McInally 74); Roy Aitken (Newcastle United, for Bett 89). *Manager:* Andy Roxburgh.

Argentina: Nery Pumpido (captain); Sergio Batista, Edgardo Bauza, Roberto Sensini, Oscar Ruggeri; Nestor Fabbri, Gabriel Calderon, Jose Basualdo; Jorge Burruchaga, Jorge Valdano, Claudio Caniggia. *Substitutes:* Abel Balbo (for Valdano 46); Pedro Troglio (for Burruchaga 49); Pedro Monzon (for Ruggeri 59). *Coach:* Carlos Bilardo.

Scorer: Scotland: McKimmie 32

25 April 1990 Friendly Hampden Park Attendance: 21,868

521 SCOTLAND 0, East Germany 1
Referee: Neil Midgley (England)

Scotland: Andy Goram (Hibernian); Richard Gough (Rangers), Gary Gillespie (Liverpool), Craig Levein (Hearts), Alex McLeish (Aberdeen, captain), Murdo MacLeod (Borussia Dortmund); Stuart McCall (Everton), Gary McAllister (Leicester City), John Collins (Hibernian); Gordon Durie (Chelsea), Maurice Johnston (Rangers). *Substitutes:* Paul McStay (Celtic, for Gillespie 57); Ally McCoist (Rangers, for Durie 68). *Manager:* Andy Roxburgh.

East Germany: Perry Brautigam; Heiko Peschke, Stefan Boger, Hendryk Herzog, Matthias Lindner; Dirk Schuster, Matthias Sammer, Jorg Stubner; Rainer Ernst (captain), Ulf Kirsten, Thomas Doll. *Substitute:* Stefan Buttner (for Stubner 85). *Coach:* Eduard Geyer.

Scorer: East Germany: Doll 73 (pen)

16 May 1990 Friendly Pittodrie, Aberdeen Attendance: 23,000

522 SCOTLAND 1, Egypt 3
Referee: Rune Pedersen (Norway)

Scotland: Bryan Gunn (Norwich City); Stewart McKimmie (Aberdeen), Richard Gough (Rangers), Alex McLeish (Aberdeen, captain), Maurice Malpas (Dundee United); Jim Bett (Aberdeen), Gary Gillespie (Liverpool), Paul McStay (Celtic), Davie Cooper (Motherwell); Gordon Durie (Chelsea), Ally McCoist (Rangers). *Substitutes:* Stuart McCall (Everton, for McKimmie 46); Craig Levein (Hearts, for McLeish 89). *Manager:* Andy Roxburgh.

Egypt: Ahmed Shoubier; Ibrahim Hassan, Hisham Yakin, Raba Yassin, Hani Ramzy; Ahmed El-Kas, Magdi Abdelghani, Ahmed Ramzy; Ismail Youssef, Gamal Abdelhamid (captain), Hossam Hassan. *Substitutes:* Thabet El-Batal (for El-Kas 46); Ala's Mayoub (for Abdelghani 60). *Coach:* Mahmoud El-Gohary.

Scorers: Egypt: Abdelhamid 15; Hossam Hassan 28; Youssef 83   Scotland: McCoist 73

19 May 1990 Friendly Hampden Park Attendance: 25,142

523 SCOTLAND 1, Poland 1
Referee: Joe Worrall (England)

Scotland: Andy Goram (Hibernian); Richard Gough (Rangers), Gary Gillespie (Liverpool), Craig Levein (Hearts), Maurice Malpas (Dundee United); Stuart McCall (Everton), Roy Aitken (Newcastle United, captain), Gary McAllister (Leicester City), Murdo MacLeod (Borussia Dortmund); Ally McCoist (Rangers), Maurice Johnston (Rangers). *Substitutes:* John Collins (Hibernian, for MacLeod 65); Alan McInally (Bayern Munich, for Johnston 73); Paul McStay (Celtic, for McAllister 83). *Manager:* Andy Roxburgh.

Poland: Jaroslaw Bako; Dariusz Kubicki, Dariusz Wdowczyk, Zbigniew Kaczmarek (captain), Damian Lukasic; Waldemar Prusik, Piotr Czachowski, Janusz Nawrocki; Jacek Ziober, Dariusz Dziekanowski, Roman Kosecki. *Substitutes:* Piotr Soczynski (for Lukasic 46); Leszek Pisz (for Nawrocki 70). *Coach:* Andrzej Strejlau.

Scorers: Scotland: Johnston 42   Poland: Gillespie 59 (own goal)

28 May 1990 Friendly Ta'Qali Stadium, Valletta Attendance: 3,000

524 Malta 1, SCOTLAND 2
Referee: Carlo Longhi (Italy)

Scotland: Andy Goram (Hibernian); David McPherson (Hearts), Gary Gillespie (Liverpool), Richard Gough (Rangers), Maurice Malpas (Dundee United); Jim Bett (Aberdeen), Paul McStay (Celtic), Roy Aitken (Newcastle United, captain), Stuart McCall (Everton); Alan McInally (Bayern Munich), Maurice Johnston (Rangers). *Substitutes:* Craig Levein (Hearts, for Gillespie 40); Jim Leighton (Manchester United, for Goram 46); Gary McAllister (Leicester City, for Bett 46); Ally McCoist (Rangers, for Johnston 69); John Collins (Hibernian, for McStay 80). *Manager:* Andy Roxburgh.

Malta: Reginald Cini; Silvio Vella, David Carabott, John Buttigieg, Joseph Galea; Jesmond Zerafa, Kristian Laferla, Raymond Vella (captain); Martin Gregory, Bernard Licari, Michael Degiorgio. *Substitutes:* Edwin Camilleri (for Galea 46); Joseph Zarb (for Gregory 62); Charles Scerri (for Licari 77). *Coach:* Horst Heese (West Germany).

Scorers: Scotland: McInally 5, 81   Malta: Degiorgio 43

11 June 1990   World Cup finals (group stage)   Stadio Luigi Ferraris, Genoa   Attendance: 30,867

525 Costa Rica 1, SCOTLAND 0
Referee: Juan Carlos Loustau (Argentina)

Scotland (4-4-2):

- 56 Jim Leighton (Manchester United);
- 5 David McPherson (Hearts)
- 50 Richard Gough (Rangers)
- 70 Alex McLeish (Aberdeen)
- 35 Maurice Malpas (Dundee United);
- 26 Jim Bett (Aberdeen)
- 47 Paul McStay (Celtic)
- 54 Roy Aitken (Newcastle United, captain)
- 6 Stuart McCall (Everton);
- 8 Alan McInally (Bayern Munich)
- 34 Maurice Johnston (Rangers)

Defeat to the lowest-rated side in the group in the opening match was the last thing Scottish fans were expecting, but it was no more than the lacklustre display merited. Costa Rica were really just competent and only threatened occasionally on the break, but they got the goal that mattered. Cayasso, who had also come close during a rare attack in the first half, clipped the ball over keeper Jim Leighton's body after a backheel flick from Jara in the 49th minute. Scotland tried hard to at least restore parity but nothing seemed to go right, and missed chances by both strikers Alan McInally and Maurice Johnston just about summed up the day.

Substitutes: 5 Stewart McKimmie (Aberdeen, for Gough 46); 24 Ally McCoist (Rangers, for Bett 74)

Manager: Andy Roxburgh

Costa Rica: Luis Conejo; German Chavarria, Roger Flores (captain), Mauricio Montero, Jose Chavez; Hector Marchena, Juan Cayasso, Ronald Gonzalez; Oscar Ramirez, Roger Gomez, Claudio Jara. *Substitute:* Hernan Medford (for Jara 85). *Trainer:* Bora Milutinovic (Yugoslavia).

Scorer: Costa Rica: Juan Cayasso 49

---

16 June 1990   World Cup finals (group stage)   Stadio Luigi Ferraris, Genoa   Attendance: 31,823

526 Sweden 1, SCOTLAND 2
Referee: Carlos Maciel (Paraguay)

Scotland (4-3-3):

- 57 Jim Leighton (Manchester United);
- 6 David McPherson (Hearts)
- 6 Craig Levein (Hearts)
- 71 Alex McLeish (Aberdeen)
- 36 Maurice Malpas (Dundee United);
- 16 Murdo MacLeod (Borussia Dortmund)
- 55 Roy Aitken (Newcastle United, captain)
- 7 Stuart McCall (Everton);
- 7 Gordon Durie (Chelsea)
- 2 Robert Fleck (Norwich City)
- 35 Maurice Johnston (Rangers)

After the shocker against Costa Rica, Scotland produced the form to see off a difficult Swedish side in the second group match. It was a tough, uncompromising display which the Swedes could not match, and afterwards coach Olle Nordin sportingly described their opponents' style as "hard but fair". A strong start led to a goal in just 10 minutes, when Stuart McCall finished off a Murdo MacLeod corner which had been headed on by David McPherson. Scotland's grip on the game continued throughout the remainder of the first half and into the second, but it took until the 81st minute for them to make the game relatively safe. After captain Roy Aitken was brought down in the box Maurice Johnston scored from the resultant penalty kick. There was still time for some late drama, as first Johnny Ekstrom missed two chances and then Stromberg scored. The Scots saw out the game, however, and qualification hopes were restored.

Substitutes: 48 Paul McStay (Celtic, for Durie 74); 25 Ally McCoist (Rangers, for Fleck 84)

Manager: Andy Roxburgh

Sweden: Thomas Ravelli; Roland Nilsson, Stefan Schwarz, Peter Larsson, Glenn Hysen (captain); Anders Limpar, Jonas Thern, Joakim Nilssen; Klas Ingesson, Thomas Brolin, Stefan Pettersson. *Substitutes:* Johnny Ekstrom (for Pettersson 65); Glenn Stromberg (for Larsson 74). *Trainer:* Olle Nordin.

Scorers: Scotland: McCall 10; Johnston 81 (pen)   Sweden: Stromberg 85

Maurice Johnston (right) scores what turned out to be the decisive second goal against Sweden.

The team which lost narrowly to Brazil at the 1990 World Cup. Back (from left): Maurice Malpas, David McPherson, Jim Leighton, Alex McLeish, Ally McCoist, Maurice Johnston. Front: Roy Aitken, Paul McStay, Stuart McCall, Stewart McKimmie, Murdo MacLeod.

20 June 1990 World Cup finals (group stage) Delle Alpi, Torino Attendance: 62,502

527 Brazil 1, SCOTLAND 0

Referee: Helmut Kohl (Austria)

Scotland (4-4-2)
- 58 Jim Leighton (Manchester United);
- 6 Stewart McKimmie (Aberdeen)
- 7 David McPherson (Hearts)
- 72 Alex McLeish (Aberdeen)
- 37 Maurice Malpas (Dundee United);
- 8 Stuart McCall (Everton)
- 49 Paul McStay (Celtic)
- 56 Roy Aitken (Newcastle United, captain)
- 17 Murdo MacLeod (Borussia Dortmund);
- 26 Ally McCoist (Rangers)
- 36 Maurice Johnston (Rangers)

Substitutes: 12 Gary Gillespie (Liverpool, for MacLeod 39);
3 Robert Fleck (Norwich City, for McCoist 77)

Manager: Andy Roxburgh

Brazil: Claudio Taffarel; Jorginho, Branco, Ricardo Rocha, Ricardo Gomes (captain); Mauro Galvao, Alemao, Dunga; Valda, Romario, Careca. *Substitute:* Luis Muller (for Romario 64). *Trainer:* Sebastiao Lazaroni.

Scorer: Brazil: Muller 81

A point would have been enough for the Scots to make it to the next stages, following the excellent win over Sweden, but unfortunately a late goal after a Jim Leighton error ultimately extinguished any hopes. It was an excellent performance up until then, defending well and matching the Brazilians in most aspects of play. There were few chances, however, the best being a fine header by captain Roy Aitken which was cleared off the line by Branco with keeper Taffarel beaten. With nine minutes remaining Leighton, who had played well, let a speculative shot from Dunga slip from his grasp. Careca was the first to react and fed substitute Muller who had an easy task to score. Most of the Scottish team had steady games with perhaps Dundee United full back Maurice Malpas being the pick of the bunch.

1990 FIFA WORLD CUP GROUP C

	P	W	D	L	F	A	Pts
Brazil	3	3	0	0	4	1	6
Costa Rica	3	2	0	1	3	2	4
Scotland	3	1	0	2	2	2	2
Sweden	3	0	0	3	3	6	0

12 September 1990 European Championship qualifying Hampden Park Attendance: 12,801

528 SCOTLAND 2, Romania 1

Referee: Ildefonso Urizar Aspitarte (Spain)

Scotland: Andy Goram (Hibernian); Stewart McKimmie (Aberdeen), Brian Irvine (Aberdeen), Alex McLeish (Aberdeen), Maurice Malpas (Dundee United); Murdo MacLeod (Borussia Dortmund), Paul McStay (Celtic, captain), Gary McAllister (Leeds United), Robert Connor (Aberdeen); John Robertson (Hearts), Ally McCoist (Rangers). *Substitutes:* Tom Boyd (Motherwell, for Connor 59); Pat Nevin (Everton, for McAllister 73). *Manager:* Andy Roxburgh.

Romania: Silviu Lung (captain); Dan Petrescu, Michael Klein, Emil Sandoi, Gheorghe Popescu; Dorin Mateut, Ionut Lupescu, Iosif Rotariu; Gheorghe Hagi, Marius Lacatus, Rodion Camataru. *Substitutes:* Florin Raducioiu (for Camataru 63); Ioan Sabau (for Mateut 79). *Coach:* Gheorghe Constantin.

Scorers: Romania: Camataru 13 Scotland: Robertson 37; McCoist 75

17 October 1990   European Championship qualifying   Hampden Park   Attendance: 27,740

529 SCOTLAND 2, Switzerland 1
Referee: Esa Palsi (Finland)

Scotland: Andy Goram (Hibernian); Stewart McKimmie (Aberdeen), David McPherson (Hearts), Alex McLeish (Aberdeen, captain), Tom Boyd (Motherwell); Steve Nicol (Liverpool), Gary McAllister (Leeds United), Stuart McCall (Everton), Murdo MacLeod (Hibernian); John Robertson (Hearts), Ally McCoist (Rangers). *Substitutes:* Gordon Durie (Chelsea, for Boyd 68); John Collins (Celtic, for McAllister 79). *Manager:* Andy Roxburgh.

Switzerland: Philipp Walker; Peter Schepull, Blaise Piffaretti, Dominique Herr, Andre Egli; Thomas Bickel, Heinz Hermann (captain), Alain Sutter; Kubilay Turkyilmaz, Adrian Knup, Stephane Chapuisat. *Substitutes:* Frederic Chassot (for Schepull 73); Beat Sutter (for Piffaretti 80). *Coach:* Gheorghe Constantin.

Scorers: Scotland: Robertson 34 (pen); McAllister 51   Switzerland: Knup 65 (pen)

14 November 1990   European Championship qualifying   Vasil Levski Stadion, Sofia   Attendance: 42,000

530 Bulgaria 1, SCOTLAND 1
Referee: Friedrich Kaupe (Austria)

Scotland: Andy Goram (Hibernian); Stewart McKimmie (Aberdeen), David McPherson (Hearts), Gary Gillespie (Liverpool), Maurice Malpas (Dundee United, captain); Jim McInally (Dundee United), Gary McAllister (Leeds United), Brian McClair (Manchester United), Tom Boyd (Motherwell); Gordon Durie (Chelsea), Ally McCoist (Rangers). *Substitute:* Pat Nevin (Everton, for Durie 59). *Manager:* Andy Roxburgh.

Bulgaria: Borislav Mihailov; Pavel Dochev, Kalin Bankov, Zlatko Yankov, Dimitar Mladenov; Kostadin Yanchev, Georgi Yordanov, Krasimir Balakov; Hristo Stoichkov (captain), Nasko Sirakov, Lyuboslav Penev. *Substitutes:* Nikolai Todorov (for Yanchev 53); Emil Kostadinov (for Balakov 75). *Coach:* Ivan Vutsov.

Scorers: Scotland: McCoist 9   Bulgaria: Todorov 70

6 February 1991   Friendly   Ibrox, Glasgow   Attendance: 20,673

531 SCOTLAND 0, Soviet Union 1
Referee: Peter Mikkelsen (Denmark)

Scotland: Andy Goram (Hibernian); Steve Nicol (Liverpool), Richard Gough (Rangers, captain), Alex McLeish (Aberdeen), Maurice Malpas (Dundee United); Gordon Strachan (Leeds United), Paul McStay (Celtic), Stuart McCall (Everton), Tom Boyd (Motherwell); Robert Fleck (Norwich City), Ally McCoist (Rangers). *Substitutes:* David McPherson (Hearts, for McLeish 46); Murdo MacLeod (Hibernian, for Boyd 46); Gary McAllister (Leeds United, for McCall 69); Gordon Durie (Chelsea, for Fleck 75). *Manager:* Andy Roxburgh.

Soviet Union: Aleksandr Uvarov; Alexei Chernishov, Vasilij Kulkov, Akhrik Tsveiba, Sergei Gorlukovich; Andrei Konchelskis, Igor Shalimov, Sergei Aleinikov; Igor Dobrovolski (captain), Sergei Yuran, Aleksandr Mostovoi. *Substitutes:* Igor Kolivanov (for Yuran 62); Dmitri Kuznetsov (for Mostovoi 69). *Coach:* Anatoliy Byshovetz.

Scorer: Soviet Union: Kuznetsov 88

27 March 1991   European Championship qualifying   Hampden Park   Attendance: 33,119

532 SCOTLAND 1, Bulgaria 1
Referee: Erik Fredriksson (Sweden)

Scotland: Andy Goram (Hibernian); David McPherson (Hearts), Richard Gough (Rangers), Alex McLeish (Aberdeen, captain), Maurice Malpas (Dundee United); Gordon Strachan (Leeds United), Paul McStay (Celtic), Jim McInally (Dundee United), Brian McClair (Manchester United); Gordon Durie (Chelsea), Ally McCoist (Rangers). *Substitutes:* John Collins (Celtic, for Strachan 80); John Robertson (Hearts, for Durie 80). *Manager:* Andy Roxburgh.

Bulgaria: Borislav Mihailov (captain); Pavel Dochev, Trifon Ivanov, Zlatko Yankov, Nikolai Iliev; Ilian Kiriakov, Krasimir Balakov, Nasko Sirakov, Georgi Yordanov, Emil Kostadinov, Lyuboslav Penev. *Substitutes:* Petar Aleksandrov (for Sirakov 86); Lachezar Tanev (for Balakov 86). *Coach:* Ivan Vutsov.

Scorers: Scotland: Collins 83   Bulgaria: Kostadinov 89

1 May 1991   European Championship qualifying   Stadio di Serraville, Serraville   Attendance: 3,512

533 San Marino 0, SCOTLAND 2
Referee: Besnik Kaimi (Albania)

Scotland: Andy Goram (Hibernian); Stewart McKimmie (Aberdeen), Steve Nicol (Liverpool), David McPherson (Hearts), Maurice Malpas (Dundee United); Gordon Strachan (Leeds United, captain), Gary McAllister (Leeds United), Stuart McCall (Everton), Brian McClair (Manchester United); Kevin Gallacher (Coventry City), Gordon Durie (Chelsea). *Substitutes:* Pat Nevin (Everton, for McClair 57); John Robertson (Hearts, for Nicol 74). *Manager:* Andy Roxburgh.

San Marino: Pierluigi Benedettini; Claudio Canti, Bruno Muccioli, Luca Gobbi, William Guerra (captain); Paulo Zanotti, Massimo Ceccoli, Marco Mazza, Fabio Francini; Paolo Mazza, Valdes Pasolini. *Substitutes:* Ivano Toccaceli (for Zanotti 60); Ivan Matteoni (for Pasolini 79). *Coach:* Giorgio Leoni.

Scorers: Scotland: Strachan 63 (pen); Durie 66

11 September 1991   European Championship qualifying   Wankdorf Stadion, Berne   Attendance: 48,000

534 Switzerland 2, SCOTLAND 2
Referee: Tullio Lanese (Italy)

Scotland: Andy Goram (Rangers); Stewart McKimmie (Aberdeen), Steve Nicol (Liverpool), Dave McPherson (Hearts), Maurice Malpas (Dundee United); Gordon Strachan (Leeds United, captain), Stuart McCall (Rangers), Tom Boyd (Chelsea); Maurice Johnston (Rangers), Gordon Durie (Tottenham Hotspur), Ally McCoist (Rangers). *Substitutes:* Gary McAllister (Leeds United, for Johnston 43); Brian McClair (Manchester United, for McKimmie 70). *Manager:* Andy Roxburgh.

Switzerland: Stefan Huber; Marc Hottiger, Christophe Ohrel, Dominique Herr, Marcel Heldmann; Ciriaco Sforza, Heinz Hermann (captain), Alain Sutter; Kubilay Turkyilmaz, Adrian Knup, Stephane Chapuisat. *Substitutes:* Thomas Bickel (for Alain Sutter 60); Beat Sutter (for Heldmann 67). *Coach:* Ulrich Stielike (Germany).

Scorers: Switzerland: Chapuisat 29; Hermann 38   Scotland: Durie 47; McCoist 83

16 October 1991 European Championship qualifying Steaua Stadionul, Bucharest Attendance: 30,000

535 Romania 1, SCOTLAND 0
Referee: Aron Scmidhuber (Germany)

Scotland: Andy Goram (Rangers); Stewart McKimmie (Aberdeen), David MacPherson (Hearts), Craig Levein (Hearts), Maurice Malpas (Dundee United); Gordon Strachan (Leeds United, captain), Stuart McCall (Rangers), Mike Galloway (Celtic), Tom Boyd (Chelsea); Brian McClair (Manchester United), Gordon Durie (Tottenham Hotspur). *Substitutes:* Kevin Gallacher (Coventry City, for Boyd 58); Roy Aitken (St Mirren, for Galloway 70). *Manager:* Andy Roxburgh.

Romania: Silviu Lung; Dan Petrescu, Michael Klein, Emil Sandoi, Gheorghe Popescu; Marius Lacatus, Ionut Lupescu, Daniel Timofte; Daniel Munteanu, Gheorghe Hagi (captain), Florin Raducioiu. *Substitutes:* Ion Timofte (for Daniel Timofte 62); Ilie Dumitrescu (for Raducioiu 75). *Coach:* Mircea Radulescu.

Scorer: Romania: Hagi 73 (pen)

---

13 November 1991 European Championship qualifying Hampden Park Attendance: 35,170

536 SCOTLAND 4, San Marino 0
Referee: Rune Pedersen (Norway)

Scotland (4-3-3):

- 18 Andy Goram (Rangers);
- 15 Dave McPherson (Hearts)
- 8 Craig Levein (Hearts)
- 53 Richard Gough (Rangers, captain)
- 45 Maurice Malpas (Dundee United);
- 53 Paul McStay (Celtic)
- 10 Gary McAllister (Leeds United)
- 14 Stuart McCall (Rangers);
- 5 John Robertson (Hearts)
- 15 Gordon Durie (Tottenham Hotspur)
- 33 Ally McCoist (Rangers)

A comfortable home victory against group minnows San Marino put the Scots in with a good chance of making it to the European Championships for the first time. Romania could still have gone equal at the top of the table had they beaten Bulgaria in the final match, but thankfully that game ended in a draw. Paul McStay and Richard Gough, both gaining their 53rd caps, each scored before Gordon Durie made it 3-0 before half-time. The Scottish players, not for the first time, seemed to take their foot off the gas in the second half, but the prolific Ally McCoist managed to add a fourth goal in the 62nd minute following a McStay pass.

Substitutes: 38 Maurice Johnston (Rangers, for McPherson 46); 7 Kevin Gallacher (Coventry City, for Levein 60)

Manager: Andy Roxburgh

San Marino: Pierluigi Benedettini; Claudio Canti, Bruno Muccioli, Luca Gobbi, William Guerra (captain); Loris Zanotti, Marco Mazza, Massimo Bonini; Fabio Francini, Paolo Mazza, Valdes Pasolini. *Substitutes:* Marco Montironi (for Gobbi 46); Pierangelo Manzaroli (for Pasolini 66). *Trainer:* Georgio Leoni.

Scorers: Scotland: McStay 10; Gough 31; Durie 37; McCoist 62

EUROPEAN CHAMPIONSHIP QUALIFYING GROUP TWO

	P	W	D	L	F	A	Pts
Scotland	8	4	3	1	14	7	11
Switzerland	8	4	2	2	19	7	10
Romania	8	4	2	2	13	7	10
Bulgaria	8	3	3	2	15	8	9
San Marino	8	0	0	8	1	33	0

---

19 February 1991 Friendly Hampden Park Attendance: 13,651

537 SCOTLAND 1, Northern Ireland 0
Referee: Joe Worrall (England)

Scotland: Henry Smith (Hearts); Stewart McKimmie (Aberdeen), David McPherson (Hearts), Richard Gough (Rangers), David Robertson (Rangers); Gordon Strachan (Leeds United, captain), Gary McAllister (Leeds United), Brian McClair (Manchester United), Maurice Malpas (Dundee United); Keith Wright (Hibernian), Ally McCoist (Rangers). *Substitutes:* Gordon Durie (Tottenham Hotspur, for McKimmie 46); Kevin Gallacher (Coventry City, for McCoist 46); John Collins (Celtic, for McClair 70); John Robertson (Hearts, for Wright 78). *Manager:* Andy Roxburgh.

Northern Ireland: Tommy Wright; Mal Donaghy, Gerry Taggart, Alan McDonald (captain), Nigel Worthington; Kevin Wilson, Danny Wilson, Jim Magilton, Kingsley Black; Michael Hughes, Colin Clarke. *Substitutes:* Ian Dowie (for Clarke 46); Michael O'Neill (for Kevin Wilson 81); Steven Morrow (for Taggart 85). *Manager:* Billy Bingham.

Scorer: Scotland: McCoist 11

---

25 March 1992 Friendly Hampden Park Attendance: 9,275

538 SCOTLAND 1, Finland 1
Referee: Anders Frisk (Sweden)

Scotland: Andy Goram (Rangers); Stewart McKimmie (Aberdeen), David McPherson (Hearts), Tom Boyd (Celtic), Maurice Malpas (Dundee United); Gordon Strachan (Leeds United, captain), Dave Bowman (Dundee United), Paul McStay (Celtic), John Collins (Celtic); John Robertson (Hearts), Gordon Durie (Tottenham Hotspur). *Substitutes:* Ally McCoist (Rangers, for Robertson 54); Gary McAllister (Leeds United, for Strachan 65). *Manager:* Andy Roxburgh.

Finland: Olavi Huttunen; Ari Heikkinen, Erikka Petaja (captain), Jari Rinne, Anders Eriksson; Kimmo Tarkkio, Ilkka Remes, Marko Myyry; Mika-Matti Paatelainen, Jari Litmanen, Petri Jarvinen. *Substitutes:* Jari Vanhala (for Tarkkio 69); Harry Nyyssonen (for Rinne 88). *Coach:* Jukka Vakkila.

Scorers: Scotland: McStay 24 Finland: Litmanen 41

---

17 May 1992 Friendly Mile High Stadium, Denver Attendance: 24,157

539 USA 0, SCOTLAND 1
Referee: Juan Pablo Escobar (Guatemala)

Scotland: Gordon Marshall (Celtic); Stewart McKimmie (Aberdeen), David McPherson (Hearts), Alan McLaren (Hearts), Maurice Malpas (Dundee United); Gary McAllister (Leeds United), Paul McStay (Celtic, captain), Stuart McCall (Rangers), Pat Nevin (Everton); Brian McClair (Manchester United), Ally McCoist (Rangers). *Substitutes:* Duncan Ferguson (Dundee United, for Nevin 50); Jim McInally (Dundee United, for McStay 68); Dave Bowman (Dundee United, for McCoist 76); Derek Whyte (Celtic, for McPherson 82). *Manager:* Andy Roxburgh.

USA: Kasey Keller; Des Armstrong, John Doyle, Fernando Clavijo, Marcelo Balboa; Janusz Michallik, Brian Quinn, Chris Henderson; Hugo Perez, Dominic Kinnear, Eric Wynalda. *Substitute:* Zachary Ibsen (for Michallik 71). *Coach:* Velibor Milutinovic (Yugoslavia).

Scorer: Scotland: Nevin 7

| 20 May 1992 | Friendly | Varsity Stadium, Toronto | Attendance: 10,872 |

540 Canada 1, SCOTLAND 3
Referee: Helder Dias (USA)

Scotland: Henry Smith (Hearts); David McPherson (Hearts), Richard Gough (Rangers, captain), Alan McLaren (Hearts), Tom Boyd (Celtic); Gary McAllister (Leeds United), Paul McStay (Celtic), Stuart McCall (Rangers); Gordon Durie (Tottenham Hotspur), Duncan Ferguson (Dundee United), Ally McCoist (Rangers). *Substitutes:* Brian McClair (Manchester United, for Ferguson 54); Maurice Malpas (Dundee United, for Durie 78); Stewart McKimmie (Aberdeen, for McCall 90). *Manager:* Andy Roxburgh.

Canada: Craig Forrest; Frank Yallop, Colin Miller, Peter Sarantopoulos, Randy Samuel; John Limniatis, Nick Dasovic, Carl Valentine; Norman Odinga, Domenico Mobilio, John Catliff. *Substitutes:* Alexander Banbury (for Mobilio 46); Nicholas Gilbert (for Limniatis 59); Lyndon Hooper (for Odinga 59); Geoffrey Aunger (for Catliff 78). *Coach:* Robert Lenarduzzi.

Scorers: Scotland: McAllister 23, 85 (pen); McCoist 65   Canada: Catliff 44

| 3 June 1992 | Friendly | Ullevaal Stadion, Oslo | Attendance: 8,786 |

541 Norway 0, SCOTLAND 0
Referee: Anders Frisk (Sweden)

Scotland: Andy Goram (Rangers); David McPherson (Hearts), Richard Gough (Rangers), Alan McLaren Hearts), Maurice Malpas (Dundee United, captain); Gary McAllister (Leeds United), Paul McStay (Celtic), Stuart McCall (Rangers), Tom Boyd (Celtic); Brian McClair (Manchester United), Ally McCoist (Rangers). *Substitutes:* Gordon Durie (Tottenham Hotspur, for McClair 46); Kevin Gallacher (Coventry City, for McCoist 46); Stewart McKimmie (Aberdeen, for Malpas 68); Jim McInally (Dundee United, for McAllister 78). *Manager:* Andy Roxburgh.

Norway: Frode Grodaas; Roger Nilsen, Tore Pedersen, Henning Berg, Rune Bratseth (captain); Stig-Inge Bjornebye, Lars Bohinen, Kjetil Rekdal; Ouvind Leonhardsen, Tore-Andre Dahlum, Frank Strandli. *Substitutes:* Erik Mykland (for Pedersen 29); Jostein Flo (for Dahlum 73); Kaare Ingebrigtsen (for Bohinen 75). *Coach:* Egil Olsen.

| 12 June 1992 | European Championship (group stage) | Ullevi, Gothenburg | Attendance: 35,720 |

542 Netherlands 1, SCOTLAND 0
Referee: Bo Karlsson (Sweden)

Scotland (4-3-3):

21 Andy Goram (Rangers);
18 Stewart McKimmie (Aberdeen)
57 Richard Gough (Rangers, captain)
21 Dave McPherson (Rangers)
51 Maurice Malpas (Dundee United);
58 Paul McStay (Celtic)
16 Gary McAllister (Leeds United)
18 Stuart McCall (Rangers);
20 Gordon Durie (Tottenham Hotspur)
24 Brian McClair (Manchester United)
39 Ally McCoist (Rangers)

Substitutes: 10 Kevin Gallacher (Coventry City, for McCoist 73);
3 Duncan Ferguson (Dundee United, for McClair 79)

Manager: Andy Roxburgh

An aura of invincibility around the Netherlands came close to being shattered in the opening tie of the Sweden tournament, as a draw would have been more than deserved. But typically, with just 13 minutes remaining Dennis Bergkamp stole in to give the Dutch both points and deflate what had been a growing sense of Scottish optimism. Richard Gough had an impressive game, dealing well with the threat of Marco van Basten, while the creativity of Paul McStay in midfield was obvious throughout. Just when the game looked like heading for a draw, the Dutch masters struck. Ruud Gullit's probing cross was touched by both van Basten and Frank Rijkaard before Bergkamp seized his opportunity to score. Although there were tough games to come against Germany and the CIS, the mood in the camp was justifiably good.

Netherlands: Johannes van Breukelen; Hubertus van Aerle, Ronald Koeman, Adrianus van Tiggelen; Frank Rijkaard, Jan Wouters, Robert Witschge, Ruud Gullit (captain); Bryan Roy, Dennis Bergkamp, Marco van Basten. *Substitutes:* Wilhelmus Joni (for Wouters 55); Aron Winter (for Bergkamp 86). *Trainer:* Rinus Michaels.

Scorer: Netherlands: Bergkamp 77

| 15 June 1992 | European Championship (group stage) | Idrottsparken, Norrkoping | Attendance: 17,800 |

543 Germany 2, SCOTLAND 0
Referee: Guy Goethals (Belgium)

Scotland (4-3-3):

22 Andy Goram (Rangers);
19 Stewart McKimmie (Aberdeen)
58 Richard Gough (Rangers, captain)
22 Dave McPherson (Rangers)
52 Maurice Malpas (Dundee United);
59 Paul McStay (Celtic)
17 Gary McAllister (Leeds United)
19 Stuart McCall (Rangers);
21 Gordon Durie (Tottenham Hotspur)
25 Brian McClair (Manchester United)
40 Ally McCoist (Rangers)

Two games played, no points and no goals scored, but there continued to be an uplifting mood among Scottish supporters who were pleased by the way their team had performed. Rarely in any of the 51 matches played since Andy Roxburgh took charge of the national side can his team have done so well in back-to-back games with nothing to show for it. The Scots were holding the Germans well when in the 29th minute Riedle took advantage of a lay-off from Klinsmann and beat Andy Goram from close range. Hopes of a comeback were extinguished two minutes into the second half when Effenberg's attempt spun off Maurice Malpas's leg and over the despairing Goram. It was a game in which the Scots got nothing, but deserved so much more.

Substitutes: 13 Pat Nevin (Everton, for Durie 54); 11 Kevin Gallacher (Coventry City, for McCoist 70)

Manager: Andy Roxburgh

Germany: Bodo Illgner; Manfred Binz, Jurgen Kohler, Guido Buchwald, Thomas Hasler; Stefan Effenberg, Matthias Sammer, Andreas Moller, Andreas Brehme (captain); Jurgen Klinsmann, Karl-Heinz Riedle. *Substitutes:* Stefan Reuter (for Riedle 68); Michael Schultz (for Reuter 75). *Trainer:* Berti Vogts.

Scorers: Germany: Riedle 29; Effenberg 47

Midfielder Paul McStay on the ball during the narrow defeat to the Netherlands at the 1992 European Championships.

18 June 1992 European Championships (group stage) Idrottsparken, Norrkoping Attendance: 14,660

544 CIS 0, SCOTLAND 3
Referee: Kurt Rothlisberger (Switzerland)

Scotland (4-3-3):
23 Andy Goram (Rangers);
20 Stewart McKimmie (Aberdeen)
59 Richard Gough (Rangers, captain)
23 Dave McPherson (Rangers)
10 Tom Boyd (Celtic);
60 Paul McStay (Celtic)
18 Gary McAllister (Leeds United)
20 Stuart McCall (Rangers);
12 Kevin Gallacher (Coventry City)
26 Brian McClair (Manchester United)
41 Ally McCoist (Rangers)

Substitutes: 8 Jim McInally (Dundee United, for McCoist 67);
14 Pat Nevin (Everton, for Gallacher 78)

Manager: Andy Roxburgh

CIS: Dmitri Kharin; Andrei Chernishev, Kakhaber Tskhadadze, Viktor Onopko, Oleg Kuznetzov; Sergei Aleynikov, Aleksei Mikhailichenko (captain), Sergei Yuran; Andrei Konchelskis, Sergei Kiryakov, Igor Dobrovolskiy. *Substitutes:* Dimitri Kuznetsov (for Aleynikov 46); Igor Korneev (for Kiryakov 46). *Trainer:* Anatoli Byshovetz.

Scorers: Scotland: McStay 6; McClair 16; McAllister 83 (pen)

All the promise was finally fulfilled as the Scots bowed out of Euro 92 in glorious style. They defeated the CIS, who had drawn with both the Netherlands and Germany, and leapfrogged them into third place in group two. The brightest of starts saw Paul McStay open the scoring in the sixth minute and when Brian McClair doubled the advantage 10 minutes later it was exactly what the team deserved. It was especially fitting for McClair as the striker finally found the net on his 26th appearance, after joking the previous day that he was destined never to open his account. There was strong running throughout the Scottish side as they kept control of proceedings in the second half. They had to wait until the 83rd minute to get a third, however, when Gary McAllister struck home a penalty after some great wing play from Pat Nevin saw him unceremoniously tripped in the box.

1992 EUROPEAN CHAMPIONSHIP GROUP TWO

	P	W	D	L	F	A	Pts
Netherlands	3	2	1	0	4	1	5
Germany	3	1	1	1	4	4	3
Scotland	3	1	0	2	3	3	2
CIS	3	0	2	1	1	4	2

9 September 1992 World Cup qualifying Wankdorf Stadion, Berne Attendance: 10,000

545 Switzerland 3, SCOTLAND 1
Referee: Mario van der Ende (Netherlands)

Scotland: Andy Goram (Rangers); Tom Boyd (Celtic), Richard Gough (Rangers, captain), David McPherson (Rangers), Maurice Malpas (Dundee United); Gary McAllister (Leeds United), Paul McStay (Celtic), Stuart McCall (Rangers), Brian McClair (Manchester United); Gordon Durie (Tottenham Hotspur), Ally McCoist (Rangers). *Substitutes:* Ian Durrant (Rangers, for McClair 57); Kevin Gallacher (Coventry City, for Boyd 75). *Manager:* Andy Roxburgh.

Switzerland: Marco Pascolo; Marc Hottiger, Yvan Quentin, Andre Egli, Alain Geiger; Christophe Ohrel, Ciriaco Sforza, Alain Sutter; Georges Bregy, Adrian Knup, Stephane Chapuisat. *Substitutes:* Beat Sutter (for Knup 86); Blaise Piffaretti (for Bregy 89). *Manager:* Roy Hodgson (England).

Scorers: Switzerland: Knup 1, 71; Bregy 81   Scotland McCoist 13

SCOTLAND AT 150: A CENTURY AND A HALF OF INTERNATIONAL FOOTBALL

14 October 1992   World Cup qualifying   Ibrox, Glasgow   Attendance: 22,583

546 SCOTLAND 0, Portugal 0
Referee: Hubert Forstinger (Austria)

Scotland: Andy Goram (Rangers); Tom Boyd (Celtic), Craig Levein (Hearts), Derek Whyte (Middlesbrough), Maurice Malpas (Dundee United); Gary McAllister (Leeds United), Paul McStay (Celtic, captain), Stuart McCall (Rangers), John Collins (Celtic); Kevin Gallacher (Coventry City), Ally McCoist (Rangers). *Substitutes:* Brian McClair (Manchester United, for Gallacher 33); Ian Durrant (Rangers, for Collins 72). *Manager:* Andy Roxburgh.

Portugal: Vitor Baia; Helder Marino, Antonio Veloso, Oceano Cruz, Fernando Couto; Joao Pinto, Jose Semedo, Antonio Andre, Vitor Paneira; Paulo Futre, Domingos Oliveira. *Substitute:* Luis Figo (for Semedo 53). *Coach:* Carlos Queiroz.

18 November 1992   World Cup qualifying   Ibrox, Glasgow   Attendance: 33,029

547 SCOTLAND 0, Italy 0
Referee: Aron Schmidhuber (Germany)

Scotland: Andy Goram (Rangers); David McPherson (Rangers), Alan McLaren (Hearts), Derek Whyte (Middlesbrough), Maurice Malpas (Dundee United); Gary McAllister (Leeds United), Paul McStay (Celtic, captain), Ian Durrant (Rangers), Tom Boyd (Celtic); Gordon Durie (Tottenham Hotspur), Ally McCoist (Rangers). *Substitutes:* Eoin Jess (Aberdeen, for Durie 71); John Robertson (Hearts, for Durrant 86). *Manager:* Andy Roxburgh.

Italy: Gianluca Pagliuca; Moreno Mannini, Alberto Di Chiara, Franco Baresi, Paolo Maldini; Alessandro Bianchi, Demetrio Albertini, Stefano Eranio; Gianluigi Lentini, Roberto Baggio, Giuseppi Signori. *Substitutes:* Alessandro Costacurta (for De Chiara 9); Roberto Donadoni (for Signori 65). *Coach:* Arrigo Sacchi.

17 February 1993   World Cup qualifying   Ibrox, Glasgow   Attendance: 35,490

548 SCOTLAND 3, Malta 0
Referee: Ilkka Koho (Finland)

Scotland: Andy Goram (Rangers); David McPherson (Rangers), Alan McLaren (Hearts), *Alex McLeish (Aberdeen, captain), Tom Boyd (Celtic); Pat Nevin (Tranmere Rovers), Gary McAllister (Leeds United), Paul McStay (Celtic), John Collins (Celtic); Eoin Jess (Aberdeen), Ally McCoist (Rangers). *Substitutes:* John Robertson (Hearts, for McPherson 64); Ian Ferguson (Rangers, for McAllister 72). *Manager:* Andy Roxburgh.

Malta: David Cluett; Silvio Vella, Richard Buhagiar, John Buttigieg, Joseph Galea; Nicholas Saliba, Joseph Brincat, Joseph Camilleri, Kristian Laferla; Stefan Sultana, Carmel Busuttil. *Substitutes:* Raymond Vella (for Sultana 74); Edwin Camilleri (for Buhagiar 83). *Coach:* Philip Psaila.

Scorers: Scotland: McCoist 15, 68; Nevin 84

*The game marked the 77th and final appearance of Alex McLeish of Aberdeen, which made him at that time the second-most capped player behind Kenny Dalglish. McLeish later went on to have two spells as manager of the team.

25 March 1993   Friendly   Ibrox, Glasgow   Attendance: 36,400

549 SCOTLAND 0, Germany 1
Referee: Leon Schelings (Belgium)

Scotland: Nicky Walker (Hearts); Stephen Wright (Aberdeen), Craig Levein (Hearts, captain), Alan McLaren (Hearts), Brian Irvine (Aberdeen), Tom Boyd (Celtic); Jim McInally (Dundee United), Dave Bowman (Dundee United), John Collins (Celtic); John Robertson (Hearts), Duncan Ferguson (Dundee United). *Substitute:* Scott Booth (Aberdeen, for Wright 63). *Manager:* Andy Roxburgh.

Germany: Andreas Kopke; Olaf Thon, Guido Buchwald, Jurgen Kohler, Thomas Hasler; Michael Zorc, Lothar Matthaus (captain), Thomas Helmer; Thomas Doll, Jurgen Klinsmann, Karl-Heinz Riedle. *Substitutes:* Stefan Effenberg (for Doll 60); Matthias Sammer (for Matthaus 88). *Coach:* Berti Vogts.

Scorer: Germany: Riedle 19

28 April 1993   World Cup qualifying   Estadio da Luz, Lisbon   Attendance: 28,000

550 Portugal 5, SCOTLAND 0
Referee: Sandor Puhl (Hungary)

Scotland: Andy Goram (Rangers); Stewart McKimmie (Aberdeen), Richard Gough (Rangers, captain), Craig Levein (Hearts), David McPherson (Rangers), Jim McInally (Dundee United); Paul McStay (Celtic), Stuart McCall (Rangers), John Collins (Celtic); Kevin Gallacher (Blackburn Rovers), Ally McCoist (Rangers). *Substitutes:* Pat Nevin (Tranmere Rovers, for Levein 59); Ian Durrant (Rangers, for Collins 75). *Manager:* Andy Roxburgh.

Portugal: Vitor Baia; Abel Xavier, Jorge Costa, Oceano Cruz, Fernando Couto; Jose Semedo, Rui Costa, Paulo Souza; Rui Barros, Paolo Futre, Jorge Cadete. *Substitutes:* Antonio Veloso (for Rui Costa 53); Domingos Oliveira (for Cadete 82). *Coach:* Carlos Queiroz.

Scorers: Portugal: Barros 5, 70; Cadete 45, 72; Futre 67

19 May 1993   World Cup qualifying   Kadriorg Stadion, Tallinn   Attendance: 5,100

551 Estonia 0, SCOTLAND 3
Referee: Tore Hollung (Norway)

Scotland: Bryan Gunn (Norwich City); Stephen Wright (Aberdeen), Brian Irvine (Aberdeen), Colin Hendry (Blackburn Rovers), Tom Boyd (Celtic); Paul McStay (Celtic, captain), Dave Bowman (Dundee United), Brian McClair (Manchester United), John Collins (Celtic); John Robertson (Hearts), Kevin Gallacher (Blackburn Rovers). *Substitutes:* Scott Booth (Aberdeen, for Robertson 61); Alan McLaren (Hearts, for Wright 80). *Manager:* Andy Roxburgh.

Estonia: Mart Poom (captain); Urmas Kaljend, Risto Kallaste, Joanus Veensalu, Marek Lemsalu; Igor Prins, Toomas Kallaste, Marko Kristal, Andrei Borissov; Sergei Bragin, Martin Reim. *Substitutes:* Urmas Hepner (for Kristal 46); Aleksander Pustov (for Veensalu 76). *Coach:* Uno Piir.

Scorers: Scotland: Gallacher 43; Collins 59; Booth 73

Chapter seven: 1990-1999

2 June 1993　　World Cup qualifying　　Pittodrie, Aberdeen　　Attendance: 14,307

552　SCOTLAND 3, Estonia 1
Referee: Atanas Ouzounov (Bulgaria)

Scotland: Bryan Gunn (Norwich City); Alan McLaren (Hearts), Colin Hendry (Blackburn Rovers), Brian Irvine (Aberdeen), Tom Boyd (Celtic); Pat Nevin (Tranmere Rovers), Paul McStay (Celtic, captain), Ian Ferguson (Rangers), John Collins (Celtic); Brian McClair (Manchester United), Kevin Gallacher (Blackburn Rovers). *Substitutes:* Scott Booth (Aberdeen, for Ferguson 55); Stewart McKimmie (Aberdeen, for McLaren 71). *Manager:* Andy Roxburgh.

Estonia: Mart Poom (captain); Urmas Kaljend, Risto Kallaste, Marek Lemsalu, Igor Prins; Toomas Kallaste, Andrei Borissov, Martin Reim, Indro Olumets; Lembit Rajala, Marko Kristal. *Substitutes:* Sergei Bragin (for Lemsalu 46); Jaanus Veensalu (for Olumets 73). *Coach:* Uno Piir.

Scorers: Scotland: McClair 18; Nevin 27, 72 (pen)　　Estonia: Bragin 57

8 September 1993　　World Cup qualifying　　Pittodrie, Aberdeen　　Attendance: 21,500

553　SCOTLAND 1, Switzerland 1
Referee: Joel Quiniou (France)

Scotland: Bryan Gunn (Norwich City); Stewart McKimmie (Aberdeen), Brian Irvine (Aberdeen), Craig Levein (Hearts), David Robertson (Rangers); Pat Nevin (Tranmere Rovers), Dave Bowman (Dundee United), Gary McAllister (Leeds United, captain), John Collins (Celtic); Scott Booth (Aberdeen), Gordon Durie (Tottenham Hotspur). *Substitutes:* Eoin Jess (Aberdeen, for Booth 70); Phil O'Donnell (Motherwell, for Bowman 75). *Manager:* Andy Roxburgh.

Switzerland: Marco Pascolo; Regis Rothenbuhler, Yvan Quentin, Dominique Herr, Alain Geiger (captain); Christophe Ohrel, Ciriaco Sforza, Alain Sutter; Georges Bregy, Adrian Knup, Stephane Chapuisat. *Substitutes:* Marco Grassi (for Rothenbuhler 60); Martin Rueda (for Bregy 85). *Coach:* Roy Hodgson (England).

Scorers: Scotland: Collins 50　　Switzerland: Bregy 69 (pen)

13 October 1993　　World Cup qualifying　　Stadio Olimpico, Rome　　Attendance: 61,178

554　Italy 3, SCOTLAND 1
Referee: Ion Craciunescu (Romania)

Scotland: Bryan Gunn (Norwich City); Stewart McKimmie (Aberdeen), Brian Irvine (Aberdeen), Alan McLaren (Hearts), Tom Boyd (Celtic); Dave Bowman (Dundee United), Gary McAllister (Leeds United, captain), Stuart McCall (Rangers); Gordon Durie (Tottenham Hotspur), Eoin Jess (Aberdeen), Kevin Gallacher (Blackburn Rovers). *Substitutes:* Ian Durrant (Rangers, for Jess 46); Paul McStay (Celtic, for Bowman 70). *Manager:* Andy Roxburgh.

Italy: Gianluca Pagliuca; Roberto Mussi, Antonio Benarrivo, Franco Baresi (captain), Alessandro Costacurta; Stefano Eranio, Dino Baggio, Giovanni Stroppa; Roberto Donadoni, Roberto Baggio, Pierluigi Casiraghi. *Substitutes:* Marco Lanna (for Mussi 68); Gianfranco Zola (for Stroppa 89). *Coach:* Arrigo Sacchi.

Scorers: Italy: Donadoni 3; Casiraghi 16; Eranio 80　　Scotland: Gallacher 18

17 November 1993　　World Cup qualifying　　Ta'Qali Stadium, Valetta　　Attendance: 7,000

555　Malta 0, SCOTLAND 2
Referee: Periklis Vassilakis (Greece)

Scotland (4-4-2):
- 59　Jim Leighton (Hibernian);
- 10　Alan McLaren (Hearts)
- 7　Brian Irvine (Aberdeen)
- 3　Colin Hendry (Blackburn Rovers)
- 1　Rob McKinnon (Motherwell);
- 6　Ian Ferguson (Rangers)
- 25　Gary McAllister (Leeds United, captain)
- 1　Billy McKinlay (Dundee United)
- 11　Ian Durrant (Rangers);
- 19　Pat Nevin (Tranmere Rovers)
- 19　Kevin Gallacher (Blackburn Rovers)

Substitutes: 5 Scott Booth (Aberdeen, for McKinlay 46); 19 Tom Boyd (Celtic, for Durrant 74)

Manager: Craig Brown

An away victory over Malta was meaningless in terms of World Cup qualification but the performance signalled better times ahead for new manager Craig Brown, officially appointed to replace previous boss Andy Roxburgh on the morning of the match. Brown predicted before the game that centre back Colin Hendry could cause aerial problems for the Maltese and it was no surprise when the Blackburn Rovers player headed home a Gary McAllister free kick to make the game safe in the second half. Before that the Scots enjoyed most of the possession but had only one goal to show for it, although it was a strike to remember. Pat Nevin took a quick free kick to McAllister and he rolled it across in the path of Billy McKinlay, who struck a superb diagonal shot to beat the Maltese keeper.

Malta: David Cluett; Silvio Vella, Richard Buhagiar, John Buttigieg, Joseph Galea; Joseph Brincat, Michael Spiteri, Kristian Laferla, Martin Gregory; Hubert Suda, Carmel Bussetil (captain). *Substitutes:* Nicholas Saliba (for Buhagiar 46); Charles Scerri (for Suda 74). *Trainer:* Pietro Ghedin (Italy).

Scorers: Scotland: McKinlay 15; Hendry 74

FIFA WORLD CUP QUALIFYING GROUP ONE

	P	W	D	L	F	A	Pts
Italy	10	7	2	1	22	7	16
Switzerland	10	6	3	1	23	6	15
Portugal	10	6	2	2	18	5	14
Scotland	10	4	3	3	14	13	11
Malta	10	1	1	8	3	23	3
Estonia	10	0	1	9	1	27	1

23 March 1994　　Friendly　　Hampden Park　　Attendance: 36,809

556　SCOTLAND 0, Netherlands 1
Referee: Kim Milton Nielsen (Denmark)

Scotland: Andy Goram (Rangers); Stewart McKimmie (Aberdeen), Alan McLaren (Hearts), Craig Levein (Hearts), Colin Hendry (Blackburn Rovers), David Robertson (Rangers); Gary McAllister (Leeds United, captain), Paul McStay (Celtic), Stuart McCall (Rangers); Pat Nevin (Tranmere Rovers), Gordon Durie (Rangers). *Substitutes:* Tom Boyd (Celtic, for Levein 46); Billy McKinlay (Dundee United, for McStay 46); John Collins (Celtic, for Robertson 65); Eoin Jess (Aberdeen, for Nevin 67). *Manager:* Craig Brown.

Netherlands: Eduard de Goeij; Ulrich van Gobbel, Frank de Boer, Frank Rijkaard (captain), Danny Blind; Gaston Taument, Wim Jonk, Robert Witschge; Bryan Roy, Dennis Bergkamp, Johannes Bosman. *Substitutes:* Hans Gillhaus (for Bosman 46); Aron Winter (for Bergkamp 46); Marc Overmars (for Taument 77). *Coach:* Dick Advocaat.

Scorer: Netherlands: Roy 23

SCOTLAND AT 150: A CENTURY AND A HALF OF INTERNATIONAL FOOTBALL

20 April 1994   Friendly   Ernst Happel Stadion, Vienna   Attendance: 35,000

557 Austria 1, SCOTLAND 2   *Referee: Hermann Albrecht (Germany)*

Scotland: Jim Leighton (Hibernian); Stewart McKimmie (Aberdeen), Alan McLaren (Hearts), Colin Hendry (Blackburn Rovers), Brian Irvine (Aberdeen), Tom Boyd (Celtic); Gary McAllister (Leeds United, captain), Billy McKinlay (Dundee United), John Collins (Celtic); John McGinlay (Bolton Wanderers), Eoin Jess (Aberdeen). *Substitutes:* Ian Ferguson (Rangers, for Boyd 46); Duncan Shearer (Aberdeen, for McGinlay 75); Pat Nevin (Tranmere Rovers, for Jess 84); Stuart McCall (Rangers, for Collins 85). *Manager:* Craig Brown.

Austria: Franz Wohlfahrt; Christian Prosenik, Walter Kogler, Walter Hochmaier, Peter Schottel; Harald Cerny, Michael Baur, Andreas Herzog (captain); Peter Stoger, Adolf Hutter, Anton Polster. *Substitutes:* Michael Konsel (for Wohlfahrt 46); Dietmar Kuhbauer (for Stoger 46); Thomas Weissenberger (for Polster 62). *Coach:* Herbert Prohaska.

Scorers: Austria: Hutter 12   Scotland: McGinlay 35, 60

27 May 1994   Friendly   Galgenwaard Stadion, Utrecht   Attendance: 22,000

558 Netherlands 3, SCOTLAND 1   *Referee: Juan Roca (Spain)*

Scotland: Jim Leighton (Hibernian); Steve Clarke (Chelsea), Brian Irvine (Aberdeen), Colin Hendry (Blackburn Rovers), Stewart McKimmie (Aberdeen); Gary McAllister (Leeds United, captain), Billy McKinlay Dundee United), Stuart McCall (Rangers), John Collins (Celtic); John McGinlay (Bolton Wanderers), Gordon Durie (Rangers). *Substitutes:* Bryan Gunn (Norwich City, for Leighton 46); Eoin Jess (Aberdeen, for Durie 46); Ian Ferguson (Rangers, for Collins 61); Duncan Shearer (Aberdeen, for McGinlay 76); Pat Nevin (Tranmere Rovers, for McKinlay 88). *Manager:* Craig Brown.

Netherlands: Eduard de Goeij; Stanley Valckx, Frank de Boer, Wim Jonk, Jan Wouters (captain); Marc Overmars, Robert Witschge, Ronald de Boer; Bryan Roy, Aron Winter, Ruud Gullit. *Substitutes:* Arthur Numan (for Ronald de Boer 46); Peter Van Vossen (for Gullit 46); Gaston Taument (for Roy 71). *Coach:* Dirk Advocaat.

Scorers: Netherlands: Roy 17; Van Vossen 61; Irvine 71 (own goal)   Scotland: Shearer 81

7 September 1994   European Championship qualifying   Olympia Stadion, Helsinki   Attendance: 12,845

559 Finland 0, SCOTLAND 2   *Referee: Ryszard Wojcik (Poland)*

Scotland: Andy Goram (Rangers); Stewart McKimmie (Aberdeen), Alan McLaren (Hearts), Colin Hendry (Blackburn Rovers), Craig Levein (Hearts), Tom Boyd (Celtic); Gary McAllister (Leeds United, captain), Paul McStay (Celtic), John Collins (Celtic); Andy Walker (Celtic), Duncan Shearer (Aberdeen). *Substitutes:* Eoin Jess (Aberdeen, for Walker 65); Stuart McCall (Rangers, for Levein 78). *Manager:* Craig Brown.

Finland: Petri Jakonen; Janne Makela, Aki Hyrylainen, Markku Kanerva, Antti Heinola; Kim Suominen, Janne Lindberg, Jari Rantanen; Mika-Matti Paatelainen, Jari Litmanen, Ari Hjelm (captain). *Substitutes:* Erik Holmgren (for Heinola 29); Petri Jarvinen (for Rantanen 41). *Coach:* Tommy Lindholm.

Scorers: Scotland: Shearer 29; Collins 66

12 October 1994   European Championship qualifying   Hampden Park   Attendance: 20,885

560 SCOTLAND 5, Faroe Islands 1   *Referee: Terje Hauge (Norway)*

Scotland: Andy Goram (Rangers); Stewart McKimmie (Aberdeen), Craig Levein (Hearts), Colin Hendry (Blackburn Rovers), Alan McLaren (Hearts), Tom Boyd (Celtic); Pat Nevin (Tranmere Rovers), Paul McStay (Celtic, captain), John Collins (Celtic); John McGinlay (Bolton Wanderers), Scott Booth (Aberdeen). *Substitutes:* Billy McKinlay (Dundee United, for Hendry 59); Andy Walker (Celtic, for Booth 70). *Manager:* Craig Brown.

Faroe Islands: Jens Knudsen; Jens Hansen, Tummas Hansen, Oli Johannesen, Ossur Hansen; Jan Dam, Magni Jarnskor, Kurt Morkore; Jan Muller, Todi Jonsson, Henning Jarnskor (captain). *Substitutes:* Djoni Joensen (for Dam 54); Janus Rasmussen (for Morkore 74). *Coach:* Allan Simonsen (Denmark).

Scorers: Scotland: McGinlay 4; Booth 34; Collins 40, 72; McKinlay 61   Faroe: Muller 75

16 November 1994   European Championship qualifying   Hampden Park   Attendance: 31,254

561 SCOTLAND 1, Russia 1   *Referee: Bo Karlsson (Sweden)*

Scotland: Andy Goram (Rangers); Stewart McKimmie (Aberdeen), Craig Levein (Hearts), Alan McLaren (Hearts), Tom Boyd (Celtic); Gary McAllister (Leeds United, captain), Billy McKinlay (Dundee United), Stuart McCall (Rangers), John Collins (Celtic); John McGinlay (Bolton Wanderers), Scott Booth (Aberdeen). *Substitutes:* John Spencer (Chelsea, for McGinlay 63); Pat Nevin (Tranmere Rovers, for McKinlay 83). *Manager:* Craig Brown.

Russia: Stanislav Cherchesov; Vasili Kulkov, Yuri Nikiforov, Sergei Gorlukovich, Igor Shalimov; Valerij Karpin, Viktor Onopko (captain), Andrei Pianitski; Andrei Konchelskis, Dmitri Radchenko, Vladislav Radimov. *Substitute:* Omar Tetradze (for Pianitski 71). *Coach:* Oleg Romantsev.

Scorers: Scotland: Booth 19   Russia: Radchenko 25

18 December 1994   European Championship qualifying   Olympia Stadhion, Athens   Attendance: 20,000

562 Greece 1, SCOTLAND 0   *Referee: John Blankenstein (Netherlands)*

Scotland: Andy Goram (Rangers); Stewart McKimmie (Aberdeen), Alan McLaren (Rangers), Colin Hendry (Blackburn Rovers), Tom Boyd (Celtic); Gary McAllister (Leeds United, captain), Billy McKinlay (Dundee United), Stuart McCall (Rangers), John Collins (Celtic); John McGinlay (Bolton Wanderers), Duncan Ferguson (Everton). *Substitutes:* John Spencer (Chelsea, for McKinlay 46); Jim Leighton (Hibernian, for Goram 77). *Manager:* Craig Brown.

Greece: Ilias Atmatzidis; Efstratios Apostolakis, Mihalis Vlahos, Theodoros Zagorakis, Yiannis Kalitzakis; Mihalis Kassapis, Nikolaos Nioplias, Panayotis Tsalouhidis; Georgios Toursounidis, Alexandros Alexandris, Nikolaos Mahlas. *Substitutes:* Spiridon Marangos (for Alexandris 72); Theofilos Karasavvidis (for Nioplias 89). *Coach:* Konstantinos Polyhroniou.

Scorer: Greece: Apostolakis 18 (pen)

Chapter seven: 1990-1999

29 March 1995   European Championship qualifying   Luzhniki Station, Moscow   Attendance: 13,939

563 Russia 0, SCOTLAND 0
Referee: Hartmut Strampe (Germany)

Scotland: Jim Leighton (Hibernian); Stewart McKimmie (Aberdeen), Alan McLaren (Rangers), Colin Hendry (Blackburn Rovers), Colin Calderwood (Tottenham Hotspur), Tom Boyd (Celtic); Gary McAllister (Leeds United, captain), Paul McStay (Celtic), John Collins (Celtic); Darren Jackson (Hibernian), John McGinlay (Bolton Wanderers). *Substitutes:* Duncan Shearer (Aberdeen, for Jackson 77); Billy McKinlay (Dundee United, for McGinlay 83). *Manager:* Craig Brown.

Russia: Dmitri Kharin; Dmitri Khlestov, Iurij Kovtun, Iurij Nikiforov, Viktor Onopko (captain); Andrei Konchelskis, Valerij Karpin, Igor Shalimov; Igor Dobrovolski, Sergei Kiriakov, Dmitri Radchenko. *Substitutes:* Nikolai Pisarev (for Radchenko 57); Vladislav Radimov (for Shalimov 69). *Coach:* Oleg Romantsev.

26 April 1995   European Championship qualifying   Olimpico, Serraville   Attendance: 1,738

564 San Marino 0, SCOTLAND 2
Referee: Loizos Loizou (Cyprus)

Scotland: Jim Leighton (Hibernian); Alan McLaren (Rangers), Colin Calderwood (Tottenham Hotspur), Colin Hendry (Blackburn Rovers), Tom Boyd (Celtic); Pat Nevin (Tranmere Rovers), Gary McAllister (Leeds United, captain), John Collins (Celtic); Darren Jackson (Hibernian), Duncan Shearer (Aberdeen), John McGinlay (Bolton Wanderers). *Substitutes:* John Spencer (Chelsea, for Shearer 67); Billy McKinlay (Dundee United, for Nevin 78). *Manager:* Craig Brown.

San Marino: Pierluigi Benedettini; Claudio Canti, Mirco Gennari, Luca Gobbi, William Guerra; Marco Mularoni, Marco Mazza, Massimo Bonini (captain); Pierangelo Manzaroli, Pierdomenico Della Valle, Nicola Bacciocchi. *Substitutes:* Ivan Matteoni (for Bonini 46); Davide Gualtieri (for Mularoni 71). *Coach:* Giorgio Leoni.

Scorers: Scotland: Collins 19; Calderwood 85

21 May 1995   Kirin Cup   Big Arch Stadium, Hiroshima   Attendance: 24,566

565 Japan 0, SCOTLAND 0
Referee: Armando Perez (Colombia)

Scotland: Jim Leighton (Hibernian, captain); Alan McLaren (Rangers), Colin Calderwood (Tottenham Hotspur), Brian Martin (Motherwell), Rob McKinnon (Motherwell); Scot Gemmill (Nottingham Forest), Paul Lambert (Motherwell), Billy McKinlay (Dundee United), Craig Burley (Chelsea); Darren Jackson (Hibernian), John Spencer (Chelsea). *Substitutes:* John Robertson (Hearts, for Lambert 37); Paul Bernard (Oldham Athletic, for Gemmill 75); Derek Whyte (Middlesbrough, for Calderwood 79). *Manager:* Craig Brown.

Japan: Kazuya Maekawa; Tetsuji Hashiratanai (captain), Aikra Narahashi, Norio Omuro, Masami Ihara; Hiroshige Yanagimoto, Rui Ramos, Motohiro Yamaguchi; Hiroaki Morishima, Kazuyoshi Miura, Masashi Nakayama. *Substitutes:* Masahiro Fukuda (for Ramos 51); Tsuyoshi Kitazawa (for Morishima 81). *Coach:* Shu Kamo.

24 May 1995   Kirin Cup   Prefectural Sports Park, Toyama   Attendance: 5,669

566 Ecuador 1, SCOTLAND 2
Referee: Masayoshi Okada (Japan)

Scotland: Jim Leighton (Hibernian, captain); Alan McLaren (Rangers), Colin Calderwood (Tottenham Hotspur), Brian Martin (Motherwell), Derek Whyte (Middlesbrough); Scot Gemmill (Nottingham Forest), Paul Bernard (Oldham Athletic), Billy McKinlay (Dundee United), Craig Burley (Chelsea); Darren Jackson (Hibernian), John Robertson (Hearts). *Substitutes:* Steven Crawford (Raith Rovers, for Jackson 62); Paul Lambert (Motherwell, for Whyte 76). *Manager:* Craig Brown.

Ecuador: Jose Cevallos; Luis Capurro, Raul Noriega, Ivan Hurtado, Wilfrido Verduga; Juan Guaman, Nixon Carcelin, Juan Garay; Hjalmar Zambrano, Diego Herrera, Eduardo Hurtado. *Substitutes:* Agustin Delgado (for Garay 46); Jose Mora (for Herrera 71). *Coach:* Francisco Maturana (Columbia).

Scorers: Scotland: Robertson 75; Crawford 83   Ecuador: Ivan Hurtado 79 (pen)

7 June 1995   European Championship qualifying   Svangaskard Stadion, Toftir   Attendance: 3,881

567 Faroe Islands 0, SCOTLAND 2
Referee: Vladimir Hrinak (Slovakia)

Scotland: Jim Leighton (Hibernian, captain); Stewart McKimmie (Aberdeen), Colin Calderwood (Tottenham Hotspur), Alan McLaren (Rangers), Rob McKinnon (Motherwell); Craig Burley (Chelsea), Billy McKinlay (Dundee United), John Collins (Celtic); Darren Jackson (Hibernian), Duncan Shearer (Aberdeen), John McGinlay (Bolton Wanderers). *Substitutes:* Scot Gemmill (Nottingham Forest, for McGinlay 75); John Robertson (Hearts, for Shearer 86). *Manager:* Craig Brown.

Faroe Islands: Jens Knudsen; Jens Hansen, Tummus Hansen, Oli Johannesen, Ossur Hansen; Julian Johnsson, Magni Jarnskor (captain), Janus Rasmussen; Henning Jarnskor, Todi Jonsson, Jens-Erik Rasmussen. *Substitutes:* Allan Joensen (for Magni Jarnskor 55); Jan Muller (for Jens-Erik Rasmussen 75). *Coach:* Allan Simonsen (Denmark).

Scorers: Scotland: McKinlay 25; McGinlay 29

16 August 1995   European Championship qualifying   Hampden Park   Attendance: 34,910

568 SCOTLAND 1, Greece 0
Referee: Peter Mikkelsen (Denmark)

Scotland: Jim Leighton (Hibernian); Stewart McKimmie (Aberdeen), Colin Calderwood (Tottenham Hotspur), Tom Boyd (Celtic), Tosh McKinlay (Celtic); Gary McAllister (Leeds United, captain), Craig Burley (Chelsea), Stuart McCall (Rangers), John Collins (Celtic); Darren Jackson (Hibernian), Duncan Shearer (Aberdeen). *Substitutes:* John Robertson (Hearts, for Jackson 71); Ally McCoist (Rangers, for Shearer 71). *Manager:* Craig Brown.

Greece: Ilias Atmatzidis; Efstratios Apostolakis (captain), Kyriakos Karataidis, Nicolaos Dabizas, Yiannis Kalitzakis; Mihalis Kassapis, Theodoros Zagorakis, Panayotis Tsalouhidis; Daniel Batista, Vassilis Tsartas, Zisis Vrizas. *Substitutes:* Nikolaos Mahlas (for Vrizas 30); Alexandros Alexandris (for Batista 51); Georgios Georgiadis (for Zagorakis 79). *Coach:* Konstantinos Polyhroniou.

Scorer: Scotland: McCoist 72

6 September 1995   European Championship qualifying   Hampden Park   Attendance: 35,505

569 SCOTLAND 1, Finland 0
Referee: Vasiliy Melnichuk (Ukraine)

Scotland: Jim Leighton (Hibernian); Stewart McKimmie (Aberdeen), Colin Calderwood (Tottenham Hotspur), Colin Hendry (Blackburn Rovers), Alan McLaren (Rangers), Tom Boyd (Celtic), Gary McAllister (Leeds United, captain), John Collins (Celtic), Tosh McKinlay (Celtic); John Spencer (Chelsea), Scott Booth (Aberdeen). *Substitutes:* Ally McCoist (Rangers, for Spencer 74); Darren Jackson (Hibernian, for Booth 80); Billy McKinlay (Dundee United, for McKimmie 88). *Manager:* Craig Brown.

Finland: Kari Laukkanen; Kari Rissanen, Rami Nieminen, Markku Kanerva, Erik Holmgren; Kim Suominen, Janne Lindberg, Marko Myyry; Petri Jarvinen, Jari Litmanen, Ari Hjelm (captain). *Substitute:* Tommi Gronlund (for Nieminen 62). *Coach:* Jukka Ikalainen.

Scorer: Scotland: Booth 10

11 October 1995   Friendly   Rasunda Stadion, Stockholm   Attendance: 19,121

570 Sweden 2, SCOTLAND 0
Referee: Manuel Diaz (Spain)

Scotland: Jim Leighton (Hibernian); Stewart McKimmie (Aberdeen), Colin Hendry (Blackburn Rovers), Alan McLaren (Rangers), Colin Calderwood (Tottenham Hotspur), Tom Boyd (Celtic); Craig Burley (Chelsea), Gary McAllister (Leeds United, captain), John Collins (Celtic); John McGinlay (Bolton Wanderers), John Robertson (Hearts). *Substitutes:* Billy McKinlay (Dundee United, for Burley 46); Eoin Jess (Aberdeen, for McGinlay 46); Darren Jackson (Hibernian, for McAllister 60); Andy Goram (Rangers, for Leighton 73); Pat Nevin (Tranmere Rovers, for Robertson 73). *Manager:* Craig Brown.

Sweden: Bengt Andersson; Mikael Nilsson, Joachim Bjorklund, Patrik Andersson (captain), Teddy Lucic; Stefan Schwarz, Niklas Alexandersson, Niklas Gudmundsson; Jorgen Pettersson, Thomas Brolin, Kennet Andersson. *Substitutes:* Martin Pringle (for Gudmundsson 70); Magnus Erlingmark (for Kennet Andersson 80); Pontus Kaamark (for Lucic 89). *Coach:* Tommy Svensson.

Scorers: Sweden: Pettersson 31; Schwarz 35

15 November 1995   European Championship qualifying   Hampden Park   Attendance: 30,306

571 SCOTLAND 5, San Marino 0
Referee: Karel Bohunek (Czech Republic)

Scotland (4-3-3):

71 Jim Leighton (Hibernian);
24 Alan McLaren (Rangers),
9 Colin Calderwood (Tottenham Hotspur),
14 Colin Hendry (Blackburn Rovers),
31 Tom Boyd (Celtic);
4 Scot Gemmill (Nottingham Forest),
37 Gary McAllister (Leeds United, captain),
29 John Collins (Celtic);
27 Pat Nevin (Tranmere Rovers),
9 Scott Booth (Aberdeen),
10 Eoin Jess (Aberdeen)

With the top two sides in group eight qualifying for the 1996 European Championships in England, Scotland easily got the three points they required to make sure of making it south of the border the following summer. The Aberdeen strike pairing of Eoin Jess and Scott Booth were chosen up front and they repaid manager Craig Brown's faith with a goal apiece in the first period, Booth's coming virtually on the stroke of half-time. The third came from substitute Ally McCoist, who had barely been on the field when he played a one-two with Pat Nevin and headed home. Nevin himself added a fourth goal 19 minutes from time and the scoring was completed by a bizarre effort in the final minute by San Marino full back Francini, heading past his keeper after Nevin had put in a low cross.

Substitutes: 49 Ally McCoist (Rangers, for McAllister 48); 15 Billy McKinlay (Blackburn Rovers, for Collins 59); 9 Darren Jackson (Hibernian, for Booth 65).

Manager: Craig Brown

San Marino: Stefano Muccioli; Federico Moroni, Mirco Gennari, Mauro Valentini, William Guerra (captain); Marco Mularoni, Marco Mazza, Fabio Francini; Pierangelo Manzaroli, Ivan Matteoni, Nicola Bacciocchi. *Substitutes:* Claudio Canti (for Mularoni 51); Paolo Montagna (for Guerra 70); Pierdomenico Della Valle (for Mazza 81). *Trainer:* Giorgio Leoni.

Scorers: Scotland: Jess 30; Booth 45; McCoist 49; Nevin 71; Francini 90 (own goal)

EUROPEAN CHAMPIONSHIP QUALIFYING GROUP EIGHT

	P	W	D	L	F	A	Pts
Russia	10	8	2	0	34	5	26
Scotland	10	7	2	1	19	3	23
Greece	10	6	0	4	23	9	18
Finland	10	5	0	5	18	18	15
Faroe Islands	10	2	0	8	10	35	6
San Marino	10	0	0	10	2	36	0

27 March 1996   Friendly   Hampden Park   Attendance: 20,608

572 SCOTLAND 1, Australia 0
Referee: Herman van Dijk (Netherlands)

Scotland: Jim Leighton (Hibernian); Craig Burley (Chelsea), Brian O'Neil (Celtic), Colin Hendry (Blackburn Rovers), Tom Boyd (Celtic); Gary McAllister (Leeds United), Paul McStay (Celtic), Billy McKinlay (Blackburn Rovers), John Collins (Celtic); John Spencer (Chelsea), Ally McCoist (Rangers, captain). *Substitutes:* Scott Booth (Aberdeen, for McStay 46); Kevin Gallacher (Blackburn Rovers, for O'Neil 46); Darren Jackson (Hibernian, for McKinlay 75); Pat Nevin (Tranmere Rovers, for McCoist 80). *Manager:* Craig Brown.

Australia: Mark Bosnich; Steven Horvat, Tony Vidmar, Tony Popovic, Alex Tobin (captain); Stephen Corica, Robert Slater, Jason van Blerk; Aurelio Vidmar, Graham Arnold, Carl Veart. *Substitute:* Daniel Tiatto (for Veart 69). *Coach:* Eddie Thomson.

Scorer: Scotland: McCoist 53

24 April 1996   Friendly   Parken Stadion, Copenhagen   Attendance: 23,031

573 Denmark 2, SCOTLAND 0
Referee: Jan Wegereef (Netherlands)

Scotland: Jim Leighton (Hibernian); Stewart McKimmie (Aberdeen), Tom Boyd (Celtic), Colin Hendry (Blackburn Rovers), Tosh McKinlay (Celtic); Gary McAllister (Leeds United, captain), Craig Burley (Chelsea), Stuart McCall (Rangers), John Collins (Celtic); John Spencer (Chelsea), Kevin Gallacher (Blackburn Rovers). *Substitutes:* Scot Gemmill (Nottingham Forest, for McCall 46); Andy Goram (Rangers, for Leighton 46); Ally McCoist (Rangers, for Spencer 72); Darren Jackson (Hibernian, for Gallacher 72); Billy McKinlay (Blackburn Rovers, for Hendry 75). *Manager:* Craig Brown.

Denmark: Peter Schmeichel; Thomas Helveg, Jens Risager, Lars Olsen, Mark Rieper; Brian Nielsen, Michael Schjonberg, Claus Thomsen; Michael Laudrup (captain), Mikkel Beck, Brian Laudrup. *Substitutes:* Mogens Krogh (for Schmeichel 46); Jacob Laursen (for Risager 81); Allan Nielsen (for Michael Laudrup 85). *Coach:* Richard Moller Nielsen.

Scorers: Denmark: Michael Laudrup 7; Brian Laudrup 27

Chapter seven: 1990-1999

26 May 1996 Friendly Willow Brook Stadium, New Britain Attendance: 8,526

574 USA 2, SCOTLAND 1
Referee: Manlio Brizio (Mexico)

Scotland: Jim Leighton (Hibernian); Colin Calderwood (Tottenham Hotspur), Colin Hendry (Blackburn Rovers, captain), Derek Whyte (Middlesbrough), Tom Boyd (Celtic); Craig Burley (Chelsea), Eoin Jess (Coventry City), Scot Gemmill (Nottingham Forest); Darren Jackson (Hibernian), Gordon Durie (Rangers), Scott Booth (Aberdeen). *Substitutes:* John Collins (Celtic, for Jackson 46); Gary McAllister (Leeds United, for Gemmill 46); John Spencer (Chelsea, for Durie 46); Stuart McCall (Rangers, for Burley 60); Nicky Walker (Partick Thistle, for Leighton 82). *Manager:* Craig Brown.

USA: Jurgen Sommer; Michael Burns, Jeffrey Agoos, Alexei Lalas, Tom Dooley; John Harkes, Marcelo Balboa, Claudio Reyna; Tabare Ramos, Cobi Jones, Eric Wynalda. *Substitutes:* Jovan Kirovski (for Dooley 53); Brian McBride (for Reyna 83). *Coach:* Steve Sampson.

Scorers: Scotland: Durie 9   USA: Wynalda 13 (pen); Jones 72

29 May 1996 Friendly Orange Bowl, Miami Attendance: 8,500

575 Colombia 1, SCOTLAND 0
Referee: Raul Dominguez (USA)

Scotland: Andy Goram (Rangers); Stewart McKimmie (Aberdeen), Colin Calderwood (Tottenham Hotspur), Colin Hendry (Blackburn Rovers), Tom Boyd (Celtic), Tosh McKinlay (Celtic); Gary McAllister (Leeds United, captain), Stuart McCall (Rangers), John Collins (Celtic); John Spencer (Chelsea), Ally McCoist (Rangers). *Substitutes:* Craig Burley (Chelsea, for Hendry 46); Kevin Gallacher (Blackburn Rovers, for McCoist 61); Eoin Jess (Coventry City, for Spencer 69). *Manager:* Craig Brown.

Columbia: Farid Mondragon; Nestor Ortiz, Antonio Moreno, Francisco Cassiani, Jorge Bemudez; Mauricio Serna, Andres Estrada, Edison Mafla; Ivan Valenciano, Freddy Rincon, Adolfo Valencia. *Substitutes:* Leonel Alvarez (for Mafla 46); Victor Aristizabal (for Valenciano 46); Faustino Asprilla (for Valencia 46); Luis Herrera (for Ortiz 46); Alexis Mendoza (for Cassiani 46); Carlos Valderrama (for Estrada 46). *Coach:* Hernan Gomez.

Scorer: Columbia: Asprilla 82

10 June 1996 European Championship (group stage) Villa Park, Birmingham Attendance: 34,363

576 Netherlands 0, SCOTLAND 0
Referee: Leif Sundell (Sweden)

Scotland (4-3-3):
37 Andy Goram (Rangers);
39 Stewart McKimmie (Aberdeen)
12 Colin Calderwood (Tottenham Hotspur)
19 Colin Hendry (Blackburn Rovers)
36 Tom Boyd (Celtic);
35 Stuart McCall (Rangers)
42 Gary McAllister (Leeds United, captain)
34 John Collins (Celtic);
23 Kevin Gallacher (Blackburn Rovers)
12 Scott Booth (Aberdeen)
29 Gordon Durie (Rangers)

Substitutes: 10 John Spencer (Chelsea, for Booth 46);
18 Billy McKinlay (Blackburn Rovers, for Gallacher 56);
10 Craig Burley (Chelsea, for McKimmie 85)

Manager: Craig Brown

The Scots emerged with great credit after an opening match against one of the competition favourites which threatened to overwhelm them at times. Manager Craig Brown altered his formation from the usual five-man defence to a flat back four and despite a few nervy moments his players recorded an excellent start to the campaign. The Dutch had their chances, of course, and were particularly aggrieved when John Collins appeared to handle the ball on the goal-line and nothing was given. However, Scotland had moments too when they could have won the match, with captain Gary McAllister twice drawing fine saves from keeper van der Sar. It was a result which made the trip to Wembley a few days later not the intimidating venture it seemed earlier.

Netherlands: Edwin van der Sar; Michael Reiziger, Johan de Kock, Winston Bogarde, Ronald de Boer (captain); Edgar Davids, Clarence Seedorf, Richard Witschge; Gaston Taument, Dennis Bergkamp, Jordi Cruyff. *Substitutes:* Patrick Kluivert (for Taument 62); Phillip Cocu (for Witschge 78); Aron Winter (for de Boer 78). *Trainer:* Guus Hiddink.

Ready to take on England at Wembley in 1996. Back (from left): Tosh McKinlay, Gordon Durie, Colin Hendry, Stuart McCall, Andy Goram, Colin Calderwood. Front: John Collins, Stewart McKimmie, Gary McAllister, Tom Boyd, John Spencer.

| 15 June 1996 | European Championship (group stage) | Wembley | Attendance: 76,864 |

577 England 2, SCOTLAND 0

Referee: Pierluigi Pairetto (Italy)

Scotland (5-3-2):

38 Andy Goram (Rangers);
40 Stewart McKimmie (Aberdeen)
13 Colin Calderwood (Tottenham Hotspur)
20 Colin Hendry (Blackburn Rovers)
37 Tom Boyd (Celtic)
5 Tosh McKinlay (Celtic);
36 Stuart McCall (Rangers)
43 Gary McAllister (Leeds United, captain)
35 John Collins (Celtic);
11 John Spencer (Chelsea)
30 Gordon Durie (Rangers)

Substitutes: 53 Ally McCoist (for Spencer 66);
11 Craig Burley (Chelsea, for McKinlay 81);
13 Eoin Jess (Coventry City, for Durie 84)

Manager: Craig Brown

A clinical display from the hosts, including a sparkling individual goal from the mercurial Paul Gascoigne of Rangers, deprived Scotland of the result they craved and left them needing to beat Switzerland in the final group match to make it to the knockout stages. The game was fairly even in the first half, with the Scots harassing and chasing to great effect, and the break arrived with the score still blank. Seven minutes after the re-start Alan Shearer showed why he is rated one of England's greatest ever strikers, ghosting in at the back post to finish off a fine cross from full back Gary Neville. With 76 minutes on the clock Scotland were given the chance they wanted when Tony Adams fouled Gordon Durie in the box. Captain Gary McAllister stepped up, hit the ball fiercely, but keeper David Seaman made one of his best saves by diving and pushing it over the bar. To compound the moment, England went up to the other end and Gascoigne, after flicking the ball over Colin Hendry, rifled it past a helpless Andy Goram. The Geordie's celebration was memorable but hardly what the Scots needed.

England: David Seaman; Gary Neville, Tony Adams (captain), Gareth Southgate, Stuart Pearce; Darren Anderton, Paul Ince, Paul Gascoigne; Steve McManaman, Alan Shearer, Teddy Sheringham. *Substitutes:* Jamie Redknapp (for Pearce 46); Steve Stone (for Ince 79); Sol Cambell (for Redknapp 86). *Manager:* Terry Venables.

Scorers: England: Shearer 52; Gascoigne 78

| 18 June 1996 | European Championship (group stage) | Villa Park, Birmingham | Attendance: 34,926 |

578 Switzerland 0, SCOTLAND 1

Referee: Vaclav Krondl (Czech Republic)

Scotland (5-3-2):

39 Andy Goram (Rangers);
12 Craig Burley (Chelsea)
14 Colin Calderwood (Tottenham Hotspur)
21 Colin Hendry (Blackburn Rovers)
38 Tom Boyd (Celtic)
6 Tosh McKinlay (Celtic);
37 Stuart McCall (Rangers)
44 Gary McAllister (Leeds United, captain)
36 John Collins (Celtic);
31 Gordon Durie (Rangers)
54 Ally McCoist (Rangers)

Substitutes: 13 Scott Booth (Aberdeen, for McKinlay 59);
12 John Spencer (Chelsea, for McCoist 84)

Manager: Craig Brown

The challenge for Scotland was clear – they needed to beat Switzerland, score as many goals as possible in the process, but also hope that England would defeat the Netherlands in the other remaining group A match. And with a few minutes remaining, Ally McCoist having given the Scots a precious 1-0 lead and word filtering though that England were 4-0 ahead, the knockout stages were looming. Not so, however, as a late Dutch goal inevitably meant the usual outcome in a major championship – Scotland were eliminated on goal difference. The match itself was never a great one, with the Swiss only threatening occasionally and the Scots missing chances. But in the 37th minute McCoist, who had himself squandered a couple of opportunities, scored his 19th and surely most memorable international goal. When the pass from Gary McAllister came to him at the edge of the box the Rangers forward hit a superb first-time shot with his right foot which flew past the helpless Swiss keeper. As the game neared an end McAllister, Gordon Durie and Scott Booth all came close but could not provide the finishing touch which would have put their side through.

Switzerland: Marco Pascolo; Marc Hottiger, Ramon Vega, Stephane Henchoz, Yvan Quentin; Johann Vogel, Marcel Koller, Ciriaco Sforza (captain); Kubilay Turkyilmaz, Christophe Bonvin, Stephane Chapuisat. *Substitutes:* Raphael Wicky (for Koller 46); Sebastian Fournier (for Chapuisat 46); Alexandre Comisetti (for Quentin 81). *Trainer:* Arthur Borges (Portugal).

Scorer: Scotland: McCoist 37

1996 EUROPEAN CHAMPIONSHIP GROUP A

	P	W	D	L	F	A	Pts
England	3	2	1	0	7	2	7
Netherlands	3	1	1	1	3	4	4
Scotland	3	1	1	1	1	2	4
Switzerland	3	0	1	2	1	4	1

| 31 August 1996 | World Cup qualifying | Ernst Happel Stadion, Vienna | Attendance: 29,500 |

579 Austria 0, SCOTLAND 0

Referee: Michel Piraux (Belgium)

Scotland: Andy Goram (Rangers); Craig Burley (Chelsea), Colin Calderwood (Tottenham Hotspur), Colin Hendry (Blackburn Rovers), Tom Boyd (Celtic), Tosh McKinlay (Celtic); Stuart McCall (Rangers), Gary McAllister (Coventry City, captain), John Collins (Monaco); Duncan Ferguson (Everton), Ally McCoist (Rangers). *Substitute:* Gordon Durie (Rangers, for McCoist 69). *Manager:* Craig Brown.

Austria: Michael Konsel; Markus Schopp, Peter Schottel, Anton Pfeffer, Wolfgang Feiersinger; Stefan Marasek, Dietmar Kuhbauer, Andreas Herzog; Andreas Heraf, Dieter Ramusch, Anton Polster (captain). *Substitutes:* Herfried Sabitzer (for Polster 67); Andreas Ogris (for Ramusch 76). *Coach:* Herbert Prohaska.

Chapter seven: 1990-1999

| 5 October 1996 | World Cup qualifying | Daugava Stadion, Riga | Attendance: 9,500 |

580 Latvia 0, SCOTLAND 2
Referee: Jiri Ulrich (Czech Republic)

Scotland: Andy Goram (Rangers); Craig Burley (Chelsea), Colin Calderwood (Tottenham Hotspur), Derek Whyte (Middlesbrough), Tom Boyd (Celtic), Tosh McKinlay (Celtic); Stuart McCall (Rangers), Gary McAllister (Coventry City, captain), John Collins (Monaco); Darren Jackson (Hibernian), John Spencer (Chelsea). *Substitutes:* Paul Lambert (Borussia Dortmund, for McCall 46); Billy Dodds (Aberdeen, for Spencer 59); Jackie McNamara (Celtic, for McKinlay 80). *Manager:* Craig Brown.

Latvia: Olegs Karavajevs; Igors Troitskis, Mihails Zemlinskis, Igors Stepanovs, Iurijs Sevlakovs (captain); Imants Bleidelis, Valerijs Ivanovs, Vitalijs Astafjevs; Vits Rimkus, Vladimirs Babicevs, Marians Pahars. *Substitutes:* Andrejs Stolcers (for Babicevs 46); Rolands Bulders (for Rimkus 79). *Coach:* Janis Gilis.

Scorers: Scotland: Collins 18; Jackson 78

| 10 November 1996 | World Cup qualifying | Ibrox, Glasgow | Attendance: 46,738 |

581 SCOTLAND 1, Sweden 0
Referee: Jose-Maria Garcia (Spain)

Scotland: Jim Leighton (Hibernian); Jackie McNamara (Celtic), Colin Calderwood (Tottenham Hotspur), Colin Hendry (Blackburn Rovers, captain), Tom Boyd (Celtic), Tosh McKinlay (Celtic); Craig Burley (Chelsea), Billy McKinlay (Blackburn Rovers), John Collins (Monaco); Darren Jackson (Hibernian), John McGinlay (Bolton Wanderers). *Substitutes:* Paul Lambert (Borussia Dortmund, for McNamara 46); Kevin Gallacher (Blackburn Rovers, for Jackson 78); Ally McCoist (Rangers, for McGinlay 85). *Manager:* Craig Brown.

Sweden: Thomas Ravelli; Roland Nilsson, Gary Sundgren, Patrik Andersson, Joachim Bjorklund; Stefan Schwarz, Par Zetterberg, Jonas Thern (captain); Niklas Alexandersson, Jesper Blomqvist, Martin Dahlin. *Substitutes:* Kennet Andersson (for Dahlin 17); Henrik Larsson (for Alexandersson 69); Andreas Andersson (for Zetterberg 77). *Coach:* Tommy Svensson.

Scorer: Scotland: McGinlay 8

| 11 February 1997 | World Cup qualifying | Stade Louis II, Monaco | Attendance: 4,000 |

582 Estonia 0, SCOTLAND 0
Referee: Miroslav Radoman (Yugoslavia)

Scotland: Andy Goram (Rangers); Jackie McNamara (Celtic), Colin Calderwood (Tottenham Hotspur), Colin Hendry (Blackburn Rovers), Tom Boyd (Celtic); Paul McStay (Celtic), Gary McAllister (Coventry City, captain), John Collins (Monaco); Kevin Gallacher (Blackburn Rovers), John McGinlay (Bolton Wanderers), Duncan Ferguson (Everton). *Substitutes:* Ian Ferguson (Rangers, for McStay 63); Ally McCoist (Rangers, for McGinlay 73); Tosh McKinlay (Celtic, for McNamara 74). *Manager:* Craig Brown.

Estonia: Mart Poom (captain); Urmas Kirs, Urmas Rooba, Marek Lemsalu, Sergei Hohlov-Simson; Viktor Alonen, Meelis Rooba, Martin Reim; Liivo Leetma, Marko Kristal, Indrek Zelinski. *Substitutes:* Mati Pari (for Meelis Rooba 67); Andres Oper (for Leetma 75). *Coach:* Teitur Thordarson (Iceland).

| 29 March 1997 | World Cup qualifying | Rugby Park, Kilmarnock | Attendance: 17,996 |

583 SCOTLAND 2, Estonia 0
Referee: Bernd Heynemann (Germany)

Scotland: Jim Leighton (Hibernian); Craig Burley (Chelsea), Colin Calderwood (Tottenham Hotspur), Colin Hendry (Blackburn Rovers), Tom Boyd (Celtic), Tosh McKinlay (Celtic); Scot Gemmill (Nottingham Forest), Paul McStay (Celtic), Gary McAllister (Coventry City, captain); Darren Jackson (Hibernian), Kevin Gallacher (Blackburn Rovers). *Substitutes:* Billy McKinlay (Blackburn Rovers, for Hendry 64); John McGinlay (Bolton Wanderers, for Jackson 83). *Manager:* Craig Brown.

Estonia: Mart Poom (captain); Urmas Kirs, Janek Meet, Marek Lemsalu, Sergei Hohlov-Simson; Mati Pari, Kristen Viikmae, Martin Reim; Andres Oper, Marko Kristal, Indrek Zelinski. *Substitutes:* Meelis Rooba (for Pari 54); Liivo Leetma (for Viikmae 72); Argo Arbeiter (for Zelinski 81). *Coach:* Teitur Thordarson (Iceland).

Scorers: Scotland: Boyd 26; Meet 52 (own goal)

| 2 April 1997 | World Cup qualifying | Celtic Park, Glasgow | Attendance: 43,295 |

584 SCOTLAND 2, Austria 0
Referee: Nikolay Levnikov (Russia)

Scotland (5-3-2):

77 Jim Leighton (Hibernian);
17 Craig Burley (Chelsea)
20 Colin Calderwood (Tottenham Hotspur)
26 Colin Hendry (Blackburn Rovers)
44 Tom Boyd (Celtic)
12 Tosh McKinlay (Celtic);
49 Gary McAllister (Coventry City, captain)
5 Paul Lambert (Borussia Dortmund)
41 John Collins (Monaco);
16 Darren Jackson (Hibernian)
27 Kevin Gallacher (Blackburn Rovers)

Substitutes: 13 John McGinlay (Bolton Wanderers, for Jackson 73); 58 Ally McCoist (Rangers, for Gallacher 86); 76 Paul McStay (Celtic, for McAllister 88)

Manager: Craig Brown

Austria were swept aside as Scotland surged seven points clear in the qualification group for the 1998 World Cup in France. With Hampden Park being redeveloped the five home matches were played at different club grounds with Celtic Park staging two and the others at Ibrox, Rugby Park and Pittodrie. The atmosphere was tremendous in the east end of Glasgow for this particular match, in which manager Craig Brown got his homework spot on. His deployment of Paul Lambert to mark Austria's most dangerous player, Andreas Hertzog, as Lambert had done when Borussia Dortmund defeated Werder Bremen 4-0 in the Bundesliga, proved vital in shutting down the opposition midfield. The Scots were well on top and both goals came from Kevin Gallacher, the first from close range and the other a spectacular strike from the edge of the penalty box. Keeper Jim Leighton had little to do as Austria rarely threatened.

Austria: Michael Konsel; Markus Schopp, Peter Schottel, Anton Pfeffer, Wolfgang Feiersinger; Arnold Wetl, Franz Aigner, Andreas Herzog; Andreas Heraf, Peter Stoger, Anton Polster (captain). *Substitutes:* Walter Kogler (for Schottel 46); Ivica Vastic (for Stoger 67); Andreas Ogris (for Aigner 81). *Coach:* Herbert Prohaska.

Scorer: Scotland: Gallacher 24, 77

Lining up at Valletta before the close victory over Malta in 1997. From left: Gary McAllister, Jim Leighton, Christian Dailly, Brian McAllister, John Collins, Tom Boyd, David Hopkin, Craig Burley, Kevin Gallacher, Tosh McKinlay, Darren Jackson.

| 30 April 1997 | World Cup qualifying | Ullevi Stadion, Gothenburg | Attendance: 40,302 |

585 Sweden 2, SCOTLAND 1   *Referee: Pierluigi Collina (Italy)*

Scotland: Jim Leighton (Hibernian); Craig Burley (Chelsea), Colin Calderwood (Tottenham Hotspur), Colin Hendry (Blackburn Rovers), Tom Boyd (Celtic), Tosh McKinlay (Celtic); *Gary McAllister (Coventry City, captain), Paul Lambert (Borussia Dortmund), John Collins (Monaco); Darren Jackson (Hibernian), Kevin Gallacher (Blackburn Rovers). *Substitutes:* Gordon Durie (Rangers, for Jackson 66); Scot Gemmill (Nottingham Forest, for McKinlay 68). *Manager:* Craig Brown.

Sweden: Thomas Ravelli; Gary Sundgren, Pontus Kaamark, Patrik Andersson, Joachim Bjorklund; Stefan Schwarz, Par Zetterberg, Jonas Thern (captain); Andreas Andersson, Kennet Andersson, Martin Dahlin. *Substitute:* Haakan Mild (for Schwarz 12). *Coach:* Tommy Svensson.

Scorers: Sweden: Kennet Andersson 43, 63   Scotland: Gallacher 83

*Captain Gary McAllister became the 19th player to reach 50 caps, eventually finishing on a total of 57.

| 27 May 1997 | Friendly | Rugby Park, Kilmarnock | Attendance: 8,000 |

586 SCOTLAND 0, Wales 1   *Referee: Alan Snoddy (Northern Ireland)*

Scotland: Neil Sullivan (Wimbledon); Tom Boyd (Celtic), David Weir (Hearts), Christian Dailly (Derby County), Brian McAllister (Wimbledon); Scot Gemmill (Nottingham Forest), Gary McAllister (Coventry City, captain), Tosh McKinlay (Celtic); Billy Dodds (Aberdeen), Darren Jackson (Hibernian), Kevin Gallacher (Blackburn Rovers). *Substitutes:* John Spencer (Queens Park Rangers, for Jackson 46); Jackie McNamara (Celtic, for Dailly 74); Jim Leighton (Hibernian, for Sullivan 80); Simon Donnelly (Celtic, for Gallacher 80). *Manager:* Craig Brown.

Wales: Andrew Marriott; Steven Jenkins, Paul Trollope, Robert Page, Kit Symons; Robbie Savage, Mark Pembridge, Gary Speed; John Robinson, John Hartson, Dean Saunders. *Substitutes:* Paul Jones (for Marriott 46); Simon Haworth (for Hartson 71); Marcus Browning (for Robinson 88); Lee Jones (for Saunders 88). *Manager:* Bobby Gould.

Scorer: Wales: Hartson 46

| 1 June 1997 | Friendly | Ta'Qali Stadium, Valletta | Attendance: 3,500 |

587 Malta 2, SCOTLAND 3   *Referee: Stefano Braschi (Italy)*

Scotland: Jim Leighton (Hibernian); Craig Burley (Chelsea), Christian Dailly (Derby County), Tom Boyd (Celtic), Brian McAllister (Wimbledon); David Hopkin (Crystal Palace), Gary McAllister (Coventry City, captain), John Collins (Monaco), Tosh McKinlay (Celtic); Darren Jackson (Hibernian), Kevin Gallacher (Blackburn Rovers). *Substitutes:* David Weir (Hearts, for Brian McAllister 46); Gordon Durie (Rangers, for Gallacher 56); Scot Gemmill (Nottingham Forest, for Hopkin 56); Simon Donnelly (Celtic, for Collins 84). *Manager:* Craig Brown.

Malta: Mario Muscat; Lawrence Attard, Jeffrey Chetcuti, Silvio Vella, Darren Debono; Ivan Zammit, Joseph Brincat, David Carabott; Nicholas Saliba, Gilbert Agius, Hubert Suda. *Substitutes:* Stefan Sultana (for Suda 46); Noel Turner (for Attard 53); Stefan Giglio (for Vella 75); David Camilleri (for Agius 75). *Coach:* Milorad Kosanovic (Yugoslavia).

Scorers: Scotland: Dailly 4; Jackson 44, 81   Malta: Suda 17; Sultana 57

| 8 June 1997 | World Cup qualifying | Dynamo Stadion, Minsk | Attendance: 14,000 |

588 Belarus 0, SCOTLAND 1   *Referee: Ahmet Cakar (Turkey)*

Scotland: Jim Leighton (Hibernian); Craig Burley (Chelsea), Christian Dailly (Derby County), Tom Boyd (Celtic), Tosh McKinlay (Celtic); Gary McAllister (Coventry City, captain), Paul Lambert (Borussia Dortmund), David Hopkin (Crystal Palace); Darren Jackson (Hibernian), Gordon Durie (Rangers), Kevin Gallacher (Blackburn Rovers). *Substitutes:* Scot Gemmill (Nottingham Forest, for Hopkin 68); Brian McAllister (Wimbledon, for McKinlay 79); Billy Dodds (Aberdeen, for Jackson 87). *Manager:* Craig Brown.

Belarus: Andrei Satsunkevich; Eric Yakhimovich, Andrei Lavrik, Radislav Orlovsky, Sergei Shtanyuk; Andrei Khlebosolov, Miroslav Romashchenko, Andrei Ostrovsky; Sergei Gurenko, Andrei Dovnar, Sergei Gerasimets (captain). *Substitutes:* Valentin Belkevich (for Dovnar 53); Vladimir Makovsky (for Khlebosolov 61); Dmitri Balashov (for Orlovsky 66). *Coach:* Mikhail Vergeyenko.

Scorer: Gary McAllister 50 (pen)

7 September 1997　　World Cup qualifying　　　　Pittodrie, Aberdeen　　　　　　Attendance: 20,160

589 SCOTLAND 4, Belarus 1　　　　　　　　　　　　　*Referee: Mario van der Ende (Netherlands)*

Scotland: Jim Leighton (Aberdeen); Craig Burley (Celtic), Colin Calderwood (Tottenham Hotspur), Christian Dailly (Derby County), Tom Boyd (Celtic), Tosh McKinlay (Celtic); Gary McAllister (Coventry City, captain), Paul Lambert (Borussia Dortmund), John Collins (Monaco); Gordon Durie (Rangers), Kevin Gallacher (Blackburn Rovers). *Substitutes:* Ally McCoist (Rangers, for Durie 46); David Hopkin (Crystal Palace, for McAllister 50); Billy Dodds (Aberdeen, for Gallacher 84). *Manager:* Craig Brown.

Belarus: Valerij Shantolosov; Andrei Ostrovsky, Andrei Lavrik, Vyacheslav Gerashchenko, Valentin Belkevich; Alexander Kulchy, Sergei Gurenko, Andrei Dovnar; Vladimir Zhuravel, Petr Kachuro, Sergei Gerasimets (captain). *Substitutes:* Radislav Orlovsky (for Gurenko 52); Oleg Chernyavsky (for Zhuravel 65); Dmitri Balashov (for Gerasimets 77). *Coach:* Mikhail Vergeyenko.

Scorers:　Scotland: Gallacher 5, 57; Hopkin 54, 88　Belarus: Kachuro 73 (pen)

11 October 1997　　World Cup qualifying　　　　Celtic Park, Glasgow　　　　　Attendance: 47,613

590 SCOTLAND 2, Latvia 0　　　　　　　　　　　　　*Referee: Sandro Pillar (Hungary)*

Scotland (5-3-2):

83　Jim Leighton (Aberdeen);
22　Craig Burley (Celtic);
23　Colin Calderwood (Tottenham Hotspur);
28　Colin Hendry (Blackburn Rovers);
5　Christian Dailly (Derby County);
50　Tom Boyd (Celtic);
55　Gary McAllister (Coventry City, captain);
9　Paul Lambert (Borussia Dortmund);
45　John Collins (Monaco);
37　Gordon Durie (Rangers);
33　Kevin Gallacher (Blackburn Rovers).

Substitutes: 18　Tosh McKinlay (Celtic, for Boyd 81);
3　Simon Donnelly (Celtic, for Durie 84);
21　Billy McKinlay (Blackburn Rovers, for Burley 89)

Manager: Craig Brown

Latvia: Olegs Karavajevs; Igors Stepanovs, Valentins Lobanovs, Mihails Zemlinskis, Jurijs Sevlakovs (captain); Olegs Blagonadezdins, Valerijs Ivanovs, Imants Bleidelis; Marians Pahars, Vladimirs Babicevs, Aleksandrs Jelisejevs. *Substitutes:* Andrejs Stolcers (for Blagonadezdins 62); Vits Rimkus (for Jelisejevs 69). *Trainer:* Janis Gilis.

Scorers:　Scotland: Gallacher 43; Durie 80

It was a case of "France, here we come" as a routine win over Latvia secured second place in group four qualification for the World Cup finals. Kevin Gallacher scored his fifth goal of the competition in the 43rd minute, leaping to head home after the Latvian keeper failed to hold a John Collins drive. Gallacher and Gordon Durie both worked their socks off up front, as manager Craig Brown's familiar 5-3-2 formation took a firm hold on proceedings with Collins, Paul Lambert and captain Gary McAllister all outstanding in the middle of the park. Fittingly it was Durie who made the game safe with 10 minutes remaining, nodding home after Gallacher's intelligent chip had rebounded off the bar with the keeper beaten. Celtic defender Tom Boyd joined an illustrious group of players by becoming the latest to achieve a half century of caps. The achievement of getting to another major championship, the fourth of the 1990s, meant it was the most successful decade ever for Scottish international football.

FIFA WORLD CUP QUALIFYING GROUP FOUR						
	P	W	D	L	F	A	Pts
Austria	10	8	1	1	17	4	25
Scotland	10	7	2	1	15	3	23
Sweden	10	7	0	3	16	9	21
Latvia	10	3	1	6	10	14	10
Estonia	10	1	1	8	4	16	4
Belarus	10	1	1	8	5	21	4

12 November 1997　　Friendly　　　　Stade Guichard, Saint-Etienne　　　　Attendance: 19,514

591 France 2, SCOTLAND 1　　　　　　　　　　　　　*Referee: Antonio Lopez (Spain)*

Scotland: Neil Sullivan (Wimbledon); Craig Burley (Celtic), Colin Calderwood (Tottenham Hotspur), Christian Dailly (Derby County), David Weir (Hearts), Tom Boyd (Celtic); Gary McAllister (Coventry City, captain), Billy McKinlay (Blackburn Rovers), John Collins (Monaco); Gordon Durie (Rangers), Kevin Gallacher (Blackburn Rovers). *Substitutes:* Matt Elliot (Leicester City, for Weir 76); Tosh McKinlay (Celtic, for Boyd 80); Simon Donnelly (Celtic, for Gallacher 83); David Hopkin (Leeds United, for Durie 89). *Manager:* Craig Brown.

France: Fabien Barthez; Lilian Thuram, Pierre Laigle, Marcel Desailly, Laurent Blanc; Emmanuel Petit, Didier Deschamps (captain), Zinedine Zidane; Ibrahim Ba, Stephane Guivarc'h, Lilian Laslandes. *Substitutes:* Youri Djorkaeff (for Laslandes 71); Alain Boghossian (for Petit 73); Vincent Candela (for Laigle 80); Franck Gava (for Ba 80). *Coach:* Aime Jacquet.

Scorers:　France: Laigle 35; Djorkaeff 78 (pen)　　　Scotland: Durie 36

25 March 1998　　Friendly　　　　Ibrox, Glasgow　　　　Attendance: 26,468

592 SCOTLAND 0, Denmark 1　　　　　　　　　　　*Referee: Dermot Gallagher (England)*

Scotland: Jim Leighton (Aberdeen); Jackie McNamara (Celtic), Colin Calderwood (Tottenham Hotspur), Colin Hendry (Blackburn Rovers, captain), Matt Elliot (Leicester City), Tom Boyd (Celtic); Scot Gemmill (Nottingham Forest), Christian Dailly (Derby County), Billy McKinlay (Blackburn Rovers); Scott Booth (Borussia Dortmund), Darren Jackson (Celtic). *Substitutes:* Andy Goram (Rangers, for Leighton 46); Eoin Jess (Aberdeen, for Booth 46); David Weir (Hearts, for McNamara 59); Stuart McCall (Rangers, for Gemmill 69); Simon Donnelly (Celtic, for Jackson 74). *Manager:* Craig Brown.

Denmark: Mogens Krogh; Jacob Laursen, Jan Heintze, Michael Schjonberg, Marc Rieper; Thomas Helveg, Morten Wieghorst, Michael Laudrup (captain); Allan Nielsen, Brian Laudrup, Peter Moller. *Substitutes:* Rene Hendriksen (for Laursen 46); Per Frandsen (for Nielsen 62); Martin Jorgensen (for Moller 74); Bjarne Goldbaek (for Brian Laudrup 80). *Coach:* Bo Johansson (Sweden).

Scorer:　Denmark: Brian Laudrup 37

| 22 April 1998 | Friendly | Easter Road, Edinburgh | Attendance: 14,315 |

593 SCOTLAND 1, Finland 1

Referee: Herman van Dijk (Netherlands)

Scotland: Jim Leighton (Aberdeen); Christian Dailly (Derby County), Colin Calderwood (Tottenham Hotspur), Colin Hendry (Blackburn Rovers, captain), Matt Elliot (Leicester City), Derek Whyte (Aberdeen); Scot Gemmill (Nottingham Forest), Billy McKinlay (Blackburn Rovers), John Collins (Monaco); Scott Booth (Borussia Dortmund), Darren Jackson (Celtic). *Substitutes:* Kevin Gallacher (Blackburn Rovers, for Jackson 46); David Weir (Hearts, for Elliot 46); Gordon Durie (Rangers, for Calderwood 71); Paul Lambert (Celtic, for Gemmill 76); Simon Donnelly (Celtic, for Booth 76); Tom Boyd (Celtic, for Dailly 87). *Manager:* Craig Brown.

Finland: Antti Niemi; Harri Ylonen, Marko Tuomela, Jukka Koskinen, Sami Hyypia; Juha Reini, Simo Valakari, Sami Mahlio; Antti Sumiala, Jari Litmanen (captain), Jonatan Johansson. *Substitutes:* Joonas Kolkka (for Sumiala 37); Aarno Turpeinen (for Litmanen 46); Aki Riihilahti (for Reini 46); Mika-Matti Paatelainen (for Johansson 59); Tomi Kinnunen (for Tuomela 64). *Coach:* Richard Moller-Nielsen (Denmark).

Scorers: Finland: Johansson 10   Scotland: Jackson 15

| 23 May 1998 | Friendly | Giants Stadium, East Rutherford | Attendance: 56,404 |

594 Colombia 2, SCOTLAND 2

Referee: Brian Hall (USA)

Scotland: Neil Sullivan (Wimbledon); Jackie McNamara (Celtic), Colin Calderwood (Tottenham Hotspur), Colin Hendry (Blackburn Rovers, captain), Tom Boyd (Celtic); Craig Burley (Celtic), Christian Dailly (Derby County), Paul Lambert (Celtic), John Collins (Monaco); Darren Jackson (Celtic), Gordon Durie (Rangers). *Substitutes:* Scott Booth (Borussia Dortmund, for Jackson 46); Simon Donnelly (Celtic, for Durie 61); Billy McKinlay (Blackburn Rovers, for McNamara 71). *Manager:* Craig Brown.

Columbia: Miguel Calero; Ivan Cordoba, Mauricio Serna, Jose Santa, Jorge Bemudez; Harold Lozano, Carlos Valderrama (captain), Wilmer Cabrera; Faustino Asprilla, Freddy Rincon, Adolfo Valencia. *Coach:* Hernan Gomez.

Scorers: Columbia: Valderrama 22 (pen); Rincon 79   Scotland: Collins 24; Burley 33

| 30 May 1998 | Friendly | RFK Stadium, Washington DC | Attendance: 46,037 |

595 USA 0, SCOTLAND 0

Referee: Felipe Ramos (Mexico)

Scotland: Jim Leighton (Aberdeen); Tom Boyd (Celtic), Christian Dailly (Derby County), Colin Calderwood (Tottenham Hotspur), Colin Hendry (Blackburn Rovers, captain), Tosh McKinlay (Celtic); Paul Lambert (Celtic), Billy McKinlay (Blackburn Rovers), John Collins (Monaco); Darren Jackson (Celtic), Kevin Gallacher (Blackburn Rovers). *Substitutes:* Jackie McNamara (Celtic, for Tosh McKinlay 60); Craig Burley (Celtic, for Billy McKinlay 74); Simon Donnelly (Celtic, for Gallacher 82). *Manager:* Craig Brown.

USA: Kasey Keller; David Regis, Eddie Pope, Michael Burns, Tom Dooley; Chad Deering, Ernie Stewart, Tabare Ramos; Joseph-Max Moore, Cobi Jones, Roy Wegerle. *Substitutes:* Predrag Radosavljevic (for Ramos 57); Eric Wynalda (for Wegerle 62); Jeffrey Agoos (for Moore 70); Alexei Lalas (for Stewart 82). *Coach:* Steve Sampson.

| 10 June 1998 | FIFA World Cup (group stage) | Stade de France, Saint-Denis | Attendance: 80,000 |

596 Brazil 2, SCOTLAND 1

Referee: Jose-Maria Garcia (Spain)

Scotland (4-3-3):
- 87 Jim Leighton (Aberdeen);
- 11 Christian Dailly (Derby County)
- 29 Colin Calderwood (Tottenham Hotspur)
- 33 Colin Hendry (Blackburn Rovers, captain)
- 56 Tom Boyd (Celtic);
- 26 Craig Burley (Celtic)
- 13 Paul Lambert (Celtic)
- 50 John Collins (Monaco);
- 25 Darren Jackson (Celtic)
- 41 Gordon Durie (Rangers)
- 37 Kevin Gallacher (Blackburn Rovers)

Substitutes: 27 Billy McKinlay (Blackburn Rovers, for Jackson 78); 21 Tosh McKinlay (Celtic, for Dailly 85)

Manager: Craig Brown

Bad luck had dogged Scotland at the five World Cup finals in a row between 1974 and 1990, and it struck again on the return to the France tournament. In a match where they merited a draw at least, Celtic's Tom Boyd unfortunately put through his own goal in the 73rd minute to give the disappointing Brazilians an undeserved victory. It was a gala occasion for the first match after the opening ceremony where the Scottish squad took to the field in kilts. A couple of hours later they were back on the park in more regular outfits. It was the worst possible start when Brazil scored in the fourth minute when Cesar Sampaio nudged home a near-post header following a corner. The Scots created a number of chances but it took until approaching half-time before they grabbed the equaliser, John Collins scoring from the penalty spot after Kevin Gallacher had been brought down. Scotland more than matched the Brazilians in the second half but it was to count for nothing and Boyd's unfortunate moment took all the gloss off a very good display against such highly rated opponents.

Brazil: Taffarel; Cafu, Junior Baiano, Aldair, Roberto Carlos; Giovanni, Cesar Sampaio, Dunga (captain), Rivaldo; Bebeto, Ronaldo. *Substitutes:* Leonardo (for Giovanni 46); Denilson (for Bebeto 70). *Trainer:* Mario Zagallo.

Scorers: Brazil: Cesar Sampaio 4; Tom Boyd 73 (own goal)   Scotland: Collins 38 (pen)

John Collins (right) equalises against Brazil from the penalty spot.

16 June 1998   FIFA World Cup (group stage)   Parc Lescure, Bordeaux   Attendance: 30,236

597 **Norway 1, SCOTLAND 1**   *Referee: Laszlo Vagner (Hungary)*

Scotland (4-3-3):

88 Jim Leighton (Aberdeen);
12 Christian Dailly (Derby County)
30 Colin Calderwood (Tottenham Hotspur)
34 Colin Hendry (Blackburn Rovers, captain)
57 Tom Boyd (Celtic);
27 Craig Burley (Celtic)
14 Paul Lambert (Celtic)
51 John Collins (Monaco);
26 Darren Jackson (Celtic)
42 Gordon Durie (Rangers)
38 Kevin Gallacher (Blackburn Rovers)

Substitutes: 6 David Weir (Hearts, for Calderwood 60);
8 Jackie McNamara (Celtic, for Jackson 62)

Manager: Craig Brown

The second tie of the World Cup group stages was a match which Scotland should have won but could equally well have lost, so a share of the points was probably just about the right result. It all looked over when Havard Flo put Norway ahead with a header as spectators were still returning to their seats after the half-time break. However, a couple of tactical substitutions, one of which saw Craig Burley moving from wing back to midfield, saw the game level 20 minutes later. The other replacement, David Weir, placed a smart pass forward between the two Norwegian centre backs and Burley stole in to lift the ball over the keeper and into the net. The Scots swarmed forward for most of the remainder and Christian Dailly and John Collins both came close, but the game ended all square. With Norway now on two points after a draw with Morocco in their opening match, Scotland needed a win over the African side to progress to the knockout stages.

Norway: Frode Grodas (captain); Henning Berg, Dan Eggen, Ronny Johnsen, Stig Inge Bjornebye; Havard Flo, Roar Strand, Stale Solbakken, Vidar Riseth; Kjetil Rendal, Tore Andre Flo. *Substitutes:* Jahn Ivar Jakobsen (for Havard Flo 62); Egil Ostenstad (for Riseth 75); Gunnar Halle (for Berg 82). *Trainer:* Egil Roger Olsen.

Scorers: Norway: Havard Flo 46   Scotland: Burley 66

23 June 1998   FIFA World Cup (group stage)   Stade Guichard, Saint-Etiennne   Attendance: 35,500

598 **Morocco 3, SCOTLAND 0**   *Referee: Ali Bujsaim (United Arab Emirates)*

Scotland (5-3-2):

89 Jim Leighton (Aberdeen);
9 Jackie McNamara (Celtic)
7 David Weir (Hearts)
13 Christian Dailly (Derby County)
35 Colin Hendry (Blackburn Rovers, captain)
58 Tom Boyd (Celtic);
28 Craig Burley (Celtic)
15 Paul Lambert (Celtic)
52 John Collins (Monaco);
43 Gordon Durie (Rangers)
39 Kevin Gallacher (Blackburn Rovers)

Substitutes: 22 Tosh McKinlay (Celtic, for McNamara 54);
17 Scott Booth (Borussia Dortmund, for Durie 84)

Manager: Craig Brown

Of all the disappointments at a World Cup finals, and there have been a few, the defeat by Morocco which ended hopes of making the knockout stages was one of the bitterest blows to take. The mood was good going into the game and even after Salaheddine Bassir put his team ahead in the 22nd minute there were still expectations that the Scottish side could come back. They should have had a penalty when a Moroccan player handled in the box, but the referee from the United Arab Emirates, for reasons unknown to everyone except himself, waved play on. Things went from bad to worse just after half-time when first Abdeljalil Hadda made it 2-0 and then midfielder Craig Burley was sent off. A second for Bassir with a few minutes remaining rubbed salt in the wounds. But then came news that a Scottish victory wouldn't have mattered anyway, as Norway had shocked Brazil with a 2-1 win meaning they would both go through. Statistics show the Scots had more possession and corners than Morocco, and almost double the shots and efforts on target. But only one statistic matters and once again the Scottish contingent was on an earlier flight home then hoped for.

Morocco: Driss Benzekri; Abdelilah Saber, Noureddine Naybet, Gharib Amzine, Lahcen Abrami; Tahar El Khalej, Mustapha Hadji, Youssef Chippo; Smahi Triki, Salaheddine Bassir, Abdeljalil Hadda. *Substitutes:* Youssef Rossi (for Saber 72); Rachid Azzouzi (for Amzine 76); Jamal Sellami (for Chippo 87). *Trainer:* Henri Michel (France).

Scorers: Morocco: Bassir 22, 84; Hadda 47

1998 FIFA WORLD CUP GROUP A

	P	W	D	L	F	A	Pts
Brazil	3	2	0	1	6	3	6
Norway	3	1	2	0	5	4	5
Morocco	3	1	1	1	5	5	4
Scotland	3	0	1	2	2	6	1

5 September 1998   European Championship qualifying   Zalgaris Stadionas, Vilnius   Attendance: 4,000

599 **Lithuania 0, SCOTLAND 0**   *Referee: Constantin Zotta (Romania)*

Scotland: Jim Leighton (Aberdeen); Christian Dailly (Blackburn Rovers), Colin Calderwood (Tottenham Hotspur), Colin Hendry (Rangers, captain), Matt Elliot (Leicester City), Tom Boyd (Celtic); Paul Lambert (Celtic), John Collins (Everton); Darren Jackson (Celtic), Ally McCoist (Kilmarnock), Kevin Gallacher (Blackburn Rovers). *Substitutes:* Barry Ferguson (Rangers, for Jackson 56); Callum Davidson (Blackburn Rovers, for Calderwood 71); Neil McCann (Hearts, for McCoist 83). *Manager:* Craig Brown.

Lithuania: Gintaras Stauce (captain); Andrius Skerla, Deividas Semberas, Tomas Zvirgzdauskas, Virginijus Baltusnikas; Gediminas Sugzda, Raimondas Zutautus, Aidas Preiksaitis; Edgaras Jankauskas, Grazvydas Mikulenas, Aurelijus Skarbalius. *Substitutes:* Orestas Buitkus (for Sugzda 61); Vaidotas Slekys (for Mikulenas 90). *Coach:* Kestutis Latoza.

SCOTLAND AT 150: A CENTURY AND A HALF OF INTERNATIONAL FOOTBALL

10 October 1998 European Championship qualifying Tynecastle, Edinburgh Attendance: 16,930

600 SCOTLAND 3, Estonia 2
Referee: Joaquim Marques (Portugal)

Scotland: Jim Leighton (Aberdeen); Tom Boyd (Celtic), Colin Calderwood (Tottenham Hotspur), Colin Hendry (Rangers, captain), David Weir (Hearts), Callum Davidson (Blackburn Rovers); Allan Johnston (Sunderland), Billy McKinlay (Blackburn Rovers), Ian Durrant (Kilmarnock); Kevin Gallacher (Blackburn Rovers), Ally McCoist (Kilmarnock). *Substitutes:* Darren Jackson (Celtic, for Gallacher 18); Simon Donnelly (Celtic, for Calderwood 57); Billy Dodds (Dundee United, for McCoist 69). *Manager:* Craig Brown.

Estonia: Mart Poom; Urmas Kirs, Urmas Rooba, Viktor Alonen, Sergei Hohlov-Simson; Sergei Terehhov, Martin Reim (captain), Marko Kristal; Andres Oper, Maksim Smirnov, Indrek Zelinski. *Substitute:* Kristen Viikmae (for Zelinski 88). *Coach:* Teitur Thordarson (Iceland).

Scorers: Estonia: Hohlov-Simson 34; Smirnov 75   Scotland: Dodds 70, 85; Hohlov-Simson 77 (own goal)

14 October 1998 European Championship qualifying Pittodrie, Aberdeen Attendance: 18,517

601 SCOTLAND 2, Faroe Islands 1
Referee: Kostas Kapitanis (Cyprus)

Scotland: Neil Sullivan (Wimbledon); Tom Boyd (Celtic), David Weir (Hearts), Colin Hendry (Rangers, captain), Matt Elliot (Leicester City), Callum Davidson (Blackburn Rovers); Allan Johnston (Sunderland), Billy McKinlay (Blackburn Rovers), Craig Burley (Celtic); Simon Donnelly (Celtic), Billy Dodds (Dundee United). *Substitutes:* Ian Durrant (Kilmarnock, for McKinlay 46); Stephen Glass (Newcastle United, for Johnston 79). *Manager:* Craig Brown.

Faroe Islands: Jakup Mikkelsen; Oli Johannesen, Jens-Kristian Hansen (captain), Pol Thorsteinsson, Hans-Frodi Hansen; Henning Jarnskor, Julian Johnsson, Samal Joensen; John Petersen, Uni Arge, Todi Jonsson. *Substitutes:* Jakup a Borg (for Arge 68); John Hansen (for Jarnskor 79). *Coach:* Allan Simonsen (Denmark).

Scorers: Scotland: Burley 21; Dodds 45   Faroe Islands: Petersen 86 (pen)

31 March 1999 European Championship qualifying Celtic Park, Glasgow Attendance: 44,513

602 SCOTLAND 1, Czech Republic 2
Referee: Kim Milton Nielsen (Denmark)

Scotland: Neil Sullivan (Wimbledon); Craig Burley (Celtic), David Weir (Everton), Matt Elliot (Leicester City), Tom Boyd (Celtic), Callum Davidson (Blackburn Rovers); David Hopkin (Leeds United), Gary McAllister (Coventry City, captain), Paul Lambert (Celtic); Neil McCann (Rangers), Eoin Jess (Aberdeen). *Substitutes:* Allan Johnston (Sunderland, for Davidson 52); Don Hutchison (Everton, for McAllister 63). *Manager:* Craig Brown.

Czech Republic: Pavel Srnicek; Tomas Votava, Jiri Nemec (captain), Jan Suchoparek, Michal Hornak; Martin Hasek, Karel Poborsky, Pavel Nedved, Patrik Berger; Vladimir Smicer, Vratislav Lokvenc. *Substitutes:* Pavel Kuka (for Lokvenc 70); Karel Rada (for Poborsky 76); Miroslav Baranek (for Smicer 84). *Coach:* Jozef Chovanec.

Scorers: Czech Republic: Elliot 27 (own goal); Smicer 35   Scotland: Jess 68

28 April 1999 Friendly Weser Stadion, Bremen Attendance: 28,000

603 Germany 0, SCOTLAND 1
Referee: Urs Meier (Switzerland)

Scotland (4-3-3):

6 Neil Sullivan (Wimbledon);
63 Tom Boyd (Celtic)
11 David Weir (Everton)
39 Colin Hendry (Rangers, captain)
5 Callum Davidson (Blackburn Rovers);
14 Scot Gemmill (Everton)
18 Paul Lambert (Celtic)
14 Ian Durrant (Kilmarnock);
4 Allan Johnston (Sunderland)
2 Don Hutchison (Everton)
7 Billy Dodds (Dundee United)

It may have been only a friendly, but the single-goal win in Bremen was notable in that it was the first over the Germans in 42 years. Should Craig Brown's makeshift heroes now be recognised as the champions of Europe? That was the tongue-in-cheek question asked by Glenn Gibbons in his match report. Probably not, but it was still a memorable night. Don Hutchison of Everton was the man responsible for the victory, side-footing home after a fluent move involving influential midfielder Paul Lambert and left back Callum Davidson. While it might have been viewed as an unlikely result, the Scottish players were worthy of the success, with their close marking tactics basically smothering the Germans out of the match.

Substitutes: 16 Eoin Jess (Aberdeen, for Gemmill 59); 1 Paul Ritchie (Hearts, for Hendry 66); 1 Robbie Winters (Aberdeen, for Durrant 71); 12 Derek Whyte (Aberdeen, for Davidson 77); 1 Colin Cameron (Hearts, for Lambert 83); 1 Brian O'Neil (Wolfsburg, for Johnston 86)

Manager: Craig Brown

Germany: Jens Lehmann; Christian Worns, Jorg Heinrich, Lothar Matthaus, Jens Nowotny; Thomas Strunz, Jens Jeremies, Dietmar Hamann; Horst Heldt, Oliver Neuville, Oliver Bierhoff (captain). *Substitutes:* Carsten Ramelow (for Jeremies 46); Michael Ballack (for Hamann 59); Ulf Kirsten (for Bierhoff 59); Carsten Jancker (for Strunz 86). *Coach:* Erich Ribbeck.

Scorer: Scotland: Hutchison 65

5 June 1999 European Championship qualifying Svangaskard Stadion, Toftir Attendance: 1,500

604 Faroe Islands 1, SCOTLAND 1
Referee: Philippe Kalt (France)

Scotland: Neil Sullivan (Wimbledon); Tom Boyd (Celtic, captain), David Weir (Everton), Colin Calderwood (Aston Villa), Matt Elliot (Leicester City), Callum Davidson (Blackburn Rovers); Allan Johnston (Sunderland), Paul Lambert (Celtic), Ian Durrant (Kilmarnock); Billy Dodds (Dundee United), Kevin Gallacher (Blackburn Rovers). *Substitutes:* Colin Cameron (Hearts, for Durrant 46); Scot Gemmill (Everton, for Johnston 86); Eoin Jess (Aberdeen, for Gallacher 89). *Manager:* Craig Brown.

Faroe Islands: Jakup Mikkelsen; Oli Johannesen, Ossur Hansen, Pol Thorsteinsson, Hans-Frodi Hansen; Johannis Joensen, Julian Johnsson, Samal Joensen; Allan Morkore, John Petersen, Todi Jonsson (captain). *Substitutes:* Jakup a Borg (for Julian Johnsson 69); Uni Arge (for Petersen 79); John Hansen (for Ossur Hansen 86). *Coach:* Allan Simonsen (Denmark).

Scorers: Scotland: Johnston 38   Faroe Islands: Hans-Frodi Hansen 90

Chapter seven: 1990-1999

9 June 1999 European Championship qualifying Sparta Stadion, Prague Attendance: 22,000

605 Czech Republic 3, SCOTLAND 2
Referee: Helmut Krug (Germany)

Scotland: Neil Sullivan (Wimbledon); Tom Boyd (Celtic, captain), David Weir (Hearts), Colin Calderwood (Aston Villa), Paul Ritchie (Hearts), Callum Davidson (Blackburn Rovers); Allan Johnston (Sunderland), Paul Lambert (Celtic), Ian Durrant (Kilmarnock); Billy Dodds (Dundee United), Kevin Gallacher (Blackburn Rovers). *Substitute:* Eoin Jess (Aberdeen, for Durrant 70). *Manager:* Craig Brown.

Czech Republic: Pavel Srnicek; Tomas Repka, Jiri Nemec (captain), Jan Suchoparek, Michal Hornak; Martin Hasek, Karel Poborsky, Pavel Nedved, Patrik Berger; Vladimir Smicer, Vratislav Lokvenc. *Substitutes:* Miroslav Baranek (for Hasek 60); Pavel Kuka (for Lokvenc 68); Jan Koller (for Poborsky 68). *Coach:* Jozef Chovanec.

Scorers: Scotland: Ritchie 30; Johnston 62   Czech Republic: Repka 65; Kuka 75; Koller 87

4 September 1999 European Championship qualifying Kosevo Stadion, Sarajevo Attendance: 26,000

606 Bosnia/Herzegovina 1, SCOTLAND 2
Referee: Nikolay Lednikov (Russia)

Scotland: Neil Sullivan (Wimbledon); David Weir (Everton), Colin Calderwood (Aston Villa), Colin Hendry (Rangers, captain), Craig Burley (Celtic); David Hopkin (Leeds United), Barry Ferguson (Rangers), John Collins (Everton); Billy Dodds (Dundee United), Don Hutchison (Everton), Neil McCann (Rangers). *Substitutes:* Christian Dailly (Blackburn Rovers, for Calderwood 46); Ian Durrant (Kilmarnock, for Ferguson 70); Kevin Gallacher (Blackburn Rovers, for McCann 75). *Manager:* Craig Brown.

Bosnia/Herzegovina: Mirsad Dedic; Omar Joldic, Jasmin Mujdza, Muhamed Konjic (captain), Mirsad Hibic; Bakir Besirevic, Sead Halilovic, Sergej Barbarez; Marko Topic, Meho Kodro, Elvir Bolic. *Substitutes:* Edin Mujcin (for Halilovic 62); Enes Demirovic (for Mujdza 78); Senad Repuh (for Joldic 78). *Coach:* Faruk Hadzibegic.

Scorers: Scotland: Hutchison 13; Dodds 45   Bosnia/Herzegovina: Bolic 23

8 September 1999 European Championship qualifying Kadriorg Stadion, Tallinn Attendance: 4,500

607 Estonia 0, SCOTLAND 0
Referee: Fritz Stuchlik (Austria)

Scotland: Neil Sullivan (Wimbledon); Craig Burley (Celtic), David Weir (Everton), Colin Hendry (Rangers, captain), Christian Dailly (Blackburn Rovers), Callum Davidson (Blackburn Rovers); Allan Johnston (Sunderland), John Collins (Everton), Ian Durrant (Kilmarnock); Don Hutchison (Everton), Billy Dodds (Dundee United). *Substitutes:* Neil McCann (Rangers, for Johnston 54); Barry Ferguson (Rangers, for Durrant 66). *Manager:* Craig Brown.

Estonia: Mart Poom; Urmas Kirs, Erko Saviauk, Sergei Hohlov-Simson (captain), Raio Piiroja; Alvar Anniste, Martin Reim, Marko Kristal; Andres Oper, Sergei Terehhov, Ivan O'Konnel-Bronin. *Substitute:* Indrek Zelinski (for O'Konnel-Bronin 46). *Coach:* Teitur Thordarson (Iceland).

5 October 1999 European Championship qualifying Ibrox, Glasgow Attendance: 30,000

608 SCOTLAND 1, Bosnia/Herzegovina 0
Referee: Leif Sundell (Sweden)

Scotland: Neil Sullivan (Wimbledon); Craig Burley (Celtic), David Weir (Everton), Christian Dailly (Blackburn Rovers), Colin Hendry (Rangers, captain), Callum Davidson (Blackburn Rovers); David Hopkin (Leeds United), Paul Lambert (Celtic), John Collins (Everton); Billy Dodds (Dundee United), Kevin Gallacher (Newcastle United). *Substitutes:* Colin Calderwood (Aston Villa, for Hendry 37); Mark Burchill (Celtic, for Gallacher 78); Gary McSwegan (Hearts, for Dodds 89). *Manager:* Craig Brown.

Bosnia/Herzegovina: Adnan Guso; Sead Kapetanovic, Bakir Besirevic, Faruk Hujdurovic, Mirza Varesanovic; Faruk Ihtijarevic, Sergej Barbarez, Nermin Sabic; Elvir Baljic, Edin Mujcin, Elvir Bolic (captain). *Substitutes:* Marko Topic (for Ihtijarevic 77); Alen Avdic (for Mujcin 84). *Coach:* Faruk Hadzibegic.

Scorer: Scotland: Collins 25 (pen)

Captain Colin Hendry leads the players during a training session prior to the double header against Bosnia/Hezegovina and Estonia in September 1999.

9 October 1999   European Championship qualifying   Hampden Park   Attendance: 22,059

609 SCOTLAND 3, Lithuania 0   *Referee: Stephane Bre (France)*

Scotland (5-2-3):

1 Jonathan Gould (Celtic);
3 Paul Ritchie (Hearts)
17 David Weir (Everton)
18 Christian Dailly (Blackburn Rovers)
3 Brian O'Neil (Wolfsburg)
10 Callum Davidson (Blackburn Rovers);
34 Craig Burley (Celtic)
22 Paul Lambert (Celtic, captain);
5 Don Hutchison (Everton)
2 Gary McSwegan (Hearts)
2 Mark Burchill (Celtic)

Substitutes: 3 Colin Cameron (Hearts, for Burley 46);
13 Billy Dodds (Dundee United, for Burchill 78);
46 Kevin Gallacher (Newcastle United, for McSwegan 82)

Manager: Craig Brown

A fairly routine home win over Lithuania gave Scotland a play-off chance of making it to the 11th European Championships, and ultimately home and away matches with England. Don Hutchison, making his fifth appearance, was the best player on the field, opening the scoring just after half-time and generally causing a nuisance all over the place for the Lithuanians. His goal was the result of great opportunism, reacting first after a penalty by Mark Burchill had rebounded off the post. Gary McSwegan made the result fairly safe two minutes later after Burchill set him up and his Hearts team mate Colin Cameron lashed home a shot with time running out to make it 3-0. Goalkeeper Jonathan Gould, making his debut, produced a fine save to deny Lithuania when the game was still goalless. Manager Craig Brown was quick to point out the relevance of that afterwards, saying it gave the team confidence at a very important time.

Lithuania: Pavelas Leusas; Darius Zutautas, Tomas Zvirgzdauskas, Marius Skinderis (captain), Andrius Skerla; Irmantas Stumbrys, Tomas Razanauskas, Saulias Mikalajunas, Andrijus Tereskinas (captain); Vidas Dancenka, Grazvydas Mikulenas. *Substitutes:* Donatas Vencevicius (for Stumbrys 54); Darius Maciulevicius (for Dancenka 54); Arturas Fomenka (for Tereskinas 64). *Trainer:* Robertas Tautkus.

Scorers: Scotland: Hutchison 48; McSwegan 50; Cameron 88

EUROPEAN CHAMPIONSHIP QUALIFYING GROUP NINE

	P	W	D	L	F	A	Pts
Czech Republic	8	6	2	0	16	6	14
Scotland	8	4	2	2	12	12	10
Boznia/Herzegovina	8	3	3	2	10	7	9
Lithuania	8	2	2	4	10	9	6
Estonia	8	0	1	7	6	20	1

13 November 1999   European Championship qualifying (play-off)   Hampden Park   Attendance: 50,132

610 SCOTLAND 0, England 2   *Referee: Manuel Diaz (Spain)*

Scotland: Neil Sullivan (Wimbledon); Craig Burley (Celtic), David Weir (Everton), Colin Hendry (Rangers, captain), Christian Dailly (Blackburn Rovers), Paul Ritchie (Hearts); Don Hutchison (Everton), Barry Ferguson (Rangers), John Collins (Everton); Billy Dodds (Dundee United), Kevin Gallacher (Newcastle United). *Substitute:* Mark Burchill (Celtic, for Gallacher 82). *Manager:* Craig Brown.

England: David Seaman; Phil Neville, Martin Keown, Tony Adams, Sol Campbell; David Beckham, Paul Ince, Paul Scholes, Jamie Redknapp; Michael Owen, Alan Shearer (captain). *Substitute:* Andy Cole (for Owen 67). *Manager:* Kevin Keegan.

Scorer: England: Scholes 21, 42

17 November 1999   European Championship qualifying (play-off)   Wembley, London   Attendance: 76,848

611 England 0, SCOTLAND 1   *Referee: Pierluigi Collina (Italy)*

Scotland (5-2-3):

13 Neil Sullivan (Wimbledon);
36 Craig Burley (Celtic)
19 David Weir (Everton)
20 Christian Dailly (Blackburn Rovers)
44 Colin Hendry (Rangers, captain)
11 Callum Davidson (Blackburn Rovers);
5 Barry Ferguson (Rangers)
58 John Collins (Everton);
7 Don Hutchison (Everton)
15 Billy Dodds (Dundee United)
5 Neil McCann (Rangers)

Substitute: 4 Mark Burchill (Celtic, for McCann 74)

Manager: Craig Brown

Having lost the first leg in Glasgow due to two Paul Scholes goals, there was not exactly great confidence going into the second match at Wembley four days later. What happened had never been seen before in the 127-year history of Scotland-England matches – a fine Scotland victory in London but the Tartan Army left distraught. One goal was just not enough and it was the English who were heading to Euro 2000. Don Hutchison, who had another fine game for his adopted country, put supporters in dreamland with seven minutes left of the first half. And with the English players appearing strangely out of touch, including David Beckham spending most of his time defending to stem the danger from winger Neil McCann, a second goal looked likely. The best chance came with 10 minutes remaining, when Christian Dailly's header looked like taking the game into extra time. However, keeper David Seaman – remember him from three years earlier – produced another miraculous save to claw the ball out from under the crossbar. It was not to be but all the Scots played well, with Dailly, Barry Ferguson and John Collins standing out.

England: David Seaman; Phil Neville, Gareth Southgate, Tony Adams, Sol Campbell; David Beckham, Paul Ince, Paul Scholes, Jamie Redknapp; Michael Owen, Alan Shearer (captain). *Substitutes:* Emile Heskey (for Owen 63); Ray Parlour (for Scholes 89). *Manager:* Kevin Keegan.

Scorer: Scotland: Hutchison 38

CHAPTER EIGHT
2000-2009

29 March 2000   Friendly   Hampden Park   Attendance: 48,157

612 SCOTLAND 0, France 2
Referee: Rune Pedersen (Norway)

Scotland: Neil Sullivan (Wimbledon); Paul Telfer (Coventry City), Paul Ritchie (Bolton Wanderers), Christian Dailly (Blackburn Rovers), Colin Hendry (Coventry City, captain), Callum Davidson (Blackburn Rovers); Don Hutchison (Everton), Barry Ferguson (Rangers), Colin Cameron (Hearts); Billy Dodds (Rangers), Kevin Gallacher (Newcastle United). *Substitutes:* Steven Pressley (Hearts, for Ritchie 46); Neil McCann (Rangers, for Cameron 46); Allan Johnston (Sunderland, for Telfer 67); Mark Burchill (Celtic, for Gallacher 78). *Manager:* Craig Brown.

France: Ulrich Rame; Lilian Thuram, Marcel Desailly, Laurent Blanc, Bixente Lizarazu; Emmanuel Petit, Youri Djorkaeff, Didier Deschamps (captain); Ludovic Giuly, Christophe Dugarry, Thierry Henry. *Substitutes:* Johan Micoud (for Djorkaeff 46); Sylvain Wiltord (for Giuly 46); Patrick Vieira (for Deschamps 60); Robert Pires (for Dugarry 73). *Coach:* Roger Lemmere.

Scorers: France: Wiltord 53; Henry 89

26 April 2000   Friendly   Gelredome, Arnheim   Attendance: 24,500

613 Netherlands 0, SCOTLAND 0
Referee: Hartmut Strampe (Germany)

Scotland: Neil Sullivan Wimbledon); Jackie McNamara (Celtic), David Weir (Everton), Christian Dailly (Blackburn Rovers), Matt Elliot (Leicester City), Paul Ritchie (Bolton Wanderers); Craig Burley (Derby County), Paul Lambert (Celtic, captain), Neil McCann (Rangers); Don Hutchison (Everton), Billy Dodds (Rangers). *Substitutes:* Ian Durrant (Kilmarnock, for Burley 46); Mark Burchill (Celtic, for McNamara 66); Brian O'Neil (Wolfsburg, for Dailly 85). *Manager:* Craig Brown.

Netherlands: Edwin van der Sar; Andre Ooijer, Frank de Boer, Bert Konterman, Arthur Numan; Marc Overmars, Edgar Davids, Paul Bosvelt; Roy Makaay, Dennis Bergkamp, Jimmy-Floyd Hasselbaink. *Substitutes:* Boudewijn Zenden (for Overmars 46); Patrick Kluivert (for Bergkamp 46); Jeffrey Talan (for Makaay 60); Pierre van Hooijdonk (for Hasselbaink 67). *Coach:* Frank Rijkaard.

30 May 2000   Friendly   Lansdowne Road, Dublin   Attendance: 30,214

614 Republic of Ireland 1, SCOTLAND 2
Referee: Vitor Pereira (Portugal)

Scotland: Neil Sullivan (Wimbledon); Craig Burley (Derby County), Christian Dailly (Blackburn Rovers), Matt Elliot (Leicester City), Brian O'Neil (Wolfsburg), Gary Naysmith (Hearts); Barry Ferguson (Rangers), Paul Lambert (Celtic, captain), Neil McCann (Rangers); Don Hutchison (Everton), Billy Dodds (Rangers). *Substitutes:* Kevin Gallacher (Newcastle United, for Dodds 46); Allan Johnston (Sunderland, for Lambert 75); Colin Cameron (Hearts, for Ferguson 83); Ian Durrant (Kilmarnock, for Naysmith 88); Steven Pressley (Hearts, for McCann 90). *Manager:* Craig Brown.

Republic of Ireland: Alan Kelly; Stephen Carr, Kevin Kilbane, Phil Babb, Gary Breen; Jason McAteer, Stephen McPhail, Steve Finnan, Mark Kennedy; Robbie Keane, Niall Quinn (captain). *Substitutes:* Damian Duff (for McPhail 61); Terry Phelen (for Kennedy 61); Richard Dunne (for Quinn 77); Dominic Foley (for Breen 77). *Manager:* Mick McCarthy.

Scorers: Republic of Ireland: Burley 2 (own goal)   Scotland: Hutchison 15; Ferguson 29

2 September 2000   World Cup qualifying   Skonto Stadion, Riga   Attendance: 9,200

615 Latvia 0, SCOTLAND 1
Referee: Andreas Schluchter (Switzerland)

Scotland: Neil Sullivan (Tottenham Hotspur); David Weir (Everton), Colin Hendry (Coventry City, captain), Matt Elliot (Leicester City), Christian Dailly (Blackburn Rovers), Callum Davidson (Leicester City); Tom Boyd (Celtic), Barry Ferguson (Rangers), Neil McCann (Rangers); Don Hutchison (Sunderland), Billy Dodds (Rangers). *Substitutes:* Colin Cameron (Hearts, for Weir 46); Gary Naysmith (Hearts, for Davidson 46); Gary Holt (Kilmarnock, for Dodds 90). *Manager:* Craig Brown.

Latvia: Aleksandrs Kolinko; Iurijs Laizans, Valentins Lobanovs, Valerijs Ivanovs, Igors Stepanovs; Olegs Blagonadezdins, Vitalijs Astafjevs (captain), Imants Bleidelis; Andrejs Rubins, Andrejs Stolcers, Marians Pahars. *Coach:* Gary Johnson (England).

Scorer: Scotland: McCann 88

7 October 2000   World Cup qualifying   Stadio Olimpico, Serraville   Attendance: 4,377

616 San Marino 0, SCOTLAND 2
Referee: Gylfi Orrason (Iceland)

Scotland: Neil Sullivan (Tottenham Hotspur); Jackie McNamara (Celtic), Christian Dailly (Blackburn Rovers), Colin Hendry (Coventry City), Matt Elliot (Leicester City), Gary Naysmith (Hearts); Colin Cameron (Hearts), Don Hutchison (Sunderland), Neil McCann (Rangers); Billy Dodds (Rangers), Kevin Gallacher (Newcastle United, captain). *Substitutes:* David Weir (Everton, for Dailly 36); Allan Johnston (Rangers, for McCann 46); Paul Dickov (Manchester City, for Gallacher 66). *Manager:* Craig Brown.

San Marino: Federico Gasperoni; Mirco Gennari, Mauro Mariani, Luca Gobbi, Ivan Matteoni; Simone Bacciocchi, Pierangelo Manzaroli (captain), Ermanno Zonzini; Bryan Gasperoni, Riccardo Muccioli, Paolo Montagna. *Substitutes:* Marco de Luigi (for Montagna 60); Vittorio Valentini (for Matteoni 73); Pierdomenico Della Valle (for Zonzini 80). *Coach:* Gian Paolo Mazza.

Scorers: Scotland; Elliot 71; Hutchison 73

11 October 2000 World Cup qualifying Maksimir Stadion, Zagreb Attendance: 17,995

617 Croatia 1, SCOTLAND 1
Referee: Gilles Veissiere (France)

Scotland: Neil Sullivan (Tottenham Hotspur); Tom Boyd (Celtic), David Weir (Everton), Colin Hendry (Coventry City, captain), Matt Elliot (Leicester City), Gary Naysmith (Hearts); Craig Burley (Derby County), Don Hutchison (Sunderland), Colin Cameron (Hearts); Allan Johnston (Rangers), Kevin Gallacher (Newcastle United). *Substitutes:* Paul Dickov (Manchester City, for Johnston 46); Gary Holt (Kilmarnock, for Dickov 90). *Manager:* Craig Brown.

Croatia: Zeljko Pavlovic; Robert Kovac, Igor Stimac, Svonimir Soldo, Robert Jarni (captain); Daniel Saric, Robert Prosinecki, Dario Simic; Niko Kovac, Bosko Balaban, Alen Boksic. *Substitutes:* Boris Zivkovic (for Jarni 46); Igor Biscan (for Soldo 46); Davor Vugrinec (for Boksic 75). *Coach:* Miroslav Blazevic.

Scorers: Croatia: Boksic 15 Scotland: Gallacher 24

15 November 2000 Friendly Hampden Park Attendance: 30,985

618 SCOTLAND 0, Australia 2
Referee: Pascal Garibian (France)

Scotland: Jonathan Gould (Celtic); Christian Dailly (Blackburn Rovers), Brian O'Neil (Wolfsburg), Dominic Matteo (Leeds United), David Weir (Everton), Tom Boyd (Celtic, captain); Craig Burley (Derby County), Barry Ferguson (Rangers), Colin Cameron (Hearts); Don Hutchison (Sunderland), Billy Dodds (Rangers). *Substitutes:* Matt Elliot (Leicester City, for Weir 46); Neil McCann (Rangers, for Cameron 46); Colin Hendry (Coventry City, for O'Neil 58); Paul Dickov (Manchester City, for Burley 63). *Manager:* Craig Brown.

Australia: Mark Schwarzer; Tony Popovic, Shaun Murphy, Kevin Muscat, Stan Lazaridis; Brett Emerton, Josip Skoko, Paul Okon (captain), Daniel Tiatto; Paul Agostino, David Zdrilic. *Substitutes:* Mile Sterjovski (for Agostino 46); Jacob Burns (for Tiatto 67); Kasey Wehrman (for Skoko 75); Clayton Zane (for Zdrilic 89). *Trainer:* Frank Farina.

Scorers: Australia: Emerton 12; Zdrilic 66

4 March 2001 World Cup qualifying Hampden Park Attendance 37,480

619 SCOTLAND 2, Belgium 2
Referee: Kim Milton Nielsen (Denmark)

Scotland: Neil Sullivan (Tottenham Hotspur); Tom Boyd (Celtic), David Weir (Everton), Colin Hendry (Bolton Wanderers, captain), Matt Elliot (Leicester City), Dominic Matteo (Leeds United); Craig Burley (Derby County), Barry Ferguson (Rangers), Paul Lambert (Celtic); Don Hutchison (Sunderland), Billy Dodds (Rangers). *Substitute:* Kevin Gallacher (Newcastle United, for Dodds 88). *Manager:* Craig Brown.

Belgium: Geert De Vlieger; Eric Deflandre, Joos Valgaeren, Glen De Boeck, Didier Dheedene; Yves Vanderhaeghe, Marc Wilmots (captain), Bart Goor; Emile Mpenza, Walter Baseggio, Mark Hendrikx. *Substitutes:* Robert Peeters (for Hendrikx 46); Daniel Van Buyten (for Valgaeren 58); Sven Vermant (for Baseggio 79). *Trainer:* Robert Waseige.

Scorers: Scotland: Dodds 2, 29 (pen) Belgium: Wilmots 58; Van Buyten 90+2

28 March 2001 World Cup qualifying Hampden Park Attendance: 27,313

620 SCOTLAND 4, San Marino 0
Referee: Petteri Kari (Finland)

Scotland: Neil Sullivan (Tottenham Hotspur); Craig Burley (Derby County), David Weir (Everton), Colin Hendry (Bolton Wanderers, captain), Matt Elliot (Leicester City), Dominic Matteo (Leeds United); Colin Cameron (Hearts), Paul Lambert (Celtic), Don Hutchison (Sunderland); Billy Dodds (Rangers), Allan Johnston (Rangers). *Substitutes:* Tom Boyd (Celtic, for Elliot 46); Kevin Gallacher (Newcastle United, for Matteo 64); Scot Gemmill (Everton, for Cameron 83). *Manager:* Craig Brown.

San Marino: Federico Gasperoni; Simone Della Balda, Mauro Marani, Luca Gobbi, Simone Bacciocchi, Riccardo Muccioli, Ermanno Zonzini, Ivan Matteoni; Damiano Vannucci, Pierangelo Manzaroli, Andy Selva. *Substitutes:* Ivan Bugli (for Vannucci 70); Roberto Selva (for Manzaroli 81); Nicola Albani (for Della Balda 90). *Coach:* Gian Paulo Mazza.

Scorers: Scotland: Hendry 22, 33; Dodds 34; Cameron 65

25 April 2001 Friendly Zawisza Stadion, Bydgoszcz Attendance: 20,000

621 Poland 1, SCOTLAND 1
Referee: Juan Roca (Spain)

Scotland: Neil Sullivan (Tottenham Hotspur); Barry Nicholson (Dunfermline Athletic), Christian Dailly (West Ham), Tom Boyd (Celtic, captain), Callum Davidson (Leicester City); John O'Neil (Hibernian), Charlie Miller (Dundee United), Gavin Rae (Dundee), Colin Cameron (Hearts); Scott Booth (Twente Enschede), Billy Dodds (Rangers). *Substitutes:* Andy McLaren (Kilmarnock, for Cameron 46); Steven Crawford (Dunfermline Athletic, for Dodds 46); Stephen Caldwell (Newcastle United, for Charlie Miller 56); David Weir (Everton, for Davidson 72); Scot Gemmill (Everton, for O'Neil 73); Kenny Miller (Rangers, for Booth 80). *Manager:* Craig Brown.

Poland: Jerzy Dudek; Tomasz Klos, Jacek Zielinski, Tomasz Waldoch, Michal Zewlakow; Tomasz Iwan, Tomasz Hajto, Tomasz Zdebel; Marek Kozminski, Marcin Zewlakow, Pawel Kryszalowicz. *Substitutes:* Jacek Krzynowek (for Michal Zewlakow 46); Radoslaw Kaluzny (for Zielinski 46); Piotr Swierczewski (for Zdebel 58); Marcin Mieciel (for Marcin Zewlakow 63); Maciej Zurawski (for Kryszalowicz 78). *Coach:* Jerzy Engel.

Scorers: Poland: Kaluzny 49 Scotland: Booth 69 (pen)

1 September 2001 World Cup qualifying Hampden Park Attendance: 47,384

622 SCOTLAND 0, Croatia 0
Referee: Lubos Michel (Slovakia)

Scotland: Neil Sullivan (Tottenham Hotspur); Craig Burley (Derby County), David Weir (Everton), Christian Dailly (West Ham), Matt Elliot (Leicester City), Gary Naysmith (Everton); Paul Lambert (Celtic, captain), Don Hutchison (West Ham), Dominic Matteo (Leeds United); Scott Booth (Twente Enschede), Neil McCann (Rangers). *Substitutes:* Colin Cameron (Hearts, for McCann 52); Billy Dodds (Rangers, for Booth 71); Scot Gemmill (Everton, for Naysmith 85). *Manager:* Craig Brown.

Croatia: Stipe Pletikosa; Robert Kovac, Svonimir Soldo, Igor Stimac, Igor Tudor, Robert Jarni (captain); Stjepan Tomas, Robert Prosinecki, Mario Stanic; Boris Zivkovic, Bosko Balaban. *Substitutes:* Davor Suker (for Stanic 72); Davor Vugrinec (for Prosinecki 78); Igor Biscan (for Tomas 84). *Coach:* Mirko Jozic.

Chapter eight: 2000-2009

5 September 2001 World Cup qualifying Stade Roi Baudouin, Brussels Attendance: 43,500

623 Belgium 2, SCOTLAND 0
Referee: Manuel Gonzalez (Spain)

Scotland: Neil Sullivan (Tottenham Hotspur); Tom Boyd (Celtic), David Weir (Everton), Christian Dailly (West Ham), Matt Elliot (Leicester City), Gary Naysmith (Everton); Craig Burley (Derby County), Paul Lambert (Celtic, captain), Dominic Matteo (Leeds United); Don Hutchison (West Ham), Billy Dodds (Rangers). *Substitutes:* Scott Booth (Twente Enschede, for Boyd 57); Colin Cameron (Wolverhampton Wanderers, for Weir 74); Jackie McNamara (Celtic, for Burley 82). *Manager:* Craig Brown.

Belgium: Geert de Vlieger; Eric Deflandre, Glen de Boeck, Eric van Meir, Nico Van Kerckhoven; Yves Vanderhaeghe, Marc Wilmots (captain), Bart Goor; Wesley Sonck, Johan Walem, Gert Verheyen. *Substitutes:* Robert Peeters (for Sonck 82); Timmy Simons (for Walem 87). *Coach:* Robert Waseige.

Scorers: Belgium: Van Kerckhoven 28; Goor 90+2

---

6 October 2001 World Cup qualifying Hampden Park Attendance: 23,228

624 SCOTLAND 2, Latvia 1
Referee: Terje Hauge (Norway)

Scotland (4-3-3):

25 Neil Sullivan (Tottenham Hotspur);
30 David Weir (Everton)
18 Matt Elliot (Leicester City)
30 Christian Dailly (West Ham)
15 Callum Davidson (Leicester City);
2 Barry Nicholson (Dunfermline Athletic)
45 Craig Burley (Derby County, captain)
14 Colin Cameron (Wolverhampton Wanderers);
19 Don Hutchison (West Ham)
1 Dougie Freedman (Crystal Palace)
13 Neil McCann (Rangers)

Substitutes: 21 Scott Booth (Twente Enschede, for Nicholson 62);
2 Gavin Rae (Dundee, for Elliot 71);
1 Scott Severin (Hearts, for Hutchison 77)

Manager: Craig Brown

Latvia: Alesandrs Kolinko; Igors Stepanovs, Vitalijs Astafjevs (captain), Arturs Zakresevskis, Juris Laizans; Olegs Blagonadezdins, Aleksandrs Isakovs, Imants Bleidelis; Marians Pahars, Andrejs Rubins, Maris Verpakovskis. *Substitutes:* Vladimirs Kolesnicenko (for Bleidelis 75); Viktors Dobrecovs (for Rubins 83). *Trainer:* Aleksandrs Starkovs.

Scorers: Latvia: Rubins 21 Scotland: Freedman 44; Weir 54

A fairly plodding World Cup qualifying campaign ground to a halt with an unconvincing home victory over Latvia. Although the Scots only lost once in the group, in the previous match away to Belgium, the inability to score goals was obvious throughout – 10 in total including six against San Marino. Craig Brown, whose record as manager compared very favourably with others who had held the role, resigned after eight years in charge. Scotland had to come from behind after Rubins gave Latvia the lead in the 21st minute, and although Dougie Freedman and David Weir managed to get on the scoresheet it was a very disappointing performance. Keeper Neil Sullivan was the best Scottish player with a string of first-class saves, while Callum Davidson also had a steady game at left back, preventing a late Latvian equaliser with a timely tackle.

FIFA WORLD CUP QUALIFYING GROUP SIX

	P	W	D	L	F	A	Pts
Croatia	8	5	3	0	15	2	18
Belgium	8	5	2	1	25	6	17
Scotland	8	4	3	1	12	6	15
Latvia	8	1	1	6	5	16	4
San Marino	8	0	1	7	3	30	1

---

27 March 2002 Friendly Stade de France, Saint-Denis Attendance: 76,961

625 France 5, SCOTLAND 0
Referee: Jacek Granat (Poland)

Scotland (5-3-2):

26 Neil Sullivan (Tottenham Hotspur);
31 David Weir (Everton)
31 Christian Dailly (West Ham)
1 Gary Caldwell (Newcastle United)
6 Dominic Matteo (Leeds United)
1 Stephen Crainey (Celtic);
15 Colin Cameron (Wolverhampton Wanderers)
29 Paul Lambert (Celtic, captain)
14 Neil McCann (Rangers);
2 Dougie Freedman (Crystal Palace)
3 Steven Crawford (Dunfermline)

Substitutes: 3 Gary Holt (Norwich City, for Cameron 46);
19 Scot Gemmill (Everton, for Freedman 46);
1 Steven Thompson (Dundee United, for Crawford 64);
13 Jackie McNamara (Celtic, for Holt 74)

Manager: Berti Vogts (Germany)

France: Fabien Barthez; Vincent Candela, Frank Leboeuf, Marcel Desailly (captain), Bixente Lizarazu; Patrick Vieira, Emmanuel Petit, Zinedine Zidane; Sylvain Wiltord, Thierry Henry, David Trezeguet. *Substitutes:* Mikael Silvestre (for Desailly 46); Claude Makalele (for Vieira 46); Steve Marlet (for Wiltord 57); Christian Karembeu (for Candela 58); Philippe Christanval (for Leboeuf 64); Eric Carrierre (for Trezeguet 74); Youri Djorkaeff (for Zidane 81). *Trainer:* Roger Lemmere.

If new Scottish manager Berti Vogts thought his job was going to be a difficult one, that belief was well and truly rammed home as his side took an almighty hammering at the hands of France. Even allowing for the fact that the opposition was currently rated the number one side in the world, this was nothing short of a humiliation. The Scots were totally outplayed in every department as the French took a 4-0 lead before half-time. Perhaps they eased up after the break, or did Scotland manage to defend more resolutely? Whatever the case, this was not pretty. Zidane started things in the 12th minute, taking a pass and rifling the ball past a bemused Neil Sullivan, and after Trezeguet with two and Henry had made it 4-0 the game was over. Marlet eventually got a fifth near the end as captain Paul Lambert and his team mates battled away manfully.

Scorers: France: Zidane 12; Trezeguet 23, 42; Henry 32; Marlet 87

17 April 2002 Friendly Pittodrie, Aberdeen Attendance: 20,465

626 SCOTLAND 1, Nigeria 2
Referee: Tom Henning Ovrebo (Norway)

Scotland: Rab Douglas (Celtic); Robbie Stockdale (Middlesbrough), David Weir (Everton), Christian Dailly (West Ham), Stephen Crainey (Celtic), Kevin McNaughton (Aberdeen); Gareth Williams (Nottingham Forest), Paul Lambert (Celtic, captain), Scot Gemmill (Everton); Steven Thompson (Dundee United), Neil McCann (Rangers). *Substitutes:* Gary Caldwell (Hibernian, for Gemmill 46); Graham Alexander (Preston North End, for Stockdale 46); Michael Stewart (Manchester United, for Williams 64); Garry O'Connor (Hibernian, for Thompson 75); Allan Johnston (Middlesbrough, for McCann 78). *Manager:* Berti Vogts (Germany).

Nigeria: Austin Ejide; Efetobore Sodje, Joseph Yoko, Isaac Okoronkwo, Justice Christopher; Augustine "Jay Jay" Okocha (captain), Eric Ejiofor, John Utaka; Nwankwo Kanu, Julius Aghahowa, Bartholomew Ogbeche. *Substitutes:* Pius Ikedia (for Utaka 54); Mutiu Adepoju (for Christopher 78); Emeka Ifejiagwa (for Sodje 85). *Coach:* Adegboye Onigbinde.

Scorers: Scotland: Dailly 7 Nigeria: Aghahowe 41, 67

16 May 2002 Friendly Asiad Stadium, Busan Attendance: 52,384

627 South Korea 4, SCOTLAND 1
Referee: Santhan Nagalingam (Singapore)

Scotland: Neil Sullivan (Tottenham Hotspur); Maurice Ross (Rangers), Christian Dailly (West Ham, captain), David Weir (Everton), Graham Alexander (Preston North End); Allan Johnston (Middlesbrough), Gary Caldwell (Hibernian), Michael Stewart (Manchester United), Scot Gemmill (Everton); Garry O'Connor (Hibernian), Scott Dobie (West Bromwich Albion). *Substitutes:* Gareth Williams (Nottingham Forest, for O'Connor 46); Scott Severin (Hearts, for Stewart 46); Robbie Stockdale (Middlesbrough, for Alexander 63); Kevin Kyle (Sunderland, for Johnston 66). *Manager:* Berti Vogts (Germany).

South Korea: Kim Byung-Ji; Hong Myung-Bo, Choi Jin-Chul, Kim Tae-Young, Lee Young-Pyo; Lee Eul-Yong; Yoo Sang-Chul, Song Jong-Gook, Lee Chun-Soo; Hwang Seon-Hong, Park Ji-Sung. *Substitutes:* Lee Min-Sung (for Jin-Chul 46); Ahn Jung-Hwan (for Seon-Hong 46); Yoon Jung-Hwan (for Myung-Bo 65); Cha Doo-Ri (for Chun-Soo 73); Choi Tae-Uk (for Ji-Sung 73). *Coach:* Guus Hiddink (Netherlands).

Scorers: South Korea: Lee Chun-Soo 14; Ahn Jung-Hwan 56, 87; Yoon Jung-Hwan 66 Scotland: Dobie 74

20 May 2002 Hong Kong Reunification Cup Hong Kong Stadium Attendance: 3,007

628 South Africa 2, SCOTLAND 0
Referee: Sui Kee Chan (Hong Kong)

Scotland: Rab Douglas (Celtic); Robbie Stockdale (Middlesbrough), David Weir (Everton), Christian Dailly (West Ham, captain), Gary Caldwell (Hibernian), Maurice Ross (Rangers); Gareth Williams (Nottingham Forest), Scot Gemmill (Everton), Alan Johnston (Middlesbrough); Kevin Kyle (Sunderland), Scott Dobie (West Bromwich Albion). *Substitutes:* Lee Wilkie (Dundee, for Caldwell 46); James McFadden (Motherwell, for Johnston 60); Graham Alexander (Preston North End, for Stockdale 68); Scott Severin (Hearts, for Williams 77); Michael Stewart (Manchester United, for Gemmill 85). *Manager:* Berti Vogts (Germany).

South Africa: Hans Vonk; Aaron Mokoena, Lucas Radebe (captain), Pierre Issa, Bradley Carnell; Teboho Mokoena, MacBeth Sibaya, Jabu Pule, Quinton Fortune; Benedict McCarthy, Sibusiso Zuma. *Substitutes:* Cyril Nzama (for Aaron Mokoena 60); MacDonald Mukansi (for Pule 68); George Koumantarakis (for Zuma 81); Delron Buckley (for Fortune 83). *Coach:* Jomo Sono.

Scorers: South Africa: Teboho Mokoena 31; Koumantarakis 90+3

23 May 2002 Hong Kong Reunification Cup Hong Kong Stadium Attendance: 8,000

629 *Hong Kong League XI 0, SCOTLAND 4
Referee: Krishnan Ramachandran (Malaysia)

Scotland: Rab Douglas (Celtic); Robbie Stockdale (Middlesbrough), David Weir (Everton), Christian Dailly (West Ham, captain), Lee Wilkie (Dundee), Maurice Ross (Rangers); Scott Severin (Hearts), Scot Gemmill (Everton), Allan Johnston (Middlesbrough); Kevin Kyle (Sunderland), Steven Thompson (Dundee United). *Substitutes:* Scott Dobie (West Bromwich Albion, for Thompson 46); Warren Cummings (Chelsea, for Ross 46); Gareth Williams (Nottingham Forest, for Johnston 60); Paul Gallacher (Dundee United, for Douglas 76); Garry O'Connor (Hibernian, for Kyle 81); Graham Alexander (Preston North End, for Gemmill 87). *Manager:* Berti Vogts (Germany).

Hong Kong League XI: Fan Chun-Yip; Yau Kin-Wai, Christiano Cordeiro, Anilton da Conceicao, Carlo Hartwig; Gary McKeown, Shum Kwok-Pui, Chan Ho-Man, Cornelius Udebuluzor; Poon Yiu-Cheuk, Aderbal Filho. *Substitutes:* Luk Koon-Pong (for da Conceicao 33); Young Hei-Chi (for Udebuluzor 46); Chan Ka-Ki (for Chun-Yip 54); Lo Kai-Wah (for Kin-Wai 57); Young Ching-Kwong (for Ho-Man 78); Lee Wai-Man (for Yiu-Cheuk 78). *Coach:* Wong Yiu-Shun.

Scorers: Scotland: Kyle 22; Thompson 36; Dailly 50; Gemmill 72

Although the Hong Kong team was not a national representative side, the Scottish Football Association awarded caps for this match and the goals also count towards the players' totals. South Africa won the trophy and Scotland were runners-up.

21 August 2002 Friendly Hampden Park Attendance: 28,766

630 SCOTLAND 0, Denmark 1
Referee: Leslie Irvine (Northern Ireland)

Scotland: Rab Douglas (Celtic); Robbie Stockdale (Middlesbrough), David Weir (Everton), Christian Dailly (West Ham), Maurice Ross (Rangers), Kevin McNaughton (Aberdeen); Paul Lambert (Celtic, captain), Barry Ferguson (Rangers), Gary Naysmith (Everton); Kevin Kyle (Sunderland), Steven Thompson (Dundee United). *Substitutes:* Stephen Crainey (Celtic, for McNaughton 46); Scott Dobie (West Bromwich Albion, for Thompson 55); Allan Johnston (Middlesbrough, for Naysmith 71); Graham Alexander (Preston North End, for Stockdale 71); Scott Severin (Hearts, for Weir 77); Derek McInnes (West Bromwich Albion, for Lambert 81). *Manager:* Berti Vogts (Germany).

Denmark: Thomas Sorensen; Kasper Bogelund, Martin Laursen, Rene Henriksen (captain), Niclas Jensen; Dennis Rommedahl, Thomas Gravesen, Christian Poulsen; Peter Lovenkrands, Jon Dahl Tomasson, Ebbe Sand. *Substitutes:* Jan Michaelsen (for Bogelund 46); Jesper Gronkjaer (for Rommedahl 46); Claus Jensen (for Gravesen 46); Morten Wieghorst (for Laursen 68); Michael Silverbauer (for Lovenkrands 71); Steven Lustu (for Henriksen 83). *Coach:* Morten Olsen.

Scorer: Denmark: Sand 8

7 September 2002   European Championship qualifying   Svangaskard, Toftir   Attendance: 4,200

631 Faroe Islands 2, SCOTLAND 2
Referee: Jacek Granat (Poland)

Scotland: Rab Douglas (Celtic); Maurice Ross (Rangers), David Weir (Everton), Christian Dailly (West Ham), Stephen Crainey (Celtic); Paul Lambert (Celtic, captain), Barry Ferguson (Rangers), Allan Johnston (Middlesbrough); Paul Dickov (Leicester City), Kevin Kyle (Sunderland), Scott Dobie (West Bromwich Albion). *Substitutes:* Stephen Crawford (Dunfermline Athletic, for Dickov 46); Graham Alexander (Preston North End, for Ross 75); Steven Thompson (Dundee United, for Dobie 83). *Manager:* Berti Vogts (Germany).

Faroe Islands: Jens Martin Knudsen; Jens Kristian Hansen, Oli Johannesen (captain), Pol Thorsteinsson, Jon Roi Jacobsen; Hjalgrim Elttor, Frodi Benjaminsen, Julian Johnsson, Jakup a Borg; John Petersen, Christian Hogni Jacobsen. *Substitutes:* Rogvi Jacobsen (for Christian Hogni Jacobsen 75); Andrew av Flotum (for Petersen 80); Hedin a Lakjuni (for Elttor 89). *Coach:* Henrik Larsen (Denmark).

Scorers: Faroe Islands: Peterson 7, 13   Scotland: Lambert 62; Ferguson 83

12 October 2002   European Championship qualifying   Laugardalsvollur, Reykjavik   Attendance: 7,065

632 Iceland 0, SCOTLAND 2
Referee: Alain Sars (France)

Scotland: Rab Douglas (Celtic); Maurice Ross (Rangers), Lee Wilkie (Dundee), Christian Dailly (West Ham), Steven Pressley (Hearts), Gary Naysmith (Everton); Jackie McNamara (Celtic), Paul Lambert (Celtic, captain), Barry Ferguson (Rangers); Stephen Crawford (Dunfermline Athletic), Steven Thompson (Dundee United). *Substitutes:* Callum Davidson (Leicester City, for McNamara 34); Scott Severin (Hearts, for Thompson 89); Russell Anderson (Aberdeen, for Naysmith 90). *Manager:* Berti Vogts (Germany).

Iceland: Arni Arason; Bjarni Thorsteinsson, Larus Sugurdsson, Hermann Hreidarsson, Arnar Vidarsson, Brynjar Gunnarsson; Runar Kristinsson (captain), Ivar Ingimarsson; Haukur Gudnason, Helgi Sigurdsson, Eidur Gudjohnsen. *Substitutes:* Heidar Helguson (for Sigurdsson 46); Marel Baldvinsson (for Vidarsson 66); Bjarni Gudjonsson (for Gudnason 88). *Coach:* Atli Edvaldsson.

Scorers: Scotland: Dailly 6; Naysmith 63

15 October 2002   Friendly   Easter Road, Edinburgh   Attendance: 16,207

633 SCOTLAND 3, Canada 1
Referee: Luc Huyghe (Belgium)

Scotland: Paul Gallacher (Dundee United); Maurice Ross (Rangers), Russell Anderson (Aberdeen), Steven Pressley (Hearts), Lee Wilkie (Dundee), Graham Alexander (Preston North End); Paul Devlin (Birmingham City), Christian Dailly (West Ham, captain), Scot Gemmill (Everton); Steven Thompson (Dundee United), Stephen Crawford (Dunfermline Athletic). *Substitutes:* Callum Davidson (Leicester City, for Ross 46); Scott Severin (Hearts, for Gemmill 65); Ian Murray (Hibernian, for Wilkie 75); James McFadden (Motherwell, for Thompson 80); Kevin Kyle (Sunderland, for Crawford 90). *Manager:* Berti Vogts (Germany).

Canada: Lars Hirschfeld; Paul Fenwick (captain), Kevin McKenna, Richard Hastings; Chris Pozniak, Tam Nsaliwa, Daniel Imhof, Paul Stalteri, Julian de Guzman; Tomasz Radzinski, Dwayne De Rosario. *Substitute:* Davide Xausa (for Imhof 81). *Coach:* Holger Osieck.

Scorers: Canada: De Rosario 9 (pen)   Scotland: Crawford 11, 73; Thompson 49

20 November 2002   Friendly   Estadio Primeiro de Maio, Braga   Attendance: 8,000

634 Portugal 2, SCOTLAND 0
Referee: Viorel Anghelinei (Romania)

Scotland: Rab Douglas (Celtic); Maurice Ross (Rangers), Russell Anderson (Aberdeen), Steven Pressley (Hearts), Lee Wilkie (Dundee), Graham Alexander (Preston North End); Christian Dailly (West Ham), Paul Lambert (Celtic, captain), Gary Naysmith (Everton); Stephen Crawford (Dunfermline Athletic), Scott Dobie (West Bromwich Albion). *Substitutes:* Derek McInnes (West Bromwich Albion, for Anderson 24); Paul Devlin (Birmingham City, for Ross 46); Gareth Williams (Nottingham Forest, for Lambert 68); Kevin Kyle (Sunderland, for Dobie 78); Scott Severin (Hearts, for Wilkie 83). *Manager:* Berti Vogts (Germany).

Portugal: Joaquim Quim; Fernando Couto (captain), Fernando Meira, Ricardo Rocha, Sergio Conceicao; Luis Figo, Rui Costa, Rui Jorge; Tiago, Pedro Pauleta, Simao. *Substitutes:* Nelson (for Quim 46); Marco Ferreira (for Luis Figo 46); Nuno Gomes (for Pauleta 46); Pedro Mendes (for Rui Costa 58); Jorge Ribeiro (for Rui Jorge 58); Joao Neca (for Simao 78); Nuno Assis (for Tiago 83). *Coach:* Agostinho Oliveira.

Scorer: Portugal: Pauleta 7, 18

Before the friendly victory over Canada in October 2002. Back (from left): Lee Wilkie, Stephen Crawford, Paul Gallacher, Steven Pressley, Russell Anderson, Steven Thompson. Front: Graham Alexander, Maurice Ross, Paul Devlin, Scot Gemmill, Christian Dailly.

12 February 2003   Friendly   Hampden Park   Attendance: 33,337

635 SCOTLAND 0, Republic of Ireland 2
Referee: Eric Braamhaer (Netherlands)

Scotland: Neil Sullivan (Tottenham Hotspur); Graham Alexander (Preston North End), Russell Anderson (Aberdeen), Christian Dailly (West Ham), Steven Caldwell (Newcastle United), Gary Naysmith (Everton); Barry Ferguson (Rangers), Paul Lambert (Celtic, captain), Neil McCann (Rangers); Don Hutchison (West Ham), Stephen Crawford (Dunfermline Athletic). *Substitutes:* Paul Gallacher (Dundee United, for Sullivan 46); Scot Gemmill (Everton, for Lambert 46); Paul Devlin (Birmingham City, for Hutchison 46); Colin Cameron (Wolverhampton Wanderers, for Ferguson 64); Jamie Smith (Celtic, for McCann 64); Steven Thompson (Rangers, for Crawford 64). *Manager:* Berti Vogts (Germany).

Republic of Ireland: Dean Kiely; Stephen Carr, Gary Breen, John O'Shea, Ian Harte; Steven Reid, Matt Holland (captain), Mark Kinsella, Kevin Kilbane; Clinton Morrison, Gary Doherty. *Substitutes:* David Connolly (for Doherty 73); Lee Carsley (for Reid 77); Colin Healy (for Kinsella 77); Richard Dunne (for O'Shea 80); Nick Colgan (for Kiely 80); Andy O'Brien (for Breen 90). *Manager:* Brian Kerr.

Scorers: Republic of Ireland: Kilbane 7; Morrison 16

29 March 2003   European Championship qualifying   Hampden Park   Attendance: 37,938

636 SCOTLAND 2, Iceland 1
Referee: Rene Temmink (Netherlands)

Scotland: Rab Douglas (Celtic); Graham Alexander (Preston North End), Lee Wilkie (Dundee), Christian Dailly (West Ham), Steven Pressley (Hearts), Gary Naysmith (Everton); Paul Lambert (Celtic, captain), Barry Ferguson (Rangers), Don Hutchison (West Ham); Kenny Miller (Wolverhampton Wanderers), Stephen Crawford (Dunfermline Athletic). *Substitutes:* Paul Devlin (Birmingham City, for Hutchison 64); Jackie McNamara (Celtic, for Miller 81). *Manager:* Berti Vogts (Germany).

Iceland: Arni Arason; Larus Sigurdsson, Gudni Bergsson, Ivan Ingimarsson; Brynjar Gunnarsson, Bjarni Thorsteinsson, Arnar Gretarsson, Johannes Karl Gudjonsson, Arnar Vidarsson; Runar Kristinsson (captain), Eidur Gudjohnsen. *Substitutes:* Thordur Gudjonsson (for Gunnarsson 73); Indridi Sigurdsson (for Vidarsson 82); Tryggvi Gudmundsson (for Eidur Gudjohnsen 88). *Coach:* Atli Edvaldsson.

Scorers: Scotland: Miller 12; Wilkie 71   Iceland: Eidar Gudjohnsen 49

2 April 2003   European Championship qualifying   Gereno Stadionas, Kaunas   Attendance: 6,400

637 Lithuania 1, SCOTLAND 0
Referee: Fritz Stuchlik (Austria)

Scotland: Paul Gallacher (Dundee United); Graham Alexander (Preston North End), Lee Wilkie (Dundee), Christian Dailly (West Ham), Steven Pressley (Hearts), Gary Naysmith (Everton), Jackie McNamara (Celtic), Paul Lambert (Celtic, captain), Don Hutchison (West Ham); Kenny Miller (Wolverhampton Wanderers), Stephen Crawford (Dunfermline Athletic). *Substitutes:* Paul Devlin (Birmingham City, for Crawford 56); Andy Gray (Bradford City, for McNamara 78); Colin Cameron (Wolverhampton Wanderers, for Hutchison 83). *Manager:* Berti Vogts (Germany).

Lithuania: Gintaras Stauce (captain); Dainius Gleveckas, Tomas Zvirgzdauskas, Ignas Dedura, Nerijus Barasa; Igoris Morinas, Vadimas Petrenka, Deividas Semberas, Saulius Mikalajunas; Edgaras Jankauskas, Tomas Razanauskas. *Substitutes:* Arturas Fomenka (for Jankauskas 62); Darius Maciulevicius (for Petrenka 70); Orestas Buitkus (for Mikalajunas 88). *Coach:* Algimantas Liubinskas.

Scorer: Lithuania: Razanauskas 74 (pen)

30 April 2003   Friendly   Hampden Park   Attendance: 12,189

638 SCOTLAND 0, Austria 2
Referee: Nicolai Vollquartz (Denmark)

Scotland: Paul Gallacher (Dundee United); Craig Burley (Derby County), Lee Wilkie (Dundee), Steven Pressley (Hearts), Andy Webster (Hearts), Gary Naysmith (Everton); Paul Devlin (Birmingham City), Christian Dailly (West Ham, captain), Don Hutchison (West Ham); Steven Thompson (Rangers), James McFadden (Motherwell). *Substitutes:* Stephen Crawford (Dunfermline Athletic, for Thompson 46); Scot Gemmill (Everton, for Dailly 46); Kenny Miller (Wolverhampton Wanderers, for Hutchison 61); Colin Cameron (Wolverhampton Wanderers, for Burley 63); Jamie Smith (Celtic, for Devlin 84). *Manager:* Berti Vogts (Germany).

Austria: Thomas Mandl; Paul Scharner, Anton Ehmann, Martin Stranzl, Ernst Dospel; Rene Aufhauser, Markus Schopp, Thomas Flogel (captain), Michael Wagner; Roland Kirchler, Mario Haas. *Substitutes:* Ronald Brunmayr (for Haas 63); Andreas Herzog (for Kirchler 83); Mario Hieblinger (for Flogel 90+1). *Coach:* Hans Krankl.

Scorers: Austria: Kirchler 27; Haas 32

27 May 2003   Friendly   Tynecastle, Edinburgh   Attendance: 10,016

639 SCOTLAND 1, New Zealand 1
Referee: Martin Ingvarsson (Sweden)

Scotland: Rab Douglas (Celtic); Maurice Ross (Rangers), Steven Pressley (Hearts), Andy Webster (Hearts), Gary Naysmith (Everton); Jackie McNamara (Celtic), Christian Dailly (West Ham, captain), Paul Devlin (Birmingham City), James McFadden (Motherwell); Kevin Kyle (Sunderland); Stephen Crawford (Dunfermline Athletic). *Substitutes:* Graham Alexander (Preston North End, for Ross 46); Andy Gray (Bradford City, for Kyle 60); Brian Kerr (Newcastle United, for McNamara 83). *Manager:* Berti Vogts (Germany).

New Zealand: Michael Utting; David Mulligan, Chris Zoricich (captain), Ryan Nelsen, Gerard Davis; Chris Jackson, Simon Elliot, Mark Burton, Vaughan Coveny; Aaran Lines, Noah Hickey. *Substitutes:* Jason Batty (for Utting 46); Duncan Oughton (for Mulligan 46); Raf de Gregorio (for Jackson 54); Scott Smith (for Zoricich 70); Chris Bouckenooghe (for Lines 80). *Coach:* Mick Waitt.

Scorers: Scotland: Crawford 10   New Zealand: Nelsen 47

7 June 2003   European Championship qualifying   Hampden Park   Attendance: 48,047

640 SCOTLAND 1, Germany 1
Referee: Domenico Messina (Italy)

Scotland: Rab Douglas (Celtic); Maurice Ross (Rangers), Steven Pressley (Hearts), Christian Dailly (West Ham), Andy Webster (Hearts), Gary Naysmith (Everton); Paul Devlin (Birmingham City), Paul Lambert (Celtic, captain), Colin Cameron (Wolverhampton Wanderers); Kenny Miller (Wolverhampton Wanderers), Stephen Crawford (Dunfermline Athletic). *Substitutes:* Gavin Rae (Dundee, for Devlin 59); Jackie McNamara (Celtic, for Ross 74); Steven Thompson (Rangers, for Miller 89). *Manager:* Berti Vogts (Germany).

Germany: Oliver Kahn (captain); Arne Friedrich, Carsten Ramelow, Christian Worns; Torsten Frings, Berndt Schneider, Jens Jeremies, Michael Ballack, Tobias Rau; Fredi Bobic, Miroslav Klose. *Substitutes:* Paul Freier (for Rau 57); Oliver Neuville (for Klose 74); Sebastian Kehl (for Schneider 86). *Coach:* Rudi Voller.

Scorers: Germany: Bobic 22   Scotland: Miller 68

Chapter eight: 2000-2009

20 August 2003 Friendly   Ullevaal Stadion, Oslo   Attendance: 12,758

641 Norway 0, SCOTLAND 0
Referee: Mikko Vuorela (Finland)

Scotland: Rab Douglas (Celtic); Maurice Ross (Rangers), Steven Pressley (Hearts), Christian Dailly (West Ham), Andy Webster (Hearts), Gary Naysmith (Everton); Colin Cameron (Wolverhampton Wanderers), Paul Lambert (Celtic, captain), Barry Ferguson (Rangers); Stephen Crawford (Dunfermline Athletic), Don Hutchison (West Ham). *Substitutes:* Darren Fletcher (Manchester United, for Ross 60); Paul Devlin (Birmingham City, for Crawford 79); Gavin Rae (Dundee, for Cameron 84). *Manager:* Berti Vogts (Germany).

Norway: Espen Johnsen; Christer Basma, Henning Berg (captain), Claus Lundekvam, Andre Bergdolmo; Martin Andresen, Frode Johnsen, Brede Hangeland, John Arne Riise; Ole Gunnar Solskjaer, John Carew. *Substitutes:* Ronny Johnsen (for Berg 46); Trond Andersen (for Hangeland 46); Jan Gunnar Solli (for Frode Johnsen 46); Steffen Iversen (for Bergdolmo 68); Alexander Aas (for Basma 70); Havard Flo (for Carew 72). *Coach:* Nils Johan Semb.

6 September 2003 European Championship qualifying Hampden Park Attendance: 40,901

642 SCOTLAND 3, Faroe Islands 1
Referee: Darko Ceferin (Slovenia)

Scotland: Rab Douglas (Celtic); Jackie McNamara (Celtic), Lee Wilkie (Dundee), Andy Webster (Hearts), Gary Naysmith (Everton); Paul Devlin (Birmingham City), Colin Cameron (Wolverhampton Wanderers), Barry Ferguson (Blackburn Rovers, captain), Neil McCann (Southampton); Paul Dickov (Leicester City), Stephen Crawford (Dunfermline Athletic). *Substitutes:* James McFadden (Everton, for Devlin 58); Gavin Rae (Dundee, for Dickov 67); Steven Thompson (Rangers, for Crawford 75). *Manager:* Berti Vogts (Germany).

Faroe Islands: Jakup Mikkelsen; Jann Ingi Petersen, Oli Johannesen (captain), Jon Roi Jacobsen, Pol Thorsteinsson; Julian Johnsson, Frodi Benjaminsen, John Petersen, Rogvi Jacobsen; Jakup a Borg, Helgi Petersen. *Substitutes:* Tor-Ingar Akselsen (for Helgi Petersen 65); Atli Danielsen (for Johnsson 84); Christian Holst (for a Borg 84). *Coach:* Henrik Larsen (Denmark).

Scorers: Scotland: McCann 8; Dickov 45+2; McFadden 73 Faroe Islands: Johnsson 35

10 September 2003 European Championship qualifying Westfalenstadion, Dortmund Attendance: 67,000

643 Germany 2, SCOTLAND 1
Referee: Anders Frisk (Sweden)

Scotland: Rab Douglas (Celtic); Jackie McNamara (Celtic), Steven Pressley (Hearts), Christian Dailly (West Ham), Gary Naysmith (Everton); Colin Cameron (Wolverhampton Wanderers), Paul Lambert (Celtic, captain), Barry Ferguson (Blackburn Rovers), James McFadden (Everton); Steven Thompson (Rangers), Neil McCann (Southampton). *Substitutes:* Maurice Ross (Rangers, for Lambert 46); Gavin Rae (Dundee, for McFadden 53). *Manager:* Berti Vogts (Germany).

Germany: Oliver Kahn (captain); Arne Friedrich, Christian Worns, Frank Baumann, Tobias Rau; Berndt Schneider, Carsten Ramelow, Michael Ballack, Marko Rehmer; Fredi Bobic, Kevin Kuranyi. *Substitutes:* Miroslav Klose (for Bobic 76); Sebastian Kehl (for Schneider 81). *Coach:* Rudi Voller.

Scorers: Germany: Bobic 25; Ballack 50 (pen) Scotland: McCann 60

11 October 2003 European Championship qualifying Hampden Park Attendance: 50,343

644 SCOTLAND 1, Lithuania 0
Referee: Claude Colombo (France)

Scotland (4-3-3):
- 14 Rab Douglas (Celtic);
- 21 Jackie McNamara (Celtic)
- 49 Christian Dailly (West Ham)
- 13 Steven Pressley (Hearts)
- 19 Gary Naysmith (Everton);
- 19 Barry Ferguson (Blackburn Rovers, captain)
- 7 Gavin Rae (Dundee)
- 23 Colin Cameron (Wolverhampton Wanderers);
- 6 Kenny Miller (Wolverhampton Wanderers)
- 16 Steven Crawford (Dunfermline)
- 7 James McFadden (Everton)

Substitutes: 2 Darren Fletcher (Manchester United, for Cameron 66);
25 Don Hutchison (West Ham, for Miller 66);
13 Graham Alexander (Preston North End, for McFadden 89)

Manager: Berti Vogts (Germany)

Scotland crept into the play-offs for Euro 2004 courtesy of a stuttering win at Hampden over Lithuania. The draw the following day paired the Scots with the Netherlands, and it was obvious they would have to raise their game considerably if they were to have any chance of making it to the finals in Portugal. Manchester United midfielder Darren Fletcher, who many believed should have started the game, scored the only goal after being introduced in the second half. James McFadden, who was again the home side's most dangerous player, played Gary Naysmith in on the left and his cutback took a deflection into the path of Fletcher. He struck a marvellously controlled right-foot volley past the keeper into the corner of the net.

Lithuania: Gintaras Stauce (captain); Rolandas Dziaukstas, Tomas Zvirgzdauskas, Ignas Dedura, Darius Regelskis; Nerijus Barasa, Donatas Vencevicius, Tomas Razanauskas, Giedrius Barevicius; Edgaras Jankauskas, Robertas Poskus. *Substitutes:* Deividas Cesnauskis (for Barevicius 46); Ricardas Beniusis (for Regelskis 86); Darius Maciulevicius (for Vencevicius 79). *Coach:* Algimantas Liubinskas.

Scorer: Scotland: Fletcher 70

EUROPEAN CHAMPIONSHIP QUALIFYING GROUP EIGHT

	P	W	D	L	F	A	Pts
Germany	8	5	3	0	13	4	18
Scotland	8	4	2	2	12	8	14
Iceland	8	4	1	3	11	9	13
Lithuania	8	3	1	4	7	11	10
Faroe Islands	8	0	1	7	7	18	1

15 November 2003   European Championship qualifying (play-off)   Hampden Park   Attendance: 50,670

645 SCOTLAND 1, Netherlands 0
Referee: Terje Hauge (Norway)

Scotland (5-3-2):
15 Rab Douglas (Celtic);
22 Jackie McNamara (Celtic);
14 Steven Pressley (Hearts);
10 Lee Wilkie (Dundee);
50 Christian Dailly (West Ham);
20 Gary Naysmith (Everton);
20 Barry Ferguson (Blackburn Rovers, captain);
3 Darren Fletcher (Manchester United);
8 James McFadden (Everton);
6 Paul Dickov (Leicester City);
19 Neil McCann (Southampton)

Substitutes: 7 Kenny Miller (Wolverhampton Wanderers, for Dickov 66);
1 Stephen Pearson (Motherwell, for McCann 71);
26 Don Hutchison (West Ham, for McFadden 90)

Manager: Berti Vogts (Germany)

Everton player James McFadden, one of manager Berti Vogts' "cheeky boys", put his side in with a chance of making it to the European finals in Portugal with a superb goal midway through the first half. Darren Fletcher of Manchester United backheeled a pass into the path of McFadden on the right wing and he cut inside before his bending shot spun off Frank de Boer's leg before nestling in the net. The Scots were deserving of the half-time lead but in truth the Dutch should at least have earned a draw with a much improved performance after the break. The task was half-done but only the most optimistic of fans would surely believe the players would complete the job in the Netherlands four days later. The job was made more difficult as one of the game's best performers, Christian Dailly who had done a great job just in front of the back four, was ruled out by injury. The doubters proved to be correct as a completely ruthless display in Amsterdam ended in a 6-0 home victory, Ruud van Nistelroy scoring a hat-trick.

Netherlands: Edwin van der Sar; Andre Ooijer, Jap Stam, Frank de Boer (captain), Giovanni van Bronckhurst; Phillip Cocu, Andy van der Meyde, Edgar Davids; Ruud van Nistelroy, Patrick Kluivert, Marc Overmars. *Substitutes:* Clarence Seedorf (for van Bronckhurst 46); Rafael van der Vaart (for Davids 61); Roy Makaay (for Kluivert 77). *Trainer:* Dick Advocaat.

Scorer: Scotland: McFadden 22

---

19 November 2003   European Championship qualifying (play-off)   Amsterdam Arena   Attendance: 51,000

646 Netherlands 6, SCOTLAND 0
Referee: Lubos Michel (Slovakia)

Scotland: Rab Douglas (Celtic); Jackie McNamara (Celtic), Steven Pressley (Hearts), Lee Wilkie (Dundee), Gary Naysmith (Everton); Barry Ferguson (Blackburn Rovers, captain), Darren Fletcher (Manchester United), Gavin Rae (Dundee), James McFadden (Everton); Paul Dickov (Leicester City), Neil McCann (Southampton). *Substitutes:* Maurice Ross (Rangers, for Naysmith 46); Steven Crawford (Dunfermline Athletic, for Dickov 46); Kenny Miller (Wolverhampton Wanderers, for McCann 63). *Manager:* Berti Vogts (Germany).

Netherlands: Edwin van der Sar; Andre Ooijer, Michael Reiziger, Wilfred Bouma; Wesley Sneijder, Rafael van der Vaart, Phillip Cocu (captain), Edgar Davids; Marc Overmars, Andy van der Meyde, Ruud van Nistelroy. *Substitutes:* Frank de Boer (for Ooijer 46); Clarence Seedorf (for Bouma 69); Patrick Kluivert (for van Nistelroy 78). *Trainer:* Dick Advocaat.

Scorers: Netherlands: Sneijder 13; Ooijer 32; van Nistelroy 37, 51, 67; Frank de Boer 65

---

18 February 2004   Friendly   Millennium Stadium, Cardiff   Attendance: 47,124

647 Wales 4, SCOTLAND 0
Referee: Michael Ross (Northern Ireland)

Scotland: Rab Douglas (Celtic); Jackie McNamara (Celtic), Steven Caldwell (Leeds United), Christian Dailly (West Ham, captain), Paul Ritchie (Walsall), Gary Naysmith (Everton); Colin Cameron (Wolverhampton Wanderers), Darren Fletcher (Manchester United), Stephen Pearson (Celtic); Kenny Miller (Wolverhampton Wanderers), Paul Dickov (Leicester City). *Substitutes:* Graeme Murty (Reading, for Naysmith 46); James McFadden (Everton, for Pearson 46); Paul Gallacher (Blackburn Rovers, for Cameron 67); Andy Webster (Hearts, for Fletcher 85). *Manager:* Berti Vogts (Germany).

Wales: Mark Crossley; Robert Edwards, Andrew Melville, Robert Page, Danny Gabbidon; John Oster, Robbie Savage, Gary Speed (captain), Simon Davies; Robert Earnshaw, Ryan Giggs. *Substitutes:* Paul Parry (for Davies 32); Darren Ward (for Crossley 46); Gareth Taylor (for Giggs 46); Carl Fletcher (for Savage 71); Carl Robinson (for Speed 71); Kit Symons (for Melville 86). *Manager:* Mark Hughes.

Scorers: Wales: Earnshaw 1, 34, 57; Taylor 77

---

31 March 2004   Friendly   Hampden Park   Attendance: 20,433

648 SCOTLAND 1, Romania 2
Referee: Jouni Hyytia (Finland)

Scotland: Paul Gallacher (Dundee United); Christian Dailly (West Ham, captain), Steven Pressley (Hearts), Gary Caldwell (Hibernian), John Kennedy (Celtic), Graham Alexander (Preston North End); Gavin Rae (Rangers), Colin Cameron (Wolverhampton Wanderers), Neil McCann (Southampton); Kenny Miller (Wolverhampton Wanderers), Steven Thompson (Rangers). *Substitutes:* Stephen Crainey (Southampton, fo Kennedy 17); James McFadden (Everton, for Miller 51); Stephen Crawford (Dunfermline Athletic, for Thompson 63). *Manager:* Berti Vogts (Germany).

Romania: Bogdan Stelea; Flavius Stoican, Adrian Iencsi, Christian Chivu (captain), Razvan Rat; Florentin Petre, Ovidiu Petre, Daniel Pancu, Florin Cernat; Ioan Ganea, Adrian Mutu. *Substitutes:* Bogdan Lobont (for Stelea 46); Nicolae Mitea (for Florentin Petre 46); Florin Soava (for Cernat 63); Andrei Cristea (for Ganea 81); Ionel Danciulescu (for Pancu 89). *Coach:* Anghel Iordanescu.

Scorers: Romania: Chivu 36; Pancu 50   Scotland: McFadden 57

Chapter eight: 2000-2009

| 28 April 2004 | Friendly | Parken, Copenhagen | Attendance: 22,885 |

649 Denmark 1, SCOTLAND 0 *Referee: Martin Ingvarsson (Sweden)*

Scotland: Paul Gallacher (Dundee United); Gary Caldwell (Hibernian), Steven Pressley (Hearts), Christian Dailly (West Ham, captain), Malky Mackay (Norwich City), Stephen Crainey (Southampton); Colin Cameron (Wolverhampton Wanderers), Darren Fletcher (Manchester United), Gary Holt (Norwich City); Kevin Kyle (Sunderland), James McFadden (Everton). *Substitutes:* Peter Canero (Leicester City, for Holt 16); Neil McCann (Southampton, for Cameron 46). *Manager:* Berti Vogts (Germany).

Denmark: Thomas Sorensen; Thomas Helveg, Rene Henriksen (captain), Martin Laursen, Niclas Jensen; Daniel Jensen, Claus Jensen, Morten Wieghorst; Jesper Gronkjaer, Jon Dahl Tomasson, Martin Jorgensen. *Substitutes:* Asbjorn Sennels (for Niclas Jensen 46); Kenneth Perez (for Claus Jensen 46); Ebbe Sand (for Tomasson 46); Dennis Rommedahl (for Jorgensen 66); Per Kroldrup (for Henriksen 66); Martin Retov (for Wieghorst 80); Thomas Rasmussen (for Gronkjaer 83). *Coach:* Morten Olsen.

Scorer: Denmark: Sand 61

| 27 May 2004 | Friendly | Le Coq Arena, Tallinn | Attendance: 4,000 |

650 Estonia 0, SCOTLAND 1 *Referee: Tonny Poulsen (Denmark)*

Scotland: Paul Gallacher (Dundee United); David McNamee (Livingston), Steven Pressley (Hearts), Malky Mackay (Norwich City), Gary Caldwell (Hibernian), Richard Hughes (Portsmouth); Gary Holt (Norwich City), Darren Fletcher (Manchester United, captain), Nigel Quashie (Portsmouth); James McFadden (Everton), Kenny Miller (Wolverhampton Wanderers). *Substitutes:* Andy Webster (Hearts, for Pressley 46); Stephen Crawford (Dunfermline Athletic, for Miller 79); Brian Kerr (Newcastle United, for McFadden 89). *Manager:* Berti Vogts (Germany).

Estonia: Martin Kaalma; Teet Allas, Andrei Stepanov, Einar Jaager, Ragnar Klavan; Taavi Rahn, Martin Reim (captain), Kristen Viikmae, Sergei Terehhov; Andres Oper, Joel Lindpere. *Substitutes:* Tarmo Kink (for Lindpere 75); Ott Reinumae (for Terehhov 85). *Coach:* Arnoldus Pijpers.

Scorer: Scotland: McFadden 76

| 30 May 2004 | Friendly | Easter Road, Edinburgh | Attendance: 16,187 |

651 SCOTLAND 4, Trinidad & Tobago 1 *Referee: Pieter Vink (Netherlands)*

Scotland: Craig Gordon (Hearts); Jackie McNamara (Celtic), Steven Pressley (Hearts, captain), Gary Caldwell (Hibernian), Malky Mackay (Norwich City), Jamie McAllister (Livingston); Nigel Quashie (Portsmouth), Darren Fletcher (Manchester United), Gary Holt (Norwich City); James McFadden (Everton), Stephen Crawford (Dunfermline Athletic). *Substitutes:* Brian Kerr (Newcastle United, for Holt 54); Kenny Miller (Wolverhampton Wanderers, for Crawford 67); Richard Hughes (Portsmouth, for Quashie 71); Steven Caldwell (Newcastle United, for Gary Caldwell 78); David McNamee (Livingston, for Mackay 85); Andy Webster (Hearts, for McFadden 85). *Manager:* Berti Vogts (Germany).

Trinidad & Tobago: Clayton Ince; Brent Sancho, Ian Cox, Marvin Andrews; Carlos Edwards, Arnold Dwarika, Angus Eve (captain), Stokely Mason, Kenwyne Jones; Cornell Glen, Stern John. *Substitutes:* Andre Boucaud (for Glen 28); Marlon Rojas (for Jones 46); Jerren Nixon (for Dwarika 74); Kerwyn Jemmot (for Eve 81); Densill Theobald (for Edwards 90). *Coach:* Bertille St Clair.

Scorers: Scotland: Fletcher 6; Holt 12; Gary Caldwell 23; Quashie 35   Trinidad & Tobago: John 55

| 18 August 2004 | Friendly | Hampden Park | Attendance: 15,933 |

652 SCOTLAND 0, Hungary 3 *Referee: Laurent Duhamel (France)*

Scotland: David Marshall (Celtic); Gary Holt (Norwich City), Andy Webster (Hearts), Gary Caldwell (Hibernian), Steven Pressley (Hearts), Gary Naysmith (Everton); Darren Fletcher (Manchester United), Barry Ferguson (Blackburn Rovers, captain), Nigel Quashie (Portsmouth); Kenny Miller (Wolverhampton Wanderers), James McFadden (Everton). *Substitutes:* Steven Thompson (Rangers, for Caldwell 46); Stephen Crawford (Plymouth Argyle, for Miller 57); Scott Severin (Aberdeen, for Ferguson 71); Stephen Pearson (Celtic, for Fletcher 73). *Manager:* Berti Vogts (Germany).

Hungary: Gabor Kiraly; Roland Juhasz, Peter Stark, Andras Toth; Laszlo Bodnar, Csaba Feher, Balazs Molnar, Szabolcs Huszti, Zoltan Gera (captain); Sandor Torghelle, Peter Simek. *Substitutes:* Peter Kovacs (for Torghelle 25); Denes Rosa (for Feher 64); Leandro de Almeida (for Gera 76); Gabor Gyepes (for Juhasz 84); Boldizsar Bodor (for Huszti 87). *Coach:* Lothar Matthaus (Germany).

Scorers: Hungary: Huszti 45+3 (pen), 53; Marshall 72 (own goal)

| 3 September 2004 | Friendly | Estadi Ciutat de Valencia | Attendance: 15,000 |

653 *Spain 1, SCOTLAND 1 *Referee: Stephane Bre (France)*

Scotland: Craig Gordon (Hearts); Jackie McNamara (Celtic), Andy Webster (Hearts), Gary Caldwell (Hibernian), Malky Mackay (Norwich City), Gary Naysmith (Everton); Darren Fletcher (Manchester United), Barry Ferguson (Blackburn Rovers, captain), Nigel Quashie (Portsmouth); James McFadden (Everton), Stephen Crawford (Plymouth Argyle). *Substitutes:* Stephen Pearson (Celtic, for McFadden 46); Kenny Miller (Wolverhampton Wanderers, for Crawford 57); Colin Cameron (Wolverhampton Wanderers, for Fletcher 57). *Manager:* Berti Vogts (Germany).

Spain: Iker Casillas (captain); Aitor Lopez Rekarte, Carles Puyol, Carlos Marchena, Asier del Horno; Ruben Baraja, Joaquin Sanchez, Xabi Alonso, Jose Antonio Reyes; Raul Tamudo, Fernando Torres. *Substitutes:* Juan Carlos Valeron (for Baraja 46); Vicente Rodriguez (for Tamudo 46); Raul Gonzales (for Torres 46); Ivan Helguera (for Marchena 57). *Coach:* Luis Aragones.

Scorers: Scotland: McFadden 18   Spain: Raul 57 (pen)

**The match was abandoned at 59 minutes due to floodlight failure caused by a lightning storm but the players still received caps.*

| 8 September 2004 | World Cup qualifying | Hampden Park | Attendance: 38,278 |

654 SCOTLAND 0, Slovenia 0 *Referee: Claus Bo Larsen (Denmark)*

Scotland: Craig Gordon (Hearts); Jackie McNamara (Celtic), Andy Webster (Hearts), Gary Caldwell (Hibernian), Malky Mackay (Norwich City), Gary Naysmith (Everton); Darren Fletcher (Manchester United), Barry Ferguson (Blackburn Rovers, captain), Nigel Quashie (Portsmouth); James McFadden (Everton), Paul Dickov (Blackburn Rovers). *Substitutes:* Gary Holt (Norwich City, for Naysmith 59); Stephen Crawford (Plymouth Argyle, for Dickov 80). *Manager:* Berti Vogts (Germany).

Slovenia: Borut Mavric; Jalen Pokorn, Matej Mavric, Aleksander Knavs (captain), Amir Karic; Simon Seslar, Nastja Ceh, Andrej Komac, Milenko Acimovic; Zlatko Dedic, Ermin Siljak. *Substitutes:* Klemen Lavric (for Siljak 64); Goran Sukalo (for Dedic 79). *Coach:* Branko Oblak.

| 9 October 2004 | World Cup qualifying | Hampden Park | Attendance: 48,882 |

655 SCOTLAND 0, Norway 1
Referee: Paul Allaerts (Belgium)

Scotland: Craig Gordon (Hearts); Gary Caldwell (Hibernian), Russell Anderson (Aberdeen), Andy Webster (Hearts), Gary Naysmith (Everton); Gary Holt (Norwich City), Darren Fletcher (Manchester United), Barry Ferguson (Blackburn Rovers, captain), Richard Hughes (Portsmouth); James McFadden (Everton), Paul Dickov (Blackburn Rovers). *Substitutes:* Stephen Pearson (Celtic, for Hughes 63); Kenny Miller (Wolverhampton Wanderers, for Dickov 75); Steven Thompson (Rangers, for Holt 80). *Manager:* Berti Vogts (Germany).

Norway: Thomas Myhre; Andre Bergdolmo, Erik Hagen, Claus Lundekvam (captain), John Arne Riise; Jan Gunnar Solli, Tommy Svindal Larsen, Jan Derek Sorensen, Steffen Iversen, Magne Hoseth; John Carew. *Substitutes:* Morten Gamst Pedersen (for Hoseth 58); Martin Andresen (for Sorensen 73); Frode Johnsen (for Iversen 88). *Coach:* Age Hareide.

Scorer: Norway: Iversen 54 (pen)

| 13 October 2004 | World Cup qualifying | Stadionul Republican, Chisinau | Attendance: 7,000 |

656 Moldova 1, SCOTLAND 1
Referee: Kristinn Jakobsson (Iceland)

Scotland: Craig Gordon (Hearts); Gary Caldwell (Hibernian), Steven Caldwell (Sunderland), Andy Webster (Hearts), Gary Naysmith (Everton); Gary Holt (Norwich City), Darren Fletcher (Manchester United), Barry Ferguson (Blackburn Rovers, captain), Colin Cameron (Wolverhampton Wanderers); Steven Thompson (Rangers), Stephen Crawford (Plymouth Argyle). *Substitutes:* Ian Murray (Hibernian, for Naysmith 46); Kenny Miller (Wolverhampton Wanderers, for Fletcher 66); Lee McCulloch (Wigan Athletic, for Thompson 86). *Manager:* Berti Vogts (Germany).

Moldova: Evgheni Hmaruc; Serghei Lascencov, Valeriu Catinsus (captain), Ghenadie Olexici, Iurie Priganiuc, Alexei Savinov; Serghei Covalciuc, Stanislav Ivanov, Iulian Bursuc; Serghei Dadu, Serghei Rogaciov. *Substitutes:* Boris Cebotari (for Olexici 39); Iurie Miterev (for Rogaciov 86). *Coach:* Viktor Pasulko.

Scorers: Moldova: Dadu 28   Scotland: Thompson 31

| 17 November 2004 | Friendly | Easter Road, Edinburgh | Attendance: 15,071 |

657 SCOTLAND 1, Sweden 4
Referee: Jaroslav Jara (Czech Republic)

Scotland: David Marshall (Celtic); Jackie McNamara (Celtic, captain), Russell Anderson (Aberdeen), Andy Webster (Hearts), Kevin McNaughton (Aberdeen); Barry Nicholson (Dunfermline Athletic), Nigel Quashie (Portsmouth), Stephen Pearson (Celtic), Ian Murray (Hibernian); James McFadden (Everton), Kenny Miller (Wolverhampton Wanderers). *Substitutes:* Steven Hammell (Motherwell, for Webster 54); Scott Severin (Aberdeen, for McNamara 64); Stephen Crawford (Plymouth Argyle, for Miller 71); Richard Hughes (Portsmouth, for Quashie 89). *Manager:* Tommy Burns.

Sweden: Magnus Hedman; Mikael Nilsson, Olof Mellberg (captain), Teddy Lucic, Mikael Dorsin; Anders Andersson, Niclas Alexandersson, Kim Kallstrom, Christian Wilhelmsson; Marcus Allback, Fredrik Berglund. *Substitutes:* Petter Hansson (for Mellberg 46); Alexander Ostlund (for Nilsson 63); Johan Elmander (for Allback 64); Sharbel Touma (for Wilhelmsson 77); Tobias Linderoth (for Lucic 82). *Coach:* Lars Lagerback.

Scorers: Sweden: Allback 27, 49; Elmander 73; Berglund 74   Scotland: McFadden 77 (pen)

| 26 March 2005 | World Cup qualifying | Stadio Guiseppe Meazza, Milan | Attendance: 40,745 |

658 Italy 2, SCOTLAND 0
Referee: Kyros Vassaras (Greece)

Scotland: Rab Douglas (Celtic); Jackie McNamara (Celtic), David Weir (Everton), Gary Caldwell (Hibernian), Steven Pressley (Hearts), Gary Naysmith (Everton); Paul Hartley (Hearts), Barry Ferguson (Rangers, captain), Nigel Quashie (Southampton); Lee McCulloch (Wigan Athletic), Kenny Miller (Wolverhampton Wanderers). *Substitutes:* Craig Gordon (Hearts, for Douglas 39); Neil McCann (Southampton, for Hartley 76); Garry O'Connor (Hibernian, for Miller 87). *Manager:* Walter Smith.

Italy: Gianluigi Buffon; Daniele Bonera, Fabio Cannavaro (captain), Marco Materazzi, Georgio Chiellini; Mauro Camoranesi, Andrea Pirlo, Gennaro Gattuso; Francesco Totti, Alberto Gilardino, Antonio Cassano. *Substitutes:* Daniele De Rossi (for Totti 70); Luca Toni (for Cassano 82). *Coach:* Marcello Lippi.

Scorer: Italy: Pirlo 35, 84

| 4 June 2005 | World Cup qualifying | Hampden Park | Attendance: 45,317 |

659 SCOTLAND 2, Moldova 0
Referee: Eric Braamhaar (Netherlands)

Scotland: Craig Gordon (Hearts); Jackie McNamara (Celtic), David Weir (Everton), Steven Pressley (Hearts), Andy Webster (Hearts), Graham Alexander (Preston North End); Darren Fletcher (Manchester United), Barry Ferguson (Rangers, captain), Paul Hartley (Hearts); Lee McCulloch (Wigan Athletic), Kenny Miller (Wolverhampton Wanderers). *Substitutes:* Christian Dailly (West Ham, for McNamara 26); James McFadden (Everton, for McCulloch 74). *Manager:* Walter Smith.

Moldova: Evgheni Hmaruc; Serghei Lascencov, Valeriu Catinsus (captain), Ghenadie Olexici, Iurie Priganiuc, Alexei Savinov, Stanislav Ivanov, Serghei Epureanu, Vadim Boret; Serghei Dadu, Serghei Rogaciov. *Substitutes:* Alexandr Covalenco (for Lascencov 46); Serghei Covalciuc (for Catinsus 60); Viorel Frunza (for Rogaciov 82). *Coach:* Viktor Pasulko.

Scorers: Scotland: Dailly 52; McFadden 88

| 8 June 2005 | World Cup qualifying | Stadyjon Dynama, Minsk | Attendance: 28,287 |

660 Belarus 0, SCOTLAND 0
Referee: Olegario Benquerenca (Portugal)

Scotland: Craig Gordon (Hearts); Christian Dailly (West Ham), David Weir (Everton), Steven Pressley (Hearts), Andy Webster (Hearts), Graham Alexander (Preston North End); Darren Fletcher (Manchester United), Barry Ferguson (Rangers, captain), Gary Caldwell (Hibernian); Lee McCulloch (Wigan Athletic), Kenny Miller (Wolverhampton Wanderers). *Substitute:* James McFadden (Everton, for McCulloch 76). *Manager:* Walter Smith.

Belarus: Yury Zhawnow; Syarhey Hurenka (captain), Syarhey Yaskovich, Syarhey Yaskovich, Syarhey Amelyanchuk; Dzyanis Kowba, Tsimafey Kalachow, Valyantsin Byalkievich, Alyaksandr Hleb; Vital Bulyha, Syarhey Karnilenka. *Substitutes:* Vyachaslaw Hleb (for Kalachow 59); Alyaksandr Kulchy (for Bulyha 85). *Coach:* Anatoliy Baidachnyi.

Chapter eight: 2000-2009

17 August 2005 Friendly   Arnold Schwarzenegger Stadion, Graz Attendance: 13,800

661 Austria 2, SCOTLAND 2
Referee: Selcuk Dereli (Turkey)

Scotland: Craig Gordon (Hearts); Jackie McNamara (Wolverhampton Wanderers), Steven Pressley (Hearts), Steven Caldwell (Sunderland), Andy Webster (Hearts), Graham Alexander (Preston North End); Christian Dailly (West Ham, captain), Brian O'Neil (Preston North End), Nigel Quashie (Southampton); Garry O'Connor (Hibernian), Kenny Miller (Wolverhampton Wanderers). *Substitutes:* Rab Douglas (Leicester City, for Gordon 46); Russell Anderson (Aberdeen, for Pressley 46); Scott Severin (Aberdeen, for O'Neil 46); Derek Riordan (Hibernian, for Miller 46); Richard Hughes (Portsmouth, for Quashie 73). *Manager:* Walter Smith.

Austria: Helge Payer; Ronald Gercaliu, Anton Ehmann, Ernst Dospel, Emanuel Pogatetz; Markus Schopp, Dietmar Kuhbauer, Rene Aufhauser, Andreas Ivanschitz (captain); Christian Mayrleb, Ivica Vastic. *Substitutes:* Andreas Schranz (for Payer 46); Joachim Standfest (for Dospel 54); Muhammet Akagunduz (for Mayrleb 65); Sanel Kuljic (for Vastic 65); Andreas Ibertsberger (for Schopp 68); Jurgen Saumel (for Kuhbauer 78). *Coach:* Hans Krankl.

Scorers: Scotland: Miller 3; O'Connor 38 Austria: Ibertsberger 83; Standfest 86

3 September 2005 World Cup qualifying Hampden Park   Attendance: 50,185

662 SCOTLAND 1, Italy 1
Referee: Lubos Michel (Slovakia)

Scotland: Craig Gordon (Hearts); Jackie McNamara (Wolverhampton Wanderers), David Weir (Everton), Christian Dailly (West Ham), Andy Webster (Hearts), Graham Alexander (Preston North End); Darren Fletcher (Manchester United), Barry Ferguson (Rangers, captain), Paul Hartley (Hearts), Nigel Quashie (Southampton); Kenny Miller (Wolverhampton Wanderers). *Substitutes:* Neil McCann (Southampton, for Quashie 67); Craig Beattie (Celtic, for Miller 76). *Manager:* Walter Smith.

Italy: Angelo Peruzzi; Cristian Zaccardo, Fabio Cannavaro (captain), Alessandro Nesta, Gianluca Zambrotta; Daniele De Rossi, Andreas Pirlo, Gennaro Gattuso, Francesco Totti; Christian Vieri, Vincenzo Iaquinta. *Substitutes:* Fabio Grosso (for Zaccardo 46); Mauro Camoranesi (for De Rossi 60); Luca Toni (for Iaquinta 71). *Coach:* Marcello Lippi.

Scorers: Scotland: Miller 13 Italy: Grosso 75

7 September 2005 World Cup qualifying Ullevaal Stadion, Oslo Attendance: 24,904

663 Norway 1, SCOTLAND 2
Referee: Alain Hamer (Luxembourg)

Scotland: Craig Gordon (Hearts); Jackie McNamara (Wolverhampton Wanderers), David Weir (Everton), Steven Pressley (Hearts), Andy Webster (Hearts), Graham Alexander (Preston North End); Darren Fletcher (Manchester United), Barry Ferguson (Rangers, captain), Paul Hartley (Hearts), James McFadden (Everton), Kenny Miller (Wolverhampton Wanderers). *Substitutes:* Neil McCann (Southampton, for Miller 40); Craig Beattie (Celtic, for McFadden 72). *Manager:* Walter Smith.

Norway: Thomas Myhre; Jan Gunnar Solli, Vidar Riseth, Claus Lundekvam, Andre Bergdolmo, John Arne Riise; Martin Andresen (captain), Christian Grindheim, Alex Valencia, Egil Ostenstad; John Carew. *Substitutes:* Kristofer Haestad (for Solli 46); Daniel Braaten (for Valencia 46); Ole Martin Arst (for Ostenstad 46). *Coach:* Age Hareide.

Scorers: Scotland: Miller 20, 30 Norway: Arst 89

Kenny Miller (second from right) is congratulated by team mates Barry Ferguson, Graham Alexander and Andy Webster after one of his two goals which saw off Norway in the World Cup qualifying tie.

8 October 2005   World Cup qualifying   Hampden Park   Attendance: 51,105

664 SCOTLAND 0, Belarus 1
Referee: Zsolt Szabo (Hungary)

Scotland: Craig Gordon (Hearts); Graham Alexander (Preston North End), David Weir (Everton), Christian Dailly (West Ham), Steven Pressley (Hearts), Ian Murray (Rangers); Darren Fletcher (Manchester United), Barry Ferguson (Rangers, captain), Paul Hartley (Hearts); Lee McCulloch (Wigan Athletic), Kenny Miller (Wolverhampton Wanderers). *Substitute:* Shaun Maloney (Celtic, for Murray 46). *Manager:* Walter Smith.

Belarus: Vasil Khamutowski; Alyaksandr Kulchy, Uladzimir Karytska, Andrey Astrowski, Ihar Tarlowski; Dzyanis Kowba, Vital Bulyha, Alyaksandr Hleb, Tsimafey Kalachow; Andrey Lavrik (captain), Vital Kutuzaw. *Substitute:* Dzyanis Sashcheka (for Bulyha 88). *Coach:* Anatoliy Bajdachnyi.

Scorer: Belarus: Kutuzaw 5

12 October 2005   World Cup qualifying   Sportni Park, Celje   Attendance: 9,100

665 Slovenia 0, SCOTLAND 3
Referee: Rene Temmink (Netherlands)

Scotland (5-3-2):

13 Craig Gordon (Hearts);
59 Christian Dailly (West Ham, captain)
27 Steven Pressley (Hearts)
44 David Weir (Everton)
20 Andy Webster (Hearts)
21 Graham Alexander (Preston North End);
6   Paul Hartley (Hearts)
19 Darren Fletcher (Manchester United)
10 Nigel Quashie (Southampton);
23 James McFadden (Everton)
25 Kenny Miller (Wolverhampton Wanderers)

Substitutes: 16 Gary Caldwell (Hibernian, for Pressley 46);
6 Garry O'Connor (Hibernian, for Miller 46);
7 Stephen Caldwell (Sunderland, for Quashie 72)

Manager: Walter Smith

Following a disappointing World Cup qualifying campaign, during which most of the best results were surprisingly achieved away from home, Scotland finished with a straightforward and morale-boosting away success against Slovenia. The three goals were all exceptional, starting with Darren Fletcher's 25-yard drive past a bemused keeper in just the fourth minute. James McFadden made it 2-0 just after half-time with a beautiful volley following good set-up play by Nigel Quashie and Fletcher. The final goal came from Paul Hartley, in for the suspended Barry Ferguson, who found the net with a superb chip after Fletcher had again been involved. The Scots had finished third in the group but there were plenty of positives for manager Walter Smith, with a Kirin Cup tournament in Japan and the start of a European Championship campaign the following year.

Slovenia: Samir Handanovic; Matej Mavric, Bostjan Cesar, Aleksander Knavs, Robert Koren; Nastja Ceh, Andrej Komac, Anton Zlogar, Sebastjan Cimirotic; Aleksandar Rodic, Milenko Acimovic. *Substitutes:* Andrej Pecnic (for Mavric 25); Branco Ilic (for Pecnic 58); Ermin Siljak (for Rodic 54). *Coach:* Branko Oblak.

Scorers: Scotland: Fletcher 4; McFadden 47; Hartley 84

FIFA WORLD CUP QUALIFYING GROUP FIVE

	P	W	D	L	F	A	Pts
Italy	10	7	2	1	17	8	23
Norway	10	5	3	2	12	7	18
Scotland	10	3	4	3	9	7	13
Slovenia	10	3	3	4	10	13	12
Belarus	10	2	4	4	12	14	10
Moldova	10	1	2	7	5	16	5

12 November 2005   Friendly   Hampden Park   Attendance: 26,708

666 SCOTLAND 1, USA 1
Referee: Alberto Mallenco (Spain)

Scotland: Craig Gordon (Hearts); Christian Dailly (West Ham, captain), David Weir (Everton), Steven Pressley (Hearts), Andy Webster (Hearts), Graham Alexander (Preston North End); Paul Hartley (Hearts), Darren Fletcher (Manchester United), Nigel Quashie (Southampton); Neil McCann (Southampton), Garry O'Connor (Hibernian). *Substitutes:* Steven Caldwell (Sunderland, for Pressley 46); Gary Caldwell (Hibernian, for Weir 46); James McFadden (Everton, for McCann 62); Shaun Maloney (Celtic, for O'Connor 73); Scott Brown (Hibernian, for Quashie 73). *Manager:* Walter Smith.

USA: Kasey Keller (captain); Steven Cherundolo, Carlos Bocanegra, Gregg Berhalter, Jonathan Spector; Brian Carroll, Kerry Zavagnin, Eddie Gaven, DaMarcus Beasley; Joshua Wolff, Brian Ching. *Substitutes:* Santino Quaranta (for Gaven 46); Ben Olsen (for Zavagnin 46); Chris Rolfe (for Wolff 58); Heath Pearce (for Beasley 76); James Conrad (for Bocanegra 78). *Coach:* Bruce Arena.

Scorers: USA: Wolff 8 (pen)   Scotland: Webster 36

1 March 2006   Friendly   Hampden Park   Attendance: 20,952

667 SCOTLAND 1, Switzerland 3
Referee: Bruno Coue (France)

Scotland: Craig Gordon (Hearts); Christian Dailly (West Ham), David Weir (Everton), Gary Caldwell (Hibernian), Andy Webster (Hearts), Graham Alexander (Preston North End); Darren Fletcher (Manchester United), Barry Ferguson (Rangers, captain), Nigel Quashie (West Bromwich Albion); James McFadden (Everton), Kenny Miller (Wolverhampton Wanderers). *Substitutes:* Neil Alexander (Cardiff City, for Gordon 46); Gary Teale (Wigan Athletic, for Ferguson 46); Steven Caldwell (Sunderland, for Weir 46). *Manager:* Walter Smith.

Switzerland: Pascal Zuberbuhler; Philipp Degen, Philippe Senderos, Stephane Grichting, Valon Behrami; Tranquillo Barnetta, Johann Vogel (captain), Ricardo Cabanas, Raphael Wicky; Daniel Gygax, Marco Streller. *Substitutes:* Fabio Coltorti (for Zuberbuhler 46); Johan Djourou (for Behrami 46); Johan Vonlanthen (for Wicky 46); Boris Smiljanic (for Senderos 73); Mauro Lustrinelli (for Streller 73); Blerim Dzemaili (for Vogel 80). *Coach:* Jakob Kuhn.

Scorers: Switzerland: Barnetta 20; Gygax 40; Cabanas 68   Scotland: Miller 54

11 May 2006   Kirin Cup   Kobe Wing Stadium, Kobe   Attendance: 5,780

668 SCOTLAND 5, Bulgaria 1

Referee: Toru Kamikawa (Japan)

Scotland (5-3-2):
2 Neil Alexander (Cardiff City);
2 Graeme Murty (Reading)
19 Gary Caldwell (Hibernian)
47 David Weir (Everton, captain)
8 Russell Anderson (Aberdeen)
29 Gary Naysmith (Everton);
2 Gary Teale (Wigan Athletic)
22 Darren Fletcher (Manchester United)
11 Scott Severin (Aberdeen);
6 Lee McCulloch (Wigan Athletic)
1 Kris Boyd (Rangers)

Substitutes: 26 James McFadden (Everton, for Boyd 52);
10 Gavin Rae (Rangers, for Severin 69);
1 Chris Burke (Rangers, for Teale 74);
5 Ian Murray (Rangers, for McCulloch 78);
3 David McNamee (Livingston, for Murty 82)

Manager: Walter Smith

Quite often the best results are achieved when the chips are down, and that was certainly the case with Scotland's first match in the Kirin Cup. The annual competition in Japan saw the hosts and two other nations compete in a three-way tournament and the Scots, although deprived of around a dozen players due to other commitments, defeated Bulgaria in thrilling style. There were doubles for Rangers pair Kris Boyd and substitute Chris Burke, while another replacement, James McFadden, kept up his excellent international scoring record. Boyd opened the scoring in the 12th minute and restored the lead just before half-time following a Bulgarian equaliser, and then Scotland romped away after the break. With Bulgaria having beaten Japan in the first game, a point against the hosts would clinch the trophy, and a 0-0 draw was duly achieved.

Bulgaria: Stoian Kolev; Stanislav Angelov, Rosen Kirilev, Elin Topuzakov, Asen Karaslavov; Lucio Wagner, Yordan Todorov, Dimitar Telkiyski, Martin Petrov (captain); Svetoslav Todorov, Valeri Domovchiyski. *Substitutes:* Hristo Yanev (for Karaslavov 55); Nikolai Mihailov (for Kolev 71); Tsvetan Genkov (for Todorov 71); Georgi Iliev (for Domovchiyski 71). *Trainer:* Hristo Stoichkov.

Scorers: Scotland: Boyd 12, 43; McFadden 69; Burke 76, 88   Bulgaria: Yordan Todorov 26

---

13 May 2006   Kirin Cup   Saitama Stadium, Saitama   Attendance: 58,648

669 Japan 0, SCOTLAND 0

Referee: Eduardo Gonzalez (Spain)

Scotland: Neil Alexander (Cardiff City); Graeme Murty (Reading), Gary Caldwell (Hibernian), David Weir (Everton, captain), Russell Anderson (Aberdeen), Gary Naysmith (Everton); Gary Teale (Wigan Athletic), Darren Fletcher (Manchester United), Scott Severin (Hearts); Lee McCulloch (Wigan Athletic), James McFadden (Everton). *Substitutes:* Ian Murray (Rangers, for Naysmith 46); Gavin Rae (Dundee, for Severin 46); Chris Burke (Rangers, for Teale 59); Kris Boyd (Rangers, for McFadden 59); Lee Miller (Dundee United, for McCulloch 69); David McNamee (Livingston, for Murty 79). *Manager:* Walter Smith.

Japan: Yoshikatsu Kawaguchi; Tsuneyasu Miyamoto, Alessandro Santos, Yuji Nakazawa, Akira Kaji; Takashi Fukunishi, Mitsuo Ogasawara, Shinji Ono; Yasuhito Endo, Tatsuhiko Kubo, Keiji Tamada. *Substitutes:* Keisuke Tsuboi (for Nakazawa 50); Hisato Sato (for Endo 72); Seiichiro Maki (for Kubo 82). *Trainer:* Zico (Brazil).

The Kirin Cup-winning side of 2006. Back (from left): Gary Teale, Gary Caldwell, David Weir, Scott Severin, Neil Alexander, Darren Fletcher. Front: Lee McCulloch, James McFadden, Gary Naysmith, Graeme Murty, Russell Anderson.

2 September 2006   European Championship qualifying   Celtic Park, Glasgow   Attendance: 50,059

670 SCOTLAND 6, Faroe Islands 0   *Referee: Igor Yegorov (Russia)*

Scotland (4-3-3):

16 Craig Gordon (Hearts);
62 Christian Dailly (West Ham)
49 David Weir (Everton, captain)
29 Steven Pressley (Hearts)
31 Gary Naysmith (Everton);
24 Darren Fletcher (Manchester United)
8 Paul Hartley (Hearts)
13 Nigel Quashie (West Bromwich Albion);
27 Kenny Miller (Celtic)
3 Kris Boyd (Rangers)
28 James McFadden (Everton)

Substitutes: 4 Gary Teale (Wigan Athletic, for Fletcher 46);
8 Garry O'Connor (Lokomotiv Moscow, for Miller 61);
13 Scott Severin (Aberdeen, for Quashie 84)

Manager: Walter Smith

Any perceptions that the Faroe Islands was Scotland's bogey side were well and truly laid to rest on a fine afternoon in Glasgow. Walter Smith's side were offered a multitude of chances and took six of them to record their biggest victory for over 20 years. Darren Fletcher got the first in the sixth minute, stabbing a cross from Kenny Miller over the line, and James McFadden doubled the lead from the edge of the box two minutes later. Kris Boyd made it three from the penalty spot after McFadden was fouled and six minutes later a similar award was given. This time Miller was handed the ball and although he also found the net, both penalties were lucky to have been converted. Boyd made it 5-0 as the half drew to an end and although the Scots appeared to ease up after the break, substitute Garry O'Connor got a sixth with five minutes remaining.

Faroe Islands: Jakup Mikkelsen; Pauli Hansen, Oli Johannesen (captain), Atli Danielsen, Janus Joensen; Frodi Benjaminsen, Julian Johnsson, Jakup a Borg, Jonhard Frederiksberg; Rogvi Jacobsen, Christian Hogni Jacobsen. *Substitutes:* Hanus Thorleifsson (for Frederiksberg 60); Simun Samuelsen (for Johnsson 76); Kari Nielsen (for Rogvi Jacobsen 84). *Trainer:* Jogvan Martin Olsen.

Scorers: Scotland: Fletcher 6; McFadden 10; Boyd 24 (pen), 38; Miller 30 (pen); O'Connor 85

---

6 September 2006   European Championship qualifying   Darias ir Gireno, Kaunas   Attendance: 7,500

671 Lithuania 1, SCOTLAND 2   *Referee: Vladimir Hrinak (Slovakia)*

Scotland: Craig Gordon (Hearts); Christian Dailly (West Ham), David Weir (Everton, captain), Gary Caldwell (Celtic), Steven Pressley (Hearts), Gary Naysmith (Everton); Paul Hartley (Hearts), Darren Fletcher (Manchester United), Nigel Quashie (West Bromwich Albion); James McFadden (Everton), Kenny Miller (Celtic). *Substitutes:* Graham Alexander (Preston North End, for McFadden 21); Kris Boyd (Rangers, for Quashie 43); Scott Severin (Aberdeen, for Hartley 88). *Manager:* Walter Smith.

Lithuania: Zydrunas Karcemarskas; Marius Stankevicius, Andrius Skerla, Tomas Zvirgzdauskas, Rolandas Dziaukstas; Mindaugas Kalonas, Mantas Savenas, Tomas Danilevicius (captain), Aidas Preiksaitis, Saulius Mikoliunas; Robertas Poskus. *Substitutes:* Tomas Tamosauskas (for Savenas 50); Tadas Labukas (for Mikoliunas 66); Darius Miceika (for Preiksaitis 81). *Coach:* Algimantas Liubinskas.

Scorers: Scotland: Dailly 46; Miller 63   Lithuania: Miceika 85

---

7 October 2006   European Championship qualifying   Hampden Park   Attendance: 50,456

672 SCOTLAND 1, France 0   *Referee: Massimo Busacca (Switzerland)*

Scotland (5-4-1):

18 Craig Gordon (Hearts);
64 Christian Dailly (West Ham)
22 Gary Caldwell (Celtic)
31 Stephen Pressley (Celtic)
51 David Weir (Everton)
25 Graham Alexander (Preston North End);
10 Paul Hartley (Hearts)
34 Barry Ferguson (Rangers, captain)
26 Darren Fletcher (Manchester United)
8 Lee McCulloch (Wigan Athletic);
30 James McFadden (Everton)

Substitutes: 5 Gary Teale (Wigan Athletic, for McCulloch 57);
9 Garry O'Connor (Lokomotiv Moscow, for McFadden 73)

Manager: Walter Smith

In a victory which was up there with anything the Scotland team had recorded for a number of years, beaten World Cup finalists France were sent packing from Hampden Park. It was only by one goal, and the French squandered a few chances to equalise, but everyone present basked in the kind of euphoria that had not been seen for a while. Manager Walter Smith named a cautious 5-4-1 formation, with James McFadden as the lone striker, and his players gave their all on the memorable occasion. The solitary goal, midway through the second half, was scored by the unlikely figure of Gary Caldwell. An outswinging corner from the left by Paul Hartley found its way to the Celtic man on the edge of the area thanks to a decoy run to the front post by David Weir. Caldwell swung his foot and the ball was in the net. The French superstars were stunned and despite controlling the match for large periods, were unable to reply. They came close near to the end but keeper Craig Gordon showed immaculate handling to keep them out. It was indeed a result for the record books.

France: Gregory Coupet; Willy Sagnol, Lilian Thuram, Jean-Alain Boumsong, Eric Abidal; Franck Ribery, Patrick Viera (captain), Claude Makelele, Florent Malouda; David Trezeguet, Thierry Henry. *Substitutes:* Louis Saha (for Trezeguet 62); Sylvain Wiltord (for Ribery 74). *Trainer:* Raymond Domenech.

Scorer: Scotland: Caldwell 67

11 October 2006 European Championship qualifying NSC Olimpiyskyi, Kiev Attendance: 55,000
673 Ukraine 2, SCOTLAND 0
Referee: Martin Hansson (Sweden)

Scotland: Craig Gordon (Hearts); Robbie Neilson (Hearts), David Weir (Everton), Gary Caldwell (Celtic), Steven Pressley (Hearts), Graham Alexander (Preston North End); Darren Fletcher (Manchester United), Barry Ferguson (Rangers, captain), Paul Hartley (Hearts); James McFadden (Everton), Kenny Miller (Celtic). *Substitutes:* Kris Boyd (Rangers, for McFadden 75); Stephen McManus (Celtic, for Neilson 90). *Manager:* Walter Smith.

Ukraine: Oleksandr Shovkovskyi; Vyacheslav Sviderskyi, Oleksandr Kucher, Andriy Rusol, Andriy Nesmachnyi; Oleg Husiev, Anatoliy Tymoshcuk, Oleg Shelayev, Maksym Kalinichenko; Andriy Voronin, Andriy Shevchenko (captain). *Substitutes:* Artem Milevskyi (for Husiev 60); Andriy Vorobey (for Kalinichenko 78); Bohdan Shershun (for Voronin 90+3). *Coach:* Oleg Blochin.

Scorers: Ukraine: Kucher 60; Shevchenko 90 (pen)

24 March 2007 European Championship qualifying Hampden Park Attendance: 50,850
674 SCOTLAND 2, Georgia 1
Referee: Nicolai Vollquartz (Denmark)

Scotland: Craig Gordon (Hearts); Graham Alexander (Preston North End), David Weir (Rangers), Stephen McManus (Celtic), Gary Naysmith (Everton); Gary Teale (Derby County), Barry Ferguson (Rangers, captain), Paul Hartley (Celtic), Lee McCulloch (Wigan Athletic); Kenny Miller (Celtic), Kris Boyd (Rangers). *Substitutes:* Scott Brown (Hibernian, for Teale 60); Craig Beattie (Celtic, for Boyd 76); Shaun Maloney (Aston Villa, for Miller 90+2). *Manager:* Alex McLeish.

Georgia: Giorgi Lomaia; Giorgi Shashiashvili, Lasha Salukvadze, Zurab Khizanishvili, Zaali Eliava; Vladimer Burduli, Zurab Menteshashvili, Levan Tskitishvili, Levan Kobiashvili (captain); Shota Arveladze, Georgi Demetradze. *Substitutes:* Gogita Gogua (for Menteshashvili 46); Davit Siradze (for Burduli 57); Davit Mujiri (for Tskitishvili 90+2). *Coach:* Klaus Toppmoller (Germany).

Scorers: Scotland: Boyd 11; Beattie 89 Georgia: Arveladze 41

28 March 2007 European Championship qualifying Stadio San Nicola, Bari Attendance: 37,500
675 Italy 2, SCOTLAND 0
Referee: Frank De Bleeckere (Belgium)

Scotland: Craig Gordon (Hearts); Graham Alexander (Preston North End), David Weir (Rangers), Stephen McManus (Celtic), Gary Naysmith (Everton); Gary Teale (Derby County), Scott Brown (Hibernian), Barry Ferguson (Rangers, captain), Paul Hartley (Celtic); Lee McCulloch (Wigan Athletic), Kenny Miller (Celtic). *Substitutes:* Shaun Maloney (Aston Villa, for Teale 66); Kris Boyd (Rangers, for McCulloch 81); Craig Beattie (Celtic, for Brown 86). *Manager:* Alex McLeish.

Italy: Gianluigi Buffon; Massimo Oddo, Fabio Cannavaro (captain), Marco Materazzi, Gianluca Zambrotta; Gennaro Gattuso, Daniele De Rossi; Mauro Camoranesi, Simone Perrotta, Antonio Di Natale; Luca Toni. *Substitutes:* Alessandro Del Piero (for Di Natale 66); Andrea Pirlo (for Perrotta 77); Fabio Quagliarella (for Toni 87). *Coach:* Roberto Donadoni.

Scorer: Italy: Toni 12, 70

30 May 2007 Friendly Gerhard Hanappi Stadion, Vienna Attendance: 13,200
676 Austria 0, SCOTLAND 1
Referee: Zsolt Szabo (Hungary)

Scotland: Allan McGregor (Rangers); Graham Alexander (Preston North End), David Weir (Rangers), Gary Caldwell (Celtic), Gary Naysmith (Everton); Shaun Maloney (Aston Villa), Darren Fletcher (Manchester United), Barry Ferguson (Rangers, captain), Lee McCulloch (Wigan Athletic); Garry O'Connor (Lokomotiv Moscow), Kris Boyd (Rangers). *Substitutes:* Craig Gordon (Hearts, for McGregor 46); Paul Hartley (Celtic, for McCulloch 46); Christian Dailly (West Ham, for Weir 46); Charlie Adam (Rangers, for Maloney 66); Alan Hutton (Rangers, for Alexander 70); Stephen McManus (Celtic, for O'Connor 86). *Manager:* Alex McLeish.

Austria: Helge Payer; Joachim Standfest, Martin Hiden, Jurgen Patocka, Christian Fuchs; Andreas Ivanshitz (captain), Rene Aufhauser, Jurgen Saumel, Christoph Leitgeb; Roland Linz, Mario Haas. *Substitutes:* Sanel Kuljic (for Haas 59); Markus Katzer (for Fuchs 74); Yuksel Sariyar (for Aufhauser 74); Sebastian Prodl (for Hiden 88). *Coach:* Josef Hickersberger.

Scorer: Scotland: O'Connor 58

6 June 2007 European Championship qualifying Svangaskard, Toftir Attendance: 4,100
677 Faroe Islands 0, SCOTLAND 2
Referee: Georgios Kasnaferis (Greece)

Scotland: Craig Gordon (Hearts); Graham Alexander (Preston North End), David Weir (Rangers), Stephen McManus (Celtic), Gary Naysmith (Everton); Paul Hartley (Celtic), Darren Fletcher (Manchester United), Barry Ferguson (Rangers, captain), Shaun Maloney (Aston Villa); Garry O'Connor (Lokomotiv Moscow), Kris Boyd (Rangers). *Substitutes:* Gary Teale (Derby County, for Fletcher 68); Charlie Adam (Rangers, for Maloney 77); Steven Naismith (Kilmarnock, for Boyd 83). *Manager:* Alex McLeish.

Faroe Islands: Jakup Mikkelsen; Atli Danielsen, Oli Johannesen (captain), Jon Roi Jacobsen, Suni Olsen; Jakup a Borg, Frodi Benjaminsen, Mikkjal Thomassen, Christian Holst; Rogvi Jacobsen, Christian Hogni Jacobsen. *Substitutes:* Marni Djurhuus (for Johannesen 36); Simun Samuelsen (for Djurhuus 77); Andrew av Flotum (for a Borg 82). *Coach:* Jogvan Martin Olsen.

Scorers: Scotland: Maloney 31; O'Connor 35

22 August 2007 Friendly Pittodrie, Aberdeen Attendance: 13,723
678 SCOTLAND 1, South Africa 0
Referee: Martin Atkinson (England)

Scotland: Craig Gordon (Sunderland); Alan Hutton (Rangers), Russell Anderson (Sunderland), Stephen McManus (Celtic), Jay McEveley (Derby County); Scott Brown (Celtic), Gary Caldwell (Celtic), Darren Fletcher (Manchester United, captain), James McFadden (Everton); Garry O'Connor (Birmingham City), Kenny Miller (Celtic). *Substitutes:* Stephen Pearson (Derby County, for McFadden 46); Barry Robson (Dundee United, for Caldwell 57); Craig Beattie (West Bromwich Albion, for O'Connor 68); Kris Boyd (Rangers, for Miller 68); Gary Teale (Derby County, for Brown 72). *Manager:* Alex McLeish.

South Africa: Rowen Fernandez; Cyril Nzama, Aaron Mokoena (captain), Benson Mhlongo, Bradley Carnell; Steven Pienaar, Papi Zothwane, MacBeth Sibaya, Delron Buckley; Siyabonga Nkosi, Sibusiso Zuma. *Substitutes:* Siyabonga Nomvethe (for Zuma 12); Teko Modise (for Zothwane 75); Dillon Sheppard (for Buckley 75); Thembinkosi Fanteni (for Nkosi 75); Vuyo Mere (for Nzama 83). *Coach:* Carlos Alberto Parreira (Brazil).

Scorer: Scotland: Boyd 71

8 September 2007   European Championship qualifying   Hampden Park   Attendance: 51,349

679 SCOTLAND 3, Lithuania 1
Referee: Damir Skomina (Slovenia)

Scotland: Craig Gordon (Sunderland); Alan Hutton (Rangers), David Weir (Rangers), Stephen McManus (Celtic), Jay McEveley (Derby County); Gary Teale (Derby County), Scott Brown (Celtic), Darren Fletcher (Manchester United, captain), Lee McCulloch (Rangers); Kris Boyd (Rangers), Garry O'Connor (Birmingham City). *Substitutes:* James McFadden (Everton, for Teale 69); Craig Beattie (West Bromwich Albion, for O'Connor 76); Shaun Maloney (Aston Villa, for McCulloch 76). *Manager:* Alex McLeish.

Lithuania: Zydrunas Karcemarskas; Marius Stankevicius, Andrius Skerla, Tomas Zvirgzdauskas, Arunas Klimavicius, Deividas Semberas; Mindaugas Kalonas, Deividas Cesnauskis, Igoris Morinas; Tomas Danilevicius (captain), Andrius Velicka. *Substitutes:* Saulius Mikoliunas (for Morinas 47); Andrius Ksanavicius (for Velicka 47); Edgaras Jankauskas (for Stankevicius 56). *Coach:* Algimantas Liubinskas.

Scorers: Scotland: Boyd 31; McManus 77; McFadden 83   Lithuania: Danilevicius 61 (pen)

12 September 2007   European Championship qualifying   Parc de Princes, Paris   Attendance: 43,342

680 France 0, SCOTLAND 1
Referee: Konrad Plautz (Austria)

Scotland (4-5-1):

26 Craig Gordon (Sunderland);
4 Alan Hutton (Rangers)
58 David Weir (Rangers)
8 Stephen McManus (Celtic)
31 Graham Alexander (Burnley);
6 Scott Brown (Celtic)
40 Barry Ferguson (Rangers, captain)
32 Darren Fletcher (Manchester United)
16 Paul Hartley (Celtic)
13 Lee McCulloch (Rangers);
34 James McFadden (Everton)

Substitutes: 8 Stephen Pearson (Derby County, for Fletcher 26);
14 Garry O'Connor (Birmingham City, for McFadden 76)

Manager: Alex McLeish

The astonishing qualifying campaign reached new heights of exhilaration as the Scots recorded their second group victory over the World Cup finalists. As he had done four days earlier against Lithuania, James McFadden conjured up a wonderful goal, beating French keeper Landrau with a magnificent strike from well outside the penalty area. The home side applied plenty of pressure throughout but were unable to break through Alex McLeish's well-organised side, which defended resolutely at times with David Weir and particularly Stephen McManus excellent in the centre of the back four. They were well backed up by full backs Alan Hutton and Graham Alexander and goalkeeper Craig Gordon while midfielder Paul Hartley also had a fine game. McFadden's strike, about midway through the second half, saw him take the ball down, turn and hit a tremendous left-foot drive which hurtled over the keeper and under the crossbar. Qualification hopes were well and truly alive.

France: Mickael Landrau; Lassana Diarra, Lilian Thuram, Julien Escude, Eric Abidal; Franck Ribery, Patrick Viera (captain), Claude Makalele, Florent Malouda; David Trezeguet, Nicolas Anelka. *Substitutes:* Samir Nasri (for Viera 69); Karim Benzema (for Abidal 77). *Trainer:* Raymond Domenech.

Scorer: Scotland: McFadden 64

Before the memorable victory in Paris which completed a winning double over the French. Back (from left); Craig Gordon, Stephen McManus, Darren Fletcher, Alan Hutton, Paul Hartley, David Weir. Front: James McFadden, Graham Alexander, Barry Ferguson, Lee McCulloch, Scott Brown.

Chapter eight: 2000-2009

13 October 2007   European Championship qualifying   Hampden Park   Attendance: 51,366

681 SCOTLAND 3, Ukraine 1   *Referee: Pieter Vink (Netherlands)*

Scotland: Craig Gordon (Sunderland); Alan Hutton (Rangers), David Weir (Rangers), Stephen McManus (Celtic), Gary Naysmith (Sheffield United); Scott Brown (Celtic), Barry Ferguson (Rangers, captain), Stephen Pearson (Derby County), Lee McCulloch (Rangers); James McFadden (Everton), Kenny Miller (Derby County). *Substitutes:* Christian Dailly (Southampton, for McCulloch 60); Shaun Maloney (Aston Villa, for Brown 76); Garry O'Connor (Birmingham City, for McFadden 80). *Manager:* Alex McLeish.

Ukraine: Oleksandr Shovkovskyi; Volodymyr Yezerskyi, Oleksandr Kucher, Dmytro Chyhrynskyi, Andriy Nesmachnyi; Anatoliy Tymoshchuk, Oleg Husiev, Andriy Voronin, Andriy Vorobey; Oleksandr Hladkyi, Andriy Shevchenko (captain). *Substitutes:* Ruslan Rotan (for Husiev 46); Serhiy Nazarenkjo (for Vorobey 62); Oleg Shelayev (for Tymoshchuk 73). *Coach:* Oleg Blochin.

Scorers: Scotland: Miller 4; McCulloch 10; McFadden 68   Ukraine: Shevchenko 24

17 October 2007   European Championship qualifying   National Stadium, Tbilisi   Attendance: 29,377

682 Georgia 2, SCOTLAND 0   *Referee: Knut Kircher (Germany)*

Scotland: Craig Gordon (Sunderland); Graeme Murty (Reading), David Weir (Rangers), Stephen McManus (Celtic), Graham Alexander (Burnley); Darren Fletcher (Manchester United), Barry Ferguson (Rangers, captain), Stephen Pearson (Derby County), Shaun Maloney (Aston Villa); James McFadden (Everton), Kenny Miller (Derby County). *Substitutes:* Craig Beattie (West Bromwich Albion, for Miller 66); Kris Boyd (Rangers, for Pearson 66). *Manager:* Alex McLeish.

Georgia: Giorgi Makaridze; Lasha Salukvadze, Zurab Khizanishvili (captain), Malkhas Asatiani, Giorgi Shashiashvili; Zurab Menteshashvili, Jaba Kankava, Davit Kvirkvelia; Levan Kenia, Levan Mchedlidze; Davit Siradze. *Substitutes:* Ilia Kandelaki (for Kenia 79); Aleksandre Kvakhadze (for Mchedlidze 85); Lasha Jakobia (for Siradze 89). *Coach:* Klaus Toppmoller (Germany).

Scorers: Georgia: Mchedlidze 16; Siradze 64

17 November 2007   European Championship qualifying   Hampden Park   Attendance: 53,301

683 SCOTLAND 1, Italy 2   *Referee: Manuel Gonzalez (Spain)*

Scotland (4-4-2):
29 Craig Gordon (Sunderland);
6   Alan Hutton (Rangers)
61 David Weir (Rangers)
11 Stephen McManus (Celtic)
38 Gary Naysmith (Sheffield United);
8   Scott Brown (Celtic)
34 Darren Fletcher (Manchester United)
43 Barry Ferguson (Rangers, captain)
17 Paul Hartley (Celtic);
15 Lee McCulloch (Rangers)
37 James McFadden (Everton)

Substitutes: 35 Kenny Miller (Derby County, for Brown 74);
13 Kris Boyd (Rangers, for McCulloch (90+2)

Manager: Alex McLeish

To Scotland's credit, going into the final match at home to Italy there was still a chance of progressing to the European Championships in Austria and Switzerland. In the so-called "group of death" two incredible wins over France had kept qualification hopes alive, but a defeat against Georgia in the previous game meant it all hinged on the final tie. A victory would have been enough while a draw would have meant progression was unlikely. It was the worst possible start when Luca Toni headed Italy into the lead in the second minute, but the Scottish players rallied and played well throughout. Barry Ferguson scored a deserved equaliser midway through the second half and there were chances to win it but unfortunately all were squandered. Then with just a minute remaining, full back Alan Hutton had his legs taken away while attempting a clearance. The Spanish referee blew his whistle and everyone was expecting a Scottish free kick. Incredibly, the official pointed to the penalty spot and Panucci put away the spot kick. It was one of the most ludicrous decisions in the history of Scotland matches. While in the event a draw would not have been enough, it left a bitter taste in the mouths of all who witnessed it.

Italy: Gianluigi Buffon; Christian Panucci, Fabio Cannavaro (captain), Andrea Barzagli, Gianluca Zambrotta; Mauro Camoranesi, Gennaro Gattuso, Andrea Pirlo, Massimo Ambrosini; Antonio Di Natale, Luca Toni. *Substitutes:* Vincenzo Iaquinta (for Di Natale 68); Giorgio Chiellini (for Camoranesi 83); Daniele De Rossi (for Gattuso 87). *Trainer:* Roberto Donadoni.

Scorers: Scotland: Ferguson 65   Italy: Toni 2; Panucci 90+1 (pen)

FIFA WORLD CUP QUALIFYING GROUP FIVE							
	P	W	D	L	F	A	Pts
Italy	12	9	2	1	22	9	29
France	12	8	2	2	25	5	26
Scotland	12	8	0	4	21	12	24
Ukraine	12	5	2	5	18	16	17
Lithuania	12	5	1	6	11	13	16
Georgia	12	3	1	8	16	19	10
Faroe Islands	12	0	0	12	4	43	0

26 March 2008   Friendly   Hampden Park   Attendance: 28,821

684 SCOTLAND 1, Croatia 1   *Referee: Terje Hauge (Norway)*

Scotland: Craig Gordon (Sunderland); Alan Hutton (Tottenham Hotspur), Gary Caldwell (Celtic), Stephen McManus (Celtic, captain), Gary Naysmith (Sheffield United); Shaun Maloney (Aston Villa), Scott Brown (Celtic), Darren Fletcher (Manchester United), Paul Hartley (Celtic); Steven Fletcher (Hibernian), Kenny Miller (Derby County). *Substitutes:* Gavin Rae (Cardiff City, for Steven Fletcher 46); Jay McEveley (Derby County, for Naysmith 62); Gary Teale (Plymouth Argyle, for Brown 66); Russell Anderson (Plymouth Argyle, for Caldwell 70); Kris Boyd (Rangers, for Maloney 72); Graham Alexander (Burnley, for Darren Fletcher 90). *Manager:* George Burley.

Croatia: Stipe Pletikosa; Vedran Corluka, Robert Kovac, Josip Simunic, Danijel Pranjic; Darijo Srna, Niko Kovac (captain), Luka Modric, Niko Kranjcar; Mladen Petric, Ivica Olic. *Substitutes:* Ognjen Vukojevic (for Kovac 46); Igor Budan (for Olic 57); Ivan Klasnic (for Petric 58); Jerko Leko (for Srna 63); Dario Knezevic (for Kovac 73); Dario Simic (for Corluka 85). *Coach:* Slaven Bilic.

Scorers: Croatia: Kranjcar 10   Scotland: Miller 30

30 May 2008 Friendly AXA Arena, Prague Attendance: 11,314

685 Czech Republic 3, SCOTLAND 1
Referee: Eric Braamhaar (Netherlands)

Scotland: Craig Gordon (Sunderland); Kevin McNaughton (Cardiff City), Gary Caldwell (Celtic), Stephen McManus (Celtic, captain), Gary Naysmith (Sheffield United); Gavin Rae (Cardiff City), Darren Fletcher (Manchester United), James Morrison (West Bromwich Albion), Paul Hartley (Celtic), Barry Robson (Celtic); Kenny Miller (Derby County). *Substitutes:* Christian Dailly (Rangers, for McManus 57); Shaun Maloney (Aston Villa, for Morrison 68); David Clarkson (Motherwell, for Rae 71); Ross McCormack (Motherwell, for Robson 82); Christophe Berra (Hearts, for McNaughton 90). *Manager:* George Burley.

Czech Republic: Petr Cech; Zdenek Pospech, Tomas Ujfalusi (captain), Radoslav Kovac, Marek Jankulovski; Jan Polak, Tomas Galasek; Libor Sionko, Marek Matejovsky, Rudolf Skacel; Jan Koller. *Substitutes:* David Rozehnal (for Ujfalusi 46); Michal Kadlec (for Jankulovski 46); David Jarolim (for Matejovsky 46); Jaroslav Plasil (for Skacel 46); Vaclav Sverkos (for Koller 46); Tomas Sivok (for Pospech 74). *Coach:* Karel Bruckner.

Scorers: Czech Republic: Sionko 60, 90; Kadlec 84 Scotland: Clarkson 85

20 August 2008 Friendly Hampden Park Attendance: 28,072

686 SCOTLAND 0, Northern Ireland 0
Referee: Nicolai Vollquartz (Denmark)

Scotland: Craig Gordon (Sunderland); Graham Alexander (Burnley), David Weir (Rangers), Stephen McManus (Celtic, captain), Gary Naysmith (Sheffield United); Scott Brown (Celtic), Darren Fletcher (Manchester United), James Morrison (West Bromwich Albion), Kevin Thomson (Rangers); James McFadden (Birmingham City), Kenny Miller (Rangers). *Substitutes:* Allan McGregor (Rangers, for Gordon 46); Barry Robson (Celtic, for Thomson 46); Darren Barr (Falkirk, for McManus 46); Kris Commons (Derby County, for Morrison 62); Michael Stewart (Hearts, for Fletcher 69); Christophe Berra (Hearts, for Weir 72). *Manager:* George Burley.

Northern Ireland: Maik Taylor; Chris Baird, Stephen Craigen, Gareth McAuley, Jonny Evans; Ryan McGivern, Sammy Clingan, Steven Davis, Chris Brunt; David Healy, Martin Paterson. *Substitutes:* Dean Shiels (for Paterson 46); Warren Feeney (for Brunt 55); Michael O'Connor (for Clingan 58); Michael Duff (for McAuley 76). *Manager:* Nigel Worthington.

6 September 2008 World Cup qualifying Gradski Stadion, Skopje Attendance: 9,000

687 FYR Macedonia 1, SCOTLAND 0
Referee: Pavel Kralovec (Czech Republic)

Scotland: Craig Gordon (Sunderland); Graham Alexander (Burnley), Gary Caldwell (Celtic), Stephen McManus (Celtic, captain), Gary Naysmith (Sheffield United); Scott Brown (Celtic), Darren Fletcher (Manchester United), Paul Hartley (Celtic), Barry Robson (Celtic); James McFadden (Birmingham City), Kenny Miller (Rangers). *Substitutes:* Kris Commons (Derby County, for Hartley 66); Shaun Maloney (Celtic, for Robson 76); Kris Boyd (Rangers, for Miller 81). *Manager:* George Burley.

FYR Macedonia: Petar Milosevski; Nikolce Noveski, Igor Mitreski, Goce Sedloski (captain); Vlade Lazarevski, Vlatko Grozdanovski, Velice Sumulikoski, Robert Petrov; Goran Maznov, Ilco Naumoski, Goran Pandev. *Substitutes:* Vanco Trajanov (for Naumoski 69); Boban Grncarov (for Petrov 79); Darko Tasevski (for Pandev 83). *Coach:* Srecko Katanec.

Scorer: FYR Macedonia: Naumoski 5

10 September 2008 World Cup qualifying Laugardalsvollur, Reykjavik Attendance: 9,764

688 Iceland 1, SCOTLAND 2
Referee: Serge Gumienny (Belgium)

Scotland: Craig Gordon (Sunderland); Kirk Broadfoot (Rangers), Gary Caldwell (Celtic), Stephen McManus (Celtic, captain), Gary Naysmith (Sheffield United); Scott Brown (Celtic), Darren Fletcher (Manchester United), Barry Robson (Celtic), Kris Commons (Derby County); James McFadden (Birmingham City), Shaun Maloney (Celtic). *Substitutes:* Kenny Miller (Rangers, for Commons 62); Graham Alexander (Burnley, for Maloney 78); Paul Hartley (Celtic, for McFadden 80). *Manager:* George Burley.

Iceland: Kjartan Sturluson; Birkir Saevarsson, Kristjan Sigurdsson, Hermann Hreidarsson (captain), Bjarni Eiriksson; Gretar Steinsson, Aron Gunnarsson, Stefan Gislason, Emil Hallfredsson; Eidur Gudjohnsen, Heidar Helguson. *Substitutes:* Indridi Sugurdsson (for Eiriksson 46); Palmi Palmason (for Aron Gunnarsson 64); Veigar Gunnarsson (for Saevarsson 78). *Coach:* Olafur Johannesson.

Scorers: Scotland: Broadfoot 19; McFadden 59 Iceland: Gudjohnsen 77 (pen)

11 October 2008 World Cup qualifying Hampden Park Attendance: 50,205

689 SCOTLAND 0, Norway 0
Referee: Massimo Busacca (Switzerland)

Scotland: Craig Gordon (Sunderland); Kirk Broadfoot (Rangers), David Weir (Rangers), Gary Caldwell (Celtic), Gary Naysmith (Sheffield United); Scott Brown (Celtic), Darren Fletcher (Manchester United, captain), James Morrison (West Bromwich Albion), Barry Robson (Celtic); James McFadden (Birmingham City), Shaun Maloney (Celtic). *Substitutes:* Chris Iwelumo (Wolverhampton Wanderers, for McFadden 54); Steven Fletcher (Hibernian, for Morrison 56). *Manager:* George Burley.

Norway: Jon Knudsen; Jon Inge Hoiland, Kjetil Waehler, Brede Hangeland (captain), John Arne Riise; Bjorn Helge Riise, Fredrik Winsnes, Christian Grindheim, Fredrik Stromstad; Steffen Iversen, John Carew. *Substitutes:* Daniel Braaten (for Bjorn Helge Riise 56); Morten Gamst Pedersen (for Stromstad 76). *Coach:* Age Hareide.

19 November 2008 Friendly Hampden Park Attendance: 32,492

690 SCOTLAND 0, Argentina 1
Referee: Felix Brych (Germany)

Scotland: Allan McGregor (Rangers); Alan Hutton (Tottenham Hotspur), Gary Caldwell (Celtic), Stephen McManus (Celtic), Kirk Broadfoot (Rangers); Scott Brown (Celtic), Barry Ferguson (Rangers, captain), Paul Hartley (Celtic), Kris Commons (Derby County); Chris Iwelumo (Wolverhampton Wanderers), James McFadden (Birmingham City). *Substitutes:* Lee Miller (Aberdeen, for Iwelumo 46); Shaun Maloney (Celtic, for Hartley 59); Scott Robertson (Dundee United, for Ferguson 59); David Clarkson (Motherwell, for McFadden 67); Christophe Berra (Hearts, for McManus 75); Graham Alexander (Burnley, for Brown 83). *Manager:* George Burley.

Argentina: Juan Pablo Carriza; Javier Zanetti, Martin Demichelis, Gabriel Heinze, Emiliano Papa; Maxi Rodriguez, Fernando Gago, Javier Mascherano (captain), Jonas Gutierrez; Carlos Tevez, Ezequiel Lavezzi. *Substitutes:* Lucho Gonzalez (for Gutierrez 71); German Denis (for Lavezzi 75); Daniel "Cata" Diaz (for Papa 86); Jose Ernesto Sosa (for Rodriquez 90+1). *Coach:* Diego Maradona.

Scorer: Argentina: Rodriguez 8

28 March 2009   World Cup qualifying   Amsterdam Arena   Attendance: 49,552

691 Netherlands 3, SCOTLAND 0
Referee: Laurent Duhamel (France)

Scotland: Allan McGregor (Rangers); Graham Alexander (Burnley), Gary Caldwell (Celtic), Christophe Berra (Wolverhampton Wanderers), Gary Naysmith (Sheffield United); Gary Teale (Derby County), Scott Brown (Celtic), Darren Fletcher (Manchester United), Barry Ferguson (Rangers, captain), Ross McCormack (Cardiff City); Kenny Miller (Rangers). *Substitutes:* Steven Fletcher (Hibernian, for Miller 71); Alan Hutton (Tottenham Hotspur, for Alexander 73); James Morrison (West Bromwich Albion, for Teale 85). *Manager:* George Burley.

Netherlands: Maarten Stekelenburg; Gregory van der Wiel, Andre Ooijer, Joris Mathijsen, Giovanni van Bronckhurst (captain); Mark van Bommel, Nigel de Jong, Dirk Kuyt, Arjen Robben; Robin van Persie, Klaas-Jan Huntelaar. *Substitutes:* Wesley Sneijder (for van Persie 65); Stijn Schaars (for de Jong 80); Ibrahim Afellay (for Huntelaar 80). *Coach:* Bert van Marwijk.

Scorers: Netherlands: Huntelaar 30; van Persie 45+1; Kuyt 77 (pen)

1 April 2009   World Cup qualifying   Hampden Park   Attendance: 42,259

692 SCOTLAND 2, Iceland 1
Referee: Thomas Einwaller (Austria)

Scotland: Craig Gordon (Sunderland); Alan Hutton (Tottenham Hotspur), Gary Caldwell (Celtic), Stephen McManus (Celtic, captain), Gary Naysmith (Sheffield United); Ross McCormack (Cardiff City), Scott Brown (Celtic), Darren Fletcher (Manchester United), James Morrison (West Bromwich Albion); Kenny Miller (Rangers), Steven Fletcher (Hibernian). *Substitutes:* Gary Teale (Derby County, for Steven Fletcher 78); Gavin Rae (Cardiff City, for Morrison 90). *Manager:* George Burley.

Iceland: Gunnleifur Gunnleifsson; Gretar Steinsson, Kristjan Sigurdsson, Hermann Hreidarsson (captain), Bjarni Eiriksson; Palmi Palmason, Aron Gunnarsson, Helgi Danielsson, Indridi Sigurdsson; Eidur Gudjohnsen, Arnor Smarason. *Substitutes:* Eggert Jonsson (for Gunnarsson 70); Armann Bjornsson (for Indridi Sigurdsson 81). *Coach:* Olafur Johannesson.

Scorers: Scotland: McCormack 39; Steven Fletcher 65   Iceland: Indridi Sigurdsson 54

12 August 2009   World Cup qualifying   Ullevaal Stadion, Oslo   Attendance: 24,493

693 Norway 4, SCOTLAND 0
Referee: Alain Hamer (Luxembourg)

Scotland: David Marshall (Cardiff City); Alan Hutton (Tottenham Hotspur), Gary Caldwell (Celtic), Steven Caldwell (Burnley), Callum Davidson (Preston North End); Graham Alexander (Burnley), Scott Brown (Celtic), Darren Fletcher (Manchester United, captain), Kris Commons (Derby County); Ross McCormack (Cardiff City), Kenny Miller (Rangers). *Substitutes:* Christophe Berra (Wolverhampton Wanderers, for McCormack 37); James McFadden (Birmingham City, for Steven Caldwell 48); Steven Whittaker (Rangers, for Berra 79). *Manager:* George Burley.

Norway: Jon Knudsen; Tom Hogni, Kjetil Waehler, Brede Hangeland (captain), John Arne Riise; Bjorn Helge Riise, Christian Grindheim, Magne Hoseth, Morten Gamst Pedersen; Erik Huseklepp, John Carew. *Substitutes:* Steffen Iversen (for Huseklepp 76); Per Ciljan Skjelbred (for Bjorn Helge Riise 84); Thorstein Helstad (for Carew 84). *Coach:* Egil Olsen.

Scorers: Norway: John Arne Riise 35; Pedersen 45, 90; Huseklepp 60

5 September 2009   World Cup qualifying   Hampden Park   Attendance: 50,214

694 SCOTLAND 2, FYR Macedonia 0
Referee: Wolfgang Stark (Germany)

Scotland: Craig Gordon (Sunderland); Alan Hutton (Tottenham Hotspur), David Weir (Rangers), Stephen McManus (Celtic), Callum Davidson (Preston North End); Graham Alexander (Burnley), Scott Brown (Celtic), Darren Fletcher (Manchester United, captain), James McFadden (Birmingham City); Steven Fletcher (Burnley), Kenny Miller (Rangers). *Substitutes:* Steven Whittaker (Rangers, for Davidson 14); Shaun Maloney (Celtic, for Steven Fletcher 68); Paul Hartley (Bristol City, for Brown 73). *Manager:* George Burley.

FYR Macedonia: Jane Nikoloski; Nikolce Noveski, Igor Mitreski, Goce Sedloski (captain), Goran Popov; Aco Stojkov, Velice Sumulikoski, Filip Despotovski, Slavco Georgievski, Ilco Naumoski; Goran Pandev. *Substitutes:* Darko Tasevski (for Naumoski 64); Vlatko Grozdanoski (for Georgievski 69); Besart Ibraimi (for Stojkov 80). *Coach:* Mirsad Jonuz.

Scorers: Scotland: Brown 56; McFadden 80

Scott Brown celebrates with team mates (from left) Graham Alexander, Kenny Miller, Darren Fletcher and Steven Whittaker after scoring against FYR Macedonia.

9 September 2009   World Cup qualifying   Hampden Park   Attendance: 51,230

695 SCOTLAND 0, Netherlands 1
Referee: Claus Bo Larsen (Denmark)

Scotland (4-4-2):

4   David Marshall (Cardiff City);
13 Alan Hutton (Tottenham Hotspur)
65 David Weir (Rangers)
20 Stephen McManus (Celtic)
3   Steven Whittaker (Rangers);
24 Paul Hartley (Bristol City)
19 Scott Brown (Celtic)
45 Darren Fletcher (Manchester United, captain)
17 Shaun Maloney (Celtic);
2   Steven Naismith (Rangers)
45 Kenny Miller (Rangers)

Substitutes: 6 Kris Commons (Derby County, for Hartley 66);
16 Garry O'Connor (Birmingham City, for Maloney 83)

Manager: George Burley

Netherlands: Michel Vorm; Gregory van der Wiel, Andre Ooijer, Joris Mathijsen, Demy de Zeeuw, Giovanni van Bronckhurst (captain); Nigel de Jong, Wesley Sneijder; Dirk Kuyt, Robin van Persie, Arjen Robben. *Substitutes:* Eljero Elia (for Robben 72); Rafael van der Vaart (for Sneijder 77); Klaas-Jan Huntelaar (for van Persie 84). *Manager:* Bert van Marwijk.

Scorer: Netherlands: Elia 81

One of the best performances under manager George Burley was sadly not enough to salvage any hopes of making it to another World Cup. The Scots had more than enough opportunities to record a victory but were unable to take any of them and were dealt a sucker punch nine minutes from the end when Dutch substitute Elia got the only goal of the game. There was a tremendous display from Darren Fletcher in midfield, the Manchester United player working hard up and down the field in one of his best games for his country. He was ably backed by keeper David Marshall, who made a string of fine saves, and Steven Naismith up front who was unlucky not to equalise with virtually the last kick of the match.

FIFA WORLD CUP QUALIFYING GROUP NINE

	P	W	D	L	F	A	Pts
Netherlands	8	8	0	0	17	2	24
Norway	8	2	4	2	9	7	10
Scotland	8	3	1	4	6	11	10
Macedonia	8	2	1	5	5	11	7
Iceland	8	1	2	5	7	13	5

---

10 October 2009   Friendly   Nissan Stadium, Yokohama   Attendance: 61,285

696 Japan 2, SCOTLAND 0
Referee: Kim Sang-Woo (South Korea)

Scotland: Craig Gordon (Sunderland); Steven Whittaker (Rangers), Christophe Berra (Wolverhampton Wanderers), Gary Caldwell (Celtic), Stephen McManus (Celtic, captain), Lee Wallace (Hearts); Ross Wallace (Preston North End), Charlie Adam (Blackpool), Graham Dorrans (West Bromwich Albion), Craig Conway (Dundee United); Lee Miller (Aberdeen). *Substitutes:* Steven Fletcher (Burnley, for Miller 46); Don Cowie (Watford, for Wallace 46); Stephen Hughes (Norwich City, for Adam 67); Derek Riordan (Hibernian, for Conway 74). *Manager:* George Burley.

Japan: Eiji Kawashima; Atsuto Uchida, Yuki Abe, Daiki Iwamasa, Yasuyuki Konno; Hideo Hashimoto, Junichi Inamoto (captain); Naohiro Ishikawa, Kengo Nakamura, Keisuke Honda; Ryoichi Maeda. *Substitutes:* Takayuki Morimoto (for Maeda 56); Yuhei Tokunaga (for Uchida 65); Yoshito Okubo (for Hashimoto 65); Daisuke Matsui (for Ishikawa 65); Yuichi Komano (for Inamoto 81). *Coach:* Takeshi Okada.

Scorers: Japan: Berra 82 (own goal); Honda 90+1

---

14 November 2009   Friendly   Cardiff City Stadium   Attendance: 13,844

697 Wales 3, SCOTLAND 0
Referee: Cyril Zimmermann (Switzerland)

Scotland: David Marshall (Cardiff City); Alan Hutton (Tottenham Hotspur), Gary Caldwell (Celtic), Stephen McManus (Celtic), Danny Fox (Celtic); Don Cowie (Watford), Darren Fletcher (Manchester United, captain), Graham Dorrans (West Bromwich Albion), James McFadden (Birmingham City); Steven Naismith (Rangers), Kenny Miller (Rangers). *Substitutes:* Lee Wallace (Hearts, for Fox 55); Steven Fletcher (Burnley, for Miller 55); Ross McCormack (Cardiff City, for McFadden 62); Kevin Kyle (Kilmarnock, for Naismith 62); Barry Robson (Celtic, for Dorrans 71); Derek Riordan (Hibernian, for Cowie 78). *Manager:* George Burley.

Wales: Wayne Hennessey; Samuel Ricketts, Ashley Williams (captain), Craig Morgan, Lewin Nyatanga, Gareth Bale; Aaron Ramsey, David Edwards, Joe Ledley; Simon Church, Ched Evans. *Substitutes:* Sam Vokes (for Church 46); Robert Earnshaw (for Evans 46); Joe Allen (for Ramsey 56); Daniel Gabbidon (for Nyatanga 60); Andy King (for Ledley 79); David Cotterill (for Edwards 86). *Manager:* John Toshack.

Scorers: Wales: Edwards 17; Church 32; Ramsey 35

CHAPTER NINE
2010-2019

3 March 2010　　　Friendly　　　　　　　　Hampden Park　　　　　　　　Attendance: 26,530

698　SCOTLAND 1, Czech Republic 0　　　*Referee: Fredy Fautrel (France)*

Scotland: Craig Gordon (Sunderland); Alan Hutton (Sunderland), Gary Caldwell (Wigan Athletic), Andy Webster (Dundee United), Lee Wallace (Hearts); Barry Robson (Middlesbrough), Darren Fletcher (Manchester United, captain), Graham Dorrans (West Bromwich Albion), Scott Brown (Celtic), Kevin Thomson (Rangers); Kenny Miller (Rangers). *Substitutes:* Paul Hartley (Bristol City, for Thomson 46); Christophe Berra (Wolverhampton Wanderers, for Webster 46); Kris Boyd (Rangers, for Miller 63); Charlie Adam (Blackpool, for Robson 69); Steven Whittaker (Rangers, for Fletcher 83). *Manager:* Craig Levein.

Czech Republic: Jaroslav Drobny; Ondrej Kusnir, Tomas Sivok, Roman Hubnik, Michal Kadlec; Jaroslav Plasil, Mario Holek, Tomas Hubschman, Tomas Rosicky (captain); Tomas Necid, Vaclav Sverkos. *Substitutes:* Rudolf Skacel (for Rosicky 67); Jan Blazek (for Necid 67); Michal Papadopulos (for Sverkos 67); Jan Moravek (for Plasil 79); Jan Rajnoch (for Hubschman 79); Daniel Pudil (for Kusnir 87). *Coach:* Michal Bilek.

Scorer: Scotland: Brown 62

11 August 2010　　　Friendly　　　　　　　　Raasunda, Solna　　　　　　　　Attendance: 25,249

699　Sweden 3, SCOTLAND 0　　　*Referee: Gianluca Rocchi (Italy)*

Scotland: Allan McGregor (Rangers); Kirk Broadfoot (Rangers), Gary Kenneth (Dundee United), Christophe Berra (Wolverhampton Wanderers), Lee Wallace (Hearts); Barry Robson (Middlesbrough), Darren Fletcher (Manchester United, captain), Charlie Adam (Blackpool), Kevin Thomson (Middlesbrough); James McFadden (Birmingham City), Steven Fletcher (Wolverhampton Wanderers). *Substitutes:* Scott Robertson (Dundee United, for Thomson 54); Kris Boyd (Middlesbrough, for Fletcher 64); James Morrison (West Bromwich Albion, for Adam 64); Steven Whittaker (Rangers, for Broadfoot 75); Chris Iwelumo (Burnley, for Robson 78). *Manager:* Craig Levein.

Sweden: Andreas Isaksson; Mikael Lustig, Olof Mellberg, Daniel Majstorovic, Behrang Safari; Anders Svensson, Pontus Wernbloom, Johan Elmander, Ola Toivonen, Emir Bajrami; Zlatan Ibrahimovic (captain). *Substitutes:* Sebastian Larsson (for Lustig 46); Kim Kallstrom (for Wernbloom 46); Tobias Hysen (for Ibrahimovic 59); Christian Wilhelmsson (for Bajrami 64); Oscar Wendt (for Svensson 73); Marcus Berg (for Elmander 78). *Coach:* Erik Hamren.

Scorers: Sweden: Ibrahimovic 4; Bajrami 39; Toivonen 56

3 September 2010　　　European Championship qualifying　　　Dariaus ir Gireno, Kaunas　　　Attendance: 6,539

700　Lithuania 0, SCOTLAND 0　　　*Referee: Cuneyt Cakir (Turkey)*

Scotland: Allan McGregor (Rangers); Alan Hutton (Tottenham Hotspur), David Weir (Rangers), Stephen McManus (Middlesbrough), Steven Whittaker (Rangers); Lee McCulloch (Rangers), Scott Brown (Celtic), Darren Fletcher (Manchester United, captain), Barry Robson (Middlesbrough); Steven Naismith (Rangers), Kenny Miller (Rangers). *Substitutes:* James McFadden (Birmingham City, for Robson 69); James Morrison (West Bromwich Albion, for Brown 76); Christophe Berra (Wolverhampton Wanderers, for Whittaker 90). *Manager:* Craig Levein.

Lithuania: Zydrunas Karcemarskas; Ramunas Radavicius, Tadas Kijanskas, Andrius Skerla, Marius Stankevicius; Deividas Semberas, Mindaugas Panka, Edgaras Cesnauskis, Saulius Mikoliunas; Darvydas Sernas, Tomas Danilevicius (captain). *Substitutes:* Robertas Poskus (for Mikoliunas 71); Vytautas Luksa (for Sernas 80); Kestutis Ivaskevicius (for Danilevicius 90). *Coach:* Raimondas Zutautas.

7 September 2010　　　European Championship qualifying　　　Hampden Park　　　　Attendance: 37,050

701　SCOTLAND 2, Liechtenstein 1　　　*Referee: Viktor Shvetsov (Ukraine)*

Scotland: Allan McGregor (Rangers); Alan Hutton (Tottenham Hotspur), David Weir (Rangers), Stephen McManus (Middlesbrough), Lee Wallace (Hearts); Scott Brown (Celtic), *Darren Fletcher (Manchester United, captain), Lee McCulloch (Rangers), James McFadden (Birmingham City); Kenny Miller (Rangers), Kris Boyd (Middlesbrough). *Substitutes:* James Morrison (West Bromwich Albion, for McFadden 46); Barry Robson (Middlesbrough, for Wallace 54); Steven Naismith (Rangers, for Boyd 66). *Manager:* Craig Levein.

Liechtenstein: Peter Jehle; Yves Oehri, Martin Stocklasa, Michael Stocklasa, Martin Rechsteiner; Michele Polverino, Sandro Wieser; Philippe Erne, Mario Frick (captain), Franz Burgmeier; David Hasler. *Substitutes:* Ronny Buchel (for Wieser 71); Fabio D'Elia (for Frick 79); Nicolas Hasler (for David Hasler 90+2). *Coach:* Hans-Peter Zaugg.

Scorers: Liechtenstein: Frick 47　　　Scotland: Miller 63; McManus 90+7

*Darren Fletcher became the 26th player to reach 50 appearances, eventually finishing on 80 which made him Scotland's third most-capped player at the time of writing.

8 October 2010　　　European Championship qualifying　　　Synot Tip Arena, Prague　　　Attendance: 14,922

702　Czech Republic 1, SCOTLAND 0　　　*Referee: Ivan Bebec (Croatia)*

Scotland: Allan McGregor (Rangers); Alan Hutton (Tottenham Hotspur), David Weir (Rangers), Stephen McManus (Middlesbrough), Steven Whittaker (Rangers); Jamie Mackie (Queens Park Rangers), James Morrison (West Bromwich Albion), Gary Caldwell (Wigan Athletic), Darren Fletcher (Manchester United, captain), Graham Dorrans (West Bromwich Albion), Steven Naismith (Rangers). *Substitutes:* Kenny Miller (Rangers, for Caldwell 76); Chris Iwelumo (Burnley, for Mackie 76); Barry Robson (Middlesbrough, for Morrison 84). *Manager:* Craig Levein.

Czech Republic: Petr Cech; Zdenek Pospech, Marek Suchy, Roman Hubnik, Michal Kadlec; Jaroslav Plasil, Tomas Hubschman, Jan Polak, Tomas Rosicky (captain); Tomas Necid, Lukas Magera. *Substitutes:* Roman Bednar (for Magera 59); Mario Holek (for Necid 84); Jan Rajnoch (for Plasil 90+4). *Coach:* Michal Bilek.

Scorer: Czech Republic: Hubnik 69

| 12 October 2010 | European Championship qualifying | Hampden Park | Attendance: 51,322 |

703 SCOTLAND 2, Spain 3

Referee: Massimo Busacca (Switzerland)

Scotland (4-4-2):
9 Allan McGregor (Rangers);
1 Phil Bardsley (Sunderland)
69 David Weir (Rangers)
26 Stephen McManus (Middlesbrough)
9 Steven Whittaker (Rangers);
5 Graham Dorrans (West Bromwich Albion)
52 Darren Fletcher (Manchester United, captain)
10 James Morrison (West Bromwich Albion)
18 Lee McCulloch (Rangers);
7 Steven Naismith (Rangers)
51 Kenny Miller (Rangers)

The previous game, a narrow defeat in Prague, had seen manager Craig Levein ridiculed for announcing he would go in with a 4-6 formation and no designated forwards. This time round it was a braver 4-4-2 against the world champions, and Levein's men could consider themselves unlucky not to take a point. Spain led at half-time through David Villa's penalty, and Andres Iniesta increased the lead 10 minutes after the interval. That was the signal for the Scots to come roaring back, influenced by substitute Charlie Adam who had a fine match. Steven Naismith headed home in the 58th minute and when Gerard Pique put through his own goal shortly after the supporters began to sense an upset might just be on the cards. It was not to be, however, and Spanish replacement Fernando Llorente nodded in the winner.

Substitutes: 6 Charlie Adam (Blackpool, for McCulloch 46);
2 Jamie Mackie (Queens Park Rangers, for Dorrans 80);
18 Shaun Maloney (Celtic, for Morrison 88)

Manager: Craig Levein

Spain: Iker Casillas (captain); Sergio Ramos, Gerard Pique, Carles Puyol, Joan Capdevila; Xabi Alonso, Sergio Busquets, Andres Iniesta, Santi Cazorla, David Silva; David Villa. *Substitutes:* Pablo Hernandez (for Cazorla 70); Fernando Llorente (for Silva 76); Carlos Marchena (for Busquets 90). *Coach:* Vicente del Bosque.

Scorers: Spain: Villa 44 (pen); Iniesta 55; Llorente 79   Scotland: Naismith 58; Pique 66 (own goal)

| 16 November 2010 | Friendly | Pittodrie, Aberdeen | Attendance: 10,873 |

704 SCOTLAND 3, Faroe Islands 0

Referee: Pol van Boekel (Netherlands)

Scotland: Craig Gordon (Sunderland); Phil Bardsley (Sunderland), Steven Caldwell (Wigan Athletic), Danny Wilson (Liverpool), Stephen Crainey (Blackpool); Kris Commons (Derby County), Barry Bannan (Aston Villa), Darren Fletcher (Manchester United, captain), Charlie Adam (Blackpool); Shaun Maloney (Celtic), Jamie Mackie (Queens Park Rangers). *Substitutes:* James McArthur (Wigan Athletic, for Adam 55); Garry Kenneth (Dundee United, for Wilson 61); Cammy Bell (Kilmarnock, for Gordon 68); Craig Bryson (Kilmarnock, for Fletcher 68); Steven Saunders (Motherwell, for Bardsley 71); David Goodwillie (Dundee United, for Commons 76). *Manager:* Craig Levein.

Faroe Islands: Gunnar Nielsen; Jonas Tor Naes, Johan Davidsen, Erling Jacobsen, Atli Gregersen (captain); Jann Ingi Petersen; Daniel Udsen, Bogi Lokin, Joan Simun Edmundsson; Christian Holst, Hjalgrim Elttor. *Substitutes:* Rogvi Poulsen (for Holst 56); Christian Mouritsen (for Petersen 60); Tordur Thomsen (for Nielsen 68); Levi Hanssen (for Lokin 78); Pol Johannus Justinussen (for Udsen 86). *Coach:* Brian Kerr (Republic of Ireland).

Scorers: Scotland: Wilson 24; Commons 31; Mackie 45

| 9 February 2011 | Nations Cup | Aviva Stadium, Dublin | Attendance: 18,742 |

705 Northern Ireland 0, SCOTLAND 3

Referee: Tomas Connolly (Republic of Ireland)

Scotland: Allan McGregor (Rangers); Alan Hutton (Tottenham Hotspur), Steven Caldwell (Wigan Athletic), Christophe Berra (Wolverhampton Wanderers), Phil Bardsley (Sunderland); Kris Commons (Celtic), James McArthur (Wigan Athletic), James Morrison (West Bromwich Albion), Charlie Adam (Blackpool); Steven Naismith (Rangers), Kenny Miller (Bursaspor, captain). *Substitutes:* Barry Bannan (Aston Villa, for Adam 57); Mark Wilson (Celtic, for Bardsley 57); Robert Snodgrass (Leeds United, for Naismith 58); Craig Conway (Dundee United, for Commons 72); Chris Maguire (Aberdeen, for Morrison 79); Danny Wilson (Liverpool, for Miller 90). *Manager:* Craig Levein.

Northern Ireland: Jonathan Tuffey; Rory McArdle, Stephen Craigan (captain), Gareth McAuley, Chris Baird; Corry Evans, Steven Davis, Grant McCann, Niall McGinn; Rory Patterson, Paddy McCourt. *Substitutes:* Lee Hodson (for McArdle 46); David Healy (for McCann 46); Oliver Norwood (for Davis 58); Adam Thompson (for Craigan 66); Liam Boyce (for McGinn 72). *Manager:* Nigel Worthington.

Scorers: Scotland: Miller 19; McArthur 32; Commons 51

| 27 March 2011 | Friendly | Emirates Stadium, London | Attendance: 53,087 |

706 SCOTLAND 0, Brazil 2

Referee: Howard Webb (England)

Scotland: Allan McGregor (Rangers); Alan Hutton (Tottenham Hotspur), Gary Caldwell (Wigan Athletic), Christophe Berra (Wolverhampton Wanderers), Stephen Crainey (Blackpool); Scott Brown (Celtic), James McArthur (Wigan Athletic), James Morrison (West Bromwich Albion), Charlie Adam (Blackpool), Steven Whittaker (Rangers); Kenny Miller (Bursaspor, captain). *Substitutes:* Barry Bannan (Leeds United, for McArthur 57); Kris Commons (Celtic, for Whittaker 65); Danny Wilson (Liverpool, for Berra 73); Robert Snodgrass (Leeds United, for Adam 78); Craig Mackail-Smith (Peterborough United, for Miller 86); Don Cowie (Watford, for Morrison 90+2). *Manager:* Craig Levein.

Brazil: Julio Cesar; Dani Alves, Lucio (captain), Thiago Silva, Andre Santos; Lucas Leiva, Ramires, Elano, Jadson; Neymar, Leandro Damiao. *Substitutes:* Lucas Moura (for Jadson 72); Jonas Oliveira (for Leandro Damiao 79); Elias (for Elano 83); Sandro (for Lucas Leiva 86); Renato Augusto (for Neymar 90). *Coach:* Mano Menezes.

Scorer: Brazil: Neymar 43, 77 (pen)

Chapter nine: 2010-2019

25 May 2011 Nations Cup Aviva Stadium, Dublin Attendance: 3,951

707 Wales 1, SCOTLAND 3
Referee: Raymond Crangle (Northern Ireland)

Scotland (4-4-2):
12 Allan McGregor (Rangers);
11 Steven Whittaker (Rangers)
40 Gary Caldwell (Wigan Athletic)
12 Christophe Berra (Wolverhampton Wanderers)
9 Stephen Crainey (Blackpool);
24 Scott Brown (Celtic)
13 James Morrison (West Bromwich Albion)
10 Charlie Adam (Blackpool)
6 Ross McCormack (Leeds United);
9 Steven Naismith (Rangers)
54 Kenny Miller (Bursaspor, captain)

When Robert Earnshaw, who had been a serious annoyance to the Scots in recent matches, scored in the 36th minute the fans could have been forgiven for thinking "Oh no, here we go again." But a rousing second half display led to a deserved victory. James Morrison and Christophe Berra both got their first international goals, either side of Kenny Miller's 14th strike for his country. Apart from the scorers other standouts were right back Steven Whittaker and striker Steven Naismith. It was the second match of the new Nations Cup competition, also involving Northern Ireland and first hosts the Republic of Ireland. The intention was for the tournament to take place every two years, with a different host each time, but poor attendance at the inaugural event meant it was discontinued.

Substitutes: 13 Barry Robson (Middlesbrough, for Morrison 74);
4 Barry Bannan (Aston Villa, for McCormack 74); 4 Phil Bardsley (Sunderland, for Whittaker 80);
1 Russell Martin (Norwich City, for Crainey 81); 1 Grant Hanley (Blackburn Rovers, for Caldwell 86);
4 James McArthur (Wigan Athletic, for Adam 88)

Manager: Craig Levein

Wales: Glyn "Boaz" Myhill; Neal Eardley, Darcy Blake, Craig Morgan, Neil Taylor; Andy King, Andy Dorman, Owain Tudor Jones; Jermaine Easter, Robert Earnshaw (captain), Sam Vokes. *Substitutes:* Chris Gunter (for Taylor 46); Adam Matthews (for Eardley 61); Aaron Ramsey (for King 61); David Cotterill (for Dorman 61); David Vaughan (for Tudor Jones 72); Steven Morison (for Vokes 73). *Manager:* Gary Speed.

CARLING NATIONS CUP

	P	W	D	L	F	A	Pts
Republic of Ireland	3	3	0	0	9	0	9
Scotland	3	2	0	1	6	2	6
Wales	3	1	0	2	3	6	3
Northern Ireland	3	0	0	3	0	10	0

Scorers: Wales: Earnshaw 36 Scotland: Morrison 56; Miller 65; Berra 71

29 May 2011 Nations Cup Aviva Stadium, Dublin Attendance: 17,694

708 Republic of Ireland 1, SCOTLAND 0
Referee: Mark Whitby (Wales)

Scotland: Allan McGregor (Rangers); Steven Whittaker (Rangers), Grant Hanley (Norwich City), Christophe Berra (Wolverhampton Wanderers), Phil Bardsley (Sunderland); James Forrest (Celtic), Scott Brown (Celtic), Charlie Adam (Blackpool), Barry Robson (Middlesbrough); Steven Naismith (Rangers), Kenny Miller (Bursaspor, captain). *Substitutes:* Barry Bannan (Aston Villa, for Adam 63); Chris Maguire (Aberdeen, for Robson 75); Ross McCormack (Leeds United, for Forrest 85). *Manager:* Craig Levein.

Republic of Ireland: Shay Given; Paul McShane, Darren O'Dea, Stephen Kelly, Stephen Ward; Liam Lawrence, Keith Andrews, Keith Fahey, Stephen Hunt; Robbie Keane (captain), Simon Cox. *Substitutes:* Seamus Coleman (for Lawrence 62); Kevin Foley (for O'Dea 66); Keith Treacy (for Keane 83). *Manager:* Giovanni Trapattoni (Italy).

Scorer: Republic of Ireland: Keane 23

10 August 2011 Friendly Hampden Park Attendance: 17,582

709 SCOTLAND 2, Denmark 1
Referee: Marco Borg (Malta)

Scotland: Allan McGregor (Rangers); Phil Bardsley (Sunderland), Gary Caldwell (Wigan Athletic), Danny Wilson (Liverpool), Stephen Crainey (Blackpool); Robert Snodgrass (Leeds United), Scott Brown (Celtic), James Morrison (West Bromwich Albion), Charlie Adam (Liverpool); Steven Naismith (Rangers), Kenny Miller (Cardiff City, captain). *Substitutes:* Don Cowie (Cardiff City, for Brown 19); Craig Mackail-Smith (Brighton & Hove Albion, for Miller 57); Graham Dorrans (West Bromwich Albion, for Adam 58); Barry Bannan (Aston Villa, for Morrison 67); James Forrest (Celtic, for Naismith 74); Grant Hanley (Blackburn Rovers, for Snodgrass 88). *Manager:* Craig Levein.

Denmark: Thomas Sorensen; Simon Kjaer, Daniel Agger, Nicolai Boilesen, Lars Jacobsen; Christian Poulsen (captain), William Kvist, Christian Eriksen, Michael Krohn-Dehli; Dennis Rommedahl, Nicklas Bendtner. *Substitutes:* Lasse Schone (for Poulsen 46); Niki Zimling (for Rommedahl 46); Nicklas Pedersen (for Bendtner 46); Mathias Jorgensen (for Agger 58); Michael Silberbauer (for Jacobsen 73); Bashkim Kadrii (for Krohn-Dehli 76). *Coach:* Morten Olsen.

Scorers: Scotland: Kvist 22 (own goal); Snodgrass 44 Denmark: Eriksen 31

3 September 2011 European Championship qualifying Hampden Park Attendance: 51,457

710 SCOTLAND 2, Czech Republic 2
Referee: Kevin Blom (Netherlands)

Scotland: Allan McGregor (Rangers); Alan Hutton (Aston Villa), Gary Caldwell (Wigan Athletic), Christophe Berra (Wolverhampton Wanderers), Phil Bardsley (Sunderland); Scott Brown (Celtic), Darren Fletcher (Manchester United, captain), James Morrison (West Bromwich Albion), Charlie Adam (Liverpool); Steven Naismith (Rangers), Kenny Miller (Cardiff City). *Substitutes:* Danny Wilson (Liverpool, for Bardsley 76); Don Cowie (Cardiff City, for Adam 79); Barry Robson (Middlesbrough, for Naismith 86). *Manager:* Craig Levein.

Czech Republic: Jan Lastuvka; Roman Hubnik, Jan Rajnoch, Tomas Sivok, Michal Kadlec; Milan Petrzela, Tomas Hubschman, Tomas Rosicky (captain), Jaroslav Plasil, Petr Jiracek; Milan Baros. *Substitutes:* Jan Rezek (for Petrzela 56); Tomas Pekhart (for Jiracek 77); Kamil Vacek (for Baros 90+2). *Coach:* Michal Bilek.

Scorers: Scotland: Miller 45; Fletcher 82 Czech Republic: Plasil 78; Kadlec 90 (pen)

6 September 2011   European Championship qualifying   Hampden Park   Attendance: 34,071

711 SCOTLAND 1, Lithuania 0
Referee: Kristinn Jakobsson (Iceland)

Scotland: Allan McGregor (Rangers); Steven Whittaker (Rangers), Gary Caldwell (Wigan Athletic), Christophe Berra (Wolverhampton Wanderers), Phil Bardsley (Sunderland); Barry Bannan (Aston Villa), Darren Fletcher (Manchester United, captain), James Morrison (West Bromwich Albion), Don Cowie (Cardiff City); Steven Naismith (Rangers), David Goodwillie (Blackburn Rovers). *Substitutes:* Stephen Crainey (Blackpool, for Bardsley 70); Graham Dorrans (West Bromwich Albion, for Morrison 79); Robert Snodgrass (Leeds United, for Bannan 84). *Manager:* Craig Levein.

Lithuania: Zydrunas Karcemarskas; Deividas Cesnauskas, Marius Zaliukas, Arunas Klimavicius, Tadas Kijanskas; Saulius Mikoliunas, Linas Pilibaitis, Deividas Semberas (captain), Ramunas Radavicius, Darvydas Sernas; Tadas Labukas. *Substitutes:* Arvydas Novikovas (for Labukas 46); Tomas Danilevicius (for Kijanskas 61); Ricardas Beniusis (for Mikoliunas 77). *Coach:* Raimondas Zutautas.

Scorer: Scotland: Naismith 50

8 October 2011   European Championship qualifying   Rheinpark Stadion, Vaduz   Attendance: 5,636

712 Liechtenstein 0, SCOTLAND 1
Referee: Tom Harald Hagen (Norway)

Scotland: Allan McGregor (Rangers); Alan Hutton (Aston Villa), Gary Caldwell (Wigan Athletic), Christophe Berra (Wolverhampton Wanderers), Phil Bardsley (Sunderland); Barry Bannan (Aston Villa), Darren Fletcher (Manchester United, captain), James Morrison (West Bromwich Albion), Charlie Adam (Liverpool); Steven Naismith (Rangers), Craig Mackail-Smith (Brighton & Hove Albion). *Substitutes:* James Forrest (Celtic, for Bannan 73); Don Cowie (Cardiff City, for Adam 76). *Manager:* Craig Levein.

Liechtenstein: Peter Jehle; Marco Ritzberger, Martin Stocklasa, Daniel Kaufmann, Martin Rechsteiner; Rony Hanselmann, Michele Polverino, Martin Buchel, Thomas Beck; Nicolas Hasler, Mario Frick (captain). *Substitutes:* Wolfgang Kieber (for Buchel 71); Lucas Eberle (for Hanselmann 75). *Coach:* Hans-Peter Zaugg.

Scorer: Scotland: Mackail-Smith 32

11 October 2011   European Championship qualifying   Estadio Perez, Alicante   Attendance: 27,559

713 Spain 3, SCOTLAND 1
Referee: Stefan Johannesson (Sweden)

Scotland (4-4-2):
- 18 Allan McGregor (Rangers);
- 23 Alan Hutton (Tottenham Hotspur)
- 45 Gary Caldwell (Wigan Athletic)
- 17 Christophe Berra (Wolverhampton Wanderers)
- 10 Phil Bardsley (Sunderland);
- 9 Barry Bannan (Aston Villa)
- 57 Darren Fletcher (Manchester United, captain)
- 18 James Morrison (West Bromwich Albion)
- 15 Charlie Adam (Liverpool);
- 15 Steven Naismith (Rangers)
- 4 Craig Mackail-Smith (Brighton & Hove Albion)

Substitutes: 3 David Goodwillie (Blackburn Rovers, for Bannan 63); 4 James Forrest (Celtic, for Adam 63); 8 Don Cowie (Cardiff City, for Fletcher 85)

Manager: Craig Levein

Spain: Victor Valdes; Sergio Ramos, Gerard Piquet, Carles Puyol, Jordi Alba; Xavi Hernandez, David Silva, Santi Cazorla, Sergio Busquets; Pedro, David Villa. *Substitutes:* Alvaro Arbeloa (for Puyol 46); Thiago Alcantara (for Silva 55); Fernando Llorente (for Xavi 62). *Manager:* Vicente del Bosque.

Scorers: Spain: Silva 6, 44; Villa 54   Scotland: Goodwillie 66 (pen)

A classy Spanish team dealt ruthlessly with Scotland in Alicante, before a smallish crowd including a large number of tartan-clad fans. The game was basically over by half-time after David Silva had scored twice and David Villa put any doubt to bed with a third in the 54th minute. Scotland's consolation, if there was one, came when David Goodwillie converted a penalty midway through the second half. There was still a mathematical chance of a play-off place as runners-up if Lithuania could get a result against the Czech Republic, but that was never realistically going to happen. The seeds of a miserable campaign had been sown in Lithuania the previous year when the Scots could only muster a 0-0 draw, and in Prague where a strange 4-6-0 formation was defeated 1-0 by a fairly unimpressive Czech side.

EUROPEAN CHAMPIONSHIP QUALIFYING GROUP I

	P	W	D	L	F	A	Pts
Spain	8	8	0	0	26	6	24
Czech Republic	8	4	1	3	12	8	13
Scotland	8	3	2	3	9	10	11
Lithuania	8	1	2	5	4	13	5
Liechtenstein	8	1	1	6	3	17	4

11 November 2011   Friendly   Stadio Papadopoulos, Larnaca   Attendance: 1,360

714 Cyprus 1, SCOTLAND 2
Referee: Meir Levi (Israel)

Scotland: Allan McGregor (Rangers); Steven Whittaker (Rangers), Gary Caldwell (Wigan Athletic), Christophe Berra (Wolverhampton Wanderers), Phil Bardsley (Sunderland); Don Cowie (Cardiff City), Darren Fletcher (Manchester United, captain), James Morrison (West Bromwich Albion), Barry Robson (Middlesbrough); Jamie Mackie (Queens Park Rangers), Kenny Miller (Cardiff City). *Substitutes:* James McArthur (Wigan Athletic, for Fletcher 63); Craig Mackail-Smith (Brighton & Hove Albion, for Miller 63); Stephen Crainey (Blackpool, for Bardsley 74); Craig Conway (Cardiff City, for Robson 80); Jordan Rhodes (Huddersfield Town, for Mackie 87). *Manager:* Craig Levein.

Cyprus: Antonis Giorgallidis; Jason Dimitriou, Stelios Parpas, Giorgos Merkis, Nektarios Alexandrou; Athos Solomou, Marinos Satsias, Sinisa Dobrasinovic, Andreas Avraam; Giorgos Efraim, Dimitris Christofi. *Substitutes:* Anastasios Kissas (for Giorgallidis 46); Valentinos Sielis (for Dimitriou 46); Nestoras Mytidis (for Avraam 46); Marios Nicolaou (for Parpas 58); Antonis Katsis (for Alexandrou 69); Giorgos Vasiliou (for Dobrasinovic 74). *Coach:* Nikos Nioplias.

Scorers: Scotland: Miller 24; Mackie 56   Cyprus: Christofi 59

Chapter nine: 2010-2019

29 February 2012　　Friendly　　　　　　　　Stadion Bonifika, Koper　　　　　　Attendance: 3,983

715 Slovenia 1, SCOTLAND 1　　　　　　　　　　　*Referee: Aleksandar Stavrev (FYR Macedonia)*

Scotland: Allan McGregor (Rangers); Russell Martin (Norwich City), Gary Caldwell (Wigan Athletic, captain), Christophe Berra (Wolverhampton Wanderers), Charlie Mulgrew (Celtic); James Forrest (Celtic), James McArthur (Wigan Athletic), James Morrison (West Bromwich Albion), Charlie Adam (Liverpool); Jamie Mackie (Queens Park Rangers), Craig Mackail-Smith (Brighton & Hove Albion). *Substitutes:* Barry Bannan (Aston Villa, for Adam 46); Robert Snodgrass (Leeds United, for Mackail-Smith 61); Graham Dorrans (West Bromwich Albion, for Morrison 72); Kenny Miller (Cardiff City, for Mackie 81); Barry Robson (Middlesbrough, for Forrest 87). *Manager:* Craig Levein.

Slovenia: Samir Handanovic (captain); Miso Brecko, Marko Suler, Bostjan Cesar, Bojan Jokic; Andras Kirm, Aleksandar Radosavljevic, Rene Krhin, Valter Birsa, Josip Ilicic; Zlatko Dedic. *Substitutes:* Haris Vuckic (for Birsa 61); Dare Vrsic (for Ilicic 68); Zlatan Ljubijankic (for Dedic 83); Darijan Matic (for Krhin 85); Nejc Pecnik (for Kirm 89). *Coach:* Slavisa Stojanovic.

Scorers:　Slovenia: Kirm 33　　　Scotland: Berra 40

26 May 2012　　Friendly　　　　　　　　Everbank Field, Jacksonville　　　　　Attendance: 44,438

716 USA 5, SCOTLAND 1　　　　　　　　　　　　*Referee: Elmer Bonilla (El Salvador)*

Scotland: Allan McGregor (Rangers); Phil Bardsley (Sunderland), Gary Caldwell (Wigan Athletic), Andy Webster (Hearts), Charlie Mulgrew (Celtic); Barry Bannan (Aston Villa), Scott Brown (Celtic), James McArthur (Wigan Athletic), Shaun Maloney (Wigan Athletic); Matt Phillips (Blackpool), Kenny Miller (Cardiff City, captain). *Substitutes:* Don Cowie (Cardiff City, for Bannan 51); Russell Martin (Norwich City, for Bardsley 59); Steven Whittaker (Rangers, for McArthur 59); Lee Wallace (Rangers, for Mulgrew 68); Christophe Berra (Wolverhampton Wanderers, for Webster 82); Craig Mackail-Smith (Brighton & Hove Albion, for Maloney 83). *Manager:* Craig Levein.

USA: Tim Howard; Steve Cherundolo, Geoff Cameron, Carlos Bocanegra (captain), Fabian Johnson; Maurice Edu, Michael Bradley, Jermaine Jones; Landon Donovan, Terrence Boyd, Jose Torres. *Substitutes:* Oguchi Onyewu (for Bocanegra 63); Hercules Gomez (for Boyd 64); Kyle Beckerman (for Edu 64); Joe Corona (for Torres 68); Brad Guzan (for Howard 71); Edgar Castillo (for Johnson 73). *Coach:* Jurgen Klinsmann (Germany).

Scorers:　USA: Donovan 3, 60, 65; Bradley 11; Jones 70　　　Scotland: Cameron 15 (own goal)

15 August 2012　　Friendly　　　　　　　　Easter Road, Edinburgh　　　　　Attendance: 11,110

717 SCOTLAND 3, Australia 1　　　　　　　　　*Referee: Tom Harald Hagen (Norway)*

Scotland: Allan McGregor (Rangers); Alan Hutton (Aston Villa), Andy Webster (Hearts), Gary Caldwell (Wigan Athletic, captain), Christophe Berra (Wolverhampton Wanderers), Danny Fox (Southampton); Robert Snodgrass (Norwich City), James Morrison (West Bromwich Albion), Charlie Adam (Liverpool); Steven Naismith (Everton), Jordan Rhodes (Huddersfield Town). *Substitutes:* Matt Gilks (Blackpool, for McGregor 23); Shaun Maloney (Wigan Athletic, for Morrison 27); Ross McCormack (Leeds United, for Rhodes 67); Russell Martin (Norwich City, for Hutton 68); Charlie Mulgrew (Celtic, for Fox 70); Ian Black (Rangers, for Caldwell 87). *Manager:* Craig Levein.

Australia: Mark Schwarzer; Rhys Williams, Lucas Neill (captain), Sasa Ognenovski, David Carney; Luke Wilkshire, Carl Valeri, Mark Bresciano, Robbie Kruse; Alex Brosque, Brett Holman. *Substitutes:* Adam Federici (for Schwarzer 46); Scott McDonald (for Holman 46); Mile Jedinak (for Bresciano 46); Jason Davidson (for Carney 59); Ryan McGowan (for Ognenovski 79); Archibald Thompson (for Brosque 85). *Coach:* Holger Osieck.

Scorers:　Australia: Bresciano 18　　　Scotland: Rhodes 29; Davidson 63 (own goal); McCormack 76

8 September 2012　　World Cup qualifying　　　　Hampden Park　　　　　Attendance: 47,369

718 SCOTLAND 0, Serbia 0　　　　　　　　　　*Referee: Jonas Eriksson (Sweden)*

Scotland: Allan McGregor (Besiktas); Alan Hutton (Aston Villa), Andy Webster (Hearts), Gary Caldwell (Wigan Athletic, captain), Christophe Berra (Wolverhampton Wanderers), Paul Dixon (Huddersfield Town); Robert Snodgrass (Norwich City), James Morrison (West Bromwich Albion), Charlie Adam (Stoke City); Steven Naismith (Everton), Kenny Miller (Vancouver Whitecaps). *Substitutes:* James Forrest (Celtic, for Snodgrass 69); Jordan Rhodes (Blackburn Rovers, for Miller 81); Jamie Mackie (Queens Park Rangers, for Morrison 81). *Manager:* Craig Levein.

Serbia: Vladimir Stojkovic; Milan Bisevac, Marija Nastasic, Aleksandar Kolarov; Branislav Ivanovic (captain), Milos Ninkovic, Srdjan Mijailovic, Aleksandar Ignjovski, Darko Lazovic; Zoran Tosic, Filip Djuricic. *Substitutes:* Ljubomir Fejsa (for Mijailovic 46); Dusan Tadic (for Lazovic 58); Dejan Lekic (for Djuricic 83). *Coach:* Sinisa Mihajlovic.

11 September 2012　　World Cup qualifying　　　Hampden Park　　　　　Attendance: 32,430

719 SCOTLAND 1, FYR Macedonia 1　　　　　　*Referee: Sergey Karasev (Russia)*

Scotland: Allan McGregor (Besiktas); Alan Hutton (Aston Villa), Andy Webster (Hearts), Gary Caldwell (Wigan Athletic), Christophe Berra (Wolverhampton Wanderers), Paul Dixon (Huddersfield Town); James Forrest (Celtic), James Morrison (West Bromwich Albion), Shaun Maloney (Wigan Athletic); Jamie Mackie (Queens Park Rangers), Kenny Miller (Vancouver Whitecaps, captain). *Substitutes:* Charlie Adam (Stoke City, for Miller 58); Jordan Rhodes (Blackburn Rovers, for Morrison 66); Steven Naismith (Everton, for Mackie 77). *Manager:* Craig Levein.

FYR Macedonia: Martin Bogatinov; Daniel Georgievski, Vance Sikov, Nikolce Noveski, Goran Popov, Agim Ibraimi, Nikola Gligorov, Muhamed Demiri, Ivan Trickovski; Goran Pandev (captain), Mirko Ivanovski. *Substitutes:* Ferhan Hasani (for Trickovski 38); Velice Sumulikoski (for Gligorov 70); Darko Tasevski (for Ibraimi 89). *Coach:* Cedomir Janevski.

Scorers:　FYR Macedonia: Noveski 11　　　Scotland: Miller 43

| 12 October 2012 | World Cup qualifying | Cardiff City Stadium | Attendance: 23,249 |

720 Wales 2, SCOTLAND 1
Referee: Florian Meyer (Germany)

Scotland: Allan McGregor (Besiktas); Alan Hutton (Aston Villa), Gary Caldwell (Wigan Athletic), Christophe Berra (Wolverhampton Wanderers), Danny Fox (Southampton); James Morrison (West Bromwich Albion), Scott Brown (Celtic), Darren Fletcher (Manchester United, captain), Kris Commons (Celtic); Shaun Maloney (Wigan Athletic), Steven Fletcher (Sunderland). *Substitutes:* Charlie Adam (Stoke City, for Brown 46); Kenny Miller (Vancouver Whitecaps, for Morrison 84); Jamie Mackie (Queens Park Rangers, for Commons 84). *Manager:* Craig Levein.

Wales: Lewis Price; Chris Gunter, Ashley Williams (captain), Darcy Blake, Ben Davies; Joe Allen, Aaron Ramsey, David Vaughan, Joe Ledley, Gareth Bale; Steve Morison. *Substitutes:* Craig Davies (for Morison 65); Hal Robson-Kanu (for Ledley 70). *Manager:* Chris Coleman.

Scorers: Scotland: Morrison 27   Wales: Bale 80 (pen), 89

| 16 October 2012 | World Cup qualifying | Stade Roi Baudouin, Brussels | Attendance: 44,132 |

721 Belgium 2, SCOTLAND 0
Referee: Tom Harald Hagen (Norway)

Scotland: Allan McGregor (Besiktas); Alan Hutton (Aston Villa), Gary Caldwell (Wigan Athletic), Christophe Berra (Wolverhampton Wanderers), Danny Fox (Southampton); Kris Commons (Celtic), Darren Fletcher (Manchester United, captain), James Morrison (West Bromwich Albion), James McArthur (Wigan Athletic); Shaun Maloney (Wigan Athletic), Steven Fletcher (Sunderland). *Substitutes:* Jamie Mackie (Queens Park Rangers, for Commons 46); Kenny Miller (Vancouver Whitecaps, for Steven Fletcher 76); Matt Phillips (Blackpool, for Morrison 80). *Manager:* Craig Levein.

Belgium: Thibaut Courtois; Toby Alderweireld, Vincent Kompany (captain), Thomas Vermaelen, Jan Vertonghen; Axel Witsel, Kevin De Bruyne, Moussa Dembele, Dries Mertens; Nacer Chadli, Christian Benteke. *Substitutes:* Eden Hazard (for Dembele 46); Kevin Mirallas (for Mertens 56); Ilombe Mboyo (for Benteke 87). *Coach:* Marc Wilmots.

Scorers: Belgium: Benteke 68; Kompany 71

| 14 November 2012 | Friendly | Stade Josy Barthel, Luxembourg City | Attendance: 2,521 |

722 Luxembourg 1, SCOTLAND 2
Referee: Cyril Zimmerman (Switzerland)

Scotland: Matt Gilks (Blackpool); Steven Whittaker (Norwich City), Grant Hanley (Blackburn Rovers), Christophe Berra (Wolverhampton Wanderers), Paul Dixon (Huddersfield Town); Steven Naismith (Everton), Darren Fletcher (Manchester United, captain), Andrew Shinnie (Inverness Caledonian Thistle), Charlie Mulgrew (Celtic); Kenny Miller (Vancouver Whitecaps), Jordan Rhodes (Blackburn Rovers). *Substitutes:* Liam Kelly (Kilmarnock, for Mulgrew 46); Leigh Griffiths (Hibernian, for Shinnie 70); Murray Davidson (St Johnstone, for Rhodes 90+1). *Manager:* Billy Stark (caretaker).

Luxembourg: Jonathan Joubert; Tom Schnell, Guy Blaise, Ante Bukvic, Mathias Janisch; Ben Payal, Charles Leweck, Lars Krogh Gerson, Gilles Bettmer; Mario Mutsch (captain), Maurice Deville. *Substitutes:* Rene Peters (for Payal 46); Daniel da Mota (for Janisch 53); Stefano Bensi (for Deville 64); David Turpel (for Bettmer 71); Tom Laterza (for Lewek 76). *Coach:* Luc Holtz.

Scorers: Scotland: Rhodes 11, 23   Luxembourg: Krogh Gerson 47

| 6 February 2013 | Friendly | Pittodrie, Aberdeen | Attendance: 16,202 |

723 SCOTLAND 1, Estonia 0
Referee: Clement Turpin (France)

Scotland: Allan McGregor (Besiktas); Alan Hutton (Real Mallorca), Andy Webster (Hearts), Christophe Berra (Wolverhampton Wanderers), Charlie Mulgrew (Celtic); Chris Burke (Birmingham City), Scott Brown (Celtic, captain), Charlie Adam (Stoke City), Shaun Maloney (Wigan Athletic); Steven Naismith (Everton), Steven Fletcher (Sunderland). *Substitutes:* Jordan Rhodes (Blackburn Rovers, for Maloney 46); Robert Snodgrass (Norwich City, for Burke 46); James Morrison (West Bromwich Albion, for Brown 62); James McArthur (Wigan Athletic, for Adam 62); Kenny Miller (Vancouver Whitecaps, for Fletcher 67); Kris Commons (Celtic, for Naismith 75). *Manager:* Gordon Strachan.

Estonia: Sergei Pareiko; Enar Jaager, Igor Morozov, Ragnar Klavan (captain), Taijo Teniste; Sergei Mosnikov, Konstantin Vassiljev; Sander Puri, Henrik Ojamaa, Tarmo Kink; Andres Oper. *Substitutes:* Jarmo Ahjupera (for Oper 46); Siim Luts (for Puri 59); Ats Purje (for Kink 59); Gert Kams (for Ojamaa 73). *Coach:* Tarmo Ruutli.

Scorer: Scotland: Mulgrew 39

The Tartan Army is back in London after an absence of almost 14 years.

Chapter nine: 2010-2019

22 March 2013 World Cup qualifying Hampden Park Attendance: 39,365

724 SCOTLAND 1, Wales 2
Referee: Antony Gautier (France)

Scotland: Allan McGregor (Besiktas); Alan Hutton (Real Mallorca), Gary Caldwell (Wigan Athletic, captain), Grant Hanley (Blackburn Rovers), Charlie Mulgrew (Celtic); Chris Burke (Birmingham City), Graham Dorrans (West Bromwich Albion), James McArthur (Wigan Athletic), Robert Snodgrass (Norwich City); Shaun Maloney (Wigan Athletic), Steven Fletcher (Sunderland). *Substitutes:* Kenny Miller (Vancouver Whitecaps, for Fletcher 5); Charlie Adam (Stoke City, for Dorrans 63); Jordan Rhodes (Blackburn Rovers, for Burke 86). *Manager:* Gordon Strachan.

Wales: Glyn "Boaz" Myhill; Chris Gunter, Sam Ricketts, Ashley Williams (captain), Ben Davies; Jack Collison, Aaron Ramsey, Joe Ledley, Gareth Bale; Hal Robson-Kanu, Craig Bellamy. *Substitutes:* Jonathan Williams (for Bale 46); Andy King (for Collison 58); Simon Church (for Ledley 89). *Manager:* Chris Coleman.

Scorers: Scotland: Hanley 45+2   Wales: Ramsey 72 (pen); Robson-Kanu 74

26 March 2013 World Cup qualifying Stadion Karadjordje, Novi Sad Attendance: 6,500

725 Serbia 2, SCOTLAND 0
Referee: Istvan Vad (Hungary)

Scotland: David Marshall (Cardiff City); Alan Hutton (Real Mallorca), Gary Caldwell (Wigan Athletic, captain), Grant Hanley (Blackburn Rovers), Steven Whittaker (Norwich City); Shaun Maloney (Wigan Athletic), James McArthur (Wigan Athletic), Liam Bridcutt (Brighton & Hove Albion), George Boyd (Hull City); Steven Naismith (Everton), Jordan Rhodes (Blackburn Rovers). *Substitutes:* Charlie Adam (Stoke City, for McArthur 46); Chris Burke (Birmingham City, for Maloney 79); Kenny Miller (Vancouver Whitecaps, for Rhodes 79). *Manager:* Gordon Strachan.

Serbia: Vladimir Stojkovic; Branislav Ivanovic (captain), Neven Subotic, Matija Nastasic, Nenad Tomovic; Dusan Basta, Luka Milivojevic, Ljubomir Fejsa, Zoran Tosic; Filip Djuricic, Dusan Tadic. *Substitutes:* Filip Djordjevic (for Tadic 68); Radosav Petrovic (for Fejsa 85); Alen Stevanovic (for Tosic 90+3). *Coach:* Sinisa Mihajlovic.

Scorer: Serbia: Djuricic 60, 66

7 June 2013 World Cup qualifying Stadion Maksimir, Zagreb Attendance: 25,016

726 Croatia 0, SCOTLAND 1
Referee: David Fernandez Borbalan (Spain)

Scotland: Allan McGregor (Besiktas); Alan Hutton (Real Mallorca), Russell Martin (Norwich City), Grant Hanley (Blackburn Rovers), Steven Whittaker (Norwich City); Barry Bannan (Aston Villa), James McArthur (Wigan Athletic), James Morrison (West Bromwich Albion, captain), Robert Snodgrass (Norwich City); Shaun Maloney (Wigan Athletic), Leigh Griffiths (Wolverhampton Wanderers). *Substitutes:* Steven Naismith (Everton, for Bannan 64); Jordan Rhodes (Blackburn Rovers, for Griffiths 64); Craig Conway (Cardiff City, for Maloney 75). *Manager:* Gordon Strachan.

Croatia: Stipe Pletikosa; Darijo Srna (captain), Gordon Schildenfeld, Josip Simunic, Ivan Strinic; Mateo Kovacic, Jorge Sammir, Ivan Rakitic, Ivan Perisic; Ivica Olic, Mario Mandzukic. *Substitutes:* Eduardo (for Perisic 56); Nikola Kalinic (for Strinic 70); Niko Kranjcar (for Mandzukic 88). *Coach:* Igor Stimac.

Scorer: Scotland: Snodgrass 26

14 August 2013 Friendly Wembley, London Attendance: 80,485

727 England 3, SCOTLAND 2
Referee: Felix Brych (Germany)

Scotland (4-4-2):

30 Allan McGregor (Hull City);
33 Alan Hutton (Aston Villa)
6 Russell Martin (Norwich City)
8 Grant Hanley (Blackburn Rovers)
19 Steven Whittaker (Norwich City);
29 Shaun Maloney (Wigan Athletic)
28 James Morrison (West Bromwich Albion)
31 Scott Brown (Celtic, captain)
11 Robert Snodgrass (Norwich City);
8 James Forrest (Celtic)
69 Kenny Miller (Vancouver Whitecaps)

Substitutes: 7 Charlie Mulgrew (Celtic, for Forrest 67);
5 Craig Conway (Cardiff City, for Snodgrass 68);
3 Leigh Griffiths (Wolverhampton Wanderers, for Miller 73);
10 Jordan Rhodes (Blackburn Rovers, for Morrison 82);
23 Steven Naismith (Everton, for Maloney 86)

Manager: Gordon Strachan

The return of the oldest football international after a break of nearly 14 years resulted in a tight match with England just managing to emerge victorious over Gordon Strachan's Scottish side which had led twice. The visitors got off to an excellent start when James Morrison found the net in the 12th minute but Theo Walcott levelled things up with the half-hour approaching. Kenny Miller deceived defender Gary Cahill with a shimmy before scoring with a fine left-foot shot to make it 2-1 four minutes after half-time. However, after keeper Allan McGregor had made a great save from a deflection off defender Russell Martin, defensive lapses allowed Danny Welbeck and substitute Rickie Lambert to both net headers and give England a somewhat fortunate victory.

England: Joe Hart; Kyle Walker, Phil Jagielka, Gary Cahill, Leighton Baines; Steven Gerrard (captain), Tom Cleverley, Jack Wilshere; Wayne Rooney, Danny Welbeck, Theo Walcott. *Substitutes:* Frank Lampard (for Wilshere 46); Alex Oxlade-Chamberlain (for Gerrard 62); Rickie Lambert (for Rooney 67); James Milner (for Cleverley 67); Wilfried Zaha (for Walcott 75); Phil Jones (for Jagielka 84). *Manager:* Roy Hodgson.

Scorers: Scotland: Morrison 12; Miller 49   England: Walcott 29; Welbeck 53; Lambert 70

6 September 2013 World Cup qualifying Hampden Park Attendance: 40,284

728 SCOTLAND 0, Belgium 2
Referee: Paolo Tagliavento (Italy)

Scotland: David Marshall (Cardiff City); Alan Hutton (Aston Villa), Russell Martin (Norwich City), Grant Hanley (Blackburn Rovers), Steven Whittaker (Norwich City); James Forrest (Celtic), Scott Brown (Celtic, captain), Charlie Mulgrew (Celtic), Robert Snodgrass (Norwich City); Shaun Maloney (Wigan Athletic), Leigh Griffiths (Wolverhampton Wanderers). *Substitutes:* Ikechi Anya (Watford, for Snodgrass 59); Jordan Rhodes (Blackburn Rovers, for Griffiths 68); Ross McCormack (Leeds United, for Forrest 86). *Manager:* Gordon Strachan.

Belgium: Thibaut Courtois; Toby Alderweireld, Daniel Van Buyten, Nicolas Lombaerts, Jan Vertonghen (captain); Axel Witsel, Steven Defour, Kevin De Bruyne, Marouane Fellaini, Nacer Chadli; Christian Benteke. *Substitutes:* Kevin Mirallas (for Fellaini 68); Sebastien Pocognoli (for Lombaerts 76); Moussa Dembele (for Defour 87). *Coach:* Marc Wilmots.

Scorers: Belgium: Defour 38; Mirallas 89

10 September 2013 World Cup qualifying Nacionalna Arena, Skopje Attendance: 14,093

729 FYR Macedonia 1, SCOTLAND 2
Referee: Fredy Fautrel (France)

Scotland: David Marshall (Cardiff City); Alan Hutton (Aston Villa), Russell Martin (Norwich City), Grant Hanley (Blackburn Rovers), Steven Whittaker (Norwich City); Barry Bannan (Crystal Palace), Scott Brown (Celtic, captain), Charlie Mulgrew (Celtic), Ikechi Anya (Watford); Shaun Maloney (Wigan Athletic), Steven Naismith (Everton). *Substitutes:* Matt Gilks (Blackpool, for Marshall 46); James McArthur (Wigan Athletic, for Bannan 79); Lee Wallace (Rangers, for Whittaker 80). *Manager:* Gordon Strachan.

FYR Macedonia: Tome Pacovski; Daniel Georgievski, Stefan Ristovski, Nikolce Noveski, Vance Sikov; Ivan Trickovski, David Babunski, Adis Jahovic, Goran Pandev (captain); Aleksandar Trajkovski, Ostoja Stjepanovic. *Substitutes:* Darko Tasevski (for Babunski 42); Mirko Ivanovski (for Trajkovski 57); Jovan Kostovski (for Jahovic 83). *Coach:* Cedomir Janevski.

Scorers: Scotland: Anya 60; Maloney 89   FYR Macedonia: Kostovski 85

15 October 2013 World Cup qualifying Hampden Park Attendance: 30,172

730 SCOTLAND 2, Croatia 0
Referee: Ovidiu Hategan (Romania)

Scotland (4-4-2):

31 Allan McGregor (Hull City);
36 Alan Hutton (Aston Villa)
9 Russell Martin (Norwich City)
11 Grant Hanley (Blackburn Rovers)
10 Charlie Mulgrew (Celtic);
14 Barry Bannan (Crystal Palace)
34 Scott Brown (Celtic, captain)
29 James Morrison (West Bromwich Albion)
3 Ikechi Anya (Watford);
13 Robert Snodgrass (Norwich City)
25 Steven Naismith (Everton)

Substitutes: 19 Graham Dorrans (West Bromwich Albion, for Anya 77);
14 James McArthur (Wigan Athletic, for Snodgrass 82);
6 Chris Burke (Birmingham City, for Bannan 89)

Manager: Gordon Strachan

Although any chance of claiming a runners-up spot in the World Cup qualifying group had long gone, and going into this game the Scots sat second bottom of the table, there was a heightened mood of optimism under Gordon Strachan. That was proved correct with an excellent 2-0 win over Croatia, who were likely to finish second in the group. Robert Snodgrass, who had claimed the winner in the reverse fixture four months earlier, set Scotland on the way with a first-half header. And when Barry Bannan saw his penalty kick saved in the 73rd minute, Steven Naismith showed good opportunism to follow up and net the rebound. There were fine performances too from right back Alan Hutton and captain Scott Brown in the middle of the park.

Croatia: Stipe Pletikosa; Domagoj Vida, Verdan Corluka, Dejan Lovren, Ivan Strinic; Ognjen Vukojevic, Darijo Srna (captain), Niko Kranjcar, Luka Modric; Mario Mandzukic, Nicola Kalinic. *Substitutes:* Eduardo da Silva (for Kalinic 59); Ivan Perisic (for Kranjcar 68); Nikica Jelavic (for Mandzukic 80). *Coach:* Igor Stimac.

Scorers: Scotland: Snodgrass 28; Naismith 73

FIFA WORLD CUP QUALIFYING GROUP A

	P	W	D	L	F	A	Pts
Belgium	10	8	2	0	18	4	26
Croatia	10	5	2	3	12	9	17
Serbia	10	4	2	4	18	11	14
Scotland	10	3	2	5	8	12	11
Wales	10	3	1	6	9	20	10
Macedonia	10	2	1	7	7	16	7

15 November 2013 Friendly Hampden Park Attendance: 21,079

731 SCOTLAND 0, USA 0
Referee: Michael Oliver (England)

Scotland: David Marshall (Cardiff City); Alan Hutton (Aston Villa), Gordon Greer (Brighton & Hove Albion), Grant Hanley (Blackburn Rovers), Steven Whittaker (Norwich City); Barry Bannan (Crystal Palace), Scott Brown (Celtic, captain), Robert Snodgrass (Norwich City), Charlie Mulgrew (Celtic); Steven Fletcher (Sunderland), Craig Conway (Brighton & Hove Albion). *Substitutes:* Lee Wallace (Rangers, for Whittaker 69); Ross McCormack (Leeds United, for Snodgrass 69); Steven Naismith (Everton, for Bannan 81); Gary Mackay-Steven (Dundee United, for Conway 84). *Manager:* Gordon Strachan.

USA: Tim Howard (captain); Bradley Evans, Omar Gonzalez, Geoff Cameron, DaMarcus Beasley; Michael Bradley, Jermaine Jones; Alejandro Bedoya, Sacha Kljestan, Eddie Johnson; Jozy Altidore. *Substitutes:* Mikkel "Mix" Diskerud (for Jones 62); Brek Shea (for Johnson 62); Aron Johannsson (for Kljestan 62); Eric Lichaj (for Evans 72); Christopher Wondolowski (for Bedoya 81); Terrence Boyd (for Altidore 90). *Coach:* Jurgen Klinsmann (Germany).

Chapter nine: 2010-2019

| 19 November 2013 | Friendly | Aker Stadion, Molde | Attendance: 9,751 |

732 Norway 0, SCOTLAND 1   *Referee: Martin Strombergsson (Sweden)*

Scotland: David Marshall (Cardiff City); Alan Hutton (Aston Villa), Russell Martin (Norwich City), Gordon Greer (Brighton & Hove Albion), Steven Whittaker (Norwich City); Ikechi Anya (Watford), Scott Brown (Celtic, captain), Craig Bryson (Derby County), Charlie Adam (Stoke City), Robert Snodgrass (Norwich City); Steven Naismith (Everton). *Substitutes:* Barry Bannan (Crystal Palace, for Bryson 46); Craig Conway (Brighton & Hove Albion, for Anya 51); James McArthur (Wigan Athletic, for Adam 64); Christophe Berra (Ipswich Town, for Naismith 90+4). *Manager:* Gordon Strachan.

Norway: Orjan Nyland; Omar Elabdellaoui, Tore Reginiussen, Vegard Forren, Tom Hogli (captain); Per Ciljan Skjelbred, Magnus Wolff Eikrem, Ruben Yttergard Jensen, Morten Gamst Pedersen; Ola Kamara, Marcus Pedersen. *Substitutes:* Mohammed Abdellaoue (for Kamara 46); Martin Linnes (for Elabdellaoui 60); Stefan Strandberg (for Reginiussen 65); Mats Moller Daehli (for Skjelbred 67); Anders Konradsen (for Eikrem 80); Tarik Elyounoussi (for Marcus Pedersen 86). *Coach:* Per-Mathias Hogmo.

Scorer: Scotland: Brown 61

| 5 March 2014 | Friendly | Stadion Narodowy, Warsaw | Attendance: 41,652 |

733 Poland 0, SCOTLAND 1   *Referee: Alain Bieri (Switzerland)*

Scotland: David Marshall (Cardiff City); Alan Hutton (Bolton Wanderers), Russell Martin (Norwich City), Gordon Greer (Brighton & Hove Albion), Charlie Mulgrew (Celtic); Barry Bannan (Crystal Palace), Scott Brown (Celtic, captain), James Morrison (West Bromwich Albion), Ikechi Anya (Watford); Steven Fletcher (Sunderland), Ross McCormack (Leeds United). *Substitutes:* Steven Naismith (Everton, for Steven Fletcher 46); Darren Fletcher (Manchester United, for Morrison 46); Andrew Robertson (Dundee United, for Bannan 67); Phil Bardsley (Sunderland, for Hutton 67); Charlie Adam (Stoke City, for McCormack 77); Chris Burke (Birmingham City, for Anya 90+2). *Manager:* Gordon Strachan.

Poland: Wojciech Szczesny; Lukasz Piszczek (captain), Lukasz Szukala, Kamil Glik, Tomasz Brzyski; Mateusz Klich, Grzegorz Krychowiak; Waldemar Sobota, Ludovic Obraniak, Slawomir Peszko; Arkadiusz Milik. *Substitutes:* Marcin Robak (for Obraniak 74); Eugen Polanski (for Peszko 74); Lukasz Teodorczyk (for Klich 82); Tomasz Jodlowiec (for Krychowiak 88); Michal Maslowski (for Sobota 89); Marcin Komorowski (for Brzyski 90+2). *Coach:* Adam Nawalka.

Scorer: Scotland: Brown 77

| 28 May 2014 | Friendly | Craven Cottage, London | Attendance: 20,156 |

734 Nigeria 2, SCOTLAND 2   *Referee: Lee Probert (England)*

*****Scotland:** Allan McGregor (Hull City); Alan Hutton (Aston Villa), Gordon Greer (Brighton & Hove Albion), Grant Hanley (Blackburn Rovers), Andrew Robertson (Dundee United); Shaun Maloney (Wigan Athletic), Scott Brown (Celtic, captain), James Morrison (West Bromwich Albion), Charlie Mulgrew (Celtic), Ikechi Anya (Watford); Steven Naismith (Everton). *Substitutes:* Chris Martin (Derby County, for Naismith 46); George Boyd (Hull City, for Morrison 63); Craig Forsyth (Derby County, for Robertson 77); Steven Whittaker (Norwich City, for Anya 84). *Manager:* Gordon Strachan.

Nigeria: Austin Ejide; Kunle Odunlami, Azubuike Egwuekwe, Joseph Yobo (captain), Uwa Echiejile; Reuben Gabriel, Joel Obi; Michael Babatunde, Michael Uchebo, Ejike Uzoenyi; Shola Ameobi. *Substitutes:* Nosa Igiebor (for Obi 54); Peter Odemwingie (for Uchebo 55); Victor Moses (for Uzoenyi 62); Uche Nwofor (for Ameobi 62); Nnamdi Oduamadi (for Babatunde 66); Efe Ambrose (for Odunlami 75). *Coach:* Stephen Keshi.

Scorers: Scotland: Mulgrew 10; Egwuekwe 52 (own goal)   Nigeria: Uchebo 41; Nwofor 90

**For the first time ever the Scottish players wore a new change strip which had been launched in February. It was based on the primrose and pink racing colours of Lord Rosebery, former SFA honorary president, which had originally been worn in 1881.*

| 7 September 2014 | European Championship qualifying | Signal Iduna Park, Dortmund | Attendance: 60,209 |

735 Germany 2, SCOTLAND 1   *Referee: Svein Oddvar Moen (Norway)*

Scotland: David Marshall (Cardiff City); Alan Hutton (Aston Villa), Russell Martin (Norwich City), Grant Hanley (Blackburn Rovers), Steven Whittaker (Norwich City); Barry Bannan (Crystal Palace), Darren Fletcher (Manchester United, captain), James Morrison (West Bromwich Albion), Charlie Mulgrew (Celtic), Ikechi Anya (Watford); Steven Naismith (Everton). *Substitutes:* Steven Fletcher (Sunderland, for Bannan 58); James McArthur (Crystal Palace, for Darren Fletcher 58); Shaun Maloney (Wigan Athletic, for Naismith 82). *Manager:* Gordon Strachan.

Germany: Manuel Neuer (captain); Sebastian Rudy, Jerome Boateng, Benedikt Howedes, Erik Durm; Christoph Kramer, Toni Kroos; Thomas Muller, Marco Reus, Andre Schurrle; Mario Gotze. *Substitutes:* Lukas Podolski (for Schurrle 84); Matthias Ginter (for Reus 90+2). *Coach:* Joachim Low.

Scorers: Germany: Muller 18, 70   Scotland: Anya 66

| 11 October 2014 | European Championship qualifying | Ibrox, Glasgow | Attendance: 34,719 |

736 SCOTLAND 1, Georgia 0   *Referee: Miroslav Zelinka (Czech Republic)*

Scotland: David Marshall (Cardiff City); Alan Hutton (Aston Villa), Russell Martin (Norwich City), Grant Hanley (Blackburn Rovers), Andrew Robertson (Hull City); Shaun Maloney (Wigan Athletic), Scott Brown (Celtic, captain), James Morrison (West Bromwich Albion), Ikechi Anya (Watford); Steven Naismith (Everton), Steven Fletcher (Sunderland). *Substitutes:* James McArthur (Crystal Palace, for Naismith 80); Chris Martin (Derby County, for Fletcher 90). *Manager:* Gordon Strachan.

Georgia: Giorgi Loria; Ucha Lobzhanidze, Solomon Kvirkvelia, Akaki Khubutia, Gia Grigalava; Giorgi Papava, Jaba Kankava (captain), Murtaz Daushvili, Davit Kvirkvelia; Valeri Qazaishvili, Nikoloz Gelashvili. *Substitutes:* Tornike Okriashvili (for Davit Kvirkvelia 46); Irakli Dzaria (for Papava 70); Giorgi Chanturia (for Qazaishvili 80). *Coach:* Temur Ketsbaia.

Scorer: Scotland: Khubutia 28 (own goal)

The line-up which gained a battling 2-2 draw with Poland in the third European Championship qualifying match. Back (from left): Steven Fletcher, Scott Brown, Alan Hutton, Gordon Greer, David Marshall, Russell Martin. Front: Steven Whittaker, Shaun Maloney, James Morrison, Steven Naismith, Ikechi Anya.

14 October 2014   European Championship qualifying   Stadion Narodowy, Warsaw   Attendance: 55,197

737 Poland 2, SCOTLAND 2
Referee: Alberto Mallenco (Spain)

Scotland: David Marshall (Cardiff City); Alan Hutton (Aston Villa), Russell Martin (Norwich City), Gordon Greer (Brighton & Hove Albion), Steven Whittaker (Norwich City); Shaun Maloney (Wigan Athletic), Scott Brown (Celtic, captain), James Morrison (West Bromwich Albion), Ikechi Anya (Watford); Steven Naismith (Everton), Steven Fletcher (Sunderland). *Substitutes:* Chris Martin (Derby County, for Naismith 71); Darren Fletcher (Manchester United, for Steven Fletcher 71). *Manager:* Gordon Strachan.

Poland: Wojciech Szczesny; Lukasz Piszczek, Lukasz Szubala, Kamil Glik, Artur Jedrzejczyk; Kamil Grosicki, Grzegorz Krychowiak, Krzysztof Maczynski, Waldemar Sobota; Arkadiusz Milik, Robert Lewandowski (captain). *Substitutes:* Sebastian Mila (for Sobota 63); Michal Zyro (for Grosicki 89). *Coach:* Adam Nawalka.

Scorers: Poland: Maczynski 11; Milik 76   Scotland: Maloney 18; Naismith 57

14 November 2014   European Championship qualifying   Celtic Park, Glasgow   Attendance: 59,239

738 SCOTLAND 1, Republic of Ireland 0
Referee: Milorad Mazic (Serbia)

Scotland: David Marshall (Cardiff City); Steven Whittaker (Norwich City), Russell Martin (Norwich City), Grant Hanley (Blackburn Rovers), Andrew Robertson (Hull City); Shaun Maloney (Wigan Athletic), Scott Brown (Celtic, captain), Charlie Mulgrew (Celtic), Ikechi Anya (Watford); Steven Naismith (Everton), Steven Fletcher (Sunderland). *Substitutes:* Chris Martin (Derby County, for Steven Fletcher 56); Darren Fletcher (Manchester United, for Anya 88). *Manager:* Gordon Strachan.

Republic of Ireland: David Forde; Seamus Coleman, Richard Keogh, John O'Shea (captain), Stephen Ward; Aiden McGeady, Darron Gibson, Jeff Hendrick, James McClean; Jon Walters, Shane Long. *Substitutes:* Stephen Quinn (for Gibson 68); Robbie Brady (for Long 68); Robbie Keane (for Hendrick 78). *Manager:* Martin O'Neill.

Scorer: Scotland: Maloney 75

18 November 2014   Friendly   Celtic Park, Glasgow   Attendance: 49,526

739 SCOTLAND 1, England 3
Referee: Jonas Eriksson (Sweden)

Scotland: David Marshall (Cardiff City); Steven Whittaker (Norwich City), Russell Martin (Norwich City), Grant Hanley (Blackburn Rovers), Andrew Robertson (Hull City); Shaun Maloney (Wigan Athletic), Scott Brown (Celtic, captain), Charlie Mulgrew (Celtic), Ikechi Anya (Watford); Steven Naismith (Everton), Chris Martin (Derby County). *Substitutes:* Craig Gordon (Celtic, for Marshall 46); James Morrison (West Bromwich Albion, for Chris Martin 46); Darren Fletcher (Manchester United, for Brown 46); Barry Bannan (Crystal Palace, for Anya 61); Stevie May (Sheffield Wednesday, for Hanley 67); Johnny Russell (Derby County, for Maloney 81). *Manager:* Gordon Strachan.

England: Fraser Forster; Nathaniel Clyne, Gary Cahill, Chris Smalling, Luke Shaw; Alex Oxlade-Chamberlain, James Milner, Jack Wilshere, Stewart Downing; Wayne Rooney (captain), Danny Welbeck. *Substitutes:* Phil Jagielka (for Cahill 46); Adam Lallana (for Downing 46); Kieran Gibbs (for Shaw 66); Raheem Sterling (for Welbeck 67); Rickie Lambert (for Oxlade-Chamberlain 80); Ross Barkley (for Wilshere 87). *Manager:* Roy Hodgson.

Scorers: England: Oxlade-Chamberlain 32; Rooney 47, 85   Scotland: Robertson 83

Chapter nine: 2010-2019

25 March 2015   Friendly   Hampden Park   Attendance: 20,117

740   SCOTLAND 1, Northern Ireland 0
Referee: Martin Atkinson (England)

Scotland: Craig Gordon (Celtic); Steven Whittaker (Norwich City), Russell Martin (Norwich City), Gordon Greer (Brighton & Hove Albion), Craig Forsyth (Derby County); Ikechi Anya (Watford), Darren Fletcher (West Bromwich Albion, captain), James McArthur (Crystal Palace), Matt Ritchie (Bournemouth); Shaun Maloney (Chicago Fire), Steven Fletcher (Sunderland). *Substitutes:* Allan McGregor (Hull City, for Gordon 46); Steven Naismith (Everton, for Maloney 46); Christophe Berra (Ipswich Town, for Martin 46); Jordan Rhodes (Blackburn Rovers, for Steven Fletcher 63); James Morrison (West Bromwich Albion, for McArthur 63); Johnny Russell (Derby County, for Whittaker 79). *Manager:* Gordon Strachan.

Northern Ireland: Michael McGovern; Paddy McNair, Aaron Hughes, Jonny Evans (captain), Daniel Lafferty; Oliver Norwood, Chris Baird, Josh Magennis, Ben Reeves, Stuart Dallas; Will Grigg. *Substitutes:* Lee Hodson (for Baird 59); Paddy McCourt (for Grigg 59); Steven Davis (for Norwood 70); Ryan McLaughlin (for Reeves 70); Billy McKay (for Magennis 75); Luke McCullough (for Evans 81). *Manager:* Michael O'Neill.

Scorer: Scotland: Berra 86

29 March 2015   European Championship qualifying   Hampden Park   Attendance: 34,255

741   SCOTLAND 6, Gibraltar 1
Referee: Mattias Gestranius (Finland)

Scotland: David Marshall (Cardiff City); Alan Hutton (Aston Villa), Russell Martin (Norwich City), Andrew Robertson (Hull City); Matt Ritchie (Bournemouth), Scott Brown (Celtic, captain), James Morrison (West Bromwich Albion), Ikechi Anya (Watford); Steven Naismith (Everton), Steven Fletcher (Sunderland), Shaun Maloney (Chicago Fire). *Substitutes:* Gordon Greer (Brighton & Hove Albion, for Ritchie 46); Jordan Rhodes, (Blackburn Rovers, for Naismith 67); Barry Bannan (Bolton Wanderers, for Anya 74). *Manager:* Gordon Strachan.

Gibraltar: Jamie Robba; Scott Wiseman, David Artell, Ryan Casciaro, Joseph Chipolina; Lee Casciaro, Aaron Payas, Roy Chipolina (captain), Anthony Bardon, Liam Walker; Adam Priestley. *Substitutes:* Jean-Carlos Garcia (for Artell 53); Jake Gosling (for Roy Chipolina 74); Daniel Duarte (for Bardon 82). *Coach:* David Wilson.

Scorers: Scotland: Maloney 18 (pen), 34 (pen); Fletcher 29, 77, 90; Naismith 39   Gibraltar: Lee Casciaro 19

5 June 2015   Friendly   Easter Road, Edinburgh   Attendance: 14,270

742   SCOTLAND 1, Qatar 0
Referee: Sebastien Delferiere (Belgium)

Scotland: David Marshall (Cardiff City); Ikechi Anya (Watford), Gordon Greer (Brighton & Hove Albion), Charlie Mulgrew (Celtic), Craig Forsyth (Derby County); James Forrest (Celtic), Scott Brown (Celtic, captain), James McArthur (Crystal Palace), Matt Ritchie (Bournemouth); Shaun Maloney (Chicago Fire), Steven Naismith (Everton). *Substitutes:* Craig Gordon (Celtic, for Marshall 46); James Morrison (West Bromwich Albion, for McArthur 46); Leigh Griffiths (Celtic, for Naismith 59); Darren Fletcher (West Bromwich Albion, for Brown 60); Charlie Adam (Stoke City, for Maloney 60); Johnny Russell (Derby County, for Forrest 74). *Manager:* Gordon Strachan.

Qatar: Amine Lecomte-Addani; Mohammed Tresor, Mohammed Kasola, Ahmed Yasser, Abdelkarim Hassan Fadlalla; Ahmed El Sayed, Karim Boudiaf; Hassan Al Haydos (captain), Ali Assadalla, Abdulaziz Hatem; Mohammed Muntari. *Substitutes:* Almahdi Ali Mukhtar (for Hatem 54); Abdulrahman Mohammed (for Assadalla 66); Hamid Ismail (for Tresor 78); Abdulqadir Ilyas (for Muntari 78); Moayad Hassan (for Al Haydos 86). *Coach:* Jose Daniel Carreno (Uruguay).

Scorer: Scotland: Ritchie 41

13 June 2015   European Championship qualifying   Aviva Stadium, Dublin   Attendance: 49,063

743   Republic of Ireland 1, SCOTLAND 1
Referee: Nicola Rizzoli (Italy)

Scotland: David Marshall (Cardiff City); Alan Hutton (Aston Villa), Russell Martin (Norwich City), Charlie Mulgrew (Celtic), Craig Forsyth (Derby County); Shaun Maloney (Chicago Fire), Scott Brown (Celtic, captain), James Morrison (West Bromwich Albion), Matt Ritchie (Bournemouth); Steven Naismith (Everton), Steven Fletcher (Sunderland). *Substitutes:* Ikechi Anya (Watford, for Ritchie 46); James McArthur (Crystal Palace, for Brown 85); Christophe Berra (Ipswich Town, for Naismith 90+2). *Manager:* Gordon Strachan.

Republic of Ireland: Shay Given; Seamus Coleman, John O'Shea (captain), Marc Wilson, Robbie Brady; Jeff Hendrick, Glenn Whelan, James McCarthy; Jon Walters, Daryl Murphy, Wes Hoolahan. *Substitutes:* James McClean (for Whelan 68); Robbie Keane (for Hoolahan 73); Shane Long (for Murphy 80). *Manager:* Martin O'Neill.

Scorers: Republic of Ireland: Walters 38   Scotland: O'Shea 47 (own goal)

4 September 2015   European Championship qualifying   Dinamo Arena, Tbilisi   Attendance: 22,886

744   Georgia 1, SCOTLAND 0
Referee: Ovidiu Hategan (Romania)

Scotland: David Marshall (Cardiff City); Alan Hutton (Aston Villa), Russell Martin (Norwich City), Charlie Mulgrew (Celtic), Andrew Robertson (Hull City); Shaun Maloney (Hull City), Scott Brown (Celtic, captain), James Morrison (West Bromwich Albion), Ikechi Anya (Watford); Steven Naismith (Everton), Steven Fletcher (Sunderland). *Substitutes:* James Forrest (Celtic, for Naismith 59); Grant Hanley (Blackburn Rovers, for Robertson 59); Leigh Griffiths (Celtic, for Anya 75). *Manager:* Gordon Strachan.

Georgia: Nukri Revishvili; Solomon Kvirkvelia, Aleksandre Amisulashvili, Guram Kashia; Ucha Lobzhanidze, Jaba Kankava (captain), Jano Ananidze, Giorgi Navalovski; Valeri Qazaishvili, Tornike Okriashvili; Levan Mchedlidze. *Substitutes:* Giorgi Merebashvili (for Okriashvili 71); Murtaz Daushvili (for Ananidze 82); Mate Vatsadze (for Mchedlidze 90+3). *Coach:* Kakhaber Tskhadadze.

Scorer: Georgia: Qazaishvili 38

7 September 2015 European Championship qualifying Hampden Park Attendance: 50,753

745 SCOTLAND 2, Germany 3
Referee: Bjorn Kuipers (Netherlands)

Scotland: David Marshall (Cardiff City); Alan Hutton (Aston Villa), Russell Martin (Norwich City), Grant Hanley (Blackburn Rovers), Charlie Mulgrew (Celtic); James Forrest (Celtic), Scott Brown (Celtic, captain), James McArthur (Crystal Palace), James Morrison (West Bromwich Albion), Shaun Maloney (Hull City); Steven Fletcher (Sunderland). *Substitutes:* Ikechi Anya (Watford, for Maloney 60); Matt Ritchie (Bournemouth, for Forrest 81); Chris Martin (Derby County, for Brown 81). *Manager:* Gordon Strachan.

Germany: Manuel Neuer; Emre Can, Jerome Boateng, Mats Hummels, Jonas Hector; Bastian Schweinsteiger (captain), Tony Kroos; Thomas Muller, Ilkay Gundogan, Mesut Ozil; Mario Gotze. *Substitutes:* Andre Schurrle (for Gotze 86); Christoph Kramer (for Ozil 90+2). *Coach:* Joachim Low.

Scorers: Germany: Muller 18, 34; Gundogan 54 Scotland: Hummels 28 (own goal); McArthur 43

8 October 2015 European Championship qualifying Hampden Park Attendance: 49,359

746 SCOTLAND 2, Poland 2
Referee: Viktor Kassai (Hungary)

Scotland: David Marshall (Cardiff City); Alan Hutton (Aston Villa), Russell Martin (Norwich City), Grant Hanley (Blackburn Rovers), Steven Whittaker (Norwich City); James Forrest (Celtic), Scott Brown (Celtic, captain), Darren Fletcher (West Bromwich Albion), Matt Ritchie (Bournemouth); Steven Naismith (Everton), Steven Fletcher (Sunderland). *Substitutes:* Shaun Maloney (Hull City, for Naismith 69); James McArthur (Crystal Palace, for Darren Fletcher 74); Graham Dorrans (Norwich City, for Forrest 84) *Manager:* Gordon Strachan.

Poland: Lukasz Fabianski; Lukasz Piszczek, Kamil Glik, Michal Pazdan, Maciej Rybus; Grzegorz Krychowiak, Krzysztof Maczynski; Jakub Blaszczykowski, Arkadiusz Milik, Kamil Grosicki, Robert Lewandowski (captain). *Substitutes:* Tomasz Jodlowiec (for Milik 63); Jakub Wawrzyniak (for Rybus 71); Pawel Olkowski (for Blaszczykowski 83). *Coach:* Adam Nawalka.

Scorers: Poland: Lewandowski 3, 90+4 Scotland: Ritchie 45; Steven Fletcher 62

11 October 2015 European Championship qualifying Faro-Loule, Portugal Attendance: 12,401

747 Gibraltar 0, SCOTLAND 6
Referee: Aleksey Kulbakov (Belarus)

Scotland (4-4-2):

34 Allan McGregor (Hull City);
49 Alan Hutton (Aston Villa)
9 Gordon Greer (Brighton & Hove Albion)
31 Christophe Berra (Ipswich Town)
8 Andrew Robertson (Hull City);
45 Shaun Maloney (Hull City)
12 Graham Dorrans (Norwich City)
49 Scott Brown (Celtic, captain)
7 Matt Ritchie (Bournemouth);
7 Chris Martin (Derby County)
25 Steven Fletcher (Sunderland)

Substitutes: 70 Darren Fletcher (West Bromwich Albion, for Brown 63);
4 Johnny Russell (Derby County, for Ritchie 63);
41 Steven Naismith (Everton, for Martin 76)

Manager: Gordon Strachan

Gibraltar: Jamie Robba; Erin Barnett, Roy Chipolina (captain), Ryan Casciaro; Jean-Carlos Garcia, Liam Walker, Daniel Duarte, Anthony Bardon, Joseph Chipolina; Lee Casciaro, Kyle Casciaro. *Substitutes:* Brian Perez (for Daniel Duarte 57); John Paul Duarte (for Lee Casciaro 82); Michael Yome (for Kyle Casciaro 89). *Coach:* Jeffrey Wood.

Scorers: Scotland: Martin 25; Maloney 39; Steven Fletcher 52, 56, 85; Naismith 90+1

It was another six goals against the group minnows Gibraltar, and another hat trick for Steven Fletcher, but sadly nowhere near enough to claim a qualification place for the following year's European Championships. Scotland coasted to victory in Portugal, where the game was played due to Gibraltar not having a suitable venue. Striker Chris Martin got the first goal, following up Gordon Greer's header from a corner. Shaun Maloney got his fifth of the campaign with a neat finish into the top corner and then Fletcher took over with a header, a close-range effort off the post and then a powerful shot from the edge of the area to complete his treble. Substitute Steve Naismith got the sixth in stoppage time. Failing to gain more points against the Republic of Ireland and Georgia had cost the Scots though.

EUROPEAN CHAMPIONSHIP QUALIFYING GROUP I

	P	W	D	L	F	A	Pts
Germany	10	7	1	2	24	9	22
Poland	10	6	3	1	33	10	21
Rep of Ireland	10	5	3	2	19	7	18
Scotland	10	4	3	3	22	12	15
Georgia	10	3	0	7	10	16	9
Gibraltar	10	0	0	10	2	56	0

24 March 2016 Friendly Generali Arena, Prague Attendance: 14,580

748 Czech Republic 0, SCOTLAND 1
Referee: Paul McLaughlin (Republic of Ireland)

Scotland: Allan McGregor (Hull City); Alan Hutton (Aston Villa), Russell Martin (Norwich City), Christophe Berra (Ipswich Town), Andrew Robertson (Hull City); Ikechi Anya (Watford), Robert Snodgrass (Hull City), Darren Fletcher (West Bromwich Albion, captain), Kenny McLean (Aberdeen), Charlie Mulgrew (Celtic); Ross McCormack (Fulham). *Substitutes:* Barry Bannan (Sheffield Wednesday, for Robertson 58); Matt Phillips (Queens Park Rangers, for McLean 59); Tony Watt (Blackburn Rovers, for McCormack 78); Paul Caddis (Birmingham City, for Anya 87). *Manager:* Gordon Strachan.

Czech Republic: Tomas Koubek; Pavel Kaderabek, Tomas Sivok (captain), Michal Kadlec, David Limbersky; Kamil Vacek, Vladimir Darida; Borek Dockal, Martin Frydek, Josef Sural; Tomas Necid. *Substitutes:* Jiri Skalak (for Frydek 46); Daniel Kolar (for Dockal 65); Matej Vydra (for Necid 65); Lukas Marecek (for Vacek 78); Daniel Pudil (for Sural 78); Jakub Rada (for Darida 87). *Coach:* Pavel Vrba.

Scorer: Scotland: Anya 10

Chapter nine: 2010-2019

| 29 March 2016 | Friendly | Hampden Park | Attendance: 18,385 |

749 SCOTLAND 1, Denmark 0 *Referee: Svein Oddvar Moen (Norway)*

Scotland: Craig Gordon (Celtic); Steven Whittaker (Norwich City), Gordon Greer (Brighton & Hove Albion), Grant Hanley (Blackburn Rovers), Kieran Tierney (Celtic); Shaun Maloney (Hull City), *Scott Brown (Celtic, captain), John McGinn (Hibernian), Matt Ritchie (Bournemouth); Steven Fletcher (Olympique de Marseille), Leigh Griffiths (Celtic). *Substitutes:* Ikechi Anya (Watford, for Fletcher 46); Charlie Mulgrew (Celtic, for Tierney 46); Chris Martin (Derby County, for Griffiths 60); Liam Bridcutt (Leeds United, for Maloney 69); Oliver Burke (Nottingham Forest, for Ritchie 82). *Manager:* Gordon Strachan.

Denmark: Kasper Schmeichel; Henrik Dalsgaard, Simon Kjaer, Daniel Agger (captain), Riza Durmisi; Andreas Christensen, Pierre Emile Hojbjerg, Thomas Delaney, Christian Eriksen; Nicolai Jorgensen, Yussuf Poulsen. *Substitutes:* Jonas Lossl (for Schmeichel 46); Martin Braithwaite (for Poulsen 46); Erik Sviatchenko (for Agger 64); Lasse Schone (for Eriksen 81). *Coach:* Age Hareide.

Scorer: Scotland: Ritchie 8

Captain Scott Brown became the 30th player to reach 50 appearances. Alan Hutton had reached the milestone in the previous match against the Czech Republic.

| 29 May 2016 | Friendly | National Stadium, Attard, Malta | Attendance: 8,000 |

750 Italy 1, SCOTLAND 0 *Referee: Alan Mario Sant (Malta)*

Scotland: David Marshall (Cardiff City); Callum Paterson (Hearts), Russell Martin (Norwich City), Grant Hanley (Blackburn Rovers), Charlie Mulgrew (Celtic); Ikechi Anya (Watford), Darren Fletcher (West Bromwich Albion, captain), James McArthur (Crystal Palace), Matt Ritchie (Bournemouth); Matt Phillips (Queens Park Rangers), Ross McCormack (Fulham). *Substitutes:* Christophe Berra (Ipswich Town, for Paterson 46); Steven Fletcher (Olympique de Marseille, for McCormack 46); Oliver Burke (Nottingham Forest, for Phillips 70); Steven Naismith (Norwich City, for Anya 71); Craig Bryson (Derby County, for McArthur 83). *Manager:* Gordon Strachan.

Italy: Gianluigi Buffon (captain); Andrea Barzagli, Leonardo Bonucci, Giorgio Chiellini; Antonio Candreva, Alessandro Florenzi, Daniele De Rossi, Emanuele Giaccherini, Matteo Darmian; Graziano Pelle, Eder. *Substitutes:* Lorenzo Insigne (for Eder 59); Federico Bernardeschi (for Darmian 60); Marco Parolo (for Candreva 62); Jorginho (for De Rossi 67); Simone Zaza (for Pelle 68); Giacomo Bonaventura (for Giaccherini 80). *Coach:* Antonio Conte.

Scorer: Italy: Pelle 57

| 4 June 2016 | Friendly | Stade Municipal, Metz | Attendance: 25,057 |

751 France 3, SCOTLAND 0 *Referee: Sebastien Delferiere (Belgium)*

Scotland: David Marshall (Cardiff City); Russell Martin (Norwich City), Gordon Greer (Brighton & Hove Albion), Grant Hanley (Blackburn Rovers), Andrew Robertson (Hull City); Robert Snodgrass (Hull City), Darren Fletcher (West Bromwich Albion, captain), James McArthur (Crystal Palace), Matt Ritchie (Bournemouth); Shaun Maloney (Hull City), Steven Fletcher (Olympique de Marseille). *Substitutes:* Ikechi Anya (Watford, for Maloney 46); Charlie Mulgrew (Celtic, for Robertson 46); Steven Naismith (Norwich City, for Steven Fletcher 58); Stephen Kingsley (Swansea City, for Snodgrass 66); Barrie McKay (Rangers, for McArthur 84). *Manager:* Gordon Strachan.

France: Hugo Lloris (captain); Bacary Sagna, Adil Rami, Laurent Koscielny, Patrice Evra; Paul Pogba, N'Golo Kante, Blaise Matuidi; Kingsley Coman, Olivier Giroud, Dimitri Payet. *Substitutes:* Antoine Griezmann (for Coman 46); Anthony Martial (for Payet 46); Andre-Pierre Gignac (for Giroud 63); Yohan Cabaye (for Matuidi 69); Lucas Digne (for Evra 83); Moussa Sissoko (for Kante 88). *Coach:* Didier Deschamps.

Scorers: France: Giroud 8, 35; Koscielny 39

| 4 September 2016 | World Cup qualifying | National Stadium, Attard | Attendance: 15,069 |

752 Malta 1, SCOTLAND 5 *Referee: Yevhen Aranovskyi (Ukraine)*

Scotland: David Marshall (Hull City); Callum Paterson (Hearts), Russell Martin (Norwich City), Grant Hanley (Newcastle United), Andrew Robertson (Hull City); Barry Bannan (Sheffield Wednesday), Darren Fletcher (West Bromwich Albion, captain), Robert Snodgrass (Hull City), Matt Ritchie (Newcastle United); Oliver Burke (RB Leipzig), Chris Martin (Fulham). *Substitutes:* James Forrest (Celtic, for Burke 66); Steven Fletcher (Sheffield Wednesday, for Martin 69); Ikechi Anya (Derby County, for Ritchie 86). *Manager:* Gordon Strachan.

Malta: Andrew Hogg; Jonathan Caruana, Andrei Agius, Steve Borg; Ryan Scicluna, Paul Fenech, Gareth Sciberras, Luke Gambin, Joseph Zerafa; Andre Schembri (captain), Alfred Effiong. *Substitutes:* Roderick Briffa (for Schembri 66); Ryan Camilleri (for Scicluna 79); Michael Mifsud (for Effiong 89). *Coach:* Pietro Ghedin.

Scorers: Scotland: Snodgrass 10, 61 (pen), 85; Chris Martin 53; Steven Fletcher 78   Malta: Effiong 14

| 8 October 2016 | World Cup qualifying | Hampden Park | Attendance: 35,966 |

753 SCOTLAND 1, Lithuania 1 *Referee: Tobias Stieler (Germany)*

Scotland: David Marshall (Hull City); Callum Paterson (Hearts), Russell Martin (Norwich City), Grant Hanley (Newcastle United), Andrew Robertson (Hull City); Robert Snodgrass (Hull City), Darren Fletcher (West Bromwich Albion, captain), Barry Bannan (Sheffield Wednesday), Matt Ritchie (Newcastle United); Oliver Burke (RB Leipzig), Chris Martin (Fulham). *Substitutes:* James McArthur (Crystal Palace, for Fletcher 46); James Forrest (Celtic, for Burke 57); Leigh Griffiths (Celtic, for Ritchie 71). *Manager:* Gordon Strachan.

Lithuania: Ernestas Setkus; Egidijus Vaitkunas, Georgas Freidgeimas, Edvinas Girdvainis, Vaidas Slavickas; Arturas Zulpa, Mantas Kuklys, Fedor Cernych (captain), Arvydas Novikovas; Nerijus Valskis, Vykintas Slivka. *Substitutes:* Vytautas Andriuskevicius (for Slavickas 64); Karolis Chvedukas (for Zulpa 65); Mindaugas Grigaravicius (for Valskis 85). *Coach:* Edgaras Jankauskas.

Scorers: Lithuania: Cernych 59   Scotland: McArthur 89

| 11 October 2016 | World Cup qualifying | Stadion Malatinskeho, Trnava | Attendance: 11,098 |

754 Slovakia 3, SCOTLAND 0 *Referee: Martin Strombergsson (Sweden)*

Scotland: David Marshall (Hull City); Callum Paterson (Hearts), Russell Martin (Norwich City), Grant Hanley (Newcastle United), Kieran Tierney (Celtic); Robert Snodgrass (Hull City), Barry Bannan (Sheffield Wednesday), Darren Fletcher (West Bromwich Albion, captain), James McArthur (Crystal Palace), Matt Ritchie (Newcastle United); Steven Fletcher (Sheffield Wednesday). *Substitutes:* Leigh Griffiths (Celtic, for Darren Fletcher 64); Ikechi Anya (Derby County, for Ritchie 64); John McGinn (Hibernian, for Steven Fletcher 76). *Manager:* Gordon Strachan.

Slovakia: Matus Kozacic; Erik Sabo, Martin Skrtel (captain), Jan Durica, Jakub Holubek; Juraj Kucka, Milan Skriniar; Michal Duris, Marek Hamsik, Robert Mak; Adam Nemec. *Substitutes:* Marek Bakos (for Nemec 69); Dusan Svento (for Mak 80); Filip Kiss (for Hamsik 87). *Coach:* Jan Kozak.

Scorers: Slovakia: Mak 18, 56; Nemec 68

| 11 November 2016 | World Cup qualifying | Wembley, London | Attendance: 87,258 |

755 England 3, SCOTLAND 0 *Referee: Cuneyt Cakir (Turkey)*

Scotland: Craig Gordon (Celtic); Ikechi Anya (Derby County), Grant Hanley (Newcastle United), Christophe Berra (Ipswich Town), Lee Wallace (Rangers); James Forrest (Celtic), Scott Brown (Celtic), Darren Fletcher (West Bromwich Albion, captain), James Morrison (West Bromwich Albion), Robert Snodgrass (Hull City); Leigh Griffiths (Celtic). *Substitutes:* James McArthur (Crystal Palace, for Morrison 66); Callum Paterson (Hearts, for Anya 79); Matt Ritchie (Newcastle United, for Snodgrass 82). *Manager:* Gordon Strachan.

England: Joe Hart; Kyle Walker, Gary Cahill, John Stones, Danny Rose; Eric Dier, Jordan Henderson; Raheem Sterling, Wayne Rooney (captain), Adam Lallana; Daniel Sturridge. *Substitute:* Jamie Vardy (for Sturridge 74). *Manager:* Gareth Southgate.

Scorers: England: Sturridge 23; Lallana 50; Cahill 61

| 22 March 2017 | Friendly | Easter Road, Edinburgh | Attendance: 9,158 |

756 SCOTLAND 1, Canada 1 *Referee: Jakob Kehlet (Denmark)*

Scotland: Allan McGregor (Cardiff City); Ikechi Anya (Derby County), Christophe Berra (Ipswich Town), Charlie Mulgrew (Blackburn Rovers), Lee Wallace (Rangers); Tom Cairney (Fulham), Darren Fletcher (West Bromwich Albion, captain), Robert Snodgrass (West Ham); Steven Naismith (Norwich City), Chris Martin (Fulham), Oliver Burke (RB Leipzig). *Substitutes:* Andrew Robertson (Hull City, for Wallace 46); Barry Bannan (Sheffield Wednesday, for Burke 46); Jordan Rhodes (Sheffield Wednesday, for Naismith 62); Leigh Griffiths (Celtic, for Martin 62); John McGinn (Hibernian, for Cairney 76). *Manager:* Gordon Strachan.

Canada: Simon Thomas; Nikolas Ledgerwood (captain), Adam Straith, Manjrekar James, Maxim Tissot; Scott Arfield, Samuel Piette; Fraser Aird, Marco Bustos, David Hoilett; Simeon Jackson. *Substitutes:* Jayson Leutwiler (for Thomas 46); La'Vere Corbin-Ong (for Tissot 68); Benjamin Fisk (for Jackson 76); Charlie Trafford (for Arfield 90+4). *Coach:* Michael Findlay.

Scorers: Canada: Aird 11   Scotland: Naismith 35

| 26 March 2017 | World Cup qualifying | Hampden Park | Attendance: 20,435 |

757 SCOTLAND 1, Slovenia 0 *Referee: Bjorn Kuipers (Netherlands)*

Scotland: Craig Gordon (Celtic); Kieran Tierney (Celtic), Russell Martin (Norwich City), Charlie Mulgrew (Blackburn Rovers), Andrew Roberson (Hull City); Robert Snodgrass (West Ham), Scott Brown (Celtic, captain), James Morrison (West Bromwich Albion), Stuart Armstrong (Celtic); James Forrest (Celtic), Leigh Griffiths (Celtic). *Substitutes:* Steven Naismith (Norwich City, for Griffiths 50); Ikechi Anya (Derby County, for Snodgrass 75); Chris Martin (Fulham, for Morrison 82). *Manager:* Gordon Strachan.

Slovenia: Jan Oblak; Aljaz Struna, Miral Samardzic, Bostjan Cesar (captain), Bojan Jokic; Kevin Kampl, Rene Krhin, Jasmin Kurtic; Valter Birsa, Josip Ilicic, Roman Bezjak. *Substitutes:* Benjamin Verbic (for Bezjak 58); Robert Beric (for Birsa 69); Nik Omladic (for Kampl 87). *Coach:* Srecko Katanec.

Scorer: Scotland: Chris Martin 88

Leigh Griffiths (hidden) scores his second direct free kick in the final minute to put Scotland 2-1 ahead against England. Unfortunately Harry Kane's stoppage-time equaliser denied the Scots a famous victory.

Chapter nine: 2010-2019

| 10 June 2017 | World Cup qualifying | Hampden Park | Attendance: 48,520 |

758 SCOTLAND 2, England 2

Referee: Paolo Tagliavento (Italy)

Scotland (3-5-2):
47 Craig Gordon (Celtic);
36 Christophe Berra (Hearts)
27 Charlie Mulgrew (Blackburn Rovers)
4   Kieran Tierney (Celtic);
27 Ikechi Anya (Derby County)
24 Robert Snodgrass (West Ham)
53 Scott Brown (Celtic, captain)
44 James Morrison (West Bromwich Albion)
15 Andrew Robertson (Hull City);
2   Stuart Armstrong (Celtic)
13 Leigh Griffiths (Celtic)

Substitutes: 28 James McArthur (Crystal Palace, for Morrison 46);
1 Ryan Fraser (Bournemouth, for Snodgrass 67);
13 Chris Martin (Derby County, for Anya 81)

Manager: Gordon Strachan

English striker Harry Kane destroyed hopes of a famous World Cup qualifying victory when defensive frailties let him in for a stoppage-time equaliser after a pulsating Hampden encounter. It was a tie the Scots needed to win to retain any hopes of finishing second in the group, but it was not to be. The match was very tight during the first half and for over half of the second, before a lapse allowed substitute Alex Oxlade-Chamberlain to open the scoring in the 70th minute. The Scottish players raised their game after that, causing panic in the English defence, and when a free kick was conceded on the edge of the penalty area Leigh Griffiths fired a superb shot past keeper Joe Hart. Incredibly, just three minutes later, with time almost up, Griffiths repeated the feat after another foul just outside the box. It looked like all three points had been achieved but then an inability to clear in the third minute of stoppage time allowed Kane to finish off a cross from Raheem Sterling. Hearts were once again broken.

England: Joe Hart; Kyle Walker, Chris Smalling, Gary Cahill, Ryan Bertrand; Jake Livermore, Eric Dier, Adam Lallana, Dele Alli; Marcus Rashford, Harry Kane (captain). *Substitutes:* Alex Oxlade-Chamberlain (for Rashford 65); Raheem Sterling (for Alli 84); Jermaine Defoe (for Livermore 90+2). *Manager:* Gareth Southgate.

Scorers: England: Oxlade-Chamberlain 70; Kane 90+3   Scotland: Griffiths 87, 90

| 1 September 2017 | World Cup qualifying | LFF Stadionas, Vilnius | Attendance: 5,067 |

759 Lithuania 0, SCOTLAND 3

Referee: Carlos del Cerro Grande (Spain)

Scotland: Craig Gordon (Celtic); Kieran Tierney (Celtic), Christophe Berra (Hearts), Charlie Mulgrew (Blackburn Rovers), Andrew Robertson (Liverpool); James Forrest (Celtic), Scott Brown (Celtic, captain), James McArthur (Crystal Palace), Stuart Armstrong (Celtic); Matt Phillips (West Bromwich Albion), Leigh Griffiths (Celtic). *Substitutes:* Matt Ritchie (Newcastle United, for Forrest 66); Chris Martin (Derby County, for Griffiths 79); John McGinn (Hibernian, for Armstrong 85). *Manager:* Gordon Strachan.

Lithuania: Ernestas Setkus; Valdemar Borovskij, Georgas Freidgeimas, Tadas Kijanskas, Egidijus Vaitkunas; Arturas Zulpa, Mantas Kuklys, Vykintas Slivka, Arvydas Novikovas, Fedor Cernych (captain); Darvydas Sernas. *Substitutes:* Lukas Spalvis (for Zulpa 68); Ovidijus Verbickas (for Slivka 79); Deivydas Matulevicius (for Sernas 82). *Coach:* Edgaras Jankauskas.

Scorers: Scotland: Armstrong 25; Robertson 30; McArthur 72

| 4 September 2017 | World Cup qualifying | Hampden Park | Attendance: 26,371 |

760 SCOTLAND 2, Malta 0

Referee: Jakob Kehlet (Denmark)

Scotland: Craig Gordon (Celtic); Kieran Tierney (Celtic), Christophe Berra (Hearts), Charlie Mulgrew (Blackburn Rovers), Andrew Robertson (Liverpool); James Forrest (Celtic), Scott Brown (Celtic, captain), James McArthur (Crystal Palace), Stuart Armstrong (Celtic); Matt Phillips (West Bromwich Albion), Leigh Griffiths (Celtic). *Substitutes:* James Morrison (West Bromwich Albion, for McArthur 46); Grant Hanley (Norwich City, for Mulgrew 56); Chris Martin (Derby County, for Griffiths 70). *Manager:* Gordon Strachan.

Malta: Andrew Hogg; Steve Borg, Samuel Magri, Andrei Agius, Zach Muscat, Joseph Zerafa; Bjorn Kristensen, Ryan Fenech, Stephen Pisani; Andre Schembri (captain), Alfred Effiong. *Substitutes:* Luke Gambin (for Schembri 71); Paul Fenech (for Kristensen 85); Alexander Muscat (for Borg 86). *Coach:* Pietro Ghedin.

Scorers: Scotland: Berra 9; Griffiths 49

| 5 October 2017 | World Cup qualifying | Hampden Park | Attendance: 46,773 |

761 SCOTLAND 1, Slovakia 0

Referee: Milorad Mazic (Serbia)

Scotland: Craig Gordon (Celtic); Kieran Tierney (Celtic), Christophe Berra (Hearts), Charlie Mulgrew (Blackburn Rovers), Andrew Robertson (Liverpool); James Forrest (Celtic), Darren Fletcher (Stoke City, captain), James Morrison (West Bromwich Albion), Barry Bannan (Sheffield Wednesday); Matt Phillips (West Bromwich Albion), Leigh Griffiths (Celtic). *Substitutes:* Chris Martin (Derby County, for Forrest 61); James McArthur (Crystal Palace, for Fletcher 79); Ikechi Anya (Derby County, for Tierney 82). *Manager:* Gordon Strachan.

Slovakia: Martin Dubravka; Peter Pekarik, Martin Skrtel (captain), Jan Durica, Tomas Hubocan; Juraj Kucka, Jan Gregus, Marek Hamsik, Stanislav Lobotka, Robert Mak; Adam Nemec. *Substitutes:* Ondrej Duda (for Hamsik 79); Vladimir Weiss (for Nemec 79); Norbert Gyomber (for Kucka 80). *Coach:* Jan Kozak.

Scorer: Scotland: Skrtel 89 (own goal)

8 October 2017   World Cup qualifying   Stadion Stozice, Ljubljana   Attendance: 11,123

762 Slovenia 2, SCOTLAND 2   Referee: Jonas Eriksson (Sweden)

Scotland (4-4-2):

51 Craig Gordon (Celtic);
8   Kieran Tierney (Celtic)
40 Christophe Berra (Hearts)
31 Charlie Mulgrew (Blackburn Rovers)
19 Andrew Robertson (Liverpool);
8   Matt Phillips (West Bromwich Albion)
32 James McArthur (Crystal Palace)
80 Darren Fletcher (Stoke City, captain)
27 Barry Bannan (Sheffield Wednesday);
17 Chris Martin (Derby County)
17 Leigh Griffiths (Celtic)

Substitutes: 29 Ikechi Anya (Derby County, for Martin 53);
25 Robert Snodgrass (Aston Villa, for McArthur 79);
31 Steven Fletcher (Sheffield Wednesday, for Tierney 80)

Manager: Gordon Strachan

Slovenia: Jan Oblak; Aljas Struna, Miha Mevlja, Bostjan Cesar (captain), Bojan Jokic; Rajko Rotman, Jasmin Kurtic; Jan Repas, Josip Ilicic, Benjamin Verbic; Tim Matavz. *Substitutes:* Nejc Skubic (for Struna 46); Roman Bezjak (for Repas 46); Amedej Vetrih (for Matavz 89). *Manager:* Srecko Katanec.

Scorers: Scotland: Griffiths 32; Snodgrass 87   Slovenia: Bezjak 52, 72

With England having fairly easily topped group F, the Scots needed to win in Slovenia in the final match to have a chance of a play-off for the World Cup finals. Things looked good when Leigh Griffiths put them ahead in the 32nd minute, but it was against the run of play and not surprisingly Slovenia came back strongly to equalise and then deservedly take the lead. They rested on their laurels from then on, allowing Robert Snodgrass to grab an equaliser near the end. Thus the 10th qualifying campaign in a row had ended in failure, a far cry from the heady days of the 1970s and 80s. Manager Gordon Strachan made a strange comment after the match about Scottish people suffering from inferior genetics, with the players being smaller than those from other countries, before resigning from his position.

FIFA WORLD CUP QUALIFYING GROUP I

	P	W	D	L	F	A	Pts
England	10	8	2	0	18	3	26
Slovakia	10	6	0	4	17	7	18
Scotland	10	5	3	2	17	12	18
Slovenia	10	4	3	3	12	7	15
Lithuania	10	1	3	6	7	20	6
Malta	10	0	1	9	3	25	1

---

9 November 2017   Friendly   Pittodrie, Aberdeen   Attendance: 17,833

763 SCOTLAND 0, Netherlands 1   Referee: Ruddy Buquet (France)

Scotland: Craig Gordon (Celtic); Ryan Jack (Rangers), Christophe Berra (Hearts), Kieran Tierney (Celtic, captain), Andrew Robertson (Liverpool); James Forrest (Celtic), John McGinn (Hibernian), Callum McGregor (Celtic), Kenny McLean (Aberdeen); Matt Phillips (West Bromwich Albion), Ryan Christie (Aberdeen). *Substitutes:* Charlie Mulgrew (Blackburn Rovers, for Berra 46); Ryan Fraser (Bournemouth, for Forrest 71); Jason Cummings (Nottingham Forest, for McGregor 87). *Manager:* Malky Mackay (caretaker).

Netherlands: Jasper Cillessen; Timothy Fosu-Mensah, Virgil van Dyke, Karim Rebik, Nathan Ake; Georginio Wijnaldum, Daley Blind, Kevin Strootman (captain); Quincy Promes, Ryan Babel, Memphis Depay. *Substitutes:* Joel Veltman (for Fosu-Mensah 72); Steven Berghuis (for Promes 76). *Coach:* Dick Advocaat.

Scorer: Netherlands: Depay 40

---

23 March 2018   Friendly   Hampden Park   Attendance: 20,488

764 SCOTLAND 0, Costa Rica 1   Referee: Tobias Stieler (Germany)

Scotland: Allan McGregor (Hull City); Callum Paterson (Cardiff City), Grant Hanley (Norwich City), Charlie Mulgrew (Blackburn Rovers, captain), Scott McKenna (Aberdeen), Andrew Robertson (Liverpool); Tom Cairney (Fulham), Scott McTominay (Manchester United), Kevin McDonald (Fulham), Matt Ritchie (Newcastle United); Oliver McBurnie (Barnsley). *Substitutes:* Stuart Armstrong (Celtic, for McTominay 58); Callum McGregor (Celtic, for Cairney 58); Matt Phillips (West Bromwich Albion, for McBurnie 77); John McGinn (Hibernian, for Mulgrew 82); Jamie Murphy (Rangers, for Ritchie 87). *Manager:* Alex McLeish.

Costa Rica: Keylor Navas; Cristian Gamboa, Johnny Acosta, Giancarlo Gonzalez, Oscar Duarte, Bryan Oviedo; Bryan Ruiz (captain), Celso Borges, David Guzman, Daniel Colindres; Marcos Urena. *Substitutes:* Yeltsin Tejeda (for Guzman 56); Rodney Wallace (for Colindres 64); Yendrick Ruiz (for Urena 69); Ian Smith (for Gamboa 75); Francisco Calvo (for Oviedo 78). *Coach:* Oscar Ramirez.

Scorer: Costa Rica: Urena 14

---

27 March 2018   Friendly   Groupama Arena, Budapest   Attendance: 8,942

765 Hungary 0, SCOTLAND 1   Referee: Harald Lechner (Austria)

Scotland: Allan McGregor (Hull City); Ryan Fraser (Bournemouth), Jack Hendry (Celtic), Charlie Mulgrew (Blackburn Rovers, captain), Scott McKenna (Aberdeen), Andrew Robertson (Liverpool); James Forrest (Celtic), John McGinn (Hibernian), Callum McGregor (Celtic), Stuart Armstrong (Celtic); Matt Phillips (West Bromwich Albion). *Substitutes:* Barry Douglas (Wolverhampton Wanderers, for Robertson 67); Kenny McLean (Aberdeen, for Armstrong 70); Ryan Christie (Aberdeen, for Forrest 77); Callum Paterson (Cardiff City, for Fraser 82); Oliver McBurnie (Barnsley, for Phillips 84); Jason Cummings (Rangers, for McGregor 90+3). *Manager:* Alex McLeish.

Hungary: Peter Gulacsi; Attila Fiola, Kenneth Otigba, Richard Guzmics; Gergo Lovrencsics, Adam Pinter, Laszlo Kleinheisler, Szilveszter Hangya; Roland Varga, Adam Szalai, Balazs Dzsudzsak (captain). *Substitutes:* Akos Elek (for Pinter 46); Janos Szabo (for Hangya 46); Krisztian Nemeth (for Dzsudzsak 58); Mate Patkai (for Kleinheisler 67); Daniel Bode (for Szalai 77); Nemanja Nikolics (for Varga 83). *Coach:* Georges Leekens (Belgium).

Scorer: Scotland: Phillips 48

Chapter nine: 2010-2019

29 May 2018   Friendly   Estadio Nacional, Lima   Attendance: 40,000

766 Peru 2, SCOTLAND 0   *Referee: Fernando Guerrero (Mexico)*

Scotland: Jordan Archer (Millwall); Stephen O'Donnell (Kilmarnock), Charlie Mulgrew (Blackburn Rovers, captain), Scott McKenna (Aberdeen), Lewis Stevenson (Hibernian); Dylan McGeouch (Hibernian), Scott McTominay (Manchester United), John McGinn (Hibernian), Kenny McLean (Aberdeen); Jamie Murphy (Rangers), Matt Phillips (West Bromwich Albion). *Substitutes:* Oliver McBurnie (Barnsley, for Murphy 63); Callum Paterson (Cardiff City, for McGinn 63); Lewis Morgan (Celtic, for Phillips 72); Graeme Shinnie (Aberdeen, for McGeough 76); Chris Cadden (Motherwell, for McLean 87). *Manager:* Alex McLeish.

Peru: Jose Carvallo; Luis Advincula, Christian Ramos, Alberto Rodriguez (captain), Miguel Trauco; Edison Flores, Renato Tapia, Yoshimar Yotun; Andre Carrillo, Jefferson Farfan, Christian Cueva. *Substitutes:* Raul Ruidiaz (for Yotun 69); Andy Polo (for Carrillo 69); Pedro Aquino (for Cueva 80); Paolo Hurtado (for Farfan 81); Wilder Cartagena (for Tapia 84); Aldo Corzo (for Advincula 87). *Coach:* Ricardo Gareca.

Scorers: Peru: Cueva 37 (pen); Farfan 47

2 June 2018   Friendly   Estadio Azteca, Mexico City   Attendance: 70,993

767 Mexico 1, SCOTLAND 0   *Referee: Henry Bejarano (Costa Rica)*

Scotland: *Jon McLaughlin; Stephen O'Donnell (Kilmarnock), Jack Hendry (Celtic), Scott McKenna (Aberdeen, captain), Graeme Shinnie (Aberdeen); Johnny Russell (Sporting Kansas City), Dylan McGeouch (Hibernian), Kenny McLean (Aberdeen), Ryan Christie (Celtic); Callum Paterson (Cardiff City), Oliver McBurnie (Swansea City). *Substitutes:* Scott Bain (Celtic, for McLaughlin 46); Charlie Mulgrew (Blackburn Rovers, for Paterson 55); Chris Cadden (Motherwell, for McLean 55); John McGinn (Hibernian, for Christie 55); Lewis Morgan (Celtic, for McBurnie 80). *Manager:* Alex McLeish.

Mexico: Guillermo Ochoa (captain); Edson Alvarez, Hugo Ayala, Carlos Salcedo, Jesus Gallardo; Miguel Layun, Hector Herrera; Carlos Vela, Giovani dos Santos, Hirving Lozano; Raul Jimenez. *Substitutes:* Rafael Marquez (for Salcedo 46); Jonathan dos Santos (for Giovani dos Santos 57); Oribe Peralta (for Jimenez 57); Marco Fabian (for Herrera 58); Javier Aquino (for Vela 63); Jesus Corona (for Lozano 73). *Coach:* Juan Carlos Osorio.

Scorer: Mexico: Giovani dos Santos 13

Goalkeeper Jon McLaughlin's contract with Hearts expired on 31st May so he was capped against Mexico as an "unattached" player.

7 September 2018   Friendly   Hampden Park   Attendance: 20,196

768 SCOTLAND 0, Belgium 4   *Referee: Luca Banti (Italy)*

Scotland: Craig Gordon (Celtic); Ryan Fraser (Bournemouth), John Souttar (Hearts), Charlie Mulgrew (Blackburn Rovers), Kieran Tierney (Celtic), Andrew Robertson (Liverpool, captain); John McGinn (Aston Villa), Kevin McDonald (Fulham), Callum McGregor (Celtic), Stuart Armstrong (Southampton); Leigh Griffiths (Celtic). *Substitutes:* Steven Naismith (Hearts, for Griffiths 46); Robert Snodgrass (West Ham, for McDonald 53); Ryan Jack (Rangers, for Armstrong 53); Johnny Russell (Sporting Kansas City, for McGregor 68); Stephen O'Donnell (Kilmarnock, for Mulgrew 68); Graeme Shinnie (Aberdeen, for McGinn 73). *Manager:* Alex McLeish.

Belgium: Thibaut Courtois; Dedryck Boyata, Vincent Kompany, Jan Vertonghen; Timothy Castagne, Youri Tielemans, Moussa Dembele, Thorgan Hazard; Dries Mertens, Romelu Lukaku, Eden Hazard (captain). *Substitutes:* Thomas Vermaelen (for Kompany 46); Thomas Meunier (for Castagne 46); Michy Batshuayi (for Lukaku 46); Yannick Carrasco (for Mertens 46); Hans Vanaken (for Eden Hazard 55); Birger Verstraete (for Dembele 85). *Coach:* Roberto Martinez (Spain).

Scorers: Belgium: Lukaku 28; Eden Hazard 46; Batshuayi 52, 60

10 September 2018   UEFA Nations League, Group C1   Hampden Park   Attendance: 17,455

769 SCOTLAND 2, Albania 0   *Referee: Matej Jug (Slovenia)*

Scotland: Allan McGregor (Rangers); Stephen O'Donnell (Kilmarnock), John Souttar (Hearts), Charlie Mulgrew (Blackburn Rovers), Kieran Tierney (Celtic), Andrew Robertson (Liverpool, captain); John McGinn (Aston Villa), Kevin McDonald (Fulham), Callum McGregor (Celtic); Johnny Russell (Sporting Kansas City), Steven Naismith (Hearts). *Substitutes:* Stuart Armstrong (Southampton, for McDonald 46); Leigh Griffiths (Celtic, for Russell 70); Scott McTominay (Manchester United, for McGregor 79). *Manager:* Alex McLeish.

Albania: Thomas Strakosha; Elseid Hysaj (captain), Frederic Veseli, Berat Djimsiti, Egzon Binaku; Taulant Xhaka, Sabien Lilaj, Emanuele Ndoj; Enis Gavazaj, Bekim Balaj, Ledian Memushaj. *Substitutes:* Herdi Prenga (for Gavazaj 46); Rey Manaj (for Ndoj 66); Enea Mihaj (for Veseli 90+1). *Coach:* Christian Panucci (Italy).

Scorers: Scotland: Djimsiti 47 (own goal); Naismith 68

11 October 2018   UEFA Nations League, Group C1   Sammy Ofer Stadium, Haifa   Attendance: 10,234

770 Israel 2, SCOTLAND 1   *Referee: Daniel Stefanski (Poland)*

Scotland: Allan McGregor (Rangers); Stephen O'Donnell (Kilmarnock), John Souttar (Hearts), Charlie Mulgrew (Blackburn Rovers), Kieran Tierney (Celtic), Andrew Robertson (Liverpool, captain); John McGinn (Aston Villa), Kevin McDonald (Fulham), Calum McGregor (Celtic); Johnny Russell (Sporting Kansas City), Steven Naismith (Hearts). *Substitutes:* Scott McKenna (Aberdeen, for Mulgrew 46); James Forrest (Celtic, for Russell 67); Oliver McBurnie (Swansea City, for Naismith 76). *Manager:* Alex McLeish.

Israel: Ariel Harush; Sheran Yeini, Eitan Tibi, Omri Ben Harush; Eli Dasa, Dor Peretz, Bibras Natcho (captain), Beram Kayal, Taleb Tawatha; Munas Dabbur, Ben Sahar. *Substitutes:* Dia Sabi'a (for Sahar 46); Eliran Atar (for Tawatha 76); Dan Einbinder (for Kayal 82). *Coach:* Andreas Herzog (Austria).

Scorers: Scotland: Mulgrew 25 (pen)   Israel: Peretz 52; Tierney 75 (own goal)

14 October 2018   Friendly   Hampden Park   Attendance: 19,684

771 SCOTLAND 1, Portugal 3
Referee: Ruddy Buquet (France)

Scotland: Craig Gordon (Celtic); Stephen O'Donnell (Kilmarnock), Jack Hendry (Celtic), Scott McKenna (Aberdeen), Andrew Robertson (Liverpool, captain); James Forrest (Celtic), John McGinn (Aston Villa), Callum McGregor (Celtic), Stuart Armstrong (Southampton); Steven Naismith (Hearts), Oliver McBurnie (Swansea City). *Substitutes:* Graeme Shinnie (Aberdeen, for McGinn 67); Gary Mackay-Steven (Aberdeen, for McBurnie 76); Kevin McDonald (Fulham, for Armstrong 77). *Manager:* Alex McLeish.

Portugal: Beto (captain); Luis Neto, Cedric Soares, Ruben Dias, Kevin Rodrigues; Sergio Oliveira, Danilo Pereira, Bruno Fernandes; Helder Costa, Eder, Bruma. *Substitutes:* Renato Sanches (for Sergio Oliveira 56); Pedro Mendes (for Ruben Dias 56); Gedson (for Bruno Fernandes 68); Claudio Ramos (for Beto 86); William Carvalho (for Danilo Pereira 90+1); Rafa (for Bruma 90+1). *Coach:* Fernando Santos.

Scorers: Portugal: Helder Costa 44; Eder 74; Bruma 84   Scotland: Naismith 90+3

---

17 November 2018   UEFA Nations League, Group C1   Loro Borici Stadiumi, Shkoder   Attendance: 8,632

772 Albania 0, SCOTLAND 4
Referee: Vladislav Bezborodov (Russia)

Scotland (4-4-2):

41 Allan McGregor (Rangers);
10 Callum Paterson (Cardiff City)
1 David Bates (SV Hamburg)
7 Scott McKenna (Aberdeen)
27 Andrew Robertson (Liverpool, captain);
25 James Forrest (Celtic)
8 Callum McGregor (Celtic)
10 Stuart Armstrong (Southampton)
4 Ryan Christie (Celtic);
5 Ryan Fraser (Bournemouth)
32 Steven Fletcher (Sheffield Wednesday)

Substitutes: 4 Scott McTominay (Manchester United, for Armstrong 61); 13 Matt Phillips (West Bromwich Albion, for Fletcher 68); 9 Johnny Russell (Sporting Kansas City, for Fraser 72)

Manager: Alex McLeish

A home win over Albania in the newly formed UEFA Nations League had been followed by a close defeat in Israel, so it was imperative that the Scots take something from the reverse fixture with the Albanians if they were going to finish top of the group. And for a pleasant change, everything fell into place with a resounding away victory. The excellent Ryan Fraser got his side up and running, finishing off a Ryan Christie pass, and Steven Fletcher's penalty in first-half stoppage time doubled the score. After the break James Forrest, who had failed to find the net in his previous 25 appearances, took over. First he held off a defender to fire in a low shot in the 55th minute, then 12 minutes later volleyed home his second for the pick of the goals. Having finally broken his duck, he then went on and netted a hat trick in the final match against Israel which clinched a play-off place.

Albania: Etrit Berisha; Frederic Veseli, Berat Djimsiti, Mergim Mavraj (captain), Egzon Binaku; Myrto Uzuni, Ergys Kace, Taulant Xhaka, Eros Grezda; Ledian Memushaj, Rey Manaj. *Substitutes:* Ardian Ismajli (for Kace 27); Kastriot Dermaku (for Djimsiti 53); Bekim Balaj (for Manaj 62). *Coach:* Christian Panucci (Italy).

EUFA NATIONS LEAGUE GROUP C1

	P	W	D	L	F	A	Pts
Scotland	4	3	0	1	10	4	9
Israel	4	2	0	2	6	5	6
Albania	4	1	0	3	1	8	3

Scorers: Scotland: Fraser 14; Fletcher 45+2 (pen); Forrest 55, 67

---

20 November 2018   UEFA Nations League, Group C1   Hampden Park   Attendance: 21,281

773 SCOTLAND 3, Israel 2
Referee: Tobias Welz (Germany)

Scotland: Allan McGregor (Rangers); Callum Paterson (Cardiff City), David Bates (SV Hamburg), Scott McKenna (Aberdeen), Andrew Robertson (Liverpool, captain); James Forrest (Celtic), Callum McGregor (Celtic), Stuart Armstrong (Southampton), Ryan Christie (Celtic); Ryan Fraser (Bournemouth), Steven Fletcher (Sheffield Wednesday). *Substitutes:* Graeme Shinnie (Aberdeen, for Christie 76); Matt Phillips (West Bromwich Albion, for Armstrong 76); Scott McTominay (Manchester United, for Fletcher 87). *Manager:* Alex McLeish.

Israel: Ariel Harush; Sheran Yeini, Loai Taha, Omri Ben Harush; Eli Dasa, Dor Peretz, Bibras Natcho (captain), Beram Kayal, Taleb Tawatha; Munas Dabbur, Eran Zahavi. *Substitutes:* Almog Cohen (for Taha 67); Dia Sabi'a (for Peretz 73); Tomer Hemed (for Tawatha 85). *Coach:* Andreas Herzog (Austria).

Scorers: Israel: Kayal 9; Zahavi 75   Scotland: Forrest 34, 43, 64

---

21 March 2019   European Championship qualifying   Astana Arena   Attendance: 27,641

774 Kazakhstan 3, SCOTLAND 0
Referee: Srdjan Jovanovic (Serbia)

Scotland: Scott Bain (Celtic); Liam Palmer (Sheffield Wednesday), David Bates (SV Hamburg), Scott McKenna (Aberdeen), Graeme Shinnie (Aberdeen); James Forrest (Celtic), John McGinn (Aston Villa), Callum McGregor (Celtic, captain), Stuart Armstrong (Southampton); Oliver McBurnie (Swansea City), Oliver Burke (Celtic). *Substitutes:* Johnny Russell (Sporting Kansas City, for McBurnie 61); Scott McTominay (Manchester United, for McGinn 70); Marc McNulty (Hibernian, for Forrest 81). *Manager:* Alex McLeish.

Kazakhstan: Dmytro Nepohodov; Temirlan Erlanov, Evgeniy Postnikov, Serhiy Malyi; Yan Vorogovskiy, Yuriy Pertsukh, Islambek Kuat (captain), Aleksandr Merkel, Gafurzhan Suyumbaev; Baktiyar Zainutdinov, Roman Murtazaev. *Substitutes:* Bauyrzhan Turysbek (for Murtazaev 68); Eldos Akhmetov (for Erlanov 81); Serikzhan Muzhikov (for Zainutdinov 84). *Coach:* Michal Bilek (Czech Republic).

Scorers: Kazakhstan: Pertsukh 6; Vorogovskiy 10; Zainutdinov 51

Chapter nine: 2010-2019

24 March 2019   European Championship qualifying   San Marino Stadium, Serraville   Attendance: 4,077

775   **San Marino 0, SCOTLAND 2**   *Referee: Manuel Schuttengruber (Austria)*

Scotland: Scott Bain (Celtic); Stephen O'Donnell (Kilmarnock), David Bates (SV Hamburg), Scott McKenna (Aberdeen), Andrew Robertson (Liverpool, captain); Johnny Russell (Sporting Kansas City), Kenny McLean (Norwich City), Callum McGregor (Celtic), Stuart Armstrong (Southampton); Ryan Fraser (Bournemouth), Callum Paterson (Cardiff City). *Substitutes:* Marc McNulty (Hibernian, for Paterson 37); Scott McTominay (Manchester United, for McGregor 56); James Forrest (Celtic, for Armstrong 71). *Manager:* Alex McLeish.

San Marino: Elia Benedettini; Manuel Battistini, Michele Cevoli, Davide Simoncini (captain), Mirko Palazzi; Filippo Berardi, Marcello Mularoni, Enrico Golinucci, Alessandro Golinucci, Adolfo Hirsch; Matteo Vitaioli. *Substitutes:* Nicola Nanni (for Vitaioli 60); Andrea Grandoni (for Hirsch 77); Lorenzo Lunadei (for Simoncini 86). *Coach:* Franco Varrella (Italy).

Scorers: Scotland: McLean 4; Russell 74

8 June 2019   European Championship qualifying   Hampden Park   Attendance: 31,277

776   **SCOTLAND 2, Cyprus 1**   *Referee: Ola Hobber Nilsen (Norway)*

Scotland: David Marshall (Hull City); Stephen O'Donnell (Kilmarnock), Charlie Mulgrew (Blackburn Rovers), Scott McKenna (Aberdeen), Andrew Robertson (Liverpool, captain); James Forrest (Celtic), John McGinn (Aston Villa), Callum McGregor (Celtic), Kenny McLean (Norwich City); Eamonn Brophy (Kilmarnock), Ryan Fraser (Bournemouth). *Substitutes:* Oliver Burke (Celtic, for Brophy 73); Scott McTominay (Manchester United, for McGinn 79); Stuart Armstrong (Southampton, for McGregor 87). *Manager:* Steve Clarke.

Cyprus: Urko Pardo; Ioannis Kousoulos, Konstantinos Laifis, Nikolas Ioannou, Kostakis Artymatas; Andreas Makris, Michalis Ioannou, Matija Spoljaric, Renato Margaca; Pieros Sotiriou, Giorgos Efraim (captain). *Substitutes:* Anthony Georgiou (for Michalis Ioannou 66); Ioannis Kosti (for Spoljaric 70); Ioannis Pittas (for Makris 80). *Coach:* Ran Ben Shimon (Israel).

Scorers: Scotland: Robertson 61; Burke 89   Cyprus: Kousoulos 87

11 June 2019   European Championship qualifying   Stade Roi Baudouin, Brussels   Attendance: 32,482

777   **Belgium 3, SCOTLAND 0**   *Referee: Petr Ardeleanu (Czech Republic)*

Scotland: David Marshall (Hull City); Stephen O'Donnell (Kilmarnock), Charlie Mulgrew (Blackburn Rovers, captain), Scott McKenna (Aberdeen), Greg Taylor (Kilmarnock); Johnny Russell (Sporting Kansas City), Scott McTominay (Manchester United), Callum McGregor (Celtic), Kenny McLean (Norwich City), Stuart Armstrong (Southampton); Oliver Burke (Celtic). *Substitutes:* Ryan Fraser (Bournemouth, for Armstrong 32); James Forrest (Celtic, for Russell 67). *Manager:* Steve Clarke.

Belgium: Thibaut Courtois; Toby Alderweireld, Vincent Kompany, Jan Vertonghen; Thomas Meunier, Axel Witsel, Youri Tielemans, Thorgan Hazard; Kevin De Bruyne, Romelu Lukaku, Eden Hazard (captain). *Substitutes:* Dries Mertens (for Tielemans 78); Thomas Vermaelen (for Kompany 90); Yannick Carrasco (for Thorgan Hazard 90). *Coach:* Roberto Martinez (Spain).

Scorers: Belgium: Lukaku 45+1, 57; De Bruyne 90+2

6 September 2019   European Championship qualifying   Hampden Park   Attendance: 32,432

778   **SCOTLAND 1, Russia 2**   *Referee: Anastasios Sidiropoulos (Greece)*

Scotland: David Marshall (Wigan Athletic); Stephen O'Donnell (Kilmarnock), Charlie Mulgrew (Wigan Athletic), Liam Cooper (Leeds United), Andrew Robertson (Liverpool, captain); James Forrest (Celtic), Scott McTominay (Manchester United), John McGinn (Aston Villa), Callum McGregor (Celtic); Oliver McBurnie (Sheffield United), Ryan Fraser (Bournemouth). *Substitutes:* Kenny McLean (Norwich City, for Forrest 62); Ryan Christie (Celtic, for McGinn 62); Matt Phillips (West Bromwich Albion, for McTominay 78). *Manager:* Steve Clarke.

Russia: Guilherme Marinato; Mario Fernandes, Andrey Semenov, Georgiy Dzhikiya, Fedor Kidryashov; Magomed Ozdoev, Roman Zobnin; Aleksey Ionov, Aleksandr Golovin, Yuriy Zhirkov; Artem Dzyuba (captain). *Substitutes:* Dmitriy Barinov (for Zobnin 66); Aleksandr Erokhin (for Ionov 80); Ilzat Akhmetov (for Golovin 89). *Coach:* Stanislav Cherchesov.

Scorers: Scotland: McGinn 11   Russia: Dzyuba 40, O'Donnell 59 (own goal)

9 September 2019   European Championship qualifying   Hampden Park   Attendance: 25,524

779   **SCOTLAND 0, Belgium 4**   *Referee: Pawel Gil (Poland)*

Scotland: David Marshall (Wigan Athletic); Stephen O'Donnell (Kilmarnock), Charlie Mulgrew (Wigan Athletic), Liam Cooper (Leeds United), Andrew Robertson (Liverpool, captain); Robert Snodgrass (West Ham), Scott McTominay (Manchester United), Callum McGregor (Celtic), Kenny McLean (Norwich City); Ryan Christie (Celtic), Matt Phillips (West Bromwich Albion). *Substitutes:* Stuart Armstrong (Southampton, for McGregor 68); Johnny Russell (Sporting Kansas City, for Phillips 77); John McGinn (Aston Villa, for Christie 86). *Manager:* Steve Clarke.

Belgium: Thibaut Courtois; Toby Alderweireld, Thomas Vermaelen, Jan Vertonghen; Thomas Meunier, Leander Dendoncker, Youri Tielemans, Nacer Chadli; Kevin De Bruyne (captain), Dries Mertens; Romelu Lukaku. *Substitutes:* Yannick Carrasco (for Chadli 77); Yari Verschaeren (for Tielemans 86); Benito Raman (for Meunier 90). *Coach:* Roberto Martinez (Spain).

Scorers: Belgium: Lukaku 9; Vermaelen 24; Alderweireld 32; De Bruyne 82

10 October 2019   European Championship qualifying   Kuzhniki Stadium, Moscow   Attendance: 65,703

780   **Russia 4, SCOTLAND 0**   *Referee: Jakob Kehlet (Denmark)*

Scotland: David Marshall (Wigan Athletic); Liam Palmer (Sheffield Wednesday), Michael Devlin (Aberdeen), Charlie Mulgrew (Wigan Athletic), Andrew Robertson (Liverpool, captain); John McGinn (Aston Villa), John Fleck (Sheffield United), Callum McGregor (Celtic), Robert Snodgrass (West Ham); Ryan Fraser (Bournemouth), Oliver Burke (Deportivo Alaves). *Substitutes:* Lawrence Shankland (Dundee United, for Burke 46); Ryan Christie (Celtic, for Fraser 68); Stuart Armstrong (Southampton, for Fleck 81). *Manager:* Steve Clarke.

Russia: Guilherme Marinato; Mario Fernandes, Andrey Semenov, Georgiy Dzhikiya, Fedor Kudryaskov; Magomed Ozdoev, Dmitriy Barinov; Aleksey Ionov, Aleksandr Golovin, Yuriy Zhirkov; Artem Dzyuba (captain). *Substitutes:* Denis Cheryshev (for Zhirkov 66); Ilzat Akhmetov (for Ionov 79); Nikolay Komlichenko (for Dzyuba 86). *Coach:* Stanislav Cherchesov.

Scorers: Russia: Dzyuba 57, 70; Ozdoev 60; Golovin 84

13 October 2019   European Championship qualifying   Hampden Park   Attendance: 20,699

781   SCOTLAND 6, San Marino 0
Referee: Jerome Brisard (France)

Scotland: Jon McLaughlin (Sunderland); Liam Palmer (Sheffield Wednesday), Michael Devlin (Aberdeen), Stuart Findlay (Kilmarnock), Andrew Robertson (Liverpool, captain); James Forrest (Celtic), John McGinn (Aston Villa), Scott McTominay (Manchester United), Callum McGregor (Celtic), Ryan Christie (Celtic); Lawrence Shankland (Dundee United). *Substitutes:* Johnny Russell (Sporting Kansas City, for McGregor 70); Stuart Armstrong (Southampton, for McGinn 70). *Manager:* Steve Clarke.

San Marino: Aldo Simoncini; Manuel Battistini, Luca Censoni, Cristian Brolli, Alessandro D'Addario; Marcello Mularoni, Alessandro Golinucci; Alex Gasperoni (captain), Filippo Berardi, Mattia Giardi; Nicola Nanni. *Substitutes:* Andrea Grandoni (for D'Addario 46); Adolfo Hirsch (for Giardi 46); Luca Ceccaroli (for Berardi 80). *Coach:* Franco Varrella (Italy).

Scorers: Scotland: McGinn 12, 27, 45+1; Shankland 65; Findlay 67; Armstrong 87

---

16 November 2019   European Championship qualifying   GSP Stadium, Strovolos   Attendance: 7,595

782   Cyprus 1, SCOTLAND 2
Referee: Harald Lechner (Austria)

Scotland: David Marshall (Wigan Athletic); Liam Palmer (Sheffield Wednesday), Declan Gallagher (Motherwell), Scott McKenna (Aberdeen), Greg Taylor (Celtic); James Forrest (Celtic), John McGinn (Aston Villa), Ryan Jack (Rangers), Callum McGregor (Celtic), Ryan Christie (Celtic); *Steven Naismith (Hearts, captain). *Substitutes:* Oliver McBurnie (Sheffield United, for Naismith 62); Oliver Burke (Deportivo Alaves, for Forrest 72); Michael Devlin (Aberdeen, for Christie 90+2). *Manager:* Steve Clarke.

Cyprus: Urko Pardo; Jason Dimitriou, Andreas Karo, Giorgos Merkis (captain), Ioannis Kousoulos, Nikolas Ioannou; Fotis Papoulis, Charalampos Kyriakou, Ioannis Kosti, Giorgos Efraim; Pieros Sotiriou. *Substitutes:* Grigoris Kastanos (for Karo 42); Matija Spoljaric (for Efraim 74); Dimitris Theodorou (for Kyriakou 77). *Coach:* Ran Ben Shimon (Israel).

Scorers: Scotland: Christie 12; McGinn 53   Cyprus: Efraim 47

* Steven Naismith became the 32nd player to reach the 50-cap milestone. With Andy Robertson absent due to injury, Naismith was given the captain's armband. He kept the honour in the next match, which was to be his final appearance.

---

19 November 2019   European Championship qualifying   Hampden Park   Attendance: 19,515

783   SCOTLAND 3, Kazakhstan 1
Referee: Bas Nijhuis (Netherlands)

Scotland (4-5-1):

34 David Marshall (Wigan Athletic);
5 Liam Palmer (Sheffield Wednesday)
2 Declan Gallagher (Motherwell)
14 Scott McKenna (Aberdeen)
3 Greg Taylor (Celtic);
34 James Forrest (Celtic)
21 John McGinn (Aston Villa)
4 Ryan Jack (Rangers)
19 Callum McGregor (Celtic)
11 Ryan Christie (Celtic);
51 Steven Naismith (Hearts, captain)

Substitutes: 11 Oliver Burke (Deportivo Alaves, for Naismith 77); 2 John Fleck (Sheffield United, for Christie 83); 19 Stuart Armstrong (Southampton, for McGinn 90+1)

Manager: Steve Clarke

In the final match of a desperately disappointing European qualifying campaign, the Scots got some revenge for the shocking defeat in Kazakhstan some eight months previously. They did it the difficult way, coming from behind after defensive slackness gifted the visitors an opener in the 34th minute. It was a disappointing crowd as some members of the Tartan Army, who had witnessed severe maulings at the hands of both Belgium and Russia, made their feelings known. A deflected free kick by John McGinn provided the equaliser just after the break and then Steven Naismith made it 2-1 with a header. McGinn, who had a fine game, got a third in added time when he turned in a cross from left back Greg Taylor.

Kazakhstan: Dmytro Nepohodov; Aleksandr Marochkin, Serhiy Malyi, Yuriy Logvinenko; Gafurzhan Suyumbaev, Yuriy Pertsukh, Aybol Abiken, Dmitriy Shomko; Baktiyar Zainutdinov, Bauyrzhan Islamkhan (captain), Aleksey Shchetkin. *Substitutes:* Islambek Kuat (for Pertsukh 74); Maksim Fedin (for Islamkhan 74); Abat Aymbetov (for Shchetkin 83). *Coach:* Michal Bilek (Czech Republic).

Scorers: Kazakhstan: Zainutdinov 34   Scotland: McGinn 48, 90+1; Naismith 64

EUROPEAN CHAMPIONSHIP QUALIFYING GROUP I

	P	W	D	L	F	A	Pts
Belgium	10	10	0	0	40	3	30
Russia	10	8	0	2	33	8	24
Scotland	10	5	0	5	16	19	15
Cyprus	10	3	1	6	15	20	10
Kazakhstan	10	3	1	6	13	17	10
San Marino	10	0	0	10	1	51	0

CHAPTER TEN
2020-2023

4 September 2020   UEFA Nations League, Group B2   Hampden Park   *Behind closed doors

784 SCOTLAND 1, Israel 1
Referee: Slavko Vincic (Slovenia)

Scotland: David Marshall (Derby County); Scott McTominay (Manchester United), Scott McKenna (Aberdeen), Kieran Tierney (Arsenal); James Forrest (Celtic), Ryan Jack (Rangers), Callum McGregor (Celtic), Andrew Robertson (Liverpool, captain); John McGinn (Aston Villa), Lyndon Dykes (Queens Park Rangers), Ryan Christie (Celtic). *Substitutes:* Oliver Burke (West Bromwich Albion, for Dykes 74); Stuart Armstrong (Southampton, for McGinn 79). *Manager:* Steve Clarke.

Israel: Ofir Marciano; Eli Dasa, Nir Bitton, Eitan Tibi, Hatem Abd Elhamed, Taleb Tawatha; Dor Peretz, Bibras Natcho (captain), Manor Solomon; Eran Zahavi, Munas Dabbur. *Substitutes:* Yonatan Cohen (for Peretz 72); Shon Weissman (for Dabbur 79); Dan Glazer (for Solomon 90). *Coach:* Willibald Ruttensteiner.

Scorers: Scotland: Christie 45 (pen)   Israel: Zahavi 73

*This match, with others at the beginning of the 2021 UEFA Nations League, had no spectators because of the risk of contracting coronavirus.

7 September 2020   UEFA Nations League, Group B2   Andruv Stadion, Olomouc   Behind closed doors

785 *Czech Republic 1, SCOTLAND 2
Referee: Serdar Gozubuyuk (Netherlands)

Scotland: David Marshall (Derby County); Scott McTominay (Manchester United), Scott McKenna (Aberdeen), Liam Cooper (Leeds United); Liam Palmer (Sheffield Wednesday), Kenny McLean (Norwich City), John Fleck (Sheffield United), Andrew Robertson (Liverpool, captain); Stuart Armstrong (Southampton), Lyndon Dykes (Queens Park Rangers), Ryan Christie (Celtic). *Substitutes:* Callum Paterson (Cardiff City, for Dykes 67); John McGinn (Aston Villa, for Fleck 71); Callum McGregor (Celtic, for Armstrong 80). *Manager:* Steve Clarke.

Czech Republic: Ales Mandous; Tomas Holes, Roman Hubnik (captain), Vaclav Jemelka, Jaroslav Zeleny; Adam Janos, Marek Havlik; Tomas Malinsky, Lukas Budinsky, Jakub Pesek; Stanislav Tecl. *Substitutes:* Radim Breite (for Budinsky 55); Roman Potocny (for Pesek 76); Antonin Rusek (for Havlik 81). *Coach:* David Holoubek.

Scorers: Czech Republic: Pesek 12   Scotland: Dykes 27; Christie 52 (pen)

*The original Czech Republic squad had been placed in quarantine because of positive coronavirus tests. The Czech FA asked for a postponement but UEFA decided the game would go ahead. A replacement 24-man squad was named with the country's under-21 coach David Holoubek in charge.

8 October 2020   European Championship qualifying (play-off, semi-final)   Hampden Park   Behind closed doors

786 SCOTLAND 0, Israel 0
Referee: Ovidiu Hategan (Romania)

(after extra time, Scotland won 5-3 on penalty kicks)

Scotland (3-5-2):

37 David Marshall (Derby County);
15 Scott McTominay (Manchester United)
3 Declan Gallagher (Motherwell)
4 Liam Cooper (Leeds United);
12 Stephen O'Donnell (Motherwell)
6 Ryan Jack (Rangers)
24 John McGinn (Aston Villa)
22 Callum McGregor (Celtic)
37 Andrew Robertson (Liverpool, captain);
3 Lyndon Dykes (Queens Park Rangers)
10 Oliver McBurnie (Sheffield United)

History was made at a deserted Hampden Park as Scotland, participating in a penalty shootout for the first time, surprised many by actually winning it. The game was pretty much on a knife edge throughout, with few scoring chances created, and the final stages became very scrappy as a fear of losing factor became evident. Extra time came and went with the score still at 0-0. The Scots were successful with all five of their penalty kicks, John McGinn, Callum McGregor, Scott McTominay, Lawrence Shankland and Kenny McLean scoring, and won 5-3. For Israel, Zahavi's shot was saved while Bitton, Weissman and Abu Fani all scored. Next up was Serbia in the final.

Substitutes: 3 Lawrence Shankland (Dundee United, for McBurnie 73);
12 Ryan Fraser (Newcastle United, for Jack 83);
14 Callum Paterson (Sheffield Wednesday, for Dykes 90);
12 Kenny McLean (Norwich City, for O'Donnell 113)

Manager: Steve Clarke

Israel: Ofir Marciano; Eli Dasa, Nir Bitton, Eitan Tibi, Sheran Yeini, Hatem Abd Elhamed; Eyal Golasa, Bibras Natcho (captain), Manor Solomon; Munas Dabbur, Eran Zahavi. *Substitutes:* Mohammad Abu Fani (for Natcho 69); Shon Weissman (for Dabbur 83); Ilay Elmkies (for Golasa 100). *Coach:* Willibald Ruttensteiner.

Looking on anxiously during the penalty shoot-out with Israel. From left: Scott McTominay, Declan Gallagher, Kenny McLean, Andrew Robertson and Callum Paterson (hidden).

| 11 October 2020 | UEFA Nations League, Group B2 | Hampden Park | Behind closed doors |

787 SCOTLAND 1, Slovakia 0
Referee: Davide Massa (Italy)

Scotland: David Marshall (Derby County); Scott McTominay (Manchester United), Declan Gallagher (Motherwell), Andrew Considine (Aberdeen); Stephen O'Donnell (Motherwell), John McGinn (Aston Villa), John Fleck (Sheffield United), Kenny McLean (Norwich City), Andrew Robertson (Liverpool, captain); Lyndon Dykes (Queens Park Rangers), Ryan Fraser (Newcastle United). *Substitutes:* Oliver McBurnie (Sheffield United, for Dykes 72); Callum McGregor (Celtic, for Fleck 72); Callum Paterson (Sheffield Wednesday, for Fraser 85); Ryan Jack (Rangers, for McGinn 89). *Manager:* Steve Clarke.

Slovakia: Dusan Kuciak; Martin Koscelnik, Branislav Ninaj, Martin Valjent, Jakub Holubek; Matus Bero, Jan Gregus, Marek Hamsik (captain); Ivan Schranz, Robert Bozenik, Lukas Haraslin. *Substitutes:* Ondrej Duda (for Bero 22); Juraj Kucka (for Hamsik 62); Robert Mak (for Schranz 62); Pavol Safranko (for Bozenik 76); Albert Rusnak (for Haraslin 76). *Coach:* Pavel Hapal.

Scorer: Scotland: Dykes 54

| 14 October 2020 | UEFA Nations League, Group B2 | Hampden Park | Behind closed doors |

788 SCOTLAND 1, Czech Republic 0
Referee: Felix Zwayer (Germany)

Scotland: David Marshall (Derby County); Scott McTominay (Manchester United), Declan Gallagher (Motherwell), Andrew Considine (Aberdeen); Stephen O'Donnell (Motherwell), John McGinn (Aston Villa, captain), Ryan Jack (Rangers), Callum McGregor (Celtic), Greg Taylor (Celtic); Lyndon Dykes (Queens Park Rangers), Ryan Fraser (Newcastle United). *Substitutes:* Oliver McBurnie (Sheffield United, for Dykes 65); Kenny McLean (Norwich City, for Fraser 70); Paul Hanlon (Hibernian, for Taylor 79); Callum Paterson (Sheffield Wednesday, for McGinn 79). *Manager:* Steve Clarke.

Czech Republic: Tomas Vaclik; Vladimir Coufal, Ondrej Celustka, Ondrej Kudela, Jan Boril; Tomas Soucek, Alex Kral, Lukas Masopust, Vladimir Darida (captain), Lukas Provod; Matej Vydra. *Substitutes:* David Hovorka (for Celustka 20); Tomas Poznar (for Masopust 65); Petr Sevcik (for Provod 65); Pavel Kaderabek (for Kral 77); Michael Rabusic (for Vydra 77). *Coach:* Jiri Chytry.

Scorer: Scotland: Fraser 6

| 12 November 2020 | European qualifying (play-off, final) | Stadion Rajko Mitic, Belgrade | Behind closed doors |

789 Serbia 1, SCOTLAND 1
(after extra time, Scotland won 5-4 on penalty kicks)
Referee: Antonio Mateu Lahoz (Spain)

Scotland (3-5-2):
- 40 David Marshall (Derby County);
- 18 Scott McTominay (Manchester United)
- 6 Declan Gallagher (Motherwell)
- 14 Kieran Tierney (Arsenal);
- 15 Stephen O'Donnell (Motherwell)
- 27 John McGinn (Aston Villa)
- 9 Ryan Jack (Rangers)
- 25 Callum McGregor (Celtic)
- 39 Andrew Robertson (Liverpool, captain);
- 6 Lyndon Dykes (Queens Park Rangers)
- 14 Ryan Christie (Celtic)

Substitutes: 13 Oliver McBurnie (Sheffield United, for Dykes 82); 15 Kenny McLean (Norwich City, for McGinn 82); 17 Callum Paterson (Sheffield Wednesday, for Christie 87); 20 Leigh Griffiths (Celtic, for O'Donnell 116)

Manager: Steve Clarke

Having made it through on penalties against Israel, Scotland incredibly repeated the act in the UEFA Nations League final against a strong Serbian side. They should have won it in normal time but conceded a last-minute equaliser to send the game into an extra 30 minutes. It was Ryan Christie who opened the scoring in the 52nd minute, taking a pass from the hard-working Callum McGregor, turning inside and hitting a left-footed drive in off the post. The Scots defended the lead well until the final minute when slack marking allowed substitute Luka Jovic to head home a corner kick. The extra-time period remained goalless and penalty kicks would decide the outcome. Scotland scored with all five, through Leigh Griffiths, McGregor, Scott McTominay, Oliver McBurnie and Kenny McLean. Serbia were successful with the first four kicks, Tadic, Jovic, Gudelj and Katai finding the net, but the final attempt by Aleksandar Mitrovic was saved by David Marshall. Scotland therefore won 5-4 and progressed to the European Championships in England, which would be delayed a year from the original 2020 date.

Serbia: Predrag Rajkovic; Nikola Milenkovic, Stefan Mitrovic, Nemanja Gudelj; Darko Lazovic, Nemanja Maksimovic, Sasa Lukic, Filip Kostic; Dusan Tadic (captain), Sergej Milinkovic-Savic; Aleksandar Mitrovic. *Substitutes:* Filip Mladenovic (for Kostic 59); Luka Jovic (for Maksimovic 70); Aleksandar Katai (for Milinkovic-Savic 70); Uros Spajic (for Stefan Mitrovic 108). *Coach:* Ljubisa Tumbakovic.

Scorers: Scotland: Christie 52   Serbia: Jovic 90

Scott McTominay, who scored one of the successful penalty kicks, shows his emotion after beating Serbia, as his team mates celebrate in the background.

Chapter ten: 2020-2023

The starting line-up for the match against Serbia. Back (from left): Andrew Robertson, Stephen O'Donnell, Ryan Jack, Declan Gallagher, Lyndon Dykes, David Marshall. Front: Scott McTominay, Callum McGregor, John McGinn, Kieran Tierney, Ryan Christie.

15 November 2020   UEFA Nations League, Group B2   Antona Malatinskeho, Trnava   Behind closed doors

790 Slovakia 1, SCOTLAND 0
Referee: Istvan Kovacs (Romania)

Scotland: Craig Gordon (Hearts); Andrew Considine (Aberdeen), Scott McKenna (Nottingham Forest), Liam Cooper (Leeds United); Liam Palmer (Sheffield Wednesday), John McGinn (Aston Villa, captain), Kenny McLean (Norwich City), Stuart Armstrong (Southampton), Kieran Tierney (Arsenal); Ryan Christie (Celtic), Oliver McBurnie (Sheffield United). *Substitutes:* Leigh Griffiths (Celtic, for Considine 68); Lawrence Shankland (Dundee United, for Armstrong 87). *Manager:* Steve Clarke.

Slovakia: Marek Rodak; Peter Pekarik, Lubomir Satka, Milan Skriniar, Robert Mazan; Patrik Hrosovsky, Juraj Kucka, Ondrej Duda, Marek Hamsik (captain), Jan Gregus; Michal Duris. *Substitutes:* Stanislav Lobotka (for Kucka 61); Albert Rusnak (for Hamsik 68); Pavol Safranko (for Duris 90+3). *Coach:* Stefan Tarkovic.

Scorer: Slovakia: Gregus 32

18 November 2020   UEFA Nations League, Group B2   Netanya Stadium   Behind closed doors

791 Israel 1, SCOTLAND 0
Referee: Pawel Raczkowski (Poland)

Scotland (5-3-2):
41 David Marshall (Derby County);
16 Stephen O'Donnell (Motherwell)
19 Scott McTominay (Manchester United)
7 Declan Gallagher (Motherwell)
16 Kieran Tierney (Arsenal)
40 Andrew Robertson (Liverpool, captain);
29 John McGinn (Aston Villa)
10 Ryan Jack (Rangers)
26 Callum McGregor (Celtic);
16 Ryan Christie (Celtic)
7 Lyndon Dykes (Queens Park Rangers)

The strangest of qualifying group campaigns ended with a tame away defeat at the hands of now regular opponents Israel, following a similar setback against Slovakia. The Scots had up until then performed very well and twice defeated group winners the Czech Republic, albeit that the Czechs were missing their entire team on the first occasion due to a covid outbreak. The only goal of this game came in the 44th minute when Manor Solomon deceived a defender before drilling a left-foot shot past David Marshall. Too many of the Scottish players appeared out of touch, which was disappointing as it came so soon after qualifying for the following year's European Championship.

Substitutes: 15 Oliver McBurnie (Sheffield United, for Dykes 61);
22 Leigh Griffiths (Celtic, for McGinn 61);
18 Scott McKenna (Nottingham Forest, for Gallagher 73);
13 Oliver Burke (Sheffield United, for O'Donnell 73);
17 Kenny McLean (Norwich City, for McGregor 82)

Manager: Steve Clarke

Israel: Ofir Marciano; Eli Dasa, Nir Bitton, Eitan Tibi, Sheran Yeini, Sun Menachem; Bibras Natcho (captain), Neta Lavi, Manor Solomon; Eran Zahavi, Shon Weissman. *Substitutes:* Eyal Golasa (for Natcho 62); Orel Dgani (for Yeini 78); Mohammad Abu Fani (for Lavi 78); Yonatan Cohen (for Solomon 84). *Coach:* Willibald Ruttensteiner.

Scorer: Israel: Solomon 44

UEFA NATIONS LEAGUE GROUP B2

	P	W	D	L	F	A	Pts
Czech Republic	6	4	0	2	9	5	12
Scotland	6	3	1	2	5	4	10
Israel	6	2	2	2	7	7	8
Slovakia	6	1	1	4	5	10	4

25 March 2021   World Cup qualifying   Hampden Park   Behind closed doors

792 SCOTLAND 2, Austria 2   *Referee: Carlos del Cerro Grande (Spain)*

Scotland: David Marshall (Derby County); Stephen O'Donnell (Motherwell), Jack Hendry (KV Ostende), Grant Hanley (Norwich City), Kieran Tierney (Arsenal), Andrew Robertson (Liverpool, captain); John McGinn (Aston Villa), Scott McTominay (Manchester United), Stuart Armstrong (Southampton); Ryan Christie (Celtic), Lyndon Dykes (Queens Park Rangers). *Substitutes:* Che Adams (Southampton, for Armstrong 66); Callum McGregor (Celtic, for Dykes 78); Kenny McLean (Norwich City, for Christie 88). *Manager:* Steve Clarke.

Austria: Alexander Schlager; Stefan Lainer, Aleksandar Dragovic, Philipp Lienhart, David Alaba (captain); Christoph Baumgartner, Florian Grillitsch, Stefan Ilsanker, Xaver Schlager; Sasa Kalajdzic, Adrian Grbic. *Substitute:* Louis Schaub (for Grbic 68). *Coach:* Franco Foda.

Scorers: Austria: Kalajdzic 55, 80   Scotland: Hanley 71; McGinn 85

28 March 2021   World Cup qualifying   Bloomfield Stadium, Tel Aviv-Jaffa   Attendance; 5,000

793 Israel 1, SCOTLAND 1   *Referee: Deniz Aytekin (Germany)*

Scotland: David Marshall (Derby County); Stephen O'Donnell (Motherwell), Jack Hendry (KV Ostende), Grant Hanley (Norwich City), Kieran Tierney (Arsenal), Andrew Robertson (Liverpool, captain); John McGinn (Aston Villa), Scott McTominay (Manchester United), Callum McGregor (Celtic); Ryan Fraser (Newcastle United), Che Adams (Southampton). *Substitutes:* Ryan Christie (Celtic, for Hendry 46); Kenny McLean (Norwich City, for McGinn 74); Lyndon Dykes (Queens Park Rangers, for Adams 75); Stuart Armstrong (Southampton, for Fraser 86). *Manager:* Steve Clarke.

Israel: Ofir Marciano; Hatem Abd Elhamed, Eitan Tibi, Ofri Arad; Eli Dasa, Bibras Natcho (captain), Dor Peretz, Sun Menachem; Manor Solomon; Eran Zahavi, Shon Weissman. *Substitutes:* Neta Lavi (for Natcho 63); Munas Dabbur (for Weissman 74); Beram Kayal (for Menachem 79). *Coach:* Willibald Ruttensteiner.

Scorers: Israel: Peretz 44   Scotland: Fraser 56

31 March 2021   World Cup qualifying   Hampden Park   Behind closed doors

794 SCOTLAND 4, Faroe Islands 0   *Referee: Trustin Farrugia Cann (Malta)*

Scotland: Craig Gordon (Celtic); Scott McTominay (Manchester United), Grant Hanley (Norwich City), Kieran Tierney (Arsenal); Ryan Fraser (Newcastle United), John McGinn (Aston Villa), Callum McGregor (Celtic), Kenny McLean (Norwich City), Andrew Robertson (Liverpool, captain); Che Adams (Southampton), Lyndon Dykes (Queens Park Rangers). *Substitutes:* Kevin Nisbet (Hibernian, for Dykes 68); Oliver McBurnie (Sheffield United, for Adams 73); John Fleck (Sheffield United, for McGregor 73); Scott McKenna (Nottingham Forest, for Tierney 79); Liam Palmer (Sheffield Wednesday, for Fraser 79). *Manager:* Steve Clarke.

Faroe Islands: Gunnar Nielsen; Gilli Rolantsson, Gunnar Vatnhamar, Sonni Nattestad, Viljormur Davidsen; Solvi Vatnhamar, Hallur Hansson (captain), Jakup Andreasen, Brandur Henriksson; Joan Simun Edmundsson, Meinhard Olsen. *Substitutes:* Ari Jonsson (for Meinhard Olsen 58); Patrik Johannesen (for Solvi Vatnhamar 69); Klaemint Olsen (for Andreasen 69); Rogvi Baldvinsson (for Nattestad 76); Heini Vatnsdal (for Edmundsson 76). *Coach:* Hakan Ericson.

Scorers: Scotland: McGinn 7, 53; Adams 60; Fraser 70

2 June 2021   Friendly   Estadio Algarve, Loule   Behind closed doors

795 Netherlands 2, SCOTLAND 2   *Referee: Vitor Ferreira (Portugal)*

Scotland: Craig Gordon (Hearts); Jack Hendry (KV Ostende), Liam Cooper (Leeds United), Kieran Tierney (Arsenal); James Forrest (Celtic), David Turnbull (Celtic), Callum McGregor (Celtic), Stuart Armstrong (Southampton), Andrew Robertson (Liverpool, captain); Ryan Christie (Celtic), Lyndon Dykes (Queens Park Rangers). *Substitutes:* Kevin Nisbet (Hibernian, for Dykes 61); Ryan Fraser (Newcastle United, for Forrest 61); Declan Gallagher (Motherwell, for Cooper 62); Greg Taylor (Celtic, for Robertson 69); Scott McKenna (Nottingham Forest, for Tierney 69); Billy Gilmour (Chelsea, for Turnbull 81). *Manager:* Steve Clarke.

Netherlands: Tim Krul; Denzel Dumfries, Jurrien Timber, Stefan de Vrij, Matthijs de Ligt, Owen Wijndal; Georginio Wijnaldum (captain), Marten de Roon, Frenkie de Jong; Wout Weghorst, Memphis Depay. *Substitutes:* Ryan Gravenberch (for Wijnaldum 31); Davy Klaassen (for Frenkie de Jong 31); Steven Berghuis (for Timber 69); Patrick van Aanholt (for Wijndal 69); Quincy Promes (for Weghorst 69); Luuk de Jong (for de Vrij 85). *Coach:* Frank de Boer.

Scorers: Scotland: Hendry 11; Nisbet 64   Netherlands: Depay 17, 89

6 June 2021   Friendly   Stade Josy Barthel, Luxembourg City   Attendance: 1,000

796 Luxembourg 0, SCOTLAND 1   *Referee: Eldorjan Hamiti (Albania)*

Scotland: David Marshall (Derby County); Stephen O'Donnell (Motherwell), Declan Gallagher (Motherwell), Grant Hanley (Norwich City), Kieran Tierney (Arsenal), Andrew Robertson (Liverpool, captain); John McGinn (Aston Villa), Scott McTominay (Manchester United), Callum McGregor (Celtic); Lyndon Dykes (Queens Park Rangers), Che Adams (Southampton). *Substitutes:* Billy Gilmour (Chelsea, for McGregor 46); Scott McKenna (Nottingham Forest, for Gallagher 46); Ryan Fraser (Newcastle United, for Robertson 64); Nathan Patterson (Rangers, for O'Donnell 64); James Forrest (Celtic, for Gilmour 76); Kevin Nisbet (Hibernian, for Dykes 82). *Manager:* Steve Clarke.

Luxembourg: Anthony Moris; Laurent Jans (captain), Enes Mahmutovic, Vahid Selimovic, Dirk Carlson, Michael Pinto; Danel Sinani, Aldin Skenderovic, Sebastien Thill; Maurice Deville, Gerson Rodrigues. *Substitutes:* Florian Bohnert (for Deville 64); Olivier Thill (for Sinani 71); Daniel da Mota (for Skenderovic 84); Marvin Martins (for Sebastien Thill 84). *Coach:* Luc Holtz.

Scorer: Scotland: Adams 27

Chapter ten: 2020-2023

| 14 June 2021 | European Championship (group stage) | Hampden Park | Attendance: 9,847 |

797 SCOTLAND 0, Czech Republic 2 *Referee: Daniel Siebert (Germany)*

Scotland (5-3-2):

45 David Marshall (Derby County);
20 Stephen O'Donnell (Motherwell)
7   Jack Hendry (KV Ostende)
34 Grant Hanley (Norwich City)
7   Liam Cooper (Leeds United)
46 Andrew Robertson (Liverpool, captain);
34 John McGinn (Aston Villa)
24 Scott McTominay (Manchester United)
26 Stuart Armstrong (Southampton);
13 Lyndon Dykes (Queens Park Rangers)
20 Ryan Christie (Celtic)

Substitutes: 5 Che Adams (Southampton, for Christie 46);
32 Callum McGregor (Celtic, for Hendry 67); 19 Ryan Fraser (Newcastle United, for Armstrong 67);
38 James Forrest (Celtic, for O'Donnell 79); 4 Kevin Nisbet (Hibernian, for Dykes 79)

Manager: Steve Clarke

The Scots were made to pay for failing to convert several chances when, with the first half coming to end, Patrik Schick got to a corner before his marker and headed home. A couple more efforts were scorned just after the break and Jack Hendry was unlucky to see his shot come off the crossbar. But as they chased the game, the home players were dealt a killer blow. Another shot by Hendry was blocked midway inside the Czech half and Schick collected the rebound. This time he struck an audacious lob from the halfway line which looped over the advancing David Marshall and into the net. It was a bitter blow from which Scotland could not recover, although Lyndon Dykes and James Forrest both had shots blocked inside the goal area late on.

Czech Republic: Tomas Vaclic; Vladimir Coufal, Ondrej Celustka, Tomas Kalas, Jan Boril; Alex Kral, Tomas Soucek; Lukas Masopust, Vladimir Darida (captain), Jakub Jankto; Patrik Schick. *Substitutes:* Tomas Holes (for Kral 67); Matej Vydra (for Masopust 72); Adam Hlosek (for Jankto 72); Petr Sevcik (for Darida 87); Michael Krmencik (for Schick 87). *Coach:* Jaroslav Silhavy.

Scorer: Czech Republic: Schick 42, 52

| 18 June 2021 | European Championship (group stage) | Wembley, London | Attendance: 20,306 |

798 England 0, SCOTLAND 0 *Referee: Antonio Mateu Lahoz (Spain)*

Scotland (5-3-2):

46 David Marshall (Derby County);
21 Stephen O'Donnell (Motherwell)
25 Scott McTominay (Manchester United)
35 Grant Hanley (Norwich City)
22 Kieran Tierney (Arsenal)
47 Andrew Robertson (Liverpool, captain);
35 John McGinn (Aston Villa)
3   Billy Gilmour (Chelsea)
33 Callum McGregor (Celtic);
14 Lyndon Dykes (Queens Park Rangers)
6   Che Adams (Southampton)

Substitutes: 27 Stuart Armstrong (Southampton, for Gilmour 76);
5 Kevin Nisbet (Hibernian, for Adams 86)

Manager: Steve Clarke

Having got off to such a disappointing start it was imperative that Scotland took something from the encounter with the group favourites and their old foes, especially as England had begun by beating Croatia. And they rose to the occasion in fine style, with the more-fancied opposition being matched and at times outplayed. Manager Steve Clarke made four changes to the side and the replacements all stood out. Kieran Tierney came back in after injury and added his class to central defence, midfielder Callum McGregor steadied the midfield, Che Adams gave his all up front and youngster Billy Gilmour, earning his first international start, provided much evidence of his undoubted ability. There were few chances created but Clarke said he was very satisfied, particularly by the great team spirit and energy which his side displayed.

England: Jordan Pickford; Reece James, John Stones, Tyrone Mings, Luke Shaw; Kalvin Phillips, Declan Rice, Mason Mount; Phil Foden, Harry Kane (captain), Raheem Sterling. *Substitutes:* Jack Grealish (for Foden 63); Marcus Rashford (for Kane 74). *Manager:* Gareth Southgate.

John McGinn is tackled by England's Kalvin Phillips during the 0-0 draw at Wembley.

22 June 2021 European Championship (group stage) Hampden Park Attendance: 9,896

799 SCOTLAND 1, Croatia 3
Referee: Fernando Rapallini (Argentina)

Scotland (5-3-2):

- 47 David Marshall (Derby County);
- 22 Stephen O'Donnell (Motherwell)
- 26 Scott McTominay (Manchester United)
- 36 Grant Hanley (Norwich City)
- 23 Kieran Tierney (Arsenal)
- 48 Andrew Robertson (Liverpool, captain);
- 36 John McGinn (Aston Villa)
- 34 Callum McGregor (Celtic)
- 28 Stuart Armstrong (Southampton);
- 15 Lyndon Dykes (Queens Park Rangers)
- 7 Che Adams (Southampton)

Substitutes: 22 Scott McKenna (Nottingham Forest, for Hanley 33); 20 Ryan Fraser (Newcastle United, for Armstrong 70); 6 Kevin Nisbet (Hibernian, for Adams 84); 2 Nathan Patterson (Rangers, for O'Donnell 84)

Manager: Steve Clarke

Hopes of reaching the knockout stages of a major tournament for the first time were ended by Croatia, who finally found their form after losing to England and drawing with the Czech Republic. It was disappointing after the heroic display at Wembley four days previously, but no more than deserved. Nicola Vlasic finished well in the 17th minute to give Croatia the lead and when Callum McGregor rifled in an equaliser with three minutes of the first half left the hopes were rekindled. But when Luka Modric got the goal of the game in the second half there was no way back. The little midfielder showed his class as he swept home the ball with the outside of his right foot, giving keeper David Marshall no chance. The Croats rubbed salt in the wounds a quarter of an hour later when the equally impressive Ivan Perisic headed home Modric's corner. McGregor was the pick of the Scots players on a day too many of his team mates were simply unable to rise to the occasion.

Croatia: Dominik Livakovic; Josip Juranovic, Dejan Lovren, Domagoj Vida, Josko Gvardiol; Luka Modric (captain), Marcelo Brozovic, Mateo Kovacic; Nicola Vlasic, Bruno Petkovic, Ivan Perisic. *Substitutes:* Borna Barisic (for Gvardiol 70); Andrej Kramaric (for Petkovic 70); Luka Ivanusec (for Vlasic 76); Ante Rebic (for Perisic 81). *Coach:* Zlatko Dalic.

Scorers: Croatia: Vlasic 17; Modric 62; Perisic 77   Scotland: McGregor 42

2020 EUROPEAN CHAMPIONSHIP (DELAYED A YEAR DUE TO CORONAVIRUS)
GROUP D

	P	W	D	L	F	A	Pts
England	3	2	1	0	2	0	7
Croatia	3	1	1	1	4	3	4
Czech Republic	3	1	1	1	3	2	4
Scotland	3	0	1	2	1	5	1

---

1 September 2021 World Cup qualifying Parken, Copenhagen Attendance: 34,562

800 Denmark 2, SCOTLAND 0
Referee: Ovidiu Hategan (Romania)

Scotland: Craig Gordon (Hearts); Andrew Robertson (Liverpool, captain), Grant Hanley (Norwich City), Liam Cooper (Leeds United), Scott McKenna (Nottingham Forest), Kieran Tierney (Arsenal); Ryan Fraser (Newcastle United), Billy Gilmour (Norwich City), Callum McGregor (Celtic), Kenny McLean (Norwich City); Che Adams (Southampton). *Substitutes:* Lyndon Dykes (Queens Park Rangers, for McKenna 46); Ryan Christie (Bournemouth, for Adams 71); David Turnbull (Celtic, for McLean 85); Lewis Ferguson (Aberdeen, for Gilmour 90+1). *Manager:* Steve Clarke.

Denmark: Kasper Schmeichel; Daniel Wass, Joachim Andersen, Simon Kjaer (captain), Andreas Christensen, Joakim Maehle; Andreas Olsen, Pierre Emile Hojbjerg, Thomas Delaney, Mikkel Damsgaard; Yussuf Poulsen. *Substitutes:* Jonas Wind (for Poulsen 68); Jens Stryger (for Wass 85); Mohamed Daramy (for Olsen 85); Christian Norgaard (for Delaney 85); Jesper Lindstrom (for Damsgaard 90+3). *Coach:* Kasper Hjulmand.

Scorers: Denmark: Wass 14; Maehle 15

---

4 September 2021 World Cup qualifying Hampden Park Attendance: 40,869

801 SCOTLAND 1, Moldova 0
Referee: Lawrence Visser (Belgium)

Scotland: Craig Gordon (Hearts); Nathan Patterson (Rangers), Jack Hendry (Club Brugge), Grant Hanley (Norwich City), Kieran Tierney (Arsenal), Andrew Robertson (Liverpool, captain); John McGinn (Aston Villa), Billy Gilmour (Norwich City), Ryan Christie (Bournemouth); Lyndon Dykes (Queens Park Rangers), Kevin Nisbet (Hibernian). *Substitutes:* Callum McGregor (Celtic, for McGinn 65); Che Adams (Southampton, for Nisbet 65); Kenny McLean (Norwich City, for Gilmour 73); Liam Cooper (Leeds United, for Robertson 73); David Turnbull (Celtic, for Dykes 84). *Manager:* Steve Clarke.

Moldova: Christian Avram; Maxim Potirniche, Vadim Bolohan, Igor Armas (captain); Ion Jardan, Sergiu Platica, Vadim Rata, Artur Ionita, Oleg Reabciuk; Mihail Ghecev, Radu Ginsari. *Substitutes:* Cristian Dros (for Ghecev 46); Dan Spataru (for Ginsari 88); Nicky Clescenco (for Ionita 90+4). *Coach:* Roberto Bordin.

Scorer: Scotland: Dykes 14

---

7 September 2021 World Cup qualifying Ernst Happel Stadion, Vienna Attendance: 18,800

802 Austria 0, SCOTLAND 1
Referee: Georgi Kabakov (Bulgaria)

Scotland: Craig Gordon (Hearts); Stephen O'Donnell (Motherwell), Jack Hendry (Club Brugge), Grant Hanley (Norwich City), Kieran Tierney (Arsenal), Andrew Robertson (Liverpool, captain); John McGinn (Aston Villa), Billy Gilmour (Norwich City), Callum McGregor (Celtic); Lyndon Dykes (Queens Park Rangers), Che Adams (Southampton). *Substitutes:* Ryan Christie (Bournemouth, for Dykes 71); Paul McGinn (Hibernian, for O'Donnell 76); Kevin Nisbet (Hibernian, for Adams 88); Lewis Ferguson (Aberdeen, for Gilmour 88). *Manager:* Steve Clarke.

Austria: Daniel Bachmann; Christopher Trimmel, Aleksandar Dragovic, Martin Hinteregger, David Alaba (captain); Stefan Ilsanker, Florian Grillitsch, Konrad Laimer, Louis Schaub, Christoph Baumgartner; Marco Arnautovic. *Substitutes:* Michael Gregoritsch (for Ilsanker 56); Andreas Ulmer (for Grillitsch 76); Yusuf Demir (for Schaub 76); Ercan Kara (for Laimer 88). *Coach:* Franco Foda.

Scorer: Scotland: Dykes 30 (pen)

Chapter ten: 2020-2023

| 9 October 2021 | World Cup qualifying | Hampden Park | Attendance: 50,585 |

803 SCOTLAND 3, Israel 2
Referee: Szymon Marciniak (Poland)

Scotland: Craig Gordon (Hearts); Nathan Patterson (Rangers), Scott McTominay (Manchester United), Jack Hendry (Club Brugge), Kieran Tierney (Arsenal), Andrew Robertson (Liverpool, captain); John McGinn (Aston Villa), Billy Gilmour (Norwich City), Callum McGregor (Celtic); Lyndon Dykes (Queens Park Rangers), Che Adams (Southampton). *Substitutes:* Ryan Christie (Bournemouth, for Adams 67); Liam Cooper (Leeds United, for Gilmour 90+5). *Manager:* Steve Clarke.

Israel: Ofir Marciano; Eyad Abu Abaid, Nir Bitton, Ofri Arad; Eli Dasa, Bibras Natcho (captain), Dor Peretz, Sun Menachem; Munas Dabbur, Manor Solomon; Eran Zahavi. *Substitutes:* Dan Glazer (for Natcho 66); Shon Weissman (for Dabbur 66); Gadi Kinda (for Arad 74); Ofir Davidzada (for Menachem 87). *Coach:* Willibald Ruttensteiner.

Scorers: Israel: Zahavi 5; Dabbur 31   Scotland: McGinn 29; Dykes 57; McTominay 90+4

| 12 October 2021 | World Cup qualifying | Torsvollur, Torshavn | Attendance: 4,233 |

804 Faroe Islands 0, SCOTLAND 1
Referee: Matej Jug (Slovenia)

Scotland: Craig Gordon (Hearts); Jack Hendry (Club Brugge), Grant Hanley (Norwich City), Kieran Tierney (Arsenal); Ryan Fraser (Newcastle United), John McGinn (Aston Villa), Scott McTominay (Manchester United), Billy Gilmour (Norwich City), Andrew Robertson (Liverpool, captain); Lyndon Dykes (Queens Park Rangers), Ryan Christie (Bournemouth). *Substitutes:* Callum McGregor (Celtic, for Hendry 68); Nathan Patterson (Rangers, for Fraser 83); Kevin Nisbet (Hibernian, for Christie 83); Liam Cooper (Leeds United, for Gilmour 89). *Manager:* Steve Clarke.

Faroe Islands: Teitur Gestsson; Odmar Faero, Heini Vatnsdal, Sonni Nattestad; Gilli Rolantsson, Gunnar Vatnhamar, Brandur Hendriksson, Viljormur Davidsen; Hallur Hansson (captain), Joan Simun Edmundsson, Ari Jonsson. *Substitutes:* Hordur Askham (for Vatnsdal 58); Petur Knudsen (for Davidsen 59); John Frederiksen (for Hansson 90+1); Klaemint Olsen (for Edmundsson 90+5). *Coach:* Hakan Ericson.

Scorer: Scotland: Dykes 86

| 12 November 2021 | World Cup qualifying | Stadionul Zimbru, Chisinau | Attendance: 3,642 |

805 Moldova 0, SCOTLAND 2
Referee: Srdjan Jovanovic (Serbia)

Scotland: Craig Gordon (Hearts); Nathan Patterson (Rangers), Jack Hendry (Club Brugge), Liam Cooper (Leeds United), Kieran Tierney (Arsenal), Andrew Robertson (Liverpool, captain); John McGinn (Aston Villa), Billy Gilmour (Norwich City), Callum McGregor (Celtic), Stuart Armstrong (Southampton); Che Adams (Southampton). *Substitutes:* Kevin Nisbet (Hibernian, for Armstrong 75); Kenny McLean (Norwich City, for Gilmour 85); Jacob Brown (Stoke City, for Adams 85); David Turnbull (Celtic, for McGinn 90). *Manager:* Steve Clarke.

Moldova: Stanislav Namasco; Ion Jardan, Veaceslav Posmac, Vadim Bolohan; Ioan-Calin Revenco, Vadim Rata, Cristian Dros, Artur Ionita (captain), Denis Marandici; Ion Nicolaescu, Radu Ginsari. *Substitutes:* Artiom Rozgoniuc (for Bolohan 61); Victor Bogaciuc (for Dros 61); Maxim Cojocaru (for Ginsari 61); Marius Iosipoi (for Marandici 71); Artiom Puntus (for Nicolaescu 71). *Coach:* Roberto Bordin.

Scorers: Scotland: Patterson 38; Adams 65

| 15 November 2021 | World Cup qualifying | Hampden Park | Attendance: 49,527 |

806 SCOTLAND 2, Denmark 0
Referee: Alejandro Hernandez (Spain)

Scotland (5-4-1):

- 64 Craig Gordon (Hearts);
- 24 Stephen O'Donnell (Motherwell)
- 4 John Souttar (Hearts)
- 13 Liam Cooper (Leeds United)
- 30 Kieran Tierney (Arsenal)
- 55 Andrew Robertson (Liverpool, captain);
- 42 John McGinn (Aston Villa)
- 10 Billy Gilmour (Norwich City)
- 41 Callum McGregor (Celtic)
- 26 Ryan Christie (Bournemouth);
- 13 Che Adams (Southampton)

Substitutes: 24 Kenny McLean (Norwich City, for Gilmour 74); 30 Stuart Armstrong (Southampton, for Christie 79); 24 Scott McKenna (Nottingham Forest, for Robertson 80); 1 Anthony Ralston (Celtic, for Tierney 87)

Manager: Steve Clarke

Scotland gained the result necessary to secure a position in the play-off stage, reversing the score from Copenhagen a couple of months previously. It was one of the best displays seen at Hampden Park for several years, albeit against a team already qualified and missing a few players, as the Danes had up until then not dropped a point in the group. The Scottish defence was particularly secure and fittingly it was John Souttar who opened the scoring in the 35th minute, heading home a flick-on from his centre back partner Liam Cooper. The Scots controlled play for large periods with midfielder John McGinn outstanding, but it took until the last few minutes to make the game safe. Substitute Kenny McLean and Ryan Christie were both involved before the ball found Che Adams running free through the middle and he superbly rifled a shot past Danish keeper Schmeichel.

Denmark: Kasper Schmeichel; Simon Kjaer (captain), Andreas Christensen, Jannik Vestergaard; Rasmus Kristensen, Daniel Wass, Jens Jonsson, Joakim Maehle; Andreas Olsen, Andreas Cornelius, Jacob Bruun Larsen. *Substitutes:* Jens Stage (for Jonsson 56); Pione Sisto (for Larsen 56); Mikael Uhre (for Cornelius 72); Alexander Bah (for Kristensen 81); Anders Dreyer (for Wass 81). *Coach:* Kasper Hjulmand.

Scorers: Scotland: Souttar 35; Adams 86

FIFA WORLD CUP QUALIFYING GROUP F

	P	W	D	L	F	A	Pts
Denmark	10	9	0	1	30	3	27
Scotland	10	7	2	1	17	7	23
Israel	10	5	1	4	23	21	16
Austria	10	5	1	4	19	17	16
Faroe Islands	10	1	1	8	7	23	4
Moldova	10	0	1	9	5	30	1

| 24 March 2022 | Friendly | Hampden Park | Attendance: 39,090 |

807 SCOTLAND 1, Poland 1
Referee: Robert Hennessy (Republic of Ireland)

Scotland: Craig Gordon (Hearts); Nathan Patterson (Everton); Scott McTominay (Manchester United), Grant Hanley (Norwich City), Kieran Tierney (Arsenal), Greg Taylor (Celtic); John McGinn (Aston Villa, captain), Billy Gilmour (Norwich City), Callum McGregor (Celtic), Ryan Christie (Bournemouth); Che Adams (Southampton). *Substitutes:* Stephen O'Donnell (Motherwell, for Patterson 66); Aaron Hickey (Bologna, for Taylor 67); Stuart Armstrong (Southampton, for Christie 76); Ryan Jack (Rangers, for McGregor 77); Kenny McLean (Norwich City, for Gilmour 77); Jacob Brown (Stoke City, for Adams 90). *Manager:* Steve Clarke.

Poland: Lukasz Skorupski; Bartosz Salamon, Kamil Glik (captain), Jan Bednarek; Matty Cash, Szymon Zurkowski, Grzegorz Krychowiak, Arkadiusz Reca; Piotr Zielinski, Arkadiusz Milik, Jakub Moder. *Substitutes:* Krzysztof Piatek (for Milik 27); Krystian Bielik (for Salamon 44); Sebastian Szymanski (for Krychowiak 61); Kamil Grosicki (for Zielinski 71); Adam Buksa (for Bednarek 83). *Coach:* Czeslaw Michniewicz.

Scorers: Scotland: Tierney 68   Poland: Piatek 90+4 (pen)

| 29 March 2022 | Friendly | Ernst Happel Stadion, Vienna | Attendance: 6,600 |

808 Austria 2, SCOTLAND 2
Referee: Tamas Bognar (Hungary)

Scotland: Craig Gordon (Hearts); Nathan Patterson (Everton); Jack Hendry (Club Brugge), Grant Hanley (Norwich City), Kieran Tierney (Arsenal), Andrew Robertson (Liverpool, captain); John McGinn (Aston Villa), Ryan Jack (Rangers), Lewis Ferguson (Aberdeen), Stuart Armstrong (Southampton); Che Adams (Southampton). *Substitutes:* Stephen O'Donnell (Motherwell, for Patterson 57); Aaron Hickey (Bologna, for Robertson 57); Scott McTominay (Manchester United, for Jack 57); Lyndon Dykes (Queens Park Rangers, for Adams 66); Billy Gilmour (Norwich City, for Ferguson 77); Ryan Christie (Bournemouth, for Armstrong 77). *Manager:* Steve Clarke.

Norwich: Daniel Bachmann; Stefan Ilsanker, Aleksandar Dragovic (captain), Martin Hinteregger; Valentino Lazaro, Konrad Laimer, Marcel Sabitzer, Andreas Ulmer; Christoph Baumgartner, Sasa Kalajdzic, Marko Arnautovic. *Substitutes:* Marco Grull (for Laimer 59); Allesandro Schopf (for Baumgartner 59); Andreas Weimann (for Ilsanker 74); Michael Gregoritsch (for Kalajdzic 74); Patrick Pentz (for Bachmann 87); Maximilian Ullmann (for Ulmer 87). *Coach:* Franco Foda.

Scorers: Scotland: Hendry 28; McGinn 56   Austria: Gregoritsch 75; Schopf 82

| 1 June 2022 | World Cup qualifying (play-off, semi-final) | Hampden Park | Attendance: 49,772 |

809 SCOTLAND 1, Ukraine 3
Referee: Danny Makkelie (Netherlands)

Scotland (5-3-2):
- 67 Craig Gordon (Hearts);
- 3 Aaron Hickey (Bologna)
- 31 Scott McTominay (Manchester United)
- 43 Grant Hanley (Norwich City)
- 14 Liam Cooper (Leeds United)
- 57 Andrew Robertson (Liverpool, captain);
- 45 John McGinn (Aston Villa)
- 13 Billy Gilmour (Chelsea)
- 43 Callum McGregor (Celtic);
- 16 Che Adams (Southampton)
- 22 Lyndon Dykes (Queens Park Rangers)

Substitutes: 29 Ryan Christie (Bournemouth, for Dykes 46);
14 Jack Hendry (Club Brugge, for Cooper 68);
33 Stuart Armstrong (Southampton, for Gilmour 68)

Manager: Steve Clarke

A very disappointing display saw Scotland squander the chance to take on Wales in the play-off final. The Ukrainians, buoyed by unparalleled levels of sympathy following the invasion of their country by Russia, rose to the occasion and played out of their skins. The home players, on the other hand, appeared flat by comparison and unable to raise their games to the standard required. When Yaremchuk added a second goal just after the break following Yarmolenko's opener in the first half the game was basically over. Callum McGregor did give the Scots some hope by scoring with 10 minutes left but Ukraine held out comfortably and substitute Dovbyk added a deserved third goal in stoppage time. With important games looming in the UEFA Nations League, manager Steve Clarke faced the task of motivating his squad.

Ukraine: Heorhiy Bushchan; Oleksandr Karavaev, Illya Zabarnyi, Mykola Matviyenko, Vitalij Mykolenko; Taras Stepanenko; Andriy Yarmolenko (captain), Ruslan Malinovskyi, Oleksandr Zinchenko, Viktor Tsygankov; Roman Yaremchuk. *Substitutes:* Mykola Shaparenko (for Malinovskyi 72); Mykhaylo Mudryk (for Tsygankov 72); Oleksandr Zubkov (for Yarmolenko 78); Artem Dovbyk (for Yaremchuk 78); Serhiy Sydorchuk (for Stepanenko 90+3). *Coach:* Oleksandr Petrakov.

Scorers: Ukraine: Yarmolenko 33; Yaremchuk 49; Dovbyk 90+5   Scotland: McGregor 79

| 8 June 2022 | UEFA Nations League, Group B1 | Hampden Park | Attendance: 38,627 |

810 SCOTLAND 2, Armenia 0
Referee: Sebastian Gishamer (Austria)

Scotland: Craig Gordon (Hearts); Anthony Ralston (Celtic), John Souttar (Hearts), Jack Hendry (Club Brugge), Scott McKenna (Nottingham Forest), Andrew Robertson (Liverpool, captain); John McGinn (Aston Villa), Callum McGregor (Celtic), Stuart Armstrong (Southampton); Ryan Christie (Bournemouth), Che Adams (Southampton). *Substitutes:* Scott McTominay (Manchester United, for Armstrong 75); Nathan Patterson (Everton, for Ralston 75); Aaron Hickey (Bologna, for Robertson 75); Ross Stewart (Sunderland, for Christie 87); Jacob Brown (Stoke City, for Adams 87). *Manager:* Steve Clarke.

Armenia: David Yurchenko; Hovhannes Hambartsumyan, Hrayr Mkoyan, Varazdat Haroyan (captain), Arman Hovhannisyan; Khoren Bayramyan, Artak Grigoryan, Eduard Spertsyan; Tigran Barseghyan, Kamo Hovhannisyan; Sergis Adamyan. *Substitutes:* Wbeymar Angulo (for Grigoryan 46); Taron Voskanyan (for Kamo Hovhannisyan 46); Vahan Bichakhchyan (for Adamyan 46); Solomon Udo (for Spertsyan 71); Artak Dashyan (for Bayramyan 89). *Coach:* Joaquin Caparros (Spain).

Scorers: Scotland: Ralston 28; McKenna 40

Chapter ten: 2020-2023

| 11 June 2022 | UEFA Nations League, Group B1 | Aviva Stadium, Dublin | Attendance: 46,927 |

811 Republic of Ireland 3, SCOTLAND 0
Referee: Marco Di Bello (Italy)

Scotland: Craig Gordon (Hearts); Anthony Ralston (Celtic), Jack Hendry (Club Brugge), Grant Hanley (Norwich City), Scott McKenna (Nottingham Forest), Andrew Robertson (Liverpool, captain); John McGinn (Aston Villa), Scott McTominay (Manchester United), Callum McGregor (Celtic); Ryan Christie (Bournemouth), Che Adams (Southampton). *Substitutes:* Billy Gilmour (Chelsea, for Hendry 46); Stuart Armstrong (Southampton, for McGinn 59); Ross Stewart (Sunderland, for Adams 59); Jacob Brown (Stoke City, for Christie 59); John Souttar (Hearts, for McKenna 74). *Manager:* Steve Clarke.

Republic of Ireland: Caoimhin Kelleher; Nathan Collins, Shane Duffy, John Egan (captain); Josh Cullen, Alan Browne, Jayson Molumby, Jason Knight, James McClean; Michael Obafemi, Troy Parrott. *Substitutes:* Scott Hogan (for Obafemi 56); Conor Hourihane (for Knight 72); Jeff Hendrick (for Molumby 84); Callum Robinson (for Parrott 84). *Manager:* Stephen Kenny,

Scorers: Republic of Ireland: Browne 20; Parrott 28; Obafemi 51

| 14 June 2022 | UEFA Nations League, Group B1 | Republican Stadium, Yerevan | Attendance: 13,500 |

812 Armenia 1, SCOTLAND 4
Referee: Nikola Dabanovic (Montenegro)

Scotland: Craig Gordon (Hearts); Nathan Patterson (Everton), Scott McTominay (Manchester United), Jack Hendry (Club Brugge), Grant Hanley (Norwich City), Greg Taylor (Celtic); John McGinn (Aston Villa, captain), Billy Gilmour (Chelsea), Callum McGregor (Celtic), Stuart Armstrong (Southampton); Che Adams (Southampton). *Substitutes:* Lewis Ferguson (Aberdeen, for Gilmour 64); David Turnbull (Celtic, for McGinn 64); Anthony Ralston (Celtic, for Patterson 64); Jacob Brown (Stoke City, for Adams 74); Allan Campbell (Luton Town, for Hanley 86). *Manager:* Steve Clarke.

Armenia: David Yurchenko; Artak Dashyan, Hovhannes Hambartsumyan, Varazdat Haroyan (captain), Hrayr Mkoyan, Arman Hovhannisyan; Artak Grigoryan, Eduard Spertsyan; Khoren Bayramyan; Tigran Barseghyan, Vahan Bichakhchyan. *Substitutes:* Styopa Mkrtchyan (for Grigoryan 46); Wbeymar Angulo (for Spertsyan 59); Solomon Udo (for Bichakhchyan 59); Kamo Hovhannisyan (for Bayramyan 59); Artur Serobyan (for Barseghyan 84). *Coach:* Joaquin Caparros (Spain).

Scorers: Armenia: Bichakhchyan 8   Scotland: Armstrong 14, 45+1; McGinn 50; Adams 54

| 21 September 2022 | UEFA Nations League, Group B1 | Hampden Park | Attendance: 42,846 |

813 SCOTLAND 3, Ukraine 0
Referee: Maurizio Mariani (Italy)

Scotland (4-4-2):
- 71 Craig Gordon (Hearts);
- 11 Nathan Patterson (Everton)
- 18 Jack Hendry (Cremonese)
- 27 Scott McKenna (Nottingham Forest)
- 33 Kieran Tierney (Arsenal);
- 49 John McGinn (Aston Villa, captain)
- 35 Scott McTominay (Manchester United)
- 47 Callum McGregor (Celtic)
- 37 Stuart Armstrong (Southampton);
- 32 Ryan Christie (Bournemouth)
- 20 Che Adams (Southampton)

Substitutes: 5 Aaron Hickey (Brentford, for Patterson 26); 23 Ryan Fraser (Newcastle United, for Armstrong 76); 23 Lyndon Dykes (Queens Park Rangers, for Adams 76); 26 Kenny McLean (Norwich City, for Christie 85); 8 Greg Taylor (Celtic, for Tierney 85)

Manager: Steve Clarke

With a result that was just as surprising as manager Steve Clarke's decision to deploy a back four, Scotland clinched a victory over Ukraine which was both welcome and justified. It was looking like the same old story with chances being spurned until John McGinn fired home the opener with 20 minutes remaining. Then Lyndon Dykes, maybe smarting at being left out of the side, entered the fray and powered in two headers from corners taken by fellow substitute Ryan Fraser. It was a fine win with the revised defensive formation working extremely well. Nathan Patterson did well at right back, as did his replacement Aaron Hickey and Kieran Tierney in his more customary position on the other flank, while centre backs Jack Hendry and Scott McKenna coped with anything Ukraine could throw at them. Scott McTominay had probably his best game for his country in midfield, and importantly the result helped erase the memory of the World Cup play-off defeat to the same side three months earlier.

Ukraine: Anatoliy Trubin; Oleksandr Karavaev, Valeriy Bondar, Mykola Matviyenko, Bohdan Mykhaylichenko; Taras Stepanenko; Andriy Yarmolenko (captain), Oleksandr Pikhalyonok, Ruslan Malinovskyi, Mykhaylo Mudryk; Artem Dovbyk. *Substitutes:* Serhiy Sydorchuk (for Stepanenko 46); Viktor Tsygankov (for Yarmolenko 67); Roman Yaremchuk (for Dovbyk 67); Oleksandr Zubkov (for Pikhalyonok 83); Danylo Ihnatenko (for Mudryk 83). *Coach:* Oleksandr Petrakov.

Scorers: Scotland: McGinn 70; Dykes 80, 87

| 24 September 2022 | UEFA Nations League, Group B1 | Hampden Park | Attendance: 48,853 |

814 SCOTLAND 2, Republic of Ireland 1
Referee: Sandro Scharer (Switzerland)

Scotland: Craig Gordon (Hearts); Aaron Hickey (Brentford), Jack Hendry (Cremonese), Scott McKenna (Nottingham Forest), Kieran Tierney (Arsenal); John McGinn (Aston Villa, captain), Scott McTominay (Manchester United), Callum McGregor (Celtic), Stuart Armstrong (Southampton); Ryan Christie (Bournemouth), Lyndon Dykes (Queens Park Rangers). *Substitutes:* Greg Taylor (Celtic, for Tierney 42); Anthony Ralston (Celtic, for Hickey 58); Ryan Fraser (Newcastle United, for Armstrong 58); Kenny McLean (Norwich City, for Christie 85); Che Adams (Southampton, for Dykes 85). *Manager:* Steve Clarke.

Republic of Ireland: Gavin Bazunu; Nathan Collins, John Egan (captain), Dara O'Shea; Matt Doherty, Jayson Molumby, Josh Cullen, Jason Knight, James McClean; Michael Obafemi, Troy Parrott. *Substitutes:* Chiedozie Ogbene (for Obafemi 60); Seamus Coleman (for Doherty 76); Alan Browne (for Molumby 76); Callum Robinson (for Parrott 76); Robbie Brady (for McClean 83). *Manager:* Stephen Kenny.

Scorers: Republic of Ireland: Egan 18   Scotland: Hendry 49; Christie 82 (pen)

27 September 2022   UEFA Nations League, Group B1   Stadion Cracovii, Krakow   Attendance; 13,534

815 Ukraine 0, SCOTLAND 0

Referee: Anastasios Sidiropoulos (Greece)

Scotland (4-5-1):
73 Craig Gordon (Hearts);
7   Aaron Hickey (Brentford),
20 Jack Hendry (Cremonese),
1   Ryan Porteous (Hibernian),
10 Greg Taylor (Celtic);
25 Ryan Fraser (Newcastle United),
51 John McGinn (Aston Villa, captain),
13 Ryan Jack (Rangers),
49 Callum McGregor (Celtic),
28 Kenny McLean (Norwich City);
22 Che Adams (Southampton).

Substitutes: 2 Stephen Kingsley (Hearts, for Taylor 72);
34 Ryan Christie (Bournemouth, for Fraser 72);
39 Stuart Armstrong (Southampton, for Jack 72);
25 Lyndon Dykes (Queens Park Rangers, for Adams 79);
6 Anthony Ralston (Celtic, for Hickey 90+1)

Manager: Steve Clarke

Ukraine: Andriy Lunin; Oleksandr Tymchyk, Illya Zabarnyi, Mykola Matviyenko, Vitaliy Mykolenko; Ruslan Malinovskyi, Taras Stepanenko, Danylo Ihnatenko; Andriy Yarmolenko (captain), Artem Dovbyk, Mykhaylo Mudryk. *Substitutes:* Roman Yaremchuk (for Dovbyk 75); Viktor Tysgankov (for Mudryk 75); Oleksandr Zubkov (for Yarmolenko 87); Okeksandr Pikhalyonok (for Malinovskyi 87). *Coach:* Oleksandr Petrakov

The Scots, having put the memories of Dublin behind them with three successive wins over Armenia, the Republic of Ireland and Ukraine, needed a point against the latter to secure top spot in the group and a back-door route to the 2024 European Championship. It was a difficult task, made harder by the fact that at least eight defenders were missing because of injury. However, the makeshift back line really stood up to the task, not least debutant Ryan Porteous. There were several nervous moments when the Ukrainians created scoring chances, but a mixture of good luck, excellent saves by Craig Gordon and calmness in defence made sure of the draw. No goals, but a performance to be proud of, and up there with anything achieved under manager Steve Clarke.

UEFA NATIONS LEAGUE GROUP B1

	P	W	D	L	F	A	Pts
Scotland	6	4	1	1	11	5	13
Ukraine	6	3	2	1	10	4	11
Republic of Ireland	6	2	1	3	8	7	7
Armenia	6	1	0	5	4	17	3

The understrength team which achieved a fighting 0-0 draw against Ukraine in Poland to finish top of the UEFA Nations League group. Back (from left): Craig Gordon, Ryan Porteous, Jack Hendry, Kenny McLean, Ryan Jack, Ryan Fraser. Front: Aaron Hickey, Callum McGregor, Greg Taylor, John McGinn, Che Adams.

16 November 2022   Friendly   Diyarbakir Stadyumu, Diyarbakir   Attendance: 28,348

816 Turkey 2, SCOTLAND 1

Referee: Visar Kastrati (Kosovo)

Scotland: Craig Gordon (Hearts); Ryan Fraser (Newcastle United), Jack Hendry (Cremonese), Grant Hanley (Norwich City), Kieran Tierney (Arsenal), Andrew Robertson (Liverpool, captain); John McGinn (Aston Villa), Billy Gilmour (Brighton & Hove Albion), Scott McTominay (Manchester United), Stuart Armstrong (Southampton); Lyndon Dykes (Queens Park Rangers). *Substitutes:* Scott McKenna (Nottingham Forest, for Hanley 46); Calvin Ramsay (Liverpool, for Fraser 46); Ryan Christie (Bournemouth, for Armstrong 67); Ryan Jack (Rangers, for Gilmour 67); Jacob Brown (Stoke City, for Dykes 79); Lewis Ferguson (Bologna, for McTominay 79). *Manager:* Steve Clarke.

Turkey: Ugurcan Cakir; Ozan Kabak, Caglar Soyuncu, Cenk Ozkacar; Zeki Celic, Orkun Kokcu, Hakan Calhanoglu (captain), Ferdi Kadioglu; Cengiz Under, Irfan Can Kahveci; Cenk Tosun. *Substitutes:* Eren Elmali (for Kadioglu 34); Salih Ozcan (for Kokcu 46); Deniz Turuc (for Calhanoglu 68); Enes Unal (for Tosun 68); Ismail Yuksek (for Under 81); Kerem Akturkoglu (for Kahveci 81). *Coach:* Stefan Kuntz (Germany).

Scorers: Turkey: Kabak 40; Under 49   Scotland: McGinn 62

Chapter ten: 2020-2023

| 25 March 2023 | European Championship qualifying | Hampden Park | Attendance: 48,195 |

817 SCOTLAND 3, Cyprus 0
Referee: Duje Strukan (Croatia)

Scotland: Angus Gunn (Norwich City); Ryan Porteous (Watford), Grant Hanley (Norwich City), Kieran Tierney (Arsenal); Aaron Hickey (Brentford), Ryan Jack (Rangers), Callum McGregor (Celtic), Andrew Robertson (Liverpool, captain); John McGinn (Aston Villa), Stuart Armstrong (Southampton); Che Adams (Southampton). *Substitutes:* Lyndon Dykes (Queens Park Rangers, for Adams 58); Scott McTominay (Manchester United, for Armstrong 67); Ryan Christie (Bournemouth, for Jack 67); Nathan Patterson (Everton, for Hickey 80). *Manager:* Steve Clarke.

Cyprus: Demetris Demetriou; Ioannis Kousoulos, Alex Gogic, Valentin Roberge; Minas Antoniou, Charalampos Kyriakou, Kostakis Artymatas (captain), Konstantinos Laifis, Nikolas Ioannou; Grigoris Kastanos; Ioannis Pittas. *Substitutes:* Alexander Spoljaric (for Kousoulos 45); Charalampos Charalampous (for Kyriakou 68); Andronikos Kakoullis (for Pittas 68); Loizos Loizou (for Gogic 79); Marinos Tzionis (for Kastanos 79). *Manager:* Temuri Ketsbaia.

Scorers: Scotland: McGinn 21; McTominay 87, 90+3

| 28 March 2023 | European Championship qualifying | Hampden Park | Attendance: 47,976 |

818 SCOTLAND 2, Spain 0
*Referee: *Sandro Scharer (Switzerland)*

Scotland (3-4-2-1):
2 Angus Gunn (Norwich City);
3 Ryan Porteous (Watford)
48 Grant Hanley (Norwich City)
37 Kieran Tierney (Arsenal);
9 Aaron Hickey (Brentford)
39 Scott McTominay (Manchester United)
51 Callum McGregor (Celtic)
62 Andrew Robertson (Liverpool, captain);
54 John McGinn (Aston Villa)
37 Ryan Christie (Bournemouth);
28 Lyndon Dykes (Queens Park Rangers)

Substitutes: 29 Kenny McLean (Norwich City, for Christie 75);
14 Liam Cooper (Leeds United, for Tierney 76);
13 Nathan Patterson (Everton, for Hickey 82);
6 Lewis Ferguson (Bologna, for McGinn 83);
5 Lawrence Shankland (Hearts, for Dykes 89)

Manager: Steve Clarke

Scott McTominay, who had scored just once in 37 international matches before his late double against Cyprus three days earlier, repeated the act as the Scots saw off the highly fancied Spanish visitors in style. It was the kind of result which used to happen occasionally at Hampden but had not been seen for many years, and indeed the first win over Spain since Kenny Dalglish's memorable goal in 1984. Andrew Robertson took advantage of a Pedro Porro slip to set up McTominay for his opener in just seven minutes. The visitors had plenty of possession after that but failed to make it pay, and just after half-time the Manchester United man got his second following a lung-bursting run down the left by Kieran Tierney. There was some sour grapes from Spanish captain Rodri after the match, complaining about Scottish tactics, but the victory was well deserved. Everyone played their part with Tierney, Robertson, Callum McGregor and McTominay particularly outstanding.

Spain: Kepa Arrizabalaga; Pedro Porro, David Garcia, Inigo Martinez, Jose Gaya; Mikel Merino, Rodri (captain); Yeremy Pino, Dani Cellabos, Mikel Oyarzabal; Joselu. *Substitutes:* Nico Williams (for Oyarzabal 46); Jose Carvajal (for Porro 46); Iglesias (for Joselu 67); Gavi (for Cellabos 79). *Coach:* Luis de la Fuente.

Scorer: Scotland: McTominay 7, 51

* Replaced in second half by Lukas Fahndrich (Switzerland)

| 17 June 2023 | European Championship qualifying | Ullevaal Stadion, Oslo | Attendance: 25,791 |

819 Norway 1, SCOTLAND 2
Referee: Matej Jug (Slovenia)

Scotland: Angus Gunn (Norwich City); Ryan Porteous (Watford), Jack Hendry (Club Brugge), Kieran Tierney (Arsenal); Aaron Hickey (Brentford), Scott McTominay (Manchester United), Callum McGregor (Celtic), Andrew Robertson (Liverpool, captain); John McGinn (Aston Villa), Ryan Christie (Bournemouth); Lyndon Dykes (Queens Park Rangers). *Substitutes:* Liam Cooper (Leeds United, for Tierney 65); Billy Gilmour (Brighton & Hove Albion, for McGregor 78); Stuart Armstrong (Southampton, for Christie 78); Kenny McLean (Norwich City, for Porteous 79); Dominic Hyam (Blackburn Rovers, for McGinn 90+1). *Manager:* Steve Clarke.

Norway: Orjan Nyland; Leo Ostigard, Stefan Strandberg, Birger Meling, Julian Ryersen; Martin Odegaard (captain), Patrick Berg, Fredrik Aursnes; Ola Solbakken, Erling Haaland, Alexander Sorloth. *Substitutes:* Sander Berge (for Solbakken 63); Mohammed Elyounoussi (for Sorloth 79); Jorgen Strand Larsen (for Berg 84); Kristian Thorstvedt (for Aursnes 84): Mats Daehli (for Haaland 84). *Manager:* Stale Solbakken.

Scorers: Norway: Haaland 61   Scotland: Dykes 87; McLean 89

| 20 June 2023 | European Championship qualifying | Hampden Park | Attendance: 50,062 |

820 SCOTLAND 2, Georgia 0*
Referee: Istvan Vad (Hungary)

Scotland: Angus Gunn (Norwich City); Ryan Porteous (Watford), Jack Hendry (Club Brugge), Kieran Tierney (Arsenal); Aaron Hickey (Brentford), Scott McTominay (Manchester United), Billy Gilmour (Brighton & Hove Albion), Callum McGregor (Celtic), Andrew Robertson (Liverpool, captain); John McGinn (Aston Villa); Lyndon Dykes (Queens Park Rangers). *Substitutes:* John Souttar (Rangers, for Tierney 79); Ryan Jack (Rangers, for McGregor 79); Kevin Nisbet (Millwall, for Dykes 79); Kenny McLean (Norwich City, for Gilmour 86); Ryan Christie (Bournemouth, for McGinn 90+2). *Manager:* Steve Clarke.

Georgia: Giorgi Mamardashvili; Lasha Dvali, Guram Kashia (captain), Saba Kvirkvelia, Otat Kakabadze; Luka Gagnidze, Otar Kiteishvili, Nika Kvekveskiri, Saba Lobzhanidze; Georges Mikautadze, Khvicha Kvaratskhelia. *Substitutes:* Giorgi Gocholeishvili (for Dvali 56); Budu Zivzivadze (for Kvekveskiri 56); Zuriko Davitashvili (for Lobzhanidze 64). *Manager:* Willy Sagnol (France).

Scorers: Scotland: McGregor 6; McTominay 47

The match was stopped after six minutes because of a waterlogged pitch and resumed after a delay of an hour and a half.

8 September 2023   European Championship qualifying   AEK Arena, Larnaca   Attendance: 6,633

821 Cyprus 0, SCOTLAND 3   *Referee: Balazs Berke (Hungary)*

Scotland: Angus Gunn (Norwich City); Ryan Porteous (Watford), Jack Hendry (Al Ettifaq), Kieran Tierney (Arsenal); Aaron Hickey (Brentford), Billy Gilmour (Brighton & Hove Albion), Callum McGregor (Celtic), Andrew Robertson (Liverpool, captain); John McGinn (Aston Villa), Scott McTominay (Manchester United); Che Adams (Southampton). *Substitutes:* Kenny McLean (Norwich City, for Gilmour 67); Lyndon Dykes (Queens Park Rangers, for Adams 67); Stuart Armstrong (Southampton, for McGinn 83); Nathan Patterson (Everton, for Hickey 83); Ryan Christie (Bournemouth, for McTominay 90). *Manager:* Steve Clarke.

Cyprus: Joel Mall; Andreas Karo, Konstantinos Laifis, Valentin Roberge; Minas Antoniou, Charalampos Kyriakou, Ioannis Kousoulos, Charalampos Charalampous, Anderson Correia; Grigoris Kastanos, Pieros Sotiriou (captain). *Substitutes:* Michalis Ioannou (for Kousoulos 46); Ioannis Pittas (for Sotiriou 46); Stelios Andreou (for Antoniou 80); Alex Gogic (for Kyriakou 80); Andronikos Kakoullis (for Charalampous 84). *Coach:* Temuri Ketsbaia (Georgia).

Scorers: Scotland: McTominay 6; Porteous 16; McGinn 30

12 September 2023   Friendly (150th anniversary)   Hampden Park   Attendance: 49,129

822 SCOTLAND 1, England 3   *Referee: Davide Massa (Italy)*

Scotland: Angus Gunn (Norwich City); Ryan Porteous (Watford), Jack Hendry (Al Ettifaq), Kieran Tierney (Arsenal); Aaron Hickey (Brentford), Billy Gilmour (Brighton & Hove Albion), Callum McGregor (Celtic), Andrew Robertson (Liverpool, captain); John McGinn (Aston Villa), Scott McTominay (Manchester United); Che Adams (Southampton). *Substitutes:* Ryan Christie (Bournemouth, for Adams 59); Lyndon Dykes (Queens Park Rangers, for Gilmour 60); Stuart Armstrong (Southampton, for Tierney 82); Lewis Ferguson (Bologna, for McGinn 82); Ryan Jack (Rangers, for McGregor 89); Nathan Patterson (Everton, for Hickey 89). *Manager:* Steve Clarke.

England: Arron Ramsdale; Kyle Walker, Lewis Dunk, Marc Guehi, Kieran Trippier; Kalvin Phillips, Declan Rice; Phil Foden, Jude Bellingham, Marcus Rashford; Harry Kane (captain). *Substitutes:* Harry McGuire (for Guehi 46); Bukayo Saka (for Foden 71); Eberechi Eze (for Rashford 71); Conor Gallagher (for Bellingham 84); Callum Wilson (for Kane 84). *Manager:* Gareth Southgate.

Scorers: England: Foden 32; Bellingham 35; Kane 81   Scotland: McGuire 67 (own goal)

12 October 2023   European Championship qualifying   Estadio La Cartuja, Seville   Attendance: 45,623

823 Spain 2, SCOTLAND 0   *Referee: Serdar Gozubuyuk (Netherlands)*

Scotland: Angus Gunn (Norwich City); Ryan Porteous (Watford), Jack Hendry (Al Ettifaq), Scott McKenna (Nottingham Forest); Aaron Hickey (Brentford), Scott McTominay (Manchester United), Callum McGregor (Celtic), Andrew Robertson (Liverpool, captain); John McGinn (Aston Villa), Ryan Christie (Bournemouth); Lyndon Dykes (Queens Park Rangers). *Substitutes:* Nathan Patterson (Everton, for Robertson 44); Che Adams (Southampton, for Dykes 79); Stuart Armstrong (Southampton, for Christie 79); Billy Gilmour (Brighton & Hove Albion, for Porteous 87); Kenny McLean (Norwich City, for McGregor 87). *Manager:* Steve Clarke.

Spain: Unai Simon; Dani Carvajal, Robin Le Normand, Aymeric Laporte, Alejandro Balde; Gavi, Rodri, Mikel Merino; Ferran Torres, Alvaro Morata (captain), Mikel Oyarzabal. *Substitutes:* Fran Garcia (for Balde 46); Bryan Zaragoza (for Oyarzabal 46); Jesus Navas (for Carvajal 67); Oihan Sancet (for Merino 67); Joselu (for Morata 84). *Coach:* Luis de la Fuente.

Scorers: Spain: Morata 73; Sancet 86

17 October 2023   Friendly   Stade Pierre Mauroy, Lille   Attendance: 44,000

824 France 4, SCOTLAND 1   *Referee: Tobias Stieler (Germany)*

Scotland: Liam Kelly (Motherwell); Jack Hendry (Al Ettifaq), Liam Cooper (Leeds United), Scott McKenna (Nottingham Forest); Nathan Patterson (Everton), Billy Gilmour (Brighton & Hove Albion), Scott McTominay (Manchester United, captain), Greg Taylor (Celtic); Lewis Ferguson (Bologna), Kenny McLean (Norwich City); Che Adams (Southampton). *Substitutes:* Zander Clark (Hearts, for Kelly 46); Jacob Brown (Luton Town, for Adams 64); John Souttar (Rangers, for Cooper 64); Stuart Armstrong (Southampton, for Gilmour 76); Ryan Christie (Bournemouth, for McLean 76); John McGinn (Aston Villa, for Patterson 89). *Manager:* Steve Clarke.

France: Mike Maignan; Jonathan Clauss, Benjamin Pavard, Ibrahima Konate, Theo Hernandez; Eduardo Camavinga, Aurelian Tchouameni; Ousmane Dembele, Antoine Griezmann, Kylian Mbappe (captain); Olivier Giroud. *Substitutes:* Kingsley Coman (for Dembele 64); Marcus Thuram (for Giroud 64); Boubacar Kamara (for Tchouameni 76); Youssouf Fofana (for Griezmann 76); Castello Lukeba (for Konate 87); Randal Kolo Muani (for Mbappe 87). *Coach:* Didier Deschamps.

Scorers: Scotland: Gilmour 11   France: Pavard 16, 24; Mbappe 41 (pen); Coman 70

16 November 2023   European Championship qualifying   Dinamo Arena, Tbilisi   Attendance: 44,595

825 Georgia 2, SCOTLAND 2   *Referee: Aleksandar Stavrev (North Macedonia)*

Scotland: Zander Clark (Hearts); Nathan Patterson (Everton), Ryan Porteous (Watford), Scott McKenna (Nottingham Forest), Greg Taylor (Celtic); Billy Gilmour (Brighton & Hove Albion), Callum McGregor (Celtic); John McGinn (Aston Villa, captain), Scott McTominay (Manchester United), Ryan Christie (Bournemouth); Lyndon Dykes (Queens Park Rangers). *Substitutes:* Lewis Ferguson (Bologna, for Christie 46); Kenny McLean (Norwich City, for Gilmour 46); Stuart Armstrong (Southampton, for Taylor 79); Anthony Ralston (Celtic, for Patterson 79); Lawrence Shankland (Hearts, for Dykes 86). *Manager:* Steve Clarke.

Georgia: Giorgi Mamardashvili; Otar Kakabadze, Solomon Kverkvelia, Guram Kashia (captain), Luka Lochoshvili, Levan Shengelia; Georgi Chakvetadze, Nika Kvekveskiri, Giorgi Gocholeishvili; Georges Mikautadze, Khvicha Kvaratskhelia. *Substitutes:* Anzor Mekvabishvili (for Kvekveskiri 69); Budu Zivzivadze (for Mikautadze 69); Irakli Azarovi (for Shengelia 72); Aleksandre Kalandadze (for Lochoshvili 78); Zuriko Davitashvili (for Chakvetadze 78). *Coach:* Willy Sagnol (France).

Scorers: Georgia: Kvaratskhelia 15, 57   Scotland: McTominay 49; Shankland 90+3

Chapter ten: 2020-2023

19 November 2023 European Championship qualifying Hampden Park Attendance: 48,138

826 *SCOTLAND 3, Norway 3 *Referee: Horatiu Fesnic (Romania)*

Scotland (4-5-1):
3   Zander Clark (Hearts);
19 Nathan Patterson (Everton)
28 Jack Hendry (Al Ettifaq)
33 Scott McKenna (Nottingham Forest)
13 Greg Taylor (Celtic)
47 Scott McTominay (Manchester United)
58 Callum McGregor (Celtic)
62 John McGinn (Aston Villa, captain)
48 Stuart Armstrong (Southampton)
36 Kenny McLean (Norwich City);
8   Jacob Brown (Luton Town)

Substitutes: 10 Lewis Ferguson (Bologna, for McLean 70);
35 Lyndon Dykes (Queens Park Rangers, for Brown 70);
45 Ryan Christie (Bournemouth, for Armstrong 70);
18 Ryan Jack (Rangers, for McGinn 79);
7   Lawrence Shankland (Hearts, for McGregor 89)

Manager: Steve Clarke

Scotland had the luxury of having qualified for the 2024 European Championship with two games to go, and second behind Spain in the group. It could have been even better but for a defeat in Seville, where the Scots were desperately unlucky not to take something from the game, especially as Scott McTominay's magnificent goal from a free kick was ruled out by a ridiculous video assistant referee (VAR) decision. But having gained their first ever point away to Georgia it was important to finish the campaign on a high. Things started badly when defensive frailty led to Norway opening the scoring in the seventh minute, but captain John McGinn deservedly restored parity from the penalty spot 10 minutes later. Another defensive lapse led to Norway going ahead again midway through the half, through Strand Larsen, but the Scots came back strongly and forced an own goal. The game looked to be won on the hour mark when Stuart Armstrong finished off a superb move to make it 3-2, but yet another mistake at the back led to a Norwegian equaliser. On balance the visitors were worthy of a draw but for Scotland it was a stark reminder of how much they miss defensive regulars Angus Gunn, Aaron Hickey, Kieran Tierney, Ryan Porteous and captain Andrew Robertson.

Norway: Egil Selvik; Julian Ryerson, Kristoffer Ajer, Leo Ostigard, Fredrik Bjorkan; Sander Berge (captain), Patrick Berg, Fredrik Aursnes; Oscar Bobb, Jorgen Strand Larsen, Aron Donnum. *Substitutes:* Mohamed Elyounoussi (for Aursnes 60); Kristian Thorstvedt (for Donnum 60); Marcus Pedersen (for Bobb 89). *Coach:* Stale Solbakken.

Scorers: Norway: Donnum 3; Strand Larsen 20; Elyounoussi 86

Scotland: McGinn 13 (pen); Ostigard 33 (own goal); Armstrong 59

EUROPEAN CHAMPIONSHIP QUALIFYING GROUP A						
	P	W	D	L	F	A	Pts
Spain	8	7	0	1	25	5	21
Scotland	8	5	2	1	17	8	17
Norway	8	3	2	3	14	12	11
Georgia	8	2	2	4	12	18	8
Cyprus	8	0	0	8	3	28	0

*The above is an extra featured match, added to the book when reprinted to bring the European Championship qualifying group up to date.

A fine display of "tifo" signifying "We'll be coming" (to Germany in 2024), at Hampden Park before Scotland's last qualifying game against Norway. Unfortunately there was no extra motivation and following a below-par display the match finished 3-3.

Always a prized possession – a Scotland cap from 1892.
Photo courtesy of Scottish Football Museum

LIST OF PLAYERS

IN ALPHABETICAL ORDER – NAME, NUMBER OF CAPS, PERIOD AND CLUBS REPRESENTED (AT AUGUST 2023)

BOLD TYPE SIGNIFIES PLAYER WAS STILL ALIVE AT TIME OF WRITING

Name	Caps	Period	Clubs
ADAM, Charlie	26	2007-2015	Rangers, Blackpool, Liverpool, Stoke
ADAMS, Che	27	2021-2023	Southampton
ADAMS, James	3	1889-1893	Hearts
AGNEW, William	3	1907-1908	Kilmarnock
AIRD, John	4	1954	Burnley
AITKEN, Andrew	14	1901-1911	Newcastle United, Middlesbrough, Leicester Fosse
AITKEN, George	8	1949-1954	East Fife, Sunderland
AITKEN, Ralph	2	1886-1888	Dumbarton
AITKEN, Roy	57	1979-1991	Celtic, Newcastle United, St Mirren
AITKENHEAD, Walter	1	1912	Blackburn Rovers
ALBISTON, Arthur	14	1982-1986	Manchester United
ALEXANDER, David	2	1894	East Stirlingshire
ALEXANDER, Graham	40	2002-2009	Preston North End, Burnley
ALEXANDER, Neil	3	2006	Cardiff City
ALLAN, David	3	1885-1886	Queen's Park
ALLAN, George	1	1897	Liverpool
ALLAN, Henry	1	1902	Hearts
ALLAN, James	2	1887	Queen's Park
ALLAN, Thomson	2	1974	Dundee
ANCELL, Bobby	2	1936	Newcastle United
ANDERSON, Alan	5	1967	Hearts
ANDERSON, Andrew	23	1933-1938	Hearts
ANDERSON, Frederick	1	1874	Clydesdale
ANDERSON, George	1	1901	Kilmarnock
ANDERSON, Harold	1	1914	Raith Rovers
ANDERSON, John	1	1954	Leicester City
ANDERSON, Kenneth	3	1896-1898	Queen's Park
ANDERSON, Russell	11	2002-2007	Aberdeen, Sunderland, Plymouth Argyle
ANDERSON, William	6	1882-1885	Queen's Park
ANDREWS, Peter	1	1875	Eastern
ANYA, Ikechi	29	2013-2017	Watford, Derby County
ARCHER, Jordan	1	2018	Millwall
ARCHIBALD, Alex	8	1921-1932	Rangers
ARCHIBALD, Steve	27	1980-1986	Aberdeen, Tottenham Hotspur, Barcelona
ARMSTRONG, Matthew	3	1935-1936	Aberdeen
ARMSTRONG, Stuart	48	2017-2023	Celtic, Southampton
ARNOTT, Walter	14	1883-1893	Queen's Park
AULD, Bertie	3	1959-1960	Celtic
AULD, John	3	1887-1889	Third Lanark
BAIN, Scott	3	2018-2019	Celtic
BAIRD, Andrew	2	1892-1894	Queen's Park
BAIRD, Archie	1	1946	Aberdeen
BAIRD, David	3	1890-1892	Hearts
BAIRD, Hugh	1	1956	Airdrie
BAIRD, John	3	1876-1880	Vale of Leven
BAIRD, Sammy	7	1956-1958	Rangers
BAIRD, William	1	1897	St Bernard's
BANNAN, Barry	27	2010-2017	Aston Villa, Leeds United, Crystal Palace, Sheffield Wednesday
BANNON, Eamonn	11	1979-1986	Dundee United
BARBOUR, Alexander	1	1885	Renton
BARDSLEY, Phil	13	2010-2014	Sunderland
BARKER, John	2	1893-1894	Rangers
BARR, Darren	1	2008	Falkirk
BARRETT, Francis	2	1894-1895	Dundee
BATES, David	4	2018-2019	SV Hamburg
BATTLES, Bernard Snr	3	1901	Celtic
BATTLES, Bernard Jnr	1	1931	Hearts
BAULD, Willie	3	1950	Hearts
BAXTER, Jim	34	1960-1967	Rangers, Sunderland
BAXTER, Robert	3	1938-1939	Middlesbrough
BEATTIE, Andy	7	1937-1938	Preston North End
BEATTIE, Craig	7	2005-2007	Celtic, West Bromwich Albion
BEATTIE, Robert	1	1938	Preston North End
BEGBIE, Isaac	4	1890-1894	Hearts
BELL, Alexander	1	1912	Manchester United
BELL, Cammy	1	2011	Kilmarnock
BELL, John	10	1890-1900	Dumbarton, Everton, Celtic
BELL, Mark	1	1901	Hearts
BELL, Willie	2	1966	Leeds United
BENNETT, Alexander	11	1904-1913	Celtic, Rangers
BENNIE, Robert	3	1925-1926	Airdrie
BERNARD, Paul	2	1995	Oldham Athletic
BERRA, Christophe	41	2008-2017	Hearts, Wolverhampton Wanderers, Ipswich Town
BERRY, Davidson	3	1894-1899	Queen's Park
BERRY, William	4	1888-1891	Queen's Park
BETT, Jim	26	1982-1990	Rangers, Lokeren, Aberdeen
BEVERIDGE, William	3	1879-1880	Glasgow University
BLACK, Andrew	3	1937-1938	Hearts
BLACK, David	1	1889	Hurlford
BLACK, Eric	2	1987	Metz
BLACK, Ian	1	2013	Rangers
BLACK, Ian	1	1948	Southampton
BLACKBURN, John	1	1873	Royal Engineers
BLACKLAW, Adam	3	1963-1965	Burnley
BLACKLEY, John	7	1973-1977	Hibernian
BLAIR, Daniel	8	1928-1932	Clyde, Aston Villa
BLAIR, James	8	1920-1924	Sheffield Wednesday, Cardiff City
BLAIR, James	1	1946	Blackpool
BLAIR, John	1	1933	Motherwell
BLAIR, William	1	1896	Third Lanark
BLESSINGTON, James	4	1894-1896	Celtic
BLYTH, Jim	2	1978	Coventry City
BONE, Jimmy	2	1972	Norwich City
BOOTH, Scott	22	1993-2001	Aberdeen, Twente Enschede
BOWIE, James	2	1920	Rangers
BOWIE, William	1	1891	Linthouse
BOWMAN, Dave	6	1992-1993	Dundee United
BOWMAN, George	1	1892	Montrose
BOYD, James	1	1933	Newcastle United
BOYD, George	2	2013-2014	Hull City
BOYD, Kris	18	2006-2010	Rangers, Middlesbrough
BOYD, Robert	2	1889-1891	Mossend Swifts
BOYD, Tom	72	1990-2001	Motherwell, Chelsea, Celtic
BOYD, William	2	1931	Clyde
BRADSHAW, Thomas	1	1928	Bury
BRAND, Ralph	8	1960-1962	Rangers
BRANDON, Thomas	1	1896	Blackburn Rovers
BRAZIL, Alan	13	1980-1983	Ipswich Town, Tottenham Hotspur
BRECKENRIDGE, Thomas	1	1888	Hearts
BREMNER, Billy	54	1965-1975	Leeds United
BREMNER, Des	1	1976	Hibernian
BRENNAN, Frank	7	1946-1954	Newcastle United
BRESLIN, Bernard	1	1897	Hibernian
BREWSTER, George	1	1921	Everton
BRIDCUTT, Liam	2	2013-2016	Brighton & Hove Albion, Leeds United
BROADFOOT, Kirk	4	2008-2010	Rangers
BROGAN, Jim	4	1971	Celtic
BROPHY, Eamon	1	2019	Kilmarnock
BROWN, Alexander	1	1904	Middlesbrough
BROWN, Andrew	2	1890-1891	St Mirren
BROWN, Allan	14	1950-1954	East Fife, Blackpool
BROWN, Bill	28	1958-1965	Dundee, Tottenham Hotspur
BROWN, Bobby	3	1946-1952	Rangers
BROWN, George	19	1930-1938	Rangers
BROWN, Hugh	3	1946-1947	Partick Thistle
BROWN, Jacob	7	2021-2023	Stoke City, Luton Town
BROWN, Jim	1	1975	Sheffield United
BROWN, John	1	1948	Clyde
BROWN, Robert	2	1884	Dumbarton
BROWN, Robert	1	1885	Dumbarton
BROWN, Robert	1	1890	Cambuslang
BROWN, Scott	55	2005-2017	Hibernian, Celtic
BROWNING, John	1	1914	Celtic

Name	Caps	Years	Clubs
BROWNLIE, James	16	1909-1914	Third Lanark
BROWNLIE, John	7	1971-1975	Hibernian
BRUCE, Daniel	1	1890	Vale of Leven
BRUCE, Robert	1	1933	Middlesbrough
BRYSON, Craig	3	2010-2016	Kilmarnock, Derby County
BUCHAN, Martin	34	1971-1978	Aberdeen, Manchester United
BUCHANAN, John	1	1889	Cambuslang
BUCHANAN, John	2	1929-1930	Rangers
BUCHANAN, Peter	1	1937	Chelsea
BUCHANAN, Robert	1	1891	Abercorn
BUCKLEY, Patrick	3	1954	Aberdeen
BUICK, Albert	2	1902	Hearts
BURCHILL, Mark	6	1999-2000	Celtic
BURKE, Chris	7	2006-2014	Rangers, Birmingham City
BURKE, Oliver	13	2016-2021	Nottingham Forest, RB Leipzig, Deportivo Alaves, West Bromwich Albion
BURLEY, Craig	46	1995-2003	Chelsea, Celtic, Derby County
BURLEY, George	11	1979-1982	Ipswich Town
BURNS, Francis	1	1969	Manchester United
BURNS, Kenny	20	1974-1981	Birmingham City, Nottingham Forest
BURNS, Tommy	8	1981-1988	Celtic
BUSBY, Matt	1	1933	Manchester City
CADDEN, Chris	2	2018	Motherwell
CADDIS, Paul	1	2016	Birmingham City
CAIRNEY, Tom	2	2017-2018	Fulham
CAIRNS, Thomas	8	1920-1925	Rangers
CALDERHEAD, David	1	1889	Queen of the South
CALDERWOOD, Colin	36	1995-1999	Tottenham Hotspur, Aston Villa
CALDERWOOD, Robert	3	1885	Cartvale
CALDOW, Eric	40	1957-1963	Rangers
CALDWELL, Gary	55	2002-2013	Newcastle United, Hibernian, Celtic, Wigan Athletic
CALDWELL, Stephen	12	2001-2011	Newcastle United, Sunderland, Burnley, Wigan Athletic
CALLAGHAN, Patrick	1	1900	Hibernian
CALLAGHAN, Willie	7	1967-1970	Dunfermline Athletic
CAMERON, Colin	28	1999-2004	Hearts, Wolverhampton Wanderers
CAMERON, John	1	1886	Rangers
CAMERON, John	1	1896	Queen's Park
CAMERON, John	2	1904-1909	St Mirren, Chelsea
CAMPBELL, Allan	1	2022	Luton Town
CAMPBELL, Bobby	5	1947-1950	Falkirk, Chelsea
CAMPBELL, Charles	13	1874-1886	Queen's Park
CAMPBELL, Henry	1	1889	Renton
CAMPBELL, James	2	1891-1892	Kilmarnock
CAMPBELL, James	1	1913	Sheffield Wednesday
CAMPBELL, James	1	1946	Clyde
CAMPBELL, John	1	1881	South Western
CAMPBELL, John	12	1893-1903	Celtic
CAMPBELL, John	4	1899-1901	Rangers
CAMPBELL, Kenneth	8	1920-1922	Liverpool, Partick Thistle
CAMPBELL, Peter	2	1878-1879	Rangers
CAMPBELL, Peter	1	1898	Morton
CAMPBELL, Willie	5	1946-1948	Morton
CANERO, Peter	1	2004	Leicester City
CARABINE, James	3	1938-1939	Third Lanark
CARR, Willie	6	1970-1972	Coventry City
CASSIDY, Joseph	4	1921-1923	Celtic
CHALMERS, Steve	5	1964-1967	Celtic
CHALMERS, William	1	1885	Rangers
CHALMERS, William	1	1929	Queen's Park
CHAMBERS, Thomas	1	1894	Hearts
CHAPLIN, George	1	1908	Dundee
CHEYNE, Alexander	5	1929-1930	Aberdeen
CHRISTIE, Alexander	3	1898-1899	Queen's Park
CHRISTIE, Robert	1	1884	Queen's Park
CHRISTIE, Ryan	45	2017-2023	Aberdeen, Celtic, Bournemouth
CLARK, Bobby	17	1967-1973	Aberdeen
CLARK, John	4	1966-1967	Celtic
CLARK, Zander	3	2023	Hearts
CLARKE, Steve	6	1987-1994	Chelsea
CLARKSON, David	2	2008	Motherwell
CLELLAND, John	1	1891	Royal Albert
CLEMENTS, Robert	1	1891	Leith Athletic
CLUNAS, William	3	1924-1925	Sunderland
COLLIER, William	1	1922	Raith Rovers
COLLINS, Bobby	31	1950-1965	Celtic, Everton, Leeds United
COLLINS, John	58	1988-1999	Hibernian, Celtic, Monaco, Everton
COLLINS, Thomas	1	1909	Hearts
COLMAN, Donald	4	1911-1913	Aberdeen
COLQUHOUN, Eddie	11	1967-1973	West Bromwich Albion, Sheffield United
COLQUHOUN, John	2	1988	Hearts
COMBE, Bobby	3	1948	Hibernian
COMMONS, Kris	12	2008-2013	Derby County, Celtic
CONN, Alfie Snr	1	1956	Hearts
CONN, Alfie Jnr	2	1975	Tottenham Hotspur
CONNACHAN, Eddie	2	1961-1962	Dunfermline Athletic
CONNELLY, George	2	1973	Celtic
CONNOLLY, John	1	1973	Everton
CONNOR, Bobby	4	1986-1990	Dundee, Aberdeen
CONNOR, James	1	1886	Airdrie
CONNOR, James	4	1930-1934	Sunderland
CONSIDINE, Andrew	3	2020	Aberdeen
CONWAY, Craig	7	2009-2013	Dundee United, Cardiff City
COOK, William	3	1934	Bolton Wanderers
COOKE, Charlie	16	1965-1975	Dundee, Chelsea
COOPER, Davie	22	1979-1990	Rangers, Motherwell
COOPER, Liam	16	2019-2023	Leeds United
CORMACK, Peter	9	1966-1971	Hibernian, Nottingham Forest
COWAN, James	3	1896-1898	Aston Villa
COWAN, Jimmy	25	1948-1951	Morton
COWAN, William	1	1924	Newcastle United
COWIE, Don	9	2009-2012	Watford, Cardiff City
COWIE, Doug	20	1953-1958	Dundee
COX, Sammy	25	1948-1954	Rangers
CRAIG, Allan	3	1929-1932	Motherwell
CRAIG, Jim	1	1967	Celtic
CRAIG, Joe	1	1977	Celtic
CRAIG, Tully	8	1927-1930	Rangers
CRAIG, Tommy	1	1976	Newcastle United
CRAINEY, Stephen	12	2002-2011	Celtic, Southampton, Blackpool
CRAPNELL, James	9	1929-1933	Airdrie
CRAWFORD, David	3	1892-1894	St Mirren, Rangers
CRAWFORD, James	5	1931-1933	Queen's Park
CRAWFORD, Steven	25	1995-2004	Raith Rovers, Dunfermline Athletic, Plymouth Argyle
CRERAND, Pat	16	1961-1965	Celtic, Manchester United
CRINGAN, William	5	1920-1923	Celtic
CROAL, James	3	1913-1914	Falkirk
CROPLEY, Alex	2	1971	Hibernian
CROSBIE, John	2	1920-1922	Ayr United, Birmingham City
CROSS, John	1	1903	Third Lanark
CRUICKSHANK, Jim	6	1964-1975	Hearts
CRUM, Johnny	2	1936-1938	Celtic
CULLEN, Michael	1	1956	Luton Town
CUMMING, David	1	1938	Middlesbrough
CUMMING, John	9	1954-1960	Hearts
CUMMINGS, George	9	1935-1939	Partick Thistle, Aston Villa
CUMMINGS, Jason	2	2017-2018	Nottingham Forest, Rangers
CUMMINGS, Warren	1	2002	Chelsea
CUNNINGHAM, Andrew	12	1920-1927	Rangers
CUNNINGHAM, Willie	8	1954-1955	Preston North End
CURRAN, Hugh	5	1969-1971	Wolverhampton Wanderers
DAILLY, Christian	67	1997-2008	Derby County, Blackburn Rovers, West Ham, Rangers
DALGLISH, Kenny	102	1971-1986	Celtic, Liverpool
DAVIDSON, Callum	19	1998-2009	Blackburn Rovers, Leicester City, Preston North End
DAVIDSON, David	5	1878-1881	Queen's Park
DAVIDSON, James	8	1954-1955	Partick Thistle
DAVIDSON, Murray	1	2012	St Johnstone
DAVIDSON, Stewart	1	1921	Middlesbrough
DAWSON, Ally	5	1980-1983	Rangers
DAWSON, Jerry	14	1934-1939	Rangers
DEAKIN, John	1	1946	St Mirren
DEANS, Dixie	2	1974	Celtic
DELANEY, Jimmy	15	1935-1948	Celtic, Manchester United
DEVINE, Archibald	1	1910	Falkirk
DEVLIN, Michael	3	2019	Aberdeen
DEVLIN, Paul	10	2002-2003	Birmingham City
DEWAR, George	2	1888-1889	Dumbarton

List of players

DEWAR, Neil	3	1932	Third Lanark
DICK, John	1	1959	West Ham
DICKIE, Matthew	3	1897-1900	Rangers
DICKOV, Paul	10	2000-2004	Manchester City, Leicester City, Blackburn Rovers
DICKSON, Billy	5	1970-1974	Kilmarnock
DICKSON, William	1	1888	Dundee Strathmore
DIVERS, John	1	1895	Celtic
DIVERS, John	1	1938	Celtic
DIXON, Paul	3	2012	Huddersfield Town
DOBIE, Scott	6	2002	West Bromwich Albion
DOCHERTY, Tommy	25	1951-1959	Preston North End, Arsenal
DODDS, Billy	26	1996-2001	Aberdeen, Dundee United, Rangers
DODDS, Davie	2	1983	Dundee United
DODDS, Joseph	3	1914	Celtic
DOIG, John	3	1887-1903	Arbroath, Sunderland
DONACHIE, Willie	35	1972-1978	Manchester City
DONALDSON, Alexander	6	1914-1922	Bolton Wanderers
DONNACHIE, Joseph	3	1913-1914	Oldham Athletic
DONNELLY, Simon	10	1997-1998	Celtic
DORRANS, Graham	12	2009-2015	West Bromwich Albion
DOUGAL, James	1	1939	Preston North End
DOUGALL, Neil	1	1946	Birmingham City
DOUGAN, Bobby	1	1950	Hearts
DOUGLAS, Angus	1	1911	Chelsea
DOUGLAS, Barry	1	2018	Wolverhampton Wanderers
DOUGLAS, James	1	1880	Renfrew
DOUGLAS, Rab	19	2002-2005	Celtic, Leicester City
DOWDS, Peter	1	1892	Celtic
DOWNIE, Robert	1	1892	Third Lanark
DOYLE, Daniel	8	1892-1898	Celtic
DOYLE, Johnny	1	1975	Ayr United
DRUMMOND, John	14	1892-1903	Falkirk, Rangers
DUNBAR, Michael	1	1886	Cartvale
DUNCAN, Arthur	6	1975	Hibernian
DUNCAN, Douglas	14	1932-1937	Derby County
DUNCAN, David	3	1948	East Fife
DUNCAN, James	2	1878-1882	Alexandra Athletic
DUNCAN, John	1	1925	Leicester City
DUNCANSON, James	1	1946	Rangers
DUNLOP, James	1	1890	St Mirren
DUNLOP, William	1	1906	Liverpool
DUNN, James	6	1925-1928	Hibernian, Everton
DURIE, Gordon	43	1987-1998	Chelsea, Tottenham Hotspur, Rangers
DURRANT, Ian	20	1987-2000	Rangers, Kilmarnock
DYKES, James	2	1938	Hearts
DYKES, Lyndon	35	2020-2023	Queens Park Rangers
EASSON, James	3	1931-1933	Portsmouth
ELLIOT, Matt	18	1997-2001	Leicester City
ELLIS, David	1	1892	Mossend Swifts
EVANS, Allan	4	1982	Aston Villa
EVANS, Bobby	48	1848-1960	Celtic, Chelsea
EWART, John	1	1921	Bradford City
EWING, Tommy	2	1957-1958	Partick Thistle
FARM, George	10	1952-1959	Blackpool
FERGUSON, Alex	4	1967	Dunfermline
FERGUSON, Barry	45	1998-2009	Rangers, Blackburn Rovers
FERGUSON, Bobby	7	1965-1966	Kilmarnock
FERGUSON, Derek	2	1988	Rangers
FERGUSON, Duncan	7	1992-1997	Dundee United, Everton
FERGUSON, Ian	9	1988-1997	Rangers
FERGUSON, John	6	1874-1878	Vale of Leven
FERGUSON, Lewis	10	2021-2023	Aberdeen, Bologna
FERNIE, Willie	12	1954-1958	Celtic
FINDLAY, Robert	1	1898	Kilmarnock
FINDLAY, Stuart	1	2019	Kilmarnock
FITCHIE, Thomas	4	1905-1907	Arsenal, Queen's Park
FLAVELL, Bobby	2	1947	Airdrie
FLECK, John	5	2019-2021	Sheffield United
FLECK, Robert	4	1990-1992	Norwich City
FLEMING, Charles	1	1954	East Fife
FLEMING, James	3	1929-1930	Rangers
FLEMING, Robert	1	1886	Morton
FLETCHER, Darren	80	2003-2017	Manchester United, West Bromwich Albion, Stoke City
FLETCHER, Steven	33	2008-2018	Hibernian, Burnley, Wolverhampton Wanderers, Sunderland, Olympique de Marseille, Sheffield Wed'sday
FORBES, Alex	14	1947-1958	Sheffield United, Arsenal
FORBES, John	5	1884-1887	Vale of Leven
FORD, Donald	3	1973-1974	Hearts
FORREST, James	38	2011-2021	Celtic
FORREST, Jim	1	1958	Motherwell
FORREST, Jim	5	1965-1971	Rangers, Aberdeen
FORSYTH, Alex	10	1972-1975	Partick Thistle, Manchester United
FORSYTH, Campbell	4	1964	Kilmarnock
FORSYTH, Craig	4	2014-2015	Derby County
FORSYTH, Tom	22	1971-1978	Motherwell, Rangers
FOX, Danny	4	2009-2012	Celtic, Southampton
FOYERS, Robert	2	1893-1894	St Bernard's
FRASER, Doug	7	1967-1968	West Bromwich Albion
FRASER, James	1	1891	Moffat
FRASER, John	1	1907	Dundee
FRASER, Malcolm	5	1880-1883	Queen's Park
FRASER, Ryan	26	2017-2023	Bournemouth, Newcastle United
FRASER, William	2	1954	Sunderland
FREEDMAN, Dougie	2	2001-2002	Crystal Palace
FULTON, William	1	1884	Abercorn
FYFE, John	1	1895	Third Lanark
GABRIEL, Jimmy	2	1960-1963	Everton
GALLACHER, Hughie	20	1924-1935	Airdrie, Newcastle United, Chelsea, Derby County
GALLACHER, Kevin	53	1988-2001	Dundee United, Coventry City, Blackburn Rovers, Newcastle United
GALLACHER, Patrick	1	1934	Sunderland
GALLACHER, Paul	8	2002-2004	Dundee United
GALLACHER, Paul	1	2004	Blackburn Rovers
GALLAGHER, Declan	9	2019-2020	Motherwell
GALLOWAY, Mike	1	1991	Celtic
GALT, James	2	1908	Rangers
GARDINER, Ian	1	1957	Motherwell
GARDNER, David	1	1897	Third Lanark
GARDNER, Robert	5	1872-1878	Queen's Park, Clydesdale
GEMMELL, Thomas	2	1955	St Mirren
GEMMELL, Tommy	18	1966-1971	Celtic
GEMMILL, Archie	43	1971-1981	Derby County, Nottingham Forest, Birmingham City
GEMMILL, Scot	26	1995-2003	Nottingham Forest, Everton
GIBB, William	1	1873	Clydesdale
GIBSON, David	7	1963-1964	Leicester City
GIBSON, James	8	1926-1930	Partick Thistle, Aston Villa
GIBSON, Neil	14	1895-1905	Rangers, Partick Thistle
GILCHRIST, John	1	1922	Celtic
GILHOOLEY, Michael	1	1922	Hull City
GILKS, Matt	3	2012-2013	Blackpool
GILLESPIE, Gary	13	1987-1991	Liverpool
GILLESPIE, George	7	1880-1891	Rangers, Queen's Park
GILLESPIE, James	1	1898	Third Lanark
GILLESPIE, John	1	1896	Queen's Park
GILLESPIE, Robert	4	1926-1933	Queen's Park
GILLICK, Torry	5	1937-1938	Everton
GILMOUR, Billy	23	2021-2023	Chelsea, Norwich City, Brighton & Hove Albion
GILMOUR, John	1	1930	Dundee
GILZEAN, Alan	22	1963-1971	Dundee, Tottenham Hotspur
GLASS, Stephen	1	1998	Newcastle United
GLAVIN, Ronnie	1	1977	Celtic
GLEN, Archie	2	1955-1956	Aberdeen
GLEN, Robert	3	1895-1900	Renton, Hibernian
GOODWILLIE, David	3	2010-2011	Dundee United, Blackburn Rovers
GORAM, Andy	43	1985-1998	Oldham Athletic, Hibernian, Rangers
GORDON, Craig	74	2004-2022	Hearts, Sunderland, Celtic
GORDON, James	10	1912-1920	Rangers
GOSSLAND, James	1	1884	Rangers
GOUDIE, John	1	1884	Abercorn
GOUGH, Richard	61	1983-1993	Dundee United, Tottenham Hotspur, Rangers
GOULD, Jonathan	2	1999-2000	Celtic
GOURLAY, James	1	1886	Cambuslang
GOURLAY, James	1	1888	Cambuslang
GOVAN, Jock	6	1947-1948	Hibernian
GOW, Donald	1	1888	Rangers
GOW, John	1	1885	Queen's Park
GOW, John	1	1888	Rangers

—187—

Name	Caps	Years	Clubs
GRAHAM, Alexander	1	1921	Arsenal
GRAHAM, Arthur	11	1978-1981	Leeds United
GRAHAM, George	12	1971-1973	Arsenal, Manchester United
GRAHAM, John	1	1884	Annbank
GRANT, John	2	1958	Hibernian
GRANT, Peter	2	1989	Celtic
GRAY, Andy	20	1975-1985	Aston Villa, Wolverhampton Wanderers, Everton
GRAY, Andy	2	2003	Bradford City
GRAY, Archibald	1	1903	Hibernian
GRAY, Douglas	10	1928-1932	Rangers
GRAY, Eddie	12	1969-1977	Leeds United
GRAY, Frank	32	1976-1983	Leeds United, Nottingham Forest
GRAY, Woodville	1	1886	Pollokshields Athletic
GREEN, Tony	6	1971-1972	Blackpool, Newcastle United
GREER, Gordon	11	2013-2016	Brighton & Hove Albion, Blackburn Rovers
GREIG, John	44	1964-1975	Rangers
GRIFFITHS, Leigh	22	2012-2020	Wolverhampton Wanderers, Celtic
GROVES, William	3	1888-1890	Hibernian
GULLILAND, William	4	1891-1895	Queen's Park
GUNN, Angus	7	2023	Norwich City
GUNN, Bryan	6	1990-1994	Norwich City
HADDOCK, Harry	6	1954-1958	Clyde
HADDOW, David	1	1894	Rangers
HAFFEY, Frank	2	1960-1961	Celtic
HAMILTON, Alex	24	1961-1965	Dundee
HAMILTON, Alexander	4	1885-1888	Queen's Park
HAMILTON, George	5	1946-1954	Aberdeen
HAMILTON, Gladstone	1	1906	Port Glasgow Athletic
HAMILTON, James	3	1892-1893	Queen's Park
HAMILTON, James	1	1924	St Mirren
HAMILTON, Robert	11	1899-1911	Rangers, Dundee
HAMILTON, Thomas	1	1891	Hurlford
HAMILTON, Thomas	1	1932	Rangers
HAMILTON, Willie	1	1965	Hibernian
HAMMELL, Steven	1	2004	Motherwell
HANLEY, Grant	48	2011-2023	Blackburn Rovers, Newcastle United, Norwich City
HANLON, Paul	1	2020	Hibernian
HANNAH, Andrew	1	1888	Renton
HANNAH, James	1	1889	Third Lanark
HANSEN, Alan	26	1979-1987	Liverpool
HANSEN, John	2	1971-1972	Partick Thistle
HARKNESS, James	12	1927-1933	Queen's Park, Hearts
HARPER, Joe	5	1967-1978	Morton, Aberdeen, Hibernian
HARPER, Willie	11	1923-1926	Arsenal
HARRIS, Joseph	2	1921	Partick Thistle
HARRIS, Neil	1	1924	Newcastle United
HARROWER, William	3	1882-1886	Queen's Park
HARTFORD, Asa	50	1972-1982	West Bromwich Albion, Manchester City, Everton
HARTLEY, Paul	25	2005-2010	Hearts, Celtic, Bristol City
HARVEY, David	16	1972-1976	Leeds United
HASTINGS, Alexander	2	1935-1937	Sunderland
HAUGHNEY, Michael	1	1954	Celtic
HAY, David	27	1970-1974	Celtic
HAY, James	11	1905-1914	Celtic, Newcastle United
HEGARTY, Paul	8	1979-1983	Dundee United
HEGGIE, Charles	1	1886	Rangers
HENDERSON, George	1	1904	Rangers
HENDERSON, Jackie	7	1953-1958	Portsmouth, Arsenal
HENDERSON, Willie	29	1962-1971	Rangers
HENDRY, Colin	51	1993-2001	Blackburn Rovers, Rangers, Coventry City, Bolton Wanderers
HENDRY, Jack	28	2018-2023	Celtic, KV Ostende, Club Brugge, Cremonese, Al Ettifaq
HEPBURN, James	1	1891	Alloa Athletic
HEPBURN, Robert	1	1932	Ayr United
HERD, Alexander	1	1935	Hearts
HERD, David	5	1958-1961	Arsenal
HERD, George	5	1958-1960	Clyde
HERRIOT, Jim	8	1968-1969	Birmingham City
HEWIE, John	19	1956-1960	Charlton Athletic
HICKEY, Aaron	14	2022-2023	Bologna, Brentford
HIGGINS, Alexander	1	1885	Kilmarnock
HIGGINS, Alexander	4	1910-1911	Newcastle United
HIGHET, Thomas	4	1875-1878	Queen's Park
HILL, David	3	1881-1882	Rangers
HILL, David	1	1906	Third Lanark
HILL, Frank	3	1930-1931	Aberdeen
HILL, John	2	1891-1892	Hearts
HOGG, Bobby	1	1937	Celtic
HOGG, George	2	1896	Hearts
HOGG, James	1	1922	Ayr United
HOLM, Andrew	3	1882-1883	Queen's Park
HOLT, Davie	5	1963-1964	Hearts
HOLT, Gary	10	2000-2004	Kilmarnock, Norwich City
HOLTON, Jim	15	1973-1974	Manchester United
HOOD, Harry	3	1967	Clyde
HOPE, Bobby	7	1967-1968	West Bromwich Albion
HOPKIN, David	7	1997-1999	Crystal Palace, Leeds United
HOULISTON, Willie	3	1948-1949	Queen of the South
HOUSTON, Stewart	1	1975	Manchester United
HOWDEN, William	1	1905	Partick Thistle
HOWE, Robert	2	1929	Hamilton Academical
HOWIE, Hugh	1	1948	Hibernian
HOWIE, James	3	1905-1908	Newcastle United
HOWIESON, James	1	1927	St Mirren
HUGHES, Billy	1	1975	Sunderland
HUGHES, John	8	1965-1969	Celtic
HUGHES, Richard	5	2004-2005	Portsmouth
HUGHES, Stephen	1	2009	Norwich City
HUMPHRIES, Wilson	1	1952	Motherwell
HUNTER, Ally	4	1972-1973	Kilmarnock, Celtic
HUNTER, John	4	1874-1877	Third Lanark
HUNTER, John	1	1909	Dundee
HUNTER, Richard	1	1890	St Mirren
HUNTER, Willie	3	1960	Motherwell
HUSBAND, Jackie	2	1946	Partick Thistle
HUTCHISON, Don	26	1999-2003	Everton, Sunderland, West Ham
HUTCHISON, Tommy	17	1973-1975	Coventry City
HUTTON, Alan	50	2007-2016	Rangers, Tottenham Hotspur, Aston Villa, Real Mallorca, Bolton Wanderers
HUTTON, James	1	1887	St Bernard's
HUTTON, John	10	1923-1928	Aberdeen, Blackburn Rovers
HYAM, Dominic	1	2023	Blackburn Rovers
HYSLOP, Thomas	2	1896-1897	Stoke City, Rangers
IMLACH, Stewart	4	1958	Nottingham Forest
IMRIE, William	2	1929	St Johnstone
INGLIS, John	2	1883	Rangers
INGLIS, John	1	1884	Kilmarnock Athletic
IRONS, James	1	1900	Queen's Park
IRVINE, Brian	9	1990-1994	Aberdeen
IWELUMO, Chris	4	2008-2010	Wolverhampton Wanderers, Burnley
JACK, Ryan	18	2017-2023	Rangers
JACKSON, Alex	17	1925-1930	Aberdeen, Huddersfield Town
JACKSON, Andrew	2	1886-1888	Cambuslang
JACKSON, Colin	8	1975-1976	Rangers
JACKSON, Darren	28	1995-1998	Hibernian, Celtic
JACKSON, John	8	1931-1935	Partick Thistle, Chelsea
JACKSON, Thomas	6	1904-1907	St Mirren
JAMES, Alex	8	1925-1932	Preston North End, Arsenal
JARDINE, Sandy	38	1970-1979	Rangers
JARVIE, Drew	3	1971	Airdrie
JENKINSON, Thomas	1	1887	Hearts
JESS, Eoin	18	1992-1999	Aberdeen, Coventry City
JOHNSTON, Allan	18	1998-2002	Sunderland, Rangers, Middlesbrough
JOHNSTON, James	1	1888	Abercorn
JOHNSTON, John	3	1929-1932	Hearts
JOHNSTON, Leslie	2	1948	Clyde
JOHNSTON, Maurice	38	1984-1992	Watford, Celtic, Nantes, Rangers
JOHNSTON, Robert	1	1937	Sunderland
JOHNSTON, Willie	22	1965-1978	Rangers, West Bromwich Albion
JOHNSTONE, Bobby	17	1951-1956	Hibernian, Manchester City
JOHNSTONE, Derek	14	1973-1979	Rangers
JOHNSTONE, Jimmy	23	1964-1974	Celtic
JOHNSTONE, John	1	1894	Kilmarnock
JOHNSTONE, William	3	1887-1890	Third Lanark
JORDAN, Joe	52	1973-1982	Leeds United, Manchester United, AC Milan
KAY, John	6	1880-1884	Queen's Park

KEILLOR, Alexander	6	1891-1897	Montrose, Dundee
KEIR, Leitch	5	1886-1888	Dumbarton
KELLY, Hugh	1	1952	Blackpool
KELLY, James	8	1888-1893	Renton, Celtic
KELLY, John	2	1948	Barnsley
KELLY, Liam	1	2012	Kilmarnock
KELLY, Liam	1	2023	Motherwell
KELSO, Thomas	1	1914	Dundee
KELSO, Robert	8	1885-1898	Renton, Dundee
KENNAWAY, James	1	1933	Celtic
KENNEDY, Alexander	6	1875-1884	Eastern, Third Lanark
KENNEDY, Jim	6	1963-1964	Celtic
KENNEDY, John	1	1897	Hibernian
KENNEDY, John	1	2004	Celtic
KENNEDY, Samuel	1	1905	Partick Thistle
KENNEDY, Stewart	5	1975	Rangers
KENNEDY, Stuart	8	1978-1981	Aberdeen
KENNETH, Gary	2	2010	Dundee United
KER, George	5	1880-1882	Queen's Park
KER, William	2	1872-1873	Queen's Park
KERR, Andrew	2	1955	Partick Thistle
KERR, Brian	3	2003-2004	Newcastle United, Coventry City
KERR, Peter	1	1924	Hibernian
KEY, George	1	1902	Hearts
KEY, William	1	1907	Queen's Park
KING, Alexander	6	1896-1899	Hearts, Celtic
KING, James	2	1932-1933	Hamilton Academical
KING, William	1	1928	Queen's Park
KINGSLEY, Stephen	2	2016-2022	Swansea City, Hearts
KINLOCH, James	1	1922	Partick Thistle
KINNAIRD, Arthur	1	1873	The Wanderers
KINNEAR, David	1	1937	Rangers
KYLE, Kevin	10	2002-2010	Sunderland, Kilmarnock
LAMBERT, Paul	40	1995-2006	Motherwell, Borussia Dortmund, Celtic
LAMBIE, John	2	1887-1888	Queen's Park
LAMBIE, William	9	1892-1897	Queen's Park
LAMONT, Walter	1	1885	Pilgrims
LANG, Archibald	1	1880	Dumbarton
LANG, James	2	1876-1878	Clydesdale, Third Lanark
LATTA, Alexander	2	1888-1889	Dumbarton
LAW, Denis	55	1958-1974	Huddersfield Town, Manchester City, Manchester United, Torino
LAW, George	3	1910	Rangers
LAW, Thomas	2	1928-1930	Chelsea
LAWRENCE, James	1	1911	Newcastle United
LAWRENCE, Tommy	3	1963-1969	Liverpool
LAWSON, Denis	1	1923	St Mirren
LECKIE, Robert	1	1872	Queen's Park
LEGGAT, Graham	18	1956-1960	Aberdeen, Fulham
LEIGHTON, Jim	91	1982-1998	Aberdeen, Manchester United, Hibernian
LENNIE, William	2	1908	Aberdeen
LENNOX, Bobby	10	1966-1970	Celtic
LESLIE, Lawrie	5	1960-1961	Airdrie
LEVEIN, Craig	16	1990-1994	Hearts
LIDDELL, Billy	29	1946-1955	Liverpool
LIDDLE, Daniel	3	1931	East Fife
LINDSAY, David	1	1903	St Mirren
LINDSAY, John	3	1888-1893	Renton
LINDSAY, Joseph	8	1880-1886	Dumbarton
LINWOOD, Alexander	1	1949	Clyde
LITTLE, John	1	1953	Rangers
LIVINGSTONE, George	2	1906-1907	Manchester City, Rangers
LOCHHEAD, Alexander	1	1889	Third Lanark
LOGAN, James	1	1891	Ayr United
LOGAN, Thomas	1	1913	Falkirk
LOGIE, James	1	1952	Arsenal
LONEY, William	2	1910	Celtic
LONG, Hugh	1	1947	Clyde
LONGAIR, William	1	1894	Dundee
LORIMER, Peter	21	1969-1976	Leeds United
LOVE, Andrew	3	1931	Aberdeen
LOW, Alexander	1	1933	Falkirk
LOW, James	1	1891	Cambuslang
LOW, Thomas	1	1897	Rangers
LOW, Wilfred	5	1911-1920	Newcastle United
LOWE, James	1	1887	St Bernard's
LUNDIE, James	1	1886	Hibernian
LYALL, John	1	1905	Sheffield Wednesday
MACARI, Lou	24	1972-1978	Celtic, Manchester United
MACAULAY, Archibald	7	1947-1948	Brentford, Arsenal
MACAULAY, John	1	1884	Arthurlie
MACDONALD, Alex	1	1976	Rangers
MACDONALD, John	1	1886	Queen's Park
MACDOUGALL, Ted	7	1975	Norwich City
MACFADYEN, William	2	1933	Motherwell
MACFARLANE, Robert	1	1896	Morton
MACFARLANE, Alexander	5	1904-1911	Dundee
MACKAIL-SMITH, Craig	7	2011-2012	Peterborough United, Brighton & Hove Albion
MACKAY-STEVEN, Gary	2	2013-2018	Dundee United, Aberdeen
MACKAY, Dave	22	1957-1965	Hearts, Tottenham Hotspur
MACKAY, Duncan	14	1959-1962	Celtic
MACKAY, Gary	4	1987-1988	Hearts
MACKAY, Malky	5	2004	Norwich City
MACKENZIE, John	9	1953-1955	Partick Thistle
MACKIE, Jamie	9	2010-2012	Queens Park Rangers
MACKINNON, Angus	1	1874	Queen's Park
MACKINNON, William	9	1872-1879	Queen's Park
MACLEOD, Johnny	4	1961	Hibernian
MACLEOD, Murdo	20	1985-1991	Celtic, Borussia Dortmund, Hibernian
MADDEN, John	2	1893-1895	Celtic
MAGUIRE, Chris	2	2011	Aberdeen
MAIN, James	1	1909	Hibernian
MAIN, Robert	1	1937	Rangers
MALEY, William	2	1893	Celtic
MALONEY, Shaun	47	2005-2016	Celtic, Aston Villa, Wigan Athletic, Chicago Fire, Hull City
MALPAS, Maurice	55	1984-1992	Dundee United
MARSHALL, David	47	2004-2021	Celtic, Cardiff City, Hull City, Wigan Athletic, Derby County
MARSHALL, Gordon	1	1992	Celtic
MARSHALL, Harry	2	1899-1900	Celtic
MARSHALL, James	3	1932-1934	Rangers
MARSHALL, John	4	1885-1887	Third Lanark
MARSHALL, John	7	1921-1924	Middlesbrough, Llanelli
MARSHALL, Robert	2	1892-1894	Rangers
MARTIN, Brian	2	1995	Motherwell
MARTIN, Chris	17	2014-2017	Derby County, Fulham
MARTIN, Fred	6	1954-1955	Aberdeen
MARTIN, Neil	3	1965	Hibernian, Sunderland
MARTIN, Russell	29	2011-2017	Norwich City
MARTIS, John	1	1960	Motherwell
MASON, Jimmy	7	1949-1951	Third Lanark
MASSIE, Alexander	18	1932-1938	Hearts, Aston Villa
MASSON, Don	17	1976-1978	Queens Park Rangers, Derby County
MATHERS, David	1	1954	Partick Thistle
MATTEO, Dominic	6	2000-2002	Leeds United
MAXWELL, William	1	1898	Stoke City
MAY, John	5	1906-1909	Rangers
MAY, Stevie	1	2014	Sheffield Wednesday
MCADAM, James	1	1880	Third Lanark
MCALLISTER, Brian	3	1997	Wimbledon
MCALLISTER, Gary	57	1990-1999	Leicester City, Leeds United, Coventry City
MCALLISTER, Jamie	1	2004	Livingston
MCARTHUR, Daniel	3	1895-1899	Celtic
MCARTHUR, James	32	2010-2017	Wigan Athletic, Crystal Palace
MCATEE, Andrew	1	1913	Celtic
MCAULAY, James	9	1882-1887	Dumbarton
MCAULEY, Robert	2	1931	Rangers
MCAVENNIE, Frank	5	1985-1988	West Ham, Celtic
MCBAIN, Edward	1	1894	St Mirren
MCBAIN, Neil	3	1922-1924	Manchester United, Everton
MCBRIDE, Joe	2	1966	Celtic
MCBRIDE, Peter	6	1904-1909	Preston North End
MCBURNIE, Oliver	16	2018-2021	Swansea City, Barnsley, Sheffield United
MCCALL, Archie	1	1888	Renton
MCCALL, James	5	1886-1890	Renton
MCCALL, Stuart	40	1990-1998	Everton, Rangers
MCCALLIOG, Jim	10	1967-1971	Sheffield Wednesday, Wolverhampton Wanderers
MCCALLUM, Neil	1	1888	Renton

Name	Caps	Years	Clubs
MCCANN, Bert	5	1959-1961	Motherwell
MCCANN, Neil	26	1998-2005	Hearts, Rangers, Southampton
MCCARTNEY, William	1	1902	Hibernian
MCCLAIR, Brian	30	1986-1993	Celtic, Manchester United
MCCLORY, Alan	3	1926-1934	Motherwell
MCCLOY, Peter	4	1973	Rangers
MCCLOY, Philip	2	1924-1925	Ayr United
MCCOIST, Ally	61	1986-1998	Rangers, Kilmarnock
MCCOLL, Ian	14	1950-1958	Rangers
MCCOLL, Robert	13	1896-1908	Queen's Park, Newcastle United
MCCOLL, William	1	1895	Renton
MCCOMBIE, Andrew	4	1903-1905	Sunderland, Newcastle United
MCCORKINDALE, John	1	1891	Partick Thistle
MCCORMACK, Ross	13	2008-2016	Motherwell, Cardiff City, Leeds United, Fulham
MCCORMICK, Robert	1	1886	Abercorn
MCCRAE, David	2	1929	St Mirren
MCCREADIE, Andrew	2	1893-1894	Rangers
MCCREADIE, Eddie	23	1965-1969	Chelsea
MCCULLOCH, David	7	1934-1938	Hearts, Brentford, Derby County
MCCULLOCH, Lee	18	2004-2010	Wigan Athletic, Rangers
MCDONALD, Joseph	2	1955	Sunderland
MCDONALD, Kevin	5	2018-2019	Fulham
MCDOUGALL, James	2	1931	Liverpool
MCDOUGALL, John	5	1877-1879	Vale of Leven
MCDOUGALL, John	1	1926	Airdrie
MCEVELEY, Jay	3	2007-2008	Derby County
MCFADDEN, James	48	2002-2010	Motherwell, Everton, Birmingham City
MCFARLANE, William	1	1947	Hearts
MCGARR, Ernie	2	1969	Aberdeen
MCGARVEY, Frank	7	1979-1984	Liverpool, Celtic
MCGEOCH, Alexander	4	1876-1877	Dumbreck
MCGEOCH, Dylan	2	2018	Hibernian
MCGHEE, James	1	1886	Hibernian
MCGHEE, Mark	4	1983-1984	Aberdeen
MCGINLAY, John	13	1994-1997	Bolton Wanderers
MCGINN, John	62	2016-2023	Hibernian, Aston Villa
MCGINN, Paul	1	2021	Hibernian
MCGONAGLE, Peter	6	1933-1934	Celtic
MCGOWAN, James	1	1946	Partick Thistle
MCGRAIN, Danny	62	1973-1982	Celtic
MCGREGOR, Allan	42	2007-2018	Rangers, Besiktas, Hull City, Cardiff City
MCGREGOR, Callum	58	2017-2023	Celtic
MCGREGOR, John	4	1877-1880	Vale of Leven
MCGRORY, Jackie	6	1964-1967	Kilmarnock
MCGRORY, Jimmy	7	1928-1933	Celtic
MCGUIRE, William	2	1881	Beith
MCGURK, Francis	1	1933	Birmingham City
MCHARDY, Hugh	1	1885	Rangers
MCINALLY, Alan	8	1989-1990	Aston Villa, Bayern Munich
MCINALLY, Jim	10	1987-1993	Dundee United
MCINALLY, Thomas	2	1926	Celtic
MCINNES, Derek	2	2002	West Bromwich Albion
MCINNES, Thomas	1	1889	Cowlairs
MCINTOSH, William	1	1905	Third Lanark
MCINTYRE, Andrew	2	1878-1882	Vale of Leven
MCINTYRE, Hugh	1	1880	Rangers
MCINTYRE, James	1	1884	Rangers
MCKAY, Barrie	1	2016	Rangers
MCKAY, John	1	1924	Blackburn Rovers
MCKAY, Robert	1	1927	Newcastle United
MCKEAN, Bobby	1	1976	Rangers
MCKENNA, Scott	33	2018-2023	Aberdeen, Nottingham Forest
MCKENZIE, Duncan	1	1938	Brentford
MCKEOWN, Thomas	2	1889-1890	Celtic
MCKIE, James	1	1898	East Stirlingshire
MCKILLOP, Thomas	1	1938	Rangers
MCKIMMIE, Stewart	40	1989-1997	Aberdeen
MCKINLAY, Billy	29	1993-1998	Dundee United, Blackburn Rovers
MCKINLAY, Donald	2	1922	Liverpool
MCKINLAY, Tosh	22	1995-1998	Celtic
MCKINNON, Rob	3	1993-1995	Motherwell
MCKINNON, Ron	28	1965-1972	Rangers
MCKINNON, William	4	1883-1884	Dumbarton
MCLAREN, Alan	24	1992-1995	Hearts, Rangers
MCLAREN, Andy	1	2001	Kilmarnock
MCLAREN, Andrew	4	1947	Preston North End
MCLAREN, James	3	1888-1890	Celtic
MCLAREN, Alexander	5	1929-1933	St Johnstone
MCLAUGHLIN, Jon	2	2018	Sunderland
MCLEAN, Adam	4	1925-1927	Celtic
MCLEAN, David	1	1912	Sheffield Wednesday
MCLEAN, Duncan	2	1896-1897	St Bernard's
MCLEAN, George	1	1968	Dundee
MCLEAN, Kenny	36	2016-2023	Aberdeen, Norwich City
MCLEAN, Tommy	9	1967-1971	Kilmarnock
MCLEISH, Alex	77	1980-1994	Aberdeen
MCLEOD, Donald	4	1905-1906	Celtic
MCLEOD, John	5	1888-1893	Dumbarton
MCLEOD, William	1	1886	Cowlairs
MCLINTOCK, Alexander	3	1875-1880	Vale of Leven
MCLINTOCK, Frank	9	1963-1971	Leicester City, Arsenal
MCLUCKIE, Jimmy	1	1933	Manchester City
MCMAHON, Alexander	6	1892-1902	Celtic
MCMANUS, Stephen	26	2006-2010	Celtic
MCMENEMY, James	12	1905-1920	Celtic
MCMENEMY, John	1	1933	Motherwell
MCMILLAN, Ian	6	1952-1958	Airdrie, Rangers
MCMILLAN, James	1	1897	St Bernard's
MCMILLAN, Thomas	1	1887	Dumbarton
MCMULLAN, James	16	1920-1929	Partick Thistle, Manchester City
MCNAB, Alexander	2	1921	Morton
MCNAB, Colin	6	1930-1932	Dundee
MCNAB, John	1	1923	Liverpool
MCNAB, Alexander	2	1937-1938	Sunderland
MCNAIR, Alexander	15	1906-1920	Celtic
MCNAMARA, Jackie	33	1996-2005	Celtic, Wolverhampton Wanderers
MCNAMEE, David	4	2004-2006	Livingston
MCNAUGHT, Willie	5	1950-1954	Raith Rovers
MCNAUGHTON, Kevin	4	2002-2008	Aberdeen, Cardiff City
MCNEIL, Henry	10	1872-1879	Third Lanark, Queen's Park
MCNEIL, Moses	2	1876-1880	Rangers
MCNEILL, Billy	29	1961-1972	Celtic
MCNULTY, Marc	2	2019	Hibernian
MCPHAIL, Bob	17	1927-1937	Airdrie, Rangers
MCPHAIL, John	5	1949-1953	Celtic
MCPHERSON, David	1	1892	Kilmarnock
MCPHERSON, David	27	1989-1993	Hearts, Rangers
MCPHERSON, John	1	1875	Clydesdale
MCPHERSON, John	8	1879-1885	Vale of Leven
MCPHERSON, John	9	1888-1897	Kilmarnock, Cowlairs, Rangers
MCPHERSON, John	1	1891	Hearts
MCPHERSON, Robert	1	1882	Arthurlie
MCQUEEN, Gordon	30	1974-1981	Leeds United, Manchester United
MCQUEEN, Matthew	2	1890-1891	Leith Athletic
MCRORIE, Daniel	1	1930	Morton
MCSPADYEN, Alexander	2	1938-1939	Partick Thistle
MCSTAY, Paul	76	1983-1997	Celtic
MCSTAY, William	13	1921-1928	Celtic
MCSWEGAN, Gary	2	1999	Hearts
MCTAVISH, John	1	1910	Falkirk
MCTOMINAY, Scott	47	2018-2023	Manchester United
MCWATTIE, George	2	1901	Queen's Park
MCWILLIAM, Peter	8	1905-1911	Newcastle United
MEEHAN, Peter	1	1896	Celtic
MEIKLEJOHN, David	15	1922-1933	Rangers
MENZIES, Alexander	1	1906	Hearts
MERCER, Robert	2	1912-1913	Hearts
MIDDLETON, Robert	1	1930	Cowdenbeath
MILLAR, Jimmy	2	1963	Rangers
MILLAR, Archibald	1	1938	Hearts
MILLER, Charlie	1	2001	Dundee United
MILLER, James	3	1897-1898	Rangers
MILLER, John	5	1931-1934	St Mirren
MILLER, Kenny	69	2001-2013	Rangers, Wolverhampton Wanderers, Celtic, Derby County, Bursaspor, Cardiff City, Vancouver Whitecaps
MILLER, Lee	3	2006-2009	Dundee United, Aberdeen
MILLER, Peter	3	1882-1883	Dumbarton

List of players

MILLER, Thomas	3	1920-1921	Liverpool, Manchester United
MILLER, William	1	1876	Third Lanark
MILLER, William	6	1946-1947	Celtic
MILLER, Willie	65	1975-1989	Aberdeen
MILLS, William	3	1935-1936	Aberdeen
MILNE, John	2	1938-1939	Middlesbrough
MITCHELL, Bobby	2	1951	Newcastle United
MITCHELL, David	5	1890-1894	Rangers
MITCHELL, James	3	1908-1910	Kilmarnock
MOCHAN, Neil	3	1954	Celtic
MOIR, William	1	1950	Bolton Wanderers
MONCUR, Bobby	16	1968-1972	Newcastle United
MORGAN, Hugh	2	1898-1899	St Mirren, Liverpool
MORGAN, Lewis	2	2018	Celtic
MORGAN, Willie	26	1967-1974	Burnley, Manchester United
MORRIS, David	6	1923-1925	Raith Rovers
MORRIS, Henry	1	1949	East Fife
MORRISON, James	46	2008-2017	West Bromwich Albion
MORRISON, Thomas	1	1927	St Mirren
MORTON, Alan	31	1920-1932	Queen's Park, Rangers
MORTON, Hugh	2	1929	Kilmarnock
MUDIE, Jackie	17	1956-1961	Blackpool
MUIR, William	1	1907	Dundee
MUIRHEAD, Thomas	8	1922-1929	Rangers
MULGREW, Charlie	44	2012-2019	Celtic, Blackburn Rovers, Wigan Athletic
MULHALL, George	3	1959-1963	Aberdeen, Sunderland
MUNRO, Alexander	3	1936-1938	Hearts, Blackpool
MUNRO, Frank	9	1971-1975	Wolverhampton Wanderers
MUNRO, Iain	7	1979-1980	St Mirren
MUNRO, Neil	2	1888-1889	Abercorn
MURDOCH, Bobby	12	1965-1969	Celtic
MURDOCH, John	1	1931	Motherwell
MURPHY, Francis	1	1938	Celtic
MURPHY, Jamie	2	2018	Rangers
MURRAY, Ian	6	2002-2006	Hibernian, Rangers
MURRAY, James	5	1958	Hearts
MURRAY, John	1	1890	Vale of Leven
MURRAY, John	1	1895	Renton
MURRAY, Patrick	2	1896-1897	Hibernian
MURRAY, Steve	1	1971	Aberdeen
MURTY, Graeme	4	2004-2007	Reading
MUTCH, George	1	1938	Preston North End
NAISMITH, Steven	51	2007-2019	Kilmarnock, Rangers, Everton, Norwich City
NAPIER, Charles	5	1932-1937	Celtic, Derby County
NAREY, David	35	1977-1989	Dundee United
NAYSMITH, Gary	46	2000-2009	Hearts, Everton, Sheffield United
NEIL, Robert	2	1896-1900	Hibernian, Rangers
NEILL, Robert	5	1876-1880	Queen's Park
NEILSON, Robbie	1	2006	Hearts
NELLIES, Peter	2	1913-1914	Hearts
NELSON, James	4	1925-1930	Cardiff City
NEVIN, Pat	28	1986-1996	Chelsea, Everton, Tranmere Rovers
NIBLO, Thomas	1	1904	Aston Villa
NIBLOE, Joseph	11	1929-1932	Kilmarnock
NICHOLAS, Charlie	20	1983-1989	Celtic, Arsenal, Aberdeen
NICHOLSON, Barry	3	2001-2004	Dunfermline Athletic
NICOL, Steve	27	1984-1992	Liverpool
NISBET, James	3	1929	Ayr United
NISBET, Kevin	10	2021	Hibernian, Millwall
NIVEN, James	1	1885	Moffat
O'CONNOR, Gary	16	2002-2008	Hibernian, Locomotiv Moscow, Birmingham City
O'DONNELL, Francis	6	1937-1938	Preston North End, Blackpool
O'DONNELL, Phil	1	1993	Motherwell
O'DONNELL, Stephen	26	2018-2022	Kilmarnock, Motherwell
OGILVIE, Duncan	1	1933	Motherwell
O'HARE, John	13	1970-1972	Derby County
O'NEIL, Brian	7	1996-2005	Celtic, Wolfsburg, Derby County, Preston North End
O'NEIL, John	1	2001	Hibernian
ORMOND, Willie	6	1954-1959	Hibernian
O'ROURKE, Francis	1	1907	Airdrie
ORR, James	1	1892	Kilmarnock
ORR, Ronald	2	1902-1904	Newcastle United
ORR, Tommy	2	1951	Morton
ORR, William	3	1900-1904	Celtic
ORROCK, Robert	1	1913	Falkirk
OSWALD, James	3	1889-1897	Third Lanark, St Bernard's, Rangers
PALMER, Liam	8	2019-2021	Sheffield Wednesday
PARKER, Alex	15	1955-1958	Falkirk, Everton
PARLANE, Derek	12	1973-1977	Rangers
PARLANE, Robert	3	1878-1879	Vale of Leven
PATERSON, Callum	17	2016-2020	Hearts, Cardiff City, Sheffield Wednesday
PATERSON, George	2	1938-1946	Celtic
PATERSON, James	3	1931	Cowdenbeath
PATERSON, John	1	1920	Leicester City
PATON, Andrew	3	1946-1952	Motherwell
PATON, Daniel	1	1896	St Bernard's
PATON, Michael	5	1883-1886	Dumbarton
PATON, Robert	2	1879	Vale of Leven
PATRICK, John	2	1897	St Mirren
PATTERSON, Nathan	19	2021-2023	Rangers, Everton
PAUL, Harold	3	1909	Queen's Park
PAUL, William	3	1888-1890	Partick Thistle
PAUL, William	1	1891	Dykebar
PEARSON, Stephen	10	2003-2007	Motherwell, Celtic, Derby County
PEARSON, Thomas	2	1947	Newcastle United
PENMAN, Andy	4	1966-1967	Dundee
PETTIGREW, Willie	5	1976-1977	Motherwell
PHILLIPS, James	3	1877-1878	Queen's Park
PHILLIPS, Matt	16	2012-2020	Blackpool, Queens Park Rangers, West Bromwich Albion
PLENDERLEITH, Jackie	1	1960	Manchester City
PORTEOUS, Ryan	9	2022-2023	Hibernian, Watford
PORTEOUS, Willie	1	1903	Hearts
PRESSLEY, Steven	32	2000-2006	Hearts
PRINGLE, Charles	1	1921	St Mirren
PROVAN, Davie	5	1963-1965	Rangers
PROVAN, Davie	10	1979-1982	Celtic
PURSELL, Peter	1	1914	Queen's Park
QUASHIE, Nigel	14	2004-2006	Portsmouth, Southampton, West Bromwich Albion
QUINN, James	11	1905-1912	Celtic
QUINN, Pat	4	1961-1962	Motherwell
RAE, Gavin	14	2001-2009	Dundee, Rangers, Cardiff City
RAE, John	2	1889-1890	Third Lanark
RAESIDE, James	1	1906	Third Lanark
RAISBECK, Alexander	8	1900-1907	Liverpool
RALSTON, Anthony	7	2021-2023	Celtic
RAMSAY, Calvin	1	2022	Liverpool
RANKIN, Gilbert	2	1890-1891	Vale of Leven
RANKIN, Robert	3	1929	St Mirren
REDPATH, Willie	9	1948-1952	Motherwell
REID, James	3	1914-1924	Airdrie
REID, Robert	2	1937-1938	Brentford
REID, William	9	1911-1914	Rangers
REILLY, Lawrie	38	1948-1958	Hibernian
RENNIE, Henry	13	1900-1908	Hearts, Hibernian
RENNY-TAILYOUR, Henry	1	1873	Royal Engineers
RHIND, Alexander	1	1872	Queen's Park
RHODES, Jordan	14	2011-2017	Huddersfield Town, Blackburn Rovers, Middlesbrough, Sheffield Wednesday
RICHMOND, Andrew	1	1906	Queen's Park
RICHMOND, James	3	1877-1882	Clydesdale, Queen's Park
RING, Tommy	12	1953-1957	Clyde
RIOCH, Bruce	24	1975-1978	Derby County, Everton
RIORDAN, Derek	3	2005-2009	Hibernian
RITCHIE, Archibald	1	1891	East Stirlingshire
RITCHIE, Billy	1	1962	Rangers
RITCHIE, Henry	2	1923-1928	Hibernian
RITCHIE, John	1	1897	Queen's Park
RITCHIE, Matt	16	2015-2018	Bournemouth, Newcastle United
RITCHIE, Paul	7	1999-2004	Hearts, Bolton Wanderers, Walsall
ROBB, Davie	5	1971	Aberdeen
ROBB, William	2	1925-1927	Rangers, Hibernian
ROBERTSON, Andrew	67	2014-2023	Dundee United, Hull City, Liverpool

ROBERTSON, Archie	5	1955-1958	Clyde	
ROBERTSON, David	3	1992-1994	Rangers	
ROBERTSON, George	4	1910-1913	Motherwell, Sheffield Wednesday	
ROBERTSON, George	1	1937	Kilmarnock	
ROBERTSON, Hugh	1	1961	Dundee	
ROBERTSON, James	2	1931	Dundee	
ROBERTSON, Jimmy	1	1964	Tottenham Hotspur	
ROBERTSON, John	16	1898-1905	Everton, Southampton, Rangers	
ROBERTSON, John	28	1978-1983	Nottingham Forest, Derby County	
ROBERTSON, John	16	1990-1995	Hearts	
ROBERTSON, Peter	1	1903	Dundee	
ROBERTSON, Scott	2	2008-2010	Dundee United	
ROBERTSON, Thomas	4	1889-1892	Queen's Park	
ROBERTSON, Thomas	1	1898	Hearts	
ROBERTSON, William	2	1887	Dumbarton	
ROBINSON, Bobby	4	1974-1975	Dundee	
ROBSON, Barry	17	2007-2012	Dundee United, Celtic, Middlesbrough	
ROSS, Maurice	13	2002-2003	Rangers	
ROUGH, Alan	53	1976-1986	Partick Thistle, Hibernian	
ROUGVIE, Doug	1	1983	Aberdeen	
ROWAN, Archibald	2	1880-1882	Caledonian, Queen's Park	
RUSSELL, David	6	1895-1901	Hearts	
RUSSELL, John	1	1890	Cambuslang	
RUSSELL, Johnny	14	2014-2019	Derby County, Sporting Kansas City	
RUSSELL, William	2	1924-1925	Airdrie	
RUTHERFORD, Edward	1	1948	Rangers	
SAUNDERS, Steven	1	2010	Motherwell	
SAWERS, William	1	1895	Dundee	
SCARFF, Peter	1	1931	Celtic	
SCHAEDLER, Erich	1	1974	Hibernian	
SCOTT, Alex	16	1956-1966	Rangers, Everton	
SCOTT, Jim	1	1966	Hibernian	
SCOTT, Jocky	2	1971	Dundee	
SCOTT, Matthew	1	1898	Airdrie	
SCOTT, Robert	1	1894	Airdrie	
SCOULAR, Jimmy	9	1951-1952	Portsmouth	
SELLAR, William	9	1885-1893	Battlefield	
SEMPLE, William	1	1886	Cambuslang	
SEVERIN, Scott	15	2001-2006	Hearts, Aberdeen	
SHANKLAND, Lawrence	7	2019-2023	Dundee United, Hearts	
SHANKLY, Bill	5	1938-1939	Preston North End	
SHARP, Graeme	12	1985-1988	Everton	
SHARP, James	5	1904-1909	Dundee, Arsenal, Fulham	
SHAW, David	9	1946-1948	Hibernian	
SHAW, Francis	2	1884	Pollockshields Athletic	
SHAW, John	6	1946-1947	Rangers	
SHEARER, Bobby	4	1961	Rangers	
SHEARER, Duncan	7	1994-1995	Aberdeen	
SHINNIE, Andrew	1	2012	Inverness Caledonian Thistle	
SHINNIE, Graeme	6	2018-2019	Aberdeen	
SILLARS, Donald	5	1891-1895	Queen's Park	
SIMPSON, James	3	1895	Third Lanark	
SIMPSON, James	14	1934-1937	Rangers	
SIMPSON, Neil	5	1983-1988	Aberdeen	
SIMPSON, Ronnie	5	1967-1968	Celtic	
SINCLAIR, George	3	1910-1912	Hearts	
SINCLAIR, Jackie	1	1966	Leicester City	
SKENE, Leslie	1	1904	Queen's Park	
SLOAN, Thomas	1	1904	Third Lanark	
SMELLIE, Robert	6	1887-1893	Queen's Park	
SMITH, Alexander	20	1898-1911	Rangers	
SMITH, Dave	2	1966-1968	Aberdeen, Rangers	
SMITH, Eric	2	1959	Celtic	
SMITH, Gordon	19	1946-1957	Hibernian	
SMITH, Henry	3	1988-1992	Hearts	
SMITH, James	1	1872	Queen's Park	
SMITH, James	2	1934-1937	Rangers	
SMITH, Jamie	2	2003	Celtic	
SMITH, Jimmy	4	1968-1974	Aberdeen, Newcastle United	
SMITH, John	10	1877-1884	Mauchline, Edinburgh University, Queen's Park	
SMITH, John	1	1924	Ayr United	
SMITH, Nicol	12	1897-1902	Rangers	
SMITH, Robert	2	1872-1873	Queen's Park	
SMITH, Thomas	2	1934-1936	Kilmarnock, Preston North End	
SNODGRASS, Robert	28	2011-2019	Leeds United, Norwich City, Hull City, West Ham, Aston Villa	
SOMERS, Peter	4	1905-1909	Celtic	
SOMERS, William	3	1879-1880	Third Lanark, Queen's Park	
SOMERVILLE, George	1	1886	Queen's Park	
SOUNESS, Graeme	54	1974-1986	Middlesbrough, Liverpool, Sampdoria, Rangers	
SOUTTAR, John	8	2018-2023	Hearts, Rangers	
SPEEDIE, David	10	1985-1989	Chelsea, Coventry City	
SPEEDIE, Finlay	3	1903	Rangers	
SPEIRS, James	1	1908	Clyde	
SPENCER, John	14	1994-1997	Chelsea, Queens Park Rangers	
STANTON, Pat	16	1966-1974	Hibernian	
STARK, James	2	1909	Rangers	
STEEL, Billy	30	1947-1953	Morton, Derby County, Dundee	
STEELE, David	3	1923	Huddersfield Town	
STEIN, Colin	21	1968-1973	Rangers, Coventry City	
STEPHEN, James	2	1946-1947	Bradford Park Avenue	
STEVENSON, George	12	1927-1934	Motherwell	
STEVENSON, Lewis	1	2018	Hibernian	
STEWART, Allan	2	1888-1889	Queen's Park	
STEWART, Andrew	1	1894	Third Lanark	
STEWART, David	3	1893-1897	Queen's Park	
STEWART, David	1	1977	Leeds United	
STEWART, Duncan	1	1888	Dumbarton	
STEWART, George	4	1906-1907	Hibernian, Manchester City	
STEWART, Jim	2	1977-1978	Kilmarnock, Middlesbrough	
STEWART, Michael	4	2002-2008	Manchester United, Hearts	
STEWART, Ray	10	1981-1987	West Ham	
STEWART, Ross	2	2022	Sunderland	
STEWART, William	2	1898-1900	Queen's Park	
ST JOHN, Ian	21	1959-1965	Motherwell, Liverpool	
STOCKDALE, Robbie	5	2002	Middlesbrough	
STORRIER, David	3	1899	Celtic	
STRACHAN, Gordon	50	1980-1992	Aberdeen, Manchester United, Leeds United	
STURROCK, Paul	20	1981-1987	Dundee United	
SULLIVAN, Neil	28	1997-2003	Wimbledon, Tottenham Hotspur	
SUMMERS, William	1	1926	St Mirren	
SYMON, Scott	1	1938	Rangers	
TAIT, Thomas	1	1911	Sunderland	
TAYLOR, Greg	13	2019-2023	Kilmarnock, Celtic	
TAYLOR, John	4	1892-1895	Dumbarton, St Mirren	
TAYLOR, Joseph	6	1872-1876	Queen's Park	
TAYLOR, William	1	1892	Hearts	
TEALE, Gary	13	2006-2009	Wigan Athletic, Derby County	
TELFER, Paul	1	2000	Coventry City	
TELFER, William	2	1932-1933	Motherwell	
TELFER, William	1	1953	St Mirren	
TEMPLETON, Robert	11	1902-1913	Aston Villa, Newcastle United, Arsenal, Kilmarnock	
THOMPSON, Steven	16	2002-2004	Dundee United, Rangers	
THOMSON, Alexander	1	1909	Airdrie	
THOMSON, Alexander	3	1926-1932	Celtic	
THOMSON, Andrew	2	1886-1889	Arthurlie, Third Lanark	
THOMSON, Billy	7	1980-1983	St Mirren	
THOMSON, Charles	21	1904-1914	Hearts, Sunderland	
THOMSON, Charles	1	1937	Sunderland	
THOMSON, David	1	1920	Dundee	
THOMSON, Harry	2	1967	Burnley	
THOMSON, James	3	1872-1874	Queen's Park	
THOMSON, John	4	1930-1931	Celtic	
THOMSON, John	1	1932	Everton	
THOMSON, Kevin	3	2008-2010	Rangers	
THOMSON, Robert	1	1927	Falkirk	
THOMSON, Robert	1	1931	Celtic	
THOMSON, Samuel	2	1884	Rangers	
THOMSON, William	4	1892-1898	Dumbarton	
THOMSON, William	1	1896	Dundee	
THORNTON, Willie	8	1946-1954	Rangers	
TIERNEY, Kieran	41	2016-2023	Celtic, Arsenal	
TINNEY, Hugh	2	1967	Bury	
TONER, Willie	2	1958	Kilmarnock	
TOWNSEND, Jim	4	1967	Hearts	

TOWNSLEY, Thomas	1	1925	Falkirk	
TROUP, Alexander	5	1920-1926	Dundee, Everton	
TURNBULL, David	4	2021-2022	Celtic	
TURNBULL, Eddie	9	1948-1959	Hibernian	
TURNER, Thomas	1	1884	Arthurlie	
TURNER, William	2	1885-1886	Pollokshields Athletic	
URE, Ian	12	1961-1967	Dundee, Arsenal	
URQUHART, Duncan	1	1934	Hibernian	
VALLANCE, Thomas	7	1877-1881	Rangers	
VENTERS, Alexander	3	1933-1939	Cowdenbeath, Rangers	
WADDELL, Thomas	6	1891-1895	Queen's Park	
WADDELL, Willie	18	1946-1954	Rangers	
WALES, Hugh	1	1933	Motherwell	
WALKER, Andy	3	1988-1994	Celtic	
WALKER, Francis	1	1922	Third Lanark	
WALKER, George	4	1930-1931	St Mirren	
WALKER, James	1	1946	Hearts	
WALKER, John	5	1895-1904	Hearts, Rangers	
WALKER, John	9	1911-1913	Swindon Town	
WALKER, Nicky	2	1993-1996	Hearts, Partick Thistle	
WALKER, Tommy	21	1934-1939	Hearts	
WALKER, Robert	29	1900-1919	Hearts	
WALKER, William	2	1909-1910	Clyde	
WALLACE, Ian	3	1978-1979	Coventry City	
WALLACE, Lee	10	2009-2017	Hearts, Rangers	
WALLACE, Ross	1	2009	Preston North End	
WALLACE, Willie	7	1964-1969	Hearts, Celtic	
WARDHAUGH, Jimmy	2	1954-1956	Hearts	
WARK, John	29	1979-1984	Ipswich Town, Liverpool	
WATSON, Andrew	3	1881-1882	Queen's Park	
WATSON, Bobby	1	1971	Motherwell	
WATSON, James	1	1878	Rangers	
WATSON, James	6	1903-1909	Sunderland, Middlesbrough	
WATSON, James	2	1947-1952	Motherwell, Huddersfield Town	
WATSON, Philip	1	1933	Blackpool	
WATSON, William	1	1898	Falkirk	
WATT, Francis	4	1889-1891	Kilbirnie Thistle	
WATT, Tony	1	2016	Blackburn Rovers	
WATT, William	1	1887	Queen's Park	
WAUGH, William	1	1937	Hearts	
WEBSTER, Andy	28	2003-2013	Hearts, Rangers	
WEIR, Andy	6	1959-1960	Motherwell	
WEIR, David	69	1997-2010	Hearts, Everton, Rangers	
WEIR, James	4	1872-1878	Queen's Park	
WEIR, John	1	1887	Third Lanark	
WEIR, Peter	6	1980-1983	St Mirren, Aberdeen	
WHITE, John	2	1922-1923	Albion Rovers, Hearts	
WHITE, John	22	1959-1964	Falkirk, Tottenham Hotspur	
WHITE, Walter	2	1907-1908	Bolton Wanderers	
WHITELAW, Andrew	2	1887-1890	Vale of Leven	
WHITTAKER, Steven	31	2009-2016	Rangers, Norwich City	
WHYTE, Derek	12	1987-1999	Celtic, Middlesbrough, Aberdeen	
WILKIE, Lee	11	2002-2003	Dundee	
WILLIAMS, Gareth	5	2002	Nottingham Forest	
WILSON, Alexander	1	1954	Portsmouth	
WILSON, Andrew	6	1907-1914	Sheffield Wednesday	
WILSON, Andrew	12	1920-1923	Dunfermline Athletic, Middlesbrough	
WILSON, Bob	2	1971	Arsenal	
WILSON, Danny	5	2010-2011	Liverpool	
WILSON, David	1	1900	Queen's Park	
WILSON, David	1	1913	Oldham Athletic	
WILSON, Davie	22	1960-1965	Rangers	
WILSON, George	6	1904-1909	Hearts, Everton, Newcastle United	
WILSON, Hugh	1	1885	Dumbarton	
WILSON, Hugh	4	1890-1904	Newmilns, Sunderland, Third Lanark	
WILSON, Ian	5	1987-1988	Leicester City, Everton	
WILSON, James	4	1888-1891	Vale of Leven	
WILSON, Mark	1	2011	Celtic	
WILSON, Paul	1	1975	Celtic	
WILSON, Peter	4	1926-1933	Celtic	
WINTERS, Robbie	1	1999	Aberdeen	
WISEMAN, William	2	1926-1930	Queen's Park	
WOOD, George	4	1979-1982	Everton, Arsenal	
WOODBURN, Willie	24	1947-1952	Rangers	
WOTHERSPOON, David	2	1872-1873	Queen's Park	
WRIGHT, Keith	1	1992	Hibernian	
WRIGHT, Stephen	2	1993	Aberdeen	
WRIGHT, Tommy	3	1952-1953	Sunderland	
WYLIE, Thomas	1	1890	Rangers	
YEATS, Ron	2	1964-1966	Liverpool	
YORSTON, Benny	1	1930	Aberdeen	
YORSTON, Harry	1	1954	Aberdeen	
YOUNG, Alexander	2	1905-1907	Everton	
YOUNG, Alex	8	1960-1966	Hearts, Everton	
YOUNG, George	54	1946-1957	Rangers	
YOUNG, James	1	1906	Celtic	
YOUNGER, Tommy	24	1955-1958	Hibernian, Liverpool	

The outside of Hampden Park in Glasgow, home of Scottish football for well over 100 years.

MOST APPEARANCES

PLAYERS WITH AT LEAST 25 CAPS (AT AUGUST 2023)
BOLD TYPE INDICATES THE PLAYER IS STILL AVAILABLE FOR SELECTION

Kenny Dalglish with his son Paul and daughter Kelly after receiving his MBE in 1985. The following year he became the only man so far to reach 100 caps for his country. He received a knighthood in 2018.

Caps	Player(s)
102	Kenny Dalglish
91	Jim Leighton
80	Darren Fletcher
77	Alex McLeish
76	Paul McStay
74	**Craig Gordon**
72	Tom Boyd
69	Kenny Miller / David Weir
67	Christian Dailly / **Andrew Robertson**
65	Willie Miller
62	Danny McGrain / **John McGinn**
61	Richard Gough / Ally McCoist
58	John Collins / **Callum McGregor**
57	Roy Aitken / Gary McAllister
55	Denis Law / Maurice Malpas / Gary Caldwell / Scott Brown
54	George Young / Billy Bremner / Graeme Souness
53	Alan Rough / Kevin Gallacher
52	Joe Jordan
51	Colin Hendry / Steven Naismith
50	Asa Hartford / Gordon Strachan / Alan Hutton
48	Bobby Evans / James McFadden / **Grant Hanley** / **Stuart Armstrong**
47	Shaun Maloney / David Marshall / **Scott McTominay**
46	Craig Burley / Gary Naysmith / James Morrison
45	Barry Ferguson / **Ryan Christie**
44	John Greig / Charlie Mulgrew
43	Archie Gemmill / Gordon Durie / Andy Goram
42	Allan McGregor
41	Christophe Berra / **Kieran Tierney**
40	Eric Caldow / Paul Lambert / Stuart McCall / Stewart McKimmie / Graham Alexander
38	Lawrie Reilly / Sandy Jardine / Maurice Johnston / James Forrest
36	Colin Calderwood / **Kenny McLean**
35	Willie Donachie / David Narey / **Lyndon Dykes**
34	Jim Baxter / Martin Buchan
33	Jackie McNamara / **Steven Fletcher** / **Scott McKenna**
32	Frank Gray / Steven Pressley / James McArthur
31	Alan Morton / Bobby Collins / Steven Whittaker
30	Billy Steel / Gordon McQueen / Brian McClair
29	Bobby Walker / Billy Liddell / Billy McNeill / Willie Henderson / John Wark / Billy McKinlay / Ikechi Anya / Russell Martin
28	Bill Brown / Ron McKinnon / John Robertson / Pat Nevin / Darren Jackson
27	David Hay / Steve Archibald / Steve Nicol / Dave McPherson / **Barry Bannan**
26	Willie Morgan / Alan Hansen / Jim Bett / Stephen McManus / Scot Gemmill / Neil McCann / Billy Dodds / Don Hutchison / Charlie Adam / **Stephen O'Donnell** / **Ryan Fraser** / **Che Adams**
25	Jimmy Cowan / Tommy Docherty / Sammy Cox / Stephen Crawford / Paul Hartley
	Colin Cameron / Neil Sullivan / Andy Webster / Robert Snodgrass / **Jack Hendry**

TOP SCORERS

PLAYERS WITH FIVE OR MORE GOALS (AT AUGUST 2023)

BOLD TYPE INDICATES THE PLAYER IS STILL AVAILABLE FOR SELECTION

30 Denis Law Kenny Dalglish	**11** Joe Jordan	**7** John McPherson Robert Walker James Quinn Robert McPhail John Bell Joe Harper John Wark Gordon Durie Billy Dodds Shaun Maloney Kris Boyd Robert Snodgrass	**5** William Lambie John Madden John Kay William Harrower Henry McNeill Alexander Smith James McMenemy Andrew Cunningham Alan Morton George Hamilton Alex Young Alex Scott David Herd Willie Henderson Bobby Murdoch John O'Hare Lou Macari Asa Hartford Gordon McQueen Don Masson Charlie Nicholas Gordon Strachan Gary McAllister Pat Nevin Darren Fletcher **James Forrest** **Ryan Christie** **Che Adams**
23 Hughie Gallacher	**10** George Ker Billy Liddell Bobby Collins Paul McStay Steven Naismith **Steven Fletcher**		
22 Lawrie Reilly			
19 Ally McCoist			
18 Kenny Miller **John McGinn**	**9** Bobby Johnstone Jackie Mudie Ralph Brand Davie Wilson Colin Stein **Lyndon Dykes**		
15 Robert Hamilton James McFadden Andrew Wilson		**6** Joseph Lindsay John Ferguson William MacKinnon William Paul John Campbell Jimmy McGrory James Delaney Willie Waddell Allan Brown Bruce Rioch Andy Gray Davie Cooper Richard Gough Christian Dailly Don Hutchison Scott Booth	
14 Maurice Johnston	**8** Derek "Dally" Duncan Alex Jackson Tommy Walker Graham Leggat Ian St John Archie Gemmill John Robertson Kevin Gallacher **Scott McTominay**		
13 John Smith Robert McColl			
12 Billy Steel Alan Gilzean John Collins			

Denis Law, joint top scorer with 30 goals, holds the CBE he received in 2016.

The great Hughie Gallacher netted a total of 23 times in just 20 appearances.

HEAD TO HEAD AGAINST OPPOSITION

ALBANIA P2 W2 D0 L0
| 2018 | Home | W | 2-0 | UEFA Nations League |
| 2018 | Away | W | 0-4 | UEFA Nations League |

ARGENTINA P4 W1 D1 L2
1977	Away	D	1-1	Friendly
1979	Home	L	1-3	Friendly
1990	Home	W	1-0	Friendly
2008	Home	L	0-1	Friendly

ARMENIA P2 W2 D0 L0
| 2022 | Home | W | 2-0 | UEFA Nations League |
| 2022 | Away | W | 1-4 | UEFA Nations League |

AUSTRALIA P8 W6 D1 L1
1967	Away	W	0-1	Friendly
1967	Away	W	1-2	Friendly
1967	Away	W	0-2	Friendly
1985	Home	W	2-0	World Cup play-off
1985	Away	D	0-0	World Cup play-off
1996	Home	W	1-0	Friendly
2000	Home	L	0-2	Friendly
2012	Home	W	3-1	Friendly

AUSTRIA P23 W7 D8 L8
1931	Away	L	5-0	Friendly
1933	Home	D	2-2	Friendly
1937	Away	D	1-1	Friendly
1950	Home	L	0-1	Friendly
1951	Away	L	4-0	Friendly
1954	Neutral	L	1-0	World Cup finals
1955	Away	W	1-4	Friendly
1956	Home	D	1-1	Friendly
1960	Away	L	4-1	Friendly
1963	Home	W	4-1	Friendly
1968	Home	W	2-1	World Cup qualifying
1969	Away	L	2-0	World Cup qualifying
1978	Away	L	3-2	European qualifying
1979	Home	D	1-1	European qualifying
1994	Away	W	1-2	Friendly
1996	Away	D	0-0	World Cup qualifying
1997	Home	W	2-0	World Cup qualifying
2003	Home	L	0-2	Friendly
2005	Away	D	2-2	Friendly
2007	Away	W	0-1	Friendly
2021	Home	D	2-2	World Cup qualifying
2021	Away	W	0-1	World Cup qualifying
2022	Away	D	2-2	Friendly

BELARUS P4 W2 D1 L1
1997	Away	W	0-1	World Cup qualifying
1997	Home	W	4-1	World Cup qualifying
2005	Away	D	0-0	World Cup qualifying
2005	Home	L	0-1	World Cup qualifying

BELGIUM P20 W4 D3 L13
1946	Home	D	2-2	Victory international
1947	Away	L	2-1	Friendly
1948	Home	W	2-0	Friendly
1951	Away	W	0-5	Friendly
1971	Away	L	3-0	European qualifying
1971	Home	W	1-0	European qualifying
1974	Away	L	2-1	Friendly
1979	Away	L	2-0	European qualifying
1979	Home	L	1-3	European qualifying
1982	Away	L	3-2	European qualifying
1983	Home	D	1-1	European qualifying
1987	Away	L	4-1	European qualifying
1987	Home	W	2-0	European qualifying
2001	Home	D	2-2	World Cup qualifying
2001	Away	L	2-0	World Cup qualifying
2012	Away	L	2-0	World Cup qualifying
2013	Home	L	0-2	World Cup qualifying
2018	Home	L	0-4	Friendly
2019	Away	L	3-0	European qualifying
2019	Home	L	0-4	European qualifying

BOSNIA/HERZEGOVINA P2 W2 D0 L0
| 1999 | Away | W | 1-2 | European qualifying |
| 1999 | Home | W | 1-0 | European qualifying |

BRAZIL P10 W0 D2 L8
1966	Home	D	1-1	Friendly
1972	Away	L	1-0	Independence Cup
1973	Home	L	0-1	Friendly
1974	Neutral	D	0-0	World Cup finals
1977	Away	L	2-0	Friendly
1982	Neutral	L	4-1	World Cup finals
1987	Home	L	0-2	Rous Cup
1990	Neutral	L	1-0	World Cup finals
1998	Neutral	L	2-1	World Cup finals
2011	Neutral	L	0-2	Friendly

BULGARIA P6 W3 D3 L0
1978	Home	W	2-1	Friendly
1986	Home	D	0-0	European qualifying
1987	Away	W	0-1	European qualifying
1990	Away	D	1-1	European qualifying
1991	Home	D	1-1	European qualifying
2006	Neutral	W	5-1	Kirin Cup

CANADA P7 W6 D1 L0
1967	Away	W	2-7	Friendly
1983	Away	W	0-2	Friendly
1983	Away	W	0-3	Friendly
1983	Away	W	0-2	Friendly
1992	Away	W	1-3	Friendly
2002	Home	W	3-1	Friendly
2017	Home	D	1-1	Friendly

CHILE P2 W2 D0 L0
| 1977 | Away | W | 2-4 | Friendly |
| 1989 | Home | W | 2-0 | Rous Cup |

CIS P1 W1 D0 L0
| 1992 | Neutral | W | 3-0 | European Championship |

COLOMBIA P3 W0 D2 L1
1988	Home	D	0-0	Rous Cup
1996	Away	L	1-0	Friendly
1998	Home	D	2-2	Friendly

COSTA RICA P2 W0 D0 L2
| 1990 | Neutral | L | 0-1 | World Cup finals |
| 2018 | Away | L | 1-0 | Friendly |

CROATIA P6 W2 D3 L1
2000	Away	D	1-1	World Cup qualifying
2001	Home	D	0-0	World Cup qualifying
2008	Home	D	1-1	Friendly
2013	Away	W	0-1	World Cup qualifying
2013	Home	W	2-0	World Cup qualifying
2021	Home	L	1-3	European Championship

CYPRUS P9 W9 D0 L0
1968	Away	W	0-5	World Cup qualifying
1969	Home	W	8-0	World Cup qualifying
1989	Away	W	2-3	World Cup qualifying
1989	Home	W	2-1	World Cup qualifying
2011	Away	W	1-2	Friendly
2019	Home	W	2-1	European qualifying
2019	Away	W	2-1	European qualifying
2023	Home	W	3-0	European qualifying
2023	Away	W	0-3	European qualifying

CZECH REPUBLIC P10 W4 D1 L5
1999	Home	L	1-2	European qualifying
1999	Away	L	3-2	European qualifying
2008	Away	L	3-1	Friendly
2010	Home	W	1-0	Friendly
2010	Away	L	1-0	European qualifying
2011	Home	D	2-2	European qualifying
2016	Away	W	0-1	Friendly
2020	Away	W	1-2	UEFA Nations League
2020	Home	W	1-0	UEFA Nations League
2021	Neutral	L	0-2	European Championship

CZECHOSLOVAKIA P10 W5 D1 L4
1937	Away	W	1-3	Friendly
1937	Home	W	5-0	Friendly
1961	Away	L	4-0	World Cup qualifying

CZECHOSLOVAKIA (continued)

1961	Home	W	3-2	World Cup qualifying
1961	Neutral	L	2-4	World Cup play-off
1972	Neutral	D	0-0	Independence Cup
1973	Home	W	2-1	World Cup qualifying
1973	Away	L	1-0	World Cup qualifying
1976	Away	L	2-0	World Cup qualifying
1977	Home	W	3-1	World Cup qualifying

DENMARK P18 W11 D0 L7

1951	Home	W	3-1	Friendly
1952	Away	W	1-2	Friendly
1968	Away	W	0-1	Friendly
1970	Home	W	1-0	European qualifying
1971	Away	L	1-0	European qualifying
1972	Away	W	1-4	World Cup qualifying
1972	Home	W	2-0	World Cup qualifying
1975	Away	W	0-1	European qualifying
1975	Home	W	3-1	European qualifying
1986	Neutral	L	0-1	World Cup finals
1996	Away	L	2-0	Friendly
1998	Home	L	0-1	Friendly
2002	Home	L	0-1	Friendly
2004	Away	L	1-0	Friendly
2011	Home	W	2-1	Friendly
2016	Home	W	1-0	Friendly
2021	Away	L	2-0	World Cup qualifying
2021	Home	W	2-0	World Cup qualifying

EAST GERMANY P6 W2 D1 L3

1974	Home	W	3-0	Friendly
1977	Away	L	1-0	Friendly
1982	Home	W	2-0	European qualifying
1983	Away	L	2-1	European qualifying
1985	Home	D	0-0	Friendly
1990	Home	L	0-1	Friendly

ECUADOR P1 W1 D0 L0

1995	Neutral	W	2-1	Kirin Cup

EGYPT P1 W0 D0 L1

1990	Home	L	1-3	Friendly

ENGLAND P116 W41 D26 L49

1872	Home	D	0-0	Friendly
1873	Away	L	4-2	Friendly
1874	Home	W	2-1	Friendly
1875	Away	D	2-2	Friendly
1876	Home	W	3-0	Friendly
1877	Away	W	1-3	Friendly
1878	Home	W	7-2	Friendly
1879	Away	L	5-4	Friendly
1880	Home	W	5-4	Friendly
1881	Away	W	1-6	Friendly
1882	Home	W	5-1	Friendly
1883	Away	W	2-3	Friendly
1884	Home	W	1-0	Home Championship
1885	Away	D	1-1	Home Championship
1886	Home	D	1-1	Home Championship
1887	Away	W	2-3	Home Championship
1888	Home	L	0-5	Home Championship
1889	Away	W	2-3	Home Championship
1890	Home	D	1-1	Home Championship
1891	Away	L	2-1	Home Championship
1892	Home	L	1-4	Home Championship
1893	Away	L	5-2	Home Championship
1894	Home	D	2-2	Home Championship
1895	Away	L	3-0	Home Championship
1896	Home	W	2-1	Home Championship
1897	Away	W	1-2	Home Championship
1898	Home	L	1-3	Home Championship
1899	Away	L	2-1	Home Championship
1900	Home	W	4-1	Home Championship
1901	Away	D	2-2	Home Championship
1902	Home	D	2-2	Home Championship
1903	Away	W	1-2	Home Championship
1904	Home	L	0-1	Home Championship
1905	Away	L	1-0	Home Championship
1906	Home	W	2-1	Home Championship
1907	Away	D	1-1	Home Championship
1908	Home	D	1-1	Home Championship
1909	Away	L	2-0	Home Championship
1910	Home	W	2-0	Home Championship
1911	Away	D	1-1	Home Championship
1912	Home	D	1-1	Home Championship

ENGLAND (continued)

1913	Away	L	1-0	Home Championship
1914	Home	W	3-1	Home Championship
1920	Away	L	5-4	Home Championship
1921	Home	W	3-1	Home Championship
1922	Away	W	0-1	Home Championship
1923	Home	D	2-2	Home Championship
1924	Away	D	1-1	Home Championship
1925	Home	W	2-0	Home Championship
1926	Away	W	0-1	Home Championship
1927	Home	L	1-2	Home Championship
1928	Away	W	1-5	Home Championship
1929	Home	W	1-0	Home Championship
1930	Away	L	5-2	Home Championship
1931	Home	W	2-0	Home Championship
1932	Away	L	3-0	Home Championship
1933	Home	W	3-1	Home Championship
1934	Away	L	3-0	Home Championship
1935	Home	W	2-0	Home Championship
1936	Away	D	1-1	Home Championship
1937	Home	W	3-1	Home Championship
1938	Away	W	0-1	Home Championship
1939	Home	L	1-2	Home Championship
1947	Away	D	1-1	Home Championship
1948	Home	L	0-2	Home Championship
1949	Away	W	1-3	Home Championship
1950	Home	L	0-1	World Cup qualifying
1951	Away	W	2-3	Home Championship
1952	Home	L	1-2	Home Championship
1953	Away	D	2-2	Home Championship
1954	Home	L	2-4	World Cup qualifying
1955	Away	L	7-2	Home Championship
1956	Home	D	1-1	Home Championship
1957	Away	L	2-1	Home Championship
1958	Home	L	0-4	Home Championship
1959	Away	L	1-0	Home Championship
1960	Home	D	1-1	Home Championship
1961	Away	L	9-3	Home Championship
1962	Home	W	2-0	Home Championship
1963	Away	W	1-2	Home Championship
1964	Home	W	1-0	Home Championship
1965	Away	D	2-2	Home Championship
1966	Home	L	3-4	Home Championship
1967	Away	W	2-3	Home Championship
1968	Home	D	1-1	Home Championship
1969	Away	L	4-1	Home Championship
1970	Home	D	0-0	Home Championship
1971	Away	L	3-1	Home Championship
1972	Home	L	0-1	Home Championship
1973	Home	L	0-5	SFA centenary
1973	Away	L	1-0	Home Championship
1974	Home	W	2-0	Home Championship
1975	Away	L	5-1	Home Championship
1976	Home	W	2-1	Home Championship
1977	Away	W	1-2	Home Championship
1978	Home	L	0-1	Home Championship
1979	Away	L	3-1	Home Championship
1980	Home	L	0-2	Home Championship
1981	Away	W	0-1	Home Championship
1982	Home	L	0-1	Home Championship
1983	Away	L	2-0	Home Championship
1984	Home	D	1-1	Home Championship
1985	Home	W	1-0	Friendly
1986	Away	L	2-1	Friendly
1987	Home	D	0-0	Rous Cup
1988	Away	L	1-0	Rous Cup
1989	Home	L	0-2	Rous Cup
1996	Away	L	0-2	European Championship
1999	Home	L	0-2	European play-off
1999	Away	W	0-1	European play-off
2013	Away	L	3-2	Friendly
2014	Home	L	1-3	Friendly
2016	Away	L	3-0	World Cup qualifying
2017	Home	D	2-2	World Cup qualifying
2021	Away	D	0-0	European Championship
2023	Home	L	1-3	SFA 150th anniversary

ESTONIA P8 W6 D2 L0

1993	Away	W	0-3	World Cup qualifying
1993	Home	W	3-1	World Cup qualifying
1997	Away	D	0-0	World Cup qualifying
1997	Home	W	2–0	World Cup qualifying
1998	Home	W	3-2	European qualifying
1999	Away	D	0-0	European qualifying
2004	Away	W	0-1	Friendly
2013	Home	W	1-0	Friendly

—197—

FAROE ISLANDS P11 W9 D2 L0
1994	Home	W	5-1	European qualifying
1995	Away	W	0-2	European qualifying
1998	Home	W	2-1	European qualifying
1999	Away	D	1-1	European qualifying
2002	Away	D	2-2	European qualifying
2003	Home	W	3-1	European qualifying
2006	Home	W	6-0	European qualifying
2007	Away	W	0-2	European qualifying
2010	Home	W	3-0	Friendly
2021	Home	W	4-0	World Cup qualifying
2021	Away	W	0-1	World Cup qualifying

FINLAND P8 W6 D2 L0
1954	Away	W	1-2	Friendly
1964	Home	W	3-1	World Cup qualifying
1965	Away	W	1-2	World Cup qualifying
1976	Home	W	6-0	Friendly
1992	Home	D	1-1	Friendly
1994	Away	W	0-2	European qualifying
1995	Home	W	1-0	European qualifying
1998	Home	D	1-1	Friendly

FRANCE P17 W8 D0 L9
1930	Away	W	0-2	Friendly
1932	Away	W	1-3	Friendly
1948	Away	L	3-0	Friendly
1949	Home	W	2-0	Friendly
1950	Away	W	0-1	Friendly
1951	Home	W	1-0	Friendly
1958	Neutral	L	2-1	World Cup finals
1984	Away	L	2-0	Friendly
1989	Home	W	2-0	World Cup qualifying
1989	Away	L	3-0	World Cup qualifying
1997	Away	L	2-1	Friendly
2000	Home	L	0-2	Friendly
2002	Away	L	5-0	Friendly
2006	Home	W	1-0	European qualifying
2007	Away	W	0-1	European qualifying
2016	Away	L	3-0	Friendly
2023	Away	L	1-4	Friendly

GEORGIA P6 W3 D1 L2
2007	Home	W	2-1	European qualifying
2007	Away	L	2-0	European qualifying
2014	Home	W	1-0	European qualifying
2015	Away	L	1-0	European qualifying
2023	Home	W	2-0	European qualifying
2023	Away	D	2-2	European qualifying

GERMANY P17 W4 D5 L8
(*including WEST GERMANY*)
1929	Away	D	1-1	Friendly
1936	Home	W	2-0	Friendly
1957	Away	W	1-3	Friendly
1959	Home	W	3-2	Friendly
1964	Away	D	2-2	Friendly
1969	Home	D	1-1	World Cup qualifying
1969	Away	L	3-2	World Cup qualifying
1973	Home	D	1-1	SFA centenary
1974	Away	L	2-1	Friendly
1986	Neutral	L	2-1	World Cup finals
1992	Neutral	L	0-2	European Championship
1993	Home	L	0-1	Friendly
1999	Away	W	0-1	Friendly
2003	Home	D	1-1	European qualifying
2003	Away	L	2-1	European qualifying
2014	Away	L	2-1	European qualifying
2015	Home	L	2-3	European qualifying

GIBRALTAR P2 W2 D0 L0
| 2015 | Home | W | 6-1 | European qualifying |
| 2015 | Away | W | 1-6 | European qualifying |

GREECE P1 W1 D0 L1
| 1994 | Away | L | 1-0 | European qualifying |
| 1995 | Home | W | 1-0 | European qualifying |

HONG KONG P1 W1 D0 L0
| 2002 | Away | W | 0-4 | Reunification Cup |

HUNGARY P9 W3 D2 L4
1938	Home	W	3-1	Friendly
1954	Home	L	2-4	Friendly
1955	Away	L	3-1	Friendly

HUNGARY (continued)
1958	Home	D	1-1	Friendly
1960	Away	D	3-3	Friendly
1980	Away	L	3-1	Friendly
1987	Home	W	2-0	Friendly
2004	Home	L	0-3	Friendly
2018	Away	W	0-1	Friendly

ICELAND P6 W6 D0 L0
1984	Home	W	3-0	World Cup qualifying
1985	Away	W	0-1	World Cup qualifying
2002	Away	W	0-2	European qualifying
2003	Home	W	2-1	European qualifying
2008	Away	W	1-2	World Cup qualifying
2009	Home	W	2-1	World Cup qualifying

IRAN P1 W0 D1 L0
| 1978 | Neutral | D | 1-1 | World Cup finals |

IRELAND P59 W45 D7 L7
1884	Away	W	0-5	Home Championship
1885	Home	W	8-2	Home Championship
1886	Away	W	2-7	Home Championship
1887	Home	W	4-1	Home Championship
1888	Away	W	2-10	Home Championship
1889	Home	W	7-0	Home Championship
1890	Away	W	1-4	Home Championship
1891	Home	W	2-1	Home Championship
1892	Away	W	2-3	Home Championship
1893	Home	W	6-1	Home Championship
1894	Home	W	1-2	Home Championship
1895	Home	W	3-1	Home Championship
1896	Away	D	3-3	Home Championship
1897	Home	W	5-1	Home Championship
1898	Away	L	0-3	Home Championship
1899	Home	W	9-1	Home Championship
1900	Away	W	0-3	Home Championship
1901	Home	W	11-0	Home Championship
1902	Away	W	1-5	Home Championship
1903	Home	L	0-2	Home Championship
1904	Away	D	1-1	Home Championship
1905	Home	W	4-0	Home Championship
1906	Away	W	0-1	Home Championship
1907	Home	W	3-0	Home Championship
1908	Away	W	0-5	Home Championship
1909	Home	W	5-0	Home Championship
1910	Away	L	1-0	Home Championship
1911	Home	W	2-0	Home Championship
1912	Away	W	1-4	Home Championship
1913	Away	W	1-2	Home Championship
1914	Away	D	1-1	Home Championship
1920	Home	W	3-0	Home Championship
1921	Away	W	0-2	Home Championship
1922	Home	W	2-1	Home Championship
1923	Away	W	0-1	Home Championship
1924	Home	W	2-0	Home Championship
1925	Away	W	0-3	Home Championship
1926	Home	W	4-0	Home Championship
1927	Away	W	0-2	Home Championship
1928	Home	L	0-1	Home Championship
1929	Away	W	3-7	Home Championship
1930	Home	W	3-1	Home Championship
1931	Away	D	0-0	Home Championship
1931	Home	W	3-1	Friendly
1932	Away	W	0-4	Home Championship
1933	Home	L	1-2	Home Championship
1934	Away	L	2-1	Home Championship
1935	Home	W	2-1	Home Championship
1936	Away	W	1-3	Home Championship
1937	Home	D	1-1	Home Championship
1938	Away	W	0-2	Home Championship
1946	Home	D	0-0	Friendly
1947	Away	L	2-0	Home Championship
1948	Home	W	3-2	Home Championship
1949	Away	W	2-8	World Cup qualifying
1950	Home	W	6-1	Home Championship
1951	Away	W	0-3	Home Championship
1952	Home	D	1-1	Home Championship
1953	Away	W	1-3	World Cup qualifying

ISRAEL P11 W7 D2 L2
1967	Away	W	1-2	Friendly
1981	Away	W	0-1	World Cup qualifying
1981	Home	W	3-1	World Cup qualifying
1986	Away	W	0-1	Friendly

ISRAEL (continued)

Year	Venue	Result	Score	Competition
2018	Away	L	2-1	UEFA Nations League
2018	Home	W	3-2	UEFA Nations League
2020	Home	D	1-1	UEFA Nations League
2020	Home	W	0-0	*European play-off
2020	Away	L	1-0	UEFA Nations League
2021	Away	D	1-1	World Cup qualifying
2021	Home	W	3-2	World Cup qualifying

*Scotland won on penalties

ITALY P11 W1 D2 L8

Year	Venue	Result	Score	Competition
1931	Away	L	3-0	Friendly
1965	Home	W	1-0	World Cup qualifying
1965	Away	L	3-0	World Cup qualifying
1988	Away	L	2-0	Friendly
1992	Home	D	0-0	World Cup qualifying
1993	Away	L	3-1	World Cup qualifying
2005	Away	L	2-0	World Cup qualifying
2005	Home	D	1-1	World Cup qualifying
2007	Away	L	2-0	European qualifying
2007	Home	L	1-2	European qualifying
2016	Away	L	1-0	Friendly

JAPAN P3 W0 D2 L1

Year	Venue	Result	Score	Competition
1995	Away	D	0-0	Kirin Cup
2006	Away	D	0-0	Kirin Cup
2009	Away	L	2-0	Friendly

KAZAKHSTAN P2 W1 D0 L1

Year	Venue	Result	Score	Competition
2019	Away	L	3-0	European qualifying
2019	Home	W	3-1	European qualifying

LATVIA P4 W4 D0 L0

Year	Venue	Result	Score	Competition
1996	Away	W	0-2	World Cup qualifying
1997	Home	W	2-0	World Cup qualifying
2000	Away	W	0-1	World Cup qualifying
2001	Home	W	2-1	World Cup qualifying

LIECHENSTEIN P2 W2 D0 L0

Year	Venue	Result	Score	Competition
2010	Home	W	2-1	European qualifying
2011	Away	W	0-1	European qualifying

LITHUANIA P10 W6 D3 L1

Year	Venue	Result	Score	Competition
1998	Away	D	0-0	European qualifying
1999	Home	W	3-0	European qualifying
2003	Away	L	1-0	European qualifying
2003	Home	W	1-0	European qualifying
2006	Away	W	1-2	European qualifying
2007	Home	W	3-1	European qualifying
2010	Away	D	0-0	European qualifying
2011	Home	W	1-0	European qualifying
2016	Home	D	1-1	World Cup qualifying
2017	Away	W	0-3	World Cup qualifying

LUXEMBOURG P5 W4 D1 L0

Year	Venue	Result	Score	Competition
1947	Away	W	0-6	Friendly
1986	Home	W	3-0	European qualifying
1987	Away	D	0-0	European qualifying
2012	Away	W	1-2	Friendly
2021	Away	W	0-1	Friendly

MALTA P7 W6 D1 L0

Year	Venue	Result	Score	Competition
1988	Away	D	1-1	Friendly
1990	Away	W	1-2	Friendly
1993	Home	W	3-0	World Cup qualifying
1993	Away	W	0-2	World Cup qualifying
1997	Away	W	2-3	Friendly
2016	Away	W	1-5	World Cup qualifying
2017	Home	W	2-0	World Cup qualifying

MEXICO P1 W0 D0 L1

Year	Venue	Result	Score	Competition
2018	Away	L	1-0	Friendly

MOLDOVA P4 W3 D1 L0

Year	Venue	Result	Score	Competition
2004	Away	D	1-1	World Cup qualifying
2005	Home	W	2-0	World Cup qualifying
2021	Home	W	1-0	World Cup qualifying
2021	Away	W	0-2	World Cup qualifying

MOROCCO P1 W0 D0 L1

Year	Venue	Result	Score	Competition
1998	Neutral	L	0-3	World Cup finals

NETHERLANDS P20 W6 D5 L9

Year	Venue	Result	Score	Competition
1929	Away	W	0-2	Friendly
1938	Away	W	1-3	Friendly
1959	Away	W	1-2	Friendly
1966	Home	L	0-3	Friendly
1968	Away	D	0-0	Friendly
1971	Away	L	1-2	Friendly
1978	Neutral	W	3-2	World Cup finals
1982	Home	W	2-1	Friendly
1986	Away	L	1-0	Friendly
1992	Neutral	L	0-1	European Championship
1994	Home	L	0-1	Friendly
1994	Home	L	3-1	Friendly
1996	Neutral	D	0-0	European Championship
2000	Away	D	0-0	Friendly
2003	Home	W	1-0	European play-off
2003	Away	L	6-0	European play-off
2009	Away	L	3-0	World Cup qualifying
2009	Home	L	0-1	World Cup qualifying
2017	Home	L	0-1	Friendly
2021	Neutral	D	2-2	Friendly

NEW ZEALAND P2 W1 D1 L0

Year	Venue	Result	Score	Competition
1982	Neutral	W	5-2	World Cup finals
2003	Home	D	1-1	Friendly

NIGERIA P2 W0 D1 L1

Year	Venue	Result	Score	Competition
2002	Home	L	1-2	Friendly
2014	Away	D	2-2	Friendly

NORTH MACEDONIA P4 W2 D1 L1

Year	Venue	Result	Score	Competition
2008	Away	L	1-0	World Cup qualifying
2009	Home	W	2-0	World Cup qualifying
2012	Home	D	1-1	World Cup qualifying
2013	Away	W	1-2	World Cup qualifying

NORTHERN IRELAND P36 W17 D10 L9

Year	Venue	Result	Score	Competition
1954	Home	D	2-2	Home Championship
1955	Away	L	2-1	Home Championship
1956	Home	W	1-0	Home Championship
1957	Away	D	1-1	Home Championship
1958	Home	D	2-2	Home Championship
1959	Away	W	0-4	Home Championship
1960	Home	W	5-2	Home Championship
1961	Away	W	1-6	Home Championship
1962	Home	W	5-1	Home Championship
1963	Away	L	2-1	Home Championship
1964	Home	W	3-2	Home Championship
1965	Away	L	3-2	Home Championship
1966	Home	W	2-1	Home Championship
1967	Away	L	1-0	Home Championship
1969	Home	D	1-1	Home Championship
1970	Away	W	0-1	Home Championship
1971	Home	L	0-1	Home Championship
1972	Home	W	2-0	Home Championship
1973	Home	L	1-2	Home Championship
1974	Home	L	0-1	Home Championship
1975	Home	W	3-0	Home Championship
1976	Home	W	3-0	Home Championship
1977	Home	W	3-0	Home Championship
1978	Home	D	1-1	Home Championship
1979	Home	W	1-0	Home Championship
1980	Away	L	1-0	Home Championship
1981	Home	D	1-1	World Cup qualifying
1981	Home	W	2-0	Home Championship
1981	Away	D	0-0	World Cup qualifying
1982	Away	D	1-1	Home Championship
1983	Home	D	0-0	Home Championship
1983	Away	L	2-0	Home Championship
1992	Home	W	1-0	Friendly
2008	Home	D	0-0	Friendly
2011	Neutral	W	3-0	Nations Cup
2015	Home	W	1-0	Friendly

NORWAY P20 W10 D7 L3

Year	Venue	Result	Score	Competition
1929	Away	W	3-7	Friendly
1954	Home	W	1-0	Friendly
1954	Away	D	1-1	Friendly
1963	Away	L	4-3	Friendly
1963	Home	W	6-1	Friendly
1974	Away	W	1-2	Friendly
1978	Home	W	3-2	European qualifying

NORWAY (continued)
1979	Away	W	0-4	European qualifying
1988	Away	W	1-2	World Cup qualifying
1989	Home	D	1-1	World Cup qualifying
1992	Away	D	0-0	Friendly
1998	Neutral	D	1-1	World Cup finals
2003	Away	D	0-0	Friendly
2004	Home	L	0-1	World Cup qualifying
2005	Away	W	1-2	World Cup qualifying
2008	Home	D	0-0	World Cup qualifying
2009	Away	L	4-0	World Cup qualifying
2013	Away	W	0-1	Friendly
2023	Away	W	1-2	European qualifying
2023	Home	D	3-3	European qualifying

PARAGUAY P1 W0 D0 L1
| 1958 | Neutral | L | 2-3 | World Cup finals |

PERU P4 W1 D1 L2
1972	Home	W	2-0	Friendly
1978	Neutral	L	1-3	World Cup finals
1979	Home	D	1-1	Friendly
2018	Away	L	2-0	Friendly

POLAND P11 W2 D6 L3
1958	Away	W	1-2	Friendly
1960	Home	L	2-3	Friendly
1965	Away	D	1-1	World Cup qualifying
1965	Home	L	1-2	World Cup qualifying
1980	Away	L	1-0	Friendly
1990	Home	D	1-1	Friendly
2001	Away	D	1-1	Friendly
2014	Away	W	0-1	Friendly
2014	Away	D	2-2	European qualifying
2015	Home	D	2-2	European qualifying
2022	Home	D	1-1	Friendly

PORTUGAL P15 W4 D3 L8
1950	Away	D	2-2	Friendly
1955	Home	W	3-0	Friendly
1959	Away	L	1-0	Friendly
1966	Home	L	0-1	Friendly
1971	Away	L	2-0	European qualifying
1971	Home	W	2-1	European qualifying
1975	Home	W	1-0	Friendly
1978	Away	L	1-0	European qualifying
1980	Home	W	4-1	European qualifying
1980	Home	D	0-0	World Cup qualifying
1981	Away	L	2-1	World Cup qualifying
1992	Home	D	0-0	World Cup qualifying
1993	Away	L	5-0	World Cup qualifying
2002	Away	L	2-0	Friendly
2018	Home	L	1-3	Friendly

QATAR P1 W1 D0 L0
| 2015 | Home | W | 1-0 | Friendly |

REPUBLIC OF IRELAND P13 W5 D3 L5
1961	Home	W	4-1	World Cup qualifying
1961	Away	W	0-3	World Cup qualifying
1963	Away	L	1-0	Friendly
1969	Away	D	1-1	Friendly
1986	Away	D	0-0	European qualifying
1987	Home	L	0-1	European qualifying
2000	Away	W	1-2	Friendly
2003	Home	L	0-2	Friendly
2011	Away	L	1-0	Nations Cup
2014	Home	W	1-0	European qualifying
2015	Away	D	1-1	European qualifying
2022	Away	L	3-0	UEFA Nations League
2022	Home	W	2-1	UEFA Nations League

ROMANIA P6 W2 D2 L2
1975	Away	D	1-1	European qualifying
1975	Home	D	1-1	European qualifying
1986	Home	W	3-0	Friendly
1990	Home	W	2-1	European qualifying
1991	Away	L	1-0	European qualifying
2004	Home	L	1-2	Friendly

RUSSIA P4 W0 D2 L2
1994	Home	D	1-1	European qualifying
1995	Away	D	0-0	European qualifying
2019	Home	L	1-2	European qualifying
2019	Away	L	4-0	European qualifying

SAN MARINO P8 W8 D0 L0
1991	Away	W	0-2	European qualifying
1991	Home	W	4-0	European qualifying
1995	Away	W	0-2	European qualifying
1995	Home	W	5-0	European qualifying
2000	Away	W	0-2	World Cup qualifying
2001	Home	W	4-0	World Cup qualifying
2019	Away	W	0-2	European qualifying
2019	Home	W	6-0	European qualifying

SAUDI ARABIA P1 W0 D1 L0
| 1988 | Away | D | 2-2 | Friendly |

SERBIA P3 W1 D1 L1
2012	Home	D	0-0	World Cup qualifying
2013	Away	L	2-0	World Cup qualifying
2020	Away	W	1-1	*European play-off

Scotland won on penalties

SLOVAKIA P4 W2 D0 L2
2016	Away	L	3-0	World Cup qualifying
2017	Home	W	1-0	World Cup qualifying
2020	Home	W	1-0	UEFA Nations League
2020	Away	L	1-0	UEFA Nations League

SLOVENIA P5 W2 D3 L0
2004	Home	D	0-0	World Cup qualifying
2005	Away	W	0-3	World Cup qualifying
2012	Away	D	1-1	Friendly
2017	Home	W	1-0	World Cup qualifying
2017	Away	D	2-2	World Cup qualifying

SOUTH AFRICA P2 W1 D0 L1
| 2002 | Away | L | 2-0 | Reunification Cup |
| 2007 | Home | W | 1-0 | Friendly |

SOUTH KOREA P1 W0 D0 L1
| 2002 | Away | L | 4-1 | Friendly |

SOVIET UNION P4 W0 D1 L3
1967	Home	L	0-2	Friendly
1971	Away	L	1-0	Friendly
1982	Neutral	D	2-2	World Cup finals
1991	Home	L	0-1	Friendly

SPAIN P15 W4 D4 L7
1957	Home	W	4-2	World Cup qualifying
1957	Away	L	4-1	World Cup qualifying
1963	Away	W	2-6	Friendly
1965	Home	D	0-0	Friendly
1974	Home	L	1-2	European qualifying
1975	Away	D	1-1	European qualifying
1982	Away	L	3-0	Friendly
1984	Home	W	3-1	World Cup qualifying
1985	Away	L	1-0	World Cup qualifying
1988	Away	D	0-0	Friendly
2004	Away	D	1-1	Friendly
2010	Home	L	2-3	European qualifying
2011	Away	L	3-1	European qualifying
2023	Home	W	2-0	European qualifying
2023	Away	L	0-2	European qualifying

SWEDEN P12 W5 D1 L6
1952	Away	L	3-1	Friendly
1953	Home	L	1-2	Friendly
1975	Away	D	1-1	Friendly
1977	Home	W	3-1	Friendly
1980	Away	W	0-1	World Cup qualifying
1981	Home	W	2-0	World Cup qualifying
1990	Neutral	W	2-1	World Cup finals
1995	Away	L	2-0	Friendly
1996	Home	W	1-0	World Cup qualifying
1997	Away	L	2-1	World Cup qualifying
2004	Home	L	1-4	Friendly
2010	Away	L	3-0	Friendly

SWITZERLAND P16 W8 D3 L5
1931	Away	W	2-3	Friendly
1946	Home	W	3-1	Victory international
1948	Away	L	2-1	Friendly

Head to head against opposition

SWITZERLAND (continued)
1950	Home	W	3-1	Friendly
1957	Away	W	1-2	World Cup qualifying
1957	Home	W	3-2	World Cup qualifying
1973	Away	L	1-0	Friendly
1976	Home	W	1-0	Friendly
1982	Away	L	2-0	European qualifying
1983	Home	D	2-2	European qualifying
1990	Home	W	2-1	European qualifying
1991	Away	D	2-2	European qualifying
1992	Away	L	3-1	World Cup qualifying
1993	Home	D	1-1	World Cup qualifying
1996	Neutral	W	1-0	European Championship
2006	Home	L	1-3	Friendly

TRINIDAD & TOBAGO P1 W1 D0 L0
2004	Home	W	4-1	Friendly

TURKEY P2 W0 D0 L2
1960	Away	L	4-2	Friendly
2022	Away	L	2-1	Friendly

UKRAINE P5 W2 D1 L2
2006	Away	L	2-0	European qualifying
2007	Home	W	3-1	European qualifying
2022	Home	L	1-3	World Cup play-off
2022	Home	W	3-0	UEFA Nations League
2023	Neutral	D	0-0	UEFA Nations League

URUGUAY P4 W1 D1 L2
1954	Neutral	L	0-7	World Cup finals
1962	Home	L	2-3	Friendly
1983	Home	W	2-0	Friendly
1986	Neutral	D	0-0	World Cup finals

USA P7 W2 D3 L2
1952	Home	W	6-0	Friendly
1992	Away	W	0-1	Friendly
1996	Away	L	2-1	Friendly
1998	Away	D	0-0	Friendly
2005	Home	D	1-1	Friendly
2012	Away	L	5-1	Friendly
2013	Home	D	0-0	Friendly

WALES P107 W61 D23 L23
1876	Home	W	4-0	Friendly
1877	Away	W	0-2	Friendly
1878	Home	W	9-0	Friendly
1879	Away	W	0-3	Friendly
1880	Home	W	5-1	Friendly
1881	Away	W	1-5	Friendly
1882	Home	W	5-0	Friendly
1883	Away	W	0-3	Friendly
1884	Home	W	4-1	Home Championship
1885	Away	W	1-8	Home Championship
1886	Home	W	4-1	Home Championship
1887	Away	W	0-2	Home Championship
1888	Home	W	5-1	Home Championship
1889	Away	D	0-0	Home Championship
1890	Home	W	5-0	Home Championship
1891	Away	W	3-4	Home Championship
1892	Home	W	6-1	Home Championship
1893	Away	W	0-8	Home Championship
1894	Home	W	5-2	Home Championship
1895	Away	D	2-2	Home Championship
1896	Home	W	4-0	Home Championship
1897	Away	D	2-2	Home Championship
1898	Home	W	5-2	Home Championship
1899	Away	W	0-6	Home Championship
1900	Home	W	5-2	Home Championship
1901	Away	D	1-1	Home Championship
1902	Home	W	5-1	Home Championship
1903	Away	W	0-1	Home Championship
1904	Home	D	1-1	Home Championship
1905	Away	L	3-1	Home Championship
1906	Home	L	0-2	Home Championship
1907	Away	L	1-0	Home Championship
1908	Home	W	2-1	Home Championship
1909	Away	L	3-2	Home Championship
1910	Home	W	1-0	Home Championship
1911	Away	D	2-2	Home Championship
1912	Home	W	1-0	Home Championship

WALES (continued)
1913	Away	D	0-0	Home Championship
1914	Home	D	0-0	Home Championship
1920	Away	D	1-1	Home Championship
1921	Home	W	2-1	Home Championship
1922	Away	L	2-1	Home Championship
1923	Home	W	2-0	Home Championship
1924	Away	L	2-0	Home Championship
1925	Home	W	3-1	Home Championship
1925	Away	W	0-3	Home Championship
1926	Home	W	3-0	Home Championship
1927	Away	D	2-2	Home Championship
1928	Home	W	4-2	Home Championship
1929	Away	W	2-4	Home Championship
1930	Home	D	1-1	Home Championship
1931	Away	W	2-3	Home Championship
1932	Home	L	2-5	Home Championship
1933	Away	L	3-2	Home Championship
1934	Home	W	3-2	Home Championship
1935	Away	D	1-1	Home Championship
1936	Home	L	1-2	Home Championship
1937	Away	L	2-1	Home Championship
1938	Home	W	3-2	Home Championship
1946	Away	L	3-1	Home Championship
1947	Home	L	1-2	Home Championship
1948	Away	W	1-3	Home Championship
1949	Home	W	2-0	World Cup qualifying
1950	Away	W	1-3	Home Championship
1951	Home	L	0-1	Home Championship
1952	Away	W	1-2	Home Championship
1953	Home	D	3-3	World Cup qualifying
1954	Away	W	0-1	Home Championship
1955	Home	W	2-0	Home Championship
1956	Away	D	2-2	Home Championship
1957	Home	D	1-1	Home Championship
1958	Away	W	0-3	Home Championship
1959	Home	D	1-1	Home Championship
1960	Away	L	2-0	Home Championship
1961	Home	W	2-0	Home Championship
1962	Away	W	2-3	Home Championship
1963	Home	W	2-1	Home Championship
1964	Away	L	3-2	Home Championship
1965	Home	W	4-1	Home Championship
1966	Away	D	1-1	European qualifying
1967	Home	W	3-2	European qualifying
1969	Away	W	3-5	Home Championship
1970	Home	D	0-0	Home Championship
1971	Away	D	0-0	Home Championship
1972	Home	W	1-0	Home Championship
1973	Away	W	0-2	Home Championship
1974	Home	W	2-0	Home Championship
1975	Away	D	2-2	Home Championship
1976	Home	W	3-1	Home Championship
1976	Home	W	1-0	World Cup qualifying
1977	Away	D	0-0	Home Championship
1977	Away	W	0-2	World Cup qualifying
1978	Home	D	1-1	Home Championship
1979	Away	L	3-0	Home Championship
1980	Home	W	1-0	Home Championship
1981	Away	L	2-0	Home Championship
1982	Home	W	1-0	Home Championship
1983	Away	W	0-2	Home Championship
1984	Home	W	2-1	Home Championship
1985	Home	L	0-1	World Cup qualifying
1985	Away	D	1-1	World Cup qualifying
1997	Home	L	0-1	Friendly
2004	Away	L	4-0	Friendly
2009	Away	L	3-0	Friendly
2011	Neutral	W	3-1	Nations Cup
2012	Away	L	2-1	World Cup qualifying
2013	Home	L	1-2	World Cup qualifying

YUGOSLAVIA P8 W2 D5 L1
1955	Away	D	2-2	Friendly
1956	Home	W	2-0	Friendly
1958	Neutral	D	1-1	World Cup finals
1972	Neutral	D	2-2	Independence Cup
1974	Neutral	D	1-1	World Cup finals
1984	Home	W	6-1	Friendly
1988	Home	D	1-1	World Cup qualifying
1989	Away	L	3-1	World Cup qualifying

ZAIRE P1 W1 D0 L0
1974	Neutral	W	2-0	World Cup finals

—201—

THE MANAGERS

Up to 1954 the Scotland team was managed by a selection committee from the Scottish Football Association. The first man to be given the official individual role was Andy Beattie, who took charge part-time while continuing as manager of Huddersfield Town.

Beattie took the team to the 1954 World Cup finals in Switzerland and had originally selected a squad of around 20, However, the SFA only allowed him to take a travelling party of 13 players. Feeling restricted by the decisions he tendered his resignation on the day of the second match, a heavy defeat to Uruguay.

The selection committee took charge again after Scotland's elimination from the tournament, and continued until the appointment of Matt Busby of Manchester United in 1958. He was initially unable to assume the role due to injuries sustained in the Munich air disaster. Dawson Walker stepped in while Busby recovered, and was in position at the 1958 World Cup finals in Sweden. There the Scots did reasonably well, drawing with Yugoslavia and losing by a single goal to both Paraguay and France, but failed to get out of their group.

After he was well enough Busby took over, but only remained in post for two matches, and Beattie became manager for a second time in 1959.

Beattie resigned the following year to take on the manager's job at Nottingham Forest, and former Rangers and Scotland player Ian McColl was appointed. He had a good degree of success, winning Home Championships in 1962 and 1963, but stepped down in 1965 to become manager at Sunderland.

Celtic boss Jock Stein was then given the job on a part-time basis and under him the team narrowly missed out on qualification for the 1966 World Cup.

Clyde manager John Prentice was next in line, but only lasted six months and four games before leaving to take over at Dundee.

After SFA official Malcolm McDonald had done a two-match stint as caretaker boss, former Rangers and Scotland goalkeeper Bobby Brown took over the role permanently in 1967. He was the first person to be given full control of the team, as up until then the selection committee had continued to choose the players.

Brown's first game in charge saw the team record one of their finest ever results, a 3-2 victory over World Cup winners England at Wembley.

The team continued to perform well under Brown, but were drawn in a qualification group for the 1970 World Cup with West Germany. They needed to avoid defeat in Hamburg to keep their hopes alive but lost 3-2.

In 1971 Tommy Docherty, who had played for Scotland at the 1954 World Cup, was appointed to the job. He did well, only losing three times in 12 matches, but left in late 1972 to become manager of Manchester United.

Another former international player, Willie Ormond, took over from Docherty. Despite a humiliating 5-0 defeat to England in his first game in charge, Ormond's team qualified for the 1974 World Cup finals in West Germany. They performed creditably, being the only undefeated side in the entire tournament, but failed to qualify from their group on goal difference.

Ormond left to take on the manager's job at Hearts in 1977, and was succeeded by Ally MacLeod who had done well at both Ayr United and Aberdeen.

MacLeod made his presence felt straight away as his side claimed another impressive win over England at Wembley. Scotland then qualified for the 1978 World Cup finals in Argentina, with the manager famously claiming that his side might not win the competition, but would "get a medal".

MacLeod was left to rue his words as almost everything went wrong after that. The Scots were well beaten by Peru in the opening match, could only draw with Iran, and Willie Johnston was sent home after failing a drugs test.

Although Scotland rallied to defeat the Netherlands in the final group match, the three-goal victory needed to make the knockout stages was beyond them. The manager resigned a couple of months later.

Stein, who was now at Leeds United, was recruited to replace MacLeod and take charge of the team for a second time. He was successful and Scotland qualified for the 1982 World Cup finals in Spain, but again failed to get out of their group on goal difference.

The Scots missed out on qualification for the 1984 European Championship and the pressure was on Stein to get them to the World Cup finals in Mexico two years later. There were highs and lows in the group games, with a fine win over Spain at Hampden Park but a home defeat to Wales.

A point was needed from the final game against the Welsh in Cardiff in order to qualify for a play-off against Australia. A late penalty kick by Davie Cooper gave the necessary result, but tragically Stein suffered a fatal heart attack at pitch-side.

Assistant manager Alex Ferguson assumed charge for the successful home and away ties with Australia and the subsequent tournament in Mexico, but his team was again eliminated at the group stage.

The SFA decided to go down a different route after that and appointed their director of coaching Andy Roxburgh as national manager in July 1986. He had previously had success with the youth teams, including winning the 1982 European Under-18 Championship.

Roxburgh's team failed to make it to Euro 1988 but he guided them to the 1990 World Cup finals in Italy. It was the same old story, however, as Scotland failed to get beyond the group.

The Scots then qualified for Euro 1992 in Sweden, the first time they had made it to a European Championship finals, but Roxburgh resigned in 1993 after failing to get to the 1994 World Cup.

Next in charge was Craig Brown, who had been Roxburgh's assistant and also part of Ferguson's coaching team. Despite having limited resources compared with previous managers, Brown took the team to both Euro 1996 in England and the 1998 World Cup finals in France.

Scotland had a chance of getting to Euro 2000 but lost narrowly in a play-off with England, and after failing to get to the World Cup finals in 2002 the manager resigned.

The replacement for Brown was former West German international player and Germany boss Berti Vogts, the first foreigner to be appointed to the position.

Vogts reached the Euro 2004 play-offs and his team defeated the Netherlands 1-0 in the first leg at home, but were then beaten 6-0 in the return match. He continued as manager into the 2006 World Cup qualification process, but resigned after the team took just two points from the first three matches.

After Tommy Burns stood in as caretaker for one match the next man at the helm was Walter Smith, who did well but left in January 2007 to return to his former job at Rangers. His replacement Alex McLeish followed a similar path, leaving to take over at Birmingham City.

George Burley was appointed in January 2008 but lasted less than two years, and his successor Craig Levein held the position for a slightly longer stint before he was also sacked.

Billy Stark assumed the caretaker role for one game before Gordon Strachan was officially appointed to replace Levein. Strachan's team competed well but failed to qualify for both Euro 2016 and the 2018 World Cup finals.

After Strachan left the position by mutual consent in October 2017 the SFA asked director of coaching Malky Mackay to step in for one game, before turning once more to McLeish. His team secured a place in the Euro 2020 play-offs, by virtue of finishing top of their group in the newly constituted UEFA Nations League, but after a poor start to the general Euro 2020 qualifying campaign he left the position.

Kilmarnock manager Steve Clarke, another former international player, was appointed in May 2019. Successful penalty shoot-outs in the play-offs against Israel and Serbia took Scotland to Euro 2020, but despite having two games at Hampden Park they again failed to get out of the group.

Clarke took the team to the 2022 World Cup play-offs, but they lost out to Ukraine. However, winning the 2022-23 Nations League meant promotion to the A section and also guaranteed at least a play-off to Euro 2024. Near the end of 2023 the side clinched an automatic place by finishing second in their group behind Spain, so thankfully the play-off became unnecessary.

The table opposite is a list of the various managers' records. Win percentages are not included, however, as I feel it is unfair to compare statistics such as these. Willie Ormond, Ally MacLeod, Jock Stein, Alex Ferguson, Andy Roxburgh and Craig Brown led teams to either World Cups or European Championships and therefore faced superior opposition. Their successors on the other hand, until Steve Clarke more recently, all failed to reach a major tournament and many of the fixtures they oversaw were against lower-rated teams.

LIST OF SCOTLAND MANAGERS

	P	W	D	L
Andy Beattie (1954)	6	2	1	3
Dawson Walker (1958)	6	1	2	3
Matt Busby (1958)	2	1	1	0
Andy Beattie (1959-1960)	12	3	3	6
Ian McColl (1960-1965)	28	17	3	8
Jock Stein (1965-1966)	7	3	1	3
John Prentice (1966)	4	0	1	3
Malcolm McDonald (1966-1967)	2	1	1	0
Bobby Brown (1967-1971)	28	9	8	11
Tommy Docherty (1971-1972)	12	7	2	3
Willie Ormond (1973-1977)	38	18	8	12
Ally MacLeod (1977-1978)	17	7	5	5
Jock Stein (1978-1985)	61	26	12	23
Alex Ferguson (1985-1986)	10	3	4	3
Andy Roxburgh (1986-1993)	61	23	19	19
Craig Brown (1993-2002)	70	32	18	20
Berti Vogts (2002-2004)	31	8	7	16
Tommy Burns (2004)	1	0	0	1
Walter Smith (2004-2007)	16	7	4	5
Alex McLeish (2007)	10	7	0	3
George Burley (2008-2009)	14	3	3	8
Craig Levein (2009-2012)	24	10	5	9
Billy Stark (2012)	1	1	0	0
Gordon Strachan (2013-2017)	40	19	9	12
Malky Mackay (2017)	1	0	0	1
Alex McLeish (2018-2019)	12	5	0	7
Steve Clarke (2019-present)	51	26	11	14

Pensive-looking faces in the Scotland dugout during the World Cup match against Brazil in June 1998. From left: Eric Ferguson (physio), Prof Stewart Hillis (team doctor), Hugh Allan (physio and kit manager), Alan Hodgkinson (goalkeeping coach), Craig Brown (manager) and Alex Miller (assistant manager).

SCOTTISH LEAGUE XI ACTION

Apart from full international matches, various other Scottish representational fixtures have taken place over the past 150 years. These included wartime and B internationals, under-23 matches (which preceded the current under-21 system) and different types of trial games.

The most significant, however, were the many international matches undertaken by the Scottish League XI, which ran from 1892 to 1980. For a long time the annual fixture against the English Football League was second in importance only to the full internationals between the two national sides. Games also took place against the Irish League (Northern Ireland), the League of Ireland (Irish Republic), Serie A in Italy and other opposition.

After the Second World War the games against England in particular attracted very large crowds, with 84,000 watching the fixture in March 1947. The record attendance against the Irish League was 62,000 in 1949, while 67,000 witnessed the match against Serie A in 1961, some no doubt attracted by Denis Law playing for the Italian League side.

The crowds began to dwindle after that and the fixtures declined in importance. This was partly due to the establishment of regular European club competitions in the late 1950s and perhaps also because of some embarrassing mismatches, one example being the 11-0 victory over the League of Ireland in 1962.

Any remaining credibility was said to have been destroyed by the 5-0 defeat against the English Football League at Maine Road in 1974. The Scottish League side contained only a few players who would have had a realistic hope of making the full international team, while the Football League had picked a very strong side.

The final game against England took place in 1976 and the annual fixture was put in abeyance after that. The Scottish League gained a creditable 1-1 draw against the Italian League in 1978, as preparation for the 1978 World Cup finals. Games were played against both Irish leagues in 1980 but no inter-league matches have taken place since.

A Scottish League team last played in 1990, to mark the league's centenary, in a match against the full Scottish national team. With Dundee United manager Jim McLean in charge, the league select won 1-0, the only goal being a penalty by Dutch player Hans Gillhaus.

Bobby Evans of Celtic holds the record for appearances with 25, with Rangers player George Young (22) the only other to gain at least 20.

The record scorer was Willie Bauld of Hearts, with 15 goals in 13 appearances between 1949 and 1958. Just behind was Hibernian centre forward Lawrie Reilly who netted 14 goals in 14 games.

The matches against English and Italian opposition were played at either Hampden Park, Ibrox or Celtic Park, while the less attractive fixtures normally took place at other grounds around the country.

The most capped Scottish League XI player, Bobby Evans of Celtic, leads out the full international team with his English counterpart Billy Wright.

SCOTTISH LEAGUE XI RECORD

Opponent	P	W	D	L
English League	75	19	14	42
Irish League	62	56	1	5
League of Ireland	22	17	3	2
Scotland (SFA)	7	2	2	3
Southern League	5	2	1	2
Italian League	3	0	2	1
Celtic	3	2	0	1
Welsh League	1	0	0	1
Danish League	1	1	0	0
Highland League	1	1	0	0
Scottish Alliance	1	1	0	0
Division Two XI	1	1	0	0
Military XI	1	1	0	0
Sunderland	1	1	0	0
Leicester City	1	0	0	1
Cambuslang	1	1	0	0
Falkirk	1	1	0	0

MOST-CAPPED PLAYERS

Player	Caps	Years	Club
Bobby Evans	25	1948-1960	Celtic
George Young	22	1947-1956	Rangers
Bobby Collins	16	1951-1958	Celtic
Alexander McNair	15	1908-1920	Celtic
Alan Morton	15	1919-1931	Queen's Park, Rangers
James Gordon	14	1909-1920	Rangers
James Brownlie	14	1909-1919	Third Lanark
Eric Caldow	14	1957-1965	Rangers
John Greig	14	1963-1976	Rangers
James McMenemy	14	1908-1920	Celtic
Lawrie Reilly	14	1948-1956	Hibernian
Alexander Smith	14	1897-1913	Rangers
Robert Walker	14	1899-1911	Hearts
Willie Bauld	13	1949-1958	Hearts
Sammy Cox	13	1948-1953	Rangers
Alexander Archibald	12	1919-1933	Rangers
Jerry Dawson	11	1931-1941	Rangers
Neil Gibson	11	1895-1903	Rangers
Gordon Smith	11	1948-1955	Hibernian
Alexander Bennett	10	1905-1912	Celtic, Rangers
Andrew Cunningham	10	1912-1928	Kilmarnock, Rangers
Daniel Doyle	10	1892-1899	Celtic
Willie McStay	10	1919-1928	Celtic
Willie Ormond	10	1947-1958	Hibernian
George Stevenson	10	1927-1934	Motherwell

WOMEN'S INTERNATIONALS

Although this book concentrates on 150 years of the Scottish international men's team, it would be remiss not to mention the growth of the sport for women, and significantly 2023 marks the 25th anniversary since the Scottish Football Association assumed direct responsibility for women's football.

History suggests that women played as far back as the 17th century, around 200 years after men first took up the game. Scotland first played an unofficial women's international match in 1881 which resulted in a 3-0 win over England.

In the 20th century the sport began to become more popular. It was not without its problems though, and after struggling for recognition was banned by the authorities in 1921. Club sides interested in using their grounds for women's matches were subsequently denied permission by the SFA.

In 1971 the member organisations of UEFA were instructed to take control of women's football within their regions. A motion was passed 31-1, with Scotland the only member to vote against it.

The mood was changing, however. The following year saw the first official international played, which resulted in a 3-2 defeat to England. The ban was finally lifted in 1974 although it took another 24 years before the SFA agreed to take over responsibility.

In the 1970s one of the best Scottish players was Rose Reilly, who was born in Kilmarnock and played first for Ayrshire side Stewarton Thistle, won the inaugural Scottish Cup in 1971 with Stewarton and the following year moved to Westthorn. There she won the treble and also reached the final of the British women's cup, losing to Southampton.

Reilly had a strong desire to turn professional and after criticism of the authorities which earned them a lifetime ban, she and her team mate Edna Neillis moved abroad. They played first for Reims in France and then went to Italy, where they signed for ACF Milan.

Although she had played briefly for Scotland in the

Rose Reilly in her Milan strip. She played in Italy for over 20 years, winning the Serie A golden boot on two occasions.

Julie Fleeting, who gained 121 caps for her country, is the top scorer with an incredible 116 goals, a ratio of just under a goal per match.

early 70s, Reilly was selected for the Italian national team. She played in the Mundialito (an unofficial precursor to the women's world cup) and reportedly scored in the final 3-1 victory against West Germany.

Reilly eventually returned to Ayrshire to live and in 2007 she was inducted into the Scottish Football Hall of Fame. To date she is one of only two women to have received the accolade, the other being Julie Fleeting.

The women's international team standing has improved significantly in the 21st century, and in 2014 reached an all-time high of 19th place in the FIFA world rankings.

Scotland reached their first major tournament finals when they qualified for the Women's European Championships in 2017, and followed that up by making it to the World Cup two years later.

The first women's international I witnessed was in June 2017, against Romania at Falkirk Stadium. It was the penultimate home match before the Euros and resulted in a comfortable 2-0 victory.

In the Scottish side that night was centre back Vaila Barsley, who I knew of as she had Shetland connections, her mother hailing from the isles. Barsley was a tall, elegant, ball-playing defender, a bit like a female Alan Hansen, and she was one of the standouts.

Scotland were in an extremely tough group for the Euros, which were staged in the Netherlands, and suffered a humbling 6-0 defeat to England in the opening match.

The second game against Portugal saw a big improvement but sadly the team went down 2-1. Barsley, unfortunately and perhaps unfairly, lost her place for the final tie, in which the team ended on a high by defeating Spain 1-0.

To reach the World Cup of 2019, staged in France,

Scotland had finished top of their qualifying group. They saw off Switzerland (who qualified as runners-up), Poland, Albania and Belarus.

As in the tournament of two years previously, England were the opening opponents. This time the game was much closer with the Scots losing 2-1, and that was the same score in the second match which saw victory for Japan.

Despite the two defeats Scotland could still have made it through to the knockout stages if they defeated Argentina in the final group tie. That looked very likely when they stormed into a 3-0 lead with just 16 minutes remaining.

What happened next was a very unfortunate sequence of events. First the Argentinians pulled one back, which initially just looked like a deserved consolation. But when the Scottish goalkeeper put through her own goal shortly after the nerves began to jangle, and in the fourth minute of stoppage time came the equaliser.

The Scots were out of the tournament and the end result was probably as big a disappointment as anything the men's team had experienced at a World Cup finals. That's no understatement.

After the qualification for two major competitions support for the women's team has continued to grow. A record attendance of 18,555 turned up for a friendly match against Jamaica and good crowds have generally been maintained.

Arguably the finest player of the last decade and more, Arsenal captain Kim Little, announced her retirement from the national team in 2021. Her decision was something of a surprise as she was aged just 30, but had racked up well over 100 caps and had also represented the Great Britain team at the Olympics twice.

The Scots were unable to qualify for the next Euros, which were played a year later than planned in 2022 and famously won by England. They finished third in a group which saw Finland and Portugal progress to the finals.

It was the same story with qualification for the 2023 World Cup, although a step further at the play-offs. After finishing second behind Spain in the groups the Scots needed to win two more matches to reach the finals in Australia and New Zealand. They managed to defeat Austria 1-0 to get to the second stage, but unfortunately lost by the same score to the Republic of Ireland.

Kim Little, arguably Scotland's best player in recent years, retired from international football aged just 30.

Until recently the women's international team tended to play more matches than their male counterparts, and already 14 players have reached a century or more of appearances.

The list is led by former goalkeeper Gemma Fay, who racked up an amazing 203 caps, followed by midfielder Joanne Love on 191. Then come Jane Ross (146), Jennifer Beattie (143), Pauline Hamill (141), Rachel Corsie (141), Little (140), Leanne Ross (133), Megan Sneddon (130), Ifeoma Dieke (123), Fleeting (121), Rhonda Jones (117), Suzanne Grant (104) and Hayley Lauder (103).

Corsie, who is still playing and the current captain of the side, has equal prominence at the entrance to Hampden Park as men's captain Andrew Robertson with both their images emblazoned on the walls. Good luck to the women's team as they continue their journey upwards.

The Scottish women's team which defeated the Republic of Ireland 1-0 at Stark's Park, Kirkcaldy in 2017, just prior to the European Championships of that year. Back (from left): Ifeoma Dieke, Leanne Ross, Gemma Fay (captain), Caroline Weir, Vaila Barsley. Front: Leanne Crichton, Hayley Lauder, Jane Ross, Erin Cuthbert, Fiona Brown, Frankie Brown.

TEAMS OF THE DECADES

Up to this point the book has been a factual account of how the men's international team has progressed over 150 years. On the last few pages, however, I will add what in my opinion are the best line-ups from different eras. I have only chosen the decades of my own lifetime, for the following reasons. I do not feel there is enough information available prior to the 1950s on the merits of individual players, and would find it difficult in some cases to choose one over another. Many, although hugely talented, only gained a small number of caps. And obviously I did not witness any of the action, either live or via footage, so do not feel qualified to judge.

So I will begin with the 1950s, where I have selected a team in the traditional 2-3-5 formation of that time. While I did not see any of the players in action, there is enough evidence available to form an opinion. A number of players narrowly missed out, including goalkeeper Jimmy Cowan, full back John Hewie, centre half Willie Woodburn, inside forwards Eddie Turnbull and Bobby Collins, centre forward Jackie Mudie and winger Willie Ormond.

1950s TEAM

TOMMY YOUNGER

SAMMY COX — ERIC CALDOW

BOBBY EVANS — GEORGE YOUNG — TOMMY DOCHERTY

BOBBY JOHNSTONE — BILLY STEEL

GORDON SMITH — LAWRIE REILLY — BILLY LIDDELL

Selecting a side from the 1960s was probably the most difficult task of all. Although Scotland did not qualify for any major tournaments during that decade, the country was blessed with a variety of superb players in almost every position. Apologies to Eddie McCreadie, Ron McKinnon, Dave Mackay, Bobby Murdoch, Pat Crerand, Pat Stanton, Willie Henderson, Ian St John, Bobby Lennox, Charlie Cooke and others, but I have gone for the following.

1960s TEAM

BILL BROWN

ALEX HAMILTON — TOMMY GEMMELL

JOHN GREIG — BILLY MCNEILL — JIM BAXTER

JOHN WHITE — DENIS LAW

JIMMY JOHNSTONE — ALAN GILZEAN — DAVIE WILSON

TEAMS OF THE DECADES (continued)

Moving to the 1970s you will see that the majority are those who represented Scotland at the 1974 World Cup. I feel that side, although unable to get beyond the group stages, performed better than any other team in subsequent campaigns. Unlucky not to make the cut were David Harvey, Willie Donachie, Jim Holton, Gordon McQueen, Kenny Burns, Lou Macari, Asa Hartford, Peter Lorimer, Willie Morgan and Tommy Hutchison. The formation is now 4-4-2.

1970s TEAM

ALAN ROUGH

SANDY JARDINE — ALAN HANSEN — MARTIN BUCHAN — DANNY MCGRAIN

ARCHIE GEMMILL — BILLY BREMNER — DAVID HAY — EDDIE GRAY

KENNY DALGLISH — JOE JORDAN

Again it is players who played at a World Cup who make up the 1980s team, and the Scots made it to the finals two more times. Jock Stein was in charge at Spain in 1982, and sadly died when he was on the verge of taking the squad to Mexico four years later. It was not easy to narrow the choice down to 11 and honourable mentions go to Frank Gray, David Narey, Roy Aitken, Steve Nicol, John Wark, Andy Gray and John Robertson.

1980s TEAM

JIM LEIGHTON

RICHARD GOUGH — WILLIE MILLER — ALEX MCLEISH — MAURICE MALPAS

GORDON STRACHAN — GRAEME SOUNESS — PAUL MCSTAY — DAVIE COOPER

STEVE ARCHIBALD — MAURICE JOHNSTON

TEAMS OF THE DECADES (continued)

The 1990s was another very successful decade and those chosen largely formed the nucleus of the sides at the World Cups of Italy in 1990 and France in 1998. There were also appearances at successive European Championships in Sweden in 1992 and England in 1996, with the team under the control of first Andy Roxburgh and then Craig Brown. Unlucky to miss out are Paul Lambert, Murdo MacLeod, Gordon Durie and Brian McClair.

1990s TEAM

ANDY GORAM

STEWART MCKIMMIE COLIN CALDERWOOD COLIN HENDRY TOM BOYD

PAT NEVIN STUART MCCALL GARY MCALLISTER JOHN COLLINS

ALLY MCCOIST KEVIN GALLACHER

Sadly the turn of the century signalled a significant decline in the fortunes of the team. The quality of players appeared to diminish, with fewer commanding regular places with top English sides, and the performances suffered as a result. There were notable exceptions, however, and occasionally a fine result. Also worthy of consideration were Neil Sullivan, Jackie McNamara, Graham Alexander, Stephen McManus and Don Hutchison.

2000s TEAM

DAVID MARSHALL

ALAN HUTTON DAVID WEIR CHRISTIAN DAILLY GARY NAYSMITH

SCOTT BROWN BARRY FERGUSON DARREN FLETCHER SHAUN MALONEY

KENNY MILLER JAMES MCFADDEN

TEAMS OF THE DECADES (continued)

If the previous decade resulted in little success, the 2010s showed barely any improvement, albeit that under Gordon Strachan the team was a bit unlucky to miss out on a play-off for the 2018 World Cup. This team pretty much picks itself, although also in the running were defenders Gary Caldwell, Andy Webster, Russell Martin and Charlie Mulgrew and midfielders Robert Snodgrass and Charlie Adam.

2010s TEAM

ALAN MCGREGOR

STEVEN WHITTAKER — GRANT HANLEY — CHRISTOPHE BERRA — ANDREW ROBERTSON

JAMES FORREST — JAMES MCARTHUR — JAMES MORRISON — STUART ARMSTRONG

STEPHEN FLETCHER — STEVEN NAISMITH

I appreciate that it is only three years into the current decade, and some of those selected may well be replaced by the end of the 2020s, but I have gone for the following. Most of them have been chiefly responsible for getting the team into the top tier of UEFA Nations League groups, and will get the chance to play against the top countries as a result. Unlucky to miss out were Nathan Paterson, Jack Hendry, Ryan Fraser and Lyndon Dykes.

2020s TEAM

CRAIG GORDON

AARON HICKEY — RYAN PORTEOUS — SCOTT MCKENNA — KIERAN TIERNEY

JOHN MCGINN — BILLY GILMOUR — SCOTT MCTOMINAY — CALLUM MCGREGOR

CHE ADAMS — RYAN CHRISTIE

GREATEST SIDE OF MY LIFETIME

Even picking a shortlist for this side is not an easy task, but narrowing that down to 11 is much, much harder. There were only three positions where in my opinion those selected are without equals – Danny McGrain at right back and Kenny Dalglish and Denis Law up front. The midfield trio of Billy Bremner, Graeme Souness and Jim Baxter were also fairly straightforward, but after that things get much more difficult.

Starting with goalkeeper, I have gone for Andy Goram who just shades it over Craig Gordon. In the centre of defence three others were in contention – the Aberdeen duo of Willie Miller and Alex McLeish plus Alan Hansen. However, Lisbon Lions captain Billy McNeill gets the nod and alongside the Celtic legend is Martin Buchan, surely one of the most composed and stylish defenders ever to wear the dark blue.

If I was picking a left back 10 years ago it would have been Tommy Gemmell, but anyone who is good enough to play in a European Cup-winning team nowadays is surely worthy of a place. So Andrew Robertson becomes the only current player to make the line-up.

With the three midfield places and two of those up front taken care of, only one space remains. There were three or four in the running here, but Jimmy Johnstone nicks the slot just ahead of Eddie Gray, Gordon Strachan and Davie Cooper.

I have chosen five substitutes – Gordon, Gemmell, Hansen, Gray and that supreme header of a ball Alan Gilzean. Narrowly missing a place on the bench were John Greig and Joe Jordan.

To look after that side there is no way I cannot go for Jock Stein, although having Alex Ferguson and Craig Brown in tow would make for some management team.

ANDY GORAM

DANNY MCGRAIN — **BILLY MCNEILL** — **MARTIN BUCHAN** — **ANDREW ROBERTSON**

BILLY BREMNER — **GRAEME SOUNESS** — **JIM BAXTER**

JIMMY JOHNSTONE — **KENNY DALGLISH** — **DENIS LAW**

Substitutes

CRAIG GORDON — TOMMY GEMMELL — ALAN HANSEN — EDDIE GRAY — ALAN GILZEAN

While every effort has been made to ensure accuracy, there may well be errors or omissions in the book. The author would appreciate any such mistakes being brought to his attention before any subsequent reprinting. Please email jickspublishing@outlook.com with comments.

THANKS AND ACKNOWLEDGMENTS

A number of people have helped me along the way, from when the book was still a pipedream, during the research period, and on to the production stage.

Firstly, I must pay homage to the late Craig Brown for his generous foreword. He first offered to do so when on a visit to Shetland in 2019, and must have been surprised when I finally got back to him three years later. Craig was a tremendous help to me, even driving up to Glasgow from Ayrshire for our last meeting in February this year, and the book is in part a tribute to him.

I am grateful to the staff at the National Library in Edinburgh, who were very obliging during the many hours I spent there researching the archives of the *The Scotsman* newspaper.

My thanks to Richard McBrearty, curator at the Scottish Football Museum at Hampden Park in Glasgow, who kindly allowed me to use several of the older photos in the book and other images. The remaining photos were purchased from Alamy, SNS Pics and Dreamstime.

Two books proved invaluable to me in my quest for information. Firstly, Richard Keir's *Scotland: The Complete International Football Record*, and secondly, Dirk Karsdorp's *The Complete Scotland FC, 1872-2020*.

For online research I am indebted to several websites, particularly the Rec. Sport.Soccer Statistics Foundation. Some information was also gleaned from www.11v11.com, Wikipedia, and also the Scottish Football Association itself.

My friend John Thomson readily agreed to do the first proof-reading, and being a stickler for accuracy he was a great assistance.

I am indebted to The Shetland Times Ltd, my former place of work, for taking on the task of printing, and ex-colleague Jenny Henry for her own superb proof-reading skills.

I would like to thank my wife Irene, my sons Callum and Stuart, and my daughter Kirsty for putting up with my obsession with the Scottish football team, and all the support they have given me along the way.

The book is also dedicated to my late friend Bobby Elphinstone, an avid football fan like myself. He took great interest in and gave much encouragement to my project.